International Library of F
and the New Medicine

MW00824232

Volume 68

Series editors

David N. Weisstub, University of Montreal Fac. Medicine Montreal, QC, Canada
Dennis R. Cooley, North Dakota State University, History, Philosophy, and
Religious Studies, Fargo, ND, USA

The book series International Library of Ethics, Law and the New Medicine comprises volumes with an international and interdisciplinary focus. The aim of the Series is to publish books on foundational issues in (bio) ethics, law, international health care and medicine. The 28 volumes that have already appeared in this series address aspects of aging, mental health, AIDS, preventive medicine, bioethics and many other current topics. This Series was conceived against the background of increasing globalization and interdependency of the world's cultures and governments, with mutual influencing occurring throughout the world in all fields, most surely in health care and its delivery. By means of this Series we aim to contribute and cooperate to meet the challenge of our time: how to aim human technology to good human ends, how to deal with changed values in the areas of religion, society, culture and the self-definition of human persons, and how to formulate a new way of thinking, a new ethic. We welcome book proposals representing the broad interest of the interdisciplinary and international focus of the series. We especially welcome proposals that address aspects of 'new medicine', meaning advances in research and clinical health care, with an emphasis on those interventions and alterations that force us to re-examine foundational issues.

More information about this series at http://www.springer.com/series/6224

Michel Dion · David Weisstub
Jean-Loup Richet
Editors

Financial Crimes: Psychological, Technological, and Ethical Issues

 Springer

Editors
Michel Dion
Chairholder of the CIBC Research Chair in
 Financial Integrity, Faculté
 d'administration
Université de Sherbrooke
Sherbrooke, QC
Canada

Jean-Loup Richet
ESSEC
Institute for Strategic Innovation & Services
Suresnes
France

David Weisstub
Faculté de Médicine
Université de Montréal
Montreal, QC
Canada

ISSN 1567-8008   ISSN 2351-955X (electronic)
International Library of Ethics, Law, and the New Medicine
ISBN 978-3-319-32418-0   ISBN 978-3-319-32419-7 (eBook)
DOI 10.1007/978-3-319-32419-7

Library of Congress Control Number: 2016938655

Printed on acid-free paper

This Springer imprint is published by Springer Nature
The registered company is Springer International Publishing AG Switzerland

Contents

Contributors

Lishan Ai School of Political and Social Inquiry, Monash University, Melbourne, Australia

Bruce Baer Arnold Canberra Law School, University of Canberra, Canberra, Australia

F.N. Baldwin Center for International Financial Crimes Studies, University of Florida, Gainesville, FL, USA

Azad Singh Bali Division of Social Science & Division of Environment, Hong Kong University of Science and Technology, Hong Kong, China

Wendy Bonython Canberra Law School, University of Canberra, Canberra, Australia

Sara Brady Harvard Longwood Psychiatry Residency Training Program, Boston, USA

Harold J. Bursztajn Clinical and Forensic Psychiatrist, Cambridge, USA

Krishnan Chandramohan Division of Social Science & Division of Environment, Hong Kong University of Science and Technology, Hong Kong, China

Nestor Courakis Faculty of Law, University of Athens, Athens, Greece

Louis de Koker Deakin Law School, Centre for Cyber Security Research, Deakin University, Geelong, Australia

Michel Dion Chairholder of the CIBC Research Chair in Financial Integrity, Faculté d'administration, Université de Sherbrooke, Sherbrooke, Québec, Canada

Peter Enderwick Auckland University of Technology, Auckland, New Zealand

Jeffrey A. Gadboys Centre for International Financial Crimes Studies, Levin College of Law, University of Florida, Gainesville, FL, USA

Stephen Greenspan Health Science Center, University of Colorado, Boulder, CO, USA

Yaniv Hanoch Plymouth University, Plymouth, UK

Omar Sultan Haque Department of Psychology, Harvard University, Cambridge, USA; Program in Psychiatry and the Law, Harvard Medical School, Boston, USA

Andreas Kapardis Department of Law, University of Cyprus, Nicosia, Cyprus

Maria Krambia-Kapardis Cyprus University of Technology, Limassol, Cyprus

Jenny E. Ligthart Tilburg University, Tilburg, Netherlands

Nlerum S. Okogbule Rivers State University of Science and Technology, Port Harcourt, Nigeria

Erick Rabin New York University School of Law, New York, USA

Grant Richardson School of Accounting and Finance, The University of Adelaide, Adelaide, SA, Australia

Anne Sachet-Milliat ISC Paris Business School, Paris, France

Barbara Maria Sadaba Tilburg University, Tilburg, Netherlands

Jun Tang School of Statistics and Mathematics, Zhongnan University of Economics and Law, Wuhan, Hubei, China

Rene van Stralen Tilburg University, Tilburg, Netherlands

Johan Verstraeten Catholic University of Leuven, Leuven, Belgium

Stacey Wood Scripps College, Claremont, CA, USA

George W. Woods Morehouse School of Medicine, Atlanta, GA, USA

Daniel Wu Harvard University, Cambridge, USA

Xun Wu Division of Social Science & Division of Environment, Hong Kong University of Science and Technology, Hong Kong, China

Introduction

Financial Crimes, Determinants, Policy Implications—Psychological and Psychiatric Aspects

Because of the enormity of damages caused by financial crimes affecting both the physical and the mental health of individuals, families and organizations (indeed in many cases exceeding those of violent crimes), it is understandable that there is a burgeoning scientific literature that attempts to investigate various dimensions of the phenomenon, delving into the psychological profiles of victims along with perpetrators. The celebrated cases that have been in the public eye are now almost legendary, having attracted a prurient interest with the public at large. We suspect that this is due to our tendency to identify more with white-collar criminals than with other offenders, given that they are normally highly educated, well-to-do, live in similar neighbourhoods to where the researchers are, and by all that we know, are extraverted, convivial, well-spoken, and when targeted, given to persuasive rationalizations. In fact, it is an attribute of the con man to be likeable and thus it is predictable that judges and even journalists are inclined to go easy on this population, underrating their malevolent impacts, with an accompanying merciful approach to their prison sentences. In the Earl Jones case recently in Canada, observers were surprised to see that given the vastness of the theft, and the cruel consequences on vulnerable populations, the perpetrator served a mild 4 years in jail. There is a similarity in cases elsewhere.

The variables involved in doing a proper analysis of what motivates white-collar criminality have made it difficult to develop predictive models. There appears to be a consensus in this volume, although there are differences and nuances between authors in this volume as to the ultimate value of continuing along the path of articulating more precise criteria to move in the direction of prediction, that although the state-of-the-art research is not predictive it is not without utility. It certainly heightens the attention of surveillance teams and organizational leadership to think carefully in their interviewing and investigative processes about which variables might prove relevant in the case at hand. It is the insight of the Harvard research group in this volume that the only method to clarify and improve our typologies should be done on a case-by-case basis, at least for the time being.

The emphasis on categories, i.e. profiles, can be seen to enhance a reflective process in looking at mitigating circumstances, such as addressing diminished responsibility. This is not to suggest vitiating culpability, but it does assist us in addressing situations where there have been over-reaching conditions of traumatic socialization or other defects which were conducive to the criminal acts in question. The psychodynamic approach has much to offer, along with other techniques and assessment tools. Within the psychodynamic methodology, there are certain generalizations which should be kept in mind when dealing with white-collar offences —such generalizations have to be at the back of the therapists' assessment process but not demanding exclusivity or unreflective application. White-collar offenders are given to narcissism, are often charismatic, have a distinct lack of integrity, possess a fear of failing or being degraded in social terms, and above all, there is frequently a propensity to have control of situations at any expense, and even at great risk. The challenge in this category of offences is thoroughly acknowledged, namely that there is an affinity between white-collar offenders and white-collar success stories, often leading to the amusing comment that political leaders and the wealthy are regarded as sociopaths while those who do not thrive and about which we can locate defects of moral character find their way into the system as psychopaths. Nevertheless, the authors in this volume seek to define the contours where the differences are apparent and real and should be the subject of continued research.

In a number of chapters found in this volume, there is attention given to neurobiological factors. Although research on neurobiological factors is still embryonic, essays in this volume assist us in having an improved understanding of the victims of white-collar criminality, which is very relevant given the fact that the 'situation' is a critical component when other preconditions are in place to catalyse perpetrators. A greater effort should be taken by socially responsible planners to improve financial skills among the population at large, especially those who are vulnerable by dint of age, education, and monetary stability. The cases are sufficiently diverse that it is a sine qua non of analyses that they should take care in dealing with the nuances of culture, the actual level of decision-making capacity and familiarity with financial decision-making, the particularities of age, the geographical location of the victims, and the details of their relationship to the perpetrator within specific contexts. This again refers us to the need for a case-by-case analysis by utilizing models and social science research to optimize results, given the challenge or need in question.

Organizational deviance is a pertinent ingredient if we are to seek a complete understanding of how white-collar offences occur in reality. In recent years, movies and journalistic accounts have highlighted the way in which perpetrators are created out of the whole cloth of peer pressure, manipulation for gains and achievement within the hierarchies where they work, the intrinsic anomy and anger that is exacerbated by competitive and avaricious organizations, and the authoritarian structures that not only control but also dictate the fearful responses of the dependents within the specific hierarchies. From a social psychological point of view, it is useful to think about how the socialization of business executives, including within university faculties, can be adjusted to educate graduates and employees about the shortcomings of deviant practices. Given the examples of recent whistleblowing and an enlarging acceptance that white-collar crime is something to be combatted, one can be hopeful that educational institutions will try to emphasize, through case studies applied to actual courses, the way in which lines can be drawn where resistance to overseers is mandated. Restricting the teaching of ethics in schools and institutions to courses simply dedicated to the subject is insufficient to combat the tendencies towards illegality that are incorporated into institutions which remain below the radar screen. Above all, it is important to note that the majority of transgressions in white-collar criminality more than likely go unnoticed due to the internal repercussions for businesses and organizations when exposed to public criticism. Internalizing standards should ultimately be the goal for those who want to avert white-collar criminality and protect the vulnerable public.

In Chap. 1, Kapardis, Krambia-Kapardis and Courakis expound upon anti-corruption measures needed in Cyprus and Greece. They present data on how corruption results in reduced investment and reduced growth in addition to which it acts as a disincentive for innovation, development and capital investment. Furthermore, corruption has evidently a negative impact on socio-political factors such as democratization by undermining citizens' confidence in democratic institutions and the rule of law. Corruption has an impact on society and environment. In the social area moral values and principles are destroyed, democracy is undermined and institutions are corroded. Greece and Cyprus—two countries facing serious financial crisis—not surprisingly experience high perceived corruption levels and deficits in the rules of law and government accountability and transparency. They conclude by explaining how European Union and the Eurozone must act on behalf of their members to safeguard the Eurozone by encouraging the fight against corruption.

In Chap. 2, Richardson presents a cross-country study of the determinants of tax evasion. When the determinants of tax evasion are clearly identified in a systematic way by empirical analysis, appropriate policy conclusions can then be drawn, and policymakers are then in a position to design and implement measures to control and restrain its damaging effects. Richardson's research indicates that non-economic determinants have the strongest impact on tax evasion. In particular, complexity is the most important determinant of tax evasion, followed by education, income source, fairness and tax morale. With that information in mind, attempts could be made by governments to make improvements to the levels of complexity in the tax system. By enhancing the general educational knowledge of taxpayers, tax evasion is also reduced. Wage and salary income subject to withholding also represents another important curb on tax evasion. Richardson concludes that this could lead to improvements in tax revenue collection by governments.

In Chap. 3, Ligthart, Sadaba and van Stralen bring to light what determines information sharing for income tax purposes across international borders. The authors review how in recent years, tax evasion issues have been in the centre of the international tax policies debate the evasion of which constitutes a considerable loss of revenue and created an environment out of which the need for shared tax information was born. Most countries treat data on the use of information sharing with considerable confidentiality and yet the authors explore how, by sharing tax information, a country has to bear the cost of information gathering and it becomes a less attractive place to investors. But in reality they observe that countries do share tax information for reasons of reciprocity, which is one of the main drivers of information sharing among countries, and the idea that tax treaties contribute as well to the flow of information across borders.

In Chap. 4, Baldwin and Gadboys review the duty of financial institutions to investigate and report fraudulent activities. The authors note that as financial institutions face the threat of liability from both the regulators and the customers, it is reasonable to ask whether those that service the public sector's financial needs are acting out of dedicated support for a common goal or principally to avoid penalty. The authors explore how the current approach to these concerns is designed to make criminal activities unprofitable and to keep the proceeds of crime out of the hands of criminals and terrorist. These goals cannot be achieved without proactive confiscation mechanisms. Financial institutions are required to report suspicious transactions within 30–60 days and if necessary refuse to complete the transaction. The result is that either the transaction occurs (with potentially illegitimate money entering the financial system), or the funds walk away, free to search for an alternative entry point. The authors concluded that what is absent from the current system is the ability to immediately seize the funds without delay as recommended, pending determination of the legitimacy of the funds involved. Providing a financial incentive to those complying institutions could not only change the course of the problem quickly but also help to grow a legitimate response to money laundering.

In Chap. 5, Brady, Rabin, Wu, Haque, and Bursztajn present comprehensive data on the forensic psychiatric contributions to financial crime. The authors explore individual psychological dimensions of financial crimes in a given social context, the group dynamics of corrupt organizations, and the interrelationship between the two. At the individual level, the authors distinguish "mad" from "bad", through conducting psychosis between character pathology and crimes committed with deliberation and foreknowledge of their consequences. The authors present the limitations of rational choice theory as a foundation for the legal approaches to preventing acts of financial crime, understanding their meaning, responding in accordance with the fundamentals of justice. The authors conclude by presenting opportunities to set forth a psychodynamically informed forensic psychiatric perspective as an aid for sentencing of white-collar crime.

In Chap. 6, Wood, Hanoch, and Woods review the cognitive factors that result in susceptibility to financial crimes including financial literacy, numeracy and deliberative reasoning. Financial literacy has been found to be a strong predictor of retirement savings, FICO scores and savings accounts. But perhaps more important, the authors have found that a strong predictor of debt and vulnerability to be predatory lending. Those individuals who have low financial literacy are more likely to employ loss aversion, sunk costs, and confirmatory bias in the financial decision-making. Dual process models of decision-making are used to explain that decision-making can be deliberative and analytical or emotional and impulsive but in cases of investment schemes, emotional and impulsive decision-making are key. That impulsive decision-making can be increased through stress, cognitive impairment or ego depletion. Decision-making can occur in or out of awareness. Overall, the authors conclude that while anyone can be a victim of fraud, factors that impact our ability to deliberate and "do the math" increase our susceptibility to financial predators.

In Chap. 7, Greenspan and Woods explore a four-factor model of gullibility as it relates to financial fraud. The authors note that being a victim of a financial fraud is usually viewed as a form of gullibility, and that gullibility can take place at individual level or at that of a financial institution. But this gullibility is described as being external to the victim, with cognition, personality and state being internal to the person. The authors conclude that a gullible financial outcome is described as the sum of all of these factors operating on a specific victim.

In Chap. 8, Arnold and Bonython explore all of the parties involved in financial crime in tandem with a more robust psychological understanding of financial crimes. The authors purport that one mechanism for understanding the psychology of financial crime in general is to adapt the seven deadly sins, i.e. opportunity, rationalization, need, greed, emulation, anger, pleasure, fear and misjudgment. Understanding financial crime requires awareness that it involves victims and bystanders, rather than merely offenders. But this awareness has shed light on the fact that there is still a great need for comprehensive empirical data that would enable more confident assessments of the psychology of financial crime and thence more effective responses. To date the authors note that there are no comprehensive culturally independent profiling mechanisms for identification of potential and active financial criminals.

Financial Crimes (From Bribery to Tax Evasion and Money Laundering)—Ethical and Technological Aspects

Criminals are using more or less complex technological means, particularly in financial crimes. In each case, financial crimes imply ethical questioning, either about the use of technology or the way laws and regulations are covering the ethical concerns. Tax evasion and money laundering schemes actually mirror the challenge we are facing now. As they are related to drug trade, transnational crimes and bribery threaten legitimate economy and raise ethical questions about the moral responsibility of citizens, social institutions and the state. The growth of transnational crimes has been strengthened by the rise of the Internet. Many traditional crimes became widespread in various countries. In some cases, crime was linked closely to drug trade. But there are other types of crimes which are not. Criminals are widening the scope of their illegal activities and thus making investigation more difficult, if not impossible, to be launched by police officers.

Crime prevention strategies cannot be efficiently designed without taking into account the various levels of moral responsibility: international financial organizations, police organizations, judges, lawyers, accounting professionals, governments, businesses and citizens. These strategies should focus on the best ways to change the mindset of all social actors. We will not reach such an objective without taking upon ourselves our own moral responsibility. Legally focused strategies are certainly useful in preventing some types of crimes. However, changing the mindset of people cannot be realized through strict laws and regulations. Making people more aware of their moral responsibility is a much more effective means of dealing with the growth of financial crimes.

This volume focuses on three basic financial crimes that have a transnational character: tax evasion, bribery, and money laundering. Other financial crimes do not necessarily reflect an accentuated transnational character: insurance/bankruptcy fraud, government fraud, insider trading and identity theft. In contrast, antitrust practices, theft of trade secrets and cybercrime have transnational character that lead to large financial losses. They actually hinder fair competition. Due to the fact that tax evasion, bribery and money laundering are truly endangering national economies and collective well-being, this volume has focused on these three transnational crimes in particular.

Fundamentally, tax fraud threatens the public interest since it tends to reduce the qualitative and quantitative dimensions of public services (e.g. health and education). In some countries, tax evasion is illegal, while in others, it is allowed. It can be demonstrated that tax evasion often creates short-term advantages for individuals. However, in the long run, the situation is not so, in both developed and developing economies. Health and education systems could always be improved, so that people will benefit from better public services. Tax evasion limits such benefits. The state is bereft of tax revenues which are sent off-shore, particularly to tax havens. So even if tax fraud is clearly an issue of public interest, tax evasion will question the way a given country accepts losing a part of its tax revenues. In countries where tax evasion is legally permitted, citizens must be more aware that tax evasion could have side effects on their own well-being. Citizens should be involved in public interest groups and be critical of tax havens. Through consciousness-raising activities, citizens can bring pressure on their governments. If we cannot prove that tax evasion contributes to diminishing collective well-being in a given country, we should then, as an a priori belief, take for granted that it has the opposite effect. The business community could try to justify tax evasion: it would make their businesses more profitable so that national economies are strengthened. However, it will likely be impossible to check to what extent collective well-being would have been improved through tax evasion schemes. In the absence of any data to the contrary, we should claim that tax evasion 'probably' adversely affects collective interests. Although such an assertion has not been empirically proven, it has the advantage of presenting tax evasion as an ambiguous phenomenon, from a moral point of view. Moreover, the probability that tax evasion will negatively affect collective well-being will help to safeguard public interest.

Bribery is one of the most well-known financial crimes. But what does it mean to offer or solicit bribes? How could we define the structure of such bribing activities? We can analyse bribery from a sociological/anthropological viewpoint as well as from a politico-legal perspective. However in doing so, we are missing the point. Offering or soliciting bribes is an abuse of power. Offering or soliciting bribes is not a part of any job description. The victim (who receives or pays the bribe) is subjected to conditions that are not an integral part of their job description or of any other contractual duties. That is why we should define bribing as an abuse of power. Moreover, when bribes are offered or solicited in the business milieu, they constitute an unfair (antitrust) practice. If competitors are unable to pay bribes (or pay comparable amounts as their competitors), they will be excluded from the market.

Bribery makes us more aware of the Kantianism of defining financial crimes. Bribery is not a cultural issue. If we admit that bribery is culturally induced, then many forms of bribery would become morally justified. Bribery cannot be culturally justified, because the offering/soliciting of bribes implies an abuse of power and an unfair business practice. If we accept bribery as a cultural phenomenon, we then legitimize an abuse of power.

Fighting bribery implies rejecting any cultural interpretation of bribery. Of course, we could use historical, sociological, political and anthropological frameworks in order to mirror the way bribery has been developed in a given country. But such justifications are not tantamount to giving a moral justification. Moral justification deals with issues of good/evil, without any historical, sociological, political or anthropological determinism. Moral justification uses objective criteria to determine the moral character of given actions. From a philosophical standpoint, such criteria are drawn from given ethical theories: theory of virtues (Aristotle), philosophical egoism (Smith, Hobbes), utilitarianism (Bentham, Mill, Moore, Ross), Kantism, primacy of otherness (Levinas), existential ethics (Sartre), theory of justice (Rawls, Sen), and moral deliberative approaches (Habermas).

Anti-money laundering strategies are designed to set up consciousness-raising activities for various social groups and institutions. Nevertheless, there are individuals who claim that money launderers are offering more advantageous prices for their products than legitimate businesses. In short term, it could be true. However, in the long run, such enterprises have been sustained through illegality and will have put their competitors out of business. In the long term, citizens will face a financial loss, as it is often the case when we are dominated by monopolistic/oligopolistic market structures. If money laundering represents approximately 2.5 % of the gross world product (GWP)—as it was assessed by the IMF—we should then be aware of four basic issues: (1) the issue of the origin: major part of that huge sum of money comes from drug trade revenues ('dirty money'); (2) the issue of detection: dirty money could be laundered everywhere; citizens (as well as governmental agencies and ministries) cannot directly perceive such laundering activities, when dealing with businesses, groups and associations; (3) the issue of economic and political effects: dirty money is laundered into a given domestic economy; it is introducing unfair competition within legitimate businesses. Money launderers are then inevitably powerful and influence a community, often including political spheres, and they do harm to democratic institutions; (4) the issue of mutual trust: in the long run, money laundering erases given human capital, that is, the way trust has been built up through the years. So they could develop an overly suspicious perception of business activities. Societal institutions cannot survive in the long term without a human capital of mutual trust. That is exactly what money laundering erodes.

In Chap. 9, Sachet-Milliat provides insight into the idea of deviance and the unethical pressures used therein. The author states that sociological research in organizational deviance, specifically in the area of corporate crime, has shown how deviant behaviours (frauds and unethical behaviours) are not only restricted to individuals but also to organizations. The author explores how deviant organizations and their leaders use unethical and pressured management practice in their internal and institutional environment so as to change the norms of individuals' behaviours and also to transform societal norms in order for their actions to be legal and even be perceived as being legitimate. Social and political methods are used in such cases. The author's conclusion explores the way to increase resistance capacity of internal and external actors faced with unethical pressures in order to prevent the perpetuation of organizational deviance.

In Chap. 10, Wu, Chandramohan and Bali offer insight into how globalization poses both the opportunities and challenges to the fight against corruption in developing countries. On the one hand, the authors contend that globalization can accelerate the convergence of governance to international standards; on the other hand, however, globalization can increase the competition for a large number of inefficient domestic firms and thus may create high pressure for them to bribe in order to survive. The authors explore how the corporate sector is an important source for rampant corruption problems in many developing countries due to a vicious cycle of bribery practices and corruption. Improvement in corporate governance can be a critical ingredient to break the vicious cycle of bribery practices and corruption. The authors conclude that public policies targeting improved corporate governance could be effective anti-corruption strategies. More importantly, such efforts are likely to be sustained because it is self-motivated and self-driven from the perspective of firms. Government, business community and individual firms all have respective roles to play in combating bribery activities in the corporate sector. Government can significantly reduce bribery by targeting areas where firms are the most prone to bribery practices, such as integrity of court systems, business licensing requirements, quality of government service delivery and taxation. The business community can reduce the incidence of bribery by setting up rules of market competition so that bribery will not automatically increase as the level of competition rises. Individual firms can shoulder their share of responsibility through improvements in corporate governance, such as broadening the basis of ownership.

In Chap. 11, Verstraeten presents a theological definition to integrity and corruption. The author explores how etymologically the concept of corruption has a negative pre-moral connotation. Its Latin root *con-rumpere* refers to: destroying, doing harm, polluting, seducing, deterioration of morals, profanation, inciting to criminal behaviour, etc.

Verstraeten criticizes several misconceptions with regard to integrity and articulates the different degrees of responsibility in corruption, while reflecting on the development of a "counter discipline" against corruption via spirituality as a precondition for ethical behaviour. The chapter concludes on the need of virtuous communities within which civility and the intellectual and moral can be sustained in order to promote integrity.

In Chap. 12, Dion explores how differently legal jurisdictions dictate the ways in which legislators deal with bribery. The author explores the basic components of bribery as a social construct with particular emphasis on the belief that there are grey areas of morality within bribery issues as a mythical mindset. Cassirer's approach of myths could be used to unveil the basic structure of mythical beliefs. If the notion of grey areas of morality in bribery issues is a mythical idea, then strategies to fight corruption cannot remain the same. The author researches how cultural relativism could justify practices that should never be socially approved, since they put harm to the business community and even collective wealth. Cultural relativism is unable to cover all situations. But financial crimes are often described from a legal/political viewpoint. When ethical dimensions of financial crimes are unveiled, then grey areas of morality could appear. Bribery is sometimes confused with gift-giving practices, as if cultural norms of behaviour would induce such conduct. The way societal culture and morality are evoked reflects a resistance toward any moral questioning. But the author concludes how bribes constitute an abuse of power and an antitrust behaviour (and thus a dehumanizing phenomenon), while gift-giving practices are closely linked to cultural (and humanizing) norms of conduct. Rational deliberation about corrupt practices would imply that the premise (or the inner structure) of corrupt practices cannot morally justify the action itself (soliciting, offering or receiving bribes). Thus, there are no grey areas of morality within bribery issues. Due to the nature of the phenomenon itself (its inner structure), the author explains how bribery can never be morally justified.

In Chap. 13, Kapardis and Krambia-Kapardis review the 'fraud triangle' as the most popular white-collar criminal profile which subsequently was developed to comprise the components of 'pressure', 'opportunity' and 'rationalization' to account for fraud. The author's present data which finds that white-collar offending is inhibited when a firm has a working compliance programme, when managers do not perceive career benefits and, finally, when managers perceive the illegal act as highly immoral. As one would have predicted, white-collar offenders do not consider themselves criminals. In recent years, profiling has moved to a more evidence-based approach, and into mainstream forensic psychology as the new discipline of Behavioural Investigative Advice. Today this profile has been expounded upon by the authors with the ROP model. The ROP model is more comprehensive than the fraud triangle as it integrates characteristics of the individual culprit in a separate but essential component—the person, and also makes possible a very useful eclectic fraud detection model.

The authors have determined that the risk of fraud is a product of both personality and environmental or situational variables. The authors state that a feasible undertaking would be to attempt to profile at different levels of analysis (e.g. individual and organizational) and specific types of fraud offenders perpetrating specific frauds. Also, the authors conclude that future research should aim to obtain a more complex causal picture of what attributes separate fraud offenders from versatile fraud offenders and those committing common crime.

In Chap. 14, Okogbule explores the challenges faced in regulating transnational financial crimes. The author first acknowledges that globalization has promoted greater integration of states into the international economy through interconnection of markets, financial services and capital, but argues that the products of technological advancements, such as computer and the Internet, have been increasingly used and exploited by criminals in the perpetration of transnational financial crimes. The existing national and international legal instruments and mechanisms have been unable to sufficiently grapple with the problems of transnational financial crimes and more emphasis needs to be placed on enhanced preventive measures, such as increased electronic surveillance, modernization of applicable legal rules along these lines, international co-operation and the cultivation of a global ethical consensus on the subject. Since transnational financial crimes are opportunity-driven, one of the most effective ways of combating or preventing them is through the elimination or reduction of those opportunities that are frequently exploited by criminals. The author concludes that currently it is imperative that there be a formulation of a new legal framework to respond to the dictates of technological developments. In addition, the adoption of a convention dealing with specific aspects of financial crime is one way of moving the fight against these crimes forward. It is only through such approaches that humankind can maximally benefit from the promise of globalization and effectively respond to the challenges posed by transnational financial crimes.

In Chap. 15, Enderwick explores the transnational organization of the drug trade. The author notes that the illegal drugs trade is concerned with the cultivation, production, distribution and sale of substances subject to drug prohibition laws. What distinguishes the transnational drugs trade from other global industries is the highly illegal nature of its activities, the large profits earned, the immense social costs created, and the significant resources dedicated to its control and reduction. The international trade in illicit drugs, one of the largest industries in the world economy, is firmly under the control of transnational criminal organizations (TCOs). These groups have prospered under a long standing regime of drug prohibition. There are marked similarities in the ways in which both legitimate and illegitimate international businesses are organized, in part because both have responded to continuing globalization. Both types of businesses are fragmenting, partially externalizing activities, and increasing locational flexibility. The author dictates that the key ethical challenge for an industry which generates huge social, economic and health costs is whether the continuation of a 40-year war on drugs founded on prohibition is more ethically acceptable than an evidence-based approach focusing on harm reduction.

In Chap. 16, De Koker reviews anti-money laundering (AML) and counter-terrorist financing (CTF) measures which focus on the abuse by criminals of technology and new payment systems to hide the flows of illicit funds. The AML/CFT system itself, however, uses technology to monitor transactions, identify potential suspicious and unusual transactions and report them to the authorities. The AML/CTF framework gives rise to privacy risks. Mobile money systems are capable of collecting and storing large amounts of data on clients. In countries that are subject to rule of law, this data is shared with the state within a legal framework. Many mobile money models are, however, operating in the countries where the rule of law is weak. The author raises concerns regarding responsible and ethical corporate compliance with statutory information-sharing responsibilities. With increasing international consensus that millions of socially vulnerable people should be included in the formal financial system, the author expresses a need for an appropriate balancing of potentially competing interests is of increasing importance. Financial institutions should comply with the law and should support legitimate state action against crime by preventing the abuse of their services by criminals and terrorists and by reporting such instances where they occur.

In Chap. 17, Tang and Ai explore how businesses are becoming increasingly global and interconnected as they continue to engage in e-commerce. The adoption of encryption techniques and the facility for remote transfer increase extraordinarily the anonymity of electronic money. It is difficult to adequately implement customer identification and record keeping on electronic transactions, let alone carrying out the obligations of suspicious transaction report (STR) on them. The authors review that as the Internet becomes more and more a worldwide phenomenon, prepaid card system, Internet payment services, and mobile payment services are potentially subject to a wide range of vulnerabilities that can be exploited for money laundering. The authors explain how new payment technologies and digital currencies have been identified as possessing risk characteristics which pose a threat to traditional due diligence systems in the international campaign against money laundering, and limit the effectiveness of implementing internal controls in numerous areas. The authors express that in order to mitigate these risks, implementing robust CDD and verification procedures and other measures such as imposing value limits and strict monitoring systems need to take place.

Part I
Financial Crimes, Its Determinants and Policy Implications

Chapter 1
Anti-corruption Measures: The Panacea to a Financial Cliff

Maria Krambia-Kapardis and Nestor Courakis

Abstract Cyprus and Greece, both members of the EU and the Eurozone, are currently in the throes of a devastating financial crisis. Public opinion surveys carried out in Cyprus (2010, 2011, 2012), Greece (2012, 2013) and the 2014 Eurobarometer identify the perceptions of and reasons for corruption, the category profile of the offender and likely measures considered to be effective by the public and the EU Commission. Following the survey findings and a review of the legislation in both countries to identify loopholes in the system, a number of suggestions are made in an effort to rebuild trust in the 'archon' and set the 'tone at the top'. The policy implications of the suggested measures aim to improve the two countries' image so as to attract foreign investment which will lead to economic growth and the IMF and the European Central Bank will consider the financial cliff the countries are facing from a positive angle.

1.1 Introduction

As far as a *definition of corruption* is concerned, the Council of Europe's Civil Law Convention on Corruption (1999) in Article 2 states: "For the purpose of this Convention 'corruption' means requesting, offering, giving or accepting, directly or indirectly, a bribe or any other undue advantage or prospect thereof, which distorts the proper performance of any duty or behaviour required of the recipient of the bribe, the undue advantage or the prospect thereof". In a more simplified way, the definition of this legal instrument can be formulated as follows: "Corruption is the illicit and abusive behavior of a (latosensu) functionary who, within the framework of his/her duties, promotes the interests of another person (physical person or legal

M. Krambia-Kapardis (✉)
Cyprus University of Technology, Limassol, Cyprus
e-mail: maria.kapardis@cut.ac.cy

N. Courakis
Faculty of Law, University of Athens, Athens, Greece
e-mail: nestor-courakis@jurisconsults.gr

© Springer International Publishing Switzerland 2016
M. Dion et al. (eds.), *Financial Crimes: Psychological, Technological, and Ethical Issues*, International Library of Ethics, Law, and the New Medicine 68, DOI 10.1007/978-3-319-32419-7_1

entity) in view to obtain for himself or for others a direct or indirect economic benefit" (Courakis and Mannozzi 2013, 15). Transparency International's definition is wider and refers to "the abuse of entrusted power for private gain". Under this definition, corruption can include not only bribery, which is the mainstay of the legal hardcore of corruption, but also some types of embezzlement, abuse of functions and/or power, misappropriation of funds or other diversions of property. Moreover, the Association of Certified Fraud Examiners (ACFE 2010) states that corruption in businesses comprises bribery, conflict of interest, illegal gratuity and economic extortion. Bose et al. (2008) add to the list government bureaucracies, leveraging their position to further their own interests. Besides, corruption is contagious (Bose et al. 2008) and is almost always a clandestine act (Officer and Taki 2013, 71).

Corruption can be seen as a "symptom that something has gone wrong in the management of the State" (Rose-Ackerman 1999, 9). Most countries around the world, particularly those in Southern Europe are facing a serious financial crisis. Fraud and corruption increase during times of recession rather than in good time (KPMG 2011). In the difficult financial times Europe is experiencing one cannot ignore the impact corruption has on economic factors (Mauro 1995; Rose-Ackerman 2004). In fact, corruption lowers investment (Campos et al. 1999) and growth (Aghion et al. 2004; Alesina et al. 2003; Mauro 1996; Tanzi and Davoodi 1997). It has also been found that corruption is bad for development and creates disincentive effects on capital investment and innovation (Krussell and Rios-Rull 1996). Due to excessive corruption in the public sector, it is expected the cost of public expenditure will be inflated and as a result there will be low quality of public infrastructures (Bose et al. 2008; Mauro 1998). Furthermore, corruption has evidently a negative impact on socio-political factors such as democratization (Anokhin and Schulze 2009; Ashiku 2011; Barro 1996). According to the first EU Anti-Corruption Report (2014),[1] corruption costs the European economy around €120 billion per year. It also undermines "citizens' confidence in democratic institutions and the rule of law, it hurts the European economy and deprives States from much-needed tax revenue" said Cecilia Malmström, EU Commissioner of Home Affairs.[2]

Corruption has an impact on society and environment. In the social area moral values and principles are destroyed, democracy is undermined and institutions are corroded. The lack of education and awareness as far as protecting the environment as well as the lack of policies and enforcement in the field of land development,

---

[1]European Commission (2014b) EU Anti-Corruption Report. http://ec.europa.eu/dgs/home-affairs/what-we-do/policies/organized-crime-and-human-trafficking/corruption/anti-corruption-report/index_en.htm. Accessed 6 Feb 2014.

[2]European Commission (2014f) Press Release: Commission unveils first EU Anti-Corruption Report, 3 Feb 2014, IP/14/86.

land planning, pollution, arson for development purposes and lack of forestry register support corruption (Galoukas 2013). Let us next consider one measure of the level of corruption in a country, namely corruption perception surveys.

1.2   Corruption Perception Studies

Literature is scant on the measure levels of corruption in a country in comparison to others since it is difficult to quantify such a crime, because: (a) a lot goes unreported as well as undetected (dark figure) and, therefore, it is not easily measurable, and (b) different cultures, "jurisdictions, and environments have different degrees of tolerance for and definitions of corruption" (de Figueiredo 2013, 135). Thus, corruption perception studies are the closest one can get in studying corruption in a country in an effort to find ways to combat the particular crime. One must not ignore, however, that such studies are based solely on the criterion of *perception,* and there may be well founded reservations as to whether this kind of assessment, widely seen as *subjective,* can, in fact, pass a verdict on corruption in various countries. Thus, it could be argued, this assessment is merely a reflection of how a qualified sample of people *perceives* corruption in a specific country, on the basis of several factors which may shape their opinion. One key factor, for example, is the frequency with which the mass media report instances of corruption in each country. Another is the stance the media takes to corruption in a particular country, which affects just how far investigative journalism is prepared to go and how it angles its criticism. Indeed, corruption, economic crimes and white-collar crimes in general may be over represented in the media, especially when they are used as improper forms of competition in the political arena. It follows that the frequency with which the media report instances of corruption in each country may also depend on the political balance or media strategies. In addition, sociologists have shown that these factors can also deeply affect the way the public perceive crime levels and, thus, their reactions of fear and insecurity can be manipulated accordingly. What is significant is the mismatch between the public's perception of crime levels and the real figures, which are often found to be considerably lower, even allowing for the dark figure.

Thus, corruption perception studies, despite their purpose to focus the world's attention on the need to monitor corruption and to offer a map of corruption of the whole world, may not only be misleading in relation to the real dimensions of corruption in a country,[3] but may also have a negative effect on the country, as they can be used by foreign enterprises in an erroneous or even improper manner. Indeed, as the economic literature about corruption has explained to no small

---

[3]Cf. the article of Alex Cobham in Foreign Policy of July 22, 2013: http://www.foreignpolicy.com/articles/2013/07/22/corrupting_perceptions. Accessed 20 Mar 2014.

extent, corruption can also influence the economic growth of a country where direct foreign investments are concerned.[4] In these cases, the corruption perception studies may run the risk of giving distorted criteria to foreign enterprises to use as part of their decision-making process as to whether to invest in a specific country or not. It is suggested, therefore, that such studies are used in conjunction with a wider range of parameters measuring both corruption rates and the efforts in adopting anti-corruption policies at legislative and administrative level in a country. Such parameters, for instance, include the existing legal framework, the way in which this legislation is enforced (including cases of corruption revealed and/or brought before the courts), *best* administrative *practices* and the strategic guidelines a country uses to cope with its indigenous corruption. Courakis and Mannnozzi (2013, 11–12) believe that a *multifactorial corruption index* (MCI), based on up-to-date and comparable data, as well as on cross-referenced facts would be more representative and objective and, consequently, more accurate and ultimately fair to the countries in question. Cognisant of the limitations of perception studies, and due to the limited statistics on corruption and prosecution of corruption offenders, in both Cyprus and Greece, the authors will utilise various perception surveys carried out locally and internationally to demonstrate the apparent extent of corruption in both countries under review.

As concerns Cyprus, in considering corruption perception, one needs to be aware that the country has been going through a financial crisis of unprecedented proportions. In fact, Cyprus, a member of the EU and in the Eurozone, on the 25th of March 2013 the Eurogroup and IMF agreed to grant the Cyprus government €10 billion assistance and the rest of the money needed (€6.6 billion) to be taken from the depositors of the two largest banks in the island with deposits over €100,000. The Eurogroup ignored the fact that in 2010 it approved restructuring of the Greek loans which created a hole in the Cypriot banking sector of €4 billion and, interestingly enough, it also refused to accept as a guarantee for the loan the 7 trillion cubic feet energy reserves of natural gas found in the Cypriot exclusive economic zone, worth trillions of euros. Time will tell why the Eurogroup has opted for bail-in, not resorted to by the Eurogroup in the Spain, Greece, Portugal, or Ireland bailouts.

Similar financial problems, but on a larger scale, have created also in Greece an atmosphere of serious crisis and provoked the intervention, among others, of a European Commission Task Force which agreed with the Greek authorities on a Road Map for technical assistance in the field of Anti-Corruption in October 2012.[5] As a result, a National Anti-Corruption Action Plan named "Transparency" was elaborated by the Ministry of Justice, Transparency and Human Rights in

---

[4]V. Tanzi, H.R. Davoodi, *Roads to Nowhere: How Corruption in Public Investment Hurts Growth*, International Monetary Fund, 1998, p. 1.

[5]European Commision. (2012) Road Map technical assistance—for Anti Corruption. http://ec. europa.eu/commission_2010-2014/president/pdf/roadmap_en.pdf. Accessed 15 Mar 2014.

Table 1.1 Eurobarometer 2013 (EU Commission 2014e)

	EU average (%)	Greece (%)	Cyprus (%)
Corruption is a widespread problem in the country	76	99	78
Affects their daily lives	26	63	57
Favouritism and corruption hamper business competition	69	80	79
There is corruption at regional and local level	77	95	84
The only way to succeed in business is to have political connections	56	74	88
Entrepreneurs believe that bribery and the use of connections are often the easiest way to obtain a public service	73	93	85
In the past 12 months they were asked or expected to pay a bribe	4	7	3
Business people believe that corruption is a problem for their company when doing business	43	66	64
Patronage and nepotism are obstacles to business	41	67	47
The only way to succeed in business is through political connections	56	74	83
Close links between business and politics lead to corruption	84	90	90
Did not report a corruption case	74	87	88
Shadow economy (% of 2012 GDP)[a]	15	24	26

[a]European Commission (2014a–f). Shadow economy and undeclared work. http://ec.europa.eu/europe2020/pdf/themes/07_shadow_economy.pdf. Accessed 6 Feb 2014

January 2013[6] and a National Anti-Corruption Coordinator together with a Coordination Committee and an Advisory Board were appointed in June 2013 (Law Nr. 4152/2013, Paragraph IG).

> The Global Corruption Barometer (2013) survey has found that Cyprus has high perceived corruption in political parties, parliament/legislature and police. In Greece the three institutions with the highest perceived corruption level were political parties, media and parliament/legislature in this order. It was also found that 19 % of the Cypriot respondents had paid a bribe whereas in Greece it was 22 %.

Two *Eurobarometer surveys (2014)* (EU Commission 2014a, e) were carried out in preparation for the EU Anti-Corruption Report. A summary of the findings is provided in Table 1.1 and these demonstrate that in both countries there is a

---

[6]Ministry of Justice, General Secretariat for Transparency and Human Rights. (2013). Transparency National Anti-Corruption Action. http://www.ministryofjustice.gr/site/LinkClick.aspx?fileticket=KyH_7RZiUPg%3D&tabid=64. Accessed 15 Mar 2014.

perception that there is corruption and it is a widespread problem. It is alarming that there is a perception that there are close links between business and politics which lead to corruption. However, it is interesting to note that only 7 % of the respondents in Greece and 3 % in Cyprus said that in the past 12 months "they were asked or expected to pay a bribe" and, besides, that a huge majority of 87 % in Greece and 88 % in Cyprus "did not report a corruption case"!

A similar picture presented by the perception surveys is found in the Quality of Government (QoG) (University of Gothenburg 2010, 10) report which has demonstrated the level and relevance of the differences in QoG and corruption across the EU. It is stated in the report that "European countries have not shown a clear improvement in their levels of quality of government in the last two decades". The Scandinavian countries have for years been showing low corruption—high government effectiveness and bureaucratic quality and the rule of law is perceived to be very high. By contrast, Italy, France, Spain, Portugal, Greece tend to present significantly lower levels of quality of government. The quality of government ranking by the University of Gothenburg (Sweden) for the 27 EU countries is in 4 categories and details are provided in Table 1.2:

- Government Effectiveness
- Control of Corruption
- Rule of Law
- Voice and accountability.

Despite the fact that the above report is 3 years old and related to 2008, it can be argued that little improvement has taken place at least for the two countries in question, Cyprus and Greece. In particular, the pillar relating to control of corruption covered the following areas: (a) corruption in public schools, (b) corruption in public health, (c) bribery paid in return for health services, (d) bribery paid to obtain public services. Finland, Denmark, Sweden show high scores of corruption's control, whereas Greece, Romania and Bulgaria relatively low scores. These rankings have not changed if one were to compare them to the CPI index. Krambia-Kapardis (2014, 48) has demonstrated that there is a close association between scores derived by CPI and QoG ranking with r(27)-0.94, p < 0.01.

The *Corruption Perceptions Index (CPI)*, published by Transparency International, has been used by authors (Holmberg et al. 2009) and professional organisations (e.g. the Basel governance organisation), as the established source in determining corruption risk and is an acceptable measure of ranking countries as to their perceived public sector corruption. Transparency International ranks the countries according to their corruption perception levels but no insights are provided as to what the problem areas are, the aetiology of corruption and the profile of the corruption offender. Since 1995, Transparency International has been carrying out a corruption perception study (CPI) in 180 countries. It aggregates 13 different sources of corruption related data produced by the World Bank, World Justice Project, the African Development bank, the Economist Intelligence Unit and other. A country is included in the index if it is reviewed by at least three sources. The lower the CPI

Table 1.2 Quality of Government

Government effectiveness	Control of corruption	Rule of law	Voice and accountability	QoG combined rank
1. Denmark	1. Finland	1. Denmark	1. Sweden	1. Denmark
2. Sweden	2. Denmark	2. Austria	2. Netherlands	2. Sweden
3. Finland	3. Sweden	3. Sweden	3. Luxembourg	3. Finland
4. Netherlands	4. Netherlands	4. Finland	4. Denmark	4. Netherlands
5. Austria	5. Luxembourg	5. Luxembourg	5. Finland	5. Luxembourg
6. United Kingdom	6. Austria	6. Netherlands	6. Ireland	6. Austria
7. Germany	7. Germany	7. Ireland	7. Belgium	7. Germany
8. Luxembourg	8. Ireland	8. Germany	8. Austria	8. United Kingdom
9. France	9. United Kingdom	9. United Kingdom	9. Germany	9. Ireland
10. Ireland	10. France	10. Malta	10. United Kingdom	10. France
11. Belgium	11. Belgium	11. France	11. France	11. Belgium
12. Malta	12. Spain	12. Belgium	12. Malta	12. Malta
13. Cyprus	13. Portugal	13. Spain	13. Portugal	13. Spain
14. Estonia	14. Cyprus	14. Cyprus	14. Spain	14. Portugal
15. Portugal	15. Malta	15. Portugal	15. Estonia	15. Cyprus
16. Czech Republic	16. Slovenia	16. Estonia	16. Czech Republic	16. Estonia
17. Slovenia	17. Estonia	17. Slovenia	17. Slovenia	17. Slovenia
18. Spain	18. Hungary	18. Czech Republic	18. Hungary	18. Czech Republic
19. Slovakia	19. Slovakia	19. Hungary	19. Cyprus	19. Lithuania
20. Hungary	20. Poland	20. Greece	20. Italy	20. Hungary
21. Lithuania	21. Czech Republic	21. Lithuania	21. Slovakia	21. Slovakia
22. Latvia	22. Latvia	22. Latvia	22. Greece	22. Greece
23. Greece	23. Lithuania	23. Poland	23. Latvia	23. Latvia
24. Poland	24. Italy	24. Slovakia	24. Poland	24. Poland
25. Italy	25. Greece	25. Italy	25. Lithuania	25. Italy
26. Bulgaria	26. Romania	26. Romania	26. Bulgaria	26. Bulgaria
27. Romania	27. Bulgaria	27. Bulgaria	27. Romania	27. Romania

Source Data comes from the World Bank Governance Indicators (Kaufman et al. 2009—Cited by Quality of Government 2010, 23)

rank, the lower the perceived corruption in a country. In the 2013 CPI index Cyprus was ranked 31st and Greece as 80th out of over 180 countries, in the global rank and 16th and 31st (respectively) in the EU regional rank.[7] Cyprus has had a drop of two positions while Greece had managed to recover the position it had 3 years ago from 80th to 94th and back to 80th in 2013. Denmark and New Zealand shared the first position in 2013 as the countries with the lower perceived corruption levels whilst Afghanistan, Korea, Somalia last with the highest perceived corruption levels.

1.3 Corruption Perception Surveys (Cyprus)

Transparency International Cyprus (TI-C) has been administering an annual corruption perception survey since 2010, in an effort to raise awareness and capacity building on corruption issues. Utilising the corruption perception survey, Krambia-Kapardis (2013) suggested an anti-corruption measures strategy plan for the new elected government in an effort to decrease corruption and regain public confidence as well as indicate to the Eurogroup and IMF that corruption can be addressed. Regarding *methodology*, the Cyprus public opinion survey (Transparency International Cyprus 2013) reported in this paper was administered in September–December 2012 and covered 953 respondents. Questionnaires were distributed during the same months and the same places as in the 2010 and 2011 surveys, i.e. in all major towns, and some rural areas, in shopping malls, in main shopping streets and car-parks of courts and hospitals, as well as sent to the members of the Institute of Certified Public Accountants in an effort to attract professionals as well as laymen, doctors, lawyers etc. In Cyprus, all the age groups were represented in the study as follows: 18–30 year old (39 %), 31–40 (21 %), 41–50 year old (19 %), 51–60 (13 %) and 61+ (8 %). The vast majority (61 %) are university graduates, depicting the high educational standard of Cypriots. Women comprised 49 % of the respondents. As far as the place of employment is concerned, 50 % worked in the private sector, 26 % in the public and semi government sector and the rest were not working.

A list of research questions addressed in this paper is provided below to present the *survey findings* and to develop a profile of corruption in Cyprus over a 3 year period in an effort to identify the most suitable anti-corruption measures:

1. Is there corruption and what is its perceived extent in Cyprus?
2. What factors underpin corruption?
3. What is the profile/position of corrupt professionals?
4. How effective are the anti-corruption measures available?
5. Who ought to have the responsibility of combating corruption?

---

[7]Transparency International (2013). Corruption Perception Index 2013. http://www.transparency.org/cpi2013/results. Accessed 15 Mar 2014.

Regarding the first research question, most (91 %) of the Cypriot respondents believed that corruption is a major problem, it exists at national (85 %) and local (82 %) level and it will get worse due to the economic crisis (79 %). In fact, a large majority (77 %) stated that over the last 3 years they believe corruption has increased and that corruption is inevitable (73 %). It is worth noting that corruption is perceived as a major problem, increased from the previous earlier surveys (it was 70 % in 2010 and 86 % in 2011). This finding is an indication of people's increasing awareness of the corruption phenomenon and the need to be adequately addressed. Concerning the second research question, the etiology of corruption in Cyprus, the respondents blamed: (a) the politicians for not doing enough to fight corruption (88 %), (b) the lack of punitive actions (87 %), (c) lack of meritocracy (87 %), (d) the fact that corruption has become part of everyday life (87 %), (e) the lack of law enforcement by the authorities (85 %) and, finally, (f) the close link between business and politics (80 %).

As far as the third research question is concerned, Table 1.3 shows that the general public considers politicians at national level to be the most corrupt (96 %), followed by officials awarding public tenders (94 %), officials at regional level (93 %), officials at local level (93 %) and police (93 %). It is also worth noting that the category of individuals who have had the biggest increase in perceptions of corruption has been the people working in the local and regional sector (i.e. local councils) and the health sector. It is believed that the 'tone at the top' needs to be set by the politicians who are the 'archon' of a community and the rest of the citizens will follow. Thus, trust-building measures ought to concentrate on politicians at national, regional and local level.

Table 1.3 Profile of the corrupt professional—(Cyprus)

Profile of the corrupt professional	2010	2011	2012
Politicians at national level	90	93	96
Officials awarding public tenders	90	92	94
Officials issuing building permits	87	83	90
Officials at regional level	88	80	93
Officials at local level	88	81	93
People working in the police service	92	90	93
Inspectors (health, construction, food, quality, health permits)	82	80	85
Officials issuing professional services	82	77	85
People working in the judicial licenses	74	71	77
People working for the custom service	86	79	84
People working in the public health sector	83	82	89
People working in the public educational services	79	76	82
People working in the private health services	72	71	76
People working in the private educational services	67	69	70

Table 1.4 Anti-corruption measures

Anti-corruption measures	2010	2011	2012
Impartial application of the law	87	74	87
Quicker trials and decision on sentences	89	83	89
Enforce stringent punishments	82	75	82
Implement asset disclosure	81	76	85
Organize campaigns against corruption	65	55	68
Create an independent commission against corruption	73	65	76
Improve the legal framework for detection, prevention and punishment of corruption	86	80	89
Implement harsh punishment for those receiving bribery	*	87	88
Implement harsh punishment for those giving bribery	*	87	81
Implement a code of conduct for civil servants	*	70	70
Introduce a subject on anti-corruption in elementary schooling	*	71	77
Enact a whistleblowing protection legislation	*	79	81
Improve transparency and supervision of political party funding	*	*	88
Improve transparency of funding of organizations	*	*	84

*Questions not posed in the annual survey

In reference to the fourth research question and as illustrated in Table 1.4, it appears that the respondents believe that the legal framework needs to be improved as far as detection, investigation, and the courts are concerned. It is a well-known fact that criminal cases in Cyprus can take on average up to 1 year to be decided by the courts. In addition, reform of the criminal code, the law of evidence and criminal procedure in Cyprus is long overdue.

The final research question addressed the issue of who ought to have the responsibility for combating corruption. The vast majority (89 %) believe the government ought to shoulder that responsibility, followed by the political parties (87 %) and the police (84 %). Over two-thirds (69 %) believe the EU institutions should take up this responsibility to encourage national governments to enact legislation and implement measures to combat corruption. Let us next take a look at corruption perception in Greece.

1.4 Corruption Perception Surveys (Greece)

Transparency International Greece (TI-G) has been elaborating an annual national perception survey since 2007. The Greek public opinion survey 2013 reported in this paper was administered in 2013 and covered a total of 12,108 telephone interviews from all over Greece. Information about the demographics of the respondents to the Greek survey (Transparency International Greece 2012) is, unfortunately, not available. However, since 2011 there are data concerning persons who have been personally victims of corruption, even only once in the past (a percentage of 20.6 % of the 2013 survey's respondents). It is believed that this is a representative sample as is the Cypriot study. The vast majority of these victims are males, with an average age of around 50 years old, having a job and a higher education. Due to a decrease in household disposable income and the anti-corruption campaigns organized by tax authorities and NGOs, petty corruption in Greece appears to have been reduced by 15 %. In addition, State controls in the public and private sectors have become more intense and have thus also contributed to the curbing of corruption. Incidents of corruption take place primarily in the public sector (76.7 %). More people in 2013 (in comparison to 2012) have denied having paid bribes (29.6 %) to the public sector and (33 %) to the private sector. Besides, only 5.6 % of the respondents could mention incidents of corruption in public sector (e.g. hospitals, tax services and construction-licensing bodies). On the other hand, as concerns the private sector, the amount of corruption's incidents is even smaller, i.e. only 1.9 %, mainly in private hospitals. The average bribe paid out, according to the survey, was €1,226 in the public and €1,333 in the private sector.

Regarding other surveys and research on corruption in Greece, firstly, there is the research "Crime and Culture: *the Relevance of Perceptions of Corruption to Crime Prevention*", as a part of a more general project coordinated by the University of Konstanz, conducted in Greece by Professor Effi Lambropoulou (Panteion University) between January 2006 and July 2009, examining the perception of political and administrative decision makers and representation of various institutions and authorities, as a "bottom-up" procedure. The main finding of this research is that the official perception of corruption in Greece is not considerably different from the corresponding reports of international organizations, such as Transparency International, OECD and World Bank (Lambropoulou 2013, 4 and 85 ff). Furthermore, a survey on the attitudes of Greek university students towards corruption in relation to the economic crisis was conducted in 2011 by Professor Calliope Spinelli (University of Athens) and a more recent (unpublished) survey carried out in 2014 by Professor Nestor Courakis (University of Athens). According to Spinelli (2014) 68 % of the students attribute the country's economic crisis to corruption and 63 % to politicians in general. In addition, for more than 50 % of the respondents there is "considerable" or "a lot" of corruption within the Police, the City Planning Office, the Public Health Services and the Taxation Offices. Interestingly enough, the majority of the respondents (73 %) state that those who are involved in active petty bribery for health reasons should not be punished. On the contrary, almost 90 % of the students were of the opinion that both civil servants and businessmen engaged in bribery concerning public works should be punished (Spinelli 2014).

On the other hand, according to the results of the Courakis survey, 58 % of the respondents stated they would never pay a bribe in order that their case could be handled by a civil servant in a more "favorable" or speedy manner. Furthermore, the respondents considered both petty corruption and grand corruption as almost equally serious (49.2 and 48.7 % respectively). The economic crisis and austerity measures, which have diminished people's income, were given by 50 % of the respondents as the reason for the decrease in petty corruption. This is in line with the findings from Transparency International Greece (2012). Other explanations for the decrease in petty corruption have been found to be: (a) that acts of corruption are not ethically correct, (b) there has been a change in the way political leaders and judges address corruption, and (c) corrupt transactions are humiliating for those implicated. The respondents in the Courakis survey identified education from as early as kindergarten until and including the university years to be the most successful corruption prevention measure. Meritocracy in selecting and promoting civil servants is another measure suggested as being effective in preventing corruption. Furthermore, the respondents stated the following additional measures in combating corruption: (a) strict implementation of corruption laws irrespective of who the accused is; (b) arrest and conviction of laws transgressors; (c) avoidance of complicated bureaucratic and legislative procedures; (d) severe punishment; (e) raise awareness on anti-corruption through campaigns; and, finally, (f) implementation of e-governance and the so-called Centers for Serving the Citizen, i.e. state agencies which function as intermediaries between public services and citizens in preventing direct contact of civil servants and citizens in corrupt vulnerable public departments.

1.5   Legislative Framework: Greece

Concerning its legal framework against corruption, Greece has signed and promulgated into laws with increased formal validity (Article 28, Paragraph 1, of the Greek Constitution) all important international and European Conventions, as well as their Additional Protocols against corruption. In particular, Greece has given full legal force to the OECD, EU, and Council of Europe and United Nations conventions.[8] In addition, Greece has brought her national legislation in line with that provided by the aforementioned legal instruments, given that this interior legislation is based on the 'typical' provisions on active and passive bribery (Article 236 and 235 of the Criminal Code, as amended by art. One, Para IE.5 of Law-Nr. 4254/2014):

> (i)   Article 236, 'Active Bribery', provides and punishes in principle the case of a person who promises or offers to an official, either directly or through the mediation of a third party, any kind of benefits for himself/herself or for a third party, for

---

[8]Among these conventions, the following can be particularly mentioned: The Organization for Economic Co-operation and Development (OECD) Convention on Combating Bribery of Foreign Public Officials in International Business Transactions of 17.12.1997 (Law-Number 2656/1998); the European Community's Convention on Combating Bribery of Foreign Public Officials in International Business Transactions of 26.5.1997 (Greek Law Number 2802/2000); the Council of Europe's two Conventions on Corruption in Criminal Law and in Civil Law of 27.1.1999 and of 22.7.2003 respectively (Greek Law-Numbers 3560/2007 and 2957/2001); and also, the United Nations' Convention against Corruption of 31.10.2003 (Greek Law-Number 3666/2008).

future or already completed act or omission on his/her part which pertains to his/her duties or is contrary to them. The penalty for the said offence is: 1–5 years of imprisonment, also incarceration of 5–10 years if the value of the benefits is more than 120.000 €.

(ii) Article 235, 'Passive Bribery', has to do with the case of *an* official *who, in contravention of his/her duties, asks for or receives*, either directly or through the mediation of a third party, for himself/herself or for a third party, any kind of benefits or accepts the promise thereof, for future or already completed act or omission on his/her part the penalty is imprisonment of 1–5 years and, in case that the value of the benefits is more than 120.000 € or the person involved is civil servant at the Ministry of Finance, incarceration of 5–10 years.

(iii) Apart from these, there are also provisions for specific cases, i.e. when bribery is committed in favor of:

- a judge or a referee (Article 237 of the Criminal Code, punished as a felony);
- the Prime Minister, a member of the government, or the heads of Prefecture or Municipality for whatever kind of benefits and the members of Parliament or of Prefecture or Municipality in relation to their duties or member of Parliament etc. in relation to elections and votes. The same penalty is provided for members of the European Commission or of European Parliament (Article 159 of the Criminal Code, according to which these offenses are punished as a felony). Furthermore, a penalty of incarceration of 5–10 years and a fine of €15,000–150,000 is provided for persons who, within this framework, commit an active bribery (Article 159A);
- a member of the European Parliament and/or to functionaries, judges et cetera, of member-states, of international or, supranational organizations,[9] as well as when foreign officials (for example judges) are bribed by a legal person engaged in international business transactions.[10]

Furthermore, the provisions on bribery are equally applicable to cases of private-to-private bribery, mainly by virtue of Article 5 Law-Number 3560/2007. Finally, the related case of "trading in influence" is also punishable in Greece, principally on the basis of an old Law, Number 5227/1931 on intermediaries, but, also, on the basis of Article 6, Law Number 3560/2007 and Article 16, Law Number 3666/2008 (Courakis and Mannozzi 2013, 16–17). Finally, concerning the control and sanctioning mechanisms for politicians' offences (mainly for ministers and members of Parliament in particular), these are very limited, thus allowing them frequently to shelter under the umbrella of a 'scandalous' immunity. In fact, although every year since 1964, MP's and ministers have been obliged to submit a declaration regarding their assets, in practice there has been no control or verification of it until recently when, according to Article 56 of Law-Number 3979/2011, these declarations must henceforth be uploaded on the internet.

---

[9]Articles 3, 4 of Greek Law-Number 2802/2002 and Articles 3, 4 of Greek Law-Number 3560/2007.

[10]Article 2 of Greek Law-Number 2656/1998, as it was replaced by Article 9, of Greek Law-Number 3090/2002.

On the other hand, when a politician in Greece commits a crime, even a serious one, he/she does not have to follow the procedure foreseen for similar cases by the Greek justice system. This happens primarily because of the existing distinctly short prescriptions and secondly, because the Hellenic Parliament is the only organ which is deemed competent to exercise penal prosecution against its own members. It should be noted here that, as a rule, such prosecution is avoided due to a tendency of politicians to protect their own as a manifestation of an "esprit-de-corps". Nonetheless, this practice has already been roundly condemned by the European Court of Human Rights (cf. Syngelides v. Greece, 11.2.2010), as it violates the elemental principle of equal treatment before Justice, and, furthermore, it has been disputed repeatedly by GRECO (cf. Paragraph 5.1 GRECO Evaluation III, Rep. (2009) 9E, Theme II). As a result, a draft of law was promulgated and enacted as Law Number 3961/2011.[11] This Law attempts to correct some of these incongruities and extravagances, allocating more responsibilities to the judicial power pertaining to the control of politicians' offenses. Yet, the amendments are restrictive, since the whole issue is regulated directly by the Greek Constitution (Articles 61–62 and 86 of the Greek Constitution[12]), which cannot be revised in the near

---

[11]See also Law Number 4022/2011 concerning the acceleration of the procedure in cases of state officials and ministers or MP's.

[12]*Article 61 of the Greek Constitution*: (a) A Member of Parliament shall not be prosecuted or in any way interrogated for an opinion expressed or a vote cast by him in the discharge of his parliamentary duties, (b) A Member of Parliament may be prosecuted only for libel, according to the law, after leave has been granted by Parliament. The Court of Appeals shall be competent to hear the case. Such leave is deemed to be conclusively denied if Parliament does not decide within 45 days from the date the charges have been submitted to the Speaker. In case of refusal to grant leave or if the time-limit lapses without action, no charge can be brought for the act committed by the Member of Parliament, (c) This paragraph shall be applicable as of the next parliamentary session—A Member of Parliament shall not be liable to testify on information given to him or supplied by him in the course of the discharge of his duties, or on the persons who entrusted the information to him or to whom he supplied such information.

Article 62 of the Greek Constitution: During the parliamentary term the Members of Parliament shall not be prosecuted, arrested, imprisoned or otherwise confined without prior leave granted by Parliament. Likewise, a member of a dissolved Parliament shall not be prosecuted for political crimes during the period between the dissolution of Parliament and the declaration of the election of the members of the new Parliament. Leave shall be deemed not granted if Parliament does not decide within three months of the date the request for prosecution by the public prosecutor was transmitted to the Speaker. The three month limit is suspended during the Parliament's recess. No leave is required when Members of Parliament are caught in the act of committing a felony.

Article 86 of the Greek Constitution: (a) Parliament shall have the right to prefer charges on serving or former members of the Cabinet and Undersecretaries before an ad hoc court, according to the statutes on the liability of Ministers. This court is presided by the President of the Supreme Civil and Criminal Court and shall be composed of twelve judges chosen by lot by the Speaker of Parliament in public sitting from among the members of the Supreme Civil and Criminal Court and the Presidents of Civil and Criminal Courts of Appeal who held office prior to the accusation, as specified by statute; (b) Prosecution, judicial inquiry or preliminary judicial inquiry of the persons specified in paragraph (a) for actions or omissions committed during the discharge of their duties shall not be permitted without a prior resolution of Parliament. If in the course of an administrative inquiry evidence should arise which may establish responsibility of a member of the Cabinet or an

future; besides, its revision is a competence of the ministers and members of Parliament themselves—a case-in-point regarding conflict of interest, or as Juvenal remarked millennia ago, 'Who watches the watchers? (Quis custodiet ipsos custodies? Juvenal, Satire VI, lines 347–8).

1.6   Legislative Framework: Cyprus

Cyprus is signatory to a number of international anti-corruption conventions and joined the Group of States against Corruption of the Council of Europe in 1999. Conventions against corruption which have been ratified by the Republic of Cyprus have been: in 2000 the Council of Europe Criminal law Convention on Corruption, in 2004 the Council of Europe Civil Law Convention on Corruption, in 2006 the Additional Protocol to the Criminal Law Convention, and in 2008 the United Nations Convention Against Corruption. Inter alia, as a result of ratifying the aforementioned conventions: both active and passive bribery has been criminalised; at a national level the co-operation of various public officials in the fight against corruption has become possible as has co-operation between the competent authorities in the Member States; the remedy of financial compensation has become available to persons who suffer damage as a consequence of acts of corruption by public officials and initiate legal against a person or the State; and, finally, employees who report in good faith their suspicions of corruption in the public and private sector are offered protection. Active and passive bribery of public officials as specified in Sect. 1.4 of Law No. 23(III)/2000 are punishable with imprisonment for up to 7 years and or a fine of up to €17,000.

The Prevention of Corruption Law (Cap 161), introduced when Cyprus was a British colony, provides for up to 2 years' imprisonment and/or a fine independently of the context in which corruption occurs and, interestingly enough, the custodial sentence provided goes up to 7 years' and/or a fine if the is related to 'a contract or a proposal for a contract with the State or any Government Department or any public body or a sub-contract to execute any work provided in such a contract. The Criminal Code, which in large part also dates back to colonial times, includes a number of corruption-related offences, including extortion, false claims, abuse of office and the receipt of property by public officials in order to show favour and, also, the pursuit in certain circumstances of private interests by public officials.

(Footnote 12 continued)

Undersecretary in accordance with the provisions of the statute on the liability of Ministers, those in charge of the inquiry shall, after its termination, forward the evidence to Parliament through the competent Public Prosecutor. Only Parliament shall be entitled to suspend criminal prosecution; (c) Should the procedure on a motion against a Minister or Undersecretary be discontinued for any reason whatsoever, including the lapse of prescribed limitation, Parliament may, at the request of the accused person, decide the establishment of a Special Committee of Members of Parliament and senior judicial functionaries to investigate the charges, as specified by the Standing Orders.

The illegal acquisition of property by be senior public officials (including the President of the republic, Ministers, members of Parliament, judges, all the independent government officials (e.g., Attorney General, Ombudsman, Auditor General, General Accountant etc.), mayors, Chief and Assistant Chief of Police and of the National Guard became an offence with the Illicit Enrichment of Certain Public Officials Law 51(1)/2004. The same law also provides for the confiscation of assets that have been acquired by the senior public officials concerned by violating the provisions of the said law.

An important piece of legislation to tackle corruption was introduced in 1998 when corruption was made a predicate offence for the purposes of the money-laundering legislation. The law concerned was revised with the enactment of the Prevention and Fight of Money Laundering Act of 2007. Thus, somehow laundering money became an offense punishable with up to 14 years' imprisonment and/or 500,000 € fine. Earlier, in 2001, the Criminal Code was amended and under article 105A it became an offence to attempt to influence any authority, commission, collective body or member thereof, or any public officer in the performance of their duties in relation to recruitment, appointment and exercise of disciplinary powers in government agency. If found in breach of article 105A, one is liable to imprisonment of no more than 12 months or a fine of no more than 1710 €. As already mentioned above, the legal framework for the registration, financing and expenditure of political parties in Cyprus was established with Law 20(1)/2011. The Civil Servants Law prohibits civil servants from accepting gifts, travel expenses or entertainment. Similar prohibitions exist for police officers and army officers in their relevant legislation. The legal framework prohibiting bribery of foreign public officials and domestic public officials, facilitating payments, payments through intermediaries or third parties is in place through various legislations (see Neocleous et al. 2012), mentioned below.

Article 83 of the Cyprus Constitution provides for immunity to elected officials such as President, Members of Parliament and Ministers. These individuals shall not be liable to civil or criminal proceedings in respect of any statement made or vote given by them in the House of Representative. However, this has been misunderstood by the Members of Parliament and they refuse to even pay on-the-spot parking fines or even speeding fines. Exploiting another Article in the Constitution (Article 15) which states that every person has the right to respect the private and family life of another, politicians generally refuse to disclose their assets stating that any such legislation would be unconstitutional. Amendment of the aforementioned provisions of the Constitution is required in order to reduce the scope for corruption among politicians.

As far as implementing existing anti-corruption legislation is concerned, the Attorney General is tasked by the Constitution to do so in all criminal cases, including corruption and anti-money laundering legislation. To deal with corruption involving police personnel, there exists the police's own Professional Standards Department and the Independent Police Authority for Claims and Complaints Against the Police, established under Law 9(1)/2006. The Public Service Commission is has jurisdiction to deal with serious breaches of the Code of Ethics of

Public officials except those senior public officials appointed by the President of the Republic. The Public Service Commission's armoury of sanctions ranges from a fine to compulsory retirement or dismissal from employment. After examining the EU Anti-Corruption Report's assessment of corruption issues in Cyprus and Greece, a number of suggestions are made below in an effort to lower the corruption perception and at the same time build trust in politicians so as to promote electoral account-ability, democracy, and transparency. Without these trust-building measures, the country cannot gain the credibility of the EU member states, IMF and Eurogroup.

1.7 The EU Anti-corruption Report (EU Commission 2014b)

1.7.1 Issues Addressed in the Report Relating to Cyprus (EU Commission 2014d)

The report welcomes the 2003 decision of the Cypriot government to establish the Coordinating Body Against Corruption as well as the (a) harmonisation provisions on corruption across the criminal code and the more recent laws ratifying the OECD Criminal Law Convention on Corruption, (b) enforcement of a Code of Ethics for Public Officials published in June 2013, (c) the willingness of the candidates in the last presidential election to disclose their assets and the elected President's decision to ask his Ministerial Council to sign a Code of Conduct, (d) the enactment of the Political Parties Funding Act of 2012, and (e) the Code of Conduct prepared by the Treasury for procurement regulating conflicts of interest. Finally, the report makes a reference to the suggestion made by Transparency International—Cyprus (but ignored by the government) that there ought to be an Independent Commission Against Corruption with its own budget, to focus solely on preventing, detecting and investigating corruption. The report identifies the following weaknesses and gaps in the system: (a) there is no general legislation on access to information; (b) there is no Whistle-blower's Protection legislation; (c) there is no 'revolving door' legislation where elected or high ranking officers are employed in the private sector upon retirement without a 'cooling off' period, (d) the Political Parties Funding Legislation covers parties but not individual candidates; it contains neither separate provisions for the monitoring of finances related to election campaigns or of individual donations above a certain threshold, nor is timely and comprehensive publication of party accounts envisaged; there is no obligation to disclose the identity of donors or the amount of donations received from identified individuals and companies and an independent supervisory mechanism in respect of election candidate's income and expenditure is not implemented; (e) the Coordinating Body Against Corruption has not developed an anti-corruption strategy; (f) there is a close relationship between the business and political environment; and, finally, (g) there is no specific mechanism in place within contracting authorities to help detect potentially corrupt practices in different stages of the procurement process.

Despite the fact that the authorities had demonstrated commitment to prevent and address corruption by amending legislation and establishing the Coordinating Body Against Corruption, the small number of cases investigated, prosecuted or adjudicated indicates the need to strengthen the enforcement system and implement transparency. Therefore, a number of recommendations are made: (a) the strengthening of the disciplinary regime for public servants and streamlining procedures to ensure effective investigation of corruption within the police, (b) the provision of an institution with the necessary powers for the effective coordination of an anti-corruption policies, (c) introducing codes of conduct for elected and appointed officials for them to declare assets periodically and to disclose potential conflicts of interest, (d) lowering the threshold for donations to political parties, limiting the ability of state-owned companies to sponsor political events, regulating donations to election candidates and campaigns, obliging parties to publish their financial statements and accounts online (including the identity of donors), and establishing external supervision of election candidates income and expenditure; and (e) developing uniform and effective tools to prevent and detect corruption in public procurement at national and local level, including internal and external control mechanisms and risk management tools within contracting authorities.

1.7.2   Issues Addressed in the Report Relating to Greece (EU Commission 2014c)

The Commission points out numerous times in the report that Greece is committed under the Memorandum of Understanding on Economic and Financial Policies to institute effective anti-corruption policies, reform the judiciary and the public administration, public procurement, and to implement an anti-fraud strategy for EU co-funded projects. A number of measures and actions taken thus far in Greece in an effort to combat corruption are: (a) the transposing of all provisions concerning the definition of active and passive corruption in the public sector; (b) the drafting of legislation on comprehensive arrangements for the protection of whistle-blowers; (c) the development of the anti-corruption strategy; (d) the appointment of the national anti-corruption coordinator; (e) the adoption in 2010 of the law placing all public institutions under the obligation to publish their decisions relating to public procurement online; (f) the adoption of the civil service code; (g) in relation to political party financing, the appointment of a committee on expenditure control and election violations set up within Parliament including MPs from all parties and three magistrates; (h) asset disclosure of elected politicians is publicly available; and (i) setting-up a health supplies price watch, and introduction of electronic prescriptions and the centralisation of healthcare procurement.

The weaknesses or gaps identified in the Greek chapter of the EU Anti-Corruption Report are: (a) there are several areas in which Greece falls short of implementing the OECD Anti-Bribery Convention, in particular the country's limited ability to detect foreign bribery cases; (b) lobbying is not regulated in

Greece; (c) Greek media is vulnerable to potential undue pressure; (d) the internal control mechanisms within the civil service have proven ineffective, causing considerable backlogs in the system; (e) GRECO's recommendations on financing of political party relating to the need to: reinforce guarantees for tracing donations; ensure that loans are not used to circumvent party financing regulations; reinforce records and the transparency of party accounts; ensure independent auditing of political parties; strengthen independence, efficiency and transparency of the Control Committee tasked with the supervision of party and electoral campaign funding; enhance the monitoring of financial documents; and enhance the reporting and sanctioning mechanisms; (f) there are no ethical codes applicable to elected officials at central and local level; (g) MPs can be prosecuted or arrested only with prior approval of Parliament; and (h) ministers and former ministers benefit from an extensive statute of limitations regime.

A number of suggestions were made by the Commission to the Greek authorities in an effort to combat corruption, namely: (a) clientelism and favouritism in public administration require a more vigorous response; (b) ensure sufficient powers and support to enable the national anti-corruption coordinator to implement anti-corruption policies; (c) strengthen the supervision of party funding and the independence, efficiency and transparency of the Control Committee; (d) ensure a professional independent verification mechanism for asset declarations of high-level elected and appointed officials; (e) take steps to eliminate immunities; (f) reform the statute of limitations; and (g) enhance the oversight of public procurement.

1.8 General Anti-corruption Suggestions on the Basis of the Causes of Corruption: The Case of Greece

The Causes of Corruption

Whilst the measures noted above are rather specific and possible, they do not address the tone at the top. As Ashiku (2011) states, "politicians have turned political parties into their own personal instruments" (2011, 115). Thus, efforts ought to increase the levels of trust and faith the general public has in politicians and the ability of the "state and the market institutions to reliably and impartially enforce law and the rules of trade" (Anokhin and Schulze 2009, 465). In fact, Rose-Ackerman (2004) and Anokhin and Schulze (2009) argue that "the control of corruption and development of institutionalized trust plays a key role in creating an institutional context in which entrepreneurship and innovation can flourish" (2009, 486). The suggestions made in this paper aim at regaining the trust and confidence of the local and EU stakeholders at times of serious financial crisis caused by lack of transparency and accountability over the years.

Concerning the *causes of corruption* (Courakis and Mannozzi 2013) and taking into account that corruption implies violation of duties by functionaries for their personal benefit, it is evident that it can be favored or facilitated especially in societies and countries where:

a. There exists in society a more general "climate" of tolerance towards corruption, as a result of an individualistic mentality and materialist orientation which gives priority to consumer goods and underestimates social or moral values.
b. There are legal provisions which are complicated and need to be interpreted by officials or provisions which are unnecessary and create delays when they are applied. Furthermore, functionaries in certain areas of policy domains, have a wide field of discretionary power to interpret legal provisions.
c. Officials in certain areas of policy domains are not the ones solely responsible to take decisions and to sign an act, so that they can sometimes feel free to ask for direct or indirect economic benefits in view of offering services to another person (for example, in view of issuing a license).
d. Officials are appointed and/or promoted to a position of the public sector not on the basis of a meritocratic system of selection, but according to criteria of nepotism and favoritism, being therefore dependent on politicians and on clientele-relations and having, consequently, a predisposition for trading in influence and even for corruption.
e. There is direct contact between officials and private persons involved which facilitates clientele-like practices.
f. There is lack of transparency at the level of formulation of administrative acts, so that it is not easy to find out which ones are being promoted by the government. This situation can evidently favor an atmosphere of arbitrariness and immunity and arbitrariness on the part of the functionaries and can offer, as a result, opportunities for corruption.
g. There is lack of trustworthy and well-coordinated mechanisms of control and of law-enforcement and, as a result, legal provisions are ineffectively applied.

Measures taken by Greece to combat corruption are:

a. Concerning the more general climate of tolerance towards corruption, which appears mainly in individualistic and consumer-oriented societies, it can be said that such a climate is not unknown in modern Greece.[13] In particular, the average citizen in Greece does frequently tolerate situations of corruption in the belief that promoting their own personal interests is a priority. As a consequence, some Greeks may purport that, in order to achieve this individualistic objective, it is indispensable to have good relations (i.e. 'incentive corruption') with politicians, and even more so to enable trafficking with functionaries. Surely this mentality is not only a Greek phenomenon but is widespread all over developed countries. The cardinal difference is that in Greece the climate of implicit rather than explicit tolerance towards corruption is fomented by a strong bureaucratic system, which causes serious hardships to citizens and dominates

---

[13]This fact is also corroborated by the results of the Transparency International Global Corruption Barometer (GCB). http://www.transparency.org/policy_research/surveys_indices/gcb/2010.

almost every domain and facet of their life. To overturn this negative climate that affects citizens, politicians and functionaries alike, is something which requires considerable effort at various levels, but mainly in schools and other educational institutions.

b. Regarding the problem of complicated legal provisions and excessive formalism in law, which leave officials wide discretionary power for interpretation, according to the 'needs' and 'wants' of each specific transaction, it can be noted that this also is a more general problem, i.e. it affects, not only Greece, but equally every developed country which tries to cope, by means of its legislation, with complicated social and economic situations in a global yet also detailed way. Concerning Greece, in many cases of existing legislation there are provisions which are contradictory, or cover the same material in a different way, and are, thus, in need of interpretation—this happens in particular when tax legislation and town-planning legislation must be enforced. A solution could be the promulgation of concrete and clear directives, by means of circulars, through the internet and printed materials, as to how a solid interpretation of these provisions can be attained for all cases (for instance, there already exists legislation which provides 'objective criteria' or a commonly-accepted formula, on *how* to justly estimate the value of a real estate, in order to juxtapose the analogous tax levy in certain areas of policy domains, instead of allowing the competent official wide discretionary power to interpret the legal provisions.[14]). Similarly, concrete legislation could be enacted, aimed at accelerating and simplifying some sluggish bureaucratic procedures and to clarify the rights and entitlements of citizens. Such an undeviating legislation would additionally specify more transparently and accurately the proper conditions for public tenders. However, apart from these solutions, which could be manipulated on occasion by a shrewd functionary capable of finding a way to exploit the Law's weaknesses and loopholes, it would be equally advisable, as it is mentioned below, to clearly separate the officials from the implicated private persons, in order to remove the opportunity to trade influence and/or to enact illicit transactions through this contact.

c. Regarding the problems arising from the diffusion of responsibilities, it is evident that it would be necessary for the state to establish a clear job-description for each official and in particular to empower a designated functionary as responsible for having to sign a license or a certificate. In Greece there exist 'Regulations of Services' for each public agency which fail, however, to describe the clear-cut duties of each functionary in detail, except for those who are heads of units. Additionally, there are also steps being taken to reduce the necessary signatures needed for the enforcement of an administrative act. Needless to say that such a restriction of responsibilities and consequent reduction of signatures would also diminish the delays of any bureaucratic procedure which plagues the system and citizens alike.

---

[14]Cf. Article 41 of Law-Number 1249/1982 and Article 14 of Law-Number 1473/1984.

d. Concerning the case of functionaries being appointed and/or promoted to a public position as an eventual result of nepotism and/or of political clientele favoritism, it must be said that since 1994 (Law Number 2190/1994) initial access and appointments to public service in Greece are mainly realized according to a system of written competition, also known as A.S.E.P. (i.e. Α.Σ.Ε.Π.) for a number of administrative positions. By virtue of this system, the names of the candidates on their essays are concealed, so that the examiners and evaluators are not in a position to know the identity of each candidate and to thenceforth, illicitly promote some of them (by giving them better marks for example). More recently, the system of written examinations was supplemented by the provision (Law-Number 3320/2205) of a verbal interview assessing the personal capabilities of each candidate; that addendum, however, made room for subjective, preferential and, thus, unsustainable evaluations. Most probably that was the reason that the above provision was later abolished (cf. Law-Number 3812/2009). From a general point of view, the A.S.E.P. System has been credited as meritocratic as far as access to the civil service is concerned and no serious complaints against it have been raised until now. On the other hand, the system of promotions to a higher position in the public sector has sufficient formal guarantees to be considered as one which is based on objective evaluations. For example, the evaluation committee for high-ranked officials especially General Directors of Ministries, until recently was presided by an ex-judge. Nowadays, in accordance to Law-Number 3839/2010, the system has been further improved, as it was placed under the responsibility of ASEP and Ombudsman. Both systems, however, suffer from formalism and, thus, cannot be considered to be a sufficient guarantee against corruption.

e. Concerning the problem of direct contacts between functionaries and implicated private persons, it is noteworthy that since 2002 there have existed offices of the State and of Municipalities which are called "Centres for Serving Citizens" (i.e. Κ.Ε.Π in Greek, or K.E.P. in English), and which function as intermediaries between public services and citizens. So, if a citizen needs a certificate, he or she can directly address the request to a K.E.P. which is in close proximity, instead of going to the public service division concerned. In this way, there is no contact between a citizen and a public functionary who might ask for a bribe in order for instance to 'accelerate' the issuing of a certificate. It is evident that this system could be expanded to, also, cover cases of issuing a license from a town-planning agency, or to cases of making an arrangement with a tax-agency on outstanding claims of taxes, given that these cases (together with the cases of bribe-money in hospitals) are the main categories of petty-corruption in Greece today.

f. Regarding the need for transparency in administrative acts, the case is clear, as transparency is a kind of self-evident 'antidote', or even guarantee against corruption in the sense that the more transparency gains ground in public life, the less corruption can be developed there. An important step towards this direction has been made by the recent introduction of the "Transparency" project by the Greek Government (Law Number 3861/2010). According to this project, no state-act bearing any cost to the budget can be valid or executable, unless first, it has been made public knowledge, via the internet site of "Transparency",[15] and has received a code number (as evidence that it has been publicly announced through the internet). Thanks to this project, any citizen, with access to a personal computer, can have good appreciation of what is going on in the public sector and consequently, quickly gain a fair knowledge of how to act to and also to react against illicit administrative actions, such as illegal appointments and promotions of functionaries, signing of inappropriate or illegal contracts for public works, and so on.

g. Finally, regarding the repression system and the need for trustworthy and coordinated mechanisms of control and law–enforcement, Greece, as was mentioned above, has a plethora of such mechanisms functioning at various levels of its Justice System, its Police Administration and its General Public Administration. Yet, it has lacked until recently a coordinating and oversight mechanism which would integrate their various, intertwined and overlapping efforts. A noteworthy solution to this conundrum has been in 2013 the establishment of an *Independent Authority*, which undertakes the role of an 'upper hand' in the anti-corruption endeavor. A similar experiment was undertaken successfully in Hong Kong, where the so-called "Independent Committee Against Corruption" (ICAC), having been allocated a sizable budget of more than USD 90 million per annum, and enjoying legal and administrative autonomy (It can proceed to search bank accounts et cetera and must give account only to the Government of Hong Kong), managed to combat corruption efficiently.

Apart from such an Authority which coordinates anti-corruption on a general level, having also the responsibility for the overall strategy on this issue and for its scientific documentation, it would be equally important to secure a better enforcement of law on various and specific levels, and mainly on the levels of disciplinary and judicial procedures. According to several reports, produced every year by the General Supervisor of Public Administration in Greece, the Disciplinary Councils show considerable leniency towards officials for whom there is evidence of bribery. Moreover, Greek Courts proceed to the trial of allegedly corrupt functionaries with great delay, and they finally either acquit them (as a result of the difficulties to obtain evidence or to ensure witnesses who could testify against a functionary), or pronounce a light sentence on them, usually suspended with probation up to 5 years or convertible up to 5 years to a fine (Articles 100 and 82 of the Greek Criminal Code, as these articles were modified, f.ex. by Law-Nr. 3904/2010). This phenomenon of 'restricted immunity' is further connected with the criminal sanctions for bribery, which are foreseen by the Criminal Code, and which are

---

[15]Ministry of Interior Decentralisation and E-government (2010) Transparency and Openness Policies of the Greek Government "Cl@rity" Program: Every Government Decision on the Internet. http://diavgeia.gov.gr/en. Accessed 20 April 2013.

indeed rather lenient (bribery is mainly punished as a misdemeanor). Yet, this problem is not particularly worrying because in serious cases, accusations of bribery are usually combined with other, more severe ones (i.e. for infidelity, money laundering, false ascertainment, fraud, or embezzlement of public money). As a result, even ex-Ministers, who were considered immune due to special constitutional regulations, were finally prosecuted and convicted for corrupt acts committed during their term of office.

Taking into account the aforementioned observations, it would be appropriate to intensify Greek disciplinary and judicial law-enforcement mechanisms and at the same time, to promote programs of protection for witnesses who would like to testify against corruption, without the fear that this act might have any negative consequences for them (for example, they could be considered as authors of active bribery[16] or they could have ramifications with their future administrative transactions).

1.9   Suggestions for Accountability and Transparency: The Case of Cyprus

1.9.1   Suggestions for Political Accountability

Given that the politicians are perceived to be the category of people who abuse their power the most for personal gain, it is suggested that political accountability is firstly addressed. To this end, the following political accountability and transparency measures are suggested. As mentioned earlier, Article 83 of the Constitution of the Republic of Cyprus, grants immunity to the 'spoken or written words of politicians while in Parliament or office'. However, the politicians are claiming immunity and refuse to pay parking fines or speeding fines, thus taking advantage of the immunity provision. It is suggested that Article 83 of the Constitution be amended, so as to either abolish the immunity enjoyed by politicians or to enforce it only for spoken words while in Parliament. In addition, if Members of Parliament, Ministers or the President fail to take reasonable care and skill in carrying out their duties they ought to be held accountable, and Parliament ought to be able to wave immunity once an investigation into alleged criminal behavior has commenced. In addition, Article 15 of the Constitution states that information on the private life of a person cannot be disclosed. Using this provision and privileged information, it is alleged that many politicians had withdrawn funds from their accounts prior to the 'haircut on bank deposits' being announced on the 15th of March 2013. Thus, the public, and the Socialist Party, have been asking for

---

[16]Cf. however, Article 236.2 of the Greek Criminal Code.

Article 15 of the Constitution to be amended and information on the politicians and their families who used privileged information be disclosed. The idea of shaming (Braithwaite 1989) and electoral accountability (Ferraz and Finan 2011) will act as a deterrent (Ashworth 2010) for politicians, not to behave in similar ways particularly in a small country like Cyprus.

Legislations on revolving doors ought to be enacted to restrain public agents and Ministers from taking interests in a related private sector up to 3 years after they leave their positions. There have been cases where the Ministers of Finance and Education took up positions in financial institutions and private university respectively, within days of leaving their Ministry. Asset disclosure legislation ought to be enacted and a registry should be maintained at the Parliament of all assets, liabilities and other income of: (a) the President, Ministers, Ministerial General Directors, Mayors, local authority councilors, and mukhtars (elected village community leaders); and (b) their spouses and any dependent children under the ages of 25 living with them. All asset disclosure ought to be submitted when the individual firstly takes up a position and the register ought to be updated annually. A final asset disclosure ought to be submitted 1 month after the elected person or Minister leaves a post; otherwise they ought to forfeit any benefits or remunerations. Also, their registry should be made publicly available once audited by the National Audit Office, and a report ought to be provided to the Ethics Parliamentary Committee for better electoral accountability. It is suggested that the Political Party Funding Legislation N175(I)/2012 will be improved by setting up a supervisory electoral body firstly ensuring that the legislation is adhered to and regulating and disciplining political parties in line with the legislation. In addition, it is suggested that a public register is set up for the donations and sponsorships offered to political parties, in order to avoid undue influence.

All Members of Parliament and Ministers ought to disclose any conflicts of interest and should not be allowed to take part in discussions of legislation to be enacted, amendments or revisions or other actions to be taken for the issue in question. Should at a later stage be found that an MP or Minister either himself or his private clients (where one is in private practice) did have a vested interest in some legislation enacted, the Ethics Parliamentary Committee should inform the Independent Disciplinary Committee to commence investigation and the person should face disciplinary action. The decision reached by the Disciplinary Committee ought to be made publicly available for improved electoral accountability. Furthermore, the rules of conflict of interest should be adhered to also by the local councilors since they, too, make decisions whereby they may have a vested interest (e.g. zoning of an area). Parliament ought to approve the implementation of a Code of Conduct for elected officials, ministers and ministerial general directors. The Code should also apply to local councilors, regional authorities and formal training should be provided to all those who are expected to comply with it.

1.9.2 Suggestions for Institutional Setting, Law Enforcement and the Judiciary

The Judiciary in Cyprus is held in high esteem by the general public as they are generally considered incorruptible and, as indicated in Table 1.1, they are considered to be the least corrupted public entity. They are, however, grossly under-staffed and under resourced, hence the lengthy delays in court proceedings. There is currently no institutional body in Cyprus dealing solely with corruption detection, investigation, prosecution and prevention. There is no hotline available for corruption victims to raise the alarm. Thus, the need to establish an Independent Commission Against Corruption cannot be overemphasized. This body ought to have investigative powers and its own budget. It is also believed that an Anti-Corruption Commissioner should be appointed so as to regulate all policies and procedures carried out, implement a National Strategic Anti-Corruption Action Plan and ensure all anti-corruption regulations are enforced. Finally, a Whistleblower's Protection Legislation is urgently needed to protect in a meaningful way (including inclusion in the police witness protection scheme) both public and private sector employees who wish to blow the whistle on a corrupt or illegal act.

1.9.3 Suggestions to Public Administration

As illustrated in Table 1.1, civil servants are perceived to be corrupt. It is believed, once the "tone at the top" is set by the President, Ministers and MPs, then the civil servants, will follow and comply with the newly established norm of values, attitudes and behavior. A Code of Conduct has been enforced for all civil servants. However, without the appropriate framework vis-à-vis relevant training and a Disciplinary Committee the implementation of the Code will be deemed to be 'barking but not biting'. Furthermore, the findings of the Disciplinary Committee should be reported to the Public Sector Board. As far as the accountability of public spending is concerned, it is suggested that a holistic risk management approach is used by the National Audit office and the Internal Audit Department so as to ensure corruption, inherent and operational risks are identified and ratified. Integrity training should be offered to all civil servants irrespective of rank. Seminars on the Code of Conduct as well as how to resolve ethical dilemmas should be made compulsory irrespective of rank.

1.10 Conclusion

Greece and Cyprus—two countries facing serious financial crisis—not surprisingly experience high perceived corruption levels and deficits in the rules of law and government accountability and transparency. Furthermore, since corruption "breeds corruption, and the longer it persists the more endemic it becomes" (Ali and Isse 2003, 451), it is imperative the two governments implement the suggestions pointed by the EU in their anti-corruption report and in addition each government identifies anti-corruption measures and show political will to enforce zero tolerance of corruption. Once the tone at the top is set by politicians and civil servant, in due course the general public will follow the same principles and values. There is no doubt that what is really need to fight corruption effectively in both Greece and Cyprus is the political will by the government in power and the political opposition parties to act in tandem. Unlike Greece and Cyprus, trust-building measures in countries that face financial problems ought to be implemented without delay early enough, unlike Cyprus, and not wait until the country is facing a catastrophe. The European Union and the Eurozone owes it to its members to safeguard the Eurozone by encouraging the fight against corruption particularly in countries with problematic economies, like in southern Europe, rather than punish the breadwinners for failures of the system caused by the decision makers to begin with.

References

ACFE. 2010. Report to the Nations on occupational fraud and abuse. http://www.acfe.com/uploadedFiles/ACFE_Website/Content/documents/rttn-2010.pdf. Accessed 20 Mar 2013.

Aghion, P., A. Alesina, and F. Trebbi. 2004. Endogenous political institutions. *Quarterly Journal of Economics* 119(2): 565–611. doi:10.1162/0033553041382148.

Alesina, A., A. Devleeschauwer, W. Easterly, S. Kurlat, and R. Wacziarg. 2003. Fractionalization. *Journal of Economic Growth* 8(2): 155–194. doi:10.1023/A:1024471506938.

Ali, A.M., and H.S. Isse. 2003. Determinants of economic corruption: A cross-country comparison. *Cato Journal* 22(3): 449–463.

Anokhin, S., and W.S. Schulze. 2009. Entrepreneurship, innovation and corruption. *Journal of Business Venturing* 24: 465–476. doi:10.1016/j.jbusvent.2008.06.001.

Ashiku, M. 2011. Political transition, corruption in new democracies. Special Case Albania. *International Journal of Economic Research* 2(3): 111–124.

Ashworth, A. 2010. *Sentencing and criminal justice*. Cambridge: Cambridge University Press.

Association of Certified Fraud Examiners. 2010. *Report to the nations on occupational fraud and abuse*: 2010 Global Fraud Study. http://www.acfechicago.org/wfdata/files/rttn2010.pdf. Accessed 21 May 2013.

Baro, R. 1996. Democracy and growth. *Journal of Economic Growth* 1(1): 1–27.

Bose, N., S. Capasso, and A.P. Musrshid. 2008. Threshold effects of corruption: Theory and evidence. *World Development* 36: 1173–1191. doi:10.1016/j.worlddev.2007.06.022.

Braithwaite, J. 1989. *Crime, shame and reintegration*. Melbourne: Cambridge University Press.

Campos, J.E., D. Lien, and S. Pradhan. 1999. The impact of corruption on investment: Predictability matters. *World Development* 27: 1059–1067. doi:10.1016/S0305-750X(99)00040-6.

Council of Europe. 1999. Civil law convention on corruption. http://conventions.coe.int/Treaty/en/Treaties/Html/174.htm. Accessed 12 Mar 2014.

Courakis, N., and G. Mannozzi. 2013. Confronting corruption in Greece and Italy. *Honorary volume in memory of professor Dr. Chr. Dedes*, 11–44. Ant. N. Sakkoulas Publishers.

De Figueiredo, J.N. 2013. Are corruption levels accurately identified? The case of U.S. states. *Journal of Policy Modelling* 35: 134–149. doi:10.1016/j.jpolmod.2012.01.006.

European Commission. 2014a. Flash survey. http://ec.europa.eu/public_opinion/archives/flash_arch_374_361_en.htm#374. Accessed 6 Feb 2014.

European Commission. 2014b. Report from the Commission to the Council and the European Parliament, EU anti-corruption report, COM (2014)38 final, Brussels.

European Commission. 2014c. Report from the Commission to the Council and the European Parliament, EU anti-corruption report, Annex 8 Greece, COM (2014)38 final, Brussels.

European Commission. 2014d. Report from the Commission to the Council and the European Parliament, EU anti-corruption report, Annex 13 Cyprus, COM (2014)38 final, Brussels.

European Commission. 2014e. Special eurobarometer. http://ec.europa.eu/public_opinion/archives/eb_special_399_380_en.htm#397. Accessed 6 Feb 2014.

European Commission. 2014f. Press release: Commission unveils first EU anti-corruption report, 3 Feb 2014, IP/14/86.

European Commission. 2012. Road map technical assistance–for anti corruption. http://ec.europa.eu/commission_2010-2014/president/pdf/roadmap_en.pdf. Accessed 15 Mar 2014.

Ferraz, C., and F. Finan. 2011. Electoral accountability and corruption: Evidence from the audits of local governments. *American Economic Review* 101: 1274–1311. doi:10.1257/aer.101.4.1274.

Galoukas, D. 2013. Transparency: National anti-corruption plan. http://www.ministryofjustice.gr/site/LinkClick.aspx?fileticket=KyH_7RZiUPg%3D&tabid=253. Accessed 18 Jan 2014.

Holmberg, S., B. Rothstein, and M. Nasiritousi. 2009. Quality of Government: What you get. *Annual Review of Political Science* 12: 135–161. doi:10.1146/annurev-polisci-100608-104510.

KPMG. 2011. Fighting fraud during and after the financial crisis. http://www.kpmg.com/EE/et/IssuesAndInsights/ArticlesPublications/Documents/Fighting-Fraud-2011.pdf. Accessed 15 March 2013.

Krambia-Kapardis. 2013. Anti-corruption measures in Cyprus www.transparencycyprus.org/.../TIC_Suggestions_Anticorruption-Measures_english_March-13.pdf. Accessed 15 April 2013.

Krambia-Kapardis, M. 2014. Perception of political corruption as a function of legislation. *Financial Crime Journal* 21(1): 44–55.

Krusell, P., and J.V. Rios-Rull. 1996. Vested interests in a positive theory of stagnation and growth. *The Review of Economic Studies* 63: 301–329. doi:10.2307/2297854.

Lambropoulou, E. 2013. *Public vices-private virtues? Corruption and its discourse in Greece.* Saarbruecken: Lap Lambert Academic Publishing.

Mauro, P. 1995. Corruption and growth. *Quarterly Journal of Economics* 110(3): 681–712.

Mauro, P. 1996. *The effects of corruption on growth, investment, and government expenditure.* IMF Working Papers 96/98, International Monetary Fund.

Mauro, P. 1998. Corruption and the composition of government expenditure. *Journal of Public Economics* 69(1998): 263–279.

Neocleous, P., C. Stamatiou, and A. Solomou. 2012. Cyprus. In *Anti-corruption regulation 2012 in 54 jurisdictions worldwide*, ed. H.E. Moyer, 77–81. http://www.ethic-intelligence.com/compliance-tools/31-anti-bribery-and-anti-corruption-strategy/163-anti-corruption-regulation-in-54-jurisdictions-worldwide. Accessed 23 March 2014.

Officer, D., and Y. Taki. 2013. *The state we are in.* Nicosia: University of Nicosia Press.

Rose-Ackerman, S. 1999. *Corruption and government: Causes, consequences and reform.* Cambridge: Cambridge University Press.

Rose-Ackerman, S. 2004. The challenge of poor governance and corruption. Copenhagen consensus challenge paper. http://www.copenhagenconsensus.com/Admin/Public/DWSDownload.aspx?File=%2FFiles%2FFiler%2FCC04%2FPP+-+Corruption1+FINISHED.pdf. Accessed 15 Apr 2013.

Spinelli, C. 2014. Beliefs and Attitudes of Greek students towards corruption. EUCPN's Newsletter, 2014; forthcoming.

Tanzi, V., and H. Davoodi. 1997. Corruption, public investment and growth (IMF Working Paper No. 97/139). http://www.imf.org/external/pubs/ft/wp/wp97139.pdf. Accessed 18 Mar 2013.

Transparency International. 2013. 2013 CPI index. http://www.transparency.org/cpi2013/results. Accessed 15 Mar 2014.

Transparency International Cyprus. 2013. 3rd annual corruption perception survey. http://www.
    transparencycyprus.org/el/wordpress/archives/1026. Accessed 15 Feb 2014.
Transparency International Greece. 2012. National survey on corruption in Greece, public issue.
    www.publicissue.gr/en/1740/corruption-2012/. Accessed 15 Feb 2014.
University of Gothenburg. 2010. Measuring the quality of government and subnational variation.
    http://ec.europa.eu/regional_policy/sources/docgener/studies/pdf/2010_government_1.pdf.
    Accessed 20 March 2013.

Chapter 2
The Determinants of Tax Evasion: A Cross-Country Study

Grant Richardson

Abstract The aim of this study is to build on the work of Riahi-Belkaoui (J Int Account Audit Tax 13: 135–143, 2004) and systematically examine on a cross-country basis, many of the key determinants of tax evasion identified by Jackson and Milliron (J Account Literat 5: 125–165, 1986). Based on data for 45 countries, the regression results show that non-economic determinants have the strongest impact on tax evasion. In particular, complexity is the most important determinant of tax evasion. Other important determinants of tax evasion are education, income source, fairness and tax morale. Overall, the regression results indicate that the lower the level of complexity and the higher the level of education, services income source, fairness and tax morale, the lower is the level of tax evasion. The findings are robust to various cross-country control variables, an alternative measure of tax evasion and several interactions.

2.1 Introduction

Tax evasion has been the subject of a great deal of academic research in most developed countries over a long period of time (e.g., Jackson and Milliron 1986; Long and Swingen 1991; Cuccia 1994; Andreoni et al. 1998; Richardson and Sawyer 2001). However, little research has investigated the underlying determinants of tax evasion on a cross-country basis. This is disappointing because Andreoni et al. (1998) and Tan and Sawyer (2003) have argued there is a need for international and cross-country comparisons on this topic. Riahi-Belkaoui (2004) examined the association between several determinants of tax morale and tax evasion, employing data from 30 countries. He provides evidence which shows that tax evasion across countries is negatively associated with the level of economic freedom, the level of importance of the equity market, the effectiveness of competition laws and high moral norms. Notwithstanding,

G. Richardson (✉)
School of Accounting and Finance, The University of Adelaide,
10 Pulteney Street, Adelaide 5005, SA, Australia
e-mail: Grant.Richardson@adelaide.edu.au

© Springer International Publishing Switzerland 2016
M. Dion et al. (eds.), *Financial Crimes: Psychological, Technological,
and Ethical Issues*, International Library of Ethics, Law,
and the New Medicine 68, DOI 10.1007/978-3-319-32419-7_2

Riahi-Belkaoui (2004) only explored the broad link between tax evasion and some selected determinants of tax morale across countries. However, tax morale is one of many potential determinants of tax evasion. The first major tax evasion literature review by Jackson and Milliron (1986) established 14 key determinants of tax evasion. These include: age, gender, education and occupation status ('demographic' determinants), income level, income source, marginal tax rates, sanctions and probability of detection ('economic' determinants), and complexity, fairness, revenue authority contact, compliant peers and ethics or tax morale ('behavioral' determinants).

The aim of this study is to build on the work of Riahi-Belkaoui (2004) and systematically investigate on a cross-country basis, many of the key determinants of tax evasion identified by Jackson and Milliron (1986). When the determinants of tax evasion are clearly identified in a systematic way by empirical analysis, appropriate policy conclusions can then be drawn, and policymakers are then in a position to design and implement measures to control and restrain its damaging effects. Based on data for 45 countries, the regression results show that non-economic determinants have the strongest impact on tax evasion. In particular, complexity is the main determinant of tax evasion. Other significant determinants of tax evasion are education, income source, fairness and tax morale. Overall, the results of the regressions show that the lower the level of complexity and the higher the level of education, services income source, fairness and tax morale, the lower is the level of tax evasion. The findings are robust to several cross-country control variables, another tax evasion measure and various interactions.

This study makes several important contributions. First, it builds on the original work of Riahi-Belkaoui (2004) and systematically examines many of the key demographic, economic and behavioral determinants of tax evasion. It thus fills a gap in the literature by exploring the major determinants of tax evasion across countries. Second, it shows that 'mixed' models of tax evasion that include demographic, economic and behavioral tax evasion determinants offer valuable insights into tax evasion across countries. Third, it provides a sound empirical framework for further research on tax evasion internationally. Finally, it presents a key summary of multiple data sources for future international tax research.

The rest of this chapter is organized into the following sections. Section 2.2 reviews the major determinants of tax evasion as discussed in the literature and develops hypotheses. Section 2.3 describes the research design. Section 2.4 reports the empirical results. Section 2.5 concludes this chapter.

2.2 Major Determinants of Tax Evasion: Theory and Hypotheses

Why do taxpayers in some countries evade paying income taxes more frequently than taxpayers in other countries? This question can be answered by considering the major determinants of tax evasion previously identified. Jackson and Milliron (1986) provide the first detailed review on this topic, and find 14 key demographic, economic and behavioral determinants of tax evasion. This study considers the impact of ten of these: age, gender, education, income level, income source, marginal tax rates, fairness, complexity, revenue authority contact and tax morale.[1]

The chronological age of taxpayers is one of the main determinants of tax evasion (Jackson and Milliron 1986). Studies find that older taxpayers are generally more compliant than younger taxpayers (Tittle 1980; Witte and Woodbury 1985; Dubin and Wilde 1988; Feinstein 1991; Hanno and Violette 1996). Tittle (1980) explains the relationship between age and tax deviance as attributable to lifecycle variations and generational differences. Younger taxpayers are more risk-seeking, less sensitive to penalties (a lifecycle variation), and reflect the social and psychological differences related to the period in which they are raised (a generational difference).

Gender of the taxpayer has been revealed to be significant in past studies. Vogel (1974) and Mason and Calvin (1978) show that the compliance levels of female taxpayers are higher than for males. Jackson and Milliron (1986) argue that this compliance gap is shrinking over time as new generations of liberated women emerge. Other studies find different outcomes (Brooks and Doob 1990; Collins et al. 1992).

Education attainment is one more key determinant. Jackson and Milliron (1986) claim that education has two elements: the general degree of fiscal knowledge and the specific degree of knowledge about tax evasion opportunities. They claim that by enhancing the level of general fiscal knowledge, tax compliance improves due to more positive perceptions about taxation. Increased knowledge of tax evasion opportunities has a negative impact on tax compliance as it aids non-compliance (Jackson and Milliron 1986). Song and Yarbrough (1978) and Witte and Woodbury (1985) find a negative association between general education and tax evasion.

Income level is another important determinant. It usually refers to the adjusted gross income or total positive income of a taxpayer (Jackson and Milliron 1986). Mason and Lowry (1981) and Witte and Woodbury (1983) find that middle income taxpayers are generally compliant with tax laws, while low income level taxpayers and high income level taxpayers are relatively non-compliant with tax laws. Richardson and Sawyer (2001) show however that overall findings remain mixed. Income source usually refers to the type or nature of the taxpayer's income (Jackson and Milliron 1986). Schmolder's (1970) shows that when a large part of a country's labor force is engaged in agriculture and small trading, income and profit taxation is unsuccessful. Wallschutzky (1984) finds that the greatest opportunity to evade income tax exists from those who derive their income from agriculture, independent trades or self-employment, whereas the least opportunity exists for those taxpayers whose source of income is dependent on wages or salaries subject to withholding, such as from the services sector.

---

[1]Occupation status, sanctions, probability of detection and compliant peers are not considered due to the lack of available cross-country data for these determinants.

Marginal tax rates is one more key tax evasion determinant, but empirical results are mixed. Clotfelter (1983) and Mason and Calvin (1984) show a positive association between marginal tax rates and tax evasion, while Feinstein (1991) and Christian and Gupta (1993) show a negative association between them. Richardson and Sawyer (2001) claim that not controlling for the correlation between marginal tax rates and income level may cause this inconsistency. They cite the work of Feinstein (1991) who tests an economic model of tax evasion using pooled data. By pooling data from years in which different tax schedules were operating in the US, Feinstein (1991) is able to separate-out the effects of marginal tax rates and income level. The results show that higher marginal tax rates reduces tax evasion.[2]

It is generally accepted that perceptions about tax fairness and tax evasion are related (Jackson and Milliron 1986). The importance of taxpayers 'perceptions' of tax fairness should not be underestimated (Richardson and Sawyer 2001). Spicer (1974) finds a significant negative association between these, while Song and Yarbrough (1978) find a significant negative association, with 75 % of subjects stating that 'ability to pay' was more significant than 'benefits.' Hite and Roberts (1992) also find that tax fairness was significantly associated with perceptions of an improved tax system, and that tax fairness and tax evasion are negatively related.

Because tax systems have become more complex over time in many developed countries around the world, complexity has become a major tax evasion determinant (Jackson and Milliron 1986; Richardson and Sawyer 2001). Previous research, utilizing archival data (Clotfelter 1983; Long and Swingen 1988) and survey data (Vogel 1974; Milliron and Toy 1988; Collins et al. 1992) methodologies provide strong empirical evidence to show that complexity has a positive association with tax evasion. Revenue authority contact is another important determinant. Spicer and Lundstedt (1976) find that taxpayers' direct experience with the revenue authority is positively associated to increased tax resistance and tax evasion. Research by Klepper and Nagin (1989a, b) and Brooks and Doob (1990) also supports this view. In contrast, by reducing the level of contact between taxpayers and public tax officials through a self-assessment tax system, this reduces the possibility of widespread tax resistance and tax evasion (Tanzi 2000; Sarker 2003; Torgler and Murphy 2004).

While tax morale is a vague concept (Jackson and Milliron 1986), it describes the morale principles or values individuals hold about paying taxes (Torgler and Murphy 2004). Research by Spicer (1974), Spicer and Lundstedt (1976) and Tittle (1980) finds that the tax morale of individuals is negatively associated with tax evasion. Torgler (2003a) also shows that tax morale and tax evasion are negatively correlated. Moreover, Riahi-Belkaoui (2004) also provides evidence which indicates that tax evasion across countries is negatively related to selected determinants of tax morale.

---

[2]In fact, by combining data from various countries with different tax schedules, this present study is able to separate-out the effects of marginal tax rates and income level.

Following from the above discussion, it is hypothesized that:

H1   All else equal, there is a significant negative association between older taxpayers and tax evasion in a country.

H2   All else equal, there is a significant negative association between female taxpayers and tax evasion in a country.

H3   All else equal, there is a significant negative association between the general education knowledge of taxpayers and tax evasion in a country.

H4   All else equal, there is a significant positive association between low income level and high income level taxpayers, and tax evasion in a country.

H5   All else equal, there is a significant positive (negative) association between income derived from agriculture (services) and tax evasion in a country.

H6   All else equal, there is a significant negative association between high marginal tax rates and tax evasion in a country.

H7   All else equal, there is a significant negative association between perceptions of fairness and tax evasion in a country.

H8   All else equal, there is a significant positive association between complexity and tax evasion in a country.

H9   All else equal, there is a significant negative association between self-assessment and tax evasion in a country.

H10   All else equal, there is a significant negative association between tax morale and tax evasion in a country.

2.3 Research Design

2.3.1 Data Description

Data for this study are collected from a wide range of sources. The Appendix presents a comprehensive description of data used to measure the different variables used and their various sources. To achieve robustness, both objective and survey measures of the variables are employed. La Porta et al. (1999, 234) argue that this is important for subjective assessments of variables, since "within the same survey responses" to different questions may simply reflect some general underlying sentiment toward a country. When different surveys use diverse respondents, this potential risk is reduced. A brief discussion of the relevant variables used now follows.

2.3.2 Dependent Variable

The dependent variable in this study is represented by tax evasion (TEVA). Its measure is based on a country survey rating of tax evasion collected by the World Economic Forum (WEF) and published in the *Global Competitiveness Report*

(World Economic Forum 2002, 2003, 2004). While the *Global Competitiveness Report* is a valuable source of cross-country tax evasion data, using one question in this study to measure tax evasion raises concerns about reliability due to measurement error. However, measurement error can be minimized by using average data for several years (Fisman and Gatti 2002; You and Khagram 2005).[3] Thus, averaged WEF tax evasion data for several years (from 2002–2004) are used as the dependent variable instead of data for a single year to reduce the possibility of measurement error.

2.3.3 Independent Variables

The independent variables are denoted in this study by age (AGE), gender (GEND), education (EDUC), income level (ILEVEL): low income level (LILEVEL) and high income level (HILEVEL), income source (ISOURCE): agriculture income source (AISOURCE) and services income source (SISOURCE), marginal tax rates (MTR), fairness (FAIR), complexity (COMP), self-assessment (SELFA) and tax morale (MORALE). Where possible, data for these independent variables are computed as three-year averages, covering 2002–2004 so as to be consistent with the measurement of the dependent variable and to reduce the possibility of measurement error.

AGE (percentage of the population greater than 65)[4] and GEND (percentage of the population that is female) are both measured from data collected by the World Bank and published in the *2005 World Development Indicators* (World Bank 2005a). EDUC is measured by a country survey rating of the quality of a country's general education system. Data are collected by the Institute of Management Development (IMD) and published in the *World Competitiveness Year Book* (Institute of Management Development 2002, 2003, 2004). LILEVEL is measured as the proportion of household income going to the lowest 20 % of households, while HILEVEL is measured as the proportion of household income going to the highest 20 % of households. Data for each of these variables are taken from the *World Competitiveness Year Book* (Institute of Management Development 2002, 2003, 2004). AISOU is measured as the percentage of employment in the agricultural sector, while SISOU is measured as the percentage of employment in the services sector. Data for these variables are gathered from the *World Competitiveness Year Book* (Institute of Management Development 2002, 2003, 2004). MTR is measured by the top marginal income tax rate for individuals. Data for this variable are collected from the *2005 World Development Indicators*

---

[3]Assuming that measurement error has a normal distribution with a mean of zero and a variance of σ^2, averaging of N observations will decrease the variance to σ^2/N.

[4]The age of '65' has been used as the cut-off point to represent older tax payers in tax evasion research by Clotfelter (1983) and Witte and Woodbury (1985), for example.

(World Bank 2005a). FAIR is measured by a country survey rating of the fairness of tax policy. Data for this variable are gathered by the Institute of Industrial Policy Studies (IPS) and published in the *National Competitiveness Report* (Institute for Industrial Policy Studies 2002). COMP is measured by a country survey rating of complexity in the tax system. Data for this variable are collected from the *Global Competitiveness Report* (World Economic Forum 2003, 2004). SELFA is measured by a dummy variable (1 if a countryhas a self-assessment tax system, 0 otherwise) based on information provided by the Organisation for Economic Co-operation and Development (2002), PricewaterhouseCoopers (2004) and KPMG (2003). Finally, in line with Torgler (2003a, b, 2005) and Torgler and Murphy (2004), MORALE is measured by a country survey rating of tax cheating. Data for this variable are gathered from the World Values Survey (Inglehart 2003; Inglehart et al. 2004).

2.3.4 Control Variables

Because this study is undertaken at the country level of analysis, it is necessary to control for potential cross-country effects. Thus, several control variables relating to economic, political and cultural factors are included in this study. The level of economic development (EDEV) can affect tax evasion across countries (Quirk 1997; Alm and Martinez-Vazquez 2003). Quirk (1997) claims that countries in the early stages of economic development are especially prone to tax evasion. Studies of tax evasion carried out in developing countries show that it is not uncommon for 50 % or more of potential income tax to remain uncollected due to tax evasion (Gillis 1989; Richupan 1984). Das-Gupta et al. (1995) find that in India, the amount of income not subject to tax is estimated to be more than 200 % of the assessed income. EDEV is measured in this study as the natural log of GDP per capita, which is collected from the *2005 World Development Indicators* (World Bank 2005a).

Political institutions based on notions of democracy (DEMOC) can also influence tax evasion levels across countries (Pommerehne and Weck-Hannemann 1996; Alm et al. 1999). As the taxpaying public is allowed to directly participate in the democratic political process via the right to vote on tax issues, politicians are more accountable and transparent so they must take taxpayer preferences into account. This improves taxpayer confidence and can reduce country tax evasion levels (Feld and Tyran 2002; Torgler et al. 2003). DEMOC is measured based on the political rights index developed by Freedom House (2005).

Culture (CULT) and religion (RELIG) can also affect tax evasion across countries. Research by Tittle (1980) in the US finds that cultural and religious background is associated with tax evasion. Focus group research by Coleman and Freeman (1997) in Australia also shows that cultural and religious background influences tax compliance. A cross-country survey study of tax evasion by

Chan et al. (2000) in Hong Kong and the US shows that cultural background affects tax evasion. CULT is measured in this study by ethnolinguistic fractionalization, collected from Mauro (1995), while RELIG is measured by the percentages of Protestants (PROT), Catholics (CATH), Muslims (MUSL) and other denominations (OTHRD), gathered from La Porta et al. (1999).

Additional controls for legal system (LEGAL), colonial heritage (COLONY) and regional developing countries (REGION) are also included in this study. This considers whether tax evasion is driven by differences between common law system countries versus civil law system countries, colonial countries versus non-colonial countries and regional developing countries versus developed countries (Treisman 2000; Brunetti and Weader 2003). Thus, dummy variables for LEGAL, COLONY and REGION are also included in this study. LEGAL is measured by the common law system country classification of La Porta et al. (1999). COLONY is measured by the colonial heritage country classification of Barro and Lee (1994). REGION is measured by the developing country grouping classifications of: East Asia and Pacific region (EAPR), Europe and Central Asia region (EUCAR) and Latin America and the Caribbean region (LACR), collected from the *World Bank Group— Data and Statistics* (World Bank 2005b).

2.3.5 Base Regression Model

To examine the determinants of tax evasion, the following base ordinary least squares (OLS) regression equation is estimated:

$$
\begin{aligned}
TEVA_i = {} & \alpha_0 + \beta_1 AGE_i + \beta_2 GEND_i + \beta_3 EDUC_i + \beta_4 LILEVEL_i + \beta_5 HILEVEL_i + \beta_6 AISOURCE_i \\
& + \beta_7 SISOURCE_i + \beta_8 MTR_i + \beta_9 FAIR_i + \beta_{10} COMP_i + \beta_{11} SELFA_i + \beta_{12} MORALE_i + \varepsilon_i
\end{aligned}
$$

$$(6.1)$$

where: $TEVA_i$ is the tax evasion score for country i, AGE_i is the percentage of the population greater than 65 for country i, $GEND_i$ is the percentage of the population that is female for country i, EDUC is the general education score for country i, LILEVEL is the proportion of household income going to the lowest 20 % of households for country i, HILEVEL is the proportion of household income going to the highest 20 % of households for country i, AISOURCE is the percentage of employment in the agricultural sector for country i, $SISOURCE_i$ is the percentage of employment in the services sector for country i, MTR_i is the top marginal income tax rate for individuals of country i, $FAIR_i$ is the fairness score for country i, $COMP_i$ is the complexity score for country i, $SELFA_i$ is a dummy variable represented by 1 if country i has a self-assessment tax system, 0 otherwise, $MORALE_i$ is the tax morale score for country i and ε_i is the error term for country i.

2.4 Results

2.4.1 Descriptive Statistics and Correlation Results

Table 2.1 reports descriptive statistics for the variables used in this study from a cross-section of 45 countries.[5] The Pearson correlation matrix for this study's dependent and independent variables is presented in Table 2.2.

The Pearson correlation matrix shows that there are some significant associations between tax evasion and the independent variables. For example, there are fairly high correlations ($p < 0.01$) between TEVA and FAIR (r = −0.72), TEVA and COMP (r = 0.68), TEVA and SISOURCE (r = −0.61), TEVA and EDUC (r = −0.53) and TEVA and AISOURCE (r = 0.51). Correlations are also found ($p < 0.05$) between TEVA and AGE (r = −0.29), TEVA and SELFA (r = −0.27) and TEVA and MORALE (−0.24). However, no correlations are found between TEVA and GEND, TEVA and LILEVEL, TEVA and HILEVEL or TEVA and MTR.[6]

These univariate results provide some preliminary support for H1, H3, H5, H7, H8, H9 and H10. Moreover, these results also show that behavioral and demographic variables have the strongest impact on tax evasion as compared to economic variables. This is an interesting finding which shows that non-economic variables are fundamental and should be examined along with economic variables in 'mixed models' of tax evasion across countries.

2.4.2 Regression Results

Table 2.3 reports the results of the regression analysis for the base regression model (Column 1), and includes several control variables (Columns 2–8) to consider potential cross-country effects.

---

[5]The 45 countries for which data are available for the study are represented by: Argentina, Australia, Austria, Belgium, Brazil, Canada, Chile, China (PRC), Colombia, Czech Republic, Denmark, Estonia, Finland, France, Germany, Greece, Hungry, Iceland, India, Indonesia, Ireland, Italy, Japan, Korea (South), Mexico, Netherlands, New Zealand, Norway, Philippines, Poland, Portugal, Russia, Singapore, Slovak Republic, Slovenia, South Africa, Spain, Sweden, Switzerland, Taiwan, Thailand, Turkey, United Kingdom, United States and Venezuela.

[6]Significant correlations are also found between tax evasion and some of the control variables. For instance, there are reasonably high correlations ($p < 0.01$) between TEVA and EDEV (r = −0.63), TEVA and COLONY (r = −0.48) and TEVA and LEGAL (r = −0.44). Correlations are also observed ($p < 0.05$) between TEVA and PROT (r = −0.29), TEVA and EUCAR (r = 0.29) and TEVA and LACR (r = 0.28). Finally, some marginal correlations are also detected ($p < 0.10$) between TEVA and EAPR (r = 0.22) and TEVA and CATH (r = 0.21). No significant correlations are found between TEVA and DEMOC, CULT, MUSL or OTHRD.

Table 2.1 Descriptive statistics of the variables

Variable	Number	Mean	Std. Dev.	Minimum	Maximum
TEVA	45	4.33	1.13	1.80	6.10
AGE	45	11.48	4.58	3.93	18.37
GEND	45	0.51	0.01	0.48	0.53
EDUC	45	5.20	1.50	2.30	8.41
ILEVEL: LILEVEL	45	6.84	2.23	2.33	10.87
ILEVEL: HILEVEL	45	43.92	8.26	32.53	65.37
ISOURCE: AISOURCE	45	11.94	14.31	0.30	62.45
ISOURCE: SISOURCE	45	59.62	14.99	23.10	84.27
MTR	45	0.41	0.10	0.13	0.59
FAIR	45	5.43	1.56	1.30	8.00
COMP	45	4.72	1.11	1.55	6.35
SELFA	45	0.47	0.50	0	1
MORALE	45	8.31	0.88	4.82	9.82
EDEV	45	9.19	1.20	6.14	10.80
DEMOC	45	1.82	1.43	1.00	7.00
CULT	44	0.21	0.22	0.00	0.83
RELIG: PROT[†]	45	19.11	29.24	0	97.80
RELIG: CATH	45	40.44	39.24	0	96.90
RELIG: MUSL	45	5.43	16.71	0	99.20
RELIG: OTHRD	45	35.02	34.13	0.70	98.50
LEGAL	45	0.27	0.45	0	1
COLONY	45	0.24	0.43	0	1
REGION: EAPR	45	0.10	0.31	0	1
REGION: EUCAR	45	0.12	0.33	0	1
REGION: LACR	45	0.12	0.33	0	1

Variable definitions *TEVA* tax evasion, *AGE* age, *GEND* gender, *EDUC* education, *ILEVEL* income level (*LILEVEL* low income level and *HILEVEL* high income level), *ISOURCE* income source (*AISOURCE* agriculture income source and *SISOURCE* services income source), *MTR* marginal tax rates, *FAIR* fairness, *COMP* complexity, *SELFA* revenue authority contact, *MORALE* morale, *EDEV* economic development, *DEMOC* democracy, *CULT* culture, *RELIG* religion (*PROT* protestant, *CATH* catholic, *MUSL* muslim and *OTHRD* other denomination), *LEGAL* legal system, *COLONY* colonial heritage and *REGION* regional developing countries (*EAPR* East Asia and Pacific region, *EUCAR* Europe and Central Asia region and *LACR* Latin America and Caribbean region)
[†]Reference category only

Table 2.3 (Column 1) shows that the base regression model is significant at the $p < 0.01$ level (F statistic = 13.20), while the adjusted R^2 for this regression model is 0.80. In terms of the significance of the regression coefficients summarized in Table 2.3 (Column 1), the results show that COMP is the most important determinant of tax evasion ($p < 0.01$) across countries, thus H8 is supported by the results. Where a country's tax system has a high level of complexity, this increases the incidence of tax evasion. This result is consistent with prior research

Table 2.2 Pearson correlation matrix for dependent and independent variables

	1	2	3	4	5	6	7	8	9	10	11	12	13
1. TEVA	1												
2. AGE	−0.29**	1											
3. GEND	0.15	0.44***	1										
4. EDUC	−0.53***	0.26**	−0.16	1									
5. LILEVEL	0.01	0.62***	0.07	0.27**	1								
6. HILEVEL	0.16	−0.72***	−0.06	−0.38***	−0.82***	1							
7. AISOURCE	0.51***	−0.60***	−0.38***	−0.33***	−0.15	0.30**	1						
8. SISOURCE	−0.61***	0.49***	0.07	0.34***	0.15	−0.36***	−0.73***	1					
9. MTR	−0.16	0.51***	−0.08	0.23*	0.52***	−0.58***	−0.29**	0.26**	1				
10. FAIR	−0.72***	0.45***	−0.03	0.55***	0.21*	−0.34**	−0.54***	0.49***	0.33**	1			
11. COMP	0.68***	0.08	0.21*	−0.38***	0.16	−0.10	0.13	−0.20*	0.26**	−0.49***	1		
12. SELFA	−0.27**	−0.28**	−0.06	−0.16	−0.29**	0.33**	0.18*	−0.24**	−0.22*	−0.25**	0.10	1	
13. MORALE	−0.24**	−0.08	−0.38***	−0.06	0.22**	−0.31**	0.01	0.18	0.34***	0.06	−0.04	0.03	1

Variable definitions *TEVA* tax evasion, *AGE* age, *GEND* gender, *EDUC* education, *ILEVEL* income level (*LILEVEL* low income level and *HILEVEL* high income level), *ISOURCE* income source (*AISOURCE* agriculture income source and *SISOURCE* services income source), *MTR* marginal tax rates, *FAIR* fairness, *COMP* complexity, *SELFA* revenue authority contact, *MORALE* morale, *EDEV* economic development, *DEMOC* democracy, *CULT* culture, *RELIG* religion (*PROT* protestant, *CATH* catholic, *MUSL* muslim and *OTHRD* other denomination), *LEGAL* legal system, *COLONY* colonial heritage and *REGION* regional developing countries (*EAPR* East Asia and Pacific region, *EUCAR* Europe and Central Asia region and *LACR* Latin America and Caribbean region)

N = 45

*, **, *** Significant at 0.10, 0.05 and 0.01 levels, respectively

Table 2.3 Regression results (dependent variable: tax evasion, WEF)

	OLS (1)	OLS (2)	OLS (3)	OLS (4)	OLS (5)	OLS (6)	OLS (7)	OLS (8)
CONSTANT	10.263 (1.185)	13.321 (1.379)	8.833 (1.001)	13.037 (1.390)	14.063 (1.433)	14.995 (1.664)	14.995 (1.664)	13.482 (1.395)
AGE	-0.256 (-1.331)	-0.201 (-0.967)	-0.270 (-1.397)	-0.313 (-1.500)*	-0.181 (-0.795)	-0.237 (-1.263)	-0.237 (-1.263)	-0.185 (-0.877)
GEND	-0.008 (-0.065)	-0.031 (-0.234)	-0.010 (-0.076)	-0.024 (-0.179)	-0.071 (-0.488)	-0.075 (-0.562)	-0.075 (-0.562)	-0.056 (-0.388)
EDUC	-0.205 (-1.877)**	-0.192 (-1.723)**	-0.214 (-1.945)**	-0.206 (-1.721)**	-0.217 (-1.967)**	-0.142 (-1.248)*	-0.142 (-1.248)*	-0.190 (-1.637)**
LILEVEL	0.047 (0.212)	0.009 (0.039)	0.078 (0.349)	0.025 (0.100)	0.106 (0.460)	0.041 (0.185)	0.041 (0.185)	0.018 (0.075)
HIILEVEL	-0.248 (-0.859)	-0.292 (-0.982)	-0.242 (-0.837)	-0.295 (-0.952)	-0.229 (-0.785)	-0.305 (-1.074)	-0.305 (-1.074)	-0.284 (-0.831)
AISOURCE	0.012 (0.079)	0.112 (0.549)	0.042 (-0.269)	0.004 (0.022)	0.014 (0.090)	0.074 (0.480)	0.074 (0.480)	0.069 (0.396)
SISOURCE	-0.301 (-2.429)**	-0.265 (-1.978)**	-0.285 (-2.372)**	-0.351 (-2.435)**	-0.319 (-2.318)**	-0.337 (-2.732)**	-0.337 (-2.732)**	-0.330 (-2.343)**
MTR	-0.047 (-0.416)	-0.023 (-0.198)	-0.008 (-0.069)	-0.017 (-0.132)	-0.114 (-0.744)	-0.078 (-0.698)	-0.078 (-0.698)	-0.026 (-0.194)
FAIR	-0.212 (-1.820)**	-0.202 (-1.708)**	-0.203 (-1.736)**	-0.235 (-1.876)**	-0.246 (-2.035)**	-0.219 (-1.924)**	-0.219 (-1.924)**	-0.218 (-1.772)**
COMP	0.438 (4.057) ***	0.438 (4.017) ***	0.442 (4.078) ***	0.405 (3.363) ***	0.416 (3.751) ***	0.427 (4.046) ***	0.427 (4.046) ***	0.418 (3.344) ***
SELFA	-0.106 (-1.286)	-0.108 (-1.294)	-0.100 (-1.198)	-0.093 (-1.044)	-0.079 (-0.857)	-0.042 (-0.466)	-0.042 (-0.466)	-0.096 (-1.102)
MORALE	-0.245 (-2.318)**	-0.241 (-2.259)**	-0.269 (-2.424)**	-0.251 (-2.378)**	-0.222 (-1.861)**	-0.228 (-2.199)**	-0.228 (-2.199)**	-0.258 (-2.316)**
EDEV		-0.203 (-0.744)						

(continued)

Table 2.3 (continued)

	OLS (1)	OLS (2)	OLS (3)	OLS (4)	OLS (5)	OLS (6)	OLS (7)	OLS (8)
DEMOC			−0.097 (−0.925)					
CULT				−0.134 (−1.146)				
RELIG					0.077 (0.521)			
PROT†					−0.024			
CATH					(−0.208)			
MUSL					−0.085			
OTHRD					(−0.481)			
LEGAL						−0.162 (−1.509)		
COLONY							−0.162 (−1.509)	
REGION								
EAPR								0.088 (0.761)
EUCAR								0.077 (0.700)
LACR								0.103 (0.747)
N	45	45	44	45	45	45	45	45
R^2 (adjusted)	0.80	0.80	0.80	0.78	0.80	0.81	0.81	0.78
F statistic	13.20***	12.01***	12.18***	10.74***	10.60***	12.98***	12.98***	9.84***

Variable definitions *TEVA* tax evasion, *AGE* age, *GEND* gender, *EDUC* education, *ILEVEL* income level (*LILEVEL* low income level and *HILEVEL* high income level), *ISOURCE* income source (*AISOURCE* agriculture income source and *SISOURCE* services income source), *MTR* marginal tax rates, *FAIR* fairness, *COMP* complexity, *SELFA* revenue authority contact, *MORALE* morale, *EDEV* economic development, *DEMOC* democracy, *CULT* culture, *RELIG* religion (*PROT* protestant, *CATH* catholic, *MUSL* muslim and *OTHRD* other denomination), *LEGAL* legal system, *COLONY* colonial heritage and *REGION* regional developing countries (*EAPR* East Asia and Pacific region, *EUCAR* Europe and Central Asia region and *LACR* Latin America and Caribbean region). t-statistics are in parentheses. Standard errors are corrected for heteroschedasticity

*, **, *** Significant at 0.10, 0.05 and 0.01 levels, respectively

†Reference category only

(Vogel 1974; Clotfelter 1983; Long and Swingen 1988; Milliron and Toy 1988; Collins et al. 1992).

EDUC, SISOURCE, FAIR and MORALE represent the next most important determinants of tax evasion ($p < 0.05$) across countries as reported in Table 2.3 (Column 1). For EDUC, H3 is supported by the results. Where a country has a good general education system, this helps to reduce the level of tax evasion. This result is consistent with theory (Song and Yarbrough 1978; Witte and Woodbury 1985). For ISOURCE, only SISOURCE is significant, thus H5 is partially confirmed by the results. Where a country has income that is subject to withholding (e.g. services employment income), this can significantly reduce the level of tax evasion in a country (Schmolders 1970; Wallschutzky 1984). Concerning FAIR, H7 is also corroborated by the results. Where taxpayers perceive that their country's tax policy is fair, this helps to reduce the level of tax evasion. This result is also consistent with theory (Spicer 1974; Song and Yarbrough 1978; Hite and Roberts 1992). For MORALE, H10 is also confirmed by the results. Where tax morale in a country is high, this assists in reducing the level of tax evasion. This confirms Riahi-Belkaoui's (2004) findings, but using a direct measure of tax morale in this instance. Finally, for AGE, GEND, LILEVEL, HILEVEL, MTR and SELFA, no significant relationships are found with tax evasion. Therefore, H1, H2, H4, H6 and H9 are not supported by the results on a multivariate basis.

Consistent with the univariate findings reported in Table 2.2, the behavioral and demographic variables in comparison with the economic variables are found to have the strongest impact on tax evasion in the base regression model. These results show that by including not only economic variables, but also behavioral and demographic variables into mixed models of tax evasion, this provides the most compelling results. This supports the views of Cuccia (1994) and Cummings et al. (2001) who argue that by combining economic and non-economic views of tax evasion, this can lead to a better understanding of the subject.

Table 2.3 (Columns 2–8) present the results of the supplementary regression models, including some cross-country control variables. The results show that the supplementary regression models are all significant at the $p < 0.01$ level (F statistics ranging from 9.84 to 12.98), while the adjusted R^2's for these regression models (i.e. around 0.80) are relatively consistent with the adjusted R^2 for the base regression model (Column 1). This indicates that the explanatory power of the base regression model is not improved by the inclusion of cross-country control variables.

In the supplementary regression models, COMP ($p < 0.01$) remains the key determinant of tax evasion, while its regression coefficient is relatively stable across all of the supplementary regression models. SISOURCE, FAIR, MORALE and EDUC remain the next most significant determinants of tax evasion ($p < 0.05$, but EDUC does at times fall to $p < 0.10$ in some of the regressions) and have relatively stable regression coefficients. Non-economic variables are again shown to have the strongest impact on tax evasion compared to economic variables across the supplementary regressions.

For the significance of the regression coefficients of the cross-country control variables in Table 2.3 (Columns 2–8), none of the control variables relating to EDEV, DEMOC, CULT, RELIG, LEGAL, COLONY, REGION are found to be significantly related to tax evasion. This shows that the base regression model results in Table 2.3 (Column 1) described above remain robust and are not driven by cross-country differences in the levels of economic development, democracy, culture, religion, type of legal system, colonial heritage and regional developing countries.

In general, the supplementary regression model results are comparable to the base regression model results presented earlier. Thus, this study's findings, after controlling for a broad range of cross-country variables, appear to be robust.

2.4.3   Sensitivity Analysis

The regression analysis so far has made use of a specific measure of tax evasion collected by the World Economic Forum (2002, 2003, 2004). This raises the question of whether the results are characteristics of this data as tax evasion is not easily observable. The robustness of the results is tested by using an alterative measure of tax evasion based on a country survey rating gathered by the Institute of Management Development (2002, 2003, 2004). Data for this measure of tax evasion are computed as three-year averages, covering the 2002–2004 years, to reduce the possibility of measurement error. The IMD tax evasion measure has a high correlation ($r = 0.95$; $p < 0.01$) with its WEF complement, suggesting that this measure of tax evasion is sound. The results of this sensitivity analysis are summarized in Table 2.4.

The results of the sensitivity analysis using the Institute of Management Development (2002, 2003, 2004) measure of tax evasion show that the regression coefficients of COMP, EDUC, SISOURCE, FAIR and MORALE are significant and remain quite stable across the various regression model specifications which are reported in Table 2.4 (Columns 1–8). This is consistent with the earlier regression results using the WEF measure of tax evasion. However, the level of significance of some of these independent variables changes slightly when using the IMD tax evasion measure.

COMP is still the most significant determinant of tax evasion across countries ($p < 0.01$). This is followed by EDUC ($p < 0.05$ or greater) and MORALE (usually $p < 0.05$). SISOURCE and FAIR also have significant relationships with tax evasion ($p < 0.10$ or greater). For AGE, GEND, LILEVEL, HILEVEL, AISOURCE, MTR and SELFA, no significant associations are found with tax evasion. Again, non-economic variables are found to have the strongest impact on tax evasion. Finally, for the cross-country control variables of EDEV, DEMOC, CULT, RELIG, LEGAL, COLONY, REGION, none of these variables are found to have a significant relationship with tax evasion.

Table 2.4 Regression results (dependent variable: tax evasion, IMD)

	OLS (1)	OLS (2)	OLS (3)	OLS (4)	OLS (5)	OLS (6)	OLS (7)	OLS (8)
CONSTANT	15.354 (1.108)	17.775 (1.140)	15.039 (1.047)	18.546 (1.287)	19.966 (1.373)	18.511 (1.236)	18.511 (1.236)	20.949 (1.366)
AGE	-0.154 (-0.737)	-0.125 (-0.547)	-0.157 (-0.730)	-0.203 (-0.944)	-0.122 (-0.531)	-0.146 (-0.687)	-0.146 (-0.687)	-0.116 (-0.510)
GEND	-0.002 (-0.011)	-0.011 (-0.073)	-0.004 (-0.030)	-0.013 (-0.097)	-0.059 (-0.397)	-0.029 (-0.190)	-0.029 (-0.190)	-0.029 (-0.185)
EDUC	-0.309 (-2.593)**	-0.302 (-2.461)**	-0.310 (-2.542)**	-0.290 (-2.345)**	-0.322 (-2.881)***	-0.280 (-2.167)**	-0.280 (-2.167)**	-0.321 (-2.558)***
LILEVEL	0.184 (0.763)	0.205 (0.813)	0.180 (0.721)	0.217 (0.855)	0.065 (0.281)	0.225 (0.886)	0.225 (0.886)	0.255 (0.996)
HIILEVEL	-0.328 (-1.159)	-0.352 (-1.181)	-0.327 (-1.129)	-0.309 (-1.193)	-0.301 (-1.123)	-0.354 (-1.110)	-0.354 (-1.110)	-0.386 (-1.188)
AISOURCE	0.165 (0.987)	0.110 (0.489)	0.160(0.921)	0.218 (1.204)	0.165 (1.034)	0.136 (0.778)	0.136 (0.778)	0.181 (0.960)
SISOURCE	-0.212 (-1.566)*	-0.193 (-1.304)*	-0.211 (-1.527)*	-0.242 (-1.632)*	-0.195 (-1.401)*	-0.228 (-1.633)*	-0.228 (-1.633)*	-0.266 (-1.744)**
MTR	-0.085 (-0.691)	-0.072 (-0.556)	-0.079 (-0.592)	-0.102 (-0.749)	-0.114 (-0.735)	-0.099 (-0.782)	-0.099 (-0.782)	-0.050 (-0.346)
FAIR	-0.186 (-1.461)*	-0.180 (-1.385)*	-0.185 (-1.418)*	-0.199 (-1.538)*	-0.222 (-1.817)**	-0.189 (-1.466)*	-0.189 (-1.466)*	-0.209 (-1.570)*
COMP	0.375 (3.180)***	0.375 (3.123)***	0.375 (3.119)***	0.345 (2.786)***	0.331 (2.954)***	0.370 (3.091)***	0.370 (3.091)***	0.303 (2.242)**
SELFA	-0.109 (-1.210)	-0.110 (-1.198)	-0.108 (-1.171)	-0.071 (-0.781)	-0.089 (-0.946)	-0.080 (-0.776)	-0.080 (-0.776)	-0.109 (-1.160)
MORALE	-0.199 (-1.723)**	-0.197 (-1.673)**	-0.201 (-1.689)**	-0.269 (-2.479)**	-0.196 (-1.628)**	-0.191 (-1.625)*	-0.191 (-1.625)*	-0.224 (-1.852)**
EDEV		-0.110 (-0.365)						

(continued)

Table 2.4 (continued)

	OLS (1)	OLS (2)	OLS (3)	OLS (4)	OLS (5)	OLS (6)	OLS (7)	OLS (8)
DEMOC			−0.015 (−0.125)					
CULT				−0.159 (−1.328)				
RELIG								
PROT†								
CATH					0.127 (0.755)			
MUSL					0.010 (0.081)			
OTHRD					0.002 (0.009)			
LEGAL						−0.074 (−0.606)		
COLONY							−0.074 (−0.606)	
REGION								
EAPR								−0.036 (−0.290)
EUCAR								0.064 (0.536)
LACR								0.146 (0.979)
N	45	45	45	44	45	45	45	45
R^2 (adjusted)	0.76	0.75	0.75	0.77	0.79	0.75	0.75	0.74
F statistic	10.75***	9.59***	9.54***	10.03***	10.36***	9.70***	9.70***	8.19***

Variable definitions *TEVA* tax evasion, *AGE* age, *GEND* gender, *EDUC* education, *ILEVEL* income level (*LILEVEL* low income level and *HILEVEL* high income level), *ISOURCE* income source (*AISOURCE* agriculture income source and *SISOURCE* services income source), *MTR* marginal tax rates, *FAIR* fairness, *COMP* complexity, *SELFA* revenue authority contact, *MORALE* morale, *EDEV* economic development, *DEMOC* democracy, *CULT* culture, *RELIG* religion (*PROT* protestant, *CATH* catholic, *MUSL* muslim and *OTHRD* other denomination), *LEGAL* legal system, *COLONY* colonial heritage and *REGION* regional developing countries (*EAPR* East Asia and Pacific region, *EUCAR* Europe and Central Asia region and *LACR* Latin America and Caribbean region). t-statistics are in parentheses. Standard errors are corrected for heteroschedasticity

*, **, *** Significant at 0.10, 0.05 and 0.01 levels, respectively

†Reference category only

Overall, the results of the sensitivity analysis show that the associations identified in the earlier regressions are robust to an alternative measure of tax evasion.

2.4.4   Additional Analysis

Reviews of the tax evasion literature by Jackson and Milliron (1986) and Richardson and Sawyer (2001) illustrate that major interactions between the key tax evasion determinants should also be considered in empirical tax evasion research. They argue that a potential reason for some of the inconsistent findings in previous tax evasion research is that interactions between the key tax evasion determinants are not taken into account by researchers. Indeed, Table 2.2 above reports some interesting correlations between several of the key tax evasion determinants.[7] Additional analysis is thus carried out in this study to include interactions terms for AGE*GEND, AGE*ILEVEL, AGE*ISOURCE, AGE*MTR, AGE*FAIR, EDUC*FAIR, ILEVEL*MTR, ISOURCE*FAIR and FAIR*COMP in separate regression models to consider whether these interactions are significant and/or change the base regression model findings reported in Table 2.3 (Column 1). While not reported here, the additional regression analysis finds that none of these interactions are significant predictors of tax evasion ($p < 0.10$).[8] Moreover, the base regression model findings remain unchanged (with no changes in sign) after including the various interactions. This additional analysis shows that the associations identified in the earlier regressions are robust to several interactions between the independent variables.

2.5   Conclusion

While tax evasion has been a popular academic research topic in most developed countries over a long period of time, there seems to be a lack of research which considers the major determinants of tax evasion on a cross-country basis. While Riahi-Belkaoui's (2004) pioneering work is noteworthy, he concentrates on the association between selected determinants of tax morale and tax evasion. This study expanded on the work of Riahi-Belkaoui (2004) and systematically examined on a cross-country basis, many of the key determinants of tax evasion.

----

[7]Specifically, correlations ($p < 0.01$) are found between AGE and GEND ($r = 0.44$), AGE and ILEVEL (AGE and LILEVEL, $r = 0.62$; AGE and HILEVEL, $r = -0.72$), AGE and ISOURCE (AGE and AISOURCE, $r = -0.60$; AGE and SISOURCE, $r = 0.49$), AGE and MTR ($r = 0.51$), AGE and FAIR ($r = 0.45$), EDUC and FAIR ($r = 0.55$), ILEVEL and MTR (LILEVEL and MTR, $r = 0.52$; HILEVEL and MTR, $r = -0.58$), ISOURCE and FAIR (AISOURCE and FAIR, $r = -0.54$; SISOURCE and FAIR, $r = 0.49$) and FAIR and COMP ($r = -0.49$).

[8]These additional results are available from the author upon request.

The regression results show that non-economic determinants have the strongest impact on tax evasion in comparison with economic determinants. By integrating these various determinants in mixed models of tax evasion, our understanding is enhanced about tax evasion across countries. Complexity is found to be the main determinant of tax evasion. Other key determinants of tax evasion found are education, income source, fairness and tax morale. Overall, the regression results show that the lower the level of complexity and the higher the level of education, services income source, fairness and tax morale, the lower is the level of tax evasion. These results are robust to different cross-country control variables, another measure of tax evasion and several interactions.

Whilst data availability limits the conclusiveness of this study's findings, the results reported in this study may have implications for governments internationally when consideration is given to the key issue of reducing the tax evasion levels in society. For example, attempts could be made by governments to make improvements to the levels of complexity in the tax system. Tax evasion appears to be controlled by reduced levels of complexity. By enhancing the general educational knowledge of taxpayers, tax evasion is also reduced. Wage and salary income subject to withholding also represents another important curb on tax evasion. It seems that the least opportunity exists for those taxpayers whose source of income is dependent on wages or salaries subject to withholding such as in the services employment sector. Perceptions by taxpayers that tax policy is fair also lead to improvements in tax evasion levels. Finally, where tax morale is high, this also provides another key control on tax evasion. All of these insights should allow policy makers to gain a better understanding of what represents the major causes of tax evasion internationally, and design and implement appropriate measures to control and restrain its damaging effects. This could lead to improvements in tax revenue collection by governments.

This study is subject to several limitations. First, due to data unavailability, other potential tax evasion determinants such as occupation status, sanctions, probability of detection and compliant peers were not included. Hence, this study might experience omitted variable bias. Second, the sample size of 45 countries is fairly small compared to the total number of countries in the world, which means that the results may not be conclusive. However, this is a common problem of cross-country tax research generally (Fisman and Gatti 2002; Brunetti and Weader 2003; Riahi-Belkaoui 2004). Third, tax evasion was measured in this study using subjective survey ratings. This raises concerns about its reliability as it could be prone to measurement error. Data are averaged over several years to minimize the possibility of measurement error for this variable. Fourth, using survey data measures for some of the independent and control variables raises concern about measurement error for these variables. While this issue cannot be ruled out entirely, every effort was made in this study to collect data from reputable sources and use averaged data measures for each independent and control variable, where possible.

Future research on tax evasion internationally could examine several issues. First, subject to reliable cross-country data becoming available, occupation status, sanctions, probability of detection and compliant peers could be analyzed. Second, research could be carried out using increased country sample sizes so that enhanced cross-country comparisons can be made. Third, research could be undertaken utilizing improved survey measures of tax evasion and various explanatory variables (e.g. complexity, education and fairness) so that the results are more reliable and the risk of measurement error is reduced further. Finally, future research in this area could develop a greater longitudinal emphasis and analyze the impact of changes in the key tax evasion determinants and other important variables on changes in the level of tax evasion.

Appendix

Data Description and Sources

Variable	Description	Source
Tax evasion (TEVA)	• Country rating that tax evasion is minimal (on a scale from 1—strongly disagree to 7—strongly agree) averaged for 2002–2004. This scale was transformed by deducting the country score from 8 to obtaining an increasing scale of tax evasion • Country rating of tax evasion (on a scale from 0—common to 10—not common) averaged for 2002–2004. This variable was transformed to obtain an increasing scale of tax evasion	*Global Competitiveness Report* (World Economic Forum 2002, 2003, 2004) *World Competitiveness Year Book* (Institute of Management Development 2002, 2003, 2004)
Age (AGE)	Percentage of the population which is greater than 65 years of age averaged for 2002–2004	*2005 World Development Indicators* (World Bank 2005a)
Gender (GEND)	Percentage of the population which is female averaged for 2002–2004	*2005 World Development Indicators* (World Bank 2005a)
Education (EDUC)	Country rating of the quality of the education system for a competitive economy (on a scale from 1—low to 7—high) averaged for 2002–2004	*World Competitiveness Year Book* (Institute of Management Development 2002, 2003, 2004)
Income level (ILEVEL)	• Proportion of household income going to the lowest 20 % of households (LILEVEL) averaged for 2002–2004 • Proportion of household income going to the highest 20 % of households (HILEVEL) averaged for 2002–2004	*World Competitiveness Year Book* (Institute of Management Development 2002, 2003, 2004)

(continued)

(continued)

Variable	Description	Source
Income source (ISOURCE)	• Employment by sector: agriculture percentage of total employment (AISOURCE) averaged for 2002–2004 • Employment by sector: services percentage of total employment (SISOURCE) averaged for 2002–2004	*World Competitiveness Year Book* (Institute of Management Development 2002, 2003, 2004)
Marginal tax rates (MTR)	The top marginal income tax rate for individuals of a country	*2005 World Development Indicators* (World Bank 2005a)
Fairness (FAIR)	Country rating of the fairness of tax policy (on a scale from 0—low fairness to 8—high fairness) for the 2002 year	*IPS National Competitiveness Report* (Institute for Industrial Policy Studies 2002)
Complexity (COMP)	Country rating of tax system complexity (on a scale from 1—high complexity to 7—low complexity) averaged for 2003–2004	*Global Competitiveness Report* (World Economic Forum 2003, 2004)
Revenue authority contact (SELFA)	Dummy variable of 1 if the country has a self-assessment tax system, 0 otherwise	Organisation for Economic Co-operation and Development (2004) http://www.oecd.org/dataoecd/28/2/33866659.pdf PricewaterhouseCoopers (2004) KPMG (2003) http://www.kpmg.com.hk
Tax morale (MORALE)	Country rating of cheating on taxes if you have the chance (on a scale from 1—never justifiable to 10—always justifiable) averaged for the 1981, 1990, 1995 and 1999 World Value Surveys. This variable was transformed to obtain an increasing scale of tax morale	Inglehart (2003) http://nds.umdl.umich.edu/cgi/s/sda/hsda?harcWEVS+wevs Inglehart et al. (2004)
Economic development (EDEV)	Natural log of GDP per capita averaged for 2001–2003	*2005 World Development Indicators* (World Bank 2005a)
Democracy (DEMOC)	Political rights index developed by Freedom House (on a scale from 1—high political rights to 7—low political rights), averaged for 2002–2004. This index was transformed to obtain an increasing scale of democracy	Freedom House (2005) http://www.freedomhouse.org/ratings/index.htm

(continued)

(continued)

Variable	Description	Source
Culture (CULT)	Ethnolinguistic fractionalization index measures the probability that two randomly selected individuals within a country belong to the same ethnic group. It is an index between 0 and 100, with 100 denoting lower fractionalization	Mauro (1995)
Religion (RELIG)	The percentages of Protestants (PROT), Catholics (CATH), Muslims (MUSL) and Other Denominations (OTHRD) in 1980 or 1990–1995 for countries of recent formation	La Porta et al. (1999)
Legal system (LEGAL)	Dummy variable of 1 if the country is a common law system country, 0 otherwise	La Porta et al. (1999)
Colonial heritage (COLONY)	Dummy variable of 1 if the country was ever a colony, 0 otherwise	Barro and Lee (1994)
Regional developing countries (REGION)	• Dummy variable of 1 if the developing country is in the East Asia and Pacific region (EAPR), 0 otherwise • Dummy variable of 1 if the developing country is in the Europe and Central Asia region (EUCAR), 0 otherwise • Dummy variable of 1 if the developing country is in the Latin America and the Caribbean region (LACR), 0 otherwise	*World Bank Group—Data and Statistics* (World Bank 2005b) http://www.worldbank.org/data/countryclass/classgroups.htm

References

Alm, J.M., and J. Martinez-Vazquez. 2003. Institutions, paradigms, and tax evasion in developing and transition countries. In *Public finance in developing and transitional countries,* ed. J. Martinez-Vazquez and J.J. Alm Cheltenham, 146–178. UK: Edward Elgar.

Alm, J., G.H. McClelland, and W.D. Schulze. 1999. Changing the social norm of tax compliance by voting. *KYKLOS* 48: 141–171.

Andreoni, J., B. Erard, and J. Feinstein. 1998. Tax compliance. *Journal of Economic Literature* 36: 818–860.

Barro, R., and J. Lee. 1994. Sources of economic growth. *Carnegie Rochester Conference Series on Public Policy* 40: 1–46.

Brooks, N., and A.H. Doob. 1990. Tax evasion: Searching for a theory of compliant behavior. In *Securing compliance: Seven case studies*, ed. M.L. Friedland, 122–164. Toronto: University of Toronto Press.

Brunetti, A., and B. Weader. 2003. A free press is bad news for corruption. *Journal of Public Economics* 87: 1801–1824.

Chan, C.W., C.S. Troutman, and D. O'Bryan. 2000. An expanded model of taxpayer compliance: Empirical evidence from the United States and Hong Kong. *Journal of International Accounting, Auditing and Taxation* 9: 83–103.

Christian, C.W., and S. Gupta. 1993. New evidence on secondary evasion. *Journal of the American Taxation Association* 16: 72–93.

Clotfelter, C.T. 1983. Tax evasion and tax rates: An analysis of individual returns. *The Review of Economics and Statistics* 65: 363–373.

Collins, J.H., V.C. Milliron, and D.R. Toy. 1992. Determinants of tax compliance: A contingency approach. *Journal of the American Taxation Association* 14: 1–29.

Coleman, C., and L. Freeman. 1997. Cultural foundations of taxpayer attitudes to voluntary compliance. *Australian Tax Forum* 13: 311–336.

Cuccia, A.D. 1994. The economics of tax compliance: What do we know and where do we go? *Journal of Accounting Literature* 13: 81–116.

Cummings, R.G., J. Martinez-Vazquez, and M. McKee. 2001. Cross cultural comparisons of tax compliance behavior. Working Paper No. 01-3, International Studies Program, Andrew Young School of Policy Studies, Georgia State University, Atlanta, Georgia.

Das-Gupta, A., R. Lahiri, and D. Mookherjee. 1995. Income tax compliance in India: An empirical analysis. *World Development* 23: 2051–2064.

Dubin, J.A., and L.L. Wilde. 1988. An empirical analysis of federal income tax auditing and compliance. *National Tax Journal* 41: 61–74.

Feinstein, J.S. 1991. An econometric analysis of income tax evasion and its detection. *RAND Journal of Economics* 22: 14–35.

Feld, L.P., and J.R. Tyran. 2002. Tax evasion and voting: An experimental analysis. *KYKLOS* 55: 197–222.

Fisman, R., and R. Gatti. 2002. Decentralization and corruption: Evidence across countries. *Journal of Public Economics* 83: 325–345.

Freedom House. 2005. *Freedom House Country Ratings.* New York: Freedom House. http://www.freedomhouse.org/ratings/index.htm.

Gillis, M. 1989. *Tax reform in developing countries.* Durham, NC: Duke University Press.

Hanno, D.M., and G.R. Violette. 1996. An analysis of moral and social influences on tax behavior. *Behavioral Research in Accounting* 8: 57–75.

Hite, A., and M.L. Roberts. 1992. An analysis of tax reform based on taxpayers' perceptions of fairness and self-interest. *Advances in Taxation* 4: 115–137.

Inglehart, R. 2003. *Human values and social change: Findings from the values surveys.* Leiden, Boston: Brill. http://nds.umdl.umich.edu/cgi/s/sda/hsda?harcWEVS+wevs.

Inglehart, R., M. Basanez, J. Diez-Medrano, L. Halman, and R. Luijkx. 2004. *Human beliefs and values: A cross-cultural sourcebook based on the 1999–2002 value surveys.* Mexico, Siglo XXI 2004.

Institute of Management Development. 2002. *The world competitiveness yearbook.* Lausanne, Switzerland: IMD.

Institute of Management Development. 2003. *The world competitiveness yearbook.* Lausanne, Switzerland: IMD.

Institute of Management Development. 2004. *The world competitiveness yearbook.* Lausanne, Switzerland: IMD.

Institute for Industrial Policy Studies. 2002. *IPS national competitiveness report.* Seoul, South Korea: IPS.

Jackson, B.R., and V.C. Milliron. 1986. Tax compliance research: Findings, problems and prospects. *Journal of Accounting Literature* 5: 125–165.

Klepper, S., and D. Nagin. 1989a. The anatomy of tax evasion. *Journal of Law Economics and Organization* 5: 1–24.

Klepper, S., and D. Nagin. 1989b. The role of tax preparers in tax compliance. *Policy Sciences* 22: 167–194.

KPMG. 2003. *Asia pacific taxation.*Hong Kong: KPMG. http://www.kpmg.com.hk.

La Porta, R., F. Lopez-de-Silanes, A. Shleifer, and R. Vishny. 1999. The quality of government. *The Journal of Law, Economics and Organization* 15: 222–279.

Long, S., and J. Swingen. 1988. The role of legal complexity in shaping taxpayer compliance. In *Lawyers on psychology and psychologists on law*, ed. P.J. Van Koppen, P.J.D. Hessing, and G. Van den Heuvel, 127–146. Amsterdam, the Netherlands: Swets and Zeitlinger.

Long, S., and J. Swingen. 1991. Taxpayer compliance: Setting new agendas for research. *Law and Society Review* 25: 637–683.

Mason, R., and L. Calvin. 1978. A study of admitted income tax evasion. *Law and Society Review* 12: 73–89.

Mason, R., and L. Calvin. 1984. Public confidence and admitted tax evasion. *National Tax Journal* 37: 489–496.

Mason, R., and H. Lowry. 1981. *An estimate of income tax evasion in oregon.* Corvallis, Oregon: Oregon State University, Survey Research Center.

Mauro, P. 1995. Corruption and growth. *The Quarterly Journal of Economics* 110: 681–712.

Milliron, V.C., and D.R. Toy. 1988. Tax compliance: An investigation of key features. *Journal of the American Tax Association* 10: 84–104.

Organisation for Economic Co-operation and Development. 2002. *Tax database.* Paris: OECD. http://www.oecd.org/dataoecd/44/2/1942506.xls.

Organisation for Economic Co-operation and Development. 2004. *Tax administration in OECD countries.* Paris: OECD. http://www.oecd.org/dataoecd/28/2/33866659.pdf.

Pommerehne, W.W., and H. Weck-Hannemann. 1996. Tax rates, tax administration and income tax evasion in Switzerland. *Public Choice* 88: 161–170.

PricewaterhouseCoopers. 2004. *Individual taxes 2004–2005: Worldwide summaries.* New York: John Wiley.

Quirk, P.J. 1997. Money laundering: Muddying the macro economy. *Finance and Development* 34: 7–9.

Riahi-Belkaoiu, A. 2004. Relationship between tax compliance internationally and selected determinants of tax morale. *Journal of International Accounting, Auditing and Taxation* 13: 135–143.

Richardson, M., and A.J. Sawyer. 2001. A taxonomy of the tax compliance literature: Further findings, problems and prospects. *Australian Tax Forum* 16: 137–320.

Richupan, S. 1984. *Income tax evasion: A review of the measurement of techniques and some estimates for the developing countries.* Department Memorandum No. DM/84/46, The International Monetary Fund, Fiscal Affairs Department, Washington, DC.

Sarker, T.K. 2003. Improving tax compliance in developing countries via self-assessment systems —what could Bangladesh learn from Japan? *Asia-Pacific Tax Bulletin* 9: 170–176.

Schmolders, G. 1970. Survey research in public finance: A behavioral approach to fiscal theory. *Public Finance* 25: 300–306.

Song, Y., and T. Yarbrough. 1978. Tax ethics and tax attitudes: A survey. *Public Administration Review* 58: 442–452.

Spicer, M. 1974. *A behavioral model of income tax evasion.* Unpublished Ph.D. thesis, Ohio State University.

Spicer, M., and S. Lundstedt. 1976. Audit probabilities and the tax evasion decision: An experimental approach. *Journal of Economic Psychology* 2: 241–245.

Tan, L.M., and A.J. Sawyer. 2003. A synopsis of taxpayer compliance studies: Overseas vis-à-vis New Zealand. *New Zealand Journal of Taxation Law and Policy* 9: 431–454.

Tanzi, V. 2000. *Policies, institutions and the dark side of economics.* Cheltenham, UK: Edward Elgar.

Tittle, C. 1980. *Sanctions and social deviance: The question of deterrence.* New York: Praeger.

Torgler, B. 2003a. *Tax morale and tax evasion: Evidence from the United States.* WWZ Discussion Paper 02/-7, Basel, Switzerland.

Torgler, B. 2003b. Tax morale and institutions. Working Paper No. 2003-09, Center for Research in Economics, Management and the Arts, Basel, Switzerland.

Torgler, B. 2005. Tax morale in Latin America. *Public Choice* 122: 133–157.

Torgler, B., and K. Murphy. 2004. Tax morale in Australia: what shapes it and has it changed over time? *Journal of Australian Taxation* 7: 298–335.

Torgler, B., C.A. Schaltegger, and M. Schaffner. 2003. Is forgiveness divine? A cross-culture comparison of tax amnesties. *Swiss Journal of Economics and Statistics* 139: 375–396.

Treisman, D. 2000. The causes of corruption: A cross-national study. *Journal of Public Economics* 76: 399–457.

Vogel, J. 1974. Taxation and public opinion in Sweden: An interpretation of recent survey data. *National Tax Journal* 27: 499–513.

Wallschutzky, I. 1984. Possible causes of tax evasion. *Journal of Economic Psychology* 5: 371–384.

Witte, A.D., and D.F. Woodbury. 1983. The effect of tax laws and tax administration on tax compliance. Working Paper 83-1, Department of Economics, University of North Carolina, Chapel Hill, North Carolina.

Witte, A.D., and D.F. Woodbury. 1985. The effect of tax laws and tax administration on tax compliance: The case of the US individual income tax. *National Tax Journal* 38: 1–13.

World Bank. 2005a. *2005 world development indicators.* Washington, DC: World Bank.

World Bank. 2005b. *2005 world bank group—data and statistics.* Washington, DC: World Bank. http://www.worldbank.org/data/countryclass/classgroups.htm.

World Economic Forum. 2002. *The global competitiveness report 2001–2002.* Geneva: WEF.

World Economic Forum. 2003. *The global competitiveness report 2002–2003.* Geneva: WEF.

World Economic Forum. 2004. *The global competitiveness report 2003–2004.* Geneva: WEF.

You, J.S., and S. Khagram. 2005. A comparative study of inequality and corruption. *American Sociological Review* 70: 136–157.

Chapter 3
What Determines Information Sharing for Income Tax Purposes: The Swedish Case

Jenny E. Ligthart, Barbara Maria Sadaba and Rene van Stralen

Abstract The sharing of information between national tax authorities for income tax purposes has recently become a central topic in international tax policy discussions. Tax authorities share tax information with a view to stem tax evasion on residents' cross-border income under the residence principle, which prescribes taxation of residents' worldwide income. Little is known about the nature of the determinants of tax information sharing, let alone countries' experiences with information sharing. Most countries treat data on the use of information sharing with considerable confidentiality. Using a unique dataset on tax information sharing between the Swedish tax authorities and tax authorities of both industrialized and transition countries, we describe the Swedish experience and investigate the determinants of tax information sharing. Our benchmark sample presents data for the year between 1993 and 2000 for 45 countries. The information sharing process is modeled by a unilateral gravity model, where the dependent variable measures the degree to which Sweden's partner country has provided tax information. To explain any additional heterogeneity above and beyond the basic gravity pattern, we include additional control variables, time dummies, and several variables of interest. We find that the height of a country's domestic income tax rate and the lowness of the non-resident withholding tax rate increase its willingness to provide spontaneous tax information.

The authors would like to thank Jan Mattsen of the National Tax Board of Sweden for making available the data on tax information sharing.

Please note that prof. Jenny E. Ligthart has passed away.

J.E. Ligthart · B.M. Sadaba (✉) · R. van Stralen
Tilburg University, Tilburg, Netherlands
e-mail: b.m.sadaba@gmail.com

R. van Stralen
e-mail: renestralen@gmail.com

3.1 Introduction

In recent years, tax evasion issues have been in the centre of the international tax policies debate. With the increased possibilities of transferring investments and savings abroad, taxpayers can easily conceal their capital income and asset ownership from the government. Thus, the ability of governments to efficiently tax cross border capital and asset holdings is highly compromised. Although not precisely known, this constitutes a considerable loss of revenue. This situation has called for stepped up international cooperation between national tax authorities in the form of tax information sharing. International tax policies are ruled by the residence principle. Under the residence principle, income tax is ultimately payable to the country where the taxpayer resides, deducted from the taxes applicable in the country where the person (or company) generates the taxable income. It is precisely because of this principle that information sharing has become necessary. To enforce the residence principle, tax authorities of countries rely on their residents' own reports (through a system of self assessment) about their income and assets abroad. All too evident is the likelihood of misreporting. Therefore, residence countries need to have access to information about income generated in the source country. Significant efforts have been made by international organizations such as the OECD and the EU to encourage tax information sharing among countries. These efforts became clear after the EU savings tax directive went into effect in July 2005 and the OECD "harmful tax practices" project took a turn and focused on transparency issues and information exchange (OECD 1998). Other examples follow. In 2007, the European Union launched a new cooperation program—Fiscalis 2013—that enables national tax administrators to create and exchange information and expertise.[1] Also, the OECD encourages tax havens to sign bilateral tax information sharing agreements. Recently, the political pressure for non-complying and tax haven countries to sign bilateral agreements is rising and the G20 countries agreed on a set of economic sanctions against non-cooperating countries (OECD 2010). On the other hand, as of July 1, 2005, 24 EU member states automatically exchange information on individuals' interest income among each other. Specifically, all EU member states and some third countries and dependent territories are required to apply either a withholding tax or exchange tax information on the interest income of foreign citizens. However, little is known about the size and nature of information flows among countries. Not much is known about countries' incentives to exchange tax information, except for a few theoretical contributions focusing on information sharing for income tax purposes. The key theoretical challenge is to understand why countries would engage in tax information sharing. By sharing tax information, a country has to bear the cost of information gathering and it becomes a less attractive place to investors. But in reality we observe that countries do share tax information.

---

[1]European Commission, Taxation and Customs Union. http://ec.europa.eu/taxation_customs/taxation/tax_cooperation/fiscalis_programme/fiscalis2013/index_en.htm.

This apparent puzzle makes it interesting to explore the underlying reasons that bring a country to engage in information sharing activities.

Two papers present theoretical models that provide plausible determinants of tax information sharing decisions. Bacchetta and Espinosa (2000) and Huizinga and Nielsen (2003) argue that bilateral cooperation in tax information sharing may be sustained if the choice of tax rates is viewed as an infinitely-repeated game rather than a one-off move. Each country then weights the present one-off gain from not cooperating in sharing information against the loss of the other country not cooperating forever. Both papers derive the gains of defecting, providing in this way a list of potential determinants of information sharing. There exist few empirical works on tax information sharing. Notable exceptions are Ligthart and Voget (2009) and Schwarz (2009), who looks into the reasons behind the lack of countries' engagement in tax information sharing on interest income. However, the author follows an analysis that tests the effectiveness of the EU Savings Tax Directive. In an attempt to fill the theoretical-empirical gap in the literature, this paper provides an empirical test of these set of determinants suggested in the theoretical literature.

To achieve this, we use a panel data sample on tax information shared by the Swedish tax authorities for the empirical analysis. Our data set consists of a sample of 45 countries between the years 1993–2000. The approach taken bears resemblance to the popular gravity model of international trade flows. Tinbergen (1962) and Poyhonen (1963) were the first authors to apply the gravity equation to analyse international trade flows. According to this model, exports from country i to country j are explained by their economic sizes (Gross Domestic Product or Gross National Product), direct geographical distances and a set of dummies incorporating some type of institutional characteristics common to specific flows. With respect to the structure of our data, the dependent variable has many zero-valued observations. These are due to the lack of information flows with many countries of our complete sample. To deal with this feature of the data, we use the Tobit regression model. The determinants proposed in the theoretical literature will be taken up in the empirical analysis of this paper.

Our results show that some of these determinants are significant for the decision of sharing information. The height of the domestic income tax rate, the size of the marginal cost of public funds, and the share of a country's interest-bearing deposits held abroad increase a country's willingness to engage in information sharing. The remainder of this paper is organized as follows. Section 3.2 discusses a simple theoretical model that gives raise to several hypotheses to be answered in this paper. Section 3.3 analyses tax information data and describe the panel dataset used in the regression analysis. Section 3.4 presents the empirical methodology. Section 3.5 presents the estimation results and robustness checks. Section 3.6 discusses the implications of our results and finally, Sect. 3.7 concludes.

3.2   Tax Information Sharing

Before the empirical methodology is discussed, we first provide some background on the economic, operational, and institutional issues related to information exchange.

3.2.1   Incentives for Sharing

In the previous section, it was mentioned that sharing tax information conveys two drawbacks for any country: (1) the country exporting information becomes less attractive for foreign investors (because the source country helps the residence country to enforce its income taxes) and (2) it has to bear the administrative costs of information gathering which is a higher burden the less developed the country's tax administration and banking system is. Then, the question that remains is under what circumstances does self-interest drive source countries (i.e. where the capital is invested) to voluntarily supply information to residence countries? The theoretical literature has set out two opposing arguments. On the one hand, some authors (Tanzi and Zee 2001) argue that given that information sharing is incentive incompatible; that is, in a decentralized equilibrium no tax information is going to be shared voluntarily. On the other hand, some authors (Bacchetta and Espinosa 1995; Keen and Ligthart 2006a, b, 2007) have pointed out the existence of a beneficial strategic effect to information sharing. By providing tax information, the information exporting country allows the information importing country to set higher tax rates. This effect, in turn, allows the information exporting country to charge a higher tax as well without losing much of its capital imports. This beneficial strategic effect is assumed to dominate the negative effect on revenue of a reduced volume of capital flows due to higher taxes. Therefore, self-interested behaviour drives countries to cooperate on information provision. One crucial assumption of this analysis is that there are only two large countries, otherwise the strategic effect breaks down due to countries' free riding on information provided by others. Another reason for information sharing is related to repeated interaction between countries over time. Even if no two stage game strategic advantage is present, some form of bilateral cooperation can be sustained if the game is infinitely repeated.

3.2.2   Analytical Framework

Following the work of Bacchetta and Espinosa (2000) and Huizinga and Nielsen (2003) in this section we briefly describe the theoretical model that introduces the potential determinants of information sharing decisions.[2] Consider a world consisting of two small countries. Each country features a continuum of households that live for one period. The population size remains constant. Each individual is endowed with one unit of savings, which can be either invested abroad (denoted by F) or in the home country. Investment abroad involves convex and continuous transaction costs, $\sigma(F)$ with $\sigma(0) = 0$ and $\sigma''' \geq 0$, whereas investment at home does not incur any transaction costs. These transaction costs can represent the expenses of gathering extra information about legal issues, of overcoming country specific regulations, of hiring foreign employees, and so on. The net cost of investing abroad is not necessarily positive. Foreign investment bears a mobility cost, but it may yield benefits in addition to the net return (Bacchetta and Espinosa 2000). Both countries have constant-returns-to-scale production technology, yielding a constant rate of interest (r). The domestic tax authority can perfectly monitor all domestic investments, but can only monitor a constant fraction of the foreign investments made by its own residents. The degree of non-monitored investments abroad is denoted by $0 \leq k \leq 1$ for the home country. Similarly, for the foreign country, we define $0 \leq k' \leq 1$ where asterisks denote foreign variables. Individuals investing abroad are assumed not to report their foreign income to the tax authorities of their country of residence. Without assistance from the source country, the residence country has a hard time identifying those of its own residents who have saved abroad. However, the tax authorities of the source country can transmit a proportion of information on tax evaders' income (ξ and ξ' for the home and foreign country, respectively) to their country of residence. For individual investors, the probability of being monitored by the home country's tax authorities $(1 - k)$ is independent from the probability of being reported by the foreign country (ξ'). It is assumed that information transmission is costless. Domestic investment is subject to the domestic income tax (τ for the home country and τ' for the foreign country). Non-monitored foreign investment income is subject to the non-resident withholding tax only. Non-resident withholding taxes in the home (foreign) country are denoted by $t_N(t'_N)$. In accordance with the residence principle, monitored foreign investment income is taxed in the residence country at the domestic income tax rate minus a (100 %) tax credit for non-resident withholding tax paid abroad. No penalty on tax evasion applies, but this can be easily taken into account. This can be done by introducing an additional cost coefficient representing cost to investing abroad subject to the probability of being discovered. Given that investing abroad is seen as a tax evasion activity this is a straightforward way of introducing this penalty. This cost increase could create incentives for the marginal investors to keep investments in the domestic country. Households maximize a well-behaved utility function, which depends on private consumption and a public good, subject to their budget constraint. Because the government decides on public consumption, utility maximization of individuals amounts to the maximization of private consumption with respect to foreign investments. More formally, a home investor deposits

---

[2]The description follows closely Ligthart and Voget (2009).

abroad until the net marginal return on foreign investments is equal to the net marginal return on domestic investments:

$$r[1 - t'_N - (1 - k(1 - \xi'))(\tau - t'_N)] - \sigma'(F) = r(1 - \tau) \tag{3.1}$$

For the foreign investor the same rule looks like:

$$r[1 - t_N - (1 - k'(1 - \xi))(\tau' - t_N)] - \sigma'(F) = r(1 - \tau') \tag{3.2}$$

Equation (3.1) says that the home country's optimal foreign investments *(F)* turn on a comparison of the transaction costs incurred in depositing funds abroad $(\sigma'(F))$ and the taxes saved in doing so $(k'(1 - \xi)(\tau' - t_N))$. In a previous stage of the game, the tax rates are set such that $\tau - t'_N > 0$ and $\tau' - t_N > 0$, implying that an interior solution results (where $F, F' > 0$). Because a higher degree of information provision makes foreign investments less attractive, $\frac{\partial F}{\partial \xi}$ and $\frac{\partial F}{\partial \xi}$ are negative. Following Bacchetta and Espinosa (2000), a second-best world is considered in which the home government finances its public spending *(G)* entirely by distortionary taxes on interest income from domestic and foreign sources. This implies that,

$$G = \tau r(1 - F) + t_N rF' + [1 - k(1 - \xi')](\tau - t'_N)rF$$

where the first two terms refer to domestic sources. Consequently, the marginal cost of public funds (η) exceeds unity. Governments maximize welfare, which is the discounted utility of present and future generations, by choosing their income tax rate, non-resident withholding tax rate, and degree of tax information sharing. We consider the special case in which countries have set their non-resident withholding taxes cooperatively, implying that a double tax relief treaty is optimal for both countries. Subsequently, the two governments play a Nash game in income tax rates, taking into account the tax effect on households' savings allocations. After governments have set their taxes, private investors decide how much to invest abroad. We analyse countries' incentives to cooperate on tax information sharing. To simplify the analysis, the effect of information sharing on the sustainability of the double tax relief treaty is ignored. Furthermore, governments cannot enjoy one-off gains from deviating from information sharing, because it is assumed that the foreign (home) private sector cannot react to a change in $\xi(\xi')$ before the foreign (home) government does. Consequently, countries' discount rates do not play a role. If one country does not transmit information, it is 'punished' by the other country that abstains from information provision too. In this context, the following condition applies (see Eq. (13) of Bacchetta and Espinosa 2000):

$$\Omega = t_N \frac{\partial F}{\partial \xi} - [\tau - (1 - k(1 - \xi'))(\tau - t'_N)]\frac{\partial F'}{\partial \xi'} + \left(\frac{\eta - 1}{\eta}\right)k(\tau - t'_N)F > 0 \tag{3.3}$$

where Ω indicates the home country's willingness to exchange information. The first term of (3.3) represents the costs of information provision to the home country, whereas the second and third terms denote the benefits of receiving information. Factors that increase Ω make the home country more willing to exchange information. This yields a set of economic and institutional determinants for the empirical analysis, which we will discuss in turn.

3.2.3 Hypotheses to Be Tested

The theoretical framework detailed in the previous section provides the starting point for the definition of six hypotheses to be tested in the present work. We define them as follows. Huizinga and Nielsen (2003) show that countries with a high income tax rate on residents are more likely to provide information than countries with a low income tax rate. This means that the second term of (3.3) increases by $\frac{\partial F'}{\partial \xi'} < 0$.

Hypothesis 3.1 A country is more likely to cooperate on information sharing if the resident income tax rate is high.

A large non-resident withholding tax rate makes the first term of (3.3) more negative since $\frac{\partial F'}{\partial \xi'} < 0$, reducing a country's incentive to share information (Hypothesis 3.2). The additional revenue a country gets from the foreign savings of its own residents (which are brought into tax due to tax information sharing) exceeds the loss of revenue from non-resident savings (which will be relocated to information free' places).

Hypothesis 3.2 A country is more likely to cooperate on information sharing if its domestic non-resident withholding tax rate is low.

The third term of Eq. (3.3) demonstrates that countries with a sizable public sector—featuring a large marginal cost of public funds (Browning 1976)—are more likely to engage in information sharing. Intuitively, these countries derive a larger gain from the additional resources brought into tax, owing to the received tax information (Hypothesis 3.3).

Hypothesis 3.3 Countries that value public goods more than private goods (and thus feature a high marginal cost of public funds) have more incentives to share information.

Bacchetta and Espinosa (1995, 2000) state that countries with a large share of investment abroad are more eager to share information than countries where a lot of foreign capital is deposited (Hypothesis 3.4). This argument follows the analysis of Tanzi and Zee (2001), who claim that countries being net exporters of capital would place a higher value on tax information received than countries that are net importers of capital.

Hypothesis 3.4 Countries that have a large share of financial assets abroad are more eager to share information than countries where a lot of foreign capital is deposited.

The degree of monitoring that a country is able to exert plays a role in determining the amount of information shared by a country. If he country is able to monitor a large proportion of its residents' tax payers and thus prevent much of domestic tax evasion, it will be less interested in tax information sharing with other countries. More formally, the second and third terms of (3.3) are positive, where $\frac{\partial F'}{\partial \xi'} < 0$, $\frac{\partial (\partial F'/\partial \xi')}{\partial k} < 0$, and $\frac{\partial F}{\partial k} < 0$. Intuitively, there is less need for information sharing if a country can obtain most information by its own means (Hypothesis 3.5).

Hypothesis 3.5 Countries that are more able to monitor their residents' financial transactions (i.e., implying a smaller k) provide less tax information.

Keen and Ligthart (2006b) defend the idea that reciprocity can be seen as process to diminish cost, such as administration and monitoring cost, which will be shared among the countries. To test for reciprocity in our model, we will add the lagged information outflow as a regressor in our model and analyze the significance and sign of its coefficient.

Hypothesis 3.6 Reciprocity among countries may influence the information flows and may be even more important than other determinants.

3.3 Data

Our data set contains tax information sharing by the Swedish tax authorities with tax authorities of foreign countries for income tax purposes during the period 1993–2000. It is reported in Tables 3.7 and 3.8 in the appendix. The exchanged information typically includes the following items: banking records (i.e., interest income earned, account number, and contact information of paying agent), fiscal residence of an individual, and expenses recorded on a tax return. The data points refer to the annual number of completed cases of information shared spontaneously between the 2 countries. All listed countries have at least provided information to Sweden once. The countries are ranked by the annual average size of the information flows. Information flows can be decomposed into three types: (i) automatic; (ii) on request; and (iii) spontaneous. As for the first type, there was no automatically received information during this period. The annual average number of cases on which Sweden was provided information on request is 190.13 and spontaneously 223.38, which on average, means that spontaneously received information accounts for 54 %, and requested information amounts to 46 % of the total amount of information received by Sweden. The dependent variable in our econometric analysis is the number of cases per year for which a partner country's tax authority has provided information to the Swedish tax authority spontaneously. The sample of our benchmark regression consists of 45 countries. This sample includes all the 34 current OECD member countries plus the former Soviet Union countries, also known as Baltic, Russia and others (BRO). This sample contains all countries in which a tax-evading investor may consider putting his or her funds. We exclude tax havens which will be part of a broader sample of 81 countries that the OECD (2006) list consider as the most important countries regarding tax information sharing. This larger sample, which comprises all industrialized countries as well as the larger developing countries and important tax havens, will later be used to perform a robustness check.

Ranking the countries by size in our benchmark sample we observe that larger countries in terms of economic size (as measured by Gross Domestic Product per capita) provide more information to Sweden than small ones. This is confirmed by Table 3.3 in the appendix. The partial correlation coefficient between the information flows and GDP per capita is positive and equal to 0.32 for spontaneous information inflows and to 0.45 for the corresponding outflows. The table also demonstrate that there is a significant negative correlation between the distance and the information provision by partner countries. Indeed, 13 countries from the sample, which cover 73 % of the imported information by Sweden, are EU countries. On the information export side, the figure is very similar, 11 countries from the sample are EU members. To get some insight into reciprocity in information sharing which will be discussed in more detail later on, we look at the correlation coefficient between inflows and outflows of information, which is equal to 0.79. This suggests that there is a high degree of reciprocity among countries. Therefore, the correlation coefficients and their sign are in line with the literature and our economic intuition.

3.4 Empirical Methodology

As was previously discussed, the approach chosen to measure the determinants of tax information exchange can be seen as an adaptation of the gravity model of bilateral trade flows (Tinbergen 1962; Anderson 1979). From the data description it appears that large countries and those close to Sweden send more information. Therefore, in this section we apply a modified gravity model to study the determinants of spontaneous information sharing[3] where the main control variables are Gross Domestic Product—as a proxy of economic size—and the distance between partner countries and Sweden. Furthermore, we will focus on tax information inflow to Sweden that has been shared spontaneously by the partner country. We expect information shared spontaneously to provide the strongest relationship between information flows and our set of determinants. Information flows on request can present difficulties for the estimations since zero-valued observations

---

[3]Real GDP of Sweden is not included since it becomes part of the time fixed effect.

could obey to a partner country's unwillingness to share, but also to the absence of demand for tax information. Positive values also present some duality in their meaning since they could represent the maximum willingness to supply information or the maximum demand for Sweden.

The model used attempts to explain the observed variation in the dependent variable, which are the inflows of tax information shared spontaneously with Sweden. With that purpose, we use, among others, two main independent variables: the partner country's economic size, proxied by a country's real GDP per capita, and the distance between both countries' capital cities. In addition to these two variables proposed in the basic gravity model, we include several other main control variables: domestic tax rates, non-resident withholding taxes, assets abroad (measured by the ratio of foreign deposits of a country over the sum of time and demand deposits of that country's banking sector) the expenditure-to-GDP ratio, which serves as a proxy to measure the marginal cost of public funds, and the degree of monitoring by tax authorities. This latter variable is approximated by: (i) the amount of bank secrecy and bank reporting indicating if income information is automatically reported to tax authorities; and (ii) the auditing intensity, proxied by the number of auditors per taxpayer in 2004. In our additional regressions, we also include the outflow of information to check for reciprocity. In the appendix all variables and their respective sources are described in detail. To capture additional observed heterogeneity in information flows, we include geographic and demographic control variables. As geographic variables we include a dummy to identify if countries are landlocked and the logarithm of the country's total surface area to capture the country's physical size (Keen and Ligthart 2006a; Ligthart 2007).

Given that the data contain much zero-valued information flows[4] and that the model implies non-negative predicted values for the tax information inflow, a Tobit regression model to estimate the parameters is the most convenient and appropriate in this case (Wooldridge 2009). The model for country $i = 1, \ldots, N$ at time $t = 1, \ldots, T$ is specified as follows.

$$y_{it} = \begin{cases} e^{y_{it}^*} & \text{if } y_{it}^* \geq 0 \\ 0 & \text{if } y_{it}^* < 0 \end{cases} \tag{3.4}$$

where y_{it} stands for the amount of information that is shared and y_{it}^* is a latent variable. Therefore, the model can be summarized as follows.

$$y_{it}^* = \alpha_0 + \alpha_1 \ln Dist + \alpha_2 \ln GDP_{it} + \beta' x_{it} + \eta' q_{it} + \delta' d_t + \varepsilon_{it}, \tag{3.5}$$

where $\ln Dist_i$ is the logarithm of the distance between countries' capitals, $\ln GDP_{it}$ is the logarithm of the partner country's GDP per capita, x_{it} is a vector containing all the variables of interest, q_{it} encompasses all additional control variables, d_t is an annual dummy to capture time-specific effects, and ε_{it} represents the normally

---

[4]78 % of the observations in the sample are equal to zero for spontaneous information sharing.

distributed error term. According to Greene (1981, 2004a, b), fixed effects Tobit regressions, or panel Tobit are not fully adequate (reflecting the incidental parameter problem) if the time dimension of the panel is insufficiently large in relation to the country dimension. The main issue is the number of parameters which is defined as "$T + N$" and with a small time dimension, as N increases, the number of a parameters will explode. Moreover, most of the variation in our sample is across countries, but time fixed effects cannot be ignored. In order to solve these issues, we pool the observations and use clustered standard errors by country such that they are robust to correlation across time. We also include time dummies to capture any cyclical behaviour that might be present. This approach yields unbiased estimates even in the presence of unobservable country specific (random) effects.

3.5   Estimation Results

This section presents the results of the estimated models for spontaneous information sharing. For the benchmark estimation, we use a small sample of 45 countries. As a robustness check, we use a larger sample of 81 countries. In addition, we address the issues of reciprocity and the importance of legal instruments, such as, tax treaties, in enhancing information sharing.

3.5.1   The Benchmark Specification

The benchmark case consists of an estimated Tobit model for the 45 countries sample. Table 3.1 below reports the Tobit regression results explaining the flow of information from foreign tax authorities to the Swedish authorities during the period 1993–2000 for spontaneous tax information sharing. In column (1), we present our benchmark regression and in column (2)–(4) we add in turn, additional control variables, namely: auditors per taxpayer, a bank reporting dummy and a bank secrecy dummy. For all regressions in the table the coefficients on the time-specific fixed effects are omitted for clarity of exposition. Using these results, in Sect. 3.6 we discuss their implications for testing the validity of Hypotheses 3.1–3.5 proposed in the present work. In turn, Hypothesis 3.6 will be addressed with the results of complementary regressions from the robustness checks. The dependent variable, spontaneous information inflows, is included in logarithmic form to facilitate the interpretation of the results. Finally, to account for the zero valued observations when computing the logarithms, we add one to the original values of these observations which is to say that those originally zero valued observations remain so.

The benchmark regression (3.1) shows a coefficient of 0.027 for the *domestic income tax rate* which is significant at a 5 % level. In line with Hypothesis 3.1, this suggests that an increase in the foreign country's tax rate on its residents' interest income by 1 % point increases the amount of spontaneous information sent abroad

Table 3.1 Spontaneous tax information sharing: tobit regression results

Independent variables	(1)	(2)	(3)	(4)
Domestic income tax rate	0.027** (0.012)	0.029*** (0.008)	0.024** (0.009)	0.027*** (0.012)
Non-resident withholding tax rate	−41.78*** (10.96)	−43.42*** (10.50)	−52.17*** (14.03)	−41.71*** (11.17)
Expenditure-to-GDP ratio	6.43*** (2.37)	6.25*** (2.02)	6.89*** (2.53)	6.43*** (2.37)
Foreign deposit ratio	0.005*** (0.002)	0.006*** (0.001)	0.006*** (0.002)	0.005*** (0.002)
Auditing intensity	–	21.01*** (4.10)	–	–
Bank reporting dummy	–	–	−0.904*** (0.304)	–
Bank secrecy dummy	–	–	–	−1.329*** (0.309)
Real GDP per capita (in logarithms)	3.63*** (0.76)	3.23*** (0.58)	4.33*** (1.03)	3.62*** (0.77)
Distance (in logarithms)	−1.89*** (0.24)	−2.06*** (0.23)	−1.91*** (0.18)	−1.89** (0.24)
Surface area (in logarithms)	0.316** (0.142)	0.557*** (0.115)	0.365*** (0.101)	0.316** (0.142)
Landlocked dummy	−2.31*** (0.57)	−1.85*** (0.52)	−3.48*** (0.77)	−0.97 (0.63)
Observations	174	168	162	162
Censored observations	132	126	120	120
F statistic	1563.9	10,537.0	7595.7	1432.8
McFadden pseudo R squared	0.64	0.70	0.67	0.63
Log-likelihood	−58.95	−48.58	−52.43	−58.95
Time dummies	Yes	Yes	Yes	Yes

Notes The values in parentheses below the coefficients are clustered standard errors. ***, **, * denote significance at the 1, 5, 10 % level, respectively

by 2.7 %. This result is robust to the inclusion of further controls in the remaining columns. It is important to notice that the coefficients in Table 3.1 represent the marginal effects that vary across observations. Thus, Tobit estimates present an upper bound on the actual marginal effects. A country's non-resident *withholding tax* is negative and significant at a 1 % level for all four specifications. This says that an increase in non-resident withholding taxes causes a reduction in spontaneous information exchange among countries, which supports our second Hypothesis. The *expenditure-to-GDP* ratio features a positive and significant coefficient at a 1 % level. This presents strong support for Hypothesis 3.3 as the *expenditure-to-GDP ratio* serves as a proxy for the marginal cost of public funds. The ratio of deposits owned abroad over the sum of time and demand deposits—*foreign deposits ratio*— is positive and significant. This implies that the direction of impact is in line with what is expected. The coefficient on *auditor per taxpayer* is positive and significant suggesting that an increase in domestic surveillance signals the country's commitment to enhancing fiscal transparency, thus its higher willingness to share tax information abroad. In column (3) we incorporate a dummy variable capturing whether there is mandatory reporting by domestic financial institutions to the country's tax authority. The coefficient has the predicted negative sign, significant at the 1 % level. This indicates that if the fiscal authorities of a country have automatic access to bank information of taxpayers, the incentive to send information abroad is lower. Finally, in column (4) we include instead a dummy variable indicating whether statutory provisions reinforce the confidentiality between the bank and its customers. Our benchmark sample presents 5 countries that have implemented this statutory provision for bank secrecy.[5] The *Bank secrecy* dummy has the correct negative and highly significant sign. This variable takes on a value of one if the tax authorities of the country do not have access to bank information for information sharing purposes in all tax matters. Therefore, the interpretation of a negative coefficient is straightforward: countries with bank secrecy provisions will be less inclined to send information abroad since they legally provide for the requested information not to be available for tax authorities to share. The various control variables present coefficients in line with what we expected. *GDP per capita* features a positive and significant coefficient for all specifications. On the other hand, *distance* has negative and significant coefficients in all specifications. These results show support to the gravity pattern. The remaining control variables, a country's surface area or whether a country is landlocked are significant for much of the specifications. Specifically, *Landlocked* is negative and significant for almost all specifications but for column (4). *Surface Area* features positive and significant coefficients for all the specifications.

We check the appropriateness of the Tobit specification by comparing our benchmark regression with similar OLS and Probit regression models. According to Wooldridge (2002), Tobit coefficients are in line with the corresponding OLS estimates in sign and significance. Table 3.2 in the appendix presents the OLS results, which support this similarity with Tobit results in terms of sign, size and significance of the coefficients. This is also confirmed by the Probit results shown in column (5) of Table 3.3 in the appendix for the binary case which measure the extensive margin. To test for joint significance, we report the F-statistic in the last rows of all the estimation results tables. In all cases, we can reject the null hypothesis of not joint significance.

3.5.2 Robustness Analysis

To test for the robustness of our results to sample selection, we estimate our four original regressions with a broader sample of countries. We use the sample of 81 countries mentioned in the OECD (2006) report on *Tax Co-operation: Towards a Level*

---

[5]These countries are: Austria, Chile, Estonia, Slovenia and Switzerland.

Playing Field (which we refer to as OECD information list). Table 3.3 reports the results for our benchmark regression in column (1) and the extended sample in column (2). The results are very close in size, sign and significance as in the benchmark regression. One difference is the change of significance level to 10 % for *Domestic Income Tax Rate* when moving to the OECD information list sample. This enlargement of the sample causes the number of observations to increase from 174 to 185.

We also check for the sensitivity of the model to other specifications; in particular, the random effects Tobit, instead of the fixed effect model presented in column (4). Generally, the results show that the estimated coefficients remain similar in terms of size, and sign across specifications. However, much of the significance is lost. Given the strong underlying assumption of the random effects model of exogeneity between the unobserved heterogeneity contained in the errors and the regressors, these variations in the results may signal the inaccuracy of this assumption in our present case. Finally, column (3) presents the results for the case where the dependent variable is restricted to those cases where information has been shared at least once and thus it has a positive value. Same as in the other cases, estimated coefficients do not present remarkable changes and follow quite closely our benchmark specification. We can conclude that based on the data, our model is robust.

3.5.3   The Role of Tax Treaties

This section discusses the role of tax treaties as a determinant of information flows. More specifically, we will test whether having joint membership to the OECD/Council of Europe affects information flows. We also analyse whether the EU Mutual Assistance directive and the EU savings tax directive has an impact in defining the amount of spontaneous information shared. The results are presented in Table 3.4 in the appendix. When the tax treaties dummies are added to the gravity model equation, the EU Mutual Assistance pact is significant at a 10 % level. Having agreed to the EU Mutual Assistance pact increases the spontaneous information sent to other countries' authorities by 1.44 %. In contrast, the joint membership of the OECD/Council of Europe has a positive influence, but fails to be significant.

3.5.4   Reciprocity

The literature on tax information sharing discusses the importance of reciprocity as a motivation for sending tax information abroad. According to Keen and Ligthart (2006b) reciprocity could be viewed as mechanism to share the administrative costs of information sharing between countries. It is indeed the case that countries do not receive any type of monetary compensation to cover for the costs implied in sending information to the requesting country. However, given the differences in costs that information collection represents for each country, the level of reciprocity will not be homogeneous across countries. Table 3.5 in the appendix presents the estimation results for our benchmark regression with the inclusion of the logarithm of the amount of information the Swedish authorities provided to other countries. The inclusion of these variables allow to test for the presence of reciprocity on top of the motives for information sharing associated with our determinants. One problem we need to address is the endogeneity in the reciprocity variables caused by the presence of a simultaneous effect between the outflow and the inflow of the shared information. To correct for this issue, we choose an instrumental variables Tobit model. The endogenous variable is instrumented by one and two years lagged information outflows. The results show that spontaneous information outflows are highly significant at a 1 %. These results go in line with our expectations and provide support for the claim that there exists a strong reciprocity motive behind spontaneous information sharing among countries.

3.6 Discussion

From the estimation results presented above we see that the gravity model is confirmed for the case of spontaneous information inflow to Sweden. This result is robust to alternative model and sample specifications. Our Hypothesis 3.1 is fully supported by our results: the significant and positive coefficients imply that an increase in the income tax charged to residents increases the incentives of that country to share information with other countries. In other words, the larger the marginal benefit a country can obtain for taxing residents the more inclined it will be to make open disclosure of the tax related information. Hypothesis 3.2 is also strongly supported by our results since non-resident withholding tax has a negative and significant coefficient all five regressions specifications. Given that sharing information of taxpayers can create incentives for people to reallocate between countries, it is important that looses of this reallocation are not too big for the country. The size of these looses is captured by the size of the domestic non-resident withholding tax rate. This is the amount that a country can hold back from individuals producing income domestically. Therefore, the sign of the coefficients go in line with the intuition that the lower the tax, the lower the loss, and therefore, the higher incentives to share information. To test Hypothesis 3.3 we look into the coefficient of *expenditure-to-GDP* which is a proxy for a country's marginal cost of public funds. The positive and highly significant coefficients provide support for this hypothesis. Specifically, our results support the claim that an increase in the size of the public sector—higher expenditure ratio—reflects a larger marginal cost of public funds. Hypothesis 3.4 is related to the size of the individuals' wealth that is held in foreign countries. Those countries with large proportion of their assets in foreign countries will have more incentives to share information. Thus, Hypothesis 3.4 is supported by our results by the positive and significant coefficients for the *foreign depositsratio* variable. To test the validity of Hypothesis 3.5 we look at the coefficients of the three measures of fiscal supervision. The first is the number of fiscal auditors per taxpayers in each country and it is positive and highly significant. The sign of the coefficient is not what can be expected given that the hypothesis states that if the country has a high level of fiscal surveillance then it would be less inclined to share information. However, the positive sign can signal that this country is both domestically and externally committed to obtain as much fiscal information as possible. Therefore, a higher ratio of auditors per taxpayer at home is positively correlated to its information sharing with other countries. The second measure, the bank reporting dummy, is also significant but of negative sign. This presents support to Hypothesis 3.5 since the statutory obligation of reporting residents' financial transactions to the fiscal authorities makes fiscal information automatically available. This suggests that the country has fewer incentives to look for fiscal information abroad. The third variable, the bank secrecy dummy, refers to the legal protection for investors banking information. The coefficient is negative and highly significant. In this case the interpretation of this result follows a different argument. Many of the countries with this statutory provision are tax havens and therefore, essentially less inclined to engage in tax information sharing agreements with other countries. Finally, Hypothesis 3.6 is supported by the results showed in Table 3.4 in relation to the presence of reciprocity in information sharing. The coefficients for *spontaneous outflow* for the two different sets of instruments are positive and highly significant. This confirms the correlation coefficients results Table 3.6 that there is a strong effect of reciprocity in the likelihood of any country sharing information with another. Based on our results, the main policy implications are that the level of the domestic income tax rate has a strong effect on the information flows and may increase the inflow of tax information by decreasing this domestic tax. Also, an increase in the non-resident withholding tax may produce similar effects. From these two, the latter appears to have the highest impact on the amount of received information. Finally, our results indicate that reciprocity plays an important role on tax information exchange implying that countries could increase the information inflow by increasing the amount of tax information that they share spontaneously abroad.

Overall, our results offer ample support to our set of hypothesis. Some short-comings of our present work are related to data limitation issues. First, the presence of missing data may affect our estimations results by making the model less stable. However, this issue cannot be solved in the short run. Second, the category of *others* in Tables 3.7 and 3.8 provides not enough information to identify the countries contained in it.

3.7   Conclusion

Tax evasion issues and tax information sharing have been in the centre of tax policies debate. With the increased mobility of capital under the residence principle, information sharing became of critical importance for governments to be able to enforce the residence principle. However, policy makers face a trade-off between the benefits of the strategic effect of sharing information and the lost of appeal for international investors. This situation received much attention in the public economic literature, which set out to the task of identifying potential determinants of the decision of sharing information. The existing literature put forward five main potential determinants: the height of the domestic tax rate, the role of non-resident withholding taxes, the size of the marginal cost of public funds, the share of a country's interest-bearing deposits held abroad, and finally, a country's monitoring ability. In the present paper, we use spontaneous tax information inflow and outflow of Sweden to test for the significance of these determinants empirically. Additionally, we test for the role of reciprocity and regional tax treaties in the likelihood of a country's sharing of information. We find that the main five determinants are strongly significant in explaining the flows of information sharing. Furthermore, we find support for the claim that reciprocity is one of the main drivers of information sharing among countries. Finally, tax treaties contribute as well to the flow of information across borders.

Data Appendix

Spontaneous information intensity Number of cases in which the Swedish tax authority received income tax information spontaneously from country i in year t. *Source:* One-off investigation by the National Tax Board of Sweden.

Spontaneous information dummy A dummy variable taking on a value of unity if the Swedish tax authority received income tax information spontaneously from country i in year t and zero otherwise. *Source:* One-off investigation by the National Tax Board of Sweden.

Domestic Income Tax Rate (in percent) Country i's top tax on residents on interest from savings deposits in year t. The top rate applies if the tax is progressive. Wealth taxes are included by calculating an equivalent tax on interest income assuming an interest rate of 4 %. Representative taxes levied at lower levels of government are taken into account as determined by the OECD data source. For non-OECD countries with sub-national taxes, the location of the capital determines the representative sub-national government tax. *Sources:* For single-level income tax regimes, statutory personal income tax rates are from the OECD tax database (Tables I.5–I.7), available at http://www.oecd.org/ctp/taxdatabase, the World Bank's World Development Indicators available at http://econ.worldbank.org, the World Tax Database of the Office of Tax Policy Research, available at http://www.bus.umich.edu/otpr/otpr/introduction.htm, and from data provided on request by Huizinga and Nicodeme (2004). In case of dual income tax systems and wealth taxes, statutory tax rates are taken from Huizinga and Nicodeme (2004) and following sources of the International Bureau of Fiscal Documentation (IBFD): Global Tax Surveys, Europe: Individual Taxation, Europe: Private Investment Income, European Tax Surveys, Central/Eastern Europe: Taxation and Investment, Africa: Taxation and Investment, Middle East: Taxation and Investment, Canada: Taxation and Investment, Caribbean: Taxation and Investment, Latin America: Taxation and

Investment, Latin American Tax Surveys, Asia-Pacific: Taxation and Investment and the Tax News Service, available at http://www.ibfd.org/portal.

Non-resident withholding tax rate (in percent) Country i's withholding tax on (Swedish) non-residents' interest from savings deposits in year t. Where in a particular case, a treaty rate is higher than the domestic rate, the latter is applicable. Under Swedish law, no tax is withheld on interest, even where a treaty allows such tax. *Sources:* Huizinga and Nicodeme (2004) and following sources of the International Bureau of Fiscal Documentation (IBFD): Global Tax Surveys, Europe: Individual Taxation, Europe: Private Investment Income, European Tax Surveys, Central/Eastern Europe: Taxation and Investment, Africa: Taxation and Investment, Middle East: Taxation and Investment, Canada: Taxation and Investment, Caribbean: Taxation and Investment, Latin America: Taxation and Investment, Latin American Tax Surveys, Asia-Pacific: Taxation and Investment, and the Tax News Service, which are available at http://www.ibfd.org. The IBFD tax treaty database, also available at http://www.ibfd.org, allows taking treaty withholding tax rates into account that potentially undercut a country's general level of withholding tax rates.

Expenditure-to-GDP ratio (in percent) Country i's consolidated general government expenditures divided by gross domestic product (in current prices) in year t. Sources: The International Monetary Fund's International Financial Statistics, available at http://www.imf.org/external/data.htm. Alternatively, if a country's time series on expenditures is missing, we use the World Bank's World Development Indicators, available at http://econ.worldbank.org.

Deposits abroad ratio Country i's total deposits held abroad divided by the sum of time and demand deposits. *Source:* Foreign deposits are taken from Table 7b of the Bank of International Settlement's Locational Banking Statistics, available at http://www.bis.org/statistics/bankstats.htm, where US dollars have been converted to local currency using the exchange rates from the World Bank's World Development Indicators, available at http://econ.worldbank.org. Time deposits and demand deposits are taken from the International Monetary Fund's International Financial Statistics, available at http://www.imf.org/external/data.htm.

Auditors per tax payer (in logarithms) Country i'snumber of audits conducted per tax payer in the year 2004. *Source:* Number of audits: Table 27 of OECD (2007) and number of registered taxpayers: Table 30 of OECD (2007).

Bank reporting dummy A one indicates that there is mandatory (automatic) reporting by domestic financial institutions to the domestic tax administration. *Source:* Table 12 of OECD (2007).

Bank secrecy dummy A one indicates that country i features bank secrecy reinforced by statute. A zero indicates the contrary. *Source:* Column 3 of Table B1 of OECD (2006).

Gross domestic product per capita (in billions of US dollars and constant prices) Country i's gross domestic product in year t in millions (in constant prices, base year 2000). *Source:* The World Bank's World Development Indicators, available at http://econ.worldbank.org.

Distance (in logarithms) Distance in kilometers between the Swedish capital Stockholm and country i's capital. *Sources:*http://distancecalculator.globefeed.com.
Surface area Country i's surface area in thousands of square kilometers. *Sources:* CEPII dataset, available at http://www.cepii.fr/anglaisgraph/bdd/distances.htm.
Landlocked dummy A one indicates that country i has no coastline, a zero, otherwise. *Sources:* CEPII dataset, available at http://www.cepii.fr/anglaisgraph/bdd/distances.htm.
EU Treaty dummy A one indicates that country i signed a Mutual Assistance EU Treaty and zero otherwise (Binding for all member states). *Source:* data available at http://ec.europa.eu/taxation_customs/taxation/tax_cooperation/mutual_assistance/direct_tax_directive/index_en.htm.
OECD Treaty dummy A one indicates that country i has ratified the OECD Mutual Assistance Treaty and zero otherwise. *Source:* data available at http://www.oecd.org.

Table Appendix

Table 3.2 Robustness analysis for spontaneous information inflow

	Pooled tobit		Sharing at least once	Random effects tobit	Probit
	Benchmark	Broad sample			
Independent variables	(1)	(2)	(3)	(4)	(5)
Domestic income tax rate	0.027** (0.012)	0.023* (0.013)	0.030*** (0.008)	0.007 (0.016)	−0.085** (0.040)
Non-resident withholding tax rate	−41.78*** (10.96)	−63.85*** (16.77)	–	−70.67** (29.11)	−267.35*** (78.62)
Expenditure-to-GDP ratio	6.43*** (2.37)	6.43** (2.77)	2.98* (1.70)	−1.17 (1.91)	11.41* (6.84)
Foreign deposit ratio	0.005*** (0.002)	0.005*** (0.002)	0.001 (0.002)	0.003* (0.002)	0.126*** (0.045)
Real GDP per capita (in logarithms)	3.63*** (0.76)	4.02*** (0.92)	2.34** (1.01)	4.09*** (1.34)	15.89*** (3.66)
Distance (in logarithms)	−1.89*** (0.24)	−2.03*** (0.27)	−1.24*** (0.19)	−2.49*** (0.47)	−18.90*** (5.01)
Surface area (in logarithms)	0.316** (0.142)	0.387*** (0.135)	0.055 (0.092)	0.475** (0.194)	5.18*** (1.42)
Landlocked dummy	−2.31*** (0.57)	−3.54*** (0.83)	−0.659*** (0.217)	−3.60** (1.4)	−15.38*** (5.09)
Observations	174	185	42	174	174
Censored observations	132	143	–	–	–
F-statistic/Wald Chi squared	1563.9	406.7	36.23	53.75	55.38

(continued)

Table 3.2 (continued)

	Pooled tobit		Sharing at least once	Random effects tobit	Probit
	Benchmark	Broad sample			
McFadden pseudo R-squared/R-squared	0.64	0.63	0.88	–	0.81
Log-likelihood	−58.95	−62.48	–	−52.22	−17.93
Time dummies	Yes	Yes	Yes	Yes	Yes

Notes The values in parentheses below the coefficients are clustered standard errors. ***, **, * denote significance at the 1, 5, 10 % level, respectively. For the OLS case robust standard errors are used

Table 3.3 Tobit regression results for tax treaties

Independent variables	Spontaneous information flow
Real GDP per capita (in logarithms)	3.55***
	(1.01)
Distance (in logarithms)	−1.57***
	(0.40)
EU treaty	1.44*
	(0.76)
OECD treaty	0.09
	(0.71)
Observations	360
Censored observations	280
F-statistic	21.74
McFadden pseudo R squared	0.50
Log-likelihood	−161.42
Time dummies	Yes

Notes The values in parentheses below the coefficients are clustered standard errors. ***, **, * denote significance at the 1, 5, 10 % level, respectively. The results correspond to our benchmark sample of 45 countries

Table 3.4 Reciprocity in information sharing

	1-year lag	1&2-year lag
Independent variables	(1)	(2)
Domestic income tax rate	0.009	0.007
	(0.007)	(0.007)
Non-resident withholding tax rate	−43.80***	−45.14***
	(13.37)	(13.62)
Expenditure-to-GDP ratio	3.62***	3.32***
	(1.23)	(1.22)
Foreign deposit ratio	0.005**	0.006**
	(0.002)	(0.003)
Real GDP per capita (in logarithms)	2.18***	2.04***
	(0.57)	(0.58)

(continued)

Table 3.4 (continued)

	1-year lag	1&2-year lag
Distance (in logarithms)	−0.87***	−0.83***
	(0.23)	(0.23)
Surface Area (in logarithms)	0.002	−0.016
	(0.086)	(0.086)
Landlocked dummy	−1.87***	−1.92***
	(0.66)	(0.68)
Spontaneous outflow (in logarithms)	1.07***	1.136***
	(0.23)	(0.25)
Observations	174	174
Censored observations	132	132
Wald Chi squared	288.62	289.68

Notes The values in parentheses below the coefficients are two-step adjusted standard errors. ***, **, * denote significance at the 1, 5, 10 % level, respectively

Table 3.5 OLS estimation results

Independent variables	(1)	(2)	(3)	(4)
Domestic income tax rate	0.0170***	0.0178***	0.0173***	0.0175***
	(0.005)	(0.005)	(0.005)	(0.005)
Non-resident withholding tax rate	−9.39***	−6.56***	−9.62***	−10.32***
	(2.81)	(1.85)	(2.81)	(3.02)
Expenditure-to-GDP ratio	2.48***	2.22***	2.70***	2.30***
	(0.57)	(0.59)	(0.60)	(0.63)
Real GDP per capita (in logarithms)	0.381***	0.468***	0.366***	0.364***
	(0.063)	(0.073)	(0.072)	(0.061)
Distance (in logarithms)	−0.628***	−0.703***	−0.629***	−0.640***
	(0.075)	(0.089)	(0.085)	(0.074)
Surface area (in logarithms)	0.154***	0.179***	0.161***	0.136***
	(0.038)	(0.051)	(0.040)	(0.042)
Landlocked dummy	−0.543***	−0.620***	−0.579***	−0.549***
	(0.142)	(0.109)	(0.152)	(0.157)
Foreign deposit ratio	−0.002	−0.002	−0.002	−0.003*
	(0.001)	(0.001)	(0.002)	(0.002)
Auditing intensity	–	12.88***	–	–
		(3.09)		
Bank reporting dummy	–	–	−0.121	–
			(0.172)	
Bank secrecy dummy	–	–	–	−0.244
				(0.177)
Observations	174	168	162	162
R-squared	0.544	0.607	0.548	0.552

Notes The values in parentheses below the coefficients are robust standard errors. ***, **, * denote significance at the 1, 5, 10 % level, respectively

Table 3.6 Correlation matrix

	Spontaneous inflow	Spontaneous outflow	GDP per capita	Distance
Spontaneous inflow	1	–	–	–
Spontaneous outflow	0.79*	1	–	–
GDPp/c	0.32*	0.45*	1	–
Distance	−0.17*	−0.26*	−0.20*	1

*correlation coefficients significant at the 5 % level or better

Table 3.7 Tax information received by Sweden

Spontaneous information from other countries/direct taxes

	1993	1994	1995	1996	1997	1998	1999	2000	Average
Denmark	72	90	134	121	110	114	69	20	91.25
Norway	24	18	40	31	47	54	65	77	44.50
Germany	9	8	12	15	17	23	30	15	16.13
Finland	4	11	14	8	8	20	24	20	13.63
United Kingdom	8	3	2	11	14	8	18	17	10.13
France	2	1	9	5	1	1	2	2	2.88
Austria	4	2	1	2	2	1	2	1	1.88
Italy	1	1	0	4	1	0	1	2	1.25
United States	2	2	0	1	1	1	1	0	1.00
The Netherlands	1	0	0	2	0	2	2	1	1.00
Belgium	0	1	1	1	1	1	1	2	1.00
Others	1	3	6	4	5	8	6	11	5.50
Total	128	140	219	205	207	233	221	168	190.13

Source one-off investigation by the National Tax Board of Sweden: countries are ranked by the size of the average information flows

Table 3.8 Information on direct taxes provided by Sweden, 1993–2000

Spontaneous information to other countries/direct taxes

	1993	1994	1995	1996	1997	1998	1999	2000	Average
Denmark	18	30	48	62	62	44	22	31	39.63
Norway	24	9	27	35	40	79	42	45	37.63
Finland	3	10	15	24	28	27	29	60	24.50
Germany	13	28	26	27	32	24	17	26	24.13
France	7	12	11	22	21	23	5	8	13.63
United States	7	15	19	13	15	10	4	8	11.38
Poland	12	9	15	13	9	8	4	7	9.63
United Kingdom	3	9	11	11	6	2	6	11	7.38

(continued)

Table 3.8 (continued)

Spontaneous information to other countries/direct taxes

	1993	1994	1995	1996	1997	1998	1999	2000	Average
Spain	2	6	3	17	10	13	5	2	7.25
Belgium	6	3	9	12	14	5	4	4	7.13
The Netherlands	1	3	4	11	7	6	3	2	4.63
Italy	1	4	4	7	9	4	3	2	4.25
Austria	4	5	2	5	2	6	5	1	3.75
Switzerland	0	0	1	9	10	7	3	0	3.75
Estonia	0	1	1	4	1	0	1	7	1.88
Greece	0	1	0	2	7	1	1	2	1.75
Russia	0	1	0	3	4	1	2	3	1.75
Japan	0	0	1	2	4	3	0	1	1.38
Czech Republic	0	1	0	2	3	1	2	1	1.25
Hungary	0	0	0	1	2	4	1	2	1.25
Turkey	0	0	1	1	5	1	1	1	1.25
Luxembourg	0	1	2	0	3	1	1	0	1.00
Australia	0	1	1	1	0	2	2	1	1.00
Canada	0	2	2	0	2	2	0	0	1.00
Brazil	0	0	0	0	5	1	2	0	1.00
Others	1	3	8	16	24	15	8	7	10.25
Total	102	154	211	300	325	290	173	232	223.38

Source one-off investigation by the National Tax Board of Sweden: countries are ranked by the size of the average information flows

References

Anderson, J.E. 1979. A theoretical foundation for the gravity equation. *American Economic Review* 63: 106.

Bacchetta, P., and M.P. Espinosa. 1995. Information sharing and tax competition among governments. *Journal of International Economics* 39: 103–121.

Bacchetta, P., and M.P. Espinosa. 2000. Exchange-of-information clauses in international tax treaties. *International Tax and Public Finance* 7: 275–293.

Browning, E.K. 1976. The marginal cost of public funds. *The Journal of Political Economy* 283–298.

Greene, W.H. 1981. On the asymptotic bias of the ordinary least squares estimator of the tobit model. *Econometrica* 49: 505–513.

Greene, W.H. 2004a. The behaviour of the maximum likelihood estimator of limited dependent variable models in the presence of fixed effects. *Econometrics Journal* 7: 98–119.

Greene, W.H. 2004b. Fixed effects and bias due to the incidental parameters problem in the tobit model. *Econometric Reviews* 23: 125–147.

Huizinga, H.P., and G. Nicodeme. 2004. Are international deposits tax driven? *Journal of Public Economics* 88: 1093–1118.

Huizinga, H.P., and S.B. Nielsen. 2003. With holding taxes or information exchange: The taxation of international interest flows. *Journal of Public Economics* 87: 39–72.

Keen, M., and J.E. Ligthart. 2006a. Information sharing and international taxation: A primer. *International Tax and Public Finance* 13: 81–110.

Keen, M., and J.E. Ligthart. 2006b. Incentives and information exchange in international taxation. *International Tax and Public Finance* 13: 163–180.

Keen, M., and J.E. Ligthart. 2007. Revenue sharing and information exchange under non-discriminatory taxation. *Scandinavian Journal of Economics* 109: 487–504.

Ligthart, J.E. 2007. The economics of taxing cross-border savings income: An application to the EU savings tax. In *International taxation handbook*, ed. G.N. Gregoriou, and C. Read, 239–266. Amsterdam: Elsevier.

Ligthart, J.E., and J. Voget. 2009. The determinants of cross-border tax information sharing: A panel data analysis. Work in progress.

OECD. 1998. *Harmful tax competition: An emerging global issue*. Paris: OECD.

OECD. 2006 *Tax co-operation: Towards a level playing field*. Paris: OECD.

OECD. 2007 *Tax administration in OECD and selected non-OECD countries: Comparative information series 2007*. Paris: OECD.

OECD. 2010. Promoting transparency and exchange of information for tax purposes, OECD Background Information Brief.

Poyhonen, P. 1963. A tentative model for the volume of trade between countries. Weltwirtschaftliches Archiv.

Schwarz, P. 2009. Why are countries reluctant to exchange information on interest income? Participation and effectiveness of the EU Savings tax directive. *International Review of Law and Economics* 29: 97–105.

Tanzi, V., and H.H. Zee. 2001. Modern issues in the law of international taxation. In *Can information exchange be effective in taxing cross-border income flows?*, ed. K. Andersson, P. Melz, and C. Silfverberg, 259–268. Kluwer Law International: Stockholm.

Tinbergen, J. 1962. *Shaping the world economy*. New York: The Twentieth Century Fund.

Wooldridge, J.M. 2002. *Econometric analysis of cross section and panel data*. Cambridge, Massachusetts: MIT Press.

Wooldridge, J.M. 2009. *Introductory econometrics—A modern approach*, 4th edn. South-Western.

Chapter 4
The Duty of Financial Institutions to Investigate and Report Suspicions of Fraud, Financial Crime, and Corruption

F.N. Baldwin and Jeffrey A. Gadboys

Abstract This chapter provides an intensive look at the history and present status of money laundering and terrorist financing. It points out the negative impact and the ambiguity of the present focus both national and global. The chapter reviews aggressive measures to defeat terrorist financing and money laundering and recommends consideration of alternative measures including the resurrection of privatization actions. Included in the privatization is the resurrection and utilization of letters of marque and reprisal found in Article I, Section 8, Clause 11 of the United States Constitution. The chapter provides an insightful national and international history of letters of marque and reprisal.

4.1 Introduction

In this chapter, we will review the development of law and procedure aimed at controlling the flow of illicit funds within the global financial system. The current United States policies will be analyzed for their success in achieving stated goals and their impact upon financial service operations. Inherent in these policies is the concept of civil and criminal liability for failing to comply with the increasing panoply of procedures throughout the increasing financial sector. As financial institutions face the threat of liability from both the regulators and customers, it is reasonable to ask those who service the public sector's financial needs are acting out of dedicated support for a common goal or primarily to avoid penalty. In pursuing anti-money laundering objectives, one must ask: (1) whether the United

F.N. Baldwin (✉)
Center for International Financial Crimes Studies, University of Florida,
Gainesville, FL, USA
e-mail: BaldwinFN@law.ufl.edu

J.A. Gadboys
Centre for International Financial Crimes Studies, Levin College of Law,
University of Florida, Gainesville, FL, USA
e-mail: jeffgadboys@gmail.com

© Springer International Publishing Switzerland 2016   83
M. Dion et al. (eds.), *Financial Crimes: Psychological, Technological,
and Ethical Issues*, International Library of Ethics, Law,
and the New Medicine 68, DOI 10.1007/978-3-319-32419-7_4

States government is levying an unfair burden upon financial institutions, (2) should the government explore less burdensome programs of control. A revival of the constitutionally acceptable Letter of Marque which provides incentives and lesser regulatory intervention is an example of an alternative.

4.2 The Development of Global Anti-money Laundering Initiatives

"Money laundering" has numerous definitions. Accepted internationally is the definition adopted by the United Nations Convention Against Illicit Traffic in Narcotic Drugs and Psychotropic Substances (1988, The "Vienna Convention"[1]) and the United Nations Convention Against Transnational Organized Crime (2000, The "Palermo Convention"[2]).

- The conversion or transfer of property, knowing that such property is derived from any offense of offenses or from an act of participation in such offense or offenses, for the purpose of concealing or disguising the illicit origin of the property or of assisting any person who is involved in the commission of such an offense to evade the legal consequences of his actions;
- The concealment or disguise of the true nature, source, location, disposition, movement, rights with respect to, or ownership of property, knowing that such property is derived from an offense or offenses or from an act of participation in such an offense or offenses, and;
- The acquisition, possession or use of property, knowing at the time of receipt that such property was derived from an offense or offenses or from an act of participation in such offense or offenses.[3]

It is alleged that the term "money laundering" dates back to the 1930s. U.S. gangster Al Capone, was terrorizing Chicago. Capone owned Chicago's largest cleaning and dying plant. He used his laundry to clean his criminally derived funds. United States Treasury agents pursued Al Capone,[4] he disguised his illgotten gain by designating it as money honestly earned from operating laundries. At the time there was no legislation that identified "money laundering" as an offense.[5] The Swiss Banking Act of 1934 created the principle of bank secrecy. Organized crime under the direction of Meyer Lansky bought a Swiss bank. He transferred illegal assets to the bank by way of a complex system of shell companies, holding companies, and offshore accounts.[6]

---

[1]http://www.indcb/org/e/conv/1988.

[2]http://www.undcp.org/adhoc/palermo/convmain.html.

[3]See *Vienna Convention*, articles 3(b) and (c) 1; and *Palermo Convention*, article 6 (i).

[4]See Chris Mathers, *Crime School: Money Laundering*, Firefly Books, 2004, p. 21.

[5]*Id.*, p. 22.

[6]Lucy Komisar, "Tracking Terrorist Money—Too Hot for US to Handle", Pacific News Service, October 4th, 2001.

Organized crime is responsible for a large proportion of illicit money flowing through international financial channels.[7] The success of any criminal enterprise is largely determined by the extent to which the actors are able to conceal the sources and uses of their funds and to sanitize the illegal proceeds by transferring them through the international financial system. The failure of a country to maintain a robust anti-money laundering program can have devastating economic and social consequences, especially if the country's economic growth is in transition or developing. The International Monetary Fund estimates money laundering amounts to between 2 and 5 % of global domestic product. This is at least $600,000,000,000 annually. Money laundering provides the financial fuel that permits transnational criminal enterprises to conduct and expand their operations to the detriment of the safety and security of law abiding citizens.[8]

- Money launderers subvert legitimate financial mechanisms and banking relationships by using them as protective covering for the movement of criminal proceeds and the financing of crime and terrorism. By doing so, money launders threaten the safety of United States citizens; they and undermine the integrity of U.S. financial institutions and the global financial and trading systems upon which prosperity and growth depend.
- Certain jurisdictions outside the U.S. provide "offshore" banking and related facilities designed to provide anonymity. Weak financial supervisory and enforcement regimes exist. These are essential tools to disguise ownership and movement of criminal funds derived from, or used to commit, offenses ranging from narcotics trafficking, terrorism, arms smuggling, and trafficking in human beings, to financial frauds that prey on law-abiding citizens.
- Correspondent banking facilities are one of the banking mechanisms susceptible to manipulation by foreign banks. They facilitate the laundering of funds by hiding the identity of real parties-in-interest to financial institutions.
- U.S. anti-money laundering efforts are impeded by outmoded and inadequate statutory provisions that make investigations, prosecutions, forfeitures more difficult. The difficulty is increased in cases in which money laundering involves foreign persons, foreign banks, or foreign countries.[9]

In terms of direct economic impact upon developing nations, a reputation as a money laundering haven causes significant adverse consequences. Foreign financial institutions may limit their transactions with institutions from money laundering havens. They may subject these transactions to extra scrutiny making them more expensive. They may terminate correspondent or lending relationships altogether. Even legitimate businesses and enterprises may suffer money laundering havens

---

[7]FinCEN Advisory, *Report on Money Laundering Topologies*, vol. 1, no 4, 2006, p. 3.

[8]See The World Bank, *Reference Guide to Anti-Money Laundering and Combating the Financial of Terrorism*, II-I (2nd edition, 2006).

[9]Pub. L. 107–56, Title III, Section 302, October 26th, 2011. But see United States versus Union Bank for Savings and Loan (Jordan) 487, f.3d 8 (1st Cir. 2007).

from reduced access to world capital markets from higher cost due to the extra scrutiny of their ownership, organization, and control systems.[10] Regardless of the nature of the underlying "predicate crime",[11] money launderers generally resort to placement, layering and integration in the process of turning illicit proceeds into apparently legitimate assets.[12]

"Placement" refers to the process of transferring bulk currency through various schemes, including the commingling of illicit funds with legitimate business revenues, smuggling, and converting cash into deposits at banks.[13]

"Layering" is aggregating these funds and moving them through a series of transactions to mask the source, ownership and location of the funds.[14]

"Integration" refers to the return of funds to the legitimate economy for later extraction via injection into legitimate business conditions such as real estate transactions, loans from front companies, and fraudulent import/export invoicing.

4.2.1   Defining the Strategy

As the world shrinks, crime and terrorism become increasingly international in scope. The rapid advances in technology and the globalization of the financial services industry increase the complexity of the movement of illicit funds or funds intended for an illicit purpose. Modern financial systems transfer billions of dollars instantly through personal computers and satellite communications. Money is laundered through currency exchange houses, stock brokerage houses, gold dealers, casinos, automobile dealerships, insurance companies, and trading companies. Private banking facilities, offshore banking, shell corporations, free trade zones, wire systems, and trade financing all have the ability to mask illegal activities. Organized crime, as well as organized terrorists, have a choice of money laundering vehicles. They are limited only by their creativity.[15] The global attempt to control money laundering involves three dimensions: (1) national and international cooperation, (2) a firm legal and enforcement foundation, and (3) close interaction

---

[10]See *supra*, note 8, II-3.

[11]The term "predicate crime" refers to the underlying crime that makes it necessary to launder proceeds. These proceeds are divided generally into five categories: drug trafficking, other "blue collar" crimes, white-collar crimes, bribery and corruption, and terrorism.

[12]See Sarah Jane Hughes, "Cyberlaundering Poses Threats to Controls", *Money Laundering Alert*, vol. 6, no 7, 1995, p. 1.

[13]See Gerald Wyrsch, "Treasury Regulation of International Wire Transfer and Money Laundering: A Case for a Permanent Moratorium", 20 *Denv. J. In'l L. and Pol'y*, 1992, p. 515.

[14]*Id.*, p. 523.

[15]United States Dept. of State, *International Narcotics Control Strategy Report*, vol. II, March 2003, p. 3.

between the public and private sectors in order to lower compliance costs and raise the probability of achieving stated objectives.[16]

Does it work? The establishment of a robust Anti-Money Laundering (AML) program is a challenge. The challenge is due to variations in institutions, perspectives, political will, and priorities. While initiatives intended to encourage nations to adopt uniform laws are commendable, they are at times inefficient. Such laws cannot easily be transported from one legal system to another without significant expenditure of scarce resources and cultural differences adaptation.[17] As a result, compromises driven by the need to balance competing objectives must be made at all levels in a given jurisdiction.

AML efforts have two prongs: (1) prevention, and (2) enforcement.

The prevention prong has four key elements:

(1) customer due diligence,
(2) reporting,
(3) regulatory supervision, and
(4) sanctions

These are intended to limit criminal access to the financial system, alert authorities to attempts to launder money, ensure compliance with laws and regulations by financial institutions and punish for failure to implement preventive measures. The enforcement prong also has four key elements:

(1) a list of predicate offenses
(2) investigation,
(3) prosecution and punishment, and
(4) confiscation

The enumeration of predicate crimes establishes the legal basis for criminalizing money laundering.[18]

This duty is the cornerstone of public and private communication in the context of AML regulations is the affirmative duty for financial institutions to file suspicious activity reports (SARs).[19] The data transmitted via SAR is reviewed and analyzed by a designated Financial Investigation Unit (FIU). In the United States,

---

[16]See Peter Reuter and Edwin Truman, *Chasing Dirty Money*, Institute for International Economics, 2004, p. 45.

[17]Barry Rider, Director of the Institute for Advanced Legal Studies, ICC Commercial Crime Services Annual Lecture, "Organized Crime and Terrorism" (June 20th, 2002).

[18]*Id.*, p. 46–47.

[19]Annunzio-Wylie Anti-Money Laundering Act, Pub. L. No. 102–550, Title XV, 106 Stat. 4044 (1992) (codified at 31 C.F.R., Section 103.81 (a)). An affirmative duty to report criminal activity is a marked change from the general rule that American law imposes no duty to report crimes. Matthew R. Hall, "An Emerging Duty to Report Criminal Conduct: Banks, Money Laundering, and the Suspicious Activity Report", *KY.L.J.*, vol. 84, 1996, p. 643, 679. Banks are not alone; there is a growing trend that private actors must report crimes in specific instances. *Id.*, p. 644.

the FIU is FinCEN.[20] Obligations impose upon private actors, specifically bank tellers and other "front-line" employees. It is an indirect deputization of a large segment of the private financial sector. The "SAR deputized the bank, grants it prosecutorial discretion, and cloaks its report with immunity".[21]

The SAR program is based upon the premise that financial institutions are better suited than the federal government to detect large movements of money. Financial institutions must alert federal officials of any suspicious activity. The institutions must not notify persons involved in the transaction that the questionable activity has been reported.[22] To encourage efficient levels of communication, financial institutions are granted limited protection from liability.[23] SARs benefit federal officials in three primary areas: (1) detecting specific criminal acts, (2) recognizing general patterns and trends,[24] and (3) tracking and locating terrorist cells.[25]

Whether a financial institution must file a SAR is not always readily discernible. There is no bright line threshold like currency transaction reports (CTRs).[26] The subjective nature of what constitutes suspicious activity places a heavy burden on private financial institutions to analyze every transaction.[27] When determining whether suspicious activity has occurred, institutions are responsible for examining

---

[20]31 C.F.R. Section 103.18 (f). FinCEN also serves as the United States' Financial Intelligence Unit. Financial Crimes Enforcement Network, FinCEN BSA Direct Retrieval and Sharing Assessment Report, 3, July 10th, 2006. (available at: http://www.fincen.gov/bsa_direct_report_071306.pdf). FinCEN is responsible for "Managing, analyzing safeguarding, and appropriately sharing financial transaction information collected under the BSA and other authorities". *Id.*, p. 6.

[21]Matthew R. Hall, "An Emerging Duty to Report Criminal Conduct: Banks, Money Laundering, and the Suspicious Activity Report", 84 *KY L.J.*, 1996, p. 643, 679.

[22]31 C.F.R. Section 103.15–22.

[23]*Id.*

[24]Financial Crimes Enforcement Network, Guidance Preparing a Complete & Sufficient Suspicious Activity Report Narrative, November 2003, p. 1 (available at http://www.fincen.gov/sarnarrompleteguidfinal_11203.pdf). Information collected by FinCEN "not only provides law enforcement, intelligence, and regulatory agencies with leads indicative of illegal activity, it also provides the data for identifying trends and patterns, vulnerabilities and compliance-related deficiencies". Financial Crimes Enforcement Network, *The SAR Activity Review*: Trends, Tips & Issues Issue, 10, 3, May 2006 (available at http://www.fincen.gov/sarreviewissue10.pd).

[25]Using the financial system to track al-Quaeda "has proven a very effective way to locate terrorist operatives and supporters and disrupt terrorist plots". Roth et al., *supra* note 7, p. 2. Blocking and seizing terrorist finds is not the only goal, "following the money to identify terrorist operatives and sympathizers provides a particularly powerful tool in the fight against terrorist groups". *Id.* Much of the success of tracking terrorist assets remains outside the public view which may distort the effectiveness of counter-terrorist programs. *Id.*

[26]Financial institutions must file a currency transaction report for any receipt of cash that exceeds $10,000. 31 C.F.R. Section 103.22.

[27]According to John Hall, spokesman of the American Bankers Association, one of the primary reasons that suspicious activity reporting is so controversial is the subjective nature of the inquiry. Andrea Maria Cecil, SARs causing big headaches, *York Daily Record*, July 13th, 2006.

all available facts, including the background and possible purpose of the transactions.[28]

4.2.2 Role of Structured Financial Institutions

Structured financial institutions play a narrow, although integral, role within the larger war on terrorist financing.[29] When financial institutions accurately report suspicious activity, the transparency of the financial system is increased. The reporting enhances the ability of federal intelligence and law enforcement agencies to connect the dots.[30] The methodology used by money launderers is not static, nor is it confined to banks and Western financial institutions. It is subject to the resources and imagination of the launderer. The importance of financial institutions' communication to the government is illustrated by the fact that a recent examination of millions of BSA documents revealed over 80,000 specific filings with some relationship to subjects of terrorism investigations.[31] In order for the enforcement of terrorist financial legislation to be efficient, the role of financial institutions within the larger context of money laundering systems must be evaluated. After compiling data from sixteen federal agencies, on January 11, 2006, the United States Government, released the Money Laundering Threat Assessment 2006 (MLTA).[32] The MLTA recognizes nine broad categories of money laundering.[33] To effectively combat terrorist financing, the intelligence focus must broaden from traditional Western financial institutions to include more elusive and ethnic based informal systems of transferring funds. The systems include money service businesses[34] and informal financial systems such as Hawala or Hundi.[35] Some of the actions to

---

[28]31 C.F.R. Section 103.18 (a) (2) (iii).

[29]Basel Committee on Banking Supervision, *Guidance on Preparing a Complete & Sufficient Suspicious Activity Report Narrative*: http://www.bis.org.

[30]Michael Morehart, Section Chief, Terrorist Financing Operations Section, Counterterrorism Division, Federal Bureau of Investigation, quoted in Financial Times Enforcement Network, *FinCEN 2005 Annual Report*, 10, 2006 (available at http://www.fincen.gov/fincenannualreport2005.pdf).

[31]*The SAR Activity Review*, Trends, Tips & Issues Issue, 10, *supra*, note 24, p. 18.

[32]See Department of Justice, Press Release, Money Laundering Threat Assessment Released, January 11th, 2006, available at 2006 WL 52785.

[33]See generally: United States Government, Money Laundering Threat Assessment (December 2005) (available at http://www.ustreas.gov/offices/enforcement/pdf/mlta.pdf) (designating nine primary vehicles for money laundering: (1) Banking, (2) Money Service Businesses, (3) Online Payment Systems, (4) Informal Value Transfer Systems, (5) Bulk Cash Smuggling, (6) Trade-Based Money Laundering, (7) Insurance Companies, (8) Shell Companies and Trusts, (9) Casinos).

[34]Money service business are defined as 31 C.F.R. Section 103, p. 29–32.

[35]While this paper cannot begin to scratch the surface of the complexities of informal ethnic financial systems, the Money Laundering Threat Assessment devotes substantial effort to break

disrupt terrorist financing forced upon financial institutions are outside the confines of the traditional criminal justice system.[36] Several of the regulations affect the delicate balance between compliance and risk. Compliance and risk also implicate filings which can be designated as defensive in nature.

4.2.3 Defensive Filings

The "defensive filing phenomenon[37]" is a major problem with the current regulatory framework. Defensive filings are reports that financial institutions file to insulate themselves from federal civil or criminal liability.[38] Confusing standards, the resulting fines of several million dollars have created a fear of failing to report all suspicious activity. A flood of "defensive" SARs has ensued.[39] This massive influx of data means that critical data transmitted by financial institutions, via SARs, may be missed or obscured based on the sheer volume of filings.[40] Some of the SARs lack quality information.

(Footnote 35 continued)

down some of the more prominent points of Hawala. See Money Laundering Threat Assessment, *supra*, note 33, p. 29–32. See Tech. Defensive Filings Cause Vulnerabilities, Credit Union J., 21, January 16th, 2006 (2006 WL 848456). "But the rapid increase in reports is a double-edged sword. While many of these reports are the result of greater vigilance, some are considered to be "defensive filings" by financial institutions, in which SARs are filed on nonsuspicious transactions out of concern about regulatory and criminal scrutiny". *Id.*

[36]"The problem with disruption is that it often involves actions that may not always be sanctioned by the law, thereby imposing upon the business community exposure to serious risks of legal liability". Rider, *supra*, note 17, p. 2. Each year in excess of 14 million BSA forms or reports are filed by more than 200,000 financial institutions. FinCEN BSA Direct Retrieval and Sharing Assessment Report, *supra*, note 29, p. 3. Adding to the sheer number of filings, 62 % of SARs revealed problems in data quality and contained incomplete, inconsistent and inappropriate information. "Starving Terrorists of Money: The Role of Middle Eastern Financial Institutions", *Joint Congress Hearing*, 109th Congress 4 (May 4th, 2005) (statement of Rep. Luis Gutierrez).

[37]Even if terrorist assets only comprise 1/10 of the total laundered money, the effective rate would only range from 0.02–5 %.

[38]Financial Crimes Enforcement Network, The SAR Activity Review, Trends, Tips & Issues Issue, 8, 3, April 2005 (available at http://www.fincen.gov/sarreviewissue8.pdf).

[39]See Tech. Defensive Filings Cause Vulnerabilities, Credit Union J., 21, January 16th, 2006 (2006 WL 848456). "But the rapid increase in reports is a double-edged sword. While many of these reports are the result of greater vigilance, some are considered to be "defensive filings" by financial institutions, in which SARs are filed on nonsuspicious transactions out of concern about regulatory and criminal scrutiny". *Id.*

[40]Each year in excess of 14 million BSA forms or reports are filed by more than 200,000 financial institutions. FinCEN BSA Direct Retrieval and Sharing Assessment Report, *supra*, note 29, p. 3. Adding to the sheer number of filings, 62 % of SARs revealed problems in data quality and contained incomplete, inconsistent and inappropriate information. "Starving Terrorists of Money: The Role of Middle Eastern Financial Institutions", *Joint Congress Hearing*, 109th Congress 4 (May 4th, 2005) (statement of Rep. Luis Gutierrez).

In essence, defensive filings serve to enlarge the proverbial haystack. It is difficult to find the needle. More than 522,000 SARs were filed by depository institutions alone in 2005. Nearly 280,000 were filed in the first 6 months of 2006.[41] SARs filed in 2005 represented an increase of almost 141,000 filings in 2004, a one-year increase of 37 %.[42] The total number of SARs filed in 2005, by all financial institutions, increased by nearly 230,000 to over 919,000.[43] By the end of 2006,[44] over 3.5 million SARs were filed since October 1st, 2001.[45] Recent figures suggest filings of close to 8 times more than SARs and 2.1 times as many as were filed in the year following 9/11. By the end of 2011, all SAR filings had increased 16 %?[46] In 2011 electronic filings generally increased by 70 % prompting the United States Federal Reserve to require mandatory E-filing of Banki Secrecy Act reports.[47]

Prior to 2001, the average annual increase of SAR filings by depository institutions in the United States was 25,083 per year. Since 2001, the average annual increase has risen to 71,173 per year,[48] although the images of 9/11 and an accompanying sense of patriotic duty may have been one impetus for the filing of SARs. It is apparent that potential fines and civil liability have also contributed greatly to this increase.[49] Even if the growth rate decreases, it is evident that every BSA report cannot be analyzed adequately. This increase in SAR filings can be attributed to a number of factors.[50] The dearth of clear guidance about how to effectively monitor activity is directly tied to the dramatic influx of SARs. Not only must financial institutions decide when it is appropriate to file a SAR, but the financial institutions must also document decisions when they decide not to file a SAR.

Overburdened bank officials, financial analysts, and other observers of the process, all share the concern over the exponential increase in volume of SAR filings. William Fox, former Director FinCEN, recognized that the volume of

---

[41]Financial Crimes Enforcement Network, The SAR Activity Review: By the Numbers, no. 73 (November 2006) (available at http://www.fincen.gov/sar_review_by_the_numbers_issue6.pdf).

[42]*Id.*

[43]*Id.*

[44]See Financial Crimes Enforcement Network Suspicious Activity Report, filings in 2nd Quarter 2001, p. 2 (September 2011).

[45]*Supra*, note 41.

[46]Id. Comparing SARs filed from April 1996 to March 1997 to the number of SARs filed from July 2005 to June 2006. See also *supra*, note 44.

[47]See FinCEN Proposes Mandatory E-Filing of BSA Reports, September 27th, 2011.

[48]*Supra*, note 46.

[49]*Id.*

[50]The rise of SAR reports may be a function of at least three factors. The least promising, although most plausible, explanation is that the filings are merely submitted to protect an institution from potential civil and criminal liability, regardless of the true suspicion level. The rise could also be contributed to effective compliance programs which have taught front line employees of financial institutions what red flags to look for and employees are detecting suspicious activity that was previously overlooked. The leasts probable explanation is that there is an actual exponential increase in suspicious activity.

defensive filings was created by "unprecedented anxiety in the financial community" regarding general BSA compliance, specifically the filing of SARs.[51] Director Fox further noted that:

> Financial institutions are increasingly convinced that the key to avoiding regulatory and criminal scrutiny under the Bank Secrecy Act is to file more reports, regardless of whether the conduct or transaction identified is suspicious. These "defensive filings" populate our database with reports that have little value, degrade the valuable reports in the database and implicate privacy concerns.[52]

Will E-filings improve or increase defensive filings?[53] The rapid increase in SAR filings[54] is directed at efforts to suppress terrorist financing. It is also an attempt to protect against liability.[55]

4.3 Compliance Risk. The Economic Impact of Financial Institutions

"Compliance risk" is generally defined as the risk of legal or regulatory sanctions, material financial loss, or the loss to reputation that a bank may suffer as a result of its failure to comply with laws, regulations, rules, related self-regulatory organization standards, and codes of conduct applicable to banking activities. The Patriot Act's legal and regulatory changes are estimated to affect 13,000 U.S. banks and securities dealers, several hundred thousand non-financial U.S. businesses, and 10,000 non-U.S. financial institutions. The common principles to manage the compliance risk of a financial institution, are:

- Compliance with the relevant AML laws of the appropriate jurisdiction;
- Knowing your customer (KYC), including the source of their wealth;
- Co-operating with various law enforcement and supervisory agencies;
- Communicating the firm's AML program via policies, procedures and staff training; and
- Continuous and sustainable money laundering risk-assessment.[56]

---

[51]The SAR Activity Review, Trends, Tips & Issues Issue, 8, *supra*, note 38, p. 3.

[52]*Id.*

[53]Increased compliance costs for ineffective programs decreases profits, increases consumer costs, consumes employee teime and leads to generally inefficient cost outlays. See generally: Philip Wellmer, "Effective Compliance Programs and Corporate Criminal Prosecutions", 27, *Cardozo Law Review*, 2005, p. 497.

[54]Defensive filings consume valuable and limited resources from attacking actionable terrorist information to sifting through superfluous data. Millions more CTRs are filed than SARs, but by applying the same time frame more than 250,000 work hours are needed to adequately assess these reports. Mallory Factor stated that, "I cannot imagine how we could follow up on 288,000 SARs", Factor, *supra*, note 21, p. 21.

[55]*The SAR Activity Review*: Trends, Tips & Issues Issue, 8, supra, note 38.

[56]http://www.worldpress.org/specials/euro/1119web_Helsinki.htm.

The most basic and crucial elements of a financial institution's AML program are the Know Your Customer component combined with the ability to identify any unusual activity that may be indicative of money laundering. The ability to mine KYC data to respond to regulatory requests is critical and requires complex data management solutions, particularly for large operations. These management solutions are expected to be able to identify higher-risk customers and thus enable their transactions to be monitored.

The complexity becomes apparent when one examines what regulatory authorities consider to be a minimum effective AML process:

- Transaction monitoring—scanning and analyzing data for potential money laundering activity;
- Watch list filtering—screening new accounts, existing customers, beneficiaries and transaction counterparties against terrorist, criminal and other blocked persons watch lists;
- Automation of regulatory reporting, filing of suspicious activity reports, currency transactions reports, or other regulatory reports; and
- A detailed audit trail to demonstrate compliance efforts to regulators, as well as to respond to subpoenas and other requests for information.

With growing regulatory demand for transactional policing and reporting, the costs of AML compliance have increased substantially over the last 3 years. A KPMG International study reported that spending on AML initiatives over a 3 year period among 224 banks in 55 countries has increased over 58 %.[57] The regions that recorded the highest increases in costs were the United States and the Middle East/Africa with 71 and 70 % respectively. Respondents to the KPMG cost study also admitted to having difficulty in estimating AML costs accurately since these costs are spread across many different functional areas (operations, compliance, risk) or regions, involve direct and indirect costs and overlap with processes that are imbedded in normal business practice (e.g. customer service).[58]

In an effort to streamline costs and improve monitoring efficiency, the FATF has proffered the adoption of a risk-based approach. With this approach, competent authorities and financial institutions are able to ensure that measures to prevent and mitigate money laundering are commensurate with the risks identified. The basic concept is that resources should be directed toward the areas of greatest risk, allowing financial institutions to exercise reasonable business judgment with respect to their customers. This is deemed as a desirable alternative to the one-size fits all approach where all institutions, customers and transactions receive equal attention and which can inadvertently lead to a "tick the box" attitude with the focus on meeting regulatory needs rather than combating money laundering.

---

[57]KPMG International, *Global Anti-Money Laundering Survey*, 14, 2007.

[58]See also The Washington Economics Group, *The Economics Impacts of International Banking in Florida*, June 5th 2006, p. 23; prepared to the Florida International Bankers Association (FIBA) Inc.

Risk is addressed in four principle areas[59]:

- Customer due diligence measures;
- Institutions's internal control systems;
- The approach to regulation and oversight by competent authorities; and
- Provisions for allowing Designated Non-Financial Businesses to apply risk determination in a similar way to financial institutions.

While a significant benefit of a properly implemented risk-based approach is that it requires people to think, the cost of due diligence has actually risen. Due diligence now requires a much more proactive approach. Firms are required to do more to monitor customer transactions. Firms must fully investigate the source of funds to trigger a response and not solely rely on threshold factors. Fundamentally, the flexibility of the risk-based approach is anathemic to the process driven banking system. In reality, customers who are classified as "low risk" naturally receive the least attention. Yet these, are the clients who if KYC and risk assessment are not continuously updated, may be receiving insufficient scrutiny, particularly in the cases where their circumstances have changed. Thus, "low risk" clients may present added costs and higher compliance risk when it comes to the need for monitoring.

4.4 The Threat of Liability

Banking managers list substantial institutional exposure to risk from BSA/AML. Enforcement actions are one of the top three industry threats.[60] The concern for legal liability among bankers is well founded, given the breadth of the money laundering laws and their periodic lack of technical coherency. The breadth and ambiguity in these laws aid law enforcement. At the same time, legitimate businesses seeking new market opportunities in emerging markets confront risks. Given the risk-based approach to transaction monitoring, what constitutes a suspicious transaction is hardly definitive. Problems emerge when banks interact with alternative asset forms like hedge funds, private equity and commodity investment firms. Problems also emerge when firms are in the process of acquiring companies in emerging markets where there may be legacy issues. The issues may relate to practices that are minor, took place a long time ago, or which are condoned locally, but are technically illegal. Despite all of the efforts at international cooperation, less than one quarter of the international financial institutions participating in the KPMG International survey are capable of monitoring a single customer's transaction and account status across multiple national borders.[61] There is no evidence that larger

---

[59]FATF/GAFT, *Guidance on the Risk-Based Approach to Combating Money Laundering and Terrorist Financing*, June 2007, p. 2.
[60]See *supra*, note 33, p. 27.
[61]See *supra*, note 17.

banks are any more capable in this respect than smaller banks. A specific example of this problem relates to "cover payments" (a type of payment made from one bank to another via correspondent banks). These may be necessary when the two banks do not have a direct banking relationship and need an intermediary to settle payments.

One of the significant characteristics of this practice is that the information on the originator(s) and beneficiary(s) is ordinarily communicated directly from the originating bank to the beneficiary bank. Generally, the correspondent banks involved are not aware of the identity of the originator, or beneficiary. Cover payments are often used where the two end banks execute multiple transactions on behalf of a client each day and find it economical to "batch process" these payments in one net transaction. This can help reduce fees and limit short-term liquidity problems. Moreover, correspondent banks cannot distinguish between cover payments that are made to settle underlying client transactions and those made to settle proprietary flows between end banks.

Banks are making greater efforts to identify politically exposed person (PEPs) who can be conduits for laundered money. The task facing banks is made more difficult by the lack of a common definition of a PEP and the fact that in some markets, business and politics are closely intertwined.

The FFIEC BSA/AML Examination Manual[62] identifies high risk factors which need to be considered in OFAC compliance, to include:

- International funds transfers;
- Nonresident alien accounts;
- Foreign customer accounts;
- Cross-border automated clearing house transactions;
- Commercial letters of credit;
- Transactional electronic banking;
- Foreign correspondent accounts;
- Payable through accounts;
- International private banking;
- Overseas branches or subsidiaries.

The enlargement of the European Union (EU) highlights additional AML risks. Many of the recent countries admitted to the EU have historically weak AML processes in place. FinCEN, pursuant to delegated authority from the Treasury Department, is responsible for determining violations under the BSA and determining what, if any, sanctions are appropriate. Entities such as banks, registered securities broker-dealers, and insurance companies that have federal function regulators, are regularly examined by the regulator for BSA compliance. Referrals for enforcement action are made to FinCEN when appropriate. The IRS is similarly authorized to examine and investigate other "financial institutions" that do not have

---

[62]Federal Financial Institutions Examination Council, *Bank Secrecy Act/Anti-Money Laundering Examination* Manual 13, 2006.

a federal function regulator. Violations of the BSA and implementing regulations can result in civil money penalties of up to $1 million per day for continuing violations and possible imprisonment. The Department of Justice may prosecute criminal violations upon referral. Departmental guidelines on criminal prosecutions of banks pursuant to the BSA, direct U.S. Attorneys not to pursue prosecutions without permission from the Criminal Division (Asset Forfeiture and Money Laundering Section). This central control has lessened the potential for uneven application of criminal prosecutions for U.S. banks. While a bank's criminal prosecution for BSA violations is unlikely, the civil penalties and defense of a civil enforcement action can be very costly in both monetary and non-monetary terms. One of many examples of civil prosecutions is indicative of the government's determined efforts to enforce the provisions of the BSA.

In January of 2005, the Riggs Bank, N.A. of Washington, D.C. agreed to plead guilty to one count of violating the BSA in connection with its failure to report suspicious monetary transactions. The transactions involved high risk customers, including former Chilean Augusto Pinochet and officials of the government of Equatorial Guinea. Between 1994 and 2002, Pinochet and his wife deposited more than $10 million into Riggs Bank. The government alleged that Riggs Bank created offshore companies and changed the name of some accounts to conceal Pinochet's ownership of the assets. Riggs Bank also maintained offshore accounts and multiple personal accounts of over $700 million for the government of Equatorial Guinea. Equatorial Guinea had been cited by the United States State Department for corruption and diversion of oil revenues to government officials. As part of its guilty plea, Riggs Bank admitted that it failed to conduct sufficient due diligence regarding the source of the deposited funds and failed to report transactions it knew or had reason to know were suspicious. Riggs Bank's guilty plea followed FinCEN's imposition of a $25 million civil fine against the institution in May 2004 for failing to design and implement a suitable AML program that would ensure timely and effective reporting of suspicious activity. The fine for Riggs Bank's most recent plea amounted to $16 million. This was considered a small penalty under the circumstances. This fine may have been influenced by a strong desire of bank regulators to conclude the investigation in order to permit the sale of the institution. Riggs Bank was in serious financial condition. Most of the criminal activity at the bank was self-disclosed by the bank's internal investigators. Self-disclosure is one of the key mitigating factors in dealing with any regulatory violation.[63]

---

[63]Terence O'Hara, "Riggs Bank Agrees to Guilty Plea and Fine", Washington Post, January 28, 2005, p. A01. The fine consisted of $25 million in civil liability for "numerous violations of the Bank Secrecy Act". See also Office of the Comptroller of the Currency, OCC News Release 2004–34, "OCC Access $25 Million Penalty Against Riggs Bank N.A.", May 13th, 2004 (available at http://www.occ.treas.gov/toolkit/newsrelease.aspx?Doc=5AOFP8K.xml). And a $16 million criminal fine. O'Hara. See also, 31 U.S.C.A. Section 5318 (g)(3); Annunzio-Wylie Abti-Money Laundering Act.

In Lopez versus First Union Bank of Florida,[64] the U.S. 11th Circuit held that a financial institution's disclosure is protected even if it ultimately turns out there was no violation of law. In order to be immune from liability, it is sufficient that the financial institution have good-faith suspicion that a law or regulation may have been violated, even if it turns out in hindsight that none existed. It is important to note that Section 314(a) provides lead information only and is not a substitute for a subpoena or other legal processes. To obtain documents from a financial institution that has reported a suspicious transaction, a law enforcement agency must still meet the same legal standards that apply to other investigations. The safe harbor provision of Section 5318 is intended to satisfy the immunity relief intended in FATF 40 Recommendation (14), and to facilitate the open communication of financial information between key elements of the AML process. However, banks still have exposure to the risk of legal liability.

Several cases dealing with the protective Annunzio-Wylie Act safe harbor provisions expose certain traps for the unwary CCO. Under the third disclosure, one "pursuant to any other authority", the U.S. 11th Circuit found that, besides Treasury Secretary's regulations, "other authority" must be pursuant to legal authority such as statute, regulation, court order or other source of law. In Lopez,[65] the court refused to recognize the safe harbor when the disclosures were made in response to "verbal instructions" of government officials. It was held that a government official's verbal instructions do not constitute "legal authority".

In Coronado versus BankAtlantic Bancorp. Inc,[66] the United States 11th Circuit refused to recognize the first safe harbor, "a disclosure of any possible violation of law or regulation", upon a failure to show that the bank had in fact determined in good faith that there was any nexus between suspicious activity and the information it disclosed. Allegations that the bank detected suspicious activity "in" and "at" the bank could merely mean that the bank detected suspicious activity in only one account. Some 400–600 accounts were released, upon finding that the accounts had "no connection with money laundering." The court also found that the government's demand for financial records was not, by itself, sufficient to give the bank a good-faith basis to suspect possible violation of law or regulation. A financial institution can be exposed to regulatory liability for not having developed a satisfactory risk-based transaction monitoring and reporting process. At the same time, over-compliance in reporting large volumes of account activity or those lacking a clear nexus between suspicious activity and the reports generated, can strip away the protective elements of the safe harbors. The institution in fact can be caught between the desire to aggressively conduct AML processes and the risk of reporting too much. Banks must not only file complete and sufficient SARs, but those SARs must be filed with established deadlines.

---

[64]129 F. 2d 1186, 1193 (11th Cir. 1997).

[65]*Id.*, p. 1193.

[66]Coronado versus BankAtlantic Bancorp Inc., 129 F.3d 1186 (11th Cir. 1997): This case was consolidate on appeal with *Lopez versus First Union Bank of Florida.*

The Justice Department has refrained from criminally prosecuting individual bank employees as principles to money laundering resulting from a failure to recognize a suspicious transaction. The prosecution is possible. Failure to comply specifically with reporting mandates can lead potentially to findings of "willful blindness".[67] This satisfies the "knowledge" and "intent" element of the money laundering statutes and may expose institutions to criminal liability under the "doctrine of collective knowledge". Under this doctrine, all the knowledge of the individual corporate agents is collected together, and then attributed to the organization providing the mens rea for the offense.

In United States versus Bank of New England,[68] the bank was charged with violating currency transaction laws for failing to file reports on transactions by a customer who used multiple transactions with multiple accounts to avoid the $10,000 cash transactions reporting threshold.[69] At trial, the jury was instructed that "knowledge is the sum of the knowledge of all employees".[70] The bank's knowledge of the CTR requirements is the totality of what all employees knew within the scope of their employment. Thus, "flagrant organizational indifference" can be found based on the fact that individual employees collectively knew what the legal requirements were and failed as an organization to meet them. Another trap for the unwary exists within the reporting requirements of 31 U.S.C. Section 5318(g)(2). The law prohibits both the bank making the filing and FinCEN from disclosing to the customer or any third party the fact of the filing or the details of the report.[71] This approach is somewhat softer than the United Kingdom's "consent regime" in which financial institutions must normally obtain prior consent before completing any customer transaction that is deemed to be suspicious.

However, any response by a U.S. institution, other than reporting suspicion of money laundering activity, can create significant commercial and legal difficulties when delays in transactions result in economic and legal damage to bank clients or third parties. The financial institution and its legal counsel must be careful not to disclose the existence of a SAR in response to a subpoena or court order related to discovery for any legal action relevant to any transaction. An effective corporate compliance program may have a significant impact on the government's decision whether to prosecute under AML statutes. Such a program does not however, act as a legal bar to prosecution. It is not enough for a firm to develop an appropriate

---

[67]Party that willfully blinds itself to a fact can be charged with constructive notice of that fact. *U.S. versus Baxter Intern. Inc.*, 3445 F.3d 866 (11th Cir.2003) cert. denied 542 U.S. 946 (2004). See also *United States vs. Heredia*, 483 F.3d 913, cert. denied 76 U.S. L.W. 3303.

[68]821 F.2d 844 (1st Cir.), cert. denied, 484 U.S. 943 (1987).

[69]See 31 U.S.C. Section 5311–22.

[70]821 F.2d 855.

[71]See 31 C.F.R. Section 5318 (g) (1); 12 C.F.R. Section 21.11 (pertaining to national banks); 12 C.F.R. Section 208.62 (pertaining to state chartered banks that are members of the Federal Reserve System); 12 C.F.R. Section 353 (pertaining to state chartered banks that are not members of the Federal Reserve System); 12C.F.R. Section 563.108(d) (pertaining to Federal thrifts and savings associations).

risk-based compliance regime. In an environment where the level of risk is dynamic and regulatory inspections generally have the benefit of hindsight, the entire compliance effort must be recorded for validation of the firm's diligence efforts in policing its customers.

4.5 Measuring Success

The fundamental nature of money laundering requires secrecy and therefore does not lend itself to easy statistical analysis. Money launderers do not document, nor publicize, their successes or failures. Their ability to use the differences between national laws and practices to accomplish complex integration schemes makes even the collection of reliable enforcement data difficult.[72] The FATF in 1996, addressing global AML success, reported that the vast majority of members lack sufficient data to support credible estimates.[73] This remains relatively unchanged today.

In its 2007 Money Laundering Threat Assessment, the U.S. government acknowledged that the data is not developed in a systemic way, making it impossible to quantify with accuracy the relative amount of money laundering activity being interrupted by federal law enforcement agencies, let alone state and local law enforcement.[74]

Problems noted included:

- Individual tracking systems are tailored to meet particular agency priorities providing incompatible data;
- Data fields are collected by some but not all agencies;
- Disparities in definitions exist; and
- Redundancies exist where two or more agencies record the same event because the case involved a joint task force.

Some authorities statistics regarding the number of SARs filed and amounts involved in those transactions as the best evidence of an effective AML program.[75] However, the adequacy of a SAR program for a single institution, an industry group, or a country cannot be judged solely by numbers of reports submitted.[76] Subsequent amendments to the reporting provisions of the Patriot Act, as well as the expansion of reporting requirement to other financial categories, have, as noted,

---

[72]See *supra*, note 8. 1–7.

[73]FATF/GAFI, *FATF-VII Report on Monay Laundering Typologies* 2 (28 June 1996).

[74]See *supra*, note 33, p. 19.

[75]See *supra*, note 58, p. 2.

[76]See Pub. L. 91–508, 84 Stat.1118 Section 221(a)(2) amended 31 U.S.C. Section 5313(a); see also *U.S. Money Laundering Typologies* 2 (28 June 1996).

continued to increase SAR filings dramatically.[77] In 2007, the aggregate number of SARs reported in the U.S. exceeded 1,087,890.[78]

A concern with the U.S. AML program is that the increased scope and emphasis on reporting requirements generates so much data that the information becomes difficult for recipient agencies to use effectively in investigation and enforcement efforts. While the volume of filings alone may not reveal a problem, it leads to the potential that financial institutions are seeking to avoid regulatory and criminal scrutiny by filing more reports, regardless of whether the transaction is suspicious.

Since an entity is not penalized for excessive filing, institutional procedures may be biased toward submitting unnecessary reports. Such defensive filings dilute the value of the information in the BSA database.[79] Since FinCEN statistics do not provide a complete reference as to the extent to which SARs directly contribute to money laundering and financial crime investigations, there is a risk that the value of FinCEN reporting is under-recognized. Since SAR information is an investigative tool alone, and can not be used for evidentiary purposes, FinCEN is challenged to sustain the relevance of SAR data. Law enforcement agencies, who may gain benefit from SAR information early in an investigation, may overlook the ultimate utility of the SAR information during the course of a lengthy investigation. Attempts at completing a cost/benefit analysis have been undertaken where circumstances support sufficient isolation of factors and responses.[80]

In 2005, the City of London commissioned a study assessing the perceived the perceived costs and benefits of the United Kingdom's Anti-Money Laundering Requirements compared with other jurisdictions, including the U.S.[81] While this study also lacked sufficiently hard cost/benefit data to satisfy a quantitative analytical standard, a cost-benefit approach was applied to perceptive responses from financial institutions and individual participants in the U.K. This was accomplished by approximating the cost of AML at the national level and assessing the perceived benefits from that expenditure. The correlation between aggregate costs at the national level and perceived benefits at the participant level is a tenuous one.

The London study was beneficial in isolating the perceptions of cost and presented the following results[82]:

- AML costs as a proportion of national GDP in the UK are significantly higher than most other jurisdictions. They are 25 % higher than in the US;
- Two-thirds of UK respondents said that AML requirements were too severe relative to the risks of money laundering;

---

[77]FinCEN, SAR Activity Review (January 2008), http://www.fincen.org.

[78]Id.

[79]Statement of William Fox, former director of FinCEN, http://www.fincen.org; Director's Forum.

[80]FATF/GAFI, *Third Mutual Evaluation Report on Anti-Money Laundering and Combating the Financing of Terrorism*, 298, 23 June 2006.

[81]Mark Yeandle et al., "Anti-Money Laundering Requirements: Costs, Benefits and Perceptions", 8, *City Research Series* 6 (June 2005).

[82]Id., p. 32.

- UK companies largely comply with AML requirements in order to avoid sanctions and not as a matter of good business practice or AML effectiveness;
- The rigorous implementation of international AML requirements has not had a pronounced impact on competitiveness;
- High AML costs reduce the perception of AML effectiveness.

Many of the respondents in the London survey perceived few AML related benefits to the organization. Benefits were acknowledged to the country as a whole. However, there is also a belief that the UK is approaching a "tipping point" where past, current and future costs of AML legislation are perceived to be greater than the benefits.[83] This suggests opposition to further efforts at AML legislation.

An interesting cost/benefit relationship has been exposed by Professor Barry Rider of the University of London. A high level of financial oversight and its incumbent costs do not necessarily render a jurisdiction unattractive to criminal enterprise.[84] Quite possible, the inverse is true. Criminal organizations need a secure place to hold their wealth so that the clean money generated by their laundering processes can be afforded by the benefits of a stable currency and low risk economic environment. What good is it to go to the trouble generating illegal wealth only to see it diminished through the financial negatives of a corrupt economic system of a third world financial structure? There is little doubt that AML policies have significantly altered how banks and core financial institutions approach their clients, their responsibilities, and conduct business. While the global AML effort may be protecting the integrity of banks and core financial institutions in key financial centers, there is no indication that these efforts have reduced the total volume of criminal proceeds being laundered globally.

4.6   The Fundamental Conflict

It is common legal theory that the "cost of punishment" must outweigh the "benefit of the crime" if the punishment is to act as a deterrent. But what if the perceived benefit is outweighed by the cost? What then is the value of the deterrent? If belief within the financial community that the costs of AML efforts are not worth the returns in financial security, attitudes to comply at the margins will increase and organizations will institute the least cost alternatives in approaching suspicious transactions. This can lead to a forfeiting of the intelligence opportunity in identifying, reporting, and seizing criminal proceeds. What will remain is merely a data collection process churning endless amounts of information with little real effort on national goals. While the costs of compliance are a significant concern to financial

---

[83]*Id.*, p. 4.

[84]Professor Barry Rider, "The Financial War Against Crime and Terror", 21, Queen's College, Cambridge (June 2005).

institutions, the lack of immediate feedback and investigative response is what leads to a crisis of confidence within the AML structure.[85]

In the London survey, only 8 % of respondents familiar with UK and international AML requirements said that feedback was "Effective" or "Very Effective".[86] In its Third Mutual Evaluation Report on Anti-Money Laundering in the U.S., FATF found that the effectiveness of FinCEN was impeded by the workload of 14 million reports, of which 70 % are still filed in paper formata. FATF also found that SAR filings are often done 30–60 days after detection and lack adequate or timely feedback to reporting institutions.[87] In addition to the financial community, the general public and money launderers in particular, need to see that the regulations and their enforcement are successful. Seeing successful enforcement will increase the perceived likelihood of being caught. This fear has been shown to be a most effective deterrent.[88]

What exists is a gap between the AML policy level on the one hand, and enforcement of AML objectives at the operational level.[89] Ultimately, regulators feel that the detection of money laundering will inevitably come as a result of activity within the private sector.[90] This recognizes that policy influences behavior, however, to achieve AML success, one must provide the right tools to those who are in the best position to use them. Within this consideration, the government must take a much more radical approach to the problem if it truly intends to meet its multiple objectives of reducing predicate crimes, terrorist financing, corruption, and kleptocracy. That radical approach needs to clearly provide incentives to those who are on the front lines of the AML fight and provide the ability to stop laundering transactions at the initial point of entry into the legitimate financial system.

4.7   Conclusion

The current approach to Anti-Money Laundering (AML) is designed to make criminal activities unprofitable. It attempts to keep the proceeds of crime out of the hands of criminals and terrorist. These goals cannot be achieved without proactive confiscation mechanisms. Traditional privateers disrupted the enemy by crippling its economic standing.[91] Economic interruption of criminal financial networks

---

[85]See *supra*, note 66, p. 26.

[86]*Id.*, p. 50.

[87]See *supra*, note 80, p. 301.

[88]See *supra*, note 81, p. 50.

[89]See *supra*, note 80, p. 301.

[90]See *supra*, note 81, p. 34.

[91]See Larry J. Sechrest, Privateering and National Defense: Naval Warfare for Private Profit, 7–9 Indep. Inst., 2001: available at http://www.independent.org/pdf/working_papers/41_privateering.pdf.

could be radically enhanced by providing financial institutions with the ability to disrupt financial transactions through timely seizure without fear of liability or economic loss. This desired effect is exactly what is provided by a letter of marque. The letter of marque historically immunized its possessor from liability by attaching state authorization to the confiscation action of select private actors.

FATF has provided guidance for the application of procedures for "Provisional Measures and Confiscation". When assessing FATF 40 compliance, countries determine that, "Laws and other measures should provide for provisional measures, including freezing and/or seizing of property, to prevent any dealing, transfer or disposal of property subject to confiscation".[92] In a formal Interpretative Note for the implementation of Special Recommendation 3 (relating to the seizure of terrorist funds), FATF directs that the freezing of funds or other assets should be done "without delay and without giving prior notice to the persons or entities concerned".[93] This goes to the heart of the problem with the current reporting based system. Financial institutions are required to report suspicious transactions within 30–60 days and if necessary refuse to complete the transaction. The result is that either the transaction occurs with potentially illegitimate money entering the financial system, or the funds walk away, free to search for an alternative entry point. What is absent from the current system is the ability to immediately seize the funds without delay as recommended, pending determination of the legitimacy of the funds involved. It is the delay in response that undermines the effectiveness of the current system.

FATF Interpretative Note 3 develops three levels of provisional action:

(1) freezing
(2) seizure
(3) confiscation (or forfeiture).[94]

"Freezing" refers to a competent authority blocking or restraining assets from being moved or otherwise dispersed. The "frozen" funds remain the property of the owner under the administration of the financial institution (or other entity) until appropriate determination. This denies use the assets for any prohibited purpose. "Seizure" means that the competent authority has authority to take control of the assets, which remain the property of the original owner, however, possession, administration, and management of the assets are taken over by the competent authority pending determination of rightful status. "Confiscation" (or "forfeiture") means the permanent deprivation of assets by order of a competent authority or a court through a judicial or administrative procedure.

---

[92]FATF-GAFI, *Methodology for Assessing Compliance with the FATF 40 Recommendations and FATF 9 Special Recommendations*, 15, February 2008; available at http://www.fatf-gafi.org/dataoecd/16/54/40339628.pdf.

[93]FATF-GAFI, *Interpretative Notes to the FATF 40 Recommendations and FATF 9 Special Recommendations*, 4; available at http://www.fatf-gafi.org/dataoecd/53/32/34262136.pdf.

[94]*Id.*, p. 2.

Under a present day letter of marque concept, Congress would direct the Treasury Department to develop standards and procedures which would license and commission qualified financial institutions to "freeze" funds up determining that a reasonable basis exists to initiate action under the freezing mechanism. The regulatory procedures would also provide an efficient and timely communication of "freeze events" to FinCEN for analysis and investigative follow-up. Similar to OFAC "blocked account" transactions, frozen funds could be segregated in an interest-bearing account (at a commercially reasonable rate) pending review and investigation.[95] Once frozen, these suspicious funds would be subject to attachment for criminal or civil proceedings consistent with current asset forfeiture laws. Notification of a "freeze event" would need to comply with the standards of the Civil Asset Reform Act of 2000 (CAFRA) which provides notification criteria, waivers of notification and provisions for "innocent owner defense".[96]

The additional purpose of the letter of marque is to create a financial incentive for commercial organizations to interrupt money laundering crimes. Given the huge volume of transactions, only the private sector has the manpower and assets to properly identify, trace and evaluate property which is subject to seizure. While the BSA provides both criminal and civil penalties for failure to comply with reporting procedures, there has been no link made to a private right of action for a financial institution against a money launderer since the harm is not considered to affect the individual entity. However, there is a history of success in inspiring private action on behalf of the government in criminal fraud cases commonly referred to as "Qui Tam" actions.[97] Similar to qui tam actions under the False Claims Act (FCA),[98] statutory authority could be developed which grants commissioned financial institutions the right to serve as "private attorneys general" and bring forward civil suits on behalf of government. Given that the financial institution would be the original source of the information, those institutions would be qualified as "relators". As such, they would receive a financial incentive to take the action by receiving a percentage of the monetary recovery. Currently, under the FCA, if the government does not join in the action, then relators receive 25–30 % of the recovery. The recovery is 15–25 % if the government join in the action.[99] Given the sizeable estimates of illegal fund transfers, this could provide a powerful incentive and deliver the power of profit motive to the AML fight.

Mr. Darryl F. Smith, 3Lw (Levin College of Law), assisted in the research and preparation of this chapter.

---

[95]See Stefan Cassella, U.S. DOJ, address Georgetown University: "Forfeiture Assets Under the USA Patriot Act, 2001" (March 18, 2002) and address 25th Cambridge International Symposium on Economic Crime: "The Case of Civil Forfeiture: Why in Rem Proceedings are an Essential Tool for Recovering the Proceeds of Crime", September 7th, 2007. See p. 136.

[96]See Civil Asset Forfeiture Reform Act of 2000, Pub. L. No. 106–185, 114 Stat. 2000; as amending 18 U.S.C. 981.

[97]The term "qui tam" is derived from the Latin phrase "qui tam pro domino rege quam pro seipse", which means "he who sues for the king as for himself".

[98]31 U.S.C. 13729–3733.

[99]See 31 U.S.C. Section 3730 (d).

Part II
Psychological and Psychiatric Aspects of Financial Crimes

Chapter 5
Forensic Psychiatric Contributions to Understanding Financial Crime

Sara Brady, Erick Rabin, Daniel Wu, Omar Sultan Haque and Harold J. Bursztajn

Abstract Forensic psychiatric evaluation and consultation can make significant contributions to understanding, preventing, and responding to financial crimes. Drawing on forensic psychiatric principles and experience, and research and analysis from related fields of inquiry, this chapter explores the individual psychological dimensions of financial crimes in their social context, the group dynamics of corrupt organizations, and the interrelationship between the two. At the individual level, there is a need to distinguish "mad" from "bad," i.e., psychosis from character pathology and crimes committed with deliberation and foreknowledge of their consequences. In this context we explore the limitations of rational choice theory as a foundation for the legal approaches to preventing acts of financial crime, understanding their meaning, responding in accordance with the fundamentals of justice. We also address the limitations of classic actuarial responses to the prevention and postvention acts of financial crime. From a forensic psychiatric perspective the prevention and postvention of acts of financial crime needs to be on a case by case basis. In any given case a forensic psychiatric analysis may make reference to such psychopathology and character traits as manic-depressive illness

S. Brady (✉)
Harvard Longwood Psychiatry Residency Training Program, Boston, USA
e-mail: sjbrady@bidmc.harvard.edu

E. Rabin
New York University School of Law, New York, USA
e-mail: erick.rabin@gmail.com

D. Wu
Harvard University, Cambridge, USA

O.S. Haque
Department of Psychology, Harvard University, Cambridge, USA
e-mail: omarsultanhaque@gmail.com

O.S. Haque
Program in Psychiatry and the Law, Harvard Medical School, Boston, USA

H.J. Bursztajn
Clinical and Forensic Psychiatrist, Cambridge, USA
e-mail: hbursztajn@hms.harvard.edu

© Springer International Publishing Switzerland 2016
M. Dion et al. (eds.), *Financial Crimes: Psychological, Technological, and Ethical Issues*, International Library of Ethics, Law, and the New Medicine 68, DOI 10.1007/978-3-319-32419-7_5

and narcissitic grandiosity, Freud's notion of "criminals from a sense of guilt," and antisocial personality disorder. The forensic psychiatric evaluation of any act of financial crime needs to ask how it is most likely to be the product of individual or institutional psychopathology, character traits, or states of desire. While we will discuss prevention of financial crime in future work, this chapter concludes via setting forth a psychodynamically informed forensic psychiatric perspective as an aid for sentencing of white-collar crime.

5.1 Introduction

As the organizer of one of the biggest financial frauds led by a single person, Bernie Madoff was known to be a likeable, industrious person. His childhood friends responded in shock when news broke that his celebrated asset management firm was, in fact, a Ponzi scheme that squandered $50 billion and led to the closing of several hospitals and philanthropies (Creswell and Thomas 2009). Before pleading guilty to 11 federal felonies, including securities fraud, money laundering, and theft from an employee benefit plan, Madoff was widely viewed as a hero who rose from modest means to financial success. To regulators, Madoff championed himself as a protector of smaller investors and worked closely with regulators to level Wall Street's playing field. How was Madoff so successful? Authorities note that the Securities and Exchange Commission audited his private management firm several times, but these investigators found nothing amiss. Some, like Gregg McCrary, a former special agent with the F.B.I, say Madoff exhibited some of the characteristics of a psychopath, including great skill at manipulating victims and managing impressions well. McCrary explains, "People like [Madoff] become chameleons. They know what people want, and they give it to them." However, we now know that Madoff did not act alone. Nine of Madoff's associates pled guilty, and five more were convicted. United States attorney Preet Bharara, whose office brought the case against Madoff, is quoted in the *New York Times*: "These convictions, along with the prior guilty pleas of nine other defendants, demonstrate what we have believed from the earliest stages of the investigation: This largest-ever Ponzi scheme could not have been the work of one person" (Abrams and Henriques 2014).

This chapter aims to provide a more scholarly and thorough review of how to deepen our understanding of the mind-set whereby one person can work alone or in concert with confederates to systematically commit financial crimes. We will draw from multiple perspectives gained from demography to forensic psychiatry in order to understand the psychology of cases such as the Madoff Ponzi scheme, and how can we better understand the causes of white-collar financial crimes and their prevention in the future. Although the Madoff case garnered the most publicity, numerous additional, high-profile financial crimes transpired within the last 20 years, drawing into focus the prevalence of similar transgressions. Enron's President Jeffrey Skilling and Chief Financial Officer Andrew Fastow employed numerous fraudulent and deceptive accounting practices to conceal company losses while simultaneously increasing not only stock prices, but also their own personal profits. As stock values continued to soar, Enron's directors perpetuated fraudulent practices in order to maintain high prices and achieve financial gains. In one famous and illustrative exchange, investigative financial analysts examining Enron's unconventional accounting methods requested balance sheets and earning statements, to which Skilling infamously responded "Well thank you very much, we appreciate that ... asshole" (McLean and Elkind 2003). Exposure of Enron's fraudulent acts and subsequent price drop led to $63.4 billion in lost assets and numerous guilty pleas based upon charges of securities and wire frauds. Numerous additional companies and individuals were implicated in the 90 s, including Worldcom and the "Wolf of Wall Street" Jordan Belfort, whose use of fake stock trades totaled $1 billion. Again, due to the prevalence and cost of these crimes, greater understanding of the intrinsic motivations must be sought. We can assess financial crime by focusing either on the offense or on the offender. Similarly, we can assess offenders either as institutions or as individuals. At the institutional level, several key factors necessitate examination: monetary incentives that encourage short-term financial growth, corporate governance mechanisms that demand immediate quarterly profits at the expense of long-term growth (e.g., executive hiring, pay-for-performance), organizational flaws that can permit or enable financial crime to occur, and conflicts of interest that exist among regulators, politicians, and financiers. However, we will focus the discussion on attributes of the *individual* who commits financial crimes, as the *individual* possesses the necessary agency and will for the commission of any and all financial crime. As such, this chapter will review the psychology and neurobiology of white-collar criminals. We will briefly introduce legal definitions of financial crime and segue into a discussion of traditional economic analysis theory of financial criminals' motivations. Finally, we will explore the important and fertile territory of contemporary psychiatry as a powerful means to understand financial crime. We conclude by substantiating the importance of forensic psychiatry as a promising methodology for preventing financial crime ex ante and remedying such incidents ex post. We aim to demonstrate that forensic psychiatric approaches can provide data to manage the risk of repeat offences. Using personal history, dynamic risk factors (such as attitudes, mental state, and social support), and actuarial instruments, forensic psychiatrists can monitor and contribute to rehabilitation of white-collar criminals and their victims.

Financial crime is a relatively new concept. It was first recognized as a distinct object of inquiry in 1939, when the sociologist Edwin Sutherland coined the term "white collar crime" to describe offenses committed by "respectable or at least respected business and professional men" (Sutherland 1940). Financial crimes characteristically involve some form of deceit, concealment, or abuse of trust, and tend to be committed by people in positions of authority, whether professional, governmental, or otherwise. There is no definitive list of offenses that comprise financial crime. Rather, the "white collar crime" label attaches to an evolving set of non-violent, financially motivated offenses. Some of the most common examples include:

- Credit Card Fraud: attempting to secure a loan with dishonest application
- Embezzlement: taking company funds meant for other purposes, and using them for personal gain
- Securities Fraud: providing investors with untrue stock information meant to impact their purchasing decisions
- Antitrust Violations: attempting to fix or regulate prices of services or merchandise
- Bribery: offering, giving, receiving, or soliciting something of value in order to influence the action of an official
- Extortion: obtaining property from another induced by wrongful use of actual or threatened force, violence, or fear, or under color of official right
- Perjury, False Statements, and False Claims: knowingly making false statements that cover up crimes and obstruct justice
- Mail and Wire Fraud: using a government-regulated means of communication to deceive others
- Tax Fraud: deceiving the government in order to avoid or decrease the amount of taxes paid
- Securities Fraud: intentionally inducing investors to make purchase or sale decisions on the basis of material misstatements or omissions of information
- Antitrust Violations: practices that unlawfully restrain trade, fix prices, etc.
- Money Laundering: moving illicit gains into legitimate channels in order to disguise the money's illegal source
- Forgery: creating a false written document or altering a genuine one with the intent to defraud
- Identity Theft: unlawfully using another's personally identifying information.

5.1.1 Rational Choice Theory

Popular psychology often assumes that financial crimes are motivated by greed alone. Similarly, academic analysis uses a traditional rational choice model. Under a traditional rational choice theory of financial crime, *homo economicus* will choose to act illegally if and when the benefits of doing so exceed the product of the probability of getting convicted of financial crime multiplied by the penalty associated with that crime. "[All] human behavior can be viewed as involving participants who maximize their utility from a stable set of preferences and accumulate an optimal amount of information and other inputs in a variety of markets" (Becker 1976). The limits of this model have been made apparent by behavioral economics, and the untruth of its assumptions has been vigorously challenged (Tversky and Kahneman 1981). Nonetheless, rational choice theory retains a level of popularity among legal academics, and it continues to shape legal arguments and policy decisions. Even under ideal conditions, many forms of financial crime are difficult to explain under this model because they involve benefits that the corporation accrues, rather than benefitting the employee who enacts the illegal behavior. Excluding incidental stock ownership, what direct economic benefits would an employee possibly gain by committing a crime that adds to the corporation's bottom line? Undeterred, rational choice devotees insist that promotions, prestige, pay-for-performance, and the like all factor into rational self-interest from an economic point of view. Fair enough—but these views also place great weight on the notion that individuals leading big firms are proficient at weighing risks and, as such, are likely to be rational in doing cost-benefit analyses of their personal actions. Moreover, they are quick to highlight that corporate crime often requires multiple individuals to coordinate their actions and so cannot be conducted in the heat of passion. Yet, as per the old Spanish proverb, revenge is a dish best served cold. Similarly, financial crime may involve cold-blooded calculations purported by the individual, and, therefore, does not eliminate passion, conviction, and the psychological.

5.2   Approaches from Psychiatry and Psychology

5.2.1   Psychoanalysis

From psychoanalytic perspective, Freud suggested that "unconscious guilt" is central to explaining why people commit crimes. He writes in the Ego and the Id (1923): "In many criminals, especially youthful ones, it is possible to detect a very powerful sense of guilt which existed before the crime, and is therefore not its result but its motive. It is as if it was a relief to be able to fasten this unconscious sense of guilt on to something real and immediate." Anna Freud described a developmental theory of psychopathology as evolving through states, and specifically included the harnessing of aggression and component affects. She also provided a developmental model of antisocial and narcissistic personality disorder (1949) which focused upon early failures by an absent, neglectful, or ambivalent primary object (the parent). Combining the two theories, analysts assert that crime is an outward manifestation of core tension and conflict among different aspects of the self. However, psychoanalytically informed observations while helpful clinically and forensically as a starting point for understanding some individuals' motives and capacities, are not generalizable beyond any individual examination.

While psychoanalytic profiles of white-collar criminals cannot be tested in a standardized fashion, Poortinga et al. (2006) hypothesized that white-collar defendants referred for psychiatric evaluation have higher rates of affective disorders (especially mania) and problem gambling and lower rates of substance abuse and psychotic disorders than do controls. They examined the clinical, forensic and socio-demographic characteristics of all white-collar crime defendants referred to the evaluation unit of a state psychiatric unit for forensic evaluation. During a 12-year period, they took more than 29,000 evaluations comparing 73 cases of "white-collar crime" (including embezzlement and health care fraud) against 73 cases of non-violent theft. White-collar defendants were found to have a higher likelihood of white race, higher education, and a lower likelihood of substance abuse than control defendants. However, controlling for race, education, and substance abuse in a regression model, neither the bipolar nor the unipolar depression rate differed statistically from that of the control group. The variance in the relationship between depression and white-collar crime was more economically accounted for by education, race, and substance abuse. What may be helpful relative to deepening one's understanding in an individual forensic psychiatric examination, therefore, may not be sufficient as a general explanation of the social psychology of white-collar crime.

5.2.2 Demographic Analyses

Demographic characteristics may be helpful in understanding observations garnered in the course of a forensic psychiatric examination. Wheeler et al. (1988a, b) conducted a descriptive study of the demographics of white-collar offenders (n = 1,342), non-white-collar offenders (n = 210), and a random US community sample, gathering data from the pre-sentence investigation reports of offenders convicted in US federal criminal courts between 1976 and 1978. The definition of white-collar crime came from Wheeler et al. (1982), which enumerated eight types of offenses that qualified as white-collar crime, noting the similarity to previously enumerated crimes in this chapter. These included:

1. Bank embezzlement (taking company funds meant for other purposes, and using them for personal gain)
2. Securities fraud (providing investors with untrue stock information meant to impact their purchasing decisions)
3. Antitrust violations (attempts to fix or regulate prices of services and merchandise)
4. Bribery (influencing a public official by promising or giving him/her something in return)
5. False statements or claims (defrauding a government agency in order to receive funds for the underserved)
6. Credit fraud (attempt to secure a loan with dishonest application)
7. Postal fraud (using a government-regulated means of communication to deceive others)
8. Tax fraud (deceiving the government in order to avoid or decrease the amount of taxes paid).

Using these criteria, Wheeler and colleagues (1988a, b) found that white-collar offenders were more likely to be Caucasian, male, older, graduated from college, and more likely to be employed, when compared to non-white-collar offenders and the community sample. Overall, descriptive results demonstrated that white-collar offenders were less likely to have an arrest history than non-white-collar offenders, and if they did have an arrest history, it was more likely to be an arrest for white-collar crime. A similar study by Benson and Moore (1992) also used the pre-sentence investigation reports of male and female federal offenders, but expanded the sample to include the years 1973–1978. Results showed that white-collar offenders were less likely to have previously used drugs or alcohol or to have demonstrated impaired academic performance than non-white-collar offenders.

Demographic studies indicate that the typical white-collar offender is a middle aged Caucasian male who graduated from high school with no major substance abuse history. However, these studies do not examine the personality traits of these individuals. Several studies explore the underlying personality characteristics present in white-collar crime offenders. Collins and Schmidt (1993) examined a 365-person sample of federal prison inmates convicted of white-collar crime and compared them to 344 individuals currently employed in upper-level positions of authority. Job titles of non-offender white-collar employees include loan bank officer, court service officer, county treasurer, fire chief, appraiser, and various other white-collar positions of employment. The study assessed the construct validity of personality scales, a personality-based integrity test, and homogenous bio-data scales as reflected in the metric's ability to discriminate white-collar criminals from other white-collar employees. More simply, these scales attempted to delineate between offenders and current employees; and if so, what traits would separate the two groups. Three instruments were administered: the California Psychological Inventory (Gough 1987), the Biodata Questionnaire (Owens and Schoenfeldt 1979), and the PDI Employee Inventory (Paajanen 1988). The California Psychological Inventory assessed traits of "responsibility," "socialization," and "self-control," noting that considerable research indicates that the responsibility and socialization scales are predictive of delinquent and other criminal behavior (Gough 1987). The Biodata Questionnaire is a systematic method of scaling life history expectancies such as extra-curricular activity, academic achievement, scientific interest and athletic participation (Owens and Schoenfeld 1979). The PDI Employee Inventory is a personality-based measure designed to predict "productive" and "counterproductive" work behavior. Paajanen (1988) describes employees with high scores on this instrument as being reliable, having good work habits, and being motivated to conform to company rules and policies. Collins and Schmidt (1993) revealed that offenders have greater tendencies toward irresponsibility, lack of dependability and disregard of rules and social norms, suggesting that lack of "social conscientiousness" is an integral character trait present in the white-collar offender compared to a non-offender white-collar employee.

5.2.3   Personality

Blickle et al. (2006) explored the differences in personality between 76 incarcerated white-collar offenders and 150 business managers, controlling for age and income. All subjects completed a self-report measure assessing social desirability, hedonism, narcissism, and conscientiousness. Self-control was measured using the Retrospective Behavioral Self-Control scale (Marcus 2003), wherein subjects read four separate scenarios within which cheating another individual was possible. If subjects chose to cheat, they were deemed to be low in self-control. Regression analysis demonstrated that white-collar offenders have higher narcissism, hedonism, lack of conscientiousness and lower self-control than their non-offender counterparts. Bucy et al. (2008) also examined the literature on personality attributes inherent in white-collar criminals. They summarized eight personality characteristics that underlie white-collar criminal activity; these include the need for control, charisma, company ambitions, lack of integrity, narcissism, fear of failure or losing social status, and lack of social conscience. Piquero et al. (2005) explored the "desire for control" in more detail within a sample of business managers and MBA students. They found that the more desirous an individual was to "have control," the more likely that individual would be to commit violations in the context of corporate decision making. Prisoners convicted of white-collar crime were interviewed by a professor of business ethics and law during which criminals attributed their crime to greed, a feeling of invincibility, and poor judgment (Ellin 2002). Using a semi-structured interview procedure, Alalehto (2003) commissioned 128 business professionals to report on the personality traits and behavior of a colleague in the music, engineering, or construction business. Particularly, the investigator instructed subjects to describe the illegal behavior of their coworker or friend if they had "close knowledge of whether or not the person committed the economic crime, regardless of whether that person was convicted of it" (p. 343). Subjects who did not know of a colleague partaking in illegal activities at work were asked, instead, to describe a co-worker who did not participate in illegal acts at work. A total of 55 white-collar offenders and 70 non-criminal white-collar professionals were described. The interview text consisted of questions examining six personality traits, such as extroversion, agreeableness, conceitedness, neuroticism, intellectualism, and negative valency. Descriptive data showed a greater number of white-collar offenders were described as extroverted (i.e., outgoing, controlling, calculating), neurotic, and less agreeable. The non-criminal white-collar professionals were conceited (i.e., diligent, frugal, refined) and more agreeable.

While the aforementioned studies elucidated differences between personality traits of white-collar offenders and non-white-collar offenders, others searched for more generalizable personality profiles of white-collar offenders. Most often, the character trait patterns exhibited by white-collar criminals fit some or all of the criteria for either narcissistic personality disorder or antisocial personality disorder.

As previously stated, narcissism has been identified as a financial offender risk factor (Bucy et al. 2008; Blickle et al. 2006). Narcissism is described as a pervasive pattern of grandiosity, a lack of empathy for others, a need for admiration, and a belief that one is superior or unique. Per Bucy et al. (2008, p. 417), white-collar offenders demonstrating narcissistic traits of extreme entitlement may not be deterred from committing fraud because they may not "fear being caught or what punishments may come their way." White-collar offenders are "extremely ambitious, obsessed with enhancing power and control, having a sense of superiority bordering on narcissism, which is fed by admiration and attention and which encourages a sense of entitlement to special privileges and resources." These individuals lack the ability to put themselves in the place of others or envision that the consequences of their actions may fall on the shoulders of numerous other people. Ken Lay, CEO of Enron, during his fraud trial "appeared arrogant, resentful of the government's investigation, remained unapologetic and indignant to the end" (Bucy et al. 2008, p. 410). Furthermore, white-collar criminals often demonstrate characteristics indicative of antisocial personality disorder, which is a pervasive pattern of disregard and violation of the rights of others and a lack in social consciousness and conventional morality wherein the perpetrator deceives, exploits and manipulates others for personal gain (Barnard 2008). An extreme version of antisocial personality disorder manifests as psychopathy. While neither the DSM-IV nor DSM-5 lists *psychopathy* as a formal diagnosis, psychopathic traits are characterized as callousness, lacking conscientiousness, antipathy, and remorselessness when violating the rights of others. It should be noted that not all individuals with antisocial personality disorder can be considered psychopaths. Based on the work of Cleckley (1941, 1988), Dr. Hare constructed the Psychopathy Check List-Revised as a risk appraisal instrument with considerable research demonstrating its usefulness for predicting criminal justice outcomes based on the traits inherent in offenders. Hare categorized psychopathic personality traits as interpersonal (superficial charm, grandiosity, deception/lying, conning and manipulative), affective (remorselessness, shallow affects, callousness, failure to accept responsibility), lifestyle (impulsivity, stimulation seeking, irresponsibility and lack of realistic goals, parasitic lifestyle) and antisocial (poor behavior controls, delinquency, criminal versatility, early behavioral problems). However, Babiak (2007) asserted that many characteristics of psychopaths may be favorable in the business or corporate domain. For instance, self-centeredness might be perceived as having "self-confidence." Babiak et al. (2010) examined the relationship between psychopathy and several work performance dimensions in a cohort of 200 corporate professionals. Psychopathy scores (as measured by the PCL-R) were found to be positively correlated with being a successful communicator, being creative and following through on new proposals, and having critical thinking skills. Not surprisingly, psychopathy scores were negatively correlated with benevolent interpersonal skills and effective managerial skills.

5.2.4   Neurobiological Approaches

Might it be possible to find out what underlies these personality traits and profiles at the level of neurobiology? Since 2000, a growing body of literature has documented neurobiological, neuropsychological, and genetic processes implicated in the etiology of antisocial and criminal behavior. To date, however, very little is known about how white-collar crime differs neurobiologically from other forms of offending. Raine et al. (2012) used a case-control design with neuroimaging to compare orienting, cortical thickness, and executive functioning between 21 white-collar criminals and 21 matched controls. They found that the white-collar criminals demonstrate better executive functions, increased and sustained orienting, increased arousal, and increased cortical thickness in multiple brain regions functioning in decision-making, social cognition, and attention. White-collar offenders showed greater cortical thickness in five circumscribed areas compared to matched controls, which include right inferior frontal gyrus, ventromedial prefrontal cortex, ventrolateral premotor area of the precentral gyrus, inferior region of the somatosensory cortex, and a broad area of the temporal pareital junction that included the right posterior superior temporal gyrus and the right inferior parietal lobule. The right inferior frontal gyrus functions to coordinate thoughts and actions in relation to internally generated goals, respond to changes in task demands, inhibit dominant responses, and resolve conflicting reasoning. Taken together, these operations produce cognitive flexibility and regulatory control. The ventromedial prefrontal cortex is associated with good decision making, sensitivity to future consequences of one's actions, and the generation of skin conductance responses. This area is also involved in the monitoring of the reward value of stimuli and giving salience to stimuli. Functional MRI studies have shown that the anterior region of this area is specifically associated with abstract rewards, such as money. Such findings support the idea that white-collar criminals, compared to other non-violent offenders, have enhanced cognitive and attentional functioning that place them at a greater likelihood of committing offenses in the workplace. However, such differences in brain functioning are not in themselves sufficient to offer a general explanation for motivation or capacity, which must take into account not only biological factors, but also psychological, social, interpersonal, and institutional contexts. In the end, there is no substitute for an individual neuropsychiatric forensic examination to address such questions as diminished capacity, specific intent, mitigation, or potential for rehabilitation or risk of reoffense.

5.2.5   Detailing the Forensic Psychiatric Approach

Now that we have reviewed common approaches in psychiatry used to understand white-collar individuals, we detail our favored method—forensic psychiatry and risk assessments—to address and mitigate white-collar financial crime.

5.2.5.1   Forensic Psychiatry and the Tool of Risk Assessments

Since the 1960s, forensic psychiatry has informally adhered to the obligation of providing both subjective and objective truth-telling when evaluating a patient, while simultaneously upholding the evaluee's rights and dignity. These points were later articulated as "the Standard Position" or truth stance defined by Paul Appelbaum in 1996 (Appelbaum 2008). However, 'objective truth' continues to be a contentious forensic legal term, as the inherent subjective experience of the evaluator influences assessment outcomes. The National Academy of Sciences commented on this issue, stating: "The simple reality is that the interpretation of forensic evidence is not always based on scientific studies to determine validity" (Committee on Identifying the Needs of the Forensic Science Community 2009, p. 8). This proves even more difficult within the field of forensic psychiatry, where conventional data, such as fingerprints and DNA, are not useful metrics. Rather, forensic psychiatry is charged with the task of demonstrating consistent and reliable results, especially within the realm of risk-assessments, such that similar conclusions could be drawn regardless of the evaluator. Over the past 30 years there has been an increased focus on improving risk assessments for violent and sexual offenders (Scott 2013).

But what should risk assessment entail? Skeem and Monahan (2011) posit that a risk assessment includes four components: (1) identifying risk factors, (2) measuring risk factors, (3) combining risk factors, and (4) producing a final risk estimate. They add that clinicians should approach this assessment on a continuum from the completely structured (or actuarial) approach to the unstructured or clinical approach. Quinsey (2006) explains the actuarial approach and enumerates and assesses the four aforementioned components of a risk assessment; an example of this type of risk assessment would be the Violence Risk Appraisal Guide (VRAG). Andrews et al. (2004) and Monahan et al. (2001) identify two risk assessment schemes that examine three risk components, which are the Classification of Violence Risk (COVR) and the Level of Service Inventory (LSI). They caution that the final risk estimate allows for inclusion of clinical impression, thus introducing unavoidable inter-rater variability. The Structured Professional Judgment assessment (SPJ) and the Historical-Clinical-Risk Management-20 (HCR-20) both structure two components of the process: both the identification and the measurement of risk factors (Webster et al. 1997). However, neither assessment goes further to structure how the individual risk factors are combined to provide an overall global risk. Finally, the last two approaches involve either assessment according to a standard list of risk factors, using this as the only structured component, or simply approaching assessment based on clinical judgment, with no specific components delineated (Skeem and Monahan 2011).

5.2.5.2   Review of Actuarial Risk Assessment Methods

Given the numerous approaches to risk assessment, we must ask whether one methodology is a superior predictor of actual violence and sexual risk than the other methodologies. Fazel et al. (2012) conducted a meta-analysis of 73 risk assessment studies, composed of 24,000 participants, which included nine commonly used risk assessment tools. They divided the tools into three categories: those designed to predict violent offending, sexual offending, or any criminal offending. The nine tools ranged from the more actuarial (including the VRAG, the Psychopathy Check List-Revised, and LSI, among others) to the more clinical (including the HCR-20). They concluded that violence risk assessment tools performed best and had higher positive predictive values than tools aimed at predicting sexual offending. Risk assessment instruments for violence and sexual offending produced high sensitivities and negative predictive values. Overall, Fazel et al. (2012) posit that there was substantial heterogeneity in the performance of these measures depending on the purpose of the risk assessment. If used to inform treatment and management decisions, then some of the instruments performed moderately well at identifying individuals at higher risk of violence. However, if used only to determine sentencing, release, or discharge decisions, the instruments were limited by their positive predictive value. They concluded that 41 % of people judged to be moderate or high risk by violence risk assessment tools went on to violently offend, 23 % of those judged to be at moderate or high risk by sexual risk assessment tools went on to sexually offend, and 52 % of those judged to be at moderate or high risk by overall risk assessment tools went on to commit any offense (Fazel et al. 2012). Another meta-analysis of 28 studies that controlled for methodological variation found that the predictive efficiencies of another nine risk assessments (which included the HCR-20, LSI-R, and VRAG) were more or less interchangeable. Yang et al. (2010) posit that each of the assessments addresses common dimensions associated with criminal risk, which include criminal history, an irresponsible lifestyle, psychopathy and criminal attitude, and substance-abuse related problems. Interestingly, Skeem et al. (2011) add that only a small proportion of violence committed by people with major mental illness is directly caused by manifestations of such illness, and that most people with mental illness have the same risk factors for violence as their non-mentally ill counterparts do.

5.2.5.3   The Limitations of Actuarial Approaches to Risk Assessment

It could be argued that more actuarial approaches to risk evaluation produce not only more accurate risk assessments, but also more inter-relater reliability as there are fewer opportunities to include an evaluator's clinical judgment. However, are these common dimensions of criminality fairly and appropriately applied when assessing individual risk as they are when applied to groups? Cooke and Michie (2010) question whether an understanding of group tendencies can assist accurate predictions in the individual case. They describe two studies; the first addresses the accuracy of diagnostic decisions and the potential range of discrepancies between two raters. The second study addresses the accuracy of prediction of future violence in the individual case. They made one broad conclusion stating that clinicians must be extremely cautious in what they claim regarding diagnoses, numerical scores, and risk potential based merely on the assessment tool examined. We could generalize this statement to other assessment tools. Cooke and Michie describe several factors that affect predictive accuracy, which include the lack of reliability in the predictor and outcome variables, the relative weakness of association between these variables, the inherent variability across individuals, and the multitudinous causes of violent crime. While we often rely on statistics to achieve meaning and significance within a group, Altman and Royston (2000) note that the "distinction between what is achievable at the group and the individual level is not well understood" (p. 454). Hart et al. (2007) also discuss the problem of moving from the general to the specific as not merely a matter of statistics; rather, it is also a matter of logic. We are making a significant inferential connection between population-level findings and individual findings. Cooke and Michie state it perfectly: "Individuals are violent for different reasons: Any one individual may be violent for different reasons on different occasions" (p. 271). That brings us to the other end of the continuum; how useful are risk assessments, and forensic evaluations as a whole, based on an individual clinician's impressions? What's more, how should these assessments be organized and for what attributes should a clinician evaluate? We discussed earlier in the chapter various personality and character traits associated with increased risk of financial crime, and how these can be identified from a variety of assessments of an individual. Going deeper, can we (and should we) as forensic psychiatrists, explore the nuanced fixtures of an individual? How do unconscious drives, defenses, themes and unspoken narratives influence a person's penchant for criminality? And are these inherent subjective findings relevant in forensic psychiatry?

5.2.5.4 The Utility of the Psychodynamic Approach

Yakeley and Adshead (2013) posit that a comprehensive forensic evaluation should include an assessment not only of the conscious cognitions (and how these influence feelings, choices, and behavior), but also of unconscious processes best explained by a psychodynamic model. They state that a psychodynamic model of therapy assumes the following:

> Healthy psychological function includes both conscious and unconscious processes and their meaning for the individual. Psychological function is relational and includes interpersonal, intersubjective, and embodied experience of both the social world and the internal world. Representations of the world are built up over time and reflect dispositions that arise from innate vulnerability and early childhood experience. These representations of both the internal and external world are dynamic; they shift and change in the context of the social relationships and group settings experienced over a lifetime. Therapists are affected by these processes as much as patients (p. 38).

Thus they argue that an individual's state of mind, with associated meanings and memories that evoke feelings of rage, grief, and shame, must be considered in addition to demographics and objective risk factors. What conventional risk assessments lack is an understanding of an individual's relationship to the world as a reflection or manifestation of their previous experiences, and how that relationship can be further affected by the interaction with the examiner, transference, or the feelings, emotions, thoughts, and beliefs that the individual projects onto the examiner, must also be considered. A psychodynamic approach argues that the individual and the examiner are engaged in a relationship that evokes and draws from previous experiences, and thus creating a new subjective experience for both. Of course, the explicit subjectivity inherent in transference and countertransference may pose a challenge for meeting the standard of objective forensic evidence. On the other hand, awareness of such potential subjectivity may paradoxically allow for greater awareness of potential bias and, ultimately, greater objectivity than psychodynamically naïve methods which confuse lack of awareness of transference and countertransference factors with a lack of bias. Ironically, less than a century ago, psychodynamic principles were used not only to explain criminal behavior but also to explain the interactions that occurred between psychiatric experts and attorneys in the courtroom (Weiss 1998). Kapoor and Williams (2012) claim that "psychodynamic formulations were difficult to prove in any setting, not least within the adversarial setting of the courtroom…[where] legal setting demanded a high degree of certainty about conclusions, provided a finite period for evaluation and promised potentially devastating consequences of error." (p. 456). Yakeley and Adshead (2013) argue that several risk factors accounted for in actuarial risk assessments actually have psychodynamic and relational aspects to them. They point out that perpetrators may act out their disorganized attachment style by attacking those who are close to them (George and Solomon 1996). These perpetrators of violence find relationships complicated and often have derogatory attitudes towards vulnerability and dependency (Hare 1999). Interpersonal relationships that trigger intense shame, guilt, anger, or grief may trigger traumatic childhood memories of rejection, which may heighten their sense of humiliation. In an individual where affect regulation is likely already impaired, a perpetrator may dissociate from these feelings or act out vengefully (Gilligan 2002). As Gilligan points out, the overwhelming shame and humiliation evoked from memory via present interpersonal relationships and objects may be enough to release unconscious control of destructive rage and fear towards the inciting objects. However, Yakeley and Adshead (2013) argue that this approach is especially salient regarding family violence and the risk to children of abusive parents. While they concede that violence may not be immediately apparent and may be hidden by oversimplification and myth, a psychodynamic evaluation best explores an abusive parent's own attachment history as a child and may provide detail into how or why the abuse occurred.

Similarly, when financial crime is delusionally based, an understanding of the psychodynamic function of the delusion may allow for its emergence from behind a barrier of shame in the forensic psychiatric evaluation process so that it can be appropriately assessed for its role in diminishing capacity to appreciate the wrongfulness of one's conduct or to form the requisite *mens rea*. It should go without saying that no psychodynamic explanation necessarily absolves or excuses criminal behavior. But it may facilitate an understanding of the individual sufficient to allow for a more objective evaluation of such factors as diminished capacity noted above. Thus even Kapoor and Williams (2012) advocate that forensic psychiatrists consider the unconscious forces at play, which may add a layer of "richness" that would otherwise be lost. Such psychodynamic richness is vital in understanding multiperson financial criminal activity such as joint criminal enterprises of the Madoff variety. Complex, sustained joint financial criminal enterprises may involve shared feelings, defense mechanisms, fantasies, and beliefs that may crisscross the boundaries amongst a company's culture, naïveté of the coconspirators, the tendency to give one's authority figures the benefit of the doubt, traumatic avoidance, denial and even cult-like shared or enabled delusions. In such instances, a psychodynamically informed assessment of factors such as shared paranoid disorder (Coletsos and Bursztajn 2012), the power dependency nature of relationships, and vulnerability to undue influence can be helpful in establishing varying degrees of capacity to appreciate the wrongfulness of one's actions and to form the *mens rea* necessary for a finding of responsibility and potential mitigating and aggravating factors.

5.3 Implications for Sentencing

The psychiatric literature above has relevance to the way important white-collar cases have been tried. As we detail below, judges have considered the offender's character as well as the impact of the offender's crimes to render verdicts. Here we will discuss implications for sentencing. In future work we will address implications for prevention of financial crime. In the 1970s, the Yale White Collar Crime Studies group conducted interviews of 51 judges that examined the rationale in sentencing white-collar offenders, as it differed from non-white collar offenders. Wheeler, Mann, and Sarat detail their findings in "Sitting in Judgment: The Sentencing of White-Collar Criminals" (1988a), detailing interviews that occurred between 1978 and 1980. The study outlined white collar crime as consisting of one of eight offenses: bank embezzlement, credit and lending institution fraud, false claims and statements, antitrust offenses, securities and exchange offenses, postal and wire fraud, IRS fraud, and bribery (Wheeler et al. 1982). The authors began with a discussion of how federal sentencing was perceived in the 1970s, wherein judges had significant discretion with no formal guidelines dictating limitations on sentencing. Judges cited their own ideologies, sentiments, and values as metrics for sentencing; often, there was a large disparity in sentencing. However, judges did ultimately consider similar factors when determining sentence (Wheeler et al. 1988a, b: pp. 9–10). Through their interviews, the authors identified three core concepts integral in sentencing regardless of crime: evaluation of the harm caused, determining the blameworthiness of the defendant, and predicting the consequence of a sentence (pp. 42–48).

The judges defined "harm caused" as the most important element in the assessment of the offense. They also determined harm caused to be as important as intent. When determining the extent of social harm caused, judges considered four major factors: (1) amount of money lost, (2) the nature of the victim, (3) spread of events over time and place, and (4) the nature of any violation of trust (p. 66). There seemed to be a consensus that amounts less than $2,000 would not require severe sanction, while six-figure losses are "serious and require incarceration" (p. 67). Judges do take the nature of the victim into account, stating that the most harmful crimes were directed towards identifiable, vulnerable victims. However, they did not translate dollar losses relative to income. For example, a $500 loss to an uninsured victim would be much more detrimental than a million-dollar loss to a bank with fidelity insurance. With regard to duration, judges viewed this as a "proxy for the repetitive and patterned nature of the offense on the one hand, the deliberate, calculating nature of the offender on the other" (p. 74). Judges examine the extent of trust violation, with particular import given to relationships wherein the victim appropriately expects the alleged perpetrator to act benevolently on their behalf. Judges assessed "blameworthiness" by looking beyond formal *mens rea* to make moral judgments that incorporated the defendant's conduct both before and after the crime (p. 87). The absence of prior convictions was vital, except in cases where there was evidence of long non-convicted offending; the judges believed that people deserve a chance to reform. However, prior convictions signified patterned deliberate and scheming behavior. They noted that a prior criminal record, while significantly less common with white-collar criminals, might be the most significant factor in the assessment (p. 88). Judges evaluated blameworthiness by considering whether a defendant lied, attempted to cover up a crime, expressed contrition, or cooperated with proceedings (p. 100). They focused on evidence that suggested defendant's knowledge and intent, degree of deliberateness or scheming, and relative culpability among multiple parties. Some argue, "motive may... be relevant as a method to distinguish between the relative blameworthiness of individuals at sentencing" (Hessick 2006). Interestingly, judges examined static character traits of the defendants when assessing blameworthiness; they stated that "simplemindedness" and "a history of community service" are considered in mitigation (p. 101). Again, the degree to which a criminal appeared deceiving, self-serving, and malevolent exacerbated the severity of the crime and subsequently impacted sentencing.

Finally, judges evaluated the impact of sentences both on the community and on the offender. They explored the doctrine of utilitarianism as the foundation for the modern concept of deterrence. Under the utilitarian philosophy, laws that specify punishment for criminal conduct should be designed to deter future criminal conduct. For the individual, deterrence included a measure of incapacitation for the offender and a penalty that would deter the individual from future crimes (pp. 124–126). Judges believed the white-collar offender suffered substantial punishment from the impact of the criminal process; a view not extended to common crime defendants. Judges found significant the loss of respectability, loss of career, and the impact on families. One judge explained that a white-collar criminal who was convicted often lost his job, his home, and his family, all of which added up to a substantial punishment. The judge further explained, "the ordinary street criminal hasn't suffered that kind of loss" (p. 145). More concerning were the parallels the judges drew between themselves and the criminals; most were white men of reputable stature and education. One must question the extent to which these similarities exerted an unconscious identification with the defendant not present with non-white collar criminals. Overall, while the study refuted the premise that there were no agreed upon principles underlying the structure of sentencing, the authors end by challenging existing sentencing guidelines as insufficient to accommodate the concepts of harm, blameworthiness, and consequence.

Due to the inconsistencies in sentencing for white-collar crime prior to the 1980s, Congress passed the Sentencing Reform Act of 1984 which not only created the United States Sentencing Commission, which set forth guidelines to direct federal sentencing, but also created a new statutory system of organizational fines, increasing all criminal fines for organizations and distinguishing between individual and organizational penalties not previously delineated. Prior to the Reform Act, judges were subject to minimal control over discretion, and usually un-waivered by previous sentencing case law. Several statutory provisions taken together describe how courts must now determine the appropriate sentence for an organization or individual. The most significant of these is 18 U.S.C. § 3553 (a), which listed several relevant factors such as "the nature and circumstances of the offense and the history and characteristics of the defendant," that judges must take into account during sentencing. Section 3553 (A) also required courts to "impose a sentence sufficient, but not greater than necessary, to comply with the purposes set forth in paragraph 2," which state said purposes as follows: (1) to reflect the seriousness of the offense, to promote respect for the law, and to provide just punishment for the offense, (2) to afford adequate deterrence to criminal conduct, (3) to protect the public from further crimes of the defendant, and (4) to provide the defendant with needed educational or vocational training, medical care, or other correctional treatment in the most effective manner (18 U.S.C. § 3553 1984). Per § 3553 (b), it required judges to impose a sentence within the guideline range unless they found an aggravating or mitigating factor not adequately taken into consideration by the Sentencing Commission. Overall, the goal of the Federal Sentencing Guidelines was to provide uniformity and to "require short but certain terms of confinement for many white-collar offenders, including tax, insider trading, and antitrust offender, who previously would likely have received only probation" (Breyer 1988).

However, in *United States v Booker* (2005), the Supreme Court held that courts violate individuals' right to a jury trial when they sentence individuals using judge-found facts in combination with mandatory sentencing guidelines articulated by the Sentencing Commission. The provision that made the guidelines mandatory was 18 U.S.C 3553, which does not distinguish between the organizational guidelines and individual guidelines. Thus, the *Booker* Court invalidated this provision, holding that the combination of judicial fact-find and mandatory sentencing guidelines violated individual defendants' Sixth Amendment rights (543 U.S. 2005). Finally, *Booker*'s outcome rendered all of the guidelines non-mandatory. While the opinion rendered in *Booker* might suggest that sentencing would return to pre-Reform inconsistency, several cases post-*Booker* suggest that judges continue to consider the sentencing guidelines in addition to other, less actuarial details when rendering a sentence. In *United States v Ranum*, post-*Booker* in 2005, the defendant was a bank officer who made a series of loans to a promising shipping company, but lied to the bank committee about the company's reserves. He was charged with misapplication of funds and false statements. After conviction at trial, he faced a federal sentencing guideline range of 37–45 months in custody. Judge Adelman of Wisconsin found mitigating factors in the nature of the offense: the defendant was not motivated by personal gain, and the case was unusual in that the shipping company had promise. He also found mitigating factors in the nature of the offender: he was 50 years old, with no criminal record, had health problems, and took care of his elderly and ill parents. Community support also showed his good character, and this case had cost the defendant another job. Moreover, imprisonment would do no good to the defendant and society. Ultimately, Judge Adelman declined to follow the guidelines and instead imposed a sentence which was sufficient, but not greater than necessary, to satisfy the purposes of sentencing, and incidentally less than dictated by the sentencing guidelines (353 U.S. 2005). While there is ongoing debate about the consistency of white-collar sentencing, judges continue to consider harm, blameworthiness, and social impact when sentencing. The sentence rendered in the *Ranum* case highlights the importance of motivation, intent, and global character of the defendant when determining punishment, and influences the assessment of risk of future crime in order to enact appropriate deterrence.

5.4 Conclusion

Although we have confined our analysis to financial crime, we note in passing that forensic psychology and psychiatry hold the potential to make significant contributions to contemporary understanding of *civil* instances of financial wrongdoing. From a larger perspective, it is important to note that only a subset of financial criminals is actually recognized as such. Criminality is about more than just transgression: it also requires detection, prosecution, and conviction. What distinguishes wrongdoers who get caught and convicted from those who do not is a function of many factors, including the size and scope of the act, the charging policies on the books and the practices on the ground of law-enforcement organizations such as the Department of Justice. But among the relevant factors are the developmental history, personality and individual differences, demographics, and overall psychiatric profile of the actor. Similarly, there are different levels of responsibility depending on the perpetrators' capacity to appreciate the wrongfulness of their conduct and their intent, or *mens rea* (Goldstein and Bursztajn 2011).

These are used to establish levels of culpability. Thus, as noted above, a psycho-dynamically informed forensic neuropsychiatric evaluation can also reveal potential mitigating or aggravating factors as are used as aids in sentencing (Bursztajn et al. 1994).

References

Abrams, R., and D.B. Henriques. 2014. *Jury says 5 Madoff employees knowingly aided swindle of clients' billions*. New York Times (March 25, 2014), B1.

Alalehto, T. 2003. Economic crime: Does personality matter? *International Journal of Offender Therapy and Comparative Criminology* 47(3): 335–355.

Altman, D.G., and P. Royston. 2000. What do we mean by validating a prognostic model? *Statistics in Medicine* 19: 453–473.

Andrews, D., J. Bonta, and J. Wormith. 2004. *Manual for the Level of Service/Case Management Inventory (LS/CMI)*. Toronto: Multi-Health Systems.

Appelbaum, P.S. 2008. Ethics and forensic psychiatry: Translating principles into practice. *Journal of the American Academy of Psychiatry and Law* 36: 195–200.

Babiak, P. 2007. From darkness into the Light: Psychopathy in industrial and organizational psychology. In *The psychopath: Theory research and practice*, ed. H. Herve, and J.C. Yuille, 411–428. Mahwah, NJ: Lawrence Erlbaum Associates Publishers.

Babiak, P., C. Neumann, and R. Hare. 2010. Corporate psychopathy: Talking the walk. *Behavioral Sciences and the Law* 28(2): 174–193.

Barnard, J.W. 2008. Securities fraud, recidivism, and deterrence. *Pennsylvania State Law Review* 113(1): 189–227.

Becker, G.S. 1976. *The economic approach to human behavior*. Chicago: University of Chicago Press.

Benson, M.L., and E. Moore. 1992. Are white-collar and common offenders the same? An empirical and theoretical critique of a recently proposed general theory of crime. *Journal of Research in Crime and Delinquency* 29: 251–272.

Blickle, G., P. Fassbender, U. Klein, A. Schlegel, et al. 2006. Some personality correlates of business white-collar crime. *Applied Psychology International Review* 55: 220–233.

Breyer, S. 1988. The Federal Sentencing Guidelines and the key compromises upon which they rest, 17. *Hofstra Law Review* 1: 20–21.

Bucy, P.H., E. Formby, M.S. Raspanti, and K.E. Rooney. 2008. Why do they do it?—the motives, mores and character of white-collar criminals. *St. Johns Law Review* 82: 401–571.

Bursztajn, H.J., A.E. Scherr, and A. Brodsky. 1994. The rebirth of forensic psychiatry in light of recent historical trends in criminal responsibility. *Psychiatric Clinics of North America* 17: 611–635.

Cleckley, H. 1941. *The mask of sanity*. St. Louis, MO: Mosby.

Cleckley, H. 1988. *The mask of sanity*, 5th ed. Augusta, GA: Cleckley, E.

Coletsos, I.C., and H.J. Bursztajn. 2012. Shared paranoid disorder. In *The 5-minute clinical consult*, 20th ed, ed. F.J. Domino, 1200–1201. Philadelphia: Lippincott Williams & Wilkins.

Collins, J.M., and F.L. Schmidt. 1993. Personality, integrity, and white-collar crime: A construct validity study. *Personnel Psychology* 46: 295–311.

Committee on Identifying the Needs of the Forensic Science Community, Committee on Science, Technology, and Law Policy and Global Affairs, Committee on Applied and Theoretical Statistics, Division on Engineering and Physical Sciences. 2009. *Strengthening forensic science in the United States: A path forward*. Washington, DC: The National Academies Press.

Cooke, D., and C. Michie. 2010. Limitations of diagnostic precision and predictive utility in the individual case: A challenge for forensic practice. *Law and Human Behavior* 34: 259–274.

Creswell, J., and L. Thomas. 2009. *The talented Mr. Madoff*. New York Times (January 24, 2009).

Ellin, A. 2002. Scared straight in business school. New York Times (January 13, 2002) Ed.7.

Fazel, S., J.P. Singh, and M. Grann. 2012. Use of risk assessment instruments to predict violence and antisocial behavior in 73 samples involving 24,827 people: Systematic review and meta-analysis. *BMJ* 345: 1–12.

Freud, A. 1949. Certain types and stages of social maladjustment. In *Searchlight on delinquency*, ed. K.R. Eissler. New York: New International Press.

Freud, S. 1923. *The Ego and the Id*. London: Hogarth.

George, C., and J. Solomon. 1996. Representational models of relationships: Links between care giving and attachment. *Infant Mental Health Journal* 17: 198–216.

Gilligan, J. 2002. *Violence: Reflections on our deadliest epidemic*. London: Jessica Kingsley Publishers.

Goldstein, A.M., and H.J. Bursztajn. 2011. Capital litigation: Special considerations. In *Handbook of forensic assessment: Psychological and psychiatric perspectives*, ed. E.Y. Drogin, F. Drogin, M. Dattilio, R.L. Sadoff, and T.G. Gutheil, 145–170. Hoboken, NJ: Wiley.

Gough, H.G. 1987. *California Psychological Inventory administrator's guide*. Palo Alto CA: Consulting Psychologists Press.

Hare, R.D. 1999. Psychopathy as a risk factor for violence. *Psychiatric Quarterly* 70: 181–197.

Hart, S.D., C. Michie, and D.J. Cooke. 2007. The precision of actuarial risk assessment instruments: Evaluating the "Margins of Error "of group versus individual predictions of violence. *British Journal of Psychiatry* 170(49): 60–65.

Hessick, C. 2006. Motive's role in criminal punishment, 80 S. *California Law Review* 89: 95.

Pub. L. No. 98–473, 98 Stat. 1987 (1984) (codified at 18 U.S.C. § §3551–3673 (2000) and 28 U.S.C. § § 991–998 (2000)).

Kapoor, R., and A. Williams. 2012. An unwelcome guest: The unconscious mind in the courtroom. *Journal of the American Academy of Psychiatry and Law* 40(4): 456–461.

Marcus, B. 2003. An empirical examination of the construct validity of two alternative self-control measures. *Educational and Psychological Measurement* 63: 674–706.

McLean, B., and P. Elkind. 2003. *The smartest guys in the room: The amazing rise and scandalous fall of enron*. New York: Portfolio.

Monahan, J., H. Steadman, E. Silver, et al. 2001. *Rethinking risk assessment: The MacArthur study of mental disorder and violence*. New York: Oxford University Press.

Owens, W.A., and L.F. Schoenfeldt. 1979. Toward a classification of persons. *Journal of Applied Psychology* 65: 569–607.

Paajanen, G.E. 1988. *The prediction of counterproductive behavior by individual and organizational variables*. Doctoral Dissertation, University of Minnesota.

Piquero, N.L., M.L. Exum, and S.S. Simpson. 2005. Integrating the desire-for-control and rational choice in a corporate crime context. *Justice Quarterly* 22(2): 252–280.

Poortinga, E., C. Lemmen, and M.D. Jibson. 2006. A case control study: White-collar defendants compared with other defendants charged with other nonviolent theft. *Journal of the American Academy of Psychiatry and Law* 34: 82–89.

Quinsey, V.L. 2006. *Violent offenders: Appraising and managing risk*, 2nd ed. Washington, DC: American Psychological Association.

Raine, A., W.S. Laufer, Y. Yang, K.L. Narr, P. Thompson, and A.W. Toga. 2012. Increased executive functioning, attention, and cortical thickness in white-collar criminals. *Human Brain Mapping* 33(12): 2932–2940.

Scott, C. 2013. Believing doesn't make it so: Forensic education and the search for truth. *Journal of the American Academy of Psychiatry and Law* 41: 18–32.

Skeem, J.L., and J. Monahan. 2011. Current directions in violence risk assessment. *Current Directions in Psychological Science* 20: 38–42.

Skeem, J.L., S.M. Manchak, and J.K. Peterson. 2011. Correctional policy for offenders with mental illness: Creating a new paradigm for recidivism reduction. *Law and Human Behavior* 35: 110–126.

Sutherland, Edwin H. 1940. White-collar criminality. *American Sociological Review* 5(February): 1–12.

Tversky, A., and D. Kahneman. 1981. The farming of decision and the psychology of choice. *Science* 211(4481): 453–548.

United States v. Booker 543 U.S. 220, 245 (2005).

United States v. Ranum, 353 F. Supp. 2d 984 (E.D. Wis. 2005).

Webster, C., K. Douglas, D. Eaves, et al. 1997. *HCR-20: Assessing risk for violence (version 2).* Vancouver, British Columbia, Canada: Simon Fraser University.

Weiss, J.M. 1998. Some reflections on countertransference in the treatment of criminals. *Psychiatry* 61: 172–177.

Wheeler, S., D. Weisburd, and N. Bode. 1982. Sentencing the white-collar offender: Rhetoric and reality. *American Sociological Review* 47: 641–659.

Wheeler, S., K. Mann, and A. Sarat. 1988a. *Sitting in judgment: The sentencing of white-collar criminals.* New Haven: Yale University Press.

Wheeler, S., D. Weisburd, E. Waring, et al. 1988b. White-collar crimes and criminals. *Am Crim Law Rev* 25: 331–358.

Yakeley, J., and G. Adshead. 2013. Locks, keys, and security of mind: Psychodynamic approaches to forensic psychiatry. *Journal of the American Academy of Psychiatry and Law* 41(1): 38–45.

Yang, M., S.C. Wong, and J. Coid. 2010. The efficacy of violence prediction: A meta-analytic comparison of nine risk assessment tools. *Psychological Bulletin* 136(5): 740–767.

Chapter 6
Cognitive Factors to Financial Crime Victimization

Stacey Wood, Yaniv Hanoch and George W. Woods

Abstract This chapter will address cognitive factors that result in susceptibility to financial crimes including financial literacy, numeracy, and deliberative reasoning. Financial literacy has been found to be a strong predictor of retirement savings, FICO scores, and savings accounts. Perhaps more importantly, financial literacy has been found to be a strong predictor of debt and vulnerability to predatory lending. Individuals low in numeracy, or literacy for numbers, tend to be more likely to employ heuristics such as loss aversion, sunk costs, and confirmatory bias in the financial decision making. Dual process models of decision making explain that decision making can be deliberative and analytical or emotional and impulsive. In general, investment schemers tend to employ techniques to engage more emotional or impulsive decision making. Factors that increase the likelihood of impulsive decision-making versus deliberative decision-making will be discussed (stress, ego depletion, cognitive impairment).

6.1 Introduction

Mr. Bill Warner is an 85-year old African-American widower with some mild cognitive impairment. His wife passed away a couple of years ago. Bill wanted to remain in his fine home, but needed some assistance. Since that time, his adult children have hired in home caregivers to help Bill with cooking and housekeeping. His daughter lives out of state and his son lives about 2 h away. His caregivers,

S. Wood (✉)
Scripps College, Claremont, CA, USA
e-mail: swood@ScrippsCollege.edu

Y. Hanoch
Plymouth University, Plymouth, UK
e-mail: Yaniv.Hanoch@gmail.com

G.W. Woods
Morehouse School of Medicine, Atlanta, GA, USA
e-mail: gwoods@georgewoodsmd.com

© Springer International Publishing Switzerland 2016   129
M. Dion et al. (eds.), *Financial Crimes: Psychological, Technological,*
and Ethical Issues, International Library of Ethics, Law,
and the New Medicine 68, DOI 10.1007/978-3-319-32419-7_6

became "like family" to him. Over time, Bill increasingly relied on his caregivers for assistance, including with his financial matters. During a visit, his adult daughter noted some art work missing from the home and some bruising on Bill's forearms. He reported that he had given the art to the caregivers in exchange for extra help around his home. He also reported that the bruising happened during his bathing. When pressed for a response, he reported that the caregivers could be a little rough. But he quickly added that he desperately wanted to stay in his home, and did not want new caregivers. His daughter also learned that over 50 K had been drained from his account, mainly through numerous suspicious ATM withdrawals.

Cases such as Bill Warner's are becoming increasingly common. Financial crimes, however, can occur at any stage of the lifespan. Con artists and other opportunists are equal opportunity predators. However, different vulnerabilities exist that can be exploited depending upon the nature of the transactions. This chapter will present a framework for thinking about financial decision-making, and then discuss certain case types that increase the risk of financial exploitation.

6.2 Dual Process Models and Decision-Making

Work in behavioral economics has emphasized that decision-making is not a unitary construct, and that different cognitive systems underlie different types of decision-making. In general these models have emphasized two systems: one system that is unconscious, quick, effortless, and rigid. The second system relates to more deliberative types of decisions where one can explicitly weigh pros and cons. This system is slower, but able to learn. Based on Kahneman's research, humans are not able to process most information in their environments, and as such become cognitive misers, utilizing the cheap efficient system 1 when faced with most daily decisions. Humans reserve the resource intense deliberative system for more complex and important decisions. In that sense humans are often in default mode throughout routine and overlearned aspects of their day. In default mode our mind can wander and we are less attentive to the environment around us. However, when needed we can bring ourselves back into System 2 and use our resources to deliberate, monitor errors, and analyze the components of a situation (Fig. 6.1).

System 1	System 2
Heuristic	Can Learn
Fast	Slow
Automatic	Effortful
Rigid	Flexible
Emotional	Analytical

Fig. 6.1 Comparison of *System 1* and *System 2* decision making

In Kahneman's book, *Thinking Fast and Slow* (2011), the author uses this classic example to illustrate the differences between System 1 and System 2 decision-making. "A bat and a ball cost $1.10, the bat costs one dollar more than the ball. How much does the ball cost? (p. 44). A number comes easily to your mind (10 c), but next do the math and you can see that it does not add up. To arrive at the correct answer, you must engage System 2 and inhibit the intuitive response that comes automatically. Interestingly, Kahneman reports that 50 % of students at Ivy League universities make this error, and up to 80 % of students at other universities report the incorrect answer. This example also helps to illustrate the dissociation between optimal decision making and general intellectual abilities. Even very bright college students are not immune to succumbing to their intuitive impulses. Humans do have an error monitoring system (anterior cingulate cortex) that can provide back up when we act impulsively and catch our mistakes, but often we are not aware of the errors we are making.

In terms of financial decision making, staying in default mode and relying on intuitive decision-making places us at increased risk for making errors. These errors may be small (counting change) or quite serious (underestimating ARM mortgages, purchasing financial products with poor terms). In general, individuals will be more susceptible to fraud when they are in this default mode, not really doing the math and not monitoring their own errors. The default mode is also less susceptible to cognitive deterioration. As decisions become more complex, more cognitive systems are brought into play. Working memory, sequencing ability, understanding of social context, even reading facial and other social cues may play a part in more complex decision making. These are the very types of cognitive systems most vulnerable to gullibility and naivete, as well as brain dysfunction.

6.2.1 Ego Depletion and Impulsivity

Ego depletion is a construct borrowed here from social psychology that refers to the finding that "willpower" is a finite resource that can be depleted (Baumeister et al. 2008; Vohs and Faber 2007). A typical experimental design to elicit depletion would be to ask a group of participants to engage in a task that requires self-control (such as checking a document line by line, or making a choice) and later asking the participants about how much studying versus TV watching they had engaged in since the study. These studies have documented that depleting ego on one type of task can impair willpower in a different domain, even several hours later (Inzlicht and Gutsell 2007). Thus, individuals who are in a state of ego depletion may have difficulty evidencing self-control later on. This construct has become important in the psychology of understanding self-control. There is some evidence that regions such as the anterior cingulate cortex, involved in error monitoring and control are part of the neural circuitry of control and ego depletion (Inzlicht and Gutsell 2007).

A number of investigators have extended this line of work to examine the link between ego depletion and risk taking. Interestingly, the literature provides mixed results. On the one hand, a number of investigators (Carr and Steele 2010; Kostek and Ashrafioun 2013; Unger and Stahlberg 2011), using different gambling tasks, report that ego depletion leads to risk aversion. They suggest (e.g., Unger and Stahlberg 2011), for example, that people become too 'exhausted' to engage in risk taking behaviour; that is, they lack the necessary mental resources needed to deal with negative consequences associated with risky options. In contrasts, other researchers report precisely the opposite picture. Heilman et al. (2010) have found that individuals who were ego depleted were more likely to exhibit risk taking and sensation seeking behaviour. In this case, the researchers argue that ego depletion reduces individuals ability to resist risky options, in other words people are less able to exert self-control and thus resists the risky option. It may also be that depleted individuals are simply less adept at identifying and assessing risky situations. Factors other than ego depletion and risk becomes relevant when examining this literature. Repetitive tasks may often lead to decreased attention, a confounding factor in this paradigm.

Novel extensions of this line of investigation has led researchers to examine whether ego depletion (or self-control) is associated with financial knowledge, financial monitoring, use of heuristics (or system 1), and perhaps most importantly, the ability to detect deception. While these domains of research are still in their neophyte stages, they are revealing some interesting findings. First, in accordance with Kahneman's work, Pohl et al. (2013) have shown that ego depleted individuals are more likely to use simple decision heuristics. When it comes to financial monitoring, Oaten and Cheng (2007) were able to demonstrate that ego depletion reduces the capacity to monitor ones financial behavior. Howlett et al. (2008), in a similar vein, found that participants who were ego depleted were less likely to report intention to participate in a company sponsored retirement plan. Finally, a study by Reinhard et al. (2013) has nicely illustrated the possible effects of ego depletion on the ability to detect deception—a key factor in fraudulent behavior. In two studies among college students, Reinhard et al. found that those who were ego depleted were less likely to detect deception. It should be noted, however, that the above research was mainly conducted with young adults. To our knowledge, no similar studies have been conducted with older individuals. That being said, there is no reason to believe that older adults will fare differently that their younger counterparts. In fact, it is feasible that older adults will be at a greater disadvantage.

To date, this literature does not differentiate among the various types of decision making that must be paired with ego depletion. Deciding whether to decide on a retirement plan takes much more complex decision making potentially than simpler decision making tasks. Nevertheless, the construct of ego depletion intuitively implicates decreased cognitive reserves available, which reasonably would lead to poorer decision making processes. Ego depletion may be the result of stressful events, but are the end results of those stressful events, which results in a different trajectory than stress alone (McEwen 1998; Martin et al. 2009).

6.2.2 Stress and Financial Decision-Making

How does stress impact financial decision-making? In general, stress results in an inverse U-shape relationship between arousal and performance. When arousal is either very low or very high performance tends to deteriorate. The effects of arousal have been studied on day-traders performance. Their results showed that traders who experienced greater positive or negative arousal towards monetary gains and losses exhibited significantly *worse* trading performance. Other research has demonstrated that participants who are stressed are more likely to take risks when encountering gambles that could result in losses. In trying to explain their results, the researchers have argued that in stressful situations *we are less able to use our rational and deliberative abilities in the decision making process*. Interestingly, in a survey among American households, more than 75 % of respondents indicated that financial concerns were a key contributor to their stress levels (American Psychological Association 2009). It is reasonable to assume, thus, that those who require fast loans are precisely the ones who are experiencing financial stress. Recent research has found that when low income individuals are faced with a financial decision-making task, they demonstrate reduced cognitive capacity overall. The general idea is that low income individuals face additional cognitive demands because they consistently have to "do the math" for every financial transaction. Because these individuals may be living pay check to pay check, they need to be more careful in spending their money. Individuals with even slightly more income, can "round up" and have some margin for errors in their day to day decision making. As a result, these individuals begin with some depletion and fewer resources overall.

Given these minimal resources, one might ask whether or not there is much risk for exploitation. Sadly, precisely because of these limitations, low income individuals are targeted by predatory lenders and con artists. Low income individuals are frequently described as "unbanked" and instead use non traditional financial services such as payday loans. These services have much higher fees and significantly higher interest rates (often exceeding 100 % APR for payday loans). While not necessarily fraudulent or deceptive, this class of financial services is very expensive. Low income individuals who use these services have been reported to have lower financial literacy as a group and are more susceptible to poor financial decision making. Although payday lending, car title laons and the like are marketed as a one time, short term loan, the majority of borrowers "renew" the loan increasing the fees and interests to exorbitant amounts that are much higher then "banked" individuals will pay out.

Scams targeting lower income consumers often take advantage of lower financial literacy targeting domains such as tax returns and foreclosure relief. In these scams, individuals are promised some large return in exchange for a fee. Of course, no papers are ever filed and the promised financial relief never appears. An especially egregious form of this scam preys on individuals who may be in the country illegally or are currently pursuing citizenship and as such are very unlikely to report these scams to law enforcement.

6.3 Cognitive Factors Related to Financial Decision-Making

High levels of numeracy or literacy for numbers is a cognitive skill that has been linked to strong decision-making. High-numeracy adults are at greater ease in using numeric information and utilize the correct numerical principles. Low-numeracy individuals, on the other hand, "are left with information that is less complete and less understood, lacking in the complexity and richness available to the more numerate" (2006, p. 412). What this means in everyday terms is that individuals who are low in numeracy are more susceptible to using cognitive short cuts such as heuristics in their decision-making and less "able to do the math" to make the optimal financial decision. This difference in abilities plays out across a wide range of financial products, such as health insurance, stocks, housing, saving, and borrowing (e.g. Wood et al. 2011). In contrast, we know that the majority of the population is having difficulties with numbers.

The pioneering work of Lusardi and colleagues (e.g., Lusardi and Mitchell 2007, 2011) provides further support for the finding that as a group consumers struggle with the comprehension of questions that involve interest rates. The results of the U.S. Financial Capability Study (Lusardi and Mitchell 2011), asked participants a number of financial questions, such as how much money a person will have after 5 years if they had $100 in a savings account and the interest rate was 2 % per year and were provided with the following prompts: more than $102.00; exactly 102; less than $102; and refuse to answer. About 65 % of respondents are able to get this answer correct which is surprisingly small given its simplicity and the lack of a requirement to complete calculations. More concerning, about 13.5 % of the participants indicated that they were unable to answer this question. As a result when faced with a loan with a high APR, arguably a more difficult calculation than the example above, the majority of consumers (not only subprime) are simply unable to calculate the total costs on their own. The (in)ability to correctly answer these simple questions is vital for any discussion of consumers' ability to understand financial data and make informed decisions, as calculations about compound interest is part and parcel of any decision about saving and borrowing. In one investigation, participants were asked the following question: "Suppose you owe $1,000 on your credit card and the interest rate you are charged is 20 % per year compounded annually. If you didn't pay anything off, at this interest rate, how many years would it take for the amount you owe to double? (i) 2 years; (ii) Less than 5 years; (iii) 5–10 years; (iv) More than 10 years; (v) Do not know;(vi) Prefer not to answer." Only roughly a third of the sample was able to correctly answer this question. Perhaps more importantly, 40 % of the participants overestimated the time it would take for the debt to double (Lusardi and Tufano 2009). What might be the side-effect of low numeracy? Repeated studies have shown that higher numeracy is linked to greater investment in the stock market, better retirement planning, higher accumulation of wealth, lower rates of mortgage and loan defaults, and higher probability of paying credit card payment in full. Those with low numeracy, on the other hand, tend to pay fees and rely more heavily on high-cost methods of borrowing. One can argue that a large portion of the population simply does not have adequate numeracy and financial literacy levels; numeracy is one of the best predictors for retirement saving and investment, and that numeracy is correlated to an understanding of many financial services. In conclusion, a large survey of American consumers indicates poor understanding of certain key financial terms such as interest.

Research from psychology and economics has highlighted certain cognitive skills as being critical to sound financial decision making. These include executive functioning, or the ability to direct goal oriented behavior, numeracy (literacy for numbers), and financial literacy (understanding of key financial principles). Work on financial literacy (Lusardi 2007, 2009, 2013) has found that individuals high on financial literacy tend to have better credit ratings, higher savings at retirement, and lower levels of debt. Financial literacy is typically assessed using 3–4 item scales that examine constructs such as simple and compound interest and portfolio diversification. Numeracy or literacy for number has been found to be related to efficient decision making in a number of decision domains including medical decision-making and financial decision-making. According to Ellen Peters and colleagues, individuals high in numeracy engage in decision-making differently than those low in numeracy. Numeracy is typically assessed using an 11 item scale (Lipkus) that assesses information such as an understanding of probability. Although subjective numeracy scales have demonstrated some promise as well (i.e. Do you skip over numbers in a sentence? (Rolison et al. 2012). What is truly important about numeracy is the understanding that unlike financial literacy that is assessing knowledge and skills relevant to good financial decision making, numeracy appears to relate to a decisional style. Individuals high in numeracy engage with numbers differently and derive more information than individuals low in numeracy. Individuals low in numeracy therefore are more likely to "go with their gut", and rely on heuristics in their decision making. In a preliminary study, Wood (2013) has reported that individuals low in numeracy were significantly more likely to be victims of financial exploitation than individuals high in numeracy (American Society of Criminology 2013).

Executive control includes many subabilities critical for decision-making capacity and has been linked to prefrontal cortex. Executive functioning includes working memory, self awareness, sequential thinking, understanding of social context and social cues (Bechara et al. 1998; Strauss and Allen 2009); and also play a part in being able to get the gestalt, the bigger picture, an attribute commonly required in financial decisions. Sizing up the entity offering the financial relationship, weighing and deliberating your own financial strengths and weaknesses, understanding the sequential nature of the financial arrangement; each of these steps requires relatively intact executive functioning. Individuals with even subtle declines in executive functioning are at greater risk for exploitation often before others become aware of their deficits and need for intervention. Further, individuals with impaired executive functioning typically lack insight into their own limitations.

Work in the related area of financial capacity in older adults highlights the importance of executive functioning and mathematical reasoning in sound financial decision making. A conceptual framework developed by Daniel Marson and his colleagues (2000) suggests that financial capacity is comprised of three types of knowledge, including declarative knowledge (sources of income), skills (like checkbook balancing), and judgment. Based on a series of studies in people with mild cognitive impairment (MCI) and moderate dementia, the following neuropsychological measures have been linked to financial incapacity: arithmetic abilities (assessed with the WRAT), executive functioning, and verbal memory. Decline in arithmetic skills was linked with impairments in financial capacity even in early stages of Alzheimer's disease and suggests that financial capacity may be impacted earlier than other types of decisional capacities (Sherod et al. 2009; Martin et al. 2009).

6.4 Undue Influence

Undue influence (UI) refers to a relational dynamic that can occur between an individual of strong mind and an individual of 'weak" mind that involves unfair persuasion. It has been used in a variety of legal settings, including in cases of elder financial exploitation (Peisah et al. 2009). Although legal definitions vary, definitions typically require some combination of the following aspects, (1) that there is a confidential/intimate relationship, (2) that there are a variety of factors that increase the susceptibility of the elder (physical dependence, depression, cognitive impairment, etc.), (3) that there is a power differential that results in susceptibility to coercion, and (4) that the coercion results in financial or testamentary decisions are suspicious (i.e., not proportionate to services provided) (Peisah et al. 2009; Sparr and Garr 1992). Theoretical frameworks have included work from social psychology (science of persuasion, Cialdini 2008), work with cult members, and those drawing from work on domestic violence (Wood and Liu 2012). These theoretical accounts share an element of a power differential between the alleged influencer and the older adult. Models of undue influence highlight the importance of the social and relational dynamics that are frequently a component of financial fraud and exploitation.

Cognitive decline is not necessarily a factor in undue influence cases, as UI is considered a separate construct from decisional capacity. That is, it is possible to unduly influence someone who is cognitively intact. But, in the majority of undue influence cases involving older adults, there is some indication of at least temporary cognitive decline. For example, individuals who are depressed following a loss exhibit poor memory and concentration and may not be able to engage deliberate reasoning. Individuals who are recovering from a medical condition or those on medication may also have periods of time that they are not able to readily engage their cognitive abilities. Many individuals with mild cognitive impairment (MCI) retain their abilities to function independently but demonstrate significant declines in memory and executive functioning. In general, even mild cognitive impairment increases the risk of susceptibility to undue influence (Wood and Liu 2012). There is limited empirical work in the area of UI. However, recently, Mary Joy Quinn and colleagues completed a study to examine definitions and applications of UI in the California probate courts based on the observation that UI while used is not clearly defined (Quinn et al. 2010). The report reviews definitions of UI in all 50 states. The report highlights that UI can exist even in cases where the elder is clearly of sound mind. The authors conducted a chart review of 25 cases in San Francisco Superior Court selected because probate court investigators or researchers had determined that there were elements of UI in the case. This report represents an attempt to quantify characteristics of cases of UI. The preliminary data from the Quinn study (2010) describes a population that was half male and half female, less likely to be married, more likely to live in some sort of living facility versus in independent homes, cognitively impaired, and frequently experiencing multiple other impairments. Impairments in executive functioning, judgment, and insight are commonly noted. Alleged abusers were noted to be friends, neighbors, family members, or scam artists (25 %). In this small sample there were no cases of person in authority (fiduciary, pastor, etc.) accused of abuse. In summary, although conceptually UI and cognitive impairment are independent constructs, at least in this preliminary sample, cognitive impairment was ubiquitous, underlying the common sense belief that it is easier to influence individuals who are not mentally intact (Sparr and Garr 1992). More research on UI is needed to more fully characterize the cognitive contributions to this type of financial exploitation.

6.5   Conclusion

In this chapter we present a framework for understanding cognitive contributions to financial crime victimization. Drawing on dual process models we suggest that risk for poor financial decision making and fraud occurs when deliberative reasoning is less likely to be engaged. In healthy individuals, most of the type decision making occurs in a default, automatic mode that is not attentive to details. In impaired individuals (depressed, mild cognitive impairment, delirium) it may be that deliberative reasoning can not be engaged. Factors that decrease our ability to engage deliberative resources such as stress and ego depletion increase our risk for poor financial decision making. Additionally we discuss the importance of numeracy and financial literacy for sound financial decision making. Low levels of financial literacy have been linked to increased debt levels and higher interest rates in financial services products. Individuals low in numeracy are less likely to engage numeric information and are more likely to rely on heuristic reasoning. Executive functioning, the ability to direct, monitor, and control behavior has also been linked to improved financial capacity.

Taken together, work on the psychology of financial decision making and financial exploitation suggests that decision making can occur in or out of awareness. Individuals difference factors related to financial knowledge and skills, as well as comfort with numbers can impact one's ability to make sound financial decisions. Financial decision-making often occurs within a social context as is the case with undue influence. Psychological factors such as persuasion and coercion interact with the cognitive contributions described above. Overall, anyone can be the victim of fraud, however factors that impact our ability to deliberate and "do the math" increase our susceptibility to financial predators.

References

Assessment of Older Adults with Diminished Capacity. 2008. In ed. S. Wood and J. Moye. American Psychological Association/American Bar Association: Washington DC.

Baumeister, R.F., E.A. Sparks, T.F. Stillman, and K.D. Vohs. 2008. Free will in consumer behavior: Self-control, ego depletion, and choice. *Journal of Consumer Psychology* 18: 4–13.

Bechara, A., H. Damasio, et al. 1998. Dissociation of working memory from decision making within the human prefrontal cortex. *The Journal of Neuroscience* 18(1): 428–437.

Carr, P.B., and C.M. Steele. 2010. Stereotype threat affects financial decision-making. *Psychological Science* 21(10): 1411–1416. doi:10.1177/0956797610384146.

Glueck, S. 2013. A criminologist looks at social work. *American Society of Criminology* 11(2). doi:10.1086/632015.

Heilman, R.M., L.G. Crisan, D. Houser, M. Miclea, and A.C. Miu. 2010. Emotion regulation and decision-making under risk and uncertainty. *Emotion* 10(2): 257–265. doi:10.1037/a0018489.

Howlett, E., J. Kees, and E. Kemp. 2008. Retirement savings, financial literacy and time preferences in Germany. http://www.uu.nl/SiteCollectionDocuments/REBO/REBO_USE/REBO_USE_OZZ/Abstract_one_page.pdf.

Inzlicht, M., and J.N. Gutsell. 2007. Running on empty: neural signals for self-control failure. *Psychological Science* 18(11): 933–937. doi:10.1111/j.1467-9280.2007.02004.x.

Kahneman, D. 2011. *Thinking fast and slow*. New York: Farrar, Strauss, & Giroux.

Kostek, J., and L. Ashrafioun. 2013. Tired winners: the effects of cognitive resources and prior winning on risky decision making. *Journal of Gambling Studies*, Advance online publication.

Lo, A.W., D.V. Repin, and B.N. Steenbarger. 2005. Fear and greed in financial markets: A clinical study of day-traders. *American Economic Review* 95: 352–359.

Lipkus, I., G. Samsa, and B.K. Rimer. 2001. General performance on a numeracy scale among highly educated samples. *Medical Decision Making* 21: 37–44.

Lusardi, A., and O.S. Mitchell. 2007. Baby Boomer retirement security: The roles of planning, financial literacy, and housing wealth. *Journal of Monetary Economics* 54: 205–224.

Lusardi, A., and O.S. Mitchell. 2011. *Financial literacy and retirement planning in the US*. NBER working paper 17108.

Lusardi, A., and P. Tufano. March 2009. *Debt literacy, financial experiences, and overindebtedness*. NBER Working paper.

Mani, A., S. Mullainathan, E. Shafir, and J. Zhao. 2013. Poverty impedes cognitive function. *Science* 341: 976–980.

Martin, E.I., K.J. Ressler, et al. 2009. The neurobiology of anxiety disorders: brain imaging, genetics, and psychoneuroendocrinology. *The Psychiatric clinics of North America* 32(3): 549–575.

McEwen, B.S. 1998. Protective and damaging effects of stress mediators. *The New England Journal of Medicine* 338(3): 171–179.

Oaten, and Cheng. n.d. Improvements in self-control from financial monitoring. Retrieved from Peisah, C., et al. 2009. "The wills of older people: Risk factors for undue influence". *International Psychogeriatrics* 21: 7–15.

Oaten, M. and Cheng, K. (2007). Improvements in Self-Control from Financial Monitoring. *Journal of EconomicPsychology* 57(4): 487–501. doi:10.1016/j.joep.2006.11.003

Peters, E., D. Västfjäll, P. Slovic, C.K. Mertz, K. Mazzocco, and S. Dickert. 2006. Numeracy and decision making. *Psychological Science* 17(5): 407–413.

Pohl, R.F., E. Erdfelder, B.E. Hilbig, L. Liebke, and D. Stahlberg. 2013. Effort reduction after self-control depletion: The role of cognitive resources in use of simple heuristics. *Journal of Cognitive Psychology* 25(3): 267–276.

Porcelli, A.J., and M.R. Delgado. 2009. Acute stress modulates risk taking in financial decision-making. *Psychological Science* 20(3): 278–283.

Reinhard, M., M. Scharmach, and P. Müller. 2013. It's not what you are, it's what you know: experience, beliefs, and the detection of deception in employment interviews. *Journal of Applied Social Psychology* 43(3): 467–479. doi:10.1111/j.1559-1816.2013.01011.x.

Rolison, J., S. Wood, and Y. Hanoch. 2012. Risky decision making in younger and older adults: The role of learning. *Psychology and Aging* 27(1): 129–140.

Sherod, M.G., H.R. Griffith, J. Copeland, K. Belue, S. Krzywanski, E.Y. Zamrini, L.E. Harrell, D. G. Clark, J.C. Brockington, R.E. Powers, and D.C. Marson. 2009. Neurocognitive predictors of financial capacity across the dementia spectrum: Normal aging, mild cognitive impairment, and Alzheimer's disease. *Journal of the International Neuropsychological Society* 15(2): 258–267. doi:10.1017/S1355617709090365.

Sparr, J.E., and A.S. Garr. 1992. Assessing competency to make a will. *American Journal of Psychiatry* 149(2): 169–174.

Strauss, G.P., and D.N. Allen. 2009. Positive and negative emotions uniquely capture attention. *Applied neuropsychology* 16(2): 144–149.

Unger, A., and D. Stahlberg. 2011. Ego-depletion and risk behavior: Too exhausted to take a risk. *Social Psychology* 42: 28–38.

Vohs, K., and R. Faber. 2007. Spent resources: Self-regulatory resource availability affects impulse buying. *Journal of Consumer Research* 5(33): 537–547.

Wood, S., Y. Hanoch, A. Barnes, P-J. Liu, J. Cummings, C. Bhattacharya, and T. Rice. 2011. Numeracy and medicare part D: The importance of choice & literacy for numbers in optimizing decision making for Medicare's prescription drug program. *Psychology and Aging* 26(2): 295–307. doi:10.1037/a0022028.

Wood, S. 2013. *Cognitive contributions to financial elder exploitation, American society of criminology*. Georgia: Atlanta.

Wood, S., and P. Liu. 2012. Undue influence and financial capacity: A clinical perspective. *Generations Journal of the American Society on Aging* 36: 53–58.

Chapter 7
Personal and Situational Contributors to Fraud Victimization: Implications of a Four-Factor Model of Gullible Investing

Stephen Greenspan and George W. Woods

Abstract Being a victim of a financial fraud is a form of gullibility, which can be described as induced social risk-awareness. A four-factor explanatory model of gullibility is described, with one of these factors (Situation) being external to the victim, and three (Cognition, Personality and State) being internal to the person. A linear (neo-psychodynamic) interactive model is proposed, in which a gullible financial outcome is described as the sum of all of these factors operating on a specific victim. A non-linear and transactional "cusp-catastrophe" version of this model is also described, but for now use of the model remains descriptive and rooted in a static linear mode. Three case studies are used to illustrate the model and its possible utility: (a) a case in Montreal in which an unlicensed financial advisor named Earl Jones took advantage of the social vulnerability and naïve trust of elderly women; (b) a case involving an internet inheritance scheme associated with Nigerian "419" scams; and (c) the massive Bernard Madoff scandal. In addition to being used to analyze the gullible investing behavior of individuals, the model is also used to shed light on the gullible actions of financial institutions, with particular focus on René-Thierry Magon de La Villehuchet, the head of one of the victimized Madoff feeder funds, who tragically took his own life after his fund was wiped out.

7.1 Introduction

Being victimized in a financial fraud is a "foolish act," by which we mean a behavior that fails to anticipate risk, in this case the risk of being swindled (Greenspan 2009a). Foolish acts can be practical (ignoring the risk of a physical

S. Greenspan (✉)
Health Science Center, University of Colorado, Boulder, CO, USA
e-mail: stephen.greenspan@gmail.com

G.W. Woods
University of California, Berkeley, CA, USA
e-mail: gwoods@georgewoodsmd.com

© Springer International Publishing Switzerland 2016   141
M. Dion et al. (eds.), *Financial Crimes: Psychological, Technological, and Ethical Issues*, International Library of Ethics, Law, and the New Medicine 68, DOI 10.1007/978-3-319-32419-7_7

consequence, such as falling off an unsecured ladder) or they can be social (ig-noring the risk of a social consequence, such as when telling an insulting or inappropriate joke). Social foolishness can come in two forms: induced or non-induced: the latter (non-induced) comes solely out of one's own foolish impulse; an example would be showing pornography to a child, something for which the social consequence could range from chastisement to a substantial prison sentence. Induced social foolishness occurs as a result of some pressure, often involving deception, by one or more other people.

Another word for induced social foolishness is "gullibility" (Greenspan 2009b; Greenspan et al. 2011). Victims of financial fraud can be described as gullible, in that they put trust in a person, or a scheme, which should not have been trusted. Gullibility (induced social foolishness) is typically viewed as a personality trait—as in "John is so gullible, that his trust is always being exploited"—or as a quasi-diagnostic category, as in "John's gullibility indicates that he has a dependent personality disorder and may need conservatorship in order to protect his savings from disappearing." In this paper, we focus more narrowly on gullibility/foolishness as a specific act or set of linked acts. That is because a generally competent or non-gullible person (i.e., the majority of people reading this paper) are capable of being defrauded on any given occasion, and it only takes one such episode to be ruined financially. Having a trusting personality can obviously be a contributing factor to a financial gullibility episode, but in the majority of cases, one's personality alone is not enough to explain why someone is defrauded. That is because, in our view, there are four broad factors which contribute to a gullible outcome, and personality is only one of those factors and, in many instances, is the least important of those factors. In subsequent sections, we describe this four factor model and illustrate it with various examples of financial gullibility.

7.2 Model of Human Gullibility

An explanatory model of gullible (induced socially foolish) action was described in the first author's book *Annals of Gullibility* (2009b) and is depicted in Fig. 7.1 below. In this model, gullible action is viewed as an outcome which occurs as the

Fig. 7.1 Main effects model of gullible behavior

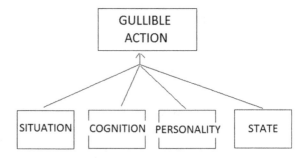

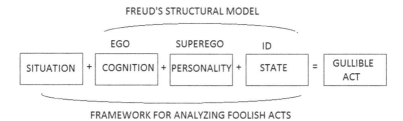

FREUD'S STRUCTURAL MODEL

FRAMEWORK FOR ANALYZING FOOLISH ACTS

Fig. 7.2 An interactive (Neo-Psychodynamic) formulation of the gullibility model

result of the independent contribution of four broad factors. The four broad factors each can be sub-divided further; some of the sub-factors are described and illustrated briefly under each of the four headings below. One factor (Situation) is external to the actor, while the other three factors (Cognition, Personality and State) are internal to the person. This version of the theory can be considered a "Main Effects" model, in that each of the four factors can be portrayed as independently bringing about a gullible outcome. However, we believe that an interactive version of the model (see Fig. 7.2), in which the factors work in complementary fashion, better explains gullible behavior.

To illustrate the meaning of the four elements in the model, we shall present an actual case of financial fraud, which took place in Montreal, Quebec over a 17-year period, before it was exposed in 2009. The perpetrator of the fraud was an unlicensed financial advisor named Earl Jones (age 67 at the time of his arrest) who operated a Ponzi scheme which mainly preyed on elderly women (many of whom were made destitute when their retirement accounts and even homes–through improperly obtained mortgage contracts–disappeared). A Ponzi scheme is a fraud where invested money is pocketed by the schemer and investors who wish to redeem their money are actually paid out of proceeds from new investors. As long as new investments are expanding at a healthy rate, the schemer is able to keep the fraud going. The scheme gets its name from Charles Ponzi (Zuckoff 2005), an Italian immigrant to Boston, who in 1920 came up with the idea of promising huge returns (50 % in 45 days) based supposedly on an arbitrage plan (buying in one market and selling in another) involving international postal reply coupons. Supposedly, the profits came from differences in exchange rates between the selling and the receiving country (where they could be cashed in). A craze ensued, and Ponzi pocketed many millions of dollars, mostly from fellow Italian immigrants (which is why Ponzi schemes are typically described as "affiliation scams"). The scheme collapsed when newspaper articles, and government officials, began to raise questions about it (pointing out, for example, that there were not nearly enough such postal reply coupons in circulation) and a run occurred.

In the case of the scheme operated by Earl Jones, a conservative estimate is that over 150 victims were swindled out of approximately $51 million (Dearing 2009).

That is small potatoes by modern Ponzi standards, but it still had devastating consequences for the victims, most of who had their modest but essential nest eggs wiped out. (Just recently are some of the victims or their estates beginning to get some of their money back). Earl Jones received a sentence of 11 years and was released after only four, which has prompted legislators to recommend changes in the Canadian criminal code to mandate tougher sentences (and reduced granting of early release) for white collar criminals. A respected financial institution, the Royal Bank of Canada (RBC), has been subjected to hefty fines and lawsuit settlements, as a result of its failure to exercise fiduciary responsibility to elderly clients (most of whom had accounts in a single RBC branch in West Montreal) and also to properly investigate the many questionable transactions of Mr. Jones, who operated his financial scheme out of the same bank and who used his connection to the bank as a way of validating the legitimacy of his operation. As with most Ponzi schemers, Mr. Jones got many victims from word of mouth and personal relationships (his own brother and sister-in-law were among his biggest victims), but his basic modus *operandi* was to give "free" financial planning workshops at retirement facilities where most of his victims resided. As with Bernard Madoff, Jones promised modest but still very respectable annual returns (8 % in the case of Jones, a little higher for Madoff), in up as well as down years. The main difference is that Madoff's victims were mostly rich and financially sophisticated, while Jones' victims were mostly middle class and financially naïve. Size of the losses aside, Jones' scam might have been even more invidious, as—working with an estate lawyer confederate—Jones typically took complete control of the victims' financial lives and even managed to divert behests away from intended beneficiaries when clients passed away (Bruemmer 2009).

7.2.1 Situation

The first element in the model, and the only one external to the actor, is termed "Situation." It encompasses the problem posed to the actor, and all of the environmental elements–including the attractiveness and complexity of the scheme, the personality and persuasiveness of the schemer, and the role of other people—which contribute to influencing the victim. Situation is a major force in every gullibility episode and the situation with a Ponzi, or other forms of fraudulent schemes, is that other people appear to be benefiting from it and by example encouraging you to jump on the bandwagon. Such modeling tells you the action is safe and too good to miss out on. An aspect of situation with the Montreal scam that was missing with the dour Madoff, is that Jones was by all accounts a charmer, whose warmth, friendliness and use of humor put victims at ease and made them feel comfortable having him handle their money. Another aspect of situation is that many of Jones' victims were widows, and lacked the company of a perhaps more financially knowledgeable spouse to advise them. A cohort effect may have been operating as well, in that most of these victims likely grew up in a time period when it was considered rude to suspect the motives of people who seemed "nice."

7.2.2 Cognition

The second element in the model, Cognition, refers to one's ability to understand the scheme and evaluate it. A differentiated treatment of the various cognitive factors which contribute to financial victimization is presented by Wood (2014), in a companion chapter in this volume. People who are financially knowledgeable or good at spotting implausible claims or signs of dissembling, are better able to resist getting sucked into a risky acivity, especially when they are morally questionable (Snow 2009). In the case of the Jones scam, few of the mostly elderly victims possessed any independent financial knowledge that might have given them pause. That is aside from the possibility that some of the victims were likely showing some signs of dementia. It is well-understood that a common adaptation in people with cognitive decline is to go along with whatever others suggest or are doing (Mordekar and Spence 2008).

7.2.3 Personality

The third element in the model, Personality, refers to behavioral dispositions—such as impulsivity, interpersonal trust and overconfidence—that can push one into a gullible act. Obviously, personalities of investors vary quite widely, but a risky personality adaptation that elderly people make, especially as they begin to lose confidence in their analytic powers, is to become dependent on others (such as authoritative frauds like Earl Jones) to help them make complicated decisions). Thus, a tendency to be trusting (which likely existed in many of the victims to begin with), became exaggerated as they began to experience some loss of cognitive ability. Rotter (1980), one of the few major personality theorists to study gullible behavior, referred to gullibility as "naïve trust," by which he meant trust that is not tempered with cognitive awareness of the risks in a particular situation. Thus, one cannot view personality or cognition as independent forces, as they work together—along with the next element in the model—state—to explain any particular gullible act.

7.2.4 State

The fourth element in the model, State, refers to aspects of one's biological self-regulatory system which (as with emotions such as fear) can motivate one to behave foolishly or which (as with physical depletions such as exhaustion or intoxication) can reduce one's ability to show good judgment or to reflect on one's actions. In the case of the Jones scam, a major state motivator was undoubtedly the relief victims must have felt at being assured that their financial futures would be secure. Related to this undoubtedly would have been the mild form of infatuation which many of the elderly female victims likely felt for the reportedly charismatic, charming and well-mannered Earl Jones (Gyulai 2009).

7.3 A Linear Interactive Perspective on Fraud Victimization

The problem with a Main Effects model is that while foolish action may be influenced by four sets of variables, these factors usually operate in a combinatory fashion, with the results not being predictable as the weights to be attached to these predictor variables are not always known, or the same across time and individuals. Furthermore, a small change in one variable can bring about a major shift in behavior. As example, adding a very slight amount of "foolishness pull" to a situation, or slightly altering a subject's affective or biological state, can bring about a dramatic change in behavior, from a typical state of non-foolishness to a single act of foolishness that could have profound consequences for the actor.

An interactive formulation of the four-factor gullibility model can be found in Fig. 7.2. In this model, a gullible act is seen not as the result of the individual factors operating separately, but as all of the four factors operating together. This formulation can be considered broadly psychodynamic, as it bears certain similarities to Sigmund Freud's "structural" (id-ego-superego) model, with Id corresponding to State, Ego corresponding to Cognition, and Personality corresponding to Superego. An element missing from Freud's structural theory is any mention of Situation. That is likely because: (a) the structural theory, which Freud later abandoned for the Topographical (levels of consciousness) theory and never fully developed, was applied to a single class of behavior—verbal parapraxes (slips of the tongue) which do not require any external stimulus, and (b) personality theorists in general have little interest in the external contexts in which personal tendencies are manifested.

7.4 Transactional Dynamic-Systems Perspective on Gullible Behavior

An even more dynamic depiction of gullibility can be considered "transactional" rather than "interactional" (Sameroff 1975). Such a perspective is depicted in Figs. 7.3 and 7.4. Such a perspective might be termed a "complexity" model of foolish or gullible action". A key aspect of this complexity is that while a confluence of forces acting within and upon an individual creates a fertile condition for the initiation of a foolish act, acting non-foolishly is still a choice available to the individual. Thus, while foolish action may be explainable, it will never be entirely

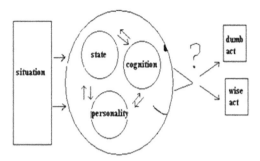

Fig. 7.3 Dynamic non-linear model of foolish action

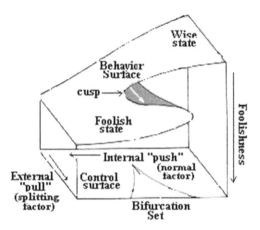

Fig. 7.4 Cusp catastrophe model showing external pull (situation) and internal push (cognition + affect/state + personality) as the control factors, and foolish action as the behavior

predictable, as depicted by the question mark in the right-hand outcome section of Fig. 7.3.

   This model helps to understand the role of temporal pressure so common in fraud episodes (as in being told "you must decide in the next 5 min to take advantage of such a fantastic opportunity"). A formulation of such a time-induced foolish action in the non-social realm can be found in a paper by Perkins (2002), who discussed the case of a truck driver who tried—with spectacularly tragic results–to get his rig across the tracks before a train got there. This case was used by Perkins to illustrate foolish behavior that can occur when there is a failure in what he termed "activity switching". Perkins makes distinctions between what he terms "true folly", "blind folly" and "plain folly". True folly occurs when someone has no awareness of the risk in a situation. In the case of the driver, this would involve not understanding the meaning of a closed railroad gate. Blind folly would involve recognizing risk but deceiving oneself as to its applicability in a given situation.

In the case of the driver, this might involve concluding that he has more than enough time to make it across. Plain folly involves recognizing the risk, but mindlessly and impulsively ignoring it. Perkins believes, because it happened so quickly, that the train-racing behavior falls in this plain folly category, but it has some qualities of blind folly as well. Perkins refers to a general systems phenomenon that he terms "self-organizing criticality" to explain the foolish behavior of the truck driver. An important aspect of this process is "emergent activity switching," which happens when forces in a system "...increase in intensity, eventually reaching a tipping point that reorganizes the system into another pattern of activity" (p. 66). Emergent activity switching is seen by Perkins as a behavioral control system that generally "...is a simple and serviceable way of guiding behavior in most circumstances" (p. 66). However, it is not a perfect mechanism and for reasons that Perkins calls "mistuning", "entrenchment" and "undermanagement", emergent activity switching can sometimes fail, resulting in foolish behavior. The notion of defective self-management of activity switching is used by Perkins as an explanation for a wide range of self-deceptions and resulting socially foolish behaviors including—in addition to impulsiveness—procrastination and vacillation. In the case of the truck driver, what Perkins thinks happened is that the driver slowed when he saw the gate come down, but he was eager to get where he was going and was already in a critical stage of impatience. An impulse built up rapidly, which offered little time for self-management. According to Perkins, this particular driver had a history of citations for reckless driving, and so "management of emergent activity switching may not have been his strength" (p. 72) anyway. The result was an impulsive act that Perkins terms "emergent folly". However, it is very likely, indeed probable, that the same driver had been in nearly identical circumstances many times in the past and had dealt with the situation non-foolishly (either by not trying to get across or doing so but having a luckier result).

One way of looking at foolish acts, including gullible investing acts, is to look at them as discontinuous transformations in state, in which an individual goes from a condition of non-foolishness to a temporary condition of foolishness. A foolish act–as opposed to, say, irrational thinking which in the right circumstance can predispose one to foolish action—is, thus, typically a sudden and infrequent behavior that represents a disequilibrium change which could be precipitated by the most minor and chance of happenings (e.g., the railroad gate coming down when it did, rather than 3 s earlier). For such discontinuities, affected by so many variables, and with such not completely predictable outcomes, a different conceptual and methodological framework is required. Such an alternative worldview may possibly be found in two non-linear systems frameworks: "chaos theory" (sometimes referred to as "complexity theory") and "catastrophe theory"(sometimes referred to as "bifurcation theory").

Chaos theory is a deterministic theory that is "a reflection of the forces operating on (and within) the system" (Carver and Scheier 1998, 250), but in which predictability isn't very good because: all of the influences on the system can't be known totally or precisely; because the influence of the forces may be non-linear, with feedback among and between the forces; or because a very small increase in one force can have very major impact on the system. Thus, the behavior of the system, "though highly determined, can give the appearance of randomness" (Carver and Scheier 1998, 251), in part because it involves oscillations in behavior that are highly irregular (as is the case with foolish acts, which typically occur irregularly). Another core aspect of chaos theory is the role of "attractors" (areas which a system approaches more frequently than others) and "repellers" (regions that seem to be actively avoided). Catastrophe theory, although emerging from a different body of mathematical theorizing (specifically, topology, a modern branch of geometry), shares many similarities with chaos theory, in that it reflects a non-linear dynamic systems worldview, and uses attractors as core concepts (Stewart and Peregoy 1983). A major difference is a focus on bifurcation, that is a sudden discontinuous state transformation (i.e. a shift from the dominance of one attractor and its replacement by the dominance of another attractor), with such a dramatic state change brought about by a small change in one or more control variables. Catastrophe theory would appear to be particularly applicable to understanding foolish action, as one can view non-foolishness as the typical equilibrium state of almost all adult humans (even those with high propensity to act foolishly), with a foolish act being a discontinuous shift to a new equilibrium brought about through the non-linear combining of four sets of variables—situation, state, personality and cognition—with a small variation in one or two of the variables making all the difference in determining whether or not an individual acts foolishly.

Catastrophe theory has been used increasingly in social and personality psychology, as in papers on impulsive "rubicon" actions (Gollwitzer 1996) brought about by an abrupt shift from a deliberative mode to an implemental mode; on the factors contributing to sudden shifts in attitudes (van der Maas et al. 2003) and on the relationship between attitudes and behavior (Flay 1978). Catastrophe theory has also been used to address clinically-relevant issues, such as child abuse (Tutzauer 1998), blaming of crime victims (Lanza 1999), coprolalic tic behavior in Tourette syndrome (Berecz 1992), violence outbursts (Milovanovic 2002), and adolescent alcohol use (Clair 1998) and smoking (Byrne et al. 2001). There are several elementary catastrophe models, named after the shape of the resulting graph, with the most commonly-used model being the "cusp catastrophe", in which there are two control variables. Figure 7.4 is a transformation of Fig. 7.3 into a cusp catastrophe model, with the three within-person factors of "cognition", "affect/state" and "personality" being collapsed into the control variable "internal push" and the "situation" factor being labeled the control variable "external pull".

The arrows are pointed in the direction of high values for these variables. Thus, high external push would be qualities of a situation (i.e., social or other attractors) that impel the person to act foolishly, while high internal pull would be those qualities of the person which also impel the person, in that situation, to act foolishly. The "Behavior Surface" is the top-most slanting plane forming the third dimension in this model, and it is on this surface that relative foolishness is depicted. The cusp is the point on the Behavior Surface at which the plane folds over onto itself in an overlapping fashion. The "Control Surface" is the bottom plane, on which the two control variables of internal push and external pull are depicted. The "Bifurcation

Set" is the shadow that the cusp on the Behavior Surface casts on the Control Surface below. It is in this zone, where the two control factors are in a relative equilibrium, that small changes in one of the control factors can, somewhat unpredictably, cause an individual to jump from non-foolish to foolish action, or vice versa.

At the top-right corner on the behavior surface, people are in a typical resting state of wisdom (i.e., non-foolishness). In catastrophe theory terminology, internal push can be considered the "normal factor". That is because, in the absence of external forces, foolish action is likely a monotonic function solely of internal push. In other words, people are very likely to behave foolishly when internal push is high and very unlikely to behave foolishly when internal push is low. An example would be someone who is highly intoxicated. In such a state, there is a very high likelihood of foolish action, even in the absence of any real external pull for such action. In catastrophe theory terminology, external pull may be considered the "splitting factor", in that external pull alone (except perhaps in the most extreme of cases, such as torture) will not cause someone to behave foolishly. Rather, at some point where external pull and internal push are in a rough balance, a slight increase in situational pressure will cause a bifurcation, in that some people will suddenly act foolishly while others will not. In catastrophe theory terminology, this region of precariousness is termed the "bifurcation set", which is the zone where the split occurs, with some people exposed to the same forces jumping suddenly from non-foolishness to foolishness, while others remain non-foolish.

The second control factor of internal push does not, obviously, remain constant, and even in a situation of relatively moderate external pull, a very strong internal push (e.g. greed, fear, limited understanding, or a tendency towards compliance) can also cause someone to fall off the non-foolishness surface onto the foolishness surface. When external pull is low, then the relationship between internal push and foolish likely remains monotonic. However, when external pull is moderate, then one can predict a bimodal distribution, where some people will respond to this pull with foolish action, while others will remain non-foolish. When both internal push and external pull factors are weak, then a person is likely to remain non-foolish. Conversely, when both internal and external forces are strong, the likelihood is high that a person will behave foolishly. The catastrophe model, in which individuals can make sudden leaps from non-foolishness to foolishness, or back again, is most likely to apply when the forces are in the middle range, say when a moderate external pull towards foolish action is counter-balanced somewhat by moderate internal forces that are resisting that pull.

An example of this can be found in a paper by Tesser (1980), in which he sought to explain sudden shifts in dating/mating (D/M) behavior as a function of love (internal push in our terms) and social pressure (external pull in our terms). Tesser was particularly interested in cases where someone who was disposed towards marrying someone was confronted by pressure, such as from parents, to break off the relationship, as well as the opposite case of someone who was disinclined to marry someone but who suddenly caved into pressure to marry. In the middle ground where internal and external forces are in a state of balance, a slight increase in external pressure could (but not necessarily) cause someone to act suddenly against his or her internal inclination. The breaking point at which bimodality occurs is in the bifurcation set, in the middle range of the graph. Tesser (1980, 396) noted that "bimodal distributions are predicted for each point in the bifurcation set and unimodal distributions for all other points on the control surface." An example, Sundem (2012) profiled a man (who we both know extremely well) who was on the fence and leaning against marrying his girlfriend, but who switched to the other side when he fell for a ploy by his mother regarding the great deal she was able to get on an engagement ring being sold cheaply by an elderly aunt. This is an example, we suppose, of a form of financial fraud, but where the outcome is not turning over money but turning over a big chunk of one's future life (to which one could presumably attach some financial value). Tesser did not label such a contrary-to-inclination action as "foolish", but we have no such hesitation. (In the above example, the coerced marriage was an unstable one, marked by years of conflict and unhappiness, before its eventual dissolution). The opposite example (deciding to break off very satisfying relationships) is reflected in works of art, such as the 1955 film *Marty* (Chayevsky 1995) and the 2004 play *Fat Pig* (LaBute 2004), depicting men who caved into pressure from friends to dump physically imperfect girlfriends they loved only to realize later what a mistake they had made.

7.5   Use of the Model in a Civil Fraud Case

At this point, the non-linear complexity model of foolish investing is not sufficiently developed to use in a quantitative predictive manner, but still can be used in descriptive fashion to shed light on why financial victims make foolish investment decisions. In the following few pages, it shall be used in that manner to illustrate how the four factors may shed some light on the fraud phenomenon from a victim standpoint. A potential use of the four-factor model, and the construct of gullibility, is in the aftermath of a fraud loss in which (as is often the case) a legitimate business such as a bank is being sued for having failed in its fiduciary duty to protect the victims from the consequences of their own naïve trust (an example is RBC being blamed in the aftermath of the Earl Jones scandal). An actual example will be used, but because the case settled just before trial, details have been altered. The case involved what has become known as a "419 scam," after the number in the criminal code covering fraud in Nigeria, the country out of which many of these scams originate (Van Wijk 2009). 419-type scams have been around for a long time, and can take many forms (the classic "Spanish Prisoner" con game depicted in the David Mamet film of the same name is an example). It usually involves financially assisting some person (who may for example be depicted as a Nigerian prince) to obtain an inheritance out of which he has been cheated. In return for this assistance, the mark is promised a sizeable payment, such as 20 or 30 % of the recovered loot. Part of the scam usually involves getting the mark to do something illegal (such as misrepresenting something to a bank) or helping the sender to do something illegal (such as evading taxes), on the assumption that victims will be reluctant to seek legal redress once they find they have been defrauded, because of fear of exposure (Zuckoff 2006). Today, 419 scams invariably are carried out over the internet, and involve a victim receiving an email message from a stranger, who often describes himself as an attorney who is seeking the assistance of the message's recipient in return for substantial monetary compensation. Using automated message generation technology, millions of people can receive the same message with individualized features added, such as the name of the target). The vast majority of recipients are smart enough to ignore the message, but it only takes a very small number of extremely gullible persons to get sucked into make this a very lucrative business for the scammers.

In the case of the man, "James Smithson", whose lawsuit one of us consulted on, the sender of the email (who claimed to be a London solicitor named "Daniel Okundo") asserted he was handling the estate of a recently deceased distant cousin of Smithson's wife, and she appeared to be the rightful beneficiary of two million dollars. In order for her to receive the money, the Smithsons would have to pay Okundo to clear up some problems. Mr. Smithson (termed by 419 scammers a *maga*, a Yoruba word for fool) was a formerly successful businessman in his early 80's, who had recently suffered a financial reverse. He was intrigued enough to call the phone number given in the message, telling his (very skeptical) wife "what do I have to lose by talking to him?" The answer, it turned out, was "a very great deal". As might be expected, the scammer, Daniel Okundo, was very charming, and Mr. Smithson—a religious man who had once been a missionary in a third world country—took to him immediately. His wife continued to try to warn him, but he ignored her, saying that this was the miracle he had been asking God to perform, to help him get back on his feet financially. Although Smithson's close friend was a prominent attorney, he refused to ask his advice as he knew that he would likely also tell him that his new friend Daniel was not to be trusted.

The scam started off on a small scale, with Smithson being asked on a few occasions to send several thousand dollars to clear up some legal complications. When the amount paid out reached $40,000, Smithson finally began to have some doubts, and he told Okundo "no more, until I start seeing some of the inherited money." Mr. Okundo replied a short time later and said "I have good news, bad news and wonderful news. The good news is that your wife's two million dollar inheritance is actually twelve million dollars. The bad news is that there are some taxes that need to be paid to claim this amount, and the taxes come to close to two million dollars. The wonderful news is that I have found an investor in Japan who will put up the entire sum in return for a sizeable interest payment, and you will not have to pay one cent towards the taxes. The arrangement that was worked out was that the two million from the Japanese investor was to be wired into Smithson's bank account and when he saw the money was there, he was to turn around and wire the two million to Okundo, who insisted that it go in and out of an account of Smithson's that was tied to a line of credit secured by his and his wife's largely paid-off home. To accomplish this, Smithson had to increase the amount of the line of credit. The reason for this, not told to Smithson of course, is that banks do not question sizeable checks as carefully when they are in a collateralized account.

While all of this was going on, there were frequent emails back and forth from well-known banks in various parts of the world. Virtually all of the emails would have aroused suspicion in a more worldly, savvy and vigilant person than Mr. Smithson. For example, one bank's email had an s added to the end of the bank name in its email address, while the famous logo in the letterhead of another bank was noticeably off center. Mr. Smithson noted none of this, and his only cautionary action was to ask his "personal banker," a young man barely out of college, to tell him what he thought of the whole plan. He told Smithson he would check with his superiors, but obviously did not as 419 scams are well-known to bankers, and Smithson's bank was a local branch of one of the biggest banks in the country. Smithson checked his bank balance online several times a day, and his vigilance paid off when to his great glee the sum of two million dollars suddenly appeared in it, wired from a bank in Japan. Smithson, being an honorable (as well as perhaps slightly greedy) person, again approached his wet-behind-the-ears personal banker and asked his assurance that the money was really in his account, and that he was free to send it off to Okundo. The banker got back to Smithson and told him the money was his and he was perfectly free to do with it as he wished. Smithson then dutifully wired the entire amount to an account of Okundo's as instructed.

A week later, Mr. Smithson was contacted by his private banker, who gave him the bad news that the check wired to them from Japan was no good, and he asked him to give back the two million dollars that the bank sent off as per his instructions. After (finally) consulting an attorney, Mr. Smithson refused this request, and the bank initiated proceedings to receive their lost funds by foreclosing on his house. Smithson's lawyer disputed that action, asserting that the bank should be held accountable for its own incompetence. A trial was scheduled, and one of us was engaged to address the gullibility issue, while an expert on bank procedures was hired to opine on several unprofessional actions by the bank, such as: (a) their initial failure to warn their client of the well-known dangers of internet inheritance schemes, (b) their rebuffing a warning from an overseas bank (which tried to return the two million, saying they strongly suspected fraud), and (c) the fact that the check from the supposed Japanese investor had several things wrong with it, including the absence of a number to clear their automated bank verification machine, and the fact that it was written on a bank that was known to have problems.

In a deposition which occurred just before the case was settled, our position was that the forty thousand, sent before Smithson brought his bank fully into the drama, was his problem, while the two million was the bank's. While we do not know the details of the confidential settlement, indications are that the bank ended up eating the majority of the loss. Our reasoning was that while Mr. Smithson 's gullibility certainly played a role in his sending the two million on to an unknown scammer, trusting the assurances of one's banker at a major financial institution, after repeated requests for such assurance, is reasonable and something that even generally non-gullible people would have done. For the purposes of illustrating the analytic utility of the gullibility model, and explaining why we opined as we did, we shall divide the case into two separate episodes, which we shall label pre-bank and post-bank.

7.5.1   Pre-bank Analysis

7.5.1.1   Situation

The situational pull in this 419 scam—an email from an unknown lawyer saying that Smithson's wife had inherited a fortune from a cousin she had never heard of—was incredibly weak, as reflected in the fact that 99.9 % of the millions who receive such messages laugh them off. Furthermore, it lacked the important element that drives most scams, which is the persuasion skills that come from a face to face interaction with a skilled con artist. Of course that equation shifted in the scammer's favor when Smithson made the fatal mistake of picking up the phone and calling him. That is because once one develops a personal relationship with someone, it becomes much more difficult to break off the relationship (Cialdini 1984), especially if one is as kind and morally agreeable a person as Smithson appears to be.

7.5.1.2   Cognition

As someone in his 80's, it is likely that Mr. Smithson had begun to show some signs of cognitive decline. One common tendency in frail elderly people (or people with brain impairment generally) is to cover up their limitations by agreeing with things said or suggested by others (Denburg et al. 2007). Regardless, Mr. Smithson showed remarkable innocence and ignorance by being one of the few email users in that time period who had never heard of internet fraud. His naivite in this regard was probably a sign in part of his age and lack of experience.

7.5.1.3   Personality

Mr. Smithson is a remarkably trusting and agreeable man. He had no meanness in his heart and had great difficulty believing others could be evil. Even after his life had been turned upside down by the disappearance of the two million dollars, Smithson continued to believe that Okundo was really who he said he was, and would come forward to clear up what was obviously a terrible misunderstanding. Smithson also obviously had a strong moral sense, in that he turned around and sent the two million forward, while many others would have kept it. In spite of his positive qualities, Smithson was very stubborn and willful, as reflected in his refusal to listen to the pleas and warnings of his wife, or his unwillingness to even listen to what his long-time friend and attorney might have to say about the scheme. He was convinced the scheme was legitimate, and would not even consider the possibility he might be mistaken.

7.5.1.4 State

A big motivator which drove Mr. Smithson's gullibility was his deep religious faith, a faith which convinced him that Okundo was a messenger from God who was sent down from Heaven to answer his prayers and reward him for his faithfulness. An equally big motivator, who explained Smithson's need for a miracle, is that he had made some risky business decisions and was now in trouble financially. Thus the money promised his wife by Okundo seemed to him to be particularly timely and necessary, and increased his otherwise high degree of gullibility to something totally off the charts.

All four factors played into Smithson's gullible susceptibility to Okundo's scam. His sense of financial desperation made him especially receptive and his religious belief in miracles and answered prayers enabled him to reframe Okundo's soliciting email as a miraculous sign. Smithson's profound ignorance of email fraud, probably reflecting to some extent his age, inexperience and perhaps some cognitive slippage, removed the protective shield that some more knowledge and experience would have provided. His cognitive limitations also showed up in ignoring or not noticing many anomalies in the email messages, such as letterhead logos and bank names that were obvious fakes. The Situational force here (an email from a stranger who likely did not exist) was a very weak force that is resisted by all but the most credulous people on the planet, but its force was enhanced when Smithson made the mistake of establishing a personal phone relationship with the scammer. Smithson's personality as a very highly trusting and agreeable person, and also someone who would not change his mind, also contributed to the decision to go ahead with this course of action.

7.5.2 Post-bank Anaysis

The same sub-factors that explain Mr. Smithson's gullibility pre-bank were also operative post-bank, so we shall keep our analysis of the post-bank phase short. The one major difference is that the situational force went from very weak (Okundo's email would have convinced virtually no one to take the next step) to very strong (the money showing up in your online bank statement and being told by a bank officer that it is yours to spend would have convinced virtually everyone). In fact, this is the main reason why one of us was prepared to testify that the pre-bank ($40,000) loss was on Smithson (because it came almost entirely from his own foolishness), while the post-bank ($2 million) loss was on the bank (because he would not have wired the money to the fictional Okundo if the bank had not passively, and to some extent actively, essentially said "go ahead, send the money overseas."

7.5.2.1   Situation

As mentioned, the bank (by vouching for the reality of the unreal $2 million) played a huge role in Smithson's post-bank gullibility, but the cleverness of the scam itself (sending a phony $2 million into a collateralized account in the hope it would show up at least temporarily in the victim's account) was extremely clever. People fall for confidence tricks because the scammers are knowledgeable about human psychology and are able to contrive scenarios that are convincing and which play on the risk-unawareness and emotional needs–such as greed–of their victims. In this case the appearance in his online bank statement of the $2 million loan from the Japanese investor was overwhelming evidence to Smithson that Okundo was telling the truth and was to be trusted.

7.5.2.2   Cognition

The average person lacks anything approaching a sophisticated understanding of how banks process and verify the legitimacy of ordinary checks, let alone international wire transfers. Only a banking expert would understand that banks can and do make mistakes, and the reasons for such mistakes. Therefore, while Smithson would have been much wiser to have waited a few days (and sought alternative assurances from higher-ups at the bank) before taking the word of a very junior local branch officer, it is very understanding, given his lack of banking expertise, that he would have assumed that when the money appeared in his account, and he was told everything looked all right, that it was actually safe for him to immediately send the money on to Okundo.

7.5.2.3   Personality

Smithson is a very honorable man, whose sense of religious duty requires him to keep his word. This explains why he did not think twice about sending the Japanese investor's money to Okundo, as he did not consider the money to be his, but rather saw it as a vehicle for facilitating the processing of his wife's inheritance. Smithson obviously also was not a reflective man, and his need to immediately act on the last stage of the process showed a certain impulsivity.

7.5.2.4   State

The haste with which Smithson sent on the money to Okundo also reflected the great deal of excitement that he felt as the process with Okundoo seemed to be nearing a successful conclusion. Again, the motor that drove this train was Smithson's desperation about feeling suddenly poorer than had previously been the case, and his great desire to rectify that problem, through God's intermediary: Daniel Okundo.

The factors that explained James Smithson's extreme pre-bank gullibility also explains his post-bank larger scale (at least from a money standpoint) gullibility, except for the fact that when the bank told him the $2 million loan actually was his to spend, the role of Situation (and the bank's legal liability) increased exponentially. While Smithson's cognitive naivite about the world of scammers and sense of trust of strangers was striking in the pre-bank phase, his naivite about bank procedures and mistakes was more understandable and commonplace in the post-bank phase. The analysis of the whole event, using the four-factor explanatory model, was apparently useful to the civil attorneys litigating this case, as we believe it could be in other cases of gullibility-driven fraud victimization.

7.6 Use of the Model to Explain Victims of Bernard Madoff

In an earlier paper, the first author (2009b) used the four-factor model to address a puzzling question that occurred to many people after the high-profile Bernard Madoff debacle, namely "how could so many intelligent people, many knowledgeable about financial matters, been dumb enough as to turn all of their money over to a master con artist running a Ponzi scheme?" The essay (Greenspan 2009c) appeared in the *Wall Street Journal* three weeks after the scandal broke (and a month after the first author's book on gullibility was released), and thus attracted a great deal of media attention. A particular irony described in the piece is that the author had invested a chunk of his retirement savings in a Madoff-linked "feeder" hedge fund. He used his own gullibility episode as a cautionary case study to illustrate the role of the four explanatory factors. A Canadian journalist, Robert Fulford (2008), humorously (at least to most people) commented on this irony in a column in which he wrote "the first Greenspan, Alan, will be remembered as the economist who didn't see it coming, while the other Greenspan, Stephen, will be remembered as the gullibility expert who forgot to read his own book."

A particularly tragic footnote to the Madoff story involved the late-night suicide in his New York office, on December 22, 2008, of René-Thierry Magon de La Villehuchet (Berenson and Saltmarsh 2009). He was an aristocratic Frenchman who managed the AIA investment group, which lost $1.4 billion dollars, including his own sizeable fortune and that of close friends and family in Europe. Being a considerate man, Mr. Magon de La Villehuchet wrapped his hands in heavy plastic garbage bags before slitting his wrists, in order not to make too big a mess for the cleaning crew to have to deal with. His honorableness is also reflected in the suicide. Regrettable as that action was, it is an indication of something relatively rare in the world of finance, which is a sense of personal responsibility for letting down one's clients (Katz 2009).

An aspect of this tragedy that is not generally known is that a few months before the Madoff scandal blew up, Mr. Magon de La Villehuchet was told that it was a scam and warned in the most urgent terms to pull all of his firm's money out. We know this because one of us was told the story by a gentleman who ran a firm hired by hedge funds to check out the legitimacy of their investments. This man had been retained by the AIA group to evaluate its sizeable investment with Madoff, and he found many red flags indicative of fraud. Although he was not granted an interview with Madoff or given details of his investment strategy (grounds for suspicion in itself), the man—someone with deep experience in financial regulation–found it extremely irregular that the investment arm of the Madoff firm (which pioneered electronic trading in its brokerage arm) used handwritten trading slips. Furthermore, these trading slips did not have time stamps, something that was a dead giveaway that Madoff's staff created paper profits by filling out the trading slips after the fact and backdating them to create illusory monthly reports that were then sent out to individual and hedge fund clients of the Madoff firm. Another thing indicating the trades did not take place, is that this man could not find evidence, from his many contacts, of any sign that such huge stock holdings actually changed hands on the indicated dates.

When Mr. Magon de La Villehuchet was given the warning to liquidate the Madoff investment, he responded irately, by saying "Bernie is a personal friend" (something that apparently was not true) and "Why should I believe you? The SEC has given him a clean bill of health and surely they know more than you do." In fact, our informant knew something that Mr. Magon de La Villehuchet did not, which is that at that time the investigative staff at the SEC was made up mainly of very young and inexperienced lawyers, bright enough to be sure but with virtually none of the skills or background in finance needed to unravel what to our informant seemed a fairly easy swindle to expose (Henriques 2012). In fact, the SEC investigation that Mr. Magon de La Villehuchet was referring to had been triggered by a lengthy letter from an investment analyst named Markopolos (2010; Zuckerman and Gauthier-Villars 2009), who pointed out all of the problems uncovered by our informant in addition to pointing out the statistical impossibility of Madoff producing such consistent returns over so many years. Furthermore, Barron's magazine (Arvedlund 2001), making many of the same points as Markopolos, had published a lengthy exposé in 2001, in which they all but publicly accused Madoff of running a fraudulent scheme. In the few days after the disclosure but before he took his own life, Mr. Magon de La Villehuchet indicated he had not known of the *Barron's* piece. But it is not likely he would have done anything even if he had. For most of the other managers of multi-billion dollar Madoff "feeder" funds surely knew of the exposé, and there is no evidence that they took the warnings seriously. For the purposes of illustrating the analytic utility of the gullibility model, and explaining why we opined as we did, we shall divide the case into two separate episodes, which we shall label: "Greenspan Gullibility" and "Magon de La Villehuchet Gullibiity."

7.6.1   Greenspan Gullibility Analysis

To avoid constant use of the awkward expression "the first author," the victim in this case will be referred to as "Greenspan" (here, we are referring to the first author of this piece, Stephen Greenspan, and not to the former Federal Reserve chairman, Alan Greenspan). In Greenspan's case, all four of the explanatory elements in the gullibility model were strongly involved, but every one of Madoff's hundreds of victims had a unique story, each with somewhat different profiles of causative weighting.

7.6.1.1   Situation

The main situational force with Greenspan, as with all Ponzi victims, is what Shiller (2000), in his book *Irrational Exuberance*, termed a social "feedback loop," in which earlier investors show the victim their past steadily increasing balance statements, and rave about what a great investment it has been. For those who invested directly with Madoff, he played the hard-to-get game described by Joe Mantagna's con artist character in Mamet's (1987) *House of Games*: "They call this a confidence game. Why? Because you give me your confidence? No, because I give you my confidence." Typically, this consisted of telling would-be investors (some of whom joined Madoff's Florida country club in the hope they could strike up a friendship) "sorry the fund is closed," only to relent when the supplicant begged him and greatly increased the size of the proposed investment. Another aspect of Situation is that most of Madoff's individual investors as well as many charitable foundation investors were, like Madoff himself, Jewish. Most Ponzi schemes can, like this one, be described as an "affiliation scam" (Sterngold 2009), as people who share an ethnic or religious identity with a scammer who typically has high status in their community (Madoff had a reputation as a Jewish philanthropist) are less likely to question his honesty.

   In the case of Greenspan, the investment was not directly with Madoff (that required a minimum investment of several million dollars), but with one of several large hedge feeder funds that turned all of its monies over to Madoff. The attraction here is that Greenspan dealt with a trusted investment adviser, a retired accountant who was a family friend and who had placed most of his own sizeable assets in the feeder fund. This adviser had several loyal friends invested through him, including one of Greenspan's closest relatives. The feeder fund, the Rye Fund, was itself part of the respected Tremont family of funds, which was part of the large Oppenheimer Group, which itself was owned by Mass Mutual, one of the largest insurance companies in the U.S. The fund was, furthermore, audited by one of the biggest accounting companies in the country. The substantial fees Greenspan paid (the usual annual hedge fund 2/20 fee (2 % of balance plus 20 % of profit) to the Rye fund plus in this case a 1 % of balance annual fee to the adviser who provided access to the feeder fund), was supposed to ensure that it was a carefully-monitored and safe investment, producing a respectable (around 10 % after fees) and secure return. In fact, all these various highly-compensated finance professionals did in return for those fees was to add up Madoff's phony monthly trading slips (without questioning the basis for the hand-written amounts) and then compare them with the phony numbers entered into the monthly balance statements produced by Madoff's high school-educated underlings toiling with historic stock market data on anti-quated computers on a locked and closely-guarded floor in Phillip Johnson's famous "lipstick" building.

7.6.1.2 Cognition

The cognitive skill needed to survive in a complex financial situation is ability to recognize risk in a proposed investment (Conquest Research Ltd 2004). Although a reasonably intelligent person (a retired college professor with a doctorate), as well as the author of a recently-published semi-scholarly book on gullibility, Greenspan was a relative ignoramus when it came to finance and lacked that skill, except perhaps in an obvious case (such as an invitation via internet from an aggrieved Nigerian prince). Greenspan readily acknowledged that he lacked the skills to actively manage his own investments, which is why he relied on funds run by and suggested by trusted advisers. This was a tactic which had worked well for him in the past and he saw no reason to doubt that it would work in this case. Unfortunately, Greenspan lacked the ability to see the dangers stemming not only from a skilled con operator, but from the incompetence, blindness and laziness of those he paid to ensure the safety of his retirement investment.

7.6.1.3 Personality

The personality trait most important in explaining gullible investing is interpersonal trust (Maister et al. 2000). Greenspan is pretty high on this trait, but it is a differ-entiated form of trust, as it depends on the context. In some settings, such as when listening to politicians or telemarketers or religious claims, Greenspan is the epit-ome of a skeptic. But when it comes to the financial suggestions of someone who is vouched for by others, Greenspan tends to put his skepticism on the shelf. This person-by-situation view of personality, espoused by Mischel (Mischel and Mendoza-Denton 2003), undoubtedly also reflects the role of Cognition, as Greenspan is more likely to be skeptical when an assertion conflicts with a topic (such as political history) where he has a great deal of content knowledge, but less likely to be skeptical when the topic (such as investment strategy) is one he knows little about. However, even this is insufficiently differentiated, as he was able a few years earlier to express deep skepticism when pitched an investment in a deep tax shelter that later was shut down by the IRS. His lack of trust in that instance reflected a personality position (Greenspan believes that excessive use of even legal tax loopholes is morally wrong) but also reflected the fact that he had read some warning articles about such schemes as well as the fact that the person pitching the scheme lacked impressive credentials.

7.6.1.4 State

A motivating state factor underlying any questionable investment, is a wish to become richer, or at any rate, to attain greater financial security (Partnoy 2014). This factor undoubtedly played a role in Greenspan's decision to invest in the Madoff feeder fund, as it seemed to answer his need for an investment with a steady decent return as he entered his retirement years. Greed is too strong a word to use here, as a truly greedy person would likely not be satisfied with a 10 % annual return. Another motivator, lesser but still explaining some small degree of the variance, is that Greenspan's had enormous regard for the charismatic financial advisor and thought it would be attractive to become a client of his.

It is not possible at this point, to place a numeric value on each of the contributing factors, or to generate a quantitative formula indicating the likelihood that Greenspan would have behaved gullibly when he was offered the opportunity to move a chunk of his retirement savings into the Madoff feeder fund. But this multi-factorial retrospective analysis helps, we believe, to explain why Greenspan was someone unlikely to resist what in retrospect was a disastrous decision. There was, however, a major secondary (ego but also to some extent financial) gain that accrued as a result of the decision and his writing about it, and that is that Greenspan went from being a relatively obscure social scientist to someone whose ideas about gullibility and foolish behavior have attained some degree of public currency (Griffin 2009).

7.6.2 Magon de La Villehuchet Gullibiity Analysis

7.6.2.1 Situation

Just as Shiller's feedback loop theory explains Greenspan's decision to invest in a feeder fund (or richer individual investors' decisions to invest directly with Madoff), it also explains the behavior of fund managers such as René-Thierry Magon de La Villehuchet to turn the AIA group into a two billion dollar Madoff feeder fund and to keep that arrangement in place even when given urgent warning that to do so was to court severe danger. In this case, there were a few early fund investors with very large Madoff positions, and they did very well for their investors and their fund managers. This news probably was shared with other fund managers, who then became motivated to emulate their colleagues and to jump on the Madoff bandwagon. The funds became especially important to Madoff, as he needed the huge multi-billion dollar infusions from hedge funds to produce enough cash to pay off the many investors who made withdrawals on a regular basis (using Madoff's firm as a kind of ATM machine). This explains in part why Madoff's scheme began to lose some of its affiliation/Jewish flavor over time, as Madoff had to some extent exhausted that ethnic resource, and had to turn to new non-Jewish sources of investment, in Europe (e.g., the AIA group) and also in Asia. It was in fact the global financial crisis in 2007–2008 that precipitated the implosion of the Madoff scheme, as fund managers began seeking to liquidate their large positions in Madoff in order to cover their losses from other investments, with the result that Madoff ran out of cash to keep his house of cards standing.

7.6.2.2 Cognition

A surprising aspect of the Madoff story is that hedge fund managers who were paid enormous fees (the typical 2/20 described earlier) did nothing for their money other than look at the phony reports from Madoff's firm and see if the increases in the net total jibed with the sums reflected in the phony undated trading slips. Although these fund managers, including Magon de La Villehuchet, were lauded for their financial acumen, in fact they got a free ride and were able to pose as more competent than they really were. Of course they were exposed as poseurs when it turns out they did nothing to earn their success and in fact their success turned out to be a massive failure. In terms of Mr. Magon de La Villehuchet's social and practical intelligence, the only thing we know is that when faced with the biggest test of his life, namely the need to decide what to do with the information that Madoff might be (and probably was) a crook, he flunked it cold.

7.6.2.3 Personality

Not enough is known about Magon de La Villehuchet to say anything about his personality, but it seems from his automatic rejection of the news that his hedge fund's enormous assets were at risk that he was somewhat rigidly defensive about accepting a piece of information that did not fit with his preconceived ideas about this very urgent matter. A social psychology formulation that applies to Magon de La Villehuchet and all of the others who refused to act on the *Barron's* article and the public accusations of Harry Markopolis is known as the theory of Cognitive Dissonance (Festinger 1957). This well-researched theory predicts that when a new fact conflicts with a held belief, one will either change the belief or else find some way of disputing or denying the reality of the fact. An example would be someone torn between buying a Mercedes versus a BMW, and who then spends a great deal of money on a BMW only to run across a report saying the Mercedes is a better car. The most typical course of behavior would be to dismiss the credentials or honesty of the author of the report and/or seek out information that extols the superior virtues of BMWs.

Of course, in the case of the Madoff investment, to accept the possibility that the informant was correct would bring with it enormous anxiety and discomfort, not to mention tremendous uncertainty and effort (for example, having to find a way of bringing comparable returns to the AIA investors that would actually involve some work and would also expose the investment incompetence of the fund's managers). Basically, this was a matter of balancing two risks: the risk that the informant was correct (in which case, the whole fund was in danger) versus the risk that the informant was wrong (in which case the danger would be ticking Madoff off and seeming rash). Obviously the latter risk paled in importance when compared to the former risk, which explains why Magon de La Villehuchet doing nothing can be described as an exercise in self-deception. In fact, these were not risks that required blind faith but could have been vetted through independent analysis and further digging by Magon de La Villehuchet or other hedge fund managers given similar news. That they did nothing reinforces the above description of these financiers as far less intelligent than they thought themselves to be, based on a definition of intelligence that includes the ability to evaluate and weigh risk. His loss of a self-image as a person of great intelligence probably explains Magon de La Villehuchet's suicide as much or more than the loss of a great deal of his own and other's money.

7.6.2.4 State

There is one huge motivator for the behavior of hedge fund managers in partnering with (and refusing to abandon) Madoff that has not been given sufficient attention. In fact, in itself it is a huge red flag that some have pointed to as an indication that at least some of the hedge fund managers might have suspected that something fishy was afoot. The motivator is that while the fund managers were charging huge fees while pretending to be actively managing their clients' money, Madoff himself only charged the funds a standard brokerage fee for buying and selling their securities (one reason the portfolio holdings were so constantly being churned by him) and his firm received no payment at all for the critical activity of managing clients' portfolios. There is absolutely no rational explanation for giving the feeder funds and other big investors such a sweetheart deal but one: Madoff needed to make investing with him so unbelievably profitable so as to make it unthinkable for the fund managers to pull out. In fact, there were a few big funds that considered going with Madoff, but they were wise and diligent enough to figure out that doing so could be a very dangerous mistake. Unfortunately, probably for legal reasons, they declined to make their conclusions public or to share them with regulatory agencies.

All four of the factors contributed to some extent to the gullibility of René-Thierry Magon de La Villehuchet and the other Madoff feeder hedge fund managers, both in the initial turning of billions over to Madoff, to their almost inexplicable refusal to consider the possibility that it was a Ponzi scheme when credible complaints about the scheme began to be made (in Magon de La Villehuchet's case from a highly expert consultant hired to check the investment out). The biggest contributor here is the fact that other, even bigger funds, were (and stayed) on board, giving the investment the seeming safety that comes from social validation.

The state (affect) motivator driving this engine (and something that should have been a huge warning sign) was the incredible sweetheart deal of being charged by Madoff only a broker fee for churning the accounts. A personality consideration was the understandable self-deception explained by the theory of cognitive dissonance (the fact that the short-term pain and effort caused by taking the warning seriously far exceeded the pain of continuing with self-delusion). Finally, this whole self-deception enterprise was propped up by the fact that these so-called financial experts were no more than bean counters who compared bogus handwritten non-time-stamped trading slips (which should have aroused suspicion) against the monthly account balance statements sent to them.

7.7   Conclusion

Most personal relationships operate on a basis of trust (Barber 1983). We trust our friends, relatives and colleagues to keep their word and to look out for our interests, and we do the same with people who appear to be honest and reputable financial advisors. Sometimes, our trust is betrayed without warning, but when it comes to financial betrayal there are usually warning signs which the least wise (such as the man who fell for an online inheritance scam) will ignore and the most wise (such the very few who suspected Madoff early) will take seriously. Survival in the social world does not require a reluctance to trust, but does require an ability to see warning signs and to take them seriously. Most interactions, whether between advisers and clients, or between financial institutions, operate on a basis of informal arrangements without written contracts or significant amounts of scrutinizing. This is as it should be, as the world would be a grim place indeed if we had to be constantly on guard against deceit. Usually trusting others works out well, and our trust is rewarded. But occasionally, we find ourselves in a situation where to be trusting is to put oneself in serious harm's way. Almost always, there are warning signs, or we possess prior knowledge of others who have been foolish enough to pursue such a transaction. An example is Mr. Smithson getting an email message from Daniel Okundo, who claimed to be an attorney handling a large inheritance from a previously unknown relative. Probably over 99 % of recipients of such a message know enough to delete it immediately. But some people, either extremely unworldly, or amazingly trusting, or seriously in need of a financial miracle, would pursue the matter further. These people are in trouble but they do not know it. For once you enter into the web of a skilled con artist, it is difficult to keep from becoming further ensnared (Ford 1999).

Foolish financial decisions do not always take place in response to an evil manipulator such as Bernard Madoff, but when they do, many quite intelligent people can be victimized, especially when others they respect and trust have also fallen into the manipulator's trap and have not yet found out what it really is. In this paper, we have used a four-factor theory of investor gullibility (induced social risk-unawareness) to shed light on an intriguing question, namely why is it that relatively vulnerable people (such as the elderly ladies who fell for Earl Jones) or relatively non-vulnerable people (such as the first author of this paper who fell for a sales pitch by an also-swindled advisor) can become victims of financial fraud.

References

Arvedlund, E.E. 2001, May 7. Don't ask, don't tell—Bernie Madoff is so secretive, he even asks investors to keep mum. *Barron's*.

Barber, B. 1983. *The logic and limits of trust*. New Brunswick, NJ: Rutgers University Press.

Berecz, J.M. 1992. *Understanding Tourette syndrome, obsessive compulsive disorder, and related problems: A developmental and catastrophe theory perspective*. New York: Springer.

Berenson, A. and M. Saltmarsh. 2009, Han. 2. Madoff investor's suicide leaves questions. In *The New York Times*, p. B1. New York.

Bruemmer, R. 2009, July 19. Uncle Earl: Is Earl Jones our Madoff?. *National Post*.

Byrne, D.G., J. Mazanov, and R.P.M. Gregson. 2001. A cusp catastrophe analysis of changes in adolescent smoking behavior in response to smoking prevention programs. *Nonlinear Dynamics, Psychology, and Life Sciences* 5(2): 115–137.

Carver, C.S., and M.F. Scheier. 1998. *On the self-regulation of behavior*. Cambridge, UK: Cambridge University Press.

Chayevsky, P. 1995. *The collected works of Paddy Chayevsky: The screen plays*, vol. 2. New York: Applause Books.

Cialdini, R.B. 1984. *Influence: The psychology of persuasion*. New York: William Morrow.

Clair, S. 1998. A cusp catastrophe model for adolescent alcohol use: An empirical test. *Nonlinear Dynamics, Psychology, and Life Sciences* 2(3): 217–241.

Conquest Research Ltd. 2004. *Consumer understanding of financial risk*. London: Financial Services Authority.

Dearing, S. 2009, July 21. The case of Canada's Earl Jones and the missing $50 million. *Digital Journal*.

Denburg, N.L., C.A. Cole, M. Hernandez, T.H. Yamada, D. Tranel, A. Bechara, and R.B. Wallace. 2007. The orbitofrontal cortex, real-world decision-making, and aging. *Annals of the New York Academy of Sciences* 1121: 480.

Festinger, L. 1957. *A theory of cognitive dissonance*. Palo Alto, CA: Stanford University Press.

Flay, B.R. 1978. Catastrophe theory in social psychology: Some applications to attitudes and behavior. *Behavioral Sciences* 78: 335–350.

Ford, C.V. 1999. *Lies! lies!! lies!!!: The psychology of deceit*. Alexandria, VA: American Psychiatric Publishing Inc.

Fulford, R. 2008, December 28. Ponzi would have been proud. *The National Post*.

Gollwitzer, P.M. 1996. The volitional benefits of planning. In *The psychology of action: Linking cognition and motivation in behavior*, ed. P.M. Gollwitzer, and J.A. Bargh, 287–312. New York: Guilford Press.

Greenspan, S. 2009a. Foolish action in adults with Intellectual Disabilities: The forgotten problem of risk-unawareness. In *International review of research in mental retardation*, ed. L.M. Glidden. New York: Elsevier.

Greenspan, S. 2009b. *Annals of gullibility: Why we are duped and how to avoid it*. Westport, CT: Praeger.

Greenspan, S. 2009c, January 3. Why we keep falling for financial scams. *Wall Street Journal*.

Greenspan, S., H.N. Switzky, and G.W. Woods. 2011. Intelligence involves risk-awareness and Intellectual Disability involves risk-unawareness: Implications of a theory of common sense. *Journal of Intellectual & Developmental Disability* 36(4): 1–33.

Griffin, G. 2009, March 3. Scam expert from CU expertly scammed. *Denver Post*.

Gyulai, L. 2009, July 15. Jones a smooth-talking flirt, friend says: Charmed "little old ladies" out of their money with promise of an eight-percent return. *Montreal Gazette*.

Henriques, D.B. 2012. *Thewizard of lies: Bernard Madoff and the death of trust*. New York: St. Martin's Press.

Katz, Alan. 2009, January 2. Madoff investor's suicide was an 'act of honor,' brother says, *Bloomberg News*.

LaBute, N. 2004. *Fat pig*. London: Faber & Faber.

Lanza, M.L. 1999. Catastrophe theory: Application of nonlinear dynamics to assault victim responses. *Journal of the American Psychiatric Nurses Association* 5(4): 117–121.

Maister, D.H., C.H. Green, and R.M. Galford. 2000. *The trusted advisor*. New York: Free Press.

Mamet, D. 1987. *House of games*. Los Angeles: Film.

Markopolos, H. 2010. *No one would listen: A true financial thriller*. New York: Wiley.

Milovanovic, D. 2002. *Critical criminology at the edge: Postmodern perspectives, integration, and applications*. Westport, CT: Praeger.

Mischel, W., and R. Mendoza-Denton. 2003. Harnessing willpower and socioemotional intelligence to enhance human agency and potential. In *A psychology of human strengths: Fundamental questions and future directions for a positive psychology*, ed. L.G. Aspinwall, and U.M. Staudinger, 245–256. Washington, DC: American Psychological Association.

Mordekar, A., and S. Spence. 2008. Personality disorder in older people: How common is it and what can be done? *Advances in Psychiatric Treatment* 14: 171–177.

Partnoy, F. 2014. *Infectious greed: How deceit and risk corrupted the financial markets*. New York: Henry Holt & Co.

Perkins, D.N. 2002. The engine of folly. In *Why smart people can be so stupid*, ed. R.J. Sternberg, 64–85. New Haven: Yale University Press.

Rotter, J.B. 1980. Interpersonal trust, trustworthiness and gullibility. *American Psychologist* 35: 1–7.

Sameroff, A. 1975. Transactional models in early social relations. *Human Development* 18: 65–79.

Shiller, R.J. 2000. *Irrational exuberance*. Princeton, NJ: Princeton University Press.

Snow, N.E. 2009. *Virtue as social intelligence: An empirically grounded theory*. New York: Routledge.

Sterngold, J. 2009, September 1. Mormons become victims in $50 million scam to sell gold bullion. Bloomberg.

Stewart, I.N., and P.L. Peregoy. 1983. Catastrophe theory modeling in psychology. *Psychological Bulletin* 94(2): 336–362.

Sundem, G. 2012. *Brain trust: 93 top scientists reveal lab-tested secrets to surfing, dating, dieting, gambling, growing man-eating plants, and more!*. New York: Crown Publishing Group.

Tesser, A. 1980. When individual dispositions and social pressure conflict: A catastrophe. *Human Relations* 33: 393–407.

Tutzauer, F. 1998. A catastrophe theory model of child abuse. *Journal of Family Issues* 5: 1–42.

van der Maas, H.R.J., R. Kolstein, and J. van der Pligt. 2003. Sudden transitions in attitudes. *Sociological Methods and Research* 32(2): 125–152.

Van Wijk, A. 2009. *Mountains of gold: Exploratory research on Nigerian 419-fraud*. Amsterdam, NLD: SWP Publishing.

Wood, S. 2014. *Cognitive factors in financial fraud victimization*. Unpublished manuscript. Claremont, CA: Scripps College.

Zuckerman, G. and D. Gauthier-Villars. 2009, February 3. A lonely lament from a whistle-blower: Mr. Markopolos regrets his failure to persuade investors. *Wall Street Journal*.

Zuckoff, M. 2005. *Ponzi's scheme: The true story of a financial legend*. New York: Random House.

Zuckoff, M. 2006. The perfect mark: How a Massachusetts psychotherapist fell for a Nigerian e-mail Scam. New Yorker, p. 6.

Chapter 8
Villains, Victims and Bystanders in Financial Crime

Bruce Baer Arnold and Wendy Bonython

Abstract White collar crime causes more pain to national economies, employees and investors than blue collar theft involving violence. Perhaps unsurprisingly, because that financial crime is often undertaken by well-educated, charming, softly spoken and socially adroit peers rather than by people who fit stereotypes about violent offenders, it has received less attention from psychologists and criminologists. This chapter considers the psychology of financial crime in terms of the criminals, their victims and bystanders such as government regulators and auditors who might be expected to prevent harms associated with figures such as Madoff, Maxwell and Stanford. It offers an overview of theories of what motivates the criminals, why some people are receptive to exploitation, and why systems of belief in gatekeeper institutions result in regulatory incapacity that inhibits effective risk identification and action to minimise that crime. The chapter highlights particular incidents since the 1880s, arguing that financial crime is a systemic problem that requires active management. It also argues that the psychology of financial crime is diverse, inducing caution about explanations purportedly enabling systematic prediction and prevention of large-scale offences.

8.1 Introduction

I've seen lots of funny men; Some will rob you with a six-gun, And some with a fountain pen.

(Guthrie 1947)

What drives a person to blatantly and repeatedly manipulate and deceive so many people for so long on such a grand scale? How can there be such a complete absence of remorse?

B.B. Arnold (✉) · W. Bonython
Canberra Law School, University of Canberra, Canberra, Australia
e-mail: Bruce.Arnold@canberra.edu.au

W. Bonython
e-mail: Wendy.Bonython@canberra.edu.au

© Springer International Publishing Switzerland 2016
M. Dion et al. (eds.), *Financial Crimes: Psychological, Technological, and Ethical Issues*, International Library of Ethics, Law, and the New Medicine 68, DOI 10.1007/978-3-319-32419-7_8

And why would such a man, after enduring public humiliation to the extent that he has - as a result of his own deeds - still crave and expect adulation from the masses, all the while denying any blame for past events.

(Verrender 2008)

Financial crime—often characterised as 'white collar crime' involving an exploitation of trust and misuse of authority, rather than violence and physical strength—causes more pain to national economies, employees and investors[1] than the 'blue collar' property offences by an 'other' that have preoccupied several generations of criminologists, law enforcement personnel and psychologists.[2] Scholars have highlighted the social distinction between 'criminals' and 'us' (Weisburd et al. 2001). Perhaps unsurprisingly, because financial crime is often undertaken by socially adroit, softly-spoken, well-educated and well-groomed 'people like us'—it has received less scholarly attention than research into criminals who fit stereotypes about violent offenders, psychological problems and social disadvantage (Moore and Milles 1990; Shover and Hochstetler 2006; Levi 1992).

This chapter considers the psychology of financial crime in terms of the criminals, their victims, and bystanders including government regulators and auditors who might be expected to prevent the harms associated with the actions of figures such as Bernard Madoff, Robert Maxwell, Ivar Krueger, Toshihide Iguchi, Therese Humbert, Bernard Ebbers, Jabez Balfour, Alan Bond, Raj Rajaratnam and Allen Stanford. A hypothesis is that the psychology of offenders—in terms of their motivations and their interactions with other people that enable them to commit financial crimes—is diverse. There is no ideal type of financial criminal and from a criminological perspective the empirical basis to substantiate theorisation since the 1920s remains weak. A consequential hypothesis is that potential victims, bystanders and regulators cannot rely on a single psychological profile for predicting and thus preventing large-scale financial crime.

The chapter thus offers an overview of theories of what motivates the criminals, why some people are receptive to exploitation, and why systems of belief in gatekeeper institutions on occasion result in regulatory incapacity that inhibits effective risk identification and minimisation. It highlights particular incidents since the 1880s. The historical perspective indicates that financial crime is a systemic problem—a function of human nature and risk taking—rather than something that is unique to our era or readily addressed through psychological forecasting. This chapter begins by discussing the concept of financial crime, noting disagreement among criminologists, legal practitioners, institutions and other stakeholders about what constitutes financial crime. In laying foundations for an exploration of

---

[1]Just one fraud committed by businessman Alan Bond was worth the same amount as all household burglary committed in Australia over 18 months (Job 1999).

[2]The concept of 'financial crime' is discussed later in this chapter. The authors have relied on the expansive definition in the 2001 International Monetary Fund 'Financial System Abuse, Financial Crime and Money Laundering', which refers to "any non-violent crime that generally results in a financial loss, including financial fraud". See also Ryder (2011). *Financial Crime in the 21st Century: Law and Policy*. Cheltenham: Edward Elgar.

psychology it argues that the concept is capacious, with criminal activity encompassing both new and traditional technologies and involving diverse demographics. The chapter illustrates that argument through reference to financial crimes in Europe, North America and Australia over the past 150 years, on the basis that although financial systems and laws change there are continuities in the behavior of financial criminals and their victims. The chapter next considers notions of profiling (including pre-employment vetting) and taxonomies of 'the financial criminal' as the basis for exclusion or detection of criminals. It argues that irrespective of the usefulness of taxonomies, information may be misread or ignored by gatekeepers and may by subverted by potential criminals. That is unsurprising, given that potential offenders have an incentive to achieve and remain in positions of trust. The third part of the chapter offers an overview of financial crime demographics, demonstrating that the attributes of potential offenders are so diverse as to both preclude comprehensive filtering and to pose questions about past stereotypes promoted by pioneering psychologists such as Lombroso. The authors then consider what is inside the head of the financial criminal, highlighting questions about sources of information for understanding criminal motivation, the extent to which some criminal activity is irrational and the usefulness of some broad analyses from mid last century.

The chapter then suggests that one mechanism for understanding the psychology of financial crime in general is to adapt the seven deadly sins, i.e. opportunity, rationalisation, need, greed, emulation, anger, pleasure, fear and misjudgment. Understanding financial crime requires awareness that it involves victims and bystanders, rather than merely offenders. We can gain insights by considering those actors—and questions of trust, subversion and victimisation—in relation to offenders. In building on that discussion the chapter then deals with the gatekeeper mindset, suggesting reasons why the psychology of crime prevention and detection personnel within and outside organizations inhibits comprehensive responses to figures such as Madoff. On the basis of the previous examination the authors suggest a wariness about notions of medicalising financial crime, because there's no single type of offence and offender and because courts have not accepted that the crime is typically attributable to a psychological disorder most appropriately addressed by therapy rather than punishment. The chapter's final section draws three conclusions regarding the crimes, the criminals and responses.

8.2   Can We Effectively Profile Financial Criminals and Victims?

It is axiomatic that financial crime involves a misuse of trust, authority and expertise in relation to individuals and organisations (Stotland 1977; Wong 2005; Braithwaite 1985; Quinney 1977; Friedrichs 1996). The notion of financial crime is capacious and encompasses activities such as embezzlement, bribery and corporate misconduct and large-scale fraud. In making sense of that crime we need to recognise that it involves a range of offenders, some of whom act on a strategic and well-considered basis and others of whom act without much thought. We also need to recognise that their success or failure involves other actors, i.e. victims, bystanders and regulators. Understanding financial crime involves understanding social, institutional and technological contexts rather than just looking at the psychology of those people who have been successfully prosecuted.

What do those financial criminals look like? What goes on inside their heads (Walters and Geyer 2004) when, like Bernie Madoff (Henriques 2011; Arvedlund 2009; Markopolos 2010) and Allen Stanford (Geis 2012), they make billions of dollars disappear in investment scams; like Robert Maxwell (Bower 1996; Greenslade 1992) they blithely loot the corporate pension fund; like Australian entrepreneur Alan Bond (Barry 2000) they gift themselves with shareholder assets; or like a succession of 'rogue traders' they illegally try to cover up a billion dollar bout of 'irrational exuberance' (Gapper 2011; Wexler 2010)? Is there a fundamental difference in the psychological attributes of petty fraudsters—for example the clerk or book-keeper engaged in a small-scale embezzlement—and someone who consciously steals a billion dollars or who criminally conceals a billion dollar loss attributable to misjudgment? The psychological processes involved in how those people understand their worlds and deal with other people (and with systems that are meant to bound risk or minimise both the incidence and seriousness of offences) is innately interesting. An awareness of motivations, inhibitions and engagement is potentially useful in building compliance mechanisms and, more ambitiously, in making recruitment decisions.

Do their victims suffer from a psychological deficit in accepting offers that were indeed too good to be true (Shichor 1998)? Are they the sort of uneducated and naive individuals who are safeguarded from themselves under consumer protection law in Australia and similar jurisdictions? What about the people in government agencies and private sector gatekeepers who appear to have misunderstood or disregarded red flags indicating that large-scale financial crime was underway (Langevoort 2009)? We need to think about minds because appearances are unenlightening. The perpetrators of financial crime sometimes look just like you and work alongside you, with managers in Australia for example diverting A$20 million (*R v O'Carrigan* [2013] QCA 327) and A$16 million (Elks 2013) of funds into personal accounts, and others embezzling smaller sums while ostensibly guarding against defalcation (Oberhardt 2007). The perpetrators may indeed look better than you: they may have an account in Vaduz or a private bank in the Caymans (Young 2012), along with the finest legal counsel and accountants that money can buy (Chenoweth 2006) and a reputation as an exemplary member of the community (Fairfax 2001; Perri and Brody 2012). Depending on the definition of financial crime, they may be teenage hackers living next door, rather than members of the Siberian cyber *mafiya* (Brenner 2002; Williams 1997; Grabosky et al. 2001). In a world where fine art and antiquities are currencies, they may instead be adding a signature to a painting that may or may not have been near an Indigenous artist or old master, but sells for several million (Alder 1999; Chappell and Polk 2008). They may be the victim's children and other loved ones, 'borrowing' that person's credit to give new meaning to the phrase 'sexually acquired debt'.

8.3   Diverse Offences, Diverse Offenders?

What is financial crime? This critical question affects how (or indeed whether) we understand criminals and potential criminals. Braithwaite's cogent 1993 'Crime and the Average American' in discussing key research suggested that financial crime encompassed offences such as embezzlement, tax fraud, securities fraud, bribery, insurance/bank fraud, postal/wire fraud and anticompetitive behaviour (Braithwaite 1991, 1993; Weisburd et al. 2001). We might infer that financial crime in all its diversity is—along with domestic violence—the crime of the average person. It may involve quite low tech or remarkably modern technologies (Harris 1987; Phelan and Chester 1997; Fay et al. 1972; Irving 1972; Worrall 2003; Soble and Dallos 1975; Jory 2005; Greenleaf 2007; Jackson and Ligertwood 2006; Graham 1990).

For some critics the activities of Madoff (Henriques 2011) and Maxwell (Bower 1996) are financial crime par excellence: large amounts of money, readily discernable offenders, behaviour such as ostentatious spending or flight and extradition that gains headlines. So too that of Bond (Barry 2000), Skase (Hoyte 2003; Clarke et al. 2003), Skilling (Watkins and Swartz 2003) and Adler (Barry 2002; Avison and Wilson 2002; Royal Commission 2003) along with peers such as Kreuger (Shaplen 1960; Partnoy 2009; Flesher and Flesher 1986), Humbert (Spurling 2000), Ponzi (Zuckoff 2005), Wright (Covick and Vickers 2003), Balfour (McKie 2004; Robb 1992), Israel (Lawson 2012), Vesco (Herzog 1987), Cornfeld (Raw et al. 1971), Savundra (Connell and Sutherland 1979), Carver (Keneley 2008) and Minkow (Akst 1990; Domanick 1989).

There is less agreement about the 'rogue trader' phenomenon (Krawiec 2000; Markham 1995). That is unsurprising because the villains are perceived to be large banks and insurance firms, rather than individuals. From a psychological perspective, discussed in more detail at the end of this chapter, it is unsurprising because some offenders and observers have relied on a 'medicalisation' model of crime and thus been quick to blame intolerable pressure, addiction, depression or other psychological justifications (Levi 2006; Lampe 1991). From a research perspective that disagreement is fostered by self-justificatory memoirs by figures such as Leeson (1996) and Jett (2004) that emphasise corporate victimisation of the offender rather than the fact that rogue traders have disregarded corporate protocols and in some instances knowingly broken the law through concealment of activity, diversion of funds and so forth.

8.4   Profiling and Prophecy

Criminal profiling is identification of actual or potential offenders on the basis of behavioral or other attributes, such as age, education, income, gender and prior convictions (Kocsis and Palermo 2006; Bartol and Bartol 2008). It may be forensic: retrospectively identifying an offender after a crime has taken place, the stuff of countless whodunits and movies (Snook et al. 2008). It may instead be predictive, attempting to identify and thereby inhibit potential criminals or exclude them from positions where they can cause a financial injury (Ramamoorti et al. 2014). It has become popular because it is founded on 'common sense' assumptions in popular culture and much public policymaking that responds to those assumptions, the same sort of assumptions that divert police resources to address the threat that you will be murdered/molested by a stranger rather than by intimates (Glassner 2000; Collins 2005; Potter and Potter 2001). It is also popular because it embodies society's faith in science (the supposed 'CSI Effect' fostered by the mass media (Tyler 2006a, b; Kocsis and Hayes 2004; Faigman 1999; Shelton 2008) or pseudo-science (Beyerstein and Beyerstein 1992; Panchasi 1996; Driver et al. 1996; Klimoski, and Rafaeli 1983; Spohn 1997), statistics (Ziliak and McCloskey 2007; Young 2004)—what Young dubbed 'voodoo criminology'.

A contention of this chapter is that predictive profiling of financial criminals has not advanced much beyond crude recruitment-level vetting (Tett et al. 1991; Walley and Smith 1998) and inferences from an individual's sweaty palms, nervous demeanour ("a claimant who adopts an inappropriately nervous or aggressive manner in talking to a claims handler may indicate a potential fraudster" Morley et al. 2006) or knowledge of claim procedures (Morse and Skajaa 2007). The 2006 Report on Gambling Motivated Fraud in Australia 1998–2007 from forensic accountants Warfield & Associates notes that "Pre-employment screening would have failed to identify problems with the overwhelming majority of perpetrators as they had no history of dishonesty prior to committing the frauds". Much profiling has been largely ineffective and will remain so in future. Individually and institutionally we are simply not very good at prognostics when dealing with people who do not have a criminal record. There are several reasons for that failure, which have a substantial basis in psychology.

The first reason that profiling is ineffective is that financial crime, in all its heterogeneity, is the crime of the average manager, people 'just like us' whose latent criminality is not signalled by homelessness (Draine et al. 2002), a marker such as a tattoo (Post 1968), the smell of despair (Schnall et al. 2008) or the overt psychological disorders and learning disabilities evident among many petty criminals (Derkzen et al. 2013; Butler et al. 2006). Another reason is because there are uncertainties about who is committing financial crimes—in particular who is not being caught or simply not being prosecuted (Shapiro 1985)—and why they are committing those crimes. A third reason is that leading executives and leading financial criminals (along with many of the most effective marketers or salespeople) often have the same attributes. Those attributes include decisiveness, persistence, risk taking, apparent sincerity, creativity, resilience, extraversion, disrespect for convention, a willingness to operate in grey areas and an indifference to the lives of employees, victims and partners.

Is profile building pointless? This chapter suggests that it is in fact useful. The process of building a profile is of value because it encourages thought about risk and opportunity rather through provision of a template against which the builder can reliably match suspects (Slovic 1987). More broadly that process should encourage an understanding of the psychology of people who are not criminals, irrespective of whether they lacked the opportunity or because their personal ethical framework inhibited egregious misbehaviour. A hard-headed look at demographics and motivations is disillusioning for anyone who believes that organisations can usefully filter all financial criminals through a simple set of psychological sieves. Experience suggests instead that major organisations, although susceptible to significant reputational and monetary loss, have often failed to use the filters at their disposal. Readers might wonder about the circumstances that allowed "high rolling gambler" Andrew Stathis—on bail after alleged $60 million drug trafficking deals —to buy and then loot the Bishopsgate Insurance Company (Grabosky 1989). Non-recognition by gatekeepers of warnings about problems are discussed in the final part of this chapter.

Sometimes prophecies are disregarded because they come from a subordinate. Some are disregarded because gatekeepers do not know to separate signal from noise—sometimes you can have too much data—or because corporate compliance is a responsibility of accountants whose conceptualisation of the world and of risk involves a language different to that used by psychologists. Data can be disregarded because of cognitive dissonance: it does not match preconceptions because for example the potential criminal is charming (Babiak and Hare 2006; Leff 1976; Maurer 1999), went to the right school, has an 'honest face' (Zebrowitz et al. 1998; Wiley 2005), a motorcycle but no tattoos (Rozycki 2007), does not blink when telling lies (Sackett and Harris 1984; Rust and Golombok 1999; Walters 1995), has an appetite for risk (Gilding 1999, 2004), provides what appeared to be a great CV or an outstanding history as an investment adviser, gives generously to charity, and has been accepted by the 'right' people—people like us. In practice we also often reward people for exhibiting the 'warning signs', such as aggression, greed and impatience with paperwork—the same signs that often denote a good dealmaker or executive (Khurana 2002). Risk management involves thinking about those signs in a context of motivation and opportunity rather than concentrating on isolated personality traits such as decisiveness or diligence. It requires an acceptance that silk ties, Zegna suits and a Harvard degree are not definitive signifiers of character, with offenders traditionally exploiting the assumptions underlying sumptuary legislation and accordingly deciding that if suspension of disbelief requires a furry hat or a uniform then buy, beg or steal that signifier (Groebner 2007; Hunt 1996).

Can we develop a productive taxonomy of financial crime demographics or motivations? Taxonomies are useful for conceptualisation, reporting and even fact-based action (Bowker and Star 1999; Clinard and Quinney 1967). It is unsurprising that they have been used for everything from basic differentiations between white collar and violent crime, civil versus criminal offences, through to consumers of ice cream, people with different blood groups or readers of Harry Potter (Patterson and Brown 2009). Exponents of 'blood type psychology', a pseudo-science now embedded in Japanese popular culture and corporate recruitment, for example claim that blue collar criminals are predominantly of the O blood group whereas white collar crime involves people with A group blood (Markus and Kitayama 1998).

One Californian body thus cogently advised that

> There is no stereotype or profile of people who perpetrate insurance fraud. The perpetrator could be a neighbor, a co-worker, an entrepreneur or a certified/licensed individual or institution. People involved in insurance fraud can be recruited by ringleaders to participate in large-scale fraud rings or they can be opportunists who try to bluff their way around the system (Advisory Task Force on Insurance Fraud 2008; Derrig and Zicko 2002).

That is consistent with observations—common in financial risk management and criminological literature—that

- financial crimes are often easier to detect in retrospect than to forecast
- financial crimes involve an interaction of opportunity, rationalisation and incentive (positive or negative)
- there is no 'ideal' or typical financial criminal, i.e. one whose appearance or activity provides a useful template for sorting sheep from wolves.

8.5   Cautions About 'Deprivation' Models

Criminologist Edwin Sutherland supposedly developed the notion of white collar crime "to drive a spike into theories that imputed poverty, defective personality or inability to delay gratification as causes of crime" (Sutherland 1983). Those theories had provided a conceptual framework for criminologists and public policymakers because they implied that societies could deal with crime by eliminating poverty through social welfare or economic growth, by education, by confinement of the insane and by 'social prophylaxis' such as sterilisation of those who carried the 'genes' for delinquency, 'theft' or 'moral idiocy' (Wetzell 2000; Largent 2007; Garton 1994).

It is clear from Australian and overseas statistics, from law reports and from a plethora of anecdotal accounts in the mass media that financial crime is not restricted to

- the 'binary proletariat' (the people behind the cash register or front counter) or to the poor
- large private sector enterprises and government agencies (Sutton and Wild 1985)
- a particular gender (Goldstraw et al. 2005), ethnic group, sexual affinity or religious faith

- people without a tertiary education or with a particular type of education
- those without a positive image in the local community, apparent for example in *R v Reginald John Rich & Craig Weston Hynes* (1997) 68 SASR 390 [1997] SASC 6639; [1997] SASC 6153
- people with a gambling or substance abuse problem
- people from a broken home or undergoing a relationship meltdown
- those who are ugly or those who are conventionally beautiful (Carré and McCormick 2008)
- those with children or other dependents versus those who are feckless or 'fancy-free.'

It has been claimed that people with specific attributes are more likely to engage in financial crime (or specific types of financial crime): for example that women are more likely to engage in petty 'front office' embezzlement, or that members of particular groups are more likely to encounter 'temptations' but lack internalised ethical/religious constraints against misbehaviour (Daly 1989; Zaplin 2007; Zeitz 1981; Dodge 2013). Strip away cultural biases and the subjectivity of those claims becomes apparent. Women, for example, appear to be underrepresented among large-scale corporate crime because they are underrepresented in the board room and the executive suite rather than because they possess a special gene for financial probity (Tupman 1994; Steffensmeier et al. 2013; Robb 2006). A 2006 BDO Kendall study in New Zealand and Australia, covering over 500 charitable organisations reported that more women than men defraud their nonprofit employers, with average loss of NZ$50,0000 relative to NZ$300,000 from a commercial enterprise (employment in the NZ nonprofit sector is heavily weighted towards women). Bigotry about particular ethnic groups having a "higher risk factor" through a "cultural predisposition" to gambling or conspicuous consumption—or the wrong blood type—is not borne out by the statistics and one analyst percipiently notes the tinge of anti-semitism evident in some commentary about Madoff and his victims (Langevoort 2009). Of course, even if the prejudice *du jour* could be justified, it does not provide an ethical approach and could be challenged by discrimination law (Engel et al. 2002).

Systematic surveillance of people who have survived the vetting process is beyond the capabilities of most organizations, poses challenges for evolving privacy regimes, and is inconsistent with contemporary corporate statements that "our people are our greatest resource". It is axiomatic that many of the reader's colleagues—and, judging by media exposes about celebrity executives—drink, gamble, disregard marriage vows, break the law (e.g. drive too fast or use recreational drugs), live beyond their means or practice the casuistry taught by the very best law and business schools. Not all of them are or will become financial criminals.

Two salient conclusions can be drawn. The first is that a 'deprivation' model is likely to be ineffective as the basis for predicting financial crime. The second is that a concentration on people with a different gender, ethno-religious affinity, cultural and educational background is likely to be perceived by courts and observers at large to be discriminatory. One response is that in seeking to understand and inhibit financial crime we should draw on what is known about how financial criminals see the world rather than looking at particular classes.

8.6   Inside the Financial Criminal's Head?

Why do people engage in financial crime? How do they see the world and, for example, deal with perceived danger of detection or harm to victims? A contention in this chapter, based on examination of the scholarly literature and of accounts by criminals, is that there is considerable uncertainty among professionals. One reason for that uncertainty, usually overlooked, is that much of what we know about motivation and criminal psychology comes from the criminals themselves. From a forensic perspective that is restrictive. Criminals lie, during and after the offence. Criminals boast. Criminals find excuses and so do their lawyers (Wheeler 1992; Mackenzie 2005; Gleeson 1995). Explanations of motivation in pleadings during civil and criminal litigation are thus biased towards what offenders and advocates consider will be persuasive, with for example reference to need rather than greed and to fear or substance abuse rather than carefully-considered planning.

From a research perspective conviction of a financial criminal does not necessarily result in honesty, and why should it? As a culture we often appear keen to be deceived twice: first through the actual crime and then in print or on screen. That is inconvenient if we are relying on tales from criminals for insights about their motivation. It is problematic for anyone seeking an identikit that forecasts future crime, rather than neatly packages what has already taken place, or merely who has been prosecuted (given indications that much financial crime in the private sector is unreported to prevent individual embarrassment or preserve corporate reputations) (Deem 2000; Fletcher 2007; Levi 2001).

What is apparent is that motivation is diverse, just like the crimes. From a historical rather than a narrowly psychological perspective people have been asking what causes someone to become a financial criminal for as long as there has been financial crime and long before there were financial institutions (Rowbotham and Stevenson 2003; Cook 2001). The answers have changed, but arguably have not become more useful. Some theorists have looked to the 'inner man' for answers to the question, assuming that criminality is innate and that what is 'bred in the bone' will appear whenever there is an opportunity. Exponents of neurocriminology are similarly experiencing limited success in retrospective and prospective identification of financial crime (Raine et al. 2012).

Physiognomists profitably peddled guidebooks and courses guaranteed to help identify a bad credit risk or a larcenous clerk. Italian criminologist Lombroso thought that financial criminals could be detected by looking at the shape of their skull: the right sort of callipers and the right sort of training would enable employers to fire a bad teller or manager before defalcation took place (Becker and Wetzell 2006; Rafter 2008; Pratt 1997). FBI head J Edgar Hoover, Henry Ford and

US billionaire Ross Perot, founder of data services giant EDS, famously assessed potential executives on the size and shape of their ears. Other gatekeepers more plausibly relied on class, family and reputation. That was predicated on the assumption that past action is a reliable indicator of future behaviour and that reports by colleagues and neighbours about sobriety, continence, domestic violence, personal hygiene and spending patterns truly reveal the past and future 'inner man' (Sandage 2005; Norris 1978). We no longer live in a village society, where the neighborhood busybody (Fitzpatrick and Gellately 1997; Ash 1997; Funder 2003) or the Nazi party blockleiter (Kater 1983; Gellately 1996; Figes 2007) knew exactly what was happening behind every lace curtain. Fear of litigation is reducing the reliability of written references as indicators of character, although people continue to rely on such documents, which may or may not have been sighted by the ostensible referee.

Enthusiasts are currently promoting tools such as psychometrics (Morgeson et al. 2007; Canhoto and Backhouse 2007; Highhouse 2002; Kapardis and Krambia-Kapardis 2006; Blinkhorn and Johnson 1990; Rieke and Guastello 1995; Ones et al. 1993; Karren and Zacharia 2007) and technologies such as magnetic resonance imaging (in the belief that the cerebral activity of financial criminals, along with that of serial killers and law-abiding gay men, may somehow be different from that of 'normal' people). It is difficult to envisage major employers insisting that company directors or front-counter staff systematically undergo examination using an MRI machine; in practice psychologists and criminologists reserve that scrutiny for practitioners of chainsaw massacres (Pridmore et al. 2005), not the executive 'rambos in pinstripes' (Byrne 1999). Other criminologists have looked at circumstances, emphasising for example the conjunction of need and opportunity (Cressey 1953). One writer for example offers the 'party theory' of property crime, a taxonomy of motivations in which some offenders engage in theft to "keep the party going" rather than merely feed the 'outer man' (or the outer woman's children).[3]

US criminologists perhaps more usefully explained fraud in terms of three factors: a supply of motivated potential offenders, the availability of suitable targets and the lack of effective control systems and capable guardians (Cohen and Felson 1979). They disagree, however, about why those offenders are motivated. Are we all potential offenders, honest only because the store-minders are vigilant (Pickett and Pickett 2002), the external watchdogs have severe sanctions, the targets are

---

[3]That taxonomy example attributes property offences to the criminal seeking to "keep things together" (crime proceeds are used for living expenses, food, shelter or child support), "keep up appearances" (the proceeds are spent in conspicuous consumption on expensive clothes, jewelry, private school fees, philanthropy or other status reinforcement) and "keep the party going" through purchase of drugs. In applying that taxonomy we might of course ask whether the party fuelled by stolen VCRs and microwave ovens is the same as that fuelled by looting an insurance company or bank, where the party might last for a whole summer in the Hamptons, Biarritz or Pearl Beach. See Topalli (2005). When Being Good Is Bad: An Expansion of Neutralization Theory. *Criminology* 43(3):797–836.

insufficiently attractive and we have been sensitised through media reports about the prosecution of the Madoff children and Maxwell children (Tyler 2006a, b)? Others such as Stotland characterise white-collar motivation as involving desire for wealth or other tangible benefits, a threat of loss (whether of those tangibles or of status), a sense of superiority (the rules do not apply to me) and an expression of power (I will show them … or show myself) (Stotland 1977). Others have differentiated between offenders with low self-control who commit crime on a non-reflexive basis when an opportunity arises, those who engage in financial crime for ego gratification (rather than for the money), and those who commit crimes "depending on personal situations in their lives" such as threat of bankruptcy or to feed a gambling habit (Benson and Moore 1992).

Levi's taxonomy divided financial crime demographics into offenders who plan their activity and those with less premeditation (Levi 1999). That is a useful differentiation from the perspective of compliance personnel and courts because financial crime is not always a strategic, sustained, carefully-calculated activity. The statistics appear to suggest that many financial offenders, particularly those dealing with small sums and without the comfort of a senior advocate on the other end of the phone, do not plan to commit a crime and to thereafter commit further crimes. Most do not have prior convictions for financial offences. Their convictions for non-financial crimes, such as domestic violence, driving under the influence or drug possession are consistent with those of many academics, medical practitioners, politicians and compliance personnel. Levi implicitly questioned the usefulness of profiling most white-collar criminals as offenders who engage in a Benthamite calculation of costs and benefits, risks and rewards, in contrast to non-financial criminals who are supposedly creatures of impulse. That has implications for corporate compliance strategies and sentencing policy founded on assumptions that financial criminals do not suffer from "inadequate impulse control" and are deterred from offences by calculating punishments signalled through statutory penalties and well-publicised judicial decisions. Subsequent researchers have perhaps pushed the impulsivity or psychopathology meme to an extreme, with one group for example drawing on psychometric tests of 150 managers in German corporations and 76 financial criminals in claiming

> Business white-collar crime is predicted by gender (males higher rates than females), low behavioral self-control, high hedonism, high narcissism, and high conscientiousness after statistically controlling for social desirability. … It is argued here that high-ranking white-collar criminals in business combine low integrity with high conscientiousness (Blickle et al. 2006).[4]

---

[4]The tests included measures of hedonism (Schwartz Value Scale), conscientiousness (NEO-FFI), narcissism (DSM-III-R), social desirability, and behavioral self-control. For a perspective see Terpstra et al. (1993). The influence of personality and demographic variables on ethical decisions related to insider trading. *The Journal of Psychology* 127(4):375–390.

A public sector auditor responded to that analysis by telling the authors "so, I'm supposed to look for actuaries who run amok if a cleaner moves the in-tray a millimetre out of place". A more positive response was "well, of course they all say that … I didn't mean to do it, so I'm not really bad". That is consistent with competing claims in court. One example is that of Raffaello Follieri, sentenced in 2008 to 54 months in a US federal prison after pleading guilty to 14 counts of wire fraud, money laundering and conspiracy. Prosecutors accused him of raising millions by claiming that special Vatican connections allowed him to buy church properties at below-market prices and redevelop them for "socially responsible" purposes. In reality he had no special rights but was simply competing against other bidders. He used investors' money to finance a lavish lifestyle, including a $37,000-a-month apartment, dinner with celebrities, designer watches and clothing. Follieri claimed that "I didn't start off with the intention of deceiving anyone. I started off with good intentions to run an honorable business and make everyone proud of me." His lawyer portrayed him as a well-intentioned businessman whose miscalculations had spun out of control, a "fundamentally good person with a generous spirit." The Assistant US Attorney characterized Follieri as a sophisticated swindler who had lured investors into something resembling a Ponzi scheme by recurrently misrepresenting his background and expertise. "It is not clear to me that investors would ever have given him a dime if they knew the truth" (Huddleston 2011).

Questions about rationality in financial crime are often persuasive (Korobkin and Ulen 2000), but perhaps we can resolve some uncertainties by abandoning a 'one size fits all' profile in favour of complex profiles that acknowledge

- diverse motivations
- the significance of opportunity
- the interaction of motivation with rationalisation (Nettler 1974)
- the potential for psychological disorders such as bipolar, depression and addiction
- the nature of particular offences (Cressey 1986; Leunes and Christensen 2003; Hirschi and Gottfredson 1987).

What starts as impulse may for example become a sustained pattern of behavior as the offender initially avoids detection, or he 'digs a deeper hole' in an effort to repay his initial embezzlement (Green 1993). Some may initially act on impulse but continue because further offending is exhilarating, is rationalised as justifiable (e.g. provides the revenue that allows the offender to secure the esteem of peers through acts of philanthropy) or allows the offender to play out resentment, anger and so forth. Unfortunately there has been no comprehensive cross-cultural longitudinal study that draws together data from in-depth interviews by psychologists or that, in the absence of such research, tabulates the justifications that are expressed in court by offenders. The following typology is thus impressionistic but of potential value in encouraging holistic management of risk, i.e. going beyond ideal types based on class and gender.

8.7 Seven Financial Deadly Sins?

Given the diversity of financial crime and disagreement among theorists it is tempting to revisit classical psychological and ethical models. In an address to the Australian Bankers Association several years ago one author of this chapter accordingly referred to the financial crime version of the Seven Deadly Sins, i.e. opportunity, rationalisation, need, greed, emulation, anger, pleasure, fear and misjudgment. We need opportunity (or perceived opportunity, given that some financial criminals clearly misunderstood whether that misbehaviour would be undetected and unprosecuted). We also need rationalisation, with offenders excusing their actions (Benson 1985) or indeed justifying them as an acceptable aspect of employment (Willott and Griffin 1999). Some offenders seem to truly believe that they have done no wrong … or persuade others that they have such belief. When the corporate liquidators are not on the doorstep we call that 'confidence', 'bravery' or charismatic leadership'. On occasion we link that belief (and an associated indifference to the effect on victims) to terms such as sociopathy (Levi 2002; Boddy 2011).

The first sin, one that has preoccupied social theorists for at least a millennium, is need. Some people engage in financial crime because they have to. They steal in order to feed themselves and their dependents, or to keep a roof over their heads …. or a roof in a suburb where there are more trees and less crime (Engdahl 2008). Some people engage in financial crime because they need to keep the business afloat, keep the bank away from the door, save themselves from the tax authorities or simply pay for goods and services. Australian and overseas law reports accordingly feature people who have engaged in financial crime to

- pay for a child's drug habit
- pay for their own drug habit (Seddon 2000)
- pay a dependant's legal bills
- buy a dependant out of a nasty situation overseas
- pay for private medical treatment

rather than tawdry tales of money blown on viagra, cocaine, sportscars and champagne (Belfort 2007). In the Australian case of *R v Campbell* [2001] NSWCCA 162 the court heard that a credit manager who embezzled almost A$2.4 million from his employer used the money for entertainment and, although impotent, spent some of it on an overseas property for a callgirl. Some of those motivations may be detected by data-mining (the symptoms of imminent financial collapse are often detectible by lenders or third parties) but others are unlikely to appear on the radar (Phua et al. 2005). The data on need-based crime is problematical. Critics have often claimed that gambling drives financial crime (Crofts 2002, 2003) and some anti-gambling advocates offer the syllogism that restricting gambling reduces financial crime, typically illustrated by anecdotal accounts. In Australia for example Renea Hughes confessed in 2007 that she had embezzled A$366,000 via false invoices and faked A$100,000 in salary claims, admitting that "every cent" went into slot machines and that she would lose sums of up to A $40,000 a month in binges that went until dawn. Pay clerk Theresa Lawson stole A $2.6 million to feed poker machines. The statistics, however, do not demonstrate a clear causal link. Research from the Australian Institute of Criminology and other bodies suggests there are grounds for caution (Sakurai and Smith 2005; Blaszczynski and McConaghy 1994).

What we might say is that gambling, particularly compulsive gambling and for large stakes, may be a warning sign. Unfortunately it is a sign that is often ignored. Most readers are familiar with accounts of eminent lawyers who embezzled trust accounts, priests who gave money to bookmakers, men with an addiction to horses (a $20 million addiction in the case of *R v Telford* [2004] SASC 248), officials who had a way with cheques (*The Queen v Gary Vaughn Norman Bird* (1988) 56 NTR 17), demure bookkeepers in small businesses and government agencies who extracted over a million dollars during a decade of otherwise exemplary service in order to feed poker machines pokies, or suburban mothers who pocketed money from the local social club (*Tuck v R* [1999] TASSC 135). Among financial elites the high roller—gaining high rewards through a willingness to embrace high risk, engaging in compulsive takeovers for the thrill of deal-making—may even be welcomed, partly because games are a feature of elite sociability. Your clerk is a gambler, you are an entrepreneur. Australian criminologist Peter Grabosky, in discussing Andrew Stathis' looting of Bishopsgate Insurance, asked "How could a high-rolling gambler on bail for alleged drug offences hoodwink the business establishment?" (Grabosky 1989). Presumably proficiency in lying and acceptance as 'one of us' through education at one of the nation's elite schools helped.

We should not forget greed. People engage in crime to buy more symbols to reassure themselves and impress their peers—a crate of Bollinger, a new Maserati, the house on the coast (*R v Campbell* [2001] NSWCCA 162), or in the case of Maxwell and Bond another publishing group and television network. Prosecution in 2007 of two Nestlé anti-fraud executives featured the claim that they stole for no other motive than 'greed' (Oberhardt 2007). Greed, like need, is a slippery concept. In terms of basic survival no-one truly needs five cars, the fifty million dollar apartment in Manhattan or a room full of Brancusis, Bacons and Warhols. A Seiko will tell the time just as efficiently as a Patek Philippe. Children have been deprived of going to Eton, Choate, or Harvard and survived to tell the tale. Greed and need are subjective. Understanding greed is a task for moralists and depth psychologists (Duffield and Grabosky 2001); watching *Citizen Kane* or biographies of Robert Maxwell and Bernard Ebbers may offer more insights for an astute viewer than a week studying financial control guidelines. Greed is problematical because it is encouraged by our financial culture: "Greed Is Good", as entrepreneur Gekko famously said and we reward chief executives for achievement that may involve unwise risk taking, operation on the borders of legality or even fraud.

Some people engage in financial crime—particularly entry-level computer-based offences—out of emulation. It is a matter of showing that I am more potent than my peers, someone who can walk through firewalls and harvest financial profiles, rather than 'this is an easy way to make a living'. It is influenced by media coverage, which illustrates opportunities and risks, and which indicates to potential offenders whether the offence is truly stigmatised (Lampe 1991; Levi 2006). Within contemporary kleptocracies such as Russia, China, Pakistan, Iraq and most of Africa emulation becomes routinised: looting the state treasury, appropriating public assets, diverting foreign aid to a personal account offshore does not pose psychological tensions for offenders because that is what their peers do as a matter of course. Data on 'copycat' offences involving payment systems is problematical. Uncertainty is further clouded by moral panics about credit card fraud and identity theft as "the crime of the millennium".

Does anger make some financial criminals tick? It is clear from a range of studies that the answer is yes. Leading forgers, such as Hebborn (1993) and Han van Meegeren (Lopez 2008), have often been motivated by anger. Their work was as much an expression of resentment as it was of making money. Robert Hughes acutely characterised *fin de siecle forger* Louis Marcy (aka Luigi Parmeggiani)—"a brilliant faker of medieval and Renaissance caskets, jewelry and reliquaries whose works entered the major museums of Europe"—as a "subversive forger", an anarchist who penned vitriolic magazine articles that reviled the capitalist art market and the purchasers of his exquisite artworks (Hughes 1990). Publishing magnate Robert Maxwell—variously dubbed a sociopath and narcissist—appears to have been very angry, reflected in his defiance of regulation and punitive approach in threatening defamation action against critics. That approach was, of course, instrumental in inhibiting exposure of his offences. Several studies of the 419 Email scam reveal that West Africans justify their activity as a righteous attack on 'colonialists' who were seen as both stupid and greedy (Kperogi and Duhé 2008; Apter 1999).

Much small-scale financial crime appears to have been driven by resentment, with employees 'compensating' themselves by taking what they thought they deserved, to equalise rewards given to other people, or to inflict a punishment on the hand that feeds (and occasionally spanks) them. Resentment is not restricted to small enterprises; it has motivated (or been used to retrospectively legitimate) some major misbehaviour (Jett 2004). Within large corporations 'helping yourself' appears to be more likely where employees believe that the organization is breaking the law or egregiously mistreating customers and suppliers, particularly where resounding statements about corporate ethics are denied through day by day practice (Clarke and Dean 2007; Green 2006). Organisations with a healthy corporate culture do not need rhetoric about 'caring & sharing'; failure to 'walk the talk' may indeed foster misbehaviour (Bryce 2002; Eichenwald 2005; Keenan 1990, 2000).

Some financial criminals are not motivated by money. They are motivated by the activity, not the outcome. Ferdinand Demara—the compulsive imposter who outshone the star of *Catch Me If You Can* in assuming the identity of real or fictitious civil engineers, police, psychologists, lawyers, teachers, Cistercian monks and scientists—for example explained his motivation as "rascality, pure rascality" (Crichton 1959). He didn't know why he did it but it felt good. Other offenders such as Abagnale (2000) and Sutton have spoken of the euphoria that comes from achievement, particularly an achievement involving evasion or subversion of authority. Offences where the criminal is not driven by stealing for financial reasons are problematic because most prevention assumes some rationality—a relationship between risk and reward. We assume that financial criminals will not engage in crime purely for pleasure, although many observers of entrepreneurs are quite comfortable with the notion that people build businesses because they enjoy building. Playing the game—what some psychologists have characterised as the ludic imperative (Buckingham and Burn 2007)—is the thing, not how many assets are accumulated by the player.

What about fear? Most of the professional literature conceptualises fear in terms of extortion. Blackmail and physical coercion do play a part in some financial crimes. In reality, however, fear usually seems to involve people further inveigling themselves, rather than extricating themselves. Several overseas studies of large scale fraud on trading desks for example indicate that the offenders such as Yasuo Hamanaka (US$2.6bn) and Jerome Kerviel (US$7.1bn) started by covering up trivial losses in order to save face, ensure they received the annual bonus or retained the job. From there it became easy to break a few more rules in the belief that losses can be turned around (Kozinn 2000; Das 2011; Kantšukov and Medvedskaja 2013; Gilligan 2011). They sometimes end by diverting funds to personal accounts because the auditor is closing in.. The same expectations can be found in board rooms and executive suites, whether in the 1890s and 1920s with Madoff-scale corporate criminals such as Balfour, Wright and Kreuger, or in the 1990s with one of Australia's largest insurers (Royal Commission 2003) and fund managers such as Madoff and Stanford.

Finally, we move to consider the sin of misjudgement.

> In the financial arena, the name of the game is money—make it now, make it fast, make a lot. To some players in this financial game, the question of whether to play fairly or unfairly, legally or illegally, is not debated. Their only issue of concern is how much, how fast, and what are the chances of being caught (Bovi 1994).

Some financial crime happens because opportunity beckons and the offenders do not expect to get caught. Sometimes they are wrong, unsurprising in a culture that rewards risk-taking (Schrand and Zechman 2013). Violent offenders with shotguns usually misjudge the odds, partly because they are easier to catch and successfully prosecute. So do IT specialists who 'borrow' the employer's credit card. Some finance personnel seem to lack basic judgment: one US government official, for example, sent US$1.2 million to 419 scammers in the belief that he would soon be richly rewarded. Alas, it was public money rather than his savings. A senior executive of leading agribusiness Archer Daniels Midland similarly started embezzling after responding to unbelievable 419 scam offers (Eichenwald 2000). Offenders who went to a private school, who wear pinstripes and who bank in the Caymans usually do not misjudge the odds. The Securities & Exchange Commission, Australian Securities & Investments Commission, Australian Competition & Consumer Commission, Federal Trade Commission and other corporate police sometimes give up because successful prosecution of smart and wealthy offenders is too difficult (Grabosky et al. 1987; Cuganesan and Lacey 2003). Sentencing may be perceived as lenient and, as in the case of Alan Bond noted above, may be less severe than those for petty theft.

8.8 Trust and Victimisation

Accounts by and about financial criminals have on occasion blamed the victims. It is common to encounter arguments that an organisation was at fault because it failed to prevent and detect misbehaviour by its staff and executives, thereby deserving the loss (sometimes further rationalised as 'victimless' because borne by insurers or customers). It is also common to see instances of victim blaming in relation to investment scams, with for example apotropaic comments that some of Madoff's investors deserved to suffer because they were extraordinarily greedy or stupid or even complicit in his scams. Victim blaming is anxiolytic for offenders (it relieves guilt) and bystanders (we are immune from ill-fortune because we are not like 'them'). In thinking about the psychology of financial crime it is more useful to consider what influences the victims and thence what could be done to protect them. Were they, for example, particularly susceptible on the basis of poor education, infirmity or other attribute? Did the offender exploit relationships within a particular ethno-religious community?

The historical perspective suggests that some victims were not in a position to meaningfully defend themselves. The collapse of the Maxwell media empire is illustrative. The charming, exuberant, aggressive and litigious Robert Maxwell looted several hundred million pounds from his employees' pension funds in order to pay for a flamboyant lifestyle, acquire assets that were grossly overvalued but impressed lenders and reinforced his sense of grandeur, and to defer collapse of a debt-ridden and badly managed conglomerate. That action resembled the behavior of Australian entrepreneur Alan Bond, whose conglomerate also collapsed. Few of Maxwell's employees were aware of the group's overall financial health and unsurprisingly assumed that gatekeepers—the ostensibly independent directors, the financial institutions and corporate rating agencies, and several government regulators (Stiles and Taylor 1993)—would either signal that something was wrong or intervene to prevent the disappearance of their jobs and savings (Department of Trade and Industry 1995). That intervention is surely one reason for the existence of the gatekeepers and a large body of law. The employees had not been given a choice about contributing to the pension fund. [That lack of agency resembles victims of state-organised or state-authorised financial crime, for example affecting citizens of the Philippines under Marcos (Chaikin and Sharman 2009), of Zaire under Mobuto (Askin and Collins 1993) and of Russia under Putin (Treisman 2008)]. In the absence of independent warnings, which were inhibited by Maxwell's use of defamation law, it is unreasonable to characterise them as gullible?

People who entrusted several billion dollars to Bernard Madoff and Allen Stanford were in a more advantageous position to discern that something was wrong. The psychological processes regarding their trust are more interesting than those of Maxwell's employees. Although they had more freedom than Maxwell printers, journalists and editors, most of the people dealing directly with Madoff and Stanford appear to have been prisoners of a belief system. Both Madoff and Stanford gained international attention as philanthropists. They attracted investment from individuals, charitable organisations and enterprises that had a reputation as being astute, providing reassurance for potential victims. The operations of both financial criminals were opaque but that was not unusual, given the opacity of many hedge funds. They offered consistently higher returns on investment but that performance was comparable with that of peers and induced perceptions among investors that the opportunity to invest was a privilege that would be denied if there were too many questions. In essence, the victims experienced a mix of reassurance and collusion.

Wilkins, Acuff and Hermanson identified victim psychology in such crimes as involving older and educated victims, a plausible story disseminated by word of mouth among people who knew each other well, demonstrated returns over several months (i.e. victims often watched peers get checks for a few months before investing themselves), low pressure promotion (no urgency to invest), and a 'good guy' promoter with a community profile for exemplary philanthropy (Wilkins et al. 2012). The betrayal of trust—the feature common to all financial crime—involved a victim psychology in which suspicions about superior returns, which might otherwise have inhibited participation was offset by a belief that criminals would not be generous and by a naive empiricism (Spalek 2001). Victims saw that peers, often peers who were authority figures, were participating. Victims often made a small initial investment, encountered no problems and accordingly made larger investments. That temporal aspect is important; running the scam for several years allowed the criminals to reassure and thereby attract potential victims who prided themselves on their astuteness and who would be suspicious of 'fly by night' offenders.

8.9   The Gatekeeper Mindset

The literature on the psychology of financial crime has one striking omission—the psychology of gatekeepers. Those gatekeepers include public and private sector regulatory agencies such as the Securities & Investments Commission (Langevoort 2009), 'analytical intermediaries' such as financial ratings services that are fundamentally important but largely self-accountable (Rousseau 2005; Fitzpatrick and Sagers 2009; Matthews 2009), pension fund managers or other trustees and financial institutions such as banks. They also include recruitment and compliance personnel within organisations, i.e. people responsible for excluding or deterring financial criminals, given that the prevention of financial crime needs a holistic approach and cannot be left to institutions that may be under-resourced and lack ready access to indications that crime is underway. It is conceivable that external and internal gatekeepers fail to anticipate and retrospectively identify financial crime because they lack that mindset. They rely on indicators—red flags—rather than understanding the psychology of offenders, a lack of understanding that is unsurprising if the offender (or potential offender) has 'executive traits'.

There is some acceptance of the notion that contemporary management styles favour what has variously been tagged as high functioning sociopathy or psychopathy, evident in the exuberance, amorality, risk-taking, self-involvement, resistance to criticism and creativity noted above. Babiak and Hare note that organisations will often disregard negative attributes such as bullying, inconsistency and consistent operation at the borders of what is legal if those executives deliver higher share prices and profits, albeit frequently on a short-term basis and in a framework that fosters creative accounting rather than sustained development (Babiak and Hare 2006). Crises privilege the sociopathic executive's need for thrills, decisiveness, exercise of authority alongside deployment of charm, and legitimacy in bending or remaking an organisation's internal rules. That is a challenge for gatekeepers, who are likely to be seen as impediments to success and lacking executive qualities. Criminals such as Madoff, Maxwell and Bond have operated outside institutional frameworks: they made their own rules, as heads of their organisations, and as noted above were not meaningfully inhibited by complaisant boards of directors.

We do not know how financial institutions and other entities are profiling their potential employees and associates, current employees and contacts, or customers. It is thus not possible to assess the effectiveness of profiling. Did criminals never get through the door? Were they deterred from crime through an overt and seamless financial control framework? Were they caught at an early stage, detected after an initial incident rather than after systemic misbehaviour? Did they exhibit warning signs … and were those signs recognised? One reason for caution is that leading organizations, facing major reputational risk and with the resources for a close scrutiny of claims by senior executives, clearly have failed to undertake basic vetting or verify claims. In Australia for example the executive known as John Friedrich was not challenged over assertions that more than A$100 million of emergency service assets were stored in several locations (Thomas 1991). Two of the most senior executives of Australia's leading telecommunications company were similarly revealed to have problematical CVs. Chris Tyler was revealed in 2000 to have been convicted of marijuana possession (with a 10-year suspended sentence), involved with a North American company that had collapsed, and responsible for a series of blunders as head of NZ Telecom's internet operations. Queried on why he had not told the board, Tyler commented that he was "never asked". The same billion dollar company had previously been embarrassed by the revelation in 1993 that Bruno Sorrentino, head of its IT arm and research laboratories (and former chief information officer of the second largest bank), had not attended London's Imperial College, let alone completed a claimed Ph.D. in physics. The head of a New Zealand broadcasting service simply invented his qualifications. In 2002 John Davy was sentenced to 8 months imprisonment in New Zealand for CV fraud. He had been controversially appointed as $NZ140,000-a-year inaugural head of the Maori Television Service. That appointment reflected supposed strong financial and management skills; Davy had no television experience, knew little of Maori culture and was unfamiliar with the language. He had claimed an MBA from the Ashland School of Business at Denver State University, an accounting certificate, experience as a member of the British Columbia Securities Commission and authorship of two books. Unfortunately the Commission had not heard of him and the 'University' was discovered to be an online diploma mill. Davy claimed that he had been 'undercover', with his academic and financial history being wiped as part of a witness protection program. In reality he had been twice declared bankrupt and had worked as an accountant in Whistler, rather than as a regulator.

Failures in vetting are evident elsewhere. Prominent German politicians have plagiarised their doctoral dissertations. Jeffrey Papows, author of Enterprise.com: *Market Leadership in the Information Age* and president of IBM's Lotus unit, resigned after *The Register* revealed:

> So he's not an orphan, his parents are alive and well. He wasn't a Marine Corps captain, he was a lieutenant. He didn't save a buddy by throwing a live grenade out of a trench. He didn't burst an eardrum when ejecting from a Phantom F4, which didn't crash, not killing his co-pilot. He's not a tae kwon do black belt, and he doesn't have a Ph.D. from Pepperdine University (Lettice 1999).

In Australia Glen Oakley rose from a mortician's assistant to become Director-General of the state Department of Business & Regional Development, partly on the strength of his academic background. Unfortunately his degrees, including a B.Sc. (Hons) and Grad Dip in Education from the University of Newcastle, MBA from UNSW and a Ph.D., were all fake (Brown 2006). Charles Sturt University more colourfully employed a man who had awarded himself a Victoria Cross, i.e. the highest military award of the UK and Australia. We might wonder whether that invention was an indicator of stupidity, a momentary misjudgment from which the offender could not resile, or a covert plea for help.

8.10 Medicalising Financial Crime?

If we regard fraud as an indicator of profound psychological distress or a disorder or associated with addiction should we conceptualise much financial crime in terms of mental illness rather than crime? In looking for psychological models of the 'financial criminal' and for a therapeutic rather than punitive or containment response to offending can we rely on a theoretical framework of the medicalisation of law, i.e. the process by which legal or non-medical states and behavior are formally conceptualised as medical problems, typically in terms of psychological disorders that should be addressed through a medical intervention rather than incarceration (Conrad 1992)?

Although detailed longitudinal statistics are unavailable, courts in Australia, the United Kingdom, Canada and United States have not been receptive to claims that financial crime is directly attributable to psychological disorders and should be excused on that basis. From a legal perspective financial crime remains a crime, rather than an illness. Arguments about impaired decision-making on the basis of depression or bipolar disorder and pleas that substance or gambling addiction as a motivation for financial crime have been taken into account in sentencing by courts (Grabosky 1990). Australian corporate criminal Rene Rivkin for example successfully referred to his bipolar disorder in seeking a lighter sentence (Main 2005). In essence, courts have typically found that financial criminals had the legally requisite intention to commit the crime, the offence was a matter of deliberation (often over several years) rather than a matter of impulse, that the offenders were able to distinguish right from wrong and that the illegal action was not determined by a psychological disorder. Implicitly, many offenders are regarded by courts as having the intelligence, education and means to seek medical help through cognitive therapy, medication or other mechanisms.

One reason courts have resisted medicalisation, for example characterisation of figures such as Maxwell and Madoff as sociopaths whose behavior should be addressed through medical treatment rather than imprisonment and financial penalties is presumably that a consensus has not emerged among health practitioners and legal practitioners. The *Diagnostic & Statistical Manual of Mental Disorders V* for example grapples with questions about addiction but necessarily sidesteps conceptualisation of crime. A more subtle reason is that conflation of financial crime with sociopathy (Black 2013) pathologises executives and other figures who may share traits with offenders but have been fortunate or have chosen to stay within the law. We sensibly prosecute and punish people who have acted illegally rather than those whose amorality, self-involvement, risk-taking and other traits has not involved a betrayal of trust or breach of law.

8.11   Conclusion

This chapter began by arguing that financial crime is important, is inherent in advanced economies and is conceptually challenging for both regulators and social scientists. One lesson of history is that financial crime is not going to disappear. Based on that history we can draw several conclusions. Those conclusions are of value for gatekeepers, particularly regulatory agencies and personnel evaluation units that conceptualise prevention of crime in terms of psychological profiling. They are also of value for scholars seeking to understand the psychology of entrepreneurship, leadership and marketing, given that financial crime involves social relationships and questions about belief and boundaries. A salient conclusion, in addressing the two hypotheses, is that psychologists, criminologists and institutional gatekeepers will benefit from acknowledging uncertainties. We need comprehensive empirical data that would enable more confident assessments of the psychology of financial crime and thence more effective responses.

The preceding paragraphs have suggested that there is no single type of financial crime and no single type of financial criminal. There is no consensus on taxonomies for the identification of financial crime and it is unlikely that a consensus will develop, with nations and the professions instead continuing to rely on categorisations that are often idiosyncratic and that provide little assistance for psychologists and other social scientists who are seeking to understand the motivations of offenders and indicators that financial crime is underway. As a result there are no comprehensive, culturally-independent profiling mechanisms for identification of potential and active financial criminals.

The shared characteristic of financial criminals is that they break the law, typically for personal financial benefit. They are otherwise quite diverse. A second finding from the instances of financial crime highlighted in the preceding pages is thus that the motivations of financial criminals varies considerably. That motivation may indeed change during the conduct of the crime and we should be wary of monocausal explanations. The motivation of some criminals appears to be simple, for example a matter of inadequate institutional boundaries interacting with an overweening sense of entitlement on the part of the offender, i.e. "just show me the money". Others mingle greed, resentment, need, defiance of authority figures and the joy of playing games or confronting extreme risks. Some offenders make a small-scale mistake that they are then impelled to compound in an effort to recoup losses, often accompanied by such severe anxiety and depression that being caught comes as a relief. Others appear to have blithely, deliberately and consistently offended whenever the opportunity arose … and continued to do so until factors outside their control, such as a market collapse, brought their activity to a halt

A third finding is that in the absence of a coherent taxonomy of offences and of motivations Australia and comparable jurisdictions have not embraced medicalisation of financial crime. A final finding is that some organizations are placing their trust—arguably misplacing their trust—in pseudo-scientific 'integrity profiling' or other personnel section mechanisms, from batteries of psychological tests centred on impulse control and diligence through to quackery about handwriting or the configuration of an individual's earlobes. Much of that appraisal is of dubious value because it is founded on problematical cultural assumptions, or because it fails to differentiate between 'leadership' attributes and 'looting' attributes.

References

Abagnale, Frank. 2000. *Catch me if you can*. New York: Broadway Books.
Advisory Task Force on Insurance Fraud. 2008. *Reducing insurance fraud in California*. Sacramento: California Department of Insurance.
Akst, Daniel. 1990. *Wonder boy: Barry minkow (the kid who swindled wall street)*. New York: Scribner.

Alder, Christine. 1999. Challenges to authenticity in the aboriginal art market. Paper presented at the art crime: Protecting art, protecting artists and protecting consumers conference, Sydney, 2–3 December 1999.

Apter, Andrew. 1999. IBB = 419: Nigerian democracy and the politics of illusion. In *civil society & the political imagination in Africa*, ed. John Comaroff, 267–308. Chicago: University of Chicago Press.

Arvedlund, Erin. 2009. *Too good to be true: The rise and fall of bernie madoff*. New York: Portfolio.

Ash, Timothy Garton. 1997. *The file: A personal history*. London: HarperCollins.

Askin, Steve, and Carole Collins. 1993. External collusion with kleptocracy: Can Zaïre recapture its stolen wealth? *Review of African Political Economy* 20(57): 72–85.

Avison, David., and David Wilson. 2002. IT Failure and the Collapse of One.Tel. In *Information Systems: The e-Business Challenge* ed. Roland Traunmuller 31–46. London: Kluwer.

Babiak, Paul, and Robert Hare. 2006. *Snakes in suits: When psychopaths go to work*. New York: HarperCollins.

Barry, Paul. 2000. *Going For broke: How bond got away with it*. Sydney: Bantam.

Barry, Paul. 2002. *Rich kids*. Sydney: Bantam.

Bartol, Curt, and Anne Bartol. 2008. *Introduction to forensic psychology*. London: SAGE.

Becker, Peter, and Richard Wetzell (eds.). 2006. *Criminals and their scientists*. Cambridge: Cambridge University Press.

Belfort, Jordan. 2007. *The wolf of wall street*. New York: Hachette.

Benson, Michael. 1985. Denying the guilty mind: Accounting for involvement in white collar crime. *Criminology* 23: 583–607.

Benson, Michael, and Elizabeth Moore. 1992. Are white-collar and common offenders the same? an empirical and theoretical critique of a recently proposed general theory of crime. *Journal of Research in Crime and Delinquency* 29(3): 251–272.

Beyerstein, Barry, and Dale Beyerstein (eds.). 1992. *The write stuff: Evaluations of graphology— the study of handwriting analysis*. Amherst: Prometheus.

Black, Donald. 2013. *Bad boys, bad men: Confronting antisocial personality disorder*. Oxford: Oxford University Press.

Blaszczynski, Alex, and Neil McConaghy. 1994. Criminal offenses in gamblers anonymous and hospital treated pathological gamblers. *Journal of Gambling Studies* 10: 99–127.

Blickle, Gerhard, Alexander Schlegel, Pantaleon Fassbender, and Uwe Klein. 2006. Some personality correlates of business white-collar crime. *Applied Psychology* 55(2): 220–233.

Blinkhorn, Steve, and Charles Johnson. 1990. The insignificance of personality testing. *Nature* 348: 671–672.

Boddy, Clive. 2011. The corporate psychopaths theory of the global financial crisis. *Journal of Business Ethics* 102: 255–259.

Bovi, David. 1994. Rule 10b-5 liability for front-running: Adding a new dimension to the 'money game'. *St. Thomas Law Review* 7: 103–125.

Bower, Tom. 1996. *Maxwell: The Final Verdict*. London: 1996.

Bowker, Geoffrey, and Susan Star. 1999. *Sorting things out: Classification and its consequences*. Cambridge: The MIT Press.

Braithwaite, John. 1985. White collar crime. *Annual Review of Sociology* 11: 1–25.

Braithwaite, John. 1991. Poverty, power, white-collar crime and the paradoxes of criminological theory. *Australian and New Zealand Journal of Criminology* 24: 40–50.

Braithwaite, John. 1993. Crime and the average American. *Law & Society Review* 27(1): 215–230.

Brenner, Susan. 2002. Organized cybercrime? how cyberspace may affect the structure of criminal relationships. *North Carolina Journal of Law & Technology* 4(1): 1–50.

Brown, George. 2006. Degrees of doubt: Legitimate, real and fake qualifications in a global market. *Journal of Higher Education Policy and Management* 28(1): 71–79.

Bryce, Robert. 2002. *Pipe dreams: Greed, ego, jealousy and the death of enron*. New York: Public Affairs.

Buckingham, David, and Andrew Burn. 2007. Game literacy in theory and practice. *Journal of Educational Multimedia and Hypermedia* 16(3): 323–349.

Butler, Tony, Gavin Andrews, Stephen Allnutt, Chika Sakashita, Nadine Smith, and John Basson. 2006. Mental disorders in Australian prisoners: A comparison with a community sample. *Australian and New Zealand Journal of Psychiatry* 40(3): 272–276.

Byrne, John. 1999. *Chainsaw: The notorious career of Al dunlap in the era of profit-at-any-price.* New York: Harper Business.

Canhoto, Ana, and James Backhouse. 2007. Profiling under conditions of ambiguity—An application in the financial services industry. *Journal of Retailing and Consumer Services* 14 (6): 408–419.

Carré, Justin, and Cheryl McCormick. 2008. In your face: Facial metrics predict aggressive behaviour in the laboratory and in varsity and professional hockey players. *Proceedings of the Royal Society* 275(1651): 2651–2656.

Chaikin, David, and J.G. Sharman. 2009. *Corruption and money laundering.* Basingstoke: Palgrave Macmillan.

Chappell, Duncan, and Kenneth Polk. 2008. Fakers and forgers, deception and dishonesty: An exploration of the murky world of art fraud. *Current Issues in Criminal Justice* 20(3): 2–20.

Chenoweth, Neil. 2006. *Packer's lunch: A rollicking tale of swiss bank accounts and money-making adventurers in the roaring '90s.* Sydney: Allen & Unwin.

Clarke, Frank, and Graeme Dean. 2007. *Indecent exposure: Gilding the corporate lily.* Cambridge: Cambridge University Press.

Clarke, Frank, Graeme Dean, and Kyle Oliver. 2003. *Corporate collapse: Accounting, regulatory and ethical failure.* Cambridge: Cambridge University Press.

Clinard, Marshall, and Richard Quinney. 1967. *Criminal behavior systems: A typology.* New York: Holt Rinehart Winston.

Cohen, Lawrence, and Marcus Felson. 1979. Social change and crime rate trends: A routine activity approach. *American Sociological Review* 44: 588–605.

Collins, Jock. 2005. Ethnic minorities and crime in Australia: Moral panic or meaningful policy responses' (Address to an office of multicultural interests seminar, 8 November 2005, Perth).

Connell, Jon., and Douglas Sutherland. 1979. *Fraud: The amazing career of Dr. Savundra.* New York: Stein & Day.

Conrad, Peter. 1992. Medicalization and social control. *Annual Review of Sociology* 18: 209–232.

Cook, James. 2001. *The arts of deception: Playing with fraud in the age of barnum.* Cambridge: Harvard University Press.

Covick, Owen, and Beverley Vickers. 2003. The Trials of whitaker wright. History of economic thought society of Australia, 16th Conference, Melbourne, 15–18 July 2003).

Cressey, Donald. 1953. *Other people's money: A study in the social psychology of embezzlement.* Glencoe: The Free Press.

Cressey, Donald. 1986. Why managers commit fraud. *Australian and New Zealand Journal of Criminology* 19: 195–209.

Crichton, Robert. 1959. *The great imposter: The amazing careers of ferdinand waldo demara.* New York: Random House.

Crofts, Penny. 2002. *Gambling and criminal behaviour: An analysis of local and district court files.* Sydney: Institute of Criminology.

Crofts, Penny. 2003. White collar punters: Stealing from the boss to gamble. *Current Issues in Criminal Justice* 15(1): 40–52.

Cuganesan, Suresh, and David Lacey. 2003. *Identity fraud in Australia: An evaluation of its nature, cost and extent.* Brisbane: SIRCA.

Daly, Kathleen. 1989. Gender and varieties of white-collar crime. *Criminology* 27: 769–794.

Das, Satyajit. 2011. *Extreme money: The masters of the universe and the cult of risk.* New York: Wiley.

Deem, Debbie. 2000. Notes from the field: Observations in working with the forgotten victims of personal financial crimes. *Journal of Elder Abuse & Neglect* 12(2): 33–48.

Department of Trade and Industry, 1995. *Mirror group newspapers PLC: Investigations under Sections 432(2) and 442 of the Companies Act 1985.*

Derkzen, Dena, Laura Booth, Kelly Taylor, and Ashley McConnell. 2013. Mental health needs of federal female offenders. *Psychological Services.* 10(1): 24–36.

Derrig, Richard, and Valerie Zicko. 2002. Prosecuting insurance fraud—A case study of the massachusetts experience in the 1990s. *Risk Management and Insurance Review* 5(7): 77–104.

Dodge, Mary. 2013. Where are the women in white collar crime. In *Routledge international handbook of crime and gender studies*, ed. Claire Renzetti, Susan Miller, and Angela Gover, 197–208. London: Routledge.

Domanick, Joe. 1989. *Faking it in America: Barry minkow and the great ZZZZ best scam.* New York: Contemporary Books.

Draine, Jeffrey, Mark Salzer, Dennis Culhane, and Trevor Hadley. 2002. The role of social disadvantage in crime, joblessness, and homelessness among persons with serious mental illness. *Psychiatric Services* 53(5): 565–573.

Driver, Russell, Ronald Buckley, and Dwight Frink. 1996. Should we write off graphology? *International Journal Of Selection And Assessment* 4(2): 78–86.

Duffield, Grace, and Peter Grabosky. 2001. The psychology of frand. *Trend and issues in crime and criminal justice* 199: 1–6.

Eichenwald, Kurt. 2000. *The informant.* New York: Broadway Books.

Eichenwald, Kurt. 2005. *Conspiracy of fools: A true story.* New York: Broadway.

Elks, Sarah. 2013. Fake prince Joel Morehu-Barlow sentenced to 14 years for theft of $16 m from Queensland Health. *The Australian* March 19.

Engdahl, Oskar. 2008. The role of money in economic crime. *British Journal of Criminology* 48 (2): 154–170.

Engel, Robin, Jennifer Calnon Robin, and Thomas Bernard. 2002. Theory and racial profiling: Shortcomings and future directions in research. *Justice Quarterly* 19(2): 249–274.

Faigman, David. 1999. *Legal alchemy: The use and misuse of science in the law.* New York: Freeman.

Fairfax, Lisa. 2001. 'With friends like these': Toward a more efficacious response to affinity-based securities and investment fraud. *Georgia Law Review* 36: 63–119.

Fay, Stephen, Lewis Chester, and Magnus Linklater. 1972. *Hoax: The inside story of the howard hughes-clifford irving affair.* London: Andre Deutsch.

Figes, Orlando. 2007. *The whisperers: Private life in stalin's Russia.* London: Allen Lane.

Fitzpatrick, Sheila, and Robert Gellately. 1997. *Accusatory practices: Denunciation in modern european history, 1789-1989.* Chicago: University of Chicago Press.

Fitzpatrick, Thomas, and Christopher Sagers. 2009. Faith-based financial regulation: A primer on oversight of credit rating organizations. *Administrative Law Review* 61(3): 557–610.

Flesher, Dale, and Tonya Flesher. 1986. Ivar Kreuger's contribution to U.S. Financial Reporting. *The Accounting Review* 61(3): 421–434.

Fletcher, Nigel. 2007. Challenges for regulating financial fraud in cyberspace. *Journal of financial crime* 14(2): 190–207.

Friedrichs, David. 1996. *Trusted criminals: White collar crime in contemporary society.* New York: Wadsworth.

Funder, Anna. 2003. *Stasiland.* London: Granta.

Gapper, John. 2011. *How to be a rogue trader.* London: Penguin.

Garton, Stephen. 1994. Sound minds and healthy bodies: Reconsidering eugenics in Australia 1914-1940. *Australian Historical Studies* 26: 163–181.

Geis, Gilbert. 2012. Unaccountable Auditors. In *How they got away with it: White collar criminals and the financial meltdown*, ed. Susan Will, Stephen Handelman and David Brotherton 83–103. New York: Columbia University Press.

Gellately, Robert. 1996. Denunciations in twentieth-century germany: Aspects of self-policing in Nazi Germany and the German democratic republic. *Journal of Modern History* 68: 931–967.

Gilding, Michael. 1999. Superwealth in Australia: Entrepreneurs, accumulation and the capitalist class. *Journal of Sociology* 35(2): 169–182.

Gilding, Michael. 2004. Entrepreneurs, elites and the ruling class: The changing structure of power and wealth in Australian society. *Australian Journal of Political Science* 39(1): 127–143.

Gilligan, George. 2011. Jérôme Kerviel the 'Rogue Trader' of Société Générale: Bad luck, bad apple, bad tree or bad orchard? *The Company Lawyer* 32(12): 355–362.

Glassner, Barry. 2000. *The culture of fear: Why Americans are afraid of the wrong thing*. New York: Perseus.

Gleeson, Murray. 1995. Individualised justice: The holy grail. *Australian Law Journal* 69: 421–432.

Goldstraw, Janice, Russell Smith, and Yuka Sakurai. 2005. Gender and serious fraud in Australia and New Zealand. *Trends and Issues in Crime and Criminal Justice* 292: 1–6.

Grabosky, Peter. 1989. The collapse of bishopsgate insurance. In *Stains on a white collar*, ed. Peter Grabosky, and Adam Sutton, 31–42. Annandale: The Federation Press.

Grabosky, Peter. 1990. Professional advisers and white collar illegality: Towards explaining and excusing professional failure. *UNSW Law Journal* 13(1): 73–96.

Grabosky, Peter, John Braithwaite, and Paul Wilson. 1987. The myth of community tolerance toward white-collar crime. *Australian and New Zealand Journal of Criminology* 20: 33–44.

Grabosky, Peter, Russell Smith, and George Demsey. 2001. *Electronic theft: Unlawful acquisition in cyberspace*. Cambridge: Cambridge University Press.

Graham, Peter. 1990. *Bureaucratic politics and technology: Computers & the Australia card*. Nathan: Centre for Australian Public Sector Management, Griffith University.

Green, Gary. 1993. White-collar crime and the study of embezzlement. *Annals of the American Academy of Political and Social Science* 525: 95–106.

Green, Stuart. 2006. *Lying, cheating and stealing: A moral theory of white-collar crime*. Oxford: Oxford University Press.

Greenleaf, Graham. 2007. Australia's proposed ID Card: Still quacking like a duck. *UNSW Law Research Series* 2007 (1): 1–15.

Greenslade, Roy. 1992. *Maxwell's fall*. New York: Simon & Schuster.

Groebner, Valentin. 2007. *Who are you? identification, deception and surveillance in early modern Europe*. New York: Zone.

Guthrie, Woody. 1947. The ballad of pretty boy floyd. In *American Folksong*, 27. New York: DISC Company of America.

Harris, Robert. 1987. *Selling Hitler*. London: Faber.

Hebborn, Eric. 1993. *Drawn to trouble: Confessions of a master forger*. New York: Random House.

Henriques, Diana. 2011. *The wizard of lies: Bernie madoff and the death of trust*. New York: Henry Holt.

Herzog, Arthur. 1987. *Vesco: From wall street to castro's cuba, the rise, fall, and exile of the king of white collar crime*. New York: Doubleday.

Highhouse, Scott. 2002. Assessing the candidate as a whole: A Historical and critical analysis of individual psychological assessment for personnel decision making. *Personnel Psychology* 55(2): 363–396.

Hirschi, Travis, and Michael Gottfredson. 1987. Causes of white-collar crime. *Criminology* 25(4): 949–974.

Hoyte, Catherine. 2003. An Australian mirage, (2003) Griffith University Ph.D. dissertation.

Huddleston, Pat. 2011. *The vigilant investor: A former SEC enforcer reveals how to fraud-proof your investments*. New York: Amacom.

Hughes, Robert. 1990. Brilliant, but not for real. *Time* (7 May).

Hunt, Alan. 1996. *Governance of the consuming passions: A history of sumptuary law*. New York: St Martins.

International Monetary Fund. 2001. Financial system abuse, financial crime and money laundering.

Irving, Clifford. 1972. *What really happened: The untold story of the hughes affair*. New York: Grove Press.

Jackson, Margaret, and Julian Ligertwood. 2006. Identity management: Is an identity card the solution for Australia? *Prometheus* 24(4): 379–387.

Jett, Joseph. 2004. *Broken bonds: My immoderate life of love, passion, war on affirmative action and Jack Welch's GE*. New York: Cambridge Matrix.

Job, Catherine. 1999. 'Crime stoppers' (Lateline, 23 March 1999) Sydney: Australian Broadcasting Corporation.

Jory, Stephen. 2005. *Loadsamoney: The true story of the world's largest ever counterfeiting ring*. London: Trafalgar Square.

Kantšukov, Mark, and Darja Medvedskaja. 2013. From dishonesty to disaster: The reasons and consequences of rogue traders' fraudulent behavior. *Advanced Series in Management* 10: 147–165.

Kapardis, Andreas, and Maria Krambia-Kapardis. 2006. Enhancing fraud prevention and detection by profiling fraud offenders. *Criminal Behaviour and Mental Health* 14(3): 189–201.

Karren, Ronald, and Larry Zacharia. 2007. Integrity tests: Critical issues. *Human Resource Management Review* 17(2): 221–234.

Kater, Michael. 1983. *The nazi party: A social profile of members and leaders, 1919-1945*. Oxford: Blackwell.

Keenan, John. 1990. Upper-level managers and whistleblowing: Determinants of perceptions of company encouragement and information about where to blow the whistle. *Journal of Business and Psychology* 5(2): 223–235.

Keenan, John. 2000. Blowing the whistle on less serious forms of fraud: A study of executives and managers. *Employee Responsibilities and Rights Journal* 12(4): 199–218.

Keneley, Monica. 2008. The curious case of the occidental and regal: The evolution of solvency and disclosure standards in the Australian life insurance industry. *Accounting History* 13(3): 313–332.

Khurana, Rakesh. 2002. *Searching for a corporate savior: The irrational quest for charismatic CEOs*. Princeton: Princeton University Press.

Klimoski, Richard, and Anat Rafaeli. 1983. Inferring personal qualities through handwriting analysis. *Journal of Occupational Psychology* 56(3): 191–202.

Kocsis, Richard, and Andrew Hayes. 2004. Believing is seeing? investigating the perceived accuracy of criminal psychological profiles. *International Journal Of Offender Therapy & Comparative Criminology* 48(2): 149–160.

Kocsis, Richard, and George Palermo. 2006. *Criminal profiling: Principles & practice*. Totowa: Humana Press.

Korobkin, Russell, and Thomas Ulen. 2000. Law and behavioral science: Removing the rationality assumption from law and economics. *California Law Review* 88(4): 1051–1144.

Kozinn, Benjamin. 2000. The great copper caper: Is market manipulation really a problem in the wake of the sumitomo debacle. *Fordham Law Review* 69: 243–285.

Kperogi, Farooq, and Sandra Duhé. 2008. A tribe migrates crime to cyberspace: Nigerian igbos in 419 E- Mail scams. In *Electronic tribes: The virtual worlds of geeks, gamers, shamans, and scammers*, ed. Tyrone Adams, and Stephen Smith, 269–288. Austin: University of Texas Press.

Krawiec, Kimberly. 2000. Accounting for greed: Unraveling the rogue trader mystery. *Oregon Law Review* 79(2): 301–330.

Lampe, Anne. 1991. Media coverage of complex commercial fraud. In *Complex commercial fraud: Proceedings of a conference held 20–23 August 1991 (AIC Conference Proceedings no. 10)* ed Peter Grabosky, Canberra: Australian Institute of Criminology.

Langevoort, Donald. 2009. The SEC and the madoff scandal: Three narratives in search of a story. *Michigan State Law Review* 4: 899–914.

Largent, Mark. 2007. *The history of coerced sterilization in the United States*. New Brunswick: Rutgers University Press.

Lawson, Guy. 2012. *Octopus: Sam israel, the secret market, and wall street's wildest con*. New York: Broadway Books.

Leeson, Nick. 1996. *Rogue trader*. London: Little, Brown.

Leff, Arthur. 1976. *Swindling and selling: The spanish prisoner & other bargains*. New York: The Free Press.

Lettice, John. 1999. Lotus chief's 'combat record' savaged by WSJ. *The Register* (30 April).

Leunes, Arnold, and Larry Christensen. 2003. A comparison of forgers with other criminals. *Journal of Community Psychology* 3(3): 285–288.

Levi, Michael. 1992. White-collar crime victimization. In *White-collar crime reconsidered*, ed. Kip Schlegel, and David Weisburd, 169–194. Dartmouth: Northeastern University Press.

Levi, Michael. 1999. Motivations and criminal careers of long-firm fraudsters. In *Fraud: Organization, motivation and control*, ed. Michael Levi. Aldershot: Ashgate.

Levi, Michael. 2001. Risky money: Regulating financial crime. In *Criminal justice, mental health and the politics of risk*, ed. Nicola Gray, Judith Laing, and Lesley Noaks, 123–148. London: Cavendish.

Levi, Michael. 2002. Suite justice or sweet charity? Some explorations of shaming and incapacitating business fraudsters. *Punishment & Society* 4(2): 147–163.

Levi, Michael. 2006. The media construction of financial white-collar crimes. *British Journal of Criminology* 46(6): 1037–1057.

Lopez, Jonathan. 2008. *The man who made vermeers: Unvarnishing the legend of master forger Han van Meegeren*. New York: Harcourt.

Mackenzie, Geraldine. 2005. *How judges sentence*. Leichhardt: The Federation Press.

Main, Andrew. 2005. *Rivkin unauthorised: The meteoric rise and tragic fall of an unorthodox money man*. Sydney: HarperCollins.

Markham, Jerry. 1995. Guarding the kraal—On the trail of the rogue trader. *Journal of Corporate Law* 21: 131–149.

Markopolos, Harry. 2010. *No one would listen: A true financial thriller*. New York: Wiley.

Markus, Hazel, and Shinobu Kitayama. 1998. The cultural psychology of personality. *Journal of Cross-Cultural Psychology* 29(1): 63–87.

Matthews, David. 2009. Ruined in a conventional way: Responses to credit ratings' role in credit crises. *Northwestern Journal of International Law & Business* 29(1): 245–274.

Maurer, David. 1999. *The big con*. New York: Anchor.

McKie, David. 2004. *Jabez: The rise & fall of a victorian rogue*. New York: Atlantic.

Moore, Elizabeth, and Michael Mills. 1990. The neglected victims and unexamined costs of white-collar crime. *Crime & Delinquency* 36(3): 408–418.

Morgeson, Frederick, Michael Campion, Robert Dipboye, John Hollenbeck, Kevin Murphy, and Neal Schmitt. 2007. Are we getting fooled again? Coming to terms with limitations in the use of personality tests for personnel selection. *Personnel Psychology* 60(4): 1029–1049.

Morley, Nicola, Linden Ball, and Thomas Ormerod. 2006. How the detection of insurance fraud succeeds and fails. *Psychology, Crime & Law* 12: 163–180.

Morse, Dexter, and Lynne Skajaa. 2007. *Tackling insurance fraud: Law and practice*. London: Informa Professional.

Nettler, Gwynn. 1974. Embezzlement without problems. *British Journal of Criminology* 14(1): 70–77.

Norris, James. 1978. *R G Dun & Co, 1841-1900: The development of credit reporting in the nineteenth century*. Westport: Greenwood Press.

Oberhardt, Mark. 2007. Managers milked Nestle of $1.6 m. *Brisbane Courier Mail* May 22.

Ones, Deniz, Chockalingam Viswesvaran, and Frank Schmidt. 1993. Comprehensive meta-analysis of integrity test validities: Findings and implications for personnel selection and theories of job performance. *Journal of Applied Psychology* 78: 679–703.

Panchasi, Roxanne. 1996. Graphology and the science of individual identity in modern france. *Configurations* 4(1): 1–32.

Partnoy, Frank. 2009. *The match king: The genius behind a century of wall street scandals*. New York: Public Affairs.

Patterson, Tony, and Stephen Brown. 2009. Never tickle a sleeping bookworm: How readers devour 'Harry Potter'. *Marketing Intelligence & Planning* 27(6): 818–832.

Perri, Frank, and Richard Brody. 2012. The optics of fraud: Affiliations that enhance offender credibility. *Journal of Financial Crime* 19(3): 305–320.

Phelan, James, and Lewis Chester. 1997. *The money: The battle for howard hughes's billions*. New York: Random House.

Phua, Clifton, Vincent, Lee, Kate, Smith, and Ross Gayler. 2005. A comprehensive survey of data mining-based fraud detection research. *Artificial Intelligence Review* 1–14.

Pickett, Spencer, and Jennifer Pickett. 2002. *Financial crime investigation and control*. New York: Wiley.

Post, Richard. 1968. Relationship of tattoos to personality disorders. *Journal of Criminal Law, Criminology & Police Science* 59(4): 516–524.

Potter, Hugh, and Lyndy Potter. 2001. The Internet, cyberporn, and sexual exploitation of children: Media moral panics and urban myths for middle-class parents? *Sexuality & Culture: An Interdisciplinary Quarterly* 5(3): 31–48.

Pratt, John. 1997. *Governing the dangerous: Dangerousness, law and social change*. Leichhardt: The Federation Press.

Pridmore, Saxby, Amber Chambers, and Milford McArthur. 2005. Neuroimaging in psychopathy. *Australian and New Zealand Journal of Psychiatry* 39(10): 856–865.

Quinney, Richard. 1977. The study of white-collar crime: Toward a reorientation in theory and practice. In *White-collar Crime*, ed. Gilbert Geis, 283–296. New York: Free Press.

Rafter, Nicole. 2008. *The criminal brain: Understanding biological theories of crime*. New York: New York University Press.

Raine, Adrian, William Laufer, Yaling Yang, Katherine Narr, Paul Thompson, and Arthur Toga. 2012. Increased executive functioning, attention, and cortical thickness in white-collar criminals. *Human Brain Mapping* 33(12): 2932–2940.

Ramamoorti, Sridhar, Daven Morrison, and Joseph Koletar. 2014. Bringing freud to fraud: Understanding the state-of-mind of the C-Level suite/white collar offender through "A-B-C" analysis. *Journal of Forensic & Investigative Accounting* 6(1): 1–20.

Raw, Charles, Bruce Page, and Godfrey Hodgson. 1971. *Do you sincerely want to be rich?: The full story of bernard cornfeld and IOS*. London: Andre Deutsch.

Rieke, Mark, and Stephen Guastello. 1995. Unresolved issues in honesty and integrity testing. *American Psychologist* 50: 458–459.

Robb, George. 1992. *White collar crime in modern England: Financial fraud and business morality 1845-1929*. Cambridge: Cambridge University Press.

Robb, George. 2006. Women and white-collar crime debates on gender, fraud and the corporate economy in England and America, 1850-1930. *The British Journal of Criminology* 46(6): 1058–1072.

Rousseau, Stephane. 2005. Enhancing the accountability of credit rating agencies: The case for a disclosure-based approach. *McGill Law Journal* 51(4): 617–664.

Rowbotham, Judith, and Kim Stevenson. 2003. *Behaving badly: Social panic and moral outrage —victorian and modern parallels*. Aldershot: Ashgate.

Royal Commission into HIH Insurance. 2003. Report of the Royal Commission into HIH Insurance.

Rozycki, Alicia. 2007. Prison tattoos as a reflection of the criminal lifestyle and predictor of recidivism, Texas Tech Ph.D. dissertation.

Rust, John, and Susan Golombok. 1999. *Modern Psychometrics: The Science of Psychological Assessment*. London: Routledge; and.

Ryder, Nicholas. 2011. *Financial crime in the 21st century: Law and policy*. Cheltenham: Edward Elgar.

Sackett, Paul, and Michael Harris. 1984. Honesty testing for personnel selection: A review and critique', 37 *Personnel Psychology* 37: 221–245.

Sakurai, Yuka, and Russell Smith. 2005. Gambling as a motivation for the commission of financial crime. *Trends and Issues in Crime and Criminal Justice* 256: 1–6.

Sandage, Scott. 2005. *Born losers: A history of failure in America*. Cambridge: Harvard University Press.

Schnall, Simone, Jennifer Benton, and Sophie Harvey. 2008. With a clean conscience: Cleanliness reduces the severity of moral judgments. *Psychological Science* 19(12): 1219–1222.

Schrand, Catherine, and Sarah Zechman. 2013. Executive overconfidence and the slippery slope to fraud. *Journal of Accounting and Economics* 53(1): 311–329.

Seddon, Toby. 2000. Explaining the drug–crime link: Theoretical, policy and research issues. *Journal of Social Policy*. 29(1): 95–107.

Shapiro, Susan. 1985. The road not taken: The elusive path to criminal prosecution for white-collar offenders. *Law & Society Review* 19(2): 179–218.

Shaplen, Robert. 1960. *Kreuger, genius and swindler*. New York: Knopf.

Shelton, Donald. 2008. The 'CSI Effect': Does it really exist? *National Institute of Justice Journal* 259: 1–8.

Shichor, David. 1998. Victimology and the victims of white-collar crime. In *Criminology on the threshold of the 21st century* ed. Hans-Dieter Schwind, Edwin Kube and Hans-Heiner Kühne 331–351. Berlin: Walter de Gruyter.

Shover, Neal, and Andrew Hochstetler. 2006. *Choosing white-collar crime*. Cambridge: Cambridge University Press.

Slovic, Paul. 1987. Perception of risk. *Science* 236: 280–285.

Snook, Brent, Richard Cullen, Craig Bennell, Paul Taylor, and Paul Gendreau. 2008. The criminal profiling illusion what's behind the smoke and mirrors? *Criminal Justice and Behavior* 35(10): 1257–1276.

Soble, Ronald, and Robert Dallos. 1975. *The impossible dream: The equity funding story, the fraud of the century*. New York: Putnam.

Spalek, Basia. 2001. White-collar victims and the issue of trust. *British criminology conference proceedings 4*, ed. Roger Tarling. London: British Society of Criminology, 1–15.

Spohn, Julie. 1997. The legal implications of graphology. *Washington University Law Quarterly* 75(3): 1307–1334.

Spurling, Hilary. 2000. *La grande therese: The greatest scandal of the century*. London: HarperCollins.

Steffensmeier, Darrell, Jennifer Schwartz, and Michael Roche. 2013. Gender and twenty-first-century corporate crime: Female involvement and the gender gap in enron-era corporate frauds. *American Sociological Review* 78(3): 448–476.

Stiles, Philip, and Bernard Taylor. 1993. Maxwell—The failure of corporate governance. *Corporate Governance: An International Review* 1(1): 34–45.

Stotland, Ezra. 1977. White collar criminals. *Journal of Social Issues* 33: 179–196.

Sutherland, Edwin. 1983. *White collar crime: The uncut version*. New Haven: Yale University Press.

Sutton, Adam, and Ronald Wild. 1985. Small business: White-collar villains or victims. *International Journal of the Sociology of Law* 13(3): 247–259.

Terpstra, David, Elizabeth Rozell, and Robert Robinson. 1993. The influence of personality and demographic variables on ethical decisions related to insider trading. *The Journal of Psychology* 127(4): 375–390.

Tett, Robert, Douglas Jackson, and Mitchell Rothstein. 1991. Personality measures as predictors of job performance: A meta-analytic review. *Personnel Psychology* 44(4): 703–741.

Thomas, Martin. 1991. *The fraud*. Richmond: Pagemasters.

Topalli, Volkan. 2005. When being good is bad: An expansion of neutralization theory. *Criminology* 43(3): 797–836.

Treisman, Daniel. 2008. Putin's silovarchs. *Orbis* 51(1): 141–153.

Tupman, Alison. 1994. Looking for 'Ms big'. *Journal of Financial Crime* 2(3): 179–186.

Tyler, Tom. 2006a. *Why people obey the law*. Princeton: Princeton University Press.

Tyler, Tom. 2006b. Viewing CSI and the threshold of guilt: Managing truth and justice in reality and fiction. *Yale Law Journal* 115: 1050–1085.

Verrender, Ian. 2008. A shark has such teeth, and it shows them pearly white. *Sydney Morning Herald*, May 31.

Walley, Liz, and Mike Smith. 1998. *Deception in Selection*. New York: Wiley.

Walters, Glenn. 1995. The psychological inventory of criminal thinking styles. *Criminal Justice and Behavior* 22(3): 307–325.

Walters, Glenn, and Matthew Geyer. 2004. Criminal thinking and identity in male white-collar offenders. *Criminal Justice and Behavior* 31(3): 263–281.

Watkins, Sherron, and Mimi Swartz. 2003. *Power failure: The inside story of the collapse of enron*. New York: Doubleday.

Weisburd, David, Elin Waring, and Ellen Chayet. 2001. *White-collar crime and criminal careers*. Cambridge: Cambridge University Press.

Wetzell, Richard. 2000. *Inventing the criminal: A history of German criminology, 1880-1945*. Chapel Hill: University of North Carolina Press.

Wexler, Mark. 2010. Financial edgework and the persistence of rogue traders. *Business and Society Review* 115(1): 1–25.

Wheeler, Stanton. 1992. The problem of white-collar crime motivation. In *White-collar crime reconsidered* ed. Shlegel, Kip and David Weisburd 108–123. Boston: Northeastern University Press.

Wiley, Susan. 2005. Deception and detection in psychiatric diagnosis. *Psychiatric Clinics of North America* 21(4): 869–893.

Wilkins, Anne, William Acuff, and Dana Hermanson. 2012. Understanding a ponzi scheme: Victims' perspectives. *Journal of Forensic and Investigative Accounting* 4(1): 1–18.

Williams, Phil (ed.). 1997. *Russian organized crime: The new threat?*. London: Frank Cass.

Willott, Sara, and Christine Griffin. 1999. Building your own lifeboat: Working-class male offenders talk about economic crime. *British Journal of Social Psychology* 38(4): 445–460.

Wong, Kam. 2005. From white-collar crime to organizational crime: An intellectual history. *Murdoch University Electronic Journal of Law* 12: 1–27.

Worrall, Simon. 2003. *The poet and the murderer: A true story of literary crime and the art of forgery*. London: 4th Estate.

Young, Jock. 2004. Mayhem and Measurement in Late Modernity. In *Crime and crime control in an integrating europe: Plenary presentations held at the third annual conference of the european society of criminology, Helsinki 2003*, ed. Kauko Aromaa, and Sami Nevala, 18–31. Helsinki: Criminal Justice Press.

Young, Mary. 2012. *Banking secrecy and offshore financial centers: Money laundering and offshore banking*. London: Routledge.

Zaplin, Ruth. 2007. *Female offenders: Critical perspectives and effective interventions*. Boston: Jones & Bartlett.

Zebrowitz, Leslie, Carrie Andreoletti, Mary Collins, So Lee, and Jeremy Young. 1998. Bright, bad, babyfaced boys: Appearance stereotypes do not always yield self-fulfilling prophecy effects. *Journal of Personality and Social Psychology* 75(5): 1300–1320.

Zeitz, Dorothy. 1981. *Women who embezzle or defraud: A study of convicted felons*. New York: Praeger.

Ziliak, Stephen, and Deirdre McCloskey. 2007. *The cult of statistical significance: How the standard error costs us jobs, justice, and lives*. Ann Arbor: University of Michigan Press.

Zuckoff, Mitchell. 2005. *Ponzi's scheme: The true story of a financial legend*. New York: Random House.

Part III
Bribery, Corporate Governance and Ethical Aspect of Financial Crime

Chapter 9
Complicity in Organizational Deviance: The Role of Internal and External Unethical Pressures

Anne Sachet-Milliat

Abstract Sociological research in organizational deviance, specifically in the area of corporate crime, has shown how deviant behaviors (frauds and unethical behaviors) are not only restricted to individuals but also to organizations. The objective of our research is to study how organizational deviance can be spread and institutionalized throughout corporate hierarchies. In order for organizational deviance to exist, be institutionalized and accepted, it must get the active or passive complicity not only from organizational members but also from institutions in charge of defining the external-legal and ethical norms. Deviant organizations and their leaders use unethical and pressured management practice in their internal and institutional environment so as to change the norms of individuals' behaviors and also to transform societal norms in order for their actions to be legal and even be perceived as being legitimate. The concept of social influence will be used to analyze the different forms of internal and external unethical pressures which help organizational deviant leaders implement them. Social influence uses various techniques such as incentives, manipulation, peer pressure, and authority. Political influence strategies carried out by deviant organizations will also be highlighted in order to understand how these organizations get the complicity of their institutional environment.

9.1 Introduction

The pioneering work of Sutherland in 1940 on white-collar crime showed that this phenomenon, far from being limited to individuals, also involved a number of companies, which consequently could be regarded as deviant actors. This view was so iconoclastic and contrary to the social and economic order of the time, it was not until the late 1970s and especially the 1980s that there arose, primarily in the United States, a current of research in sociology setting out to explore the organizational

A. Sachet-Milliat (✉)
ISC Paris Business School, Paris, France
e-mail: asachet.milliat@isc.paris.com

© Springer International Publishing Switzerland 2016
M. Dion et al. (eds.), *Financial Crimes: Psychological, Technological,
and Ethical Issues*, International Library of Ethics, Law,
and the New Medicine 68, DOI 10.1007/978-3-319-32419-7_9

201

dimension of deviance and more particularly of corporate crime, notably with the work of Reiss (1978), Ermann and Lundman (1978) and Clinard and Yeager (1980).

In line with this research, the aim of this chapter is to study the mechanisms by which organizational deviance was able to spread into different hierarchical levels and become institutionalized within companies.

By way of a preamble, the concept of organizational deviance and its characteristics will be defined by elucidating the different levels of norms (individual, group, organizational and environmental) serving as a reference point for describing the deviance of an action. Different degrees of organizational responsibility, ranging from the unintended creation of a favourable environment for fraud to deliberate attempts on the part of company management to encourage this type of behaviour, will be studied and illustrated by means of different instances of U.S. and French fraud. For it to be perpetuated and institutionalized, organizational deviance requires the more or less active complicity not only of the members of the organization but also of the actors and institutions responsible for defining external legal or ethical standards and ensuring they are adhered to. The emphasis here will be on the various forms of unethical pressures exerted by deviant organizations and their management on internal and external actors, by mobilizing in particular the concepts of social influence and corporate political strategy.

9.2 Norms and Organizational Deviance

Cheating, transgression, deviance, fraud, unethical behaviour…, the diversity of the terminology used by researchers and practitioners to study deviance phenomena illustrates their multifaceted nature within organizations and the difficulty apprehending them. In general, deviance may be defined as a departure from a socially accepted norm. It is therefore important to clarify the type of norms used to assess behaviour in organizations (Warren 2003). Indeed the value placed on deviance varies among studies in sociology and management, some pointing to its destructive nature, particularly research on business crime (see, in particular, Sutherland 1940, 1983; Cressey 1986; Clinard and Yeager 1979, 1980), and others emphasizing its beneficial effects on the organization when it is matter of deviating from inappropriate or oppressive norms through revolt, circumvention or innovation (Warren 2003; Babeau 2006; Babeau and Chanlat 2008; Courpasson and Thoenig 2008; Louart 2012; Honoré 2012).

Warren proposes evaluating individual behaviour according to two sets of norms: on the one hand, those of the reference group, which can themselves be further subdivided into informal norms, corresponding to usual behaviour, and formal standards (procedural rules, codes of conduct), referring to expected behaviour, and on the other those of society, by mobilizing the concept of hypernorms developed by Donaldson and Dunfee (1994). *Hypernorms*, defined as the beliefs and values generally shared in different cultural contexts, encompass a variety of normative approaches (law, justice, utilitarianism, duty, virtue, etc.). Warren specifies that deviance at a social level may be compliance at another level. Consequently, taking account only of the norms of the reference group is insufficient for judging the value of a behaviour.

Our reflections here will address a particular form of deviance, perpetrated more or less deliberately by organizations as an entity, with the complicity of a number of their members, not individual deviance carried out unbeknownst to the organization. We will focus on deviance the effects of which may be deemed destructive from a societal standpoint insofar as it leads to a transgression of the norms reflecting the values and ethical principles necessary for life in a community. Examples of organizational deviance abound in the business world: unlawful cartels, bribery to obtain a contract, violation of labour laws or environmental regulations, and so on. The public sphere is not immune to this phenomenon either, as evidenced by the different cases of deviance in administrations that have marked the darkest moments in our history, such as the participation of Nazi officials in the Holocaust (Hilberg 1985) or the massacre of innocent civilians by American soldiers during the Vietnam War (Kelman and Hamilton 1989). The key work on the topic, regularly republished since 1978, *Corporate and Governmental Deviance. Problems of Organizational Behavior in Contemporary Society*, by the sociologists Ermann and Lundman, thus shows the dark side of both private and public organizations.

If we transpose the Warren model to the analysis of organizational deviance, it seems necessary to take into account the articulation of four levels of norms—individual, group, organizational and environmental, since this phenomenon may be regarded as a particular form of organizational behaviour.

Firstly, at the individual level, members of an organization are characterized by different levels of ethical development (Kohlberg 1969) and frameworks of moral reasoning and by their own value system (Rokeach 1973), as is made clear by research on the cognitive dimension of ethical decision-making (Leleux 2003). Next, individuals are influenced by the norms of their work group. A number of studies on deviance have highlighted the role of the informal rules of colleagues on deviant employee behaviour (Hollinger and Clark 1982). Deviant activities are subject to regulation within the work group and to an informal consensus on standards to be adhered with regard to committing and covering up such actions. It is also important to take into account the organizational level with its various systems of norms, both formal, such as rules and procedures, and informal, as every organization is characterized by a culture composed of values and beliefs that exercise social control through being internalized by the members of the organization. Firms will differ depending on whether or not their social structure—essentially internal processes and the hierarchy—generates fraudulent behaviour (Clinard 1983). The size, distribution of responsibilities, and reporting structure of large organizations give rise to the conditions leading to organizational deviance. In addition, the nature of the organization's objectives may promote unethical or illegal behaviour. For these reasons, the offenses of organizations should be regarded as organizational behaviours (Gross 1978; Reiss 1978). Finally, the social and institutional environment produces more or less stringent norms that have a significant impact on the functioning of various organizations, whether it be a matter of the legal framework or the expectations of stakeholders with regard to ethics.

Members of organizations are thus confronted by various regulatory systems. They may have to comply with the behaviour of their group work, while at the same being deviant with regard to the rules of the organization or the law. Conversely, organizational norms may be deviant in terms of the law or ethics. Conforming to them then entails breaking the law or violating ethical principles, whereas resistance to organizational pressure becomes a behaviour in line with expectations at the societal level, while being deviant from the standpoint of the organization.

In the view of Ermann and Lundman (1978, p. 58), "*Organizational deviance, in sum, refers to action attributed to an organization which is labelled deviant because it violates the normative expectations surrounding the organization. Moreover, the action is peer and elite supported.*" The confrontation between different levels of norms is thus intrinsically linked to the fundamental characteristics of organizational deviance, since such deviance violates the norms of the actors and external institutions, finds support in the norms of a given level of the organization, and is known and supported more or less directly by the elites of the organization (Ermann and Lundman, *op. cit.*).

The analytic model proposed by Ermann and Lundman (2002) reveals different degrees of involvement and responsibility in organizational deviance on the part of management. Such deviance may not be initially planned but is produced incidentally by a lack of information, a division of work limiting responsibilities, failure of the hierarchy to enforce external standards and management practices, such as reward systems, that encourage it indirectly. In some cases organizational deviance is, however, deliberately perpetrated, as when managers explicitly encourage it by direct orders.

The Kerviel affair[1] appears to illustrate a case of deviance indirectly linked to the hierarchy in the French bank concerned, even though the individual dimension of the fraud played a major part. The former trader at Société Générale, Jérôme Kerviel, was prosecuted for taking speculative positions in the order of tens of billions of euros, masked by the use of fictitious trades, which led in early 2008 to the loss of almost €5 billion for his employer. Kerviel's line of defence remained the same throughout his trial. He claimed to have tried to "*do the best possible work*" so as "*to make money for the bank.*" He acknowledged his mistakes, but added that "*without the support and tacit consent of my superiors, none of this would have happened.*"[2] A judgment in the first instance pronounced on 5 October 2010 and confirmed on appeal in October 2012, rejected these arguments and attributed full responsibility to the trader, who was sentenced to 5 years in prison,

---

[1]The data in this case is largely derived from articles published between 2010 and 2014 on the blog "Chroniques judiciaires". By the Monde journalist Pascale Robert-Diard http://prdchroniques.blog.lemonde.fr/?s=kerviel.

[2]Comments cited by Robert Diard in Le Monde of 7 October 2010.

on three criminal charges for "*breach of trust*", "*falsehood and use of falsehood*" and "*fraudulent introduction of data into a computer system*", plus a civil payment of 4.9 billion euros in damages and interest to his former bank. However, a judgment by the Criminal Division of the Court of Cassation on 19 March 2014 overturned the civil provisions requiring the trader to pay the full damages suffered by Société Générale. The Court of Cassation took the view that civil liability for the losses were shared between the trader and his employer due to failures of internal control, without which a fraud of this magnitude would not have been possible.

Even though the trader's offences were clearly not deliberately supported his hierarchy, it seems to us that this fraud may in certain respects be characterized as organizational deviance. Indeed, apart from the failures of internal control indicated by the Court of Cassation, the delegation of decision-making and the reward systems for traders based on very generous bonuses linked to gains on financial transactions created an environment conducive to deviant behaviour. Note, too, that Jerome Kerviel was not personally enriched by the frauds he committed.

While the system of governance and senior management do not appear to be directly involved in the crimes committed by Jérôme Kerviel at Société Générale (Monin 2008), the situation is very different with regard to the fraudulent bankruptcy of Enron in 2002. This scandal represents the very archetype of organizational deviance initiated by the company's top management, covered up by all internal and external actors and institutions—which were supposed, moreover, to control abuse, and corrupting various levels of the hierarchy. Without the connivance of supervisory bodies—the board of directors, the audit firm Andersen, investment banks, the Securities and Exchange Commission, etc., whose members were beset by numerous conflicts of interest, the management abuses could have been prevented or at least corrected before the fatal sanction of the financial market intervened (U.S. Senate report 2002). The mechanisms that allowed the complicity of these various actors and organizations to be obtained therefore appear critical in the perpetuation of organizational deviance.

9.3 Institutionalization of Organizational Deviance and Complicity of Members of the Organization

The sociologists Ermann and Lundman (*op. cit.*) identify three stages of the development of organizational deviance: initiation, institutionalization and reaction.

In the initiation phase, individuals or groups identify a situation as problematic and look for solutions. The hierarchy may establish guidelines or require subordinates to implement specific actions. The initial act may not even be deviant, as in the case of a corporate network in the electrical equipment sector, that was first formed on the basis of legal cooperation and encouraged by the government, but then drifted towards illegal price fixing during the Great Depression.

In the institutionalization stage, deviant behaviour is an integral part of the functioning of the organization and often persists for reasons unrelated to those present at the outset. The participants are largely unaware of deviance and its consequences for themselves and the organization, but are caught up in a spiral of commitment. Even when the people who initiated the deviance leave their positions, their replacements find that deviant behaviour is part of their job and must either go along with it or make way for other more accommodating individuals. "*Once deviant actions are institutionalized, they become intertwined with legitimate ones, and both become routine*" (Ermann and Lundman 2002, p. 25). Institutionalized deviance continues until it is stopped either by internal reactions, especially exposure by certain members of the organization, or external reactions through the mobilization of the media, the victims or the law (Miceli and Near 1997).

The study of different cases of organizational deviance, such as the falsification by the company Goodrich of safety testing of a faulty braking system for military aircraft (Vandiver 1972), the previously mentioned Enron scandal, and the deliberate marketing by the French laboratory Servier of a dangerous drug (Sachet-Milliat 2012), shows that all these cases have in common the need for the cooperation of several members of the organizations concerned, not only to implement deviant acts but also to hide them. To understand this phenomenon better, we introduced the concept of unethical pressure to designate direct or indirect management practices aiming at encouraging or compelling an employee to commit unethical, or even fraudulent, acts contrary to his or her ethical principles, for the benefit of the organization (Sachet-Milliat 2005).

The work of psycho-sociologists on social influence seems particularly fruitful for better understanding how pressure is exerted to obtain the cooperation of employees, especially managers, in organizational deviance. Bedard et al. define social influence as "*a change in the behaviour or beliefs of an individual as a result of real or imaginary, intentional or unintentional pressure exercised by a person or group of persons*" (1999, p. 164). Different forms of expression of social influence—normative peer pressure, manipulation, the power of authority—will combine to change the individual's perceptions, judgments, attitudes or behaviour.

As we have noted above, employees' behaviour is influenced by the informal rules of their work group (Hollinger and Clark 1982). The cooperation of new members in deviance involves a socialization process (Anan et al. 2004). Upon arrival, new employees faced with unethical behaviour experience cognitive dissonance, which will be resolved by neutralization techniques provided by their peers. Newcomers usually begin with minor transgressions and then find themselves caught up in a spiral of increasingly deviant acts. In addition, once compromised, it is difficult for them to backtrack. The socialization process takes place unbeknownst to the new employees, who feel they have freedom of choice.

This illusion can be enhanced through the use of manipulative techniques by the hierarchy. Manipulation involves using methods that make employees collaborate in unethical or fraudulent acts without exerting direct pressure on them. They seem to be freely consenting (Beauvois and Joule 1987), as they are caught up in a system where fierce competition and the pursuit of profitability justify such practices. The manipulation strategy may be based on creating a trusting relationship that combines aspects of work and friendship (Anquetil 2003) and on the provision of ambiguous information that minimizes the unethical nature of the actions called for. For example in the context of public procurement, illicit payments to local politicians are not presented by the hierarchy as bribery but as funding for the campaigns required for democracy and as a common everyday practice among competitors (Prompsy 2000). Dejours (1998) borrows from Habermas the concept of *communicative distortion* to analyse the symbolic violence exerted by business leaders to make social suffering acceptable in the eyes of employees by neutralizing their moral sense. Dejours points to the discrepancy between official management discourse on the organization of work and how the job is actually experienced by employees, with its issues and shortcomings and the distress thereby induced. Communicative distortion may be the result of unintended and unconscious acts, but may also stem from a deliberate strategy based on the general denial of the reality of work and workplace distress. Managerial and commercial arguments originally intended for propaganda in relation to the outside world are also deployed internally in the name of efficiency. Specific media are used to disseminate stereotyped and simplistic messages that replace collective discussion and do not give rise to awkward questions. Along similar lines to Dejours's analysis, Pesqueux and Biefnot (2002) point to the new corporate ideological project of universalizing the managerial logic of efficiency to the detriment of collective values. Willingness by employees to compromise their ethical principles can in particular be accounted for by social conformity to norms of efficiency and commitment in relation to the company and, given their subordinate position, respect for the hierarchy.

Various studies that have tried to understand how human beings without any pathological moral sense have been able to participate in war crimes or crimes against humanity provide a valuable insight into the phenomenon of complicity in organizational deviance. Hilberg (1985) thus emphasizes the role of anti-Jewish propaganda, which depicted Jews as subhuman and the incarnation of evil in order to justify violence against them. He explains the absence of opposition from German officials through two principal mechanisms: on the one hand hiding abuses and on the other rationalizing acts while suppressing any form of criticism. A special vocabulary was used in Nazi propaganda to neutralize the scope of acts committed, with the word "*killing*" replaced by "*the final solution of the Jewish question*" and the term "*special installations*" used instead of "*killing installations*" (Hillberg 1985 *in* Ermann and Lundman 2002, p. 181).

Responsibilities are often fragmented, leading employees to cooperate in a minor way in the system while quietly doing what is defined as a normal part of their work. According to Silver and Geller (1978), compartmentalization of tasks partly explains the ease with which the complicity of Nazi officials in the Holocaust was obtained. Certain employees not directly involved in exterminating Jews were content to handle the paperwork, others were responsible for the supply of toxic gas but were unaware of its destination, and yet others organized train transport, thus routinely and efficiently contributing to a process of mass destruction alongside their normal duties (Hilberg 1985). *"The worst horrors often stem from a string of petty crimes"* (Myers 2006, p. 143).

Hilberg also shows how the Nazi administration created its own set of rules, with which members had to comply. In particular it prohibited corruption in the seizure of Jewish property and specified the methods to be used for exterminating the Jews, in order that the killing process be effective while not damaging the image of the Nazis among the German population. Officials managed the split between their personal feelings and the duties relating to their position by justifying their actions though obedience to authority and the rules.

The philosopher Arendt (1963) introduced the concept of the banality of evil to explain how the functionary Adolf Eichmann, an unremarkable personality, came to collaborate actively with Nazism and play a major part in organizing the death camps. She describes this war criminal as a zealous and obedient servant who had lost his capacity to think for himself and to distinguish right from wrong. Along similar lines, the famous Milgram experiments (1965), on how individuals submitted to demands that they gratuitously hurt other people, showed that factors related to the situation—prestige, legitimacy, proximity to authority, proximity to the victim, etc.—are much more important than the personality of the person who submits. Kelman and Hamilton (1989) in turn proposed the concept of the *crime of obedience* to describe the participation of American soldiers in the massacre of hundreds of Vietnamese civilians in My Lai village during a military operation in which they were supposed to neutralize enemy soldiers. Even though the massacre is unlikely to have been deliberately planned by the military hierarchy, the context of the Vietnam War encouraged, more or less explicitly, the destruction of the Vietnamese rural population for reasons of strategic necessity. The authors identify three social processes that led individuals to agree to participate in this type of abuse by eliminating all forms of moral inhibition, namely *authorization, routinization* and dehumanization. *"Through authorization, the situation becomes so defined that the individual is absolved of the responsibility to make personal moral choices. Through routinization, the action become so organized that there is no opportunity for raising moral questions. Through dehumanization, the actors' attitudes toward the target and toward themselves become so structured that it is neither necessary nor possible for them to view the relationship in moral terms."*

Corporate deviance is generally not as destructive as that committed in cases of genocide or war crimes, and the violence inflicted on the victims is often more symbolic than physical. Thus an employee whose employer wants to "get rid of" him or her is not physically eliminated but dismissed or forced to resign though moral harassment or fear-inducing management practices. Corporate deviance can nevertheless have serious consequences for those subject to it, in terms of their psychological and physical well-being, and in extreme cases it may even lead to death. Thus 1,138 workers, mostly women, were killed and over 2,000 were injured in the collapse on 24 April 2013 in Bangladesh of the Raza Plana building that housed a clothing factory working for major European and American brands. According to the testimony of survivors, the employees of this textile factory were forced by their employer to go to work the day the tragedy occurred, despite large cracks having appeared the previous day in the walls of the building, which had been hastily constructed with disregard for safety standards.[3] Employees are not the sole victims of corporate deviance, as is shown in the scandal of Mediator. This appetite suppressing drug was prescribed for more than thirty years to five million patients in France, even though the Servier laboratory managers were aware of its high-risk character from the outset, and of the fact that it could eventually be responsible for the deaths of over 2,100 people, according to forensic experts.[4]

It does not seem an exaggeration, in our view, to speak of real economic war crimes in those situations where innocent lives are sacrificed on the altar of efficiency and profitability, similar to the violence suffered by civilians during armed conflicts. It therefore seems appropriate to transpose the thinking from research conducted on government deviance in wartime onto deviant behaviour in the business world, although it is important to remain cautious with regard to importing conceptual frameworks for certain forms of crime such as financial fraud where the victims of illegal behaviour are more diffuse and difficult to identify and the culpability is less. The different types of deviance are characterized by varying degrees of *moral intensity*, to use the concept introduced by Jones (1991), who identified six dimensions of an ethical problem: the magnitude of the impact on others, the social consensus it is subject to, the likelihood of effects, temporality (immediate or delayed), the proximity of the persons concerned, and the concentration of the effects on a greater or lesser number of people.

By the same logic as the studies of deviance in sociology and social psychology outlined above, the unethical pressure exerted by the hierarchy on employees can take a much more direct form than manipulation, using authority to obtain obedience (Milgram 1965) or even management based on fear (Dejours 1998). The employee in fear of being side-lined or losing his job will accept being complicit in fraud through his submission to authority. The fact that unethical behaviour is dictated by someone senior in the hierarchy rather than freely adopted will tend to make the employee less feel responsible and facilitate the adoption of deviant behaviour that may be very harmful to other people. Lastly, employees may be prompted to behave unethically through assessment and compensation systems based on short-term performance regardless of the means used to obtain the results (Anan et al., *op. cit.*). In an investigation of fraud in times of crisis conducted by PricewaterhouseCoopers in 2009, 40 % of the companies questioned considered that the economic crisis created a favourable environment for fraud and 68 % said this was linked to the intensification of underlying pressures and incentives, particularly financial objectives that were harder to attain, the fear of losing one's job, and the desire to get performance bonuses.

The different forms of influence are often combined in order more effectively to obtain the complicity in deviance of members of the organization. Moreover these

---

[3]See the website of the NGO Peuples solidaires, http://www.peuples-solidaires.org/bangladesh-ranaplaza-appelurgent/.

[4]Le Monde, 17 April 2014.

pressure practices do not leave those who submit to them unscathed. Apart from the risk of prosecution, employees who commit an act contrary to their personal ethics are exposed to psychological damage that can lead to depression and, in the most severe cases, even suicide (Anquetil, *op. cit.*). The gap between the requirements of the organization and individual morality generates ethical distress (Dejours, *op. cit.*), which often ultimately leads the ending of the collaboration with the company of employees subject to it, either of their own accord or through dismissal (Anquetil, *op. cit.*). Managers seem to be increasingly powerless against the pressures exerted on them, due to increasingly individualized management practices that have undermined collective work practices (Pierson 2011).

Having explored the mechanisms for obtaining the complicity in deviance of members of an organization, we will now discuss the pressures on external actors and institutions, to ensure the continuance of organizational deviance.

9.4 The Role of Political Influence Strategies in the Perpetuation of Organizational Deviance

As shown by Ermann and Lundman (*op. cit.*), once institutionalized, the only way organizational deviance ceases in when there is a reaction either from a member of the organization or from outside. Thus in many instances organizational deviance requires, as well as the complicity of members of the organization, the cooperation, or at least the tacit consent, of the actors responsible for defining external legal and ethical standards and monitoring their application. We shall use the concept of *external unethical pressures* to designate practices, both legal and illegal, aimed at influencing the actors of the socio-institutional environment (policy makers, non-governmental organizations, the media, etc.), in order to obtain their collaboration in deviant actions, and that of *internal unethical pressures* to describe practices intended to influence members of the organization.

While some political influence practices deployed by firms, such as legislative monitoring and the provision of non-biased information to political actors, appear legitimate, others are ethically and even legally questionable: political funding of varying degrees of opacity, the manipulation of expertise and information, the "*revolving door*", influence peddling and corruption, intimidation, etc. (Stauber and Rampton 2004; Sachet-Milliat 2010).

The Enron affair demonstrates the importance of the use of political influence strategies by the heads of deviant companies to obtain regulation favourable to their interest and to adapt the external regulatory system to their deviant behaviour so that such behaviour remains legal. Thus the Texas firm employed no less than a hundred employees in its Washington-based "*Public Affairs*" department and, entirely legally, spent ten million dollars on its political activities, mainly in the form of funding election campaigns (Halimi 2002). In particular, it was the main contributor to George Bush's campaign. Republicans demonstrated their gratitude to their generous donor by deregulating the energy sector, thus providing Enron with tremendous opportunities to develop its negotiation and trading activities free of federal control (Sauviat 2002). In the words of John Sweeney, president of the AFL-CIO (American Federation of Labor and Congress of Industrial Organizations), *"The real outage is not that Enron violated the rules. The real outrage is that Enron made the rules"* (quoted St. Petersburg Times, 6 February 2002).

In the Mediator affair mentioned above, the health authorities were for over 35 years manipulated by the Servier laboratory to obtain authorization to put the dangerous drug on the market and to continue marketing it. Experts from IGAS (General Inspectorate of Social Affairs—*Inspection Générale des Affaires Sociales*) have exposed the various mechanisms that allowed it, as they put it, to *"take the health authorities to the cleaners"*: submission of flawed studies, pressures exerted, personal and family threats. The report also points to the ineffectiveness of these authorities, which failed in their role to protect public health by not adopting the precautionary principle, despite various alerts about the harmfulness of the product between 1974 and 2007.[5] Many of the experts working for AFSSAPS (French Agency for Sanitary Safety of Health Products—*Agence Française de Sécurité Sanitaire des Produits de Santé*)[6] have financial ties to pharmaceutical companies, which can lead to conflicts of interest. In particular, two former officials of the agency had close links with Servier at the time of the first alerts concerning Mediator: the former director of drug evaluation was paid nearly a million euros in consultancy fees by the laboratory and the wife of the pharmacovigilance representative, who headed the European Committee for Human Medicinal Products, was Servier's lawyer for 6 years.[7] The damning testimony of two former researchers at the Servier Laboratory, interviewed by the judges in the summer of 2011, confirm the analysis by IGAS experts in showing that studies concerning the placing on the market of Mediator were deliberately falsified from 1973 and that the company's management deliberately violated the precautionary principle in the late 1990s by trying at all costs to continue selling the drug when proof of its dangers were accumulating.[8]

Jacques Servier, the founder and chairman of the Group, along with four managers and the corporation itself, were indicted for *aggravated fraud*. In addition, there was an indictment for *manslaughter and involuntary injuries* of Jacques Servier in December 2012 and of the Agence Nationale de Sécurité du Médicament (National Security Agency of Medicines) (formerly AFSSAPS) in March 2013, on suspicion of having neglected alerts as to the dangers of the drug and having

---

[5]Le Monde, 18 January 2011.

[6]The AFSSAPS was renamed Agence Nationale de Sécurité du Médicament following the Mediator scandal.

[7]Le Monde, 20 May 2013.

[8]Minutes of hearings published by Libération of 6 September 2011.

delayed its withdrawal from the market. The trial is currently under way despite the death in April 2014 of Jacques Servier, who can consequently no longer be tried.

The complicity of politicians is also at the heart of the deadly Raza Plana accident, since most of the elected representatives of the Bangladeshi parliament have interests in the textile industry and are therefore not inclined to apply more restrictive rules in terms of working conditions and safety. According to Anu Muhammad, Professor of Economics at the University of Jahangirnagar, *"The garment trade offers easy money, a lucrative means to invest in any other sector or a route into parliament. Officially, only 29 of the 300 members of parliament are textile factory owners. But in reality, if you include those whose interests are registered under another name, there are many more. In Bangladesh, it's hard to find anyone with power who isn't linked to the world of textiles."* (Comments recorded by Ciran 2013).

These examples, among many others, illustrate the key role of political influence strategies in the perpetuation of organizational deviance and lead us to draw, by way of conclusion to our observations, a parallel between internal and external unethical pressure practices. Indeed, the forms of social influence that we deployed to account for pressure practices regarding members of the organization appear to be equally relevant for analysing the relations between deviant organizations and their environment. The analysis is summarized in the Table 9.1.

Given the intensity of unethical pressures exerted by deviant organizations, the question now arises as to the resistance of internal and external actors, which as Ermann and Lundman have shown, is the only way to stop this type of behaviour. It is therefore important to consider how to increase the resistance capacity not only of employees but also people from civil society and policy makers. Much remains to be done to ensure the independence of elected representations and state employees

Table 9.1 Internal and external unethical pressures and methods of social influence

Methods	Unethical pressure	
	Internal	External
Incentives	Evaluation and compensation system rewarding the deviance of members of the organization	Political funding/corruption/the revolving door/exchanges of favours with political actors (representatives, NGOs, the media, etc.)
Manipulation	Communicative distortion in the messages delivered internally/confusion of emotional and professional registers	Communicative distortion in information disseminated to political actors/manipulation of expertise
Use of authority	Direct orders, use of fear (threat of dismissal or demotion, harassment, etc.)	Intimidation, threat of ending funding, jobs in the constituency, etc.
Normative peer pressure	Informal pressure of colleagues	Informal pressure of economic and political elites belonging to the same social networks

faced with the political influence strategies adopted by firms. Appropriate measures include promoting the public funding of political life, prohibiting conflicts of interest, and strengthening the countervailing powers of civil society, particularly in terms of expertise. The laws guaranteeing legal protection for whistle-blowers have progressed in this sense, with many instances of deviance being exposed thanks to the courage of those who dare to publicly denounce the deviance they witness. However, despite newly introduced legislative, the scope of these laws is restricted to certain sectors and employee categories. Thus the law passed in France in April 2013, following the Médiator scandal, applies only to alerts in the areas of public health and the environment. The Whistleblower Protection Act, passed in the United States in 1989 to provide legal protection to federal employees disclosing illegal or improper government activities, ultimately leaves limited scope for action, because the information revealed must not be confidential and the disclosure must not be subject to a legal prohibition. In addition, employees of organizations related to intelligence and the executive are excluded from this protection. Furthermore, private sector employees, given unethical orders by their superiors, do not have the right to object (along the lines of the conscience clause for journalists), and ethical warning systems in place in certain major Western companies, especially those listed in New York, seem ill-suited to exposing organizational deviance involving company executives.

Faced with these regulatory shortcomings, resistance to organizational deviance ultimately relies on the ethics of actors in the private and public spheres, hence the crucial role of education. The question then arises as to the role of training institutions in raising the ethical awareness of future managers and policy makers.

As Mintzberg (2004) points out in his highly critical book on American MBA programs, ethics courses are generally confined to modules set apart from other teaching, which is mostly concerned with the acquisition of management techniques dissociated from human issues and centered on creating shareholder value. How then can one convince students of the importance of ethics in the business world, when the dominant discourse favors a calculative and technocratic conception of management? It would be desirable, first of all, for ethical issues to be integrated transversally into all management studies disciplines, in addition to courses specifically concerned with ethical thinking. Next, the teaching of business ethics should not only focus on the instrumental dimension of deploying ethical approaches in business, through tools such as ethical charters or alert systems that by and large correspond to corporate compliance to legal standards or CSR intended to guard against deviant practices on the part of employees. The collective resolution of ethical dilemmas in management, especially those involving conflicts between personal values and organizational expectations, mobilizing different philosophical approaches to ethics is in our view an effective way to develop the ethics of future managers. Indeed, this type of scenario helps create an awareness of the phenomenon of cognitive dissonance inherently linked to ethical dilemmas and reveals the neutralization techniques at work in the process of ethical decision-making. As was pointed out almost 20 years ago by McDonald and Pak (1996), it is important not to restrict ways of thinking to the utilitarian approaches still dominant in teaching techniques, especially scenario methods, and to take into account other frameworks of moral reasoning such as the Kantian approach or the ethics of responsibility. Finally, an important place should be given to what social psychology reveals regarding social influence phenomena, to enable students to identify situations where they are being manipulated or being subjected to a dis-empowering authority. In this way, by exercising their own critical judgment, they will be better able to withstand unethical pressure. As demonstrated by the philosopher Arendt (1963), the banality of evil finds fertile ground in the inability to distinguish good and evil and to resist an immoral system. In short, Universities and Business Schools should not be limited to passing on management techniques but should also have the mission of awakening the ethical awareness of future managers and their capacity to think for themselves, forming true citizens rather than simply competent employees.

9.5   Conclusion

This research aimed to investigate the mechanisms by which deviant organizations obtain the complicity both of their members as well as the external actors and institutions in charge of defining and monitoring legal and ethical standards, in order to perpetrate organizational deviance.

We introduced in our previous research the concept of unethical pressure to designate managing practices aiming at obtaining the cooperation of employees to commit deviant actions. Here, we attempted to take the analysis further by distinguishing two forms of unethical pressures: internal ones, intended to influence members of the organization and external ones, aimed at influencing the actors of the socio-institutional environment, especially policy makers and governmental institutions. In order to do so, we mobilized the work of psycho-sociologists on social influence and its various forms of expression—including normative peer pressure, manipulation, incentive and power of authority—and the concept of corporate political strategy. We also transposed the thinking from research conducted on complicity in war crime onto deviant behaviour in the business world to provide a valuable insight into the phenomenon of destructive organizational deviance. Finally, we drew a parallel between internal and external unethical pressures by comparing the various forms of social influence and the different political activities. We concluded our thinking with a questioning on the way to increase the resistance capacity of internal and external actors faced with unethical pressures in order to prevent the perpetuation of organizational deviance. Further research is needed in order to further investigate the various mechanisms that enable deviant organizations to obtain the complicity of their employees and of the actors of their socio-institutional environment by carrying out several case studies in various cultural and political environments. The psychological distress experienced by the employees that are the targets of unethical pressures and the individual and collective resistance to this psychological violence also need further attention.

References

Anan, V., B.E. Ashford, and M. Joshi. 2004. Business as usual: The acceptance and perpetuation of corruption in organizations. *Academy of Management Executive* 18(2): 39–55.

Anquetil, A. 2003. *Dilemmes éthiques en entreprise: le rôle de la faiblesse de la volonté dans la décision des cadres*, Thèse de Doctorat en Sciences cognitives, Ecole Polytechnique, Paris, juin.

Arendt, H. 1963. *Eichman in Jerusalem: A report on the banality of evil*. New York: The Viking Press.

Babeau, O. 2006. La transgression ordinaire des règles dans les cabinets de conseil en management. In *Recherches en Management et Organisation*, ed. M. Kalika and P. Romelaer. Economica, 245–260.

Babeau, O., and J.-F. Chanlat. 2008. La transgression, une dimension oubliée de l'organisation. *Revue Française de Gestion, no* 183: 201–219.

Beauvois, J.L., and R.V. Joule. 1987. *Petit traité de manipulation à l'usage des honnêtes gens*, Presses universitaires de Grenoble.

Bédard, L., Déziel J., and Lamarche L. 1999. *Introduction à la psychologie sociale*. ERPI.

Ciran, O. 2013. *Au Bangladesh les meurtriers du prêt-à-porter*. Le Monde Diplomatique (June).

Clinard, M.B. 1983. *Corporate ethics and crime*. USA: Sage Publications.

Clinard, M.B., and P.C. Yeager. 1979. *Illegal corporate behaviour*. Washington DC: US Government Printing office.

Clinard, M.B., and P.C. Yeager. 1980. *Corporate crime*. New York: Free Press.

Courpasson, D., and J.-C. Thoenig. 2008. *Quand les cadres se rebellent*. Paris: Vuibert.

Cressey, D.R. 1986. Why managers commit fraud. *Australian & New Zealand Journal of Criminology* 19: 195–209.

Dejours, C. 1998. *Souffrance en France. La banalisation de l'injustice sociale*. Paris: Editions du Seuil.

Donaldson, T., and T. Dunfee. 1994. Toward unified conception of business ethics: contracts theory. *Academy of Management Review* 19: 252–284.

Ermann, M.D., and R.J. Lundman. 1978. Deviant acts by complex organizations: Deviance and social control at the organizational level of analysis. *The Sociological Quarterly* 19(Winter): 55–67.

Ermann, M.D., and R.J. Lundman. 2002. *Corporate and governmental deviance*, 6th ed. New York: Oxford University Press.

Gross, E. 1978. Organizational crime: A theoretical perspective. In *Studies in symbolic interaction*, ed. Denzin. Greenwood, CT: JAI.

Halimi, S. 2002. *Un scandale presque légal. Enron symbole d'un système*. Le Monde Diplomatique (March).

Hilberg, R. 1985. The Nazi Holocaust. Using bureaucracies and overcoming psychological barriers to genocide. In *The destruction of the European Jews*, by Raul Hilberg. New York: Holmes & Meier (Reprinted by permission in Ermann M.D. and Lundman R.J. (Eds), *Corporate and Governmental Deviance*, Sixth Edition, Oxford University Press, New York, 2002, 167–188).

Hollinger, R.C., and J.P. Clark. 1982. Formal and informal controls of employee deviance. *The Sociological Quaterly* 23(summer): 333–343.

Honoré, L. 2012. Les jeux des normes et de la déviance. Etude du fonctionnement de services de néonatologie. Dossier *Déviance et Management, Humanisme et Entreprise* 306: 69–84 (January/February).

Jones, T. 1991. Ethical decision making by individuals in organizations: An issue-contingent model. *Academy of Management Review* 16(2): 366–396.

Kelman, H.C., and V.L. Hamilton. 1989. The My Lai massacre. Crimes of obedience and sanctioned massacres, From *Crimes of obedience: Toward a social psychology of authority and responsibility*, Yale University Press (Reprinted by permission *in* Ermann M.D. and

Lundman R.J. (Eds), *Corporate and Governmental Deviance*, Sixth Edition, Oxford University Press, New York, 2002, 195–222).

Kohlberg, L. 1969. Moral stages and moralization: The cognitive-developmental approach. In *Moral development and behaviour: theory, research, and social issues*, T. Lickona, 170–205.

Leleux, C. 2003. Théorie du développement moral chez Lawrence Kohlberg et ses critiques (Gilligan et Habermas). In *Pour une éducation postnationale*, ed. J.-M. Ferry and B. Libois, Editions de l'Université de Bruxelles, coll. "Philosophie et société", Bruxelles, 111–128.

Louart, P. 2012. Introduction. Déviance et Management - Régulations, stigmatisations, émergences créatives. *Humanisme et Entreprise* 306: 1–8 (January/February).

Mc Donald G., and P.C. Pak. 1996. It's all fair in love, war and business: Cognitive philosophies in ethical decision making. *Journal of Business Ethics* 15: 973–996.

Miceli, M., and J. Near. 1997. Whistleblowing as antisocial behavior. In *Antisocial behavior in organizations*, ed. R.A. Giacalone and Greenberg, 130–149. Thousand Oaks, CA: Sage.

Milgram, S. 1965. Some conditions of obedience and disobedience. *Human Relations* 18: 57–76.

Mintzberg, H. 2004. *Managers not MBAs. A hard look at the soft practice of managing and management development*. Berett-Koehler Publishers.

Monin, P. 2008. Légitimité, déviance, délits. Retour sur l'affaire Société Générale. Entretien avec Peter Wirtz. *Revue Française de Gestion* 183: 131–134.

Myers, D.G. 2006. *Psychologie sociale pour managers. Adapted by Nicolas Guégen*. Paris: Dunod.

Pesqueux, Y., and Y. Biéfnot. 2002. *L'éthique des affaires. Management par les valeurs et la responsabilité sociale*, Editions d'Organisation, Paris.

Pierson, F. 2011. Pour un apprentissage de la lutte et de la résistance des cadres pour limiter la souffrance au travail: les apports de la théorie de la reconnaissance d'Axel Honneth, M@n@gement, 2011/5, vol 14, 352–370.

Prompsy, J.-J. 2000. *La cour des cadres*. Paris: Les Editions de la Nerthe.

Reiss Jr, A.J. 1966. The study of deviant behaviour: Where the action is. *Ohio Valley Sociologist* 32: 1–12.

Rokeach, M. 1973. *The nature of human values*. New York: Free Press.

Sachet-Milliat, A. 2005. Ethique et management: pratiques de pression sur les cadres pour obtenir leur collaboration aux actes de délinquance d'affaires, *Revue de Gestion des Ressources Humaines*, July–August–September, 90–107.

Sachet-Milliat, A. 2010. *Les dérives éthiques des stratégies politiques des firmes*, vol. 33, 325–345. Management et Avenir (March).

Sachet-Milliat, A. 2012. Déviance organisationnelle: définition, caractéristiques et mécanismes de diffusion, numéro spécial sur *Déviance et management* de la *Revue Humanisme et Entreprise* 306: 17–32 (January/February).

Sauviat, C. 2002. *Etats-Unis: Enron, une énorme "défaillance de marché*. Chronique internationale de l'IRES, vol. 74, 3–12.

Schwartz, H. 1992. Universals in the content and structure of values: Theoretical advances and empirical tests in 20 countries. *Advances in Experimental Social Psychology* 25: 1–65.

Silver, M., and D. Geller. 1978. On the irrelevance of evil, the organization and individual action. *Journal of Social Issues* 34: 125–136.

Stauber, J., and S. Rampton. 2004. Prefaced and completed by R. Lenglet, *L'industrie du mensonge: lobbying, communication, publicité et médias*. Marseille: Agone (First Edition: *Toxic sludge is Good for you: Lies, Damn lies and the Public Relation Industry*, Common Courage Press 1995).

Sutherland, E.H. 1940. White collar criminality. *American Sociological Review* 5(1): 1–12.

Sutherland, E.H. 1983. *White collar crime, the uncut version*. New Haven: Yale University Press.

United States Senate. 2002. *The role of the board of Directors in Enron's collapse*, Report prepared by the Permanent Subcommittee on Investigation of the Committee on Governmental

Affairs, July 8, 107th Congress, 2d Session, S.PRT 107–70, US Government Printing Office, Washington.

Vandiver, K. 1972. Why should my conscience bother me. In *In the Name of Profit,* by Robert Heilbroner, Doubleday, a division of Bantam Doubleday Dell Publishing Group, Inc., (Reprinted by permission in Ermann M.D. and Lundman R.J. (Eds), *Corporate and Governmental Deviance*, Sixth Edition, Oxford University Press, New York, 2002, 146–166).

Warren, D.E. 2003. Constructive and destructive deviance in organizations. *The Academy of management Review* 28(4): 622–632.

Chapter 10
Corporate Governance and Bribery: Evidence from the World Business Environment Survey

Xun Wu, Krishnan Chandramohan and Azad Singh Bali

Abstract Corporate sector, often portrayed as the victim of corruption, is an important source of rampant corruption problems in many developing countries due to a vicious cycle of bribery practices and corruption. This vicious cycle starts when firms are forced into bribery practices because of a high level of corruption in their operating environment, but widened participation of firms in bribery practices further contributes to the perception of high corruption, which in turn makes the bribery practices even more uncontrollable. The results of our empirical study based on a unique cross-country firm-level dataset suggest that improvement in corporate governance can be a critical ingredient to break the vicious cycle of bribery practices and corruption. We find that firms controlled by individual owners and family are more likely to pay bribes than are firms governed by corporate boards, and that firms reporting higher percentage of their sales for tax purpose are less likely to be involved in corrupt exchanges. Measures adopted by government, business community and individual firms in improving corporate governance can be effective anti-corruption strategies in an environment with high level of corruption.

10.1 Introduction

Corruption continues to be a persistent and systemic problem in many parts of the world, despite enormous resources directed to anti-corruption programs. In Asia, the progress towards corruption reduction in many developing countries has stagnated over the last decade according to Corruption Perception Index (CPI) by

X. Wu (✉) · K. Chandramohan · A.S. Bali
Division of Social Science & Division of Environment, Hong Kong University of Science and Technology, Hong Kong, China
e-mail: wuxun@ust.hk

K. Chandramohan
e-mail: c.krishnan86@gmail.com

A.S. Bali
e-mail: a.bali@murdoch.edu.au

© Springer International Publishing Switzerland 2016
M. Dion et al. (eds.), *Financial Crimes: Psychological, Technological, and Ethical Issues*, International Library of Ethics, Law, and the New Medicine 68, DOI 10.1007/978-3-319-32419-7_10

Table 10.1 Corruption in selected Asian countries: corruption perception index 2001–2011

	2001		2011		2001–2011
	CPI Raw score	Rank (out of 91)	CPI Raw score	Rank (out of 174)	Annual GDP growth rate (%)
Azerbaijan	2	84	2.4	143	14.0
Bangladesh	0.4	91	2.7	120	6.0
China	3.5	57	3.6	75	10.6
India	2.7	71	3.1	95	7.6
Indonesia	1.9	88	3	100	5.5
Kazakhstan	2.7	71	2.7	120	7.7
Malaysia	5	36	4.3	60	5.0
Pakistan	2.3	79	2.5	134	4.6
Philippines	2.9	65	2.6	129	4.9
Thailand	3.2	61	3.4	80	4.1
Vietnam	2.6	75	2.9	112	7.2

Data source Transparency International and World Development Indicators

Transparency International (Table 10.1), and some of these countries have even experienced a noticeable increase in level of corruption in spite of rapid economic growth. The lack of progress towards reducing corruption raises questions about the effectiveness of anti-corruption programs.

A critical shortcoming of existing approaches towards reducing corruption is insufficient attention to the corporate role in corrupt exchanges (Vogl 1998; Wu 2005). The corporate sector can be both the victim and perpetrator of corruption: on one hand, businesses are often subjected to extortion from corrupt government officials; but on the other hand, it is not uncommon to find that businesses themselves initiate the bribery deal in order to evade their responsibilities to the public, or to undermine the efforts of their competitors. The relationship between bribery practices in corporate sector and the level of corruption can be depicted as a vicious cycle (Fig. 10.1). This vicious cycle starts when firms are forced into bribery practices because of a high level of corruption in their operating environment, but widened participation of firms in bribery practices further contributes to the perception of high corruption, which in turn makes the bribery practices even more uncontrollable.

Corporate governance can be a critical ingredient to break the vicious cycle of bribery practices and corruption. Although on the surface bribery may appear to be a low-cost, high-return activity, it carries significant risks for firms that practice it, and it is counterproductive in the long run (Wu 2005). But modern corporations are often subject to principle-agent problems and information asymmetry that make it difficult to detect bribery. Principles of good corporate governance, such as responsibility, accountability, and transparency, may not only reduce the level of bribery by solving principle-agent problems and information asymmetry, but also impose more constraints on corrupt officials by increasing the risks of being caught in corrupt exchanges.

Fig. 10.1 Vicious cycle between bribery practices and corruption

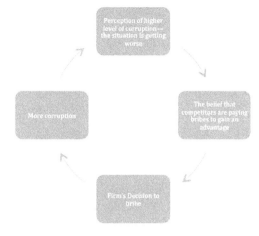

A better understanding of the linkage between corporate governance and corruption is therefore of paramount importance to a more balanced approach to corruption. While empirical studies on the causes of corruption have significantly advanced our understanding on the demand side of corruption, that is, on the motives and constraints facing public officials in corrupt practices, critical questions regarding the supply side of corruption remain unanswered. This chapter seeks to contribute to the empirical literature on corruption by focusing on corporate governance practices as potential contributing factors of bribery activities at the firm level. Using a unique cross-country firm-level dataset, we examine some distinct characteristics of bribery in corporate sector, and empirically test the relationship between firms' corporate governance practices and the level of bribery activities. Our findings suggest that better corporate governance practices can help reduce the incidence of bribery activities.

The linkage between corporate governance and corruption is especially relevant in the context of developing countries. For instance, many developing countries have embarked on various forms of market-oriented reforms to modernize their economies, and the privatization of state-owned enterprises has often been a centerpiece of such reforms. Privatization, however, presents special challenges for both the public sector governance and corporate governance in developing countries. In some developing countries, weak corporate governance has facilitated the corrupt officials in looting the already impoverished states during the process of privatization (Black et al. 2000).

Globalization also poses both the opportunities and challenges to the fight against corruption in developing countries. On one hand, globalization can accelerate the convergence of governance to international standards; on the other hand, however, globalization can increase the competition for a large number of inefficient domestic firms and thus may create high pressure for them to bribe in order to survive. In addition, the role of multinational companies in the battle against corruption should not be overlooked. While they certainly are capable of making significant impacts in improving the global business environment, some recent high profile corporate bribery scandals involving multinational companies indicate that bribery may have been used by some multinationals as a marketing strategy to penetrate into emerging markets. As a result, in an era of globalization bad corporate governance may facilitate the exporting of bribery practices across the borders, and thus may undermine the effectiveness of the global anti-corruption campaign.

10.2 Corporate Governance and Bribery: Theoretical Discussions

On the surface bribery may appear to be cost-effective for the firms because bribe payment is often a fraction of the services provided by the bribe-takers, but the seemingly justifiable bribery practices have several hidden costs for the firms in the long run. Participating in bribery activities could expose firms to substantial legal and financial risks in the future, and open the door for more extortions. Bribery also undermines the firms' strategies in developing long-term competitive advantage if they continue to rely on bribe payments to win businesses (Wu 2005).

The principal-agent problem may explain why so many firms engage in bribery activities although it is not in their best interest to be involved in such activities. The managers (the agents) might pursue their own interests at the expense of the owners and other stakeholders (the principals) of the firms (Agrawal and Knoeber 1996). For example, securing a public project by bribing public officials may increase the compensation for the managers, but the firm could be held criminally liable for such action, and the owners and other stakeholders are forced to take the blame for the managers' actions. In addition, there are multiple layers in modern corporations: even if the top management is committed to ethical business conduct, lower-level managers or employees may engage in corrupt practices to increase their short-term personal gains. For example, many multinational companies have established subsidiary companies to penetrate markets in developing countries, and there have been several high profile bribery cases involving these subsidiaries in recent years.

Coordination problems may explain another challenge in reducing bribery practices in an environment with high level of corruption: the fear of being undercut by its competitors with bribe payment forces all firms to do the same in order to survive. We can use a simple coordination game below to illustrate firms' dilemma in such situations. We assume two firms compete for a public contract, and the payoff matrix is shown in the table below. The number in the top-left corner in each cell represents the payoff for Firm A and the number in the bottom-right corner in each cell represents the payoff for Firm B. We assume that the firm involved in bribery can gain an unfair advantage over the other firm if the other doesn't bribe, but such gain would be offset by potential costs. The firm choosing not to bribe given the other firm bribes will suffer big losses as indicated by the change from 4 to 0. When both firms offer bribe (4th Scenario), no firm can gain an unfair advantage over the other, and the award of the public contract would be determined by the same probability distribution prior to the bribery; but the corrupt officials can charge higher premium for their services because demand for them are higher. This game has two equilibriums: (not bribe, not bribe) and (bribe, bribe). While the best strategy for each firm given the other firm doesn't bribe is not to bribe, the best strategy in the situation that other firm bribes is to bribe in order to avoid the worst scenario (2nd Scenario for Firm A and 3rd Scenario for Firm B).

Firm B

		Not bribe	Bribe
Firm A	Not bribe	4 1st Scenario 4	0 2nd Scenario 3
	Bribe	3 3rd Scenario 0	1 4th Scenario 1

The implications of the simple coordination game are straightforward. A firm's decision to pay bribe has negative effects on other firms in the game by decreasing their rate of success with a given bribe payment or raising the bribe amount needed for success, or both. While the individual firm's best choice is to bribe given others would do the same, this best strategy from the perspective of the individual firm leads to the worst scenario collectively for all firms involved. On the other hand, the simple coordination game shows that the equilibrium at which no firm bribes is also a stable outcome: once everyone stops to bribe, there is no incentive to defect from this equilibrium (Rose-Ackerman 2002).

Good corporate governance can lead to the reduction of bribery practices by addressing the principle-agent and the coordination problems. The principles of good corporate governance, such as accountability and transparency, not only can improve firms' operating performance, but also impose more constraints for bribery activities. In order to verify our claims empirically, we propose the following two hypotheses to explore the linkage between corporate governance and bribery.

Hypothesis 1: Corruption will be lower in firms where they are controlled by boards of directors.

In developing countries, the fact that most businesses are family-run may contribute to the complexity of dealing with bribery practices. Family-run firms are often more vulnerable to bribery pressures because they may be perceived by corrupt officials as ideal "trading" partners. Family-run firms are more likely to return past favors because of a longer continuity of management (Wu 2005). Being involved with a few families instead of a large number of firms could also reduce the chances of being exposed, as corrupt officials would only need to deal with a few individuals.

In comparison, having corporate boards also makes it more credible for the managers to commit to a "no bribe" policy when dealing with public officials who demand bribe payment. Clarke and Xu (2002) found that the level of bribe payment depends on the ability of the firms to pay instead of on the potential gains from the services provided by the corrupt officials. An independent and competent corporate board limits the firm's ability to pay bribe and can actually boost the bargaining power of the managers in dealing with corrupt officials. In addition, having a corporate board helps to deter the extortion demands from corrupt officials by increasing the risks they face because there will be more people in the know, and the chance of whistle-blowing from insiders will be increased. Increasing the accountability of corporate boards to shareholders can also help to solve the problem of the coordination game by providing firms a mechanism to signal to their competitors that they are unwilling to cope with demand from corrupt officials for bribe payment, and thus the best strategy for all firms is not to offer bribe.

Hypothesis 2: Corruption will be lower in firms that have higher standards for accounting information reporting.

Bribery often involves financial payment in one form or another, and it inevitably leaves behind a paper trail. Accounting is an information system that reports financial transaction, and auditing serves as the monitoring and internal control mechanism—together they form a critical line of defense against corrupt practices. Unusual and excessive expenditure may immediately raise the red flag on the possibility of bribery, and a departure from the routine handling of financial transactions could also catch the attention of well-trained accountants. It is thus no surprise that accountants are often closer than other professionals in detecting corrupt acts (Kimbro 2002).

First of all, better accounting practices can reduce bribery by solving the problem of information asymmetry inherent in modern corporations. The information asymmetry problem originates from the fact that agents often have some advantage over principals in their access to information, as they are closer to business operations. Clear accounting rules and implementation guidelines level the playing field between the agents and principals over information, enabling the principals to more effectively monitor and assess the behaviors of the agents.

High quality accounting practices can also help to deter bribery activities from the demand side because the bribe-extracting official would face greater risks of being caught if firms' have good accounting systems. By committing to better accounting practices, a firm is also sending a strong signal to other firms that it is determined to close the door to bribery practices, limiting the chances for predatory officials to play the firms against each other in eliciting bribes.

Last, better accounting practices can help to prevent high level of corruption ("grand corruption") for which bribes are paid in exchange for favoured treatment on contracts, concessions and privatization deals, because it would be almost impossible to hide huge payments under a well-run accounting system. While greatly outnumbered by "petty corruption", which is widespread in many developing countries, "grand corruption" often has far more destructive impact on a country's economic and political system (Rose-Ackerman 2002).

10.3   Empirical Analysis

10.3.1   Data

In contrast to the wealth of literature on corruption, few empirical studies on bribery have been conducted on the firm level. The secretive and illicit nature of bribery poses serious challenges for data collection. In recent years, however, international financial institutions have launched several large-scale cross-country surveys targeted at the firm level, such as the World Business Environment Survey (WBES) and the Business Enterprise Environment Performance Survey (BEEPS). Because these surveys address many issues related to bribery activities, they provide unique new data on firm-level bribery that can be used for empirical research (Svensson 2003; Kaufmann 1997).

The present study relies on data from the World Business Environment Survey (WBES), conducted by the World Bank, to determine the constraints that businesses confront worldwide. The surveys were carried out over a period of roughly 18 months between the end of 1998 and the middle of 2000. Data were collected mostly through personal interviews conducted at the managerial level, and 10,032 enterprises from 83 countries participated in the survey. WBES appears to be the only survey to record information on corruption and bribery from individual firms across Asian countries (BEEPS contains similar information but for 26 transitions countries in Central and East Europe).

WEBS data are particularly suitable for comparative analysis of bribery activities in Asia because 1,867 firms from 12 Asian countries participated in the survey (for details, see Table 10.2). The survey contains several important questions directly related to corruption and bribery in firms' business environment. For example, it asks the respondent/manager how often the individual firm must make "additional payment" to public officials to get things done,[1] and it elicits the amount of bribes paid as a percentage of the firm's revenues.[2]

Table 10.3 presents an overall assessment of the bribery practices in Asian firms. Fifty-four percent of Asian firms regularly pay bribes to public officials, and only

---

[1]Firms were asked: "How often do firms in my line of business have to pay some irregular 'additional payments' for government officials to get things done?" The responses were tabulated across a range: always, usually, frequently, sometimes, seldom, and never.

[2]Firms were asked: "What percentage of revenues do firms like yours pay per annum in unofficial payments to public officials?" The responses ranged across percentages: 0 %, less than 1 %, 1–2 %, 2–10 %, 10–12 %, 12–25 %, and >25 %.

Table 10.2 Coverage of world business environment survey in Asia

Country	Number of firms
Azerbaijan	128
Bangladesh	50
Cambodia	326
China	101
India	210
Indonesia	100
Kazakhstan	127
Malaysia	100
Pakistan	103
Philippines	100
Singapore	100
Thailand	422
Total	1867

Table 10.3 Bribery activities in Asian firms

	Frequently (%)	Sometimes (%)	Seldom (%)	Never (%)
Do firms have to pay some irregular "additional payments" to government officials to get things done?	54	19	10	17
Do firms know in advance about how much this "additional payment" is?	57	22	12	9
Is the service delivered as agreed if the firm pays the required "additional payment"?	77	13	5	5
Would another government officials subsequently require an additional payment for the same service if firm pays the required additional payment to a particular government official?	47	21	11	20
Can the firms go to another officials to get the correct treatment without recourse to unofficial payments if a government agent acts against the rules?	29	24	22	25

Data source WBES (2000) and author's calculation

17 % of firms have never paid any bribe. The results unquestionably reveal the highly institutionalized bribery practices in many Asian countries: firms generally know in advance the amount of bribe payments that have to be made, and the bribe-takers do deliver their services once the bribe payments are received. It is equally revealing to find that many firms have the option of not paying bribes. While the bribe-extracting officials are highly predatory, as about half of the firms report that bribery payment may lead to additional requests for bribe payments, over fifty percent of the firms do have the option of not paying the bribes. It is clear that

the corporate sector is not just a 'victim' of corruption, and many firms are in fact active and willing parties to corrupt transactions.

There are considerable variations in the levels of bribery among different countries. Table 10.4 shows the frequency of the bribery payments by firms in different countries. In Bangladesh, where bribery is the most prevalent among all countries in the sample, 96 % of firms reported that they regularly bribe public officials. In Singapore, only 2 % of firms are found to offer bribes regularly, and 90 % of firms never pay any at all. It is interesting to note that the rank of a country in the Corruption Perception Index roughly corresponds to the frequency of the bribery payments—not only suggesting that the findings are robust, but also confirming that the corporate sector is indeed the main contributor of the rampant corruption problems in Asia.

In summary, the corporate sector is an important source of prevalent corruption problems. Based on WBES results, the majority of Asian firms have been involved in bribery activities although there are significant variations across countries. Firms pay a significant portion of their sales as bribes, and bribe payments often lead to more extortion from predatory officials.

10.3.2   Econometric Models

Corresponding to the two hypotheses with regard to the relationship between corporate governance and bribery, we use two measures of corporate governance—one on the existence of corporate boards (BOARD) in controlling firms and the other on the quality of accounting practices (UNREPORT). The first measure of corporate governance is based on the overall control of the firm. The variable—BOARD—takes

Table 10.4 Incidence of bribery across Asian countries

| | Incidence of bribery | | | |
	Frequently (%)	Sometimes (%)	Seldom (%)	Never (%)
Azerbaijan	59	9	14	17
Bangladesh	94	4	2	0
Cambodia	44	27	14	15
India	55	28	6	11
Indonesia	68	23	3	6
Kazakhstan	24	35	13	28
Malaysia	20	27	7	45
Pakistan	70	17	9	4
Philippines	43	27	17	13
Singapore	2	1	7	90
Thailand	79	10	8	4
Total	54	19	10	17

Data source WBES (2000) and author's calculation

the value "1" if the firm is controlled by its board of directors/supervisory board, and "0" otherwise.

The second measure of corporate governance—UNREPORT—focuses on the quality of accounting practices across countries. It is based on the percentage of sales that was not reported for tax purpose (scale from 1 to 10, where 1 = less than 5 %, 2 = 5–10 %, 3 = 11–20 %, 4 = 21–30 %, ..., 9 = 71–80 %, 10 = more than 80 %). Higher percentage of unreported profits and wages represents more frequent occurrence of accounting irregularities which imply that it might be relatively easy to hide the expenses of bribery.

Two econometric models—probit and ordered probit—were adopted to test the hypotheses on the influence of corporate governance practices on bribery activities. The probit model focuses on firms' decisions to engage in or refrain from bribery in their business operations. The ordered probit model investigates how frequently firms are engaged in bribery. Together, these econometric models offer a multidimensional view of the dynamics of bribery activities at firm level.

The probit model assumes that the firm's bribe payment (y_i^*) is a function of a set of variables. That is,

$$y_i^* = \beta' x_i + u_i, \tag{10.1}$$

where y_i^* is assumed to be a "latent" variable that cannot be observed directly. What is observed is a dummy variable y_i defined by

$$y_i = \begin{cases} 1 & \text{if } y_i^* > 0 \\ 0 & \text{otherwise} \end{cases}. \tag{10.2}$$

The dependent variable for the probit model is I_{ij}, a dummy variable indicating whether or not firm i in country j is involved in bribery activities. I_{ij} takes 1 if the firm has engaged in bribery, and I_{ij} equals to 0 if the firm has never been involved in bribery. The likelihood function for the probit model can be expressed as follows:

$$L = \prod_{y_i=1} F(\beta' x_i) \prod_{y_i=0} [1 - F(\beta' x_i)], \tag{10.3}$$

where F is the cumulative distribution function of u.

The second econometric model, the ordered probit model, focuses on the determinants of frequency of bribery activities. The dependent variable, BRIBE, indicates how frequently firms engage in bribery (ranging from "never" to "always"). This model assumes that frequency of bribery practices (y_i^*) is a function of a set of variables, including the test variables and control variable. That is,

$$y_i^* = \beta' x_i + u_i, \tag{10.4}$$

where y_i^* is a "latent" variable that cannot be observed directly. What is observed is

$$
\begin{aligned}
y_i &= \text{"never" if } y_i^* \leq 0 \\
&= \text{"seldom" if } 0 \leq y_i^* < \mu_1 \\
&= \text{"sometimes" if } \mu_1 \leq y_i^* < \mu_2 \\
&= \text{"frequently" if } \mu_2 \leq y_i^* < \mu_3 \\
&= \text{"mostly" if } \mu_3 \leq y_i^* < \mu_4 \\
&= \text{"always" if } \mu_4 \leq y_i^* < \mu_5
\end{aligned}
\tag{10.5}
$$

The corresponding probabilities for each ordinal interval can be stated as:

$$
\begin{aligned}
\text{Prob } (y_i = \text{"never"}) &= \phi(-\beta' x_i) \\
\text{Prob } (y_i = \text{"seldom"}) &= \phi(\mu_1 = \beta' x_i) - \phi(-\beta' x_i) \\
\text{Prob } (y_i = \text{"sometimes"}) &= \phi(\mu_2 = \beta' x_i) - \phi(\mu_1 - \beta' x_i) \\
\text{Prob } (y_i = \text{"frequently"}) &= \phi(\mu_3 = \beta' x_i) - \phi(\mu_2 - \beta' x_i) \\
\text{Prob } (y_i = \text{"mostly"}) &= \phi(\mu_4 = \beta' x_i) - \phi(\mu_3 - \beta' x_i) \\
\text{Prob } (y_i = \text{"always"}) &= \phi(\mu_5 = \beta' x_i) - \phi(\mu_4 - \beta' x_i)
\end{aligned}
\tag{10.6}
$$

And log-likelihood of the model can be specified as

$$
\ln L = \sum_{i=1}^{N} \sum_{j=0.4}^{1} Z_{ij} \ln[\phi_{ij} - \phi_{i,j-1}],
\tag{10.7}
$$

where $\phi_{i,j} = \phi[\mu_j - \beta' x_i]$, $\phi_{i,j-1} = \phi[\mu_{j-1} - \beta' x_i]$ and Z_{ij} is an indicator variable which equals 1 if $y_i = j$ and 0 otherwise.

In addition to variables on corporate governance practices, a set of independent variables can be defined to measure firm characteristics, market competition, legal, and regulatory environments; and taxation. These, summarized in Table 10.5, are defined as follows.

First of all, firm characteristics such as size (SME) and growth (SALES) may affect firms' involvement in bribery. Smaller firms may have a higher propensity to bribe than large firms because they lack power to resist predatory officials' demands for bribe payments and they do not ordinarily attract much attention from government disciplinary agencies and law enforcement authorities (Svensson 2003; Herrera and Rodriguez 2003). Firms that are growing rapidly may be more vulnerable to extortion by corrupt officials because of their increasing "ability to pay." According to the "endogenous harassment" theory (Myrdal 1968), predatory officials can sort targeted firms according to their "ability to pay" and demand corresponding levels of bribe payments.

Secondly, many developing countries have introduced market-oriented reforms to open up more sectors for competition, and globalization entails competition not only

Table 10.5 Descriptive statistics of variables

Variable	Description
SME	Dummy variable. 1 = Small or medium size firm; 0 = others
BOARD	Dummy variable. 1 = firm is controlled either by board of directors; 0 = all others
UNREPORT	Categorical variable indicating percentage of total sales not reported for tax purpose (1 = less than 5 %, 2 = 5–10 %, 3 = 11–20 %, 4 = 21–30 %, 5 = 31–40, 6 = 41–50, 7 = 51–60, 8 = 61–70, 9 = 71–80 %, 10 = more than 80 %)
COMPETITION	Number of competitors
SALES	Percentage of change (increase or decrease) of the firm's sales over the last three years
COURT	The extent to which the court system is honest/uncorrupt (1 = never; 2 = seldom; 3 = sometimes; 4 = frequent; 5 = usually; 6 = always)
LICENSING	The extent to which business licensing is problematic. Scale from 1 to 4 (1 = no obstacle; 2 = minor obstacle; 3 = moderate obstacle; 4 = major obstacle)
TAXATION	The extent to which tax regulations/administration are problematic. Scale from 1 to 4 (1 = no obstacle; 2 = minor obstacle; 3 = moderate obstacle; 4 = major obstacle)
INTERPRETATION	The extent to which interpretations of regulations affecting the firm are consistent and predictable (1 = never; 2 = seldom; 3 = sometimes; 4 = frequently; 5 = mostly; 6 = always)

among local firms but also with multinational companies that may have better technology and products. These changes could have profound impacts on firms' decisions to participate in bribery and other corruption schemes. Market competition created by dismantling state monopolies may reduce bribery activities by decreasing firms' incentive to bribe. Increased market competition may also offer firms the chance to sell to new markets and thus decreases their reliance on government procurement contracts to meet sales targets. In this research, we use the number of competitors (COMPETITION) to measure the level of competition for individual firms.

Thirdly, firms' legal environment is measured by COURT, a nominal variable scaling from 1 to 6, indicating the extent to which the court system is honest and uncorrupted. The legal system provides a potential safety valve for controlling the spread of bribery practices: it imposes risks on both sides, to corrupt officials and to firms that pay bribes (Treisman 2000). However, the legal system itself is an integral part of government structure and thus subjected to the same afflictions. For example, in many Asian countries the legal system is as corrupt as other government agencies, if not more so. Firms operating within a corrupt legal environment may be more prone to bribery, for two reasons. Predatory officials have less to fear when backed by a corrupt legal system. And firms can bribe their way out of trouble when dealing with law enforcement agencies, even if their bribery activities become exposed.

Fourthly, regulation is an important policy instrument that governments can wield to combat various market failures that are pervasive in modern society, and it has assumed a heightened role in many developing countries after market-oriented reforms. However, regulation can provide a fertile breeding ground for bribery in countries with weak governance, where officials charged with regulatory responsibility are often given discretionary power (Wei 2000). The greater an official's discretionary power becomes, the more opportunities arise for extracting bribery payments. Moreover, according to the endogenous harassment theory, predatory officials may create unnecessary regulations and rules expressly in order to maximize opportunities for reaping payments. Such opaque and complex regulatory environments create various incentives for firms to pay bribes, including quick approval of registration permits or licenses, or favourable interpretations of laws and regulations. Quality of the regulatory environment is measured by LICENSING (licensing requirements) and INTERPRETATION (level of transparency in interpretation of laws and regulations).

Last, TAXATION measures firms' perceptions on the extent to which high taxes are an obstacle to business activity (ranging from "no obstacle" to "major obstacle"). Tax evasion is a common form of financial fraud among firms that are confronted with high taxes. Opportunities for tax evasion provide firms with an incentive to bribe tax collectors to overlook the fraud. And taxation subjects firms to extortion from corrupt officials who have discretionary powers to interpret and enforce laws and regulations on taxation, and this is especially true in instances where arbitrary and irregular tax-like levies are imposed by authorities (Asher 2001). One would expect that firms facing high taxes would have greater propensity to bribe.

In addition to the independent variables mentioned above, a set of dummy variables for country was also included, to control for country and international differences such as global corruption and income level. A set of industry-level dummy variables was added to control for the influence of sectors (manufactory, services, agriculture) on bribery.

10.3.3   Regression Results

The results of the two models are presented in Table 10.6. Column (1) reports the coefficients and standard errors of the estimation based on the probit model, which aims at explaining firms' decisions on whether or not to bribe. Column (2) reports the results of the ordered probit model that focus on the determinants of frequency of bribery. The results from the two models are quite similar to the estimations based on the probit model, an indication that the findings are robust.

Our results suggest that corporate governance practices play an important role in propensity to bribe. Consistent with the hypothetical prediction, firms controlled by board of directors/supervisory boards are less likely to pay bribes than are firms governed by individuals, families, or banks. In addition, the quality of firms' accounting practices has a statistically significant effect on bribery activities.

Table 10.6 Regression results		Probit model	Ordered probit model
	SME	0.228 (0.143)	0.050 (0.084)
	BOARD	−0.822*** (0.152)	−0.195** (0.091)
	UNREPORT	0.048** (0.022)	0.049*** (0.013)
	COMPETITION	0.533*** (0.079)	0.198*** (0.060)
	SALES	−0.061 (0.136)	−0.093 (0.131)
	COURT	−0.084** (0.039)	−0.097*** (0.024)
	LICENSING	0.267*** (0.075)	0.171** (0.036)
	INTERPRETATION	−0.165*** (0.058)	−0.094*** (0.032)
	TAXATION	0.248*** (0.052)	0.193*** (0.037)
	Number of observations	1179	1192
	Pseudo R^2	0.320	0.081

Note The table reports unstandardized coefficients, with standard errors in parentheses
$*p < 0.1$; $**p < 0.05$; $***p < 0.01$

The higher the percentage of sales kept "off the books", the more likely for firms to engage in bribery activities. These results are consistent with empirical studies based on country level data (Wu 2005).

The results show that the effect of market competition on bribery is both statistically and economically significant in the probit and ordered probit models, but the sign on the coefficients on COMPETITION shows that the level of competition has positive effects on bribery activities, in contrary to the theoretical prediction made earlier. One plausible explanation is that firms may acquiesce to increased bribe payments if a bidding war for desired services intensifies. Another explanation is that, in a fiercely competitive environment, firms may resort to bribery to sidestep bureaucratic red tape when delays could directly translate to loss of market shares. The findings of a positive correlation between competition and bribery activities suggest that reform initiatives to increase market competition, such as privatization and deregulation, might actually create some obstacles for anti-corruption campaign from the supply side of corruption.

Legal and regulatory environments play a significant role in determining firms' propensity to bribe. Propensity to bribe is found negatively correlated with quality of legal environment as measured by the extent to which the court system is viewed as honest and uncorrupted. Characteristics of the regulatory environment are also among key determinants of propensity to bribe: firms that report resentment over licensing requirements (LICENSING) are more likely to bribe government officials, and the opposite is true for firms that are satisfied with persistence and predictability of interpretation of laws and regulations. The level of taxes (TAXATION) are shown to be important determinants of firms' decision to bribe. Firms are more likely to bribe if they perceive high taxes are barriers to their businesses.

10.4 Conclusion

Corporate governance has emerged as a major policy concern following the financial crisis in Asia, Russia and Latin America, and the recent global economic crisis. The increased attention on corporate government should be a welcome news for the global anti-corruption campaign. Our empirical results support a theoretical projection that good corporate governance can lead to reduced level of bribery activities at the firm level.

The linkage between corporate governance and corruption suggests that the improvement in corporate governance may be a catalyst to break the vicious cycle of bribery and corruption. Shareholders and investors in countries that are experiencing a high level of corruption may receive double dividends from the improvement in corporate government. Companies with better corporate governance have better prospects of growth and command higher valuation in the market. Improvement in corporate governance may help a country with a high level of corruption to partially offset the negative impacts of the perception of corruption on the flow of capital (both financial and human capital), and the additional capital induced by good corporate government serves as catalyst for further improvement in both corporate governance and the governance of the public sector. Therefore, public policies targeting improved corporate governance could be effective anti-corruption strategies. More important, such efforts are likely to be sustained because it is self-motivated and self-driven from the perspective of firms.

Government, the business community, and individual firms all have respective roles to play in combating bribery activities in the corporate sector. Government can significantly reduce bribery by targeting areas where firms are most prone to bribery practices, such as integrity of court systems, business licensing requirements, quality of government service delivery, and taxation. The business community can reduce incidence of bribery by setting up rules of market competition so that bribery will not automatically increase as the level of competition rises. Individual firms can shoulder their share of responsibility through improvements in corporate governance, such as broadening the basis of ownership.

References

Agrawal, A., and C.R. Knoeber. 1996. Firm performance and mechanisms to control agency problems between managers and shareholders. *Journal of Financial and Quantitative Analysis* 31: 377–397.

Asher, M. G. 2001. *Design of Tax Systems and Corruption*, paper presented in a conference on "Fighting corruption: Common challenges and shared experiences", Singapore, 10–11 May, 2001.

Black, B., R. Kraakman, and A. Tarasova. 2000. Russian privatization and corporate governance: What went wrong? *Stanford Law Review* 52: 1731–1808.

Clarke, G. and L. C. Xu. 2002. Ownership, competition, and corruption: Bribe takers versus bribe payers. *World Bank Policy Research Working Paper* No. 2783.

Herrera, A. M. and P. Rodriguez. 2003. *Bribery and the nature of corruption*, Working Paper, Department of Economics, Michigan State University, MI.

Kaufmann, D. 1997. Corruption: Some myths and facts. *Foreign Policy, Summer* 1997: 114–131.

Kimbro, M.B. 2002. A cross-country empirical investigation of corruption and its relationship to economic, cultural and institutional variables: An examination of the role of accounting and financial statements quality. *Journal of Accounting Auditing and Finance* 17(4): 325–349.

Myrdal, G. 1968. *Asian drama: An inquiry into the poverty of nations*. New York: Pantheon Books.

Rose-Ackerman, S. 2002. "Grand" corruption and the ethics of global business. *Journal of Banking & Finance* 26: 1889–1918.

Svensson, J. 2003. Who must pay bribes and how much? Evidence from a cross-section of firms. *The Quarterly Journal of Economics* 118(1): 207–230.

Treisman, D. 2000. The causes of corruption: A cross-national study. *Journal of Public Economics* 76: 399–457.

Vogl, F. 1998. The supply side of global bribery. *Finance & Development* 35(2): 30–33.

Wei, S.-J. 2000. How taxing is corruption on international investors? *Review of Economics and Statistics* 82(1): 1–11.

Wu, X. 2005. Corporate governance and corruption: A cross-country analysis. *Governance: An International Journal of Policy Administration and Institutions* 18(2): 151–170.

Chapter 11
Institutionalised Corruption and Integrity: A Theological-Ethical Clarification of a Complex Issue

Johan Verstraeten

Abstract Starting from definitions of corruption and integrity, the first part of the article criticizes several misconceptions with regards to integrity. Focusing on the concepts of 'institution' and 'collective secondary actor' the second part articulates the relation between individual action and structural aspects of corruption which are theologically interpreted as 'structural sin'. The third part articulates the different degrees of responsibility in corruption. The article concludes with a reflection on developing a "counter discipline" against corruption via spirituality as precondition for ethical behaviour.

11.1 Introduction

Etymologically the concept of corruption has a negative pre-moral connotation. Its Latin root *conrumpere* refers to: destroying, doing harm, polluting, seducing, deterioration of morals, profanation, inciting to criminal behaviour, etc. Integrity, on the contrary, refers to *integritas*: wholeness, completeness, to assemble separate parts into a whole (Paine, 335). Crane and Matten (2004, 123) describe it as "adherence to moral values". According to Tom Morris (1997, 151) it involves the whole of who one is, of what one appreciates and aspires to be. A person of integrity is virtuous, and aspires to strike a balance between principles and acts (Paine, 336). She is the opposite of a chameleon, opportunist or hypocrite.

Bert Musschenga distinguishes three formal dimensions of integrity: consistency, coherency and correspondence. Consistency refers to a correspondence between acts and behaviour *at various moments in time*. Inconsistency however is to apply rules and norms arbitrarily. Coherency refers to a correspondence between acts *in different contexts and roles*. Correspondence indicates a complete concordance of words and deeds: "*to walk the talk*". Related terms are veracity and

J. Verstraeten (✉)
Catholic University of Leuven, Leuven, Belgium
e-mail: Johan.Verstraeten@theo.kuleuven.be; Johan.Verstraeten@oce.kuleuven.be

© Springer International Publishing Switzerland 2016   235
M. Dion et al. (eds.), *Financial Crimes: Psychological, Technological,*
and Ethical Issues, International Library of Ethics, Law,
and the New Medicine 68, DOI 10.1007/978-3-319-32419-7_11

sincerity. Integrity has not only a formal meaning: it gets content in a professional context as, for example, professional, administrative, civil or political integrity.

One could ask whether integrity requires all acts to be consistent and coherent without exception. Can one for example require a person to demonstrate in all aspects of his or her life a coherency between his or her actions, convictions and roles? Can one require people to behave with equal integrity in a professional context as well as in private life? At least not in politics, if we may believe Max Weber who criticizes Förster's contention that only 'good' persons make good politicians. According to Weber it is quite normal that a politician, who acts quite viciously in private, is capable of making adequate political decisions and even that he or she is an excellent politician. Examples are Winston Churchill whose private vices and vanities did not detract him from becoming a great statesman and Oscar Schindler, who despite the danger of imminent arrest, bribed Nazi leaders time and again if and when necessary to save large groups of Jews from the gas chambers. One should, however, take into account that both examples refer to exceptional circumstances. On the other hand there are examples of individuals with a strict set of personal values who pursued calamitous policies (e.g. president Diem of Vietnam a devout catholic at the head of a corrupt government).

Questions regarding the integrity of a person can, moreover, not only be based on the degree of success she attained whilst realising her goals. Both the expert who acts with integrity as the expert who act without it, can be confronted with the problem of '*moral luck*'. Consider the example of an unscrupulous politician who decides to rescue hostages using each and every means at his disposal, including the use of extreme violence without giving a second thought to the possibility that a large number of civilians might end up as 'collateral damage'. If by chance, his imprudent action ends well, he will be praised as a hero, notwithstanding his initial lack of respect for his fellow civilians. Politicians with an ethical intention, on the contrary, can fail due to unfortunate circumstances: e.g. Jimmy Carter whose presidency ended when his attempt to free the American hostages in Iran failed due to circumstances beyond his control.

11.2   Uncritical Concepts of Integrity

11.2.1   Reducing Integrity to "Role Integrity" or Compliance with Codes of Conduct

Numerous publications on business ethics emphasize the importance of *role integrity*. They are convinced that corruption can be eradicated by demanding strict compliance with role specific duties and standards—mostly written down as a corporate or professional deontology (Solomon, 215). Rules of compliance can be positively or negatively sanctioned: e.g. a code of conduct prohibiting the giving or taking of bribes.

Some authors link "*role integrity*" to fiduciary duties or fiduciary responsibility. This form of responsibility entails that one should base one's judgement and actions on objective professional criteria and not on personal opinions or interests (Paine, 335). A civil servant employed by the Inland Revenue department is obliged to apply the tax laws in order to serve the common good of a community collecting its legitimate revenue. He or she has no right to randomly interpret the laws or to grant a tax reduction in exchange for personal gain such as dinner in a luxury restaurant.

The advantage of *role integrity* and its emphasis on fiduciary duty is that these concepts take into account the specific needs and responsibilities of a particular professional group, such as it is the case with codes of conduct in banking. Such codes can be a useful tools to combat money laundering, for example, by way of determining precisely from which amount on it is mandatory to register the personal data and identity card number of the customer who wants to deposit a large amount of cash.

Professional codes of conduct, although useful and necessary in the fight against corruption, are insufficient. Integrity requires more than just the conscientious fulfilling of a professional duty or complying with a rule. The English language provides us with a distinction between "*to do things right*", i.e. fulfilling one's role duties and "*to do the right thing*", i.e. to make the right choice which is more than a matter of compliance with rules or rolemorality. Moral conduct requires, moreover, that one takes into account not only various duties but also circumstances and consequences.

One of the main deficiencies in the concept of role morality is that it grossly underestimates the conflict between different roles of conduct. For example: to a lawyer, client confidentiality is an important deontological rule. But the lawyer's professional duty to preserve client confidentiality at all cost may conflict with his or her civic duty to disclose information about cases of corruption which are fundamentally detrimental to the community. On the one hand, a company can impose on its managers a confidentiality or loyalty clause with regards to providing information to third parties, on the other hand this clause may conflict with the managers' civic duty to inform the community about shady practices or those which are to the detriment of human rights or the environment. The conflict between the duty to comply one's professional code of conduct and one's civic duty can lead to *whistle blowing* (Solomon, 217). Whenever human lives or democratic principles are at stake—or when natural catastrophes are imminent—civic duty or the duty to protect life (or in negative terms the duty to avoid harming others) may supersede acting with professional role integrity. For example: a physician may consider breaking patient confidentiality when confronted with a HIV—positive patient who refuses to inform his or her partner. In this case the life or quality of life of the partner outweigh physician-patient confidentiality. Referring to the conflict between professional duties and other duties, Mathias Nebel draws attention to a paradox: corruption can only exist because we cultivate certain values such as discretion, trust and loyalty (Nebel, 95, 96, 105). Such values and the duties they infer, have thus need of a wider framework to be judged against.

A second point of criticism with regards to reducing integrity to role integrity concerns the fact that, from the perspective of professional responsibilities, insufficient attention is paid to the narrative unity of the acting person. The aforementioned formal criteria of consistency and coherency oblige a person to avoid changing her 'morality' according to the role she has to fulfil: what matters is the integration of various roles and their related responsibilities into the narrative unity of al life based on a fundamental option. This constitutes the difference between role identity and integral integrity (Martin, 203). In a hypermodern cultural context the latter has become problematic. MacIntyre uses the image of a post—or hypermodern human being who dashes from one stage to the other; playing each time a different role, unable to see the connection between the different roles because they is not plot in their story. When various roles are not being meaningfully integrated into a meaningfully integrated life project, it become urgent to reconfigure oneself as a narrative unity.

A crucial ethical question in this respect is: to what extend can one, as an individual, act in a corrupt or semi-corrupt manner or can one tolerate corrupt practices (possibly because professional ethics requires one to keep silent), without becoming completely corrupt as a person? Morality engages the whole person and is not just a matter of separate case studies nor of isolating the act from the acting person. Hence Tom Morris' proposition: "*whenever you make a decision, whenever you act, you are never just doing, you are always becoming*" (Morris, 164).

A third problem linked to an overemphasis on professional integrity is the fact that it can lead to hypocrisy, the complete opposite of what integrity aims at.

Praxis shows us that codes of conduct for managers are sometimes no more than a tool for companies seeking to avoid moral responsibility or liability. Multinational companies oblige their mangers to sign a document via which they agree to comply with the prohibition of corruption or bribery and to act in accordance with anti-corruption laws. But the same managers are sometimes obliged—in an international context—to bribe civil servants or politicians in order to secure a contract (usually via the semi-legal practice of sending an invoice to a local 'contract facilitator'). When corruption is discovered or charges are brought, the individual manager is hold responsible and not the firm. In other words: codes of conduct can mask hypocrisy.

A fourth problem with regards to a reduction of integrity role integrity is an underestimation of the complex institutional context in which corruption flourishes. As the virtue ethicist Robert Solomon demonstrates: integrity is not only a matter of a conscientious fulfilment of role duties or integrating various roles into a narrative unity of the individual, but also of the relationship between an individual and society. A human being is not an isolated atom. He or she always forms part of a larger social fabric/whole. That whole not only encompasses the fulfilment of one's professional role. The concept to live a 'good' life as an individual, is also determined by the communities and society of which one is a part (whereby of course misconception about the good life such as loyalty to corrupt networks also play a part). People are influenced by the narrative communities to which they belong: in accordance with the values of such communities, an individual develops her own hierarchy of values (for example, a member of the Christian community will use another hierarchy of values with regards to life than an atheist who is convinced of the total autonomy of the person). I will further discuss the influence of religious communities. Here it suffice to say that wholeness or integrity always implies a relationship with others in an institutionalised context, i.e. a context of societal norms, values, expectations and influences (Solomon, 217). A negative context will have a negative influence on the individual; a positive context will have a positive influence.

11.2.2 The Uncritical 'Relativity of Values and Norms' Argument

A second simplification is to excuse on corruption on the ground that values and norms would be relative.

In a context of globalisation and cultural diversity one can justify one's actions with the proverb: "*When in Rome, do as the Romans do*" (DeGeorge, 48).

A similar form of relativism can be found in a famous speech by Mr. Herkströter, a former Shell top executive. His argument is that since different cultures value different cultural customs one cannot therefore impose strict western norms: "*What is the ethical way to proceed? Should we apply the higher-cost western standards (…). Or, should we adopt the prevailing legal standards at that site, while having clear plans to improve towards "best practice" within a reasonable time frame? That way, of course, we would risk condemnation in the West (…). Nepotism is regarded in the West with extreme ambivalence (…). In much of the rest of the world, hiring relatives and people of your own ethic group is regarded as a positive virtue (…). It is something to applaud, not criticise.*

Similarly, gifts are an essential part of doing business in some countries. In Japan for example, it would be the height of rudeness not to bring a gift when you initiate a business meeting. In the West we regard gifts, especially if they are substantial, as a form of bribery (…) At what point does a gift end and a bribe begin? And, who decides?(…) Transparency may be a virtue when we are dealing with a western democratic government (…) in some other areas of the world it may be regarded as one of the grossest forms of betrayal (…)

Those who would impose one standard on this whole globe—the moral imperialists—are clearly wrong. But, so are the moral relativists who argue that one must apply only local standards. For, as we have all learnt, what is acceptable in one country is simply not acceptable on an international level." (Herkströter, 11–12).

Herkströter has a point: one cannot indeed do business on the basis of absolute moral principles and without taking into account the local context. But that is not an excuse to condone corruption. A huge difference exists between, on the one hand, taking into account different cultural customs (for example: exchanging presents is more important in Japan than in Europe), and, on the other hand, accepting unethical practises such as using bribes to secure a sales contract. The millions of dollars paid during the seventies of the previous century by Karl Kotchian, CEO of Lockheed, to prime minister Tanaka and a number of other Japanese politicians, was something different than showing respect for Japanese etiquette. Kotchian refused to acknowledge any wrongdoing on the basis of a sort of moral reasoning (act-utilitarian reasoning) which was as follows: "bribing politicians is justified, in so far as it is, in a particular circumstance the only means to do good, in case, saving jobs". A similar argument can found among economists such as Huntington who simply claim that corruption is acceptable because it is useful "to grease the market'. Such opinions can be rejected with arguments based on deontological ethics and rule-utilitarianism.

11.3   Integrity and Corruption in a Structural Context

11.3.1   Interaction Between People and Corrupt Structures

The degree to which a person can act with integrity is influenced by his or her institutional or structural context.

Companies, organisations, administrations or corrupt networks exert a huge influence on morality and, according to Thomas Brytting, also on the moral competence of an individual. This influence not only directly occurs by means of interiorising the values or codes of conduct of the organisation, but also indirectly by way of learning habits and practices. Certain practices have influence on the rise of corrupt behaviour such as the tendency in some countries to pay public servants or employees irregularly or to pay them extremely low wages, pressuring them too seek additional sources of income in order to survive. In such a context the step to extortion or other forms of corruption is easily taken. Another source of influence is the culture in particular groups or organisations governed by 'onerta'. In such a context the duty to secrecy is often combined with reprisals in case of disclosing facts.

Patricia Werhane's concept 'collective secondary actor' elucidates the influence structures have on individual actors. Werhane (1985, 49–59) demonstrates, that a business organisation, a political party or an administration is not only an aggregate (the sum of individuals or the sum of individual acts), but also a conglomerate, a concerted action. Acts of an organisation cannot be reduced to acts of individuals. For example: when two companies 'merge', their employees don't merge. A corrupt company or a corrupt administration is more than the sum of corrupt individual acts, because such entities act as 'secondary collective actors'. Even though individuals constitute the ontological basis for such collective acts, they also act 'by order of', 'are mandated by' or 'under the influence of 'the organisation or network to which they belong. Individual acts are being orientated or directed by means of decision-making structures, customs, sanctions, regulations, expectations, codes of conduct, etc. In other words: if one wants to eradicate corrupt organisations or networks, one also needs to change the decision-making procedures and ethical codes.

In this context, I think it is more adequate to refer to the term *institutions* instead of to structures. An institution does not coincide with the physical reality of an organisation or group, but it is a collective noun for those normative patterns (or patterns of expectation) that determine or influence the collaboration or living together of persons. These normative practices are imbedded and reinforced by laws and informal customs and practices. Robert Bellah defines institutions as *patterns of expected action of individuals or groups enforced by social sanctions, both positive and negative* (Bellah, 10).

The influence institutions have on acting persons is not a one-way traffic. Collective secondary actors or institutions do not determine the action of individuals. They influence individuals, but individuals also influence institutions. Institutions and collective secondary actors only exist in so far as and because acting persons bring them to life.

One of the causes of exerting a negative influence is the fact that people who act corruptly are guilty of what one could call *institutionalized perversion*. Nebel (2006, 84) defines this as the alienation of the general to the benefit of the particular ("*aliénation du général au particulier*"). Referring to the public sector, he uses the term "privatisation of institutionalised power". Corrupt individuals do not use their power to further political goals—which would be a legitimate use—but to further their own private interests.

The damage caused by corrupt individuals to communities is articulated in interesting terms by the Italian bishops.

On the one hand, they compare corruption with theft. Theft is not only a consequence of cupidity and selfishness and as such a matter for one's personal conscience, but it is also an act which damages the community. On the other hand, the Italian bishops add that corruption is infinitely worse than theft, since it is not only an unlawful appropriation of an arbitrary good but of a *public* good. Corruption puts at stake the common good. Because corruption creates occult power structures, it results in a privatisation of the state to benefit an individual or a group (Nebel, 125). Corruption undermines the state of law and causes a fundamental crisis of trust, which is extremely detrimental to a political and economical system which operates on trust (Nebel, 125). Trust is, as Ricoeur (Le Juste, 35 as quoted by Nebel, 129) has demonstrated, an extremely important social good, implying "more than an inter-personal relation" because it constitutes "the institutional condition for every inter-personal relation" A violation of trust will engender the destruction of the bonds of solidarity (Nebel, 516). In other words, he or she who contributes to corruption has a destructive influence on the community.

11.3.2   A Theological Perspective: Corruption and Sinful Structures

The systematic and institutional aspect of corruption can be interpreted theologically in terms of 'structural sin' or 'sinful structures'. According to Mathias Nebel's these concepts are useful hermeneutic tools to bridge the gap between 'institutional context' and 'personal integrity'.

On the one hand, the concept of 'sinful structures' is a theological interpretation of the concept 'institutional injustice'. While liberation theologies tend to emphasises the structures as such, official Catholic social teaching emphasizes that individuals always remain the ontological subjects of these structures.

In this respect John Paul II's *Reconciliatio en poenitentia*, published on December 4th 1984, is a key text: "*Whenever the church speaks of situations of sin or when the condemns as social sins certain situations or the collective behaviour of certain social groups, big or small, or even of whole nations and blocs of nations, she knows and she proclaims that such cases of social sin are the result of the accumulation and concentration of many personal sins. It is a case of the very personal sins of those who cause or support evil or who exploit it; of those who are in a position to avoid, eliminate or at least limit certain social evils but who fail to do so out of laziness, fear or the conspiracy of silence, through secret complicity or indifference; of those who take refuge in the supposed impossibility of changing the world and also of those who sidestep the effort and sacrifice required, producing specious reasons of higher order. The real responsibility, then, lies with individuals. A situation-or likewise an institution, a structure, society itself-is not in itself the subject of moral acts. Hence a situation cannot in itself be good or bad.*" (John Paul II, 217).

This is a most interesting point of view since it combines personal responsibility with structural influence. The premise is that no structure, no institution can be reduced to its physical or infrastructural components, because *ultima ratio* it are always people who make a structure work: "*Aucune structure, aucune institution n'est essentiellement constituée par ses composantes matérielles, ses infrastructures. Son essence est porté par des personnes qui la font ou l'ont fait fonctionner*" (Nebel 135). Or as Rahner wrote: "*social structures and institutions are not natural facts, but the objective manifestation of freedom*" (Rahner as quoted by Mynatty, 4).

In this perspective institutions or structures are no irreversible static entities. They are always becoming. They are fashioned by acting individuals (Morris, 165) and there is always a dynamic interaction between individuals and institutions: "we form institutions and they form us". According to Robert Bellah any interpretation of institutions as objective mechanisms separate from individuals, is an ideology, in the sense of a false representation of reality.

The question now is: how do people corroborate or change sinful structures?

11.3.3   The Responsibility to Change Corrupt Structures

Corrupt structures and institution are always linked with the inward dimension of the persons contributing to them, in other words: the corrupt structures are not only external to people, they are also present in their interiority in so far as they have interiorized or accepted the rules of corrupt networks. This interiorisation is also the starting point for the question: to what extend is a person responsible for preserving or encouraging sinful structures?

Hormis Mynatty explains this by formally differentiating between an objective and a subjective component, between sinful structures as such and the social sin from which it sprung.

On the one hand there is the sinful structure as an objective fact. Here Mynatty endorses an axiom of liberation theology that moral evil or sin, is not merely a personal phenomenon but also a socio-structural reality. Evil crystallizes into social structures and institutions which systematically maintain and support evil (Mynatty, 4).

On the other hand, these 'structures of sin' only exist in so far as individuals initiate or corroborate them. An individual cannot be held responsible for every evil caused by (corrupt) structures since they take the form of a conglomerate and not of an aggregate. Nevertheless, there is an individual responsibility or guilt in so far as one is in one or other way accountable for the evil caused by the structures. Strictly speaking, individuals are only 'guilty' when carrying out an intentional or deliberate act. But in the case of participation in corrupt structures, individuals should also accept a form of responsibility. They have a duty to not to preserve the evil consequences of the structures they are confronted with. It is this contribution to the preservation or continuation of evil that is interpreted by Mynatty as 'social sin'.

The meaning of this subjective component is further articulated by Nebel in the perspective of Karl Jaspers' analysis of the problem of the collective guilt of German people's for the crimes committed by the Nazi regime. Nebel distinguishes between objective and subjective responsibility.

Objective responsibility refers to the past. It signals one's belonging to a historical community. One could therefore state that all Germans are jointly responsible for the Nazi regime, without being in the strict sense guilty of its crimes. The same applies for those born in Congo, Italy or Russia: being a member of a community where corruption is rife, that in itself constitutes a responsibility.

Nebel agrees with Mynatty that a human being cannot be held guilty for acts committed in the past, but as an individual person she is responsible for the common history of corruption that she continues by participating in it. As soon as we become aware of what's happening, our factual objective responsibility constitutes a moral duty to refuse to perpetuate this negative history. One should do all that is possible to restore past injustices and to transform the unjust institutionalised context (Nebel, 534).

Thus objective responsibility invokes subjective duty. Objective responsibility puts an individual in a position where he or she has to make a choice whether or not to become a participant in corrupt institutions, which one neither has chosen nor spontaneously deem desirable. Here one must differentiate between diverse circumstances. The possibility exists that, for instance, one becomes part of a corrupt community in an absolute way (e.g. a child born into a mafia family) The possibility also exists that one joins a corrupt system out of necessity (e.g. a civil servant who is underpaid or not paid at all and who becomes corrupt in order to survive). The possibility even exists to become accidentally or unwillingly part of a corrupt community (for example, an ambitious lawyer proud to be hired by a prestigious corporation, who discovers gradually that he is involved in fraudulent practices for which he is ultimately hold co-responsible). In such cases there remains always some space of freedom in as far as one is responsible to decide whether one continues to participate in the unethical practices or not. Even those who are victims of circumstances (e.g. our underpaid civil servants) are responsible when they continue to support the system and act as recipients of the system.

The objective responsibility opens the eyes for a subjective responsibility. This subjective responsibility doesn't concentrate on the past interactions, but on the now, the interaction in the present, the active participation itself (Nebel, 535). Here responsibility becomes a conscious choice. One decides whether or not to participate in an action coordinated with that of the other participants (Nebel, 536). Of the utmost importance is that this responsibility is both similar and different. On the one hand, there is an equality of all as collective responsibility in so far as everyone is a participant in the interaction; on the other hand this responsibility is very different according to one's role in the system.

The concept of *shared responsibility* should bring more clarity here. It needs to be distinguished from *concentrated responsibility and diffused responsibility.* In the case of *concentrated responsibility*, the leaders of an organisation or group are held responsible, but this may lead subordinates to evade their responsibility. In the case of *diffused responsibility*, everyone is held equally responsible without taking into account the different roles and degrees of responsibility. Fiala (2006, 679) therefore prefers the term *shared responsibility*: in this case everyone involved shares responsibility according to his or her position or power in the system.

Nebel (537) doesn't refer to this differentiation, but he articulates the different levels of responsibility according to the levels of implication of the acting persons. He distinguishes four levels.

- *"Instigation"* or *being urged to*: this is the level of those who exert a direct influence, because of their position as executives, on the genesis and functioning of a corrupt system or network
- *"Collaboration"* or *active participation*: in order for a corrupt network to come into being one needs the active participation of persons institutionally linked to the system
- *"Collusion"* or *occasional participation*: refers to people who in order to profit make not systematically but only occasionally use of the network

- "*Omission*": refers to a group of people who are not actively participating, but refuse to act against it.

In this manner almost everyone has a distinct but shared responsibility.

11.4 Inner Strength as a Remedy Against the Fear to Act with Integrity

The hitherto proposed solutions in our discourse on sinful structures and personal moral integrity leave a few crucial questions unanswered: why do individuals get so easily entangled in corrupt networks? Where does someone involved in a corrupt network find the strength to say no? How can membership of a religious community contribute to this process of change?

The starting point for answering these questions is the fact that one of the major causes why corrupt networks are being perpetuated is the security they offer, or negatively put, the fear of rejection, of no longer belonging to the network that activates the corrupt system; the fear to be no longer in accord with others in the system, the fear to lose status or to be side-lined.

Nebel's analysis of corruption in Northern Italy sheds an interesting light on this matter: corruption has a persistent and is systematic character.

A first striking characteristic is that organised networks of corruption are very structured and stable. They hedge against economical risks (Nebel, 98). These organised but corrupt networks succeed in providing 'certainty' and 'security' precisely because so many have been long-lasting and thoroughly compromised.

Secondly, intermediaries are charged with maintaining the stability of a corrupt system. These are people who are the liaison between corrupting and corrupted agencies. Often these are firmly entrenched civil servants nominated by a political party and they are a member of different networks (they are operating partly as a top civil servants, partly representing political interests, partly as representatives of economical interests, e.g. members of the board of company directors or supervisors). Their appointment is not based on actual economical or executive competencies or skills, but on their usefulness for the corrupt network. They continuously slink around in the grey area between their *de iure* power within the administration and their hidden de facto political-economical function on behalf of their network. They consider their public function to be a kind of personal patrimony and it can be used to further either personal or network interests. Silence and loyalty are important values cultivated. As clients or vassals they owe the system unconditional loyalty. The system embraces them, acquires in their eyes a quasi-normative status and offers them security (Nebel, 107).

Nebel's analysis also shows that participants in transversal and covert networks pursue more than economical enrichment or personal interests. They also want to belong to a group and seek their support, especially when accompanied by status and affirmation. The more the participants act as insecure individuals without an interior life (and inwardness is always something more than merely a 'self' influenced by society) they become dependent for the fulfilment of their need for security and affirmation on backslaps provided by the group to which they belong. Moreover, they will feel embraced by the network but to the point of suffocation. Consequently, participants to the system will adapt their behaviour to what they think they must do to please their employer, organisation or network, or those performing a liaison job for the corrupt network. They develop a mimetic life and become more and more dependent on those persons or institutions providing affirmation. The less confidence they have in themselves, the more they will frenetically seek affirmation and because of their dependence will be prepared to sacrifice everything, even their personal integrity, which in fact has been replaced by a false sense of integrity based on compliance with the rules of the group. The liberty to act has thus been reduced and their existence been impoverished.

Moreover, someone whose behaviour indicates dependency can easily be manipulated by toxic leaders, people who abuse the dependency of their followers and incite them to alienating actions. But toxic leaders are only able to maintain their position because and in so far as their followers obey them (literally: the wrong, external source of inspiration is being listened to, and not their own authentic moral sense).

A transformation becomes possible when people who are confronted with corruption overcome their fear of rejection by its network, when they liberate themselves from their dependency on the backslaps of the peer group. The precondition, however, is that (1) they discover their real self and a fundamental basic trust in life, and (2) they get support of an alternative community which offers them the space for a 'counter discipline' against the discipline imposed by the corrupt networks by which they are surrounded.

The first step towards liberating oneself from the grip of the corrupt system is the rediscovery of the source of authenticity. This requires what Otto Scharmer describes as 'the letting go of the downloaded self' (the self that is based on the expectations of the system or of the peer group on which an insecure person depends to 'be' someone), or, in positive terms: the peaceful discovery of the 'real' self ("I feel more quiet and present to my real self", Scharmer, 12–13). This 'real' self requires 'the courage to be', the courage to accept to be accepted, the courage to accept oneself as a complex person with strengths and weaknesses, and yet capable of resistance against injustice and corruption in so far as one become receptive for an inner strength which enables a person to do the right thing. Moral courage in this regards is not a matter of being perfect, or the effect of an overexerted effort, but of trust in life, of finding a deep sense of inner security, peace and freedom, whereby one becomes less dependent from corrupt systems for one's self-esteem. The way towards such a fundamental inner trust and self-awareness is stillness and/or prayer (Verstraeten, 131–147). It is in stillness that a new future can emerge.

Inner trust and freedom are necessary but, however, not sufficient conditions, because 'no man is an island'. The development of resilience and resistance against corruption requires the support of a virtuous community, the values and norms of which are different from those of networks of corruption. Appropriating and practicing these values and norms is a counter-discipline against the 'discipline' of corruption, not as an unbearable burden, nor as an heteronomous 'law' imposed upon somebody, but as the realisation of one's own authenticity. Because as far as the discipline of the virtuous community matches with the very personal longing for a good life (as part of the discovery of the real self), the participation in the life of the virtuous community becomes the source of a person's autonomy and integrity: "*Each human being following his or hers own road will gradually take on firm shape, and will become clearly conscious of a number of requirements. Though mostly external, they will become closely entwined with personal/intimate growth and become of such imposition from within, that if denied one denies the self*" (Légaut, 16). The internalized requirements of the virtuous community are no more those of a superficial downloaded self, seeking affirmation in a corrupt community, but the concretisation of a person's real self and thus her authenticity and integrity.

11.5 Conclusion

Corruption is in many ways corrosive for states and societies. It is, however, not a static or unchangeable reality, because it is always the cumulative product of human interaction. Consequently individuals bear a real responsibility either for the continuation or for the dismantling of corrupt networks. This responsibility can be supported by professional codes, but since they focus merely on role responsibility they are not sufficient. In order to enable people to practice a counter-discipline against corruption it is necessary that individuals integrate their different roles into a coherent life project based on a fundamental choice to contribute to the wellbeing of the society, in other words, what is required is an "integral" integrity understood as narrative unity of the person. Lonely individuals are, however, not on themselves capable of achieving this unity. They need support from communities which enable them to acquire real freedom and inner strength to resist the backslaps of corrupt networks. As such the article confirms the intuition of Alasdair Macintyre at the end of his book 'After Virtue'. In order to promote integrity we need "the construction of local forms of community within which civility and the intellectual and moral can be sustained" (MacIntyre 1985, 263). Via membership of a virtuous community, or more precisely virtuous communities-since one can belong to more than one at once, for example a socially responsible business and a religious community-, a person who discovers her real self, is enabled to stick her "hands into the spokes of the wheel of history" (Weber, 51), not as a tragic or solitary hero who shoulders an impossible task, but as someone whose resistance against corruption is the realisation of her authentic self.

References

Bellah, Robert, Richard Madsen, William Sullivan, Ann Swidler, and Steven M. Tipton. 1992. *The good society*. New York: Alfred Knopf.

Brytting, Tomas. 2000. The precondition for moral competence: Contemporary rationalisation and the creation of moral space. In *Business ethics. Broadening the perspectives*, ed. Verstraeten Johan, 81–95. Leuven: Peeters.

Crane, Andrew and Matten, Dirk. 2004. *Business ethics: A European perspective*. Oxford: Oxford University Press.

De George, Richard T. 2006. *Business ethics*. Upper Saddle River: Prentice Hall/Pearson.

Fiala, Andrew. 2006. Practical pacifism, jus in bello, and citizen responsibility: The case of Iraq. *Ethical Perspectives* 13(2006).

Herkströter, C.A.J. 1996. *Dealing with contradictory expectations–the dilemmas facing multinationals*. Amsterdam: Shell.

John, Paul II. 1985. Reconciliatio et Paenitentia, *Acta Apostolicae Sedis* 77.

Légaut, Marcel. 1977. De westerse mens op zoek naar een volledig humanisme. *Pro Mundi Vita Bulletin*, 69(1977).

Macintyre, Alasdair. 1985. *After virtue. A study in moral theory*. 2nd ed. London: Duckworth.

Martin, Mike W. 2000. *Meaningful work. Rethinking professional ethics*. Oxford: Oxford University Press.

McMahon, Thomas. 1986. Creed, cult, code and business ethics. *Journal of Business Ethics* 5(6): 453–464.

Musschenga, Bert. 2004. Integriteit. Eenheid en heelheid van de mens. Utrecht: Lemma, as summarized by the author in, http://www.Bezinningscentrum.nl/teksten/bert/inleiding-integriteit.htm.

Mynatty, Hormis. 1991. The concept of social sin. *Louvain Studies* 16(1): 3–26.

Nebel, Mathias. 2006. *La catégorie morale de péché structure*. Editions du Cerf: Essai de systématique. Paris.

Paine, Lynn Sharp. 1998. Integrity. In *Blackwell encyclopedic dictionary of business ethics*, ed. Patricia H. Werhane and R. Edward Freeman, 335–337. Oxford: Blackwell.

Scharmer, C. Otto. 2009. *Theory U. Leading from the future as it emerges. The social technology of presencing*. San Francisco: Berrett-Koehler Publishers.

Solomon, Robert. 1997. Corporate roles, personal virtues: an aristotelian approach to business ethics. In *Virtue ethics: A critical reader*, ed. Daniel Stratman, 205–226. Edinburgh: Edinburgh University Press.

Verstraeten, Johan. 2008. Responsible leadership beyond managerial rationality: The necessity of reconnecting ethics and spirituality. In *Leadership and business ethics (Issues in business ethics, 25)*, ed. Gabriel Flynn. New York: Springer.

Weber, Max. 1964. *Politik als Beruf*. Berlin: Duncker und Humblot.

Werhane, Patricia. 1985. *Persons, rights and corporations*. Englewood Cliffs: Prentice Hall.

Chapter 12
Bribery and the Grey Areas of Morality

Michel Dion

Abstract Depending on legal jurisdictions, legislators deal with bribery in a very different way. The basis components of bribery as social construct will be unveiled. Believing that there are grey areas of morality within bribery issues is embracing a mythical mindset. Cassirer's approach of myths could be used to unveil the basic structure of mythical beliefs. If the notion of grey areas of morality in bribery issues is a mythical idea, then strategies to fight corruption cannot remain the same.

12.1 Introduction

Bribery seems to be universally prohibited. In some Asian countries, bribery is often confused with gift-giving practices. That's why some authors believed that there are grey areas of morality in bribery issues. Such grey areas of morality refer to conceptions of rightness/wrongness following the cultural (moral) relativism mainstream. Cultural relativism could justify practices that should never be socially approved, since they put harm to the business community and even collective wealth. Cultural relativism is unable to cover all situations. So, which philosophical theory could help us to unveil the real frontiers between bribes and gift-giving practices? Which ethical theory could make it easier to analyze the moral dimensions of bribing activities? A non-consequentialist approach to bribery will put light on the real frontiers between bribes and gift-giving practices. Neither Aristotle nor Kant, for example, would have morally approved bribery (giving, soliciting, or receiving bribes). Looking at bribery in a non-consequentialist way implies the following philosophical choice: either the Kantian viewpoint (focusing on the use of pure reason, and thus on the primacy of moral duty), or the Aristotelian viewpoint (emphasizing the way we put basic human virtues into practice).

M. Dion (✉)
Chairholder of the CIBC Research Chair in Financial Integrity, Faculté d'administration, Université de Sherbrooke, Sherbrooke, Québec, Canada
e-mail: Michel.Dion@USherbrooke.ca

© Springer International Publishing Switzerland 2016
M. Dion et al. (eds.), *Financial Crimes: Psychological, Technological, and Ethical Issues*, International Library of Ethics, Law, and the New Medicine 68, DOI 10.1007/978-3-319-32419-7_12

12.2 The Phenomenon of Bribery and the Structural Analysis of Action

Corruption includes both bribery and extortion. However, people seem to be much more concerned with the effects of bribery than with those of extortion. Corrupt practices have national and international ramifications. They can even be analyzed from a macro-economic perspective. According to Baughn et al. (2010), wealthier countries have less propensity for international bribe-paying, although such an approach is much less evident when dealing with low-income countries. Corruption is a national and international phenomenon. On the national level, corrupt practices could involve nationals, and sometimes foreign people. On the international level (in the context of international contracts, agreements and business deals), the offer-side of bribery usually comes from wealthier countries.

The effect of culture on bribe paying could be captured in the measure of bribe-supplying country's level of domestic corruption. Sanyal and Aguvenli (2009) asserted that per capital income in the home country is the most important factor determining a firm's propensity to bribe abroad. They did not explain the reality of bribes which are provided by large business corporations (coming from wealthiest countries), when doing business in low-income countries. Those firms could safeguard their moral beliefs when doing business in rich countries, because they must comply themselves to strong anticorruption regulations. But in low-income countries, such regulations are quite soft. So, large business corporations (from rich countries) are assuming that their corporate sense of morality could be largely modified. They seem to embrace a Machiavellian way of life: we could use every effective/efficient means to safeguard our power and influence. And one of those means could be social conformism. According to David Hume (1711–1776), the basic motive of human action is to ensure social approval and to avoid social disapproval (Hume 1961). When such firms are dealing in rich countries, their corporate ethics could be rooted in social conformism: their organizational ethics could mirror the corporate will that organizational actions/decisions will receive social approval. And if it implies to give bribes, that's fine. But does such attitude actually reflect the whole reality? In some countries, the public reaction against corruption is so strong that foreign multinationals could feel the high potentiality to be socially disapproved, when going ahead with bribing practices. Nonetheless, some of those multinationals could focus on their self-interest rather than on the perception of social approval/disapproval. When dealing in low-income countries, such multinationals could make their corporate morality more egoistic, that is, centered on their self-interest.

How could corruption spread so rapidly in given societies? Some institutional, social and political factors could play a major role in the implementation of corrupt practices. In way or another, corruption negatively affects political institutions. According to Dal Bo et al. (2006), when threats (such as legal harassment, smear campaigns in the media, and physical violence) are actually present in a given country, there are more possibilities to bribe politicians. Such fact seems to be correlated to public officials of lower quality. More violent countries give birth to bad (and corrupt) politicians. Corrupt practices always have side effects related to any kind of violence. Sometimes, violence is not a side effect, but a basic component of corrupt practices. Politicians do not (and should not) evolve as if they were excluded from reality. Rather, they are deeply influenced by their external environment. If such environment is characterized by a high level of corruption, then politicians will have two basic choices: either fighting corruption (focusing on virtue), or conforming themselves to their corrupt environment (mirroring their social conformism). Authors presuppposed that politicians will imitate the actors of their external environment. Institutional and social factors could even play a major role on the way corruption is widespread in a given society. According to Li and Ouyang (2007), when corruption intensity is high, then most government officials are corrupt. The effect of a firm's bribery behavior could be increased or reduced by other firms' bribing behavior. That's what they called the synergy effect. A firm's decision to bribe (or not to bribe) could influence other firms' bribing behavior. The synergy effect could be due to organizational mimetism. DiMaggio and Powell (1991, 69–70) believed that organizations tend to model themselves after similar organizations in their field. But such organizations are perceived in their field either as more legitimate, or more successful than others.

Organizational mimetism means that some firms are much more influential than others, so that they will represent the role model: the cultural guide other firms should follow. Certainly, there are some firms influencing others about technological issues. But, is it also true for ethical issues? Champions of ethical behavior seem to be quite rare on the national and on the international scene. Champions of integrity do not suddenly appear in the short-term. On the other hand, there is no firm having stronger influence than others. Every firm could make reality changing. But how could small suppliers influence multinationals? There could be an effect of moral propagation when a given society is impregnated with religious/spiritual values (for instance, in Hindu, Buddhist, or Islamic countries). But such effect will be quite different (and sometimes inexistent) in some countries. So, religion/spirituality could not explain the synergy effect. It is hardly possible to explain how a given country could get rid of corruption through the synergy effect. So, how could 'synergy effect' explain the way countries have raised their level of corruption? The existence of the synergy effect has not been rationally proved.

Institutional, social, and political factors converge to unveil corruption as a social construct. According to Gordon and Miyake (2001), what is considered as an acceptable practice is culturally induced. However, cultural values and beliefs could be used as excuses for corrupt practices. The perception of corrupt practices is culturally induced. But such fact should never be considered as a moral justification of corrupt practices. Okogbule (2006) asserted that all societies are corrupt. What varies is the level of corruption, not its presence. Corruption is a social phenomenon that negatively affects every society. Corruption is a social construct (Bailey and Paras 2006; Shehu 2004).

Does it imply that corruption cannot be defined? Various cultures and civilizations will define corruption in very different ways. However, it does not mean that the phenomenon of corruption cannot be circumscribed. The essentials of corruption is not a set of cultural layers. Whatever societal cultures, corruption remains the same. We do not have to consider the cultural forms of corruption to understand what the phenomenon of corruption actually conveys. The sociocultural explanation of corruption should never be considered as a moral justification of corrupt practices. An explanation reveals how things happened. Explanations reflect causal relationships. An explanation can never be a moral justification. Moral justification is partly related to moral reasoning. As Velasquez (1988) observed, the process of moral reasoning implies a given moral standard and the facts that reveal the contents of the standard itself (whether it is a required, or prohibited behavior). Such process of moral reasoning actually mirrors an attitude of ethical relativism. In that way, any culture could use moral reasoning processes to morally justify corruption, as if it would be a culturally-bound phenomenon. If we distinguish moral justification from moral reasoning, then we must identify parameters of truth as the foundations of moral justification.

Moral universalism seems to be an attractive way to look at ethical issues. Ethical universalism could be effective, when dealing with basic human rights: the UN Declaration of Human Rights (1948) becomes a hyper-norm, that is, a norm overcoming any cultural/religious norm. But for other issues, ethical/cultural relativism could be a morally justified approach, since there is no universal principle determining the contents of given human behaviors. It is clearly the case for gift-giving practices. There is no universal principle imposing universal limitations (for instance, about the worth of gifts). The socially acceptable worth of gifts depends on social, cultural, political, and religious/spiritual factors. In Western countries, the limitation could be around 150–200$, while in Asian countries, it could be $2 500, or $3 000. The decisive factor is not only the social perception of the gift as gift, but above all the analysis of the circumstances of gift-giving practices. To what extent gift-giving practices could be disguised bribes? Arunthanes et al. (1994) gave three basic motives for gift-giving practices: (1) expressing one's appreciation for past client relationships; (2) creating a positive impression helping to establish initial business relationships; (3) returning a favour or expecting a favour in return for something. Indeed, the last motive rather characterizes bribe-giving practices. Gift giving is never connected to any favour the offer-side would like to ensure for himself/herself. Could we reasonably accept that bribes are business costs we must include in transaction costs? Unlike bribes, gifts could certainly be considered as business costs, since they are not immoral practices. However, offering, soliciting, or accepting bribes is immoral: it is both an antitrust behavior and an abuse of power over the victim. The antitrust behavior is self-evident, since bribery is aiming at preferential treatment. Other competitors are unable to provide such bribes and will then lose contracts. Offering or soliciting bribes is an abuse of power: we should thus focus on the relationships between the offer-side and the receiver. According to Brown and Cloke (2006), analyzing the phenomenon of corruption implies unveiling the power relationships involved in given societies/cultures as well as the roles and responsibilities of business, governments, and supra-national institutions (such as the World Bank and the IMF).

Bribery implies both an abuse of power and an antitrust behavior. That's essentially what bribery means. Abuse of power and antitrust behavior constitute the inner structure of corrupt practices. The nature of bribes makes them quite different from gifts. Unlike gifts, bribes cannot be added to business costs, at least from a moral viewpoint. If the structural components of bribery (abuse of power and antitrust behavior) are not present in a given business transaction, then gift-giving practices can be morally justified.

Is social morality a factor we should take into account? According to Hooker (2009), every culture has its own way to deal with moral deviance. Every society has a given set of moral principles, norms, and values implying given ways of moral deviance (when such principles, norms, or values are neglected/denied). Various countries could be corrupt for different reasons. They would even prohibit bribery for different motives. As Hooker (2009) said, in relationship-based cultures, life is organized around relationships with parents, friends, and bosses. Rule-based cultures seem to be more vulnerable due to cheating and to bribery. Bribery is a threat to the stability of the whole society. It denies any worth to compliance with the applicable rules (rule-based cultures), or to short-circuit stable relationships (relationship-based cultures). However, will bribery only reflect basic weaknesses characterizing a given societal culture? Both rule-based cultures and relationship-based cultures convey specific expectations about social conformism and moral deviance. Although bribery could happen in both cases and for different reasons, various social expectations will be at stake. What does corruption mean for people in the street? The meaning of corruption is the basis of social expectations toward a more or less corrupt behavior. How are bribery and extortion perceived by most people?

Khalil et al. (2010) made a clear distinction between extortion and bribery: bribery involves cooperation between corrupt parties, while extortion is antagonistic. Authors believed that extortion penalizes an agent after a good conduct, while bribery imposes some penalty for bad behavior. They perceived extortion as being a worse problem. When we carefully analyze both conducts, we find out a basic commonality: a constraint imposed on the victim. The offer-side of bribery does not actually let the other party free to accept bribes. The receiver could refuse the offer. But due to his/her financial situation (quite vulnerable, in low-income countries), the receiver could feel strong pressure to accept the offer (pressures could even come from members of his/her family). In some cases, the receiver could share his/her bribes with many members of his/her family. The constraint is then to reduce receiver's choices. In the case of extortion, the constraint is self-evident. The receiver must accept the offer. The constraint could even involve physical violence.

In the case of bribery and extortion as well, the constraint is basically a psychological violence exerted on the receiver. It expresses the will to reduce receiver's choices. This is a rational analyzis of bribery and extortion as social phenomena. The basic question is the following one: does it reflect the way people actually perceive bribery and extortion? What are the basic social expectations about corruption in a given society? Do social expectations about corrupt practices reflect some basic accepted moral values and principles?

According to Gopinath (2008), the moral perspective about corruption defines corruption as a violation of accepted values and a misuse of position of power for personal gain. The phenomenon of corruption involves an abuse of power over others (for personal gain). But does it necessarily imply to transgress socially accepted values? Certainly not. Some people claim that corruption is a way of life. Such assertion will always tend to justify corrupt practices. That's why social acceptability should never be a criterion for morally justifying corrupt practices. However, the legal/illegal character of the phenomenon suggests a consensus about social morality. Countries have very different ways to enforce and punish corruption. Most of countries would make corruption illegal. However, in some cultures, sums of money provided in given circumstances could be gifts, while in other societies, they could be considered as bribes. The legal/illegal character of the phenomenon is not a reliable criterion for identifying and defining corruption. Social values as well as legal enforcement can largely vary from culture to culture. That's why we must circumscribe the nature of the phenomenon itself. When the nature of bribery is unveiled (abuse of power and antitrust behavior), it becomes self-evident that giving, soliciting, or receiving bribes cannot be morally justified.

12.3   The Existence of Grey Areas of Morality Within Bribery Issues

Ethics has grey areas. When facing ethical dilemmas, people could adopt two traditional viewpoints: either a consequentialist, or a non-consequentialist perspective. A consequentialist viewpoint focuses on the consequences (effects) of given decisions/behaviors, either on oneself only (philosophical egoism: Smith, Hobbes), or on all people affected by such decisions/actions (utilitarianism: Bentham, Mill, Moore, Ross). A non-consequentialist viewpoint focuses either on virtues (Aristotle), or on moral duties (Kant). So, depending on the philosophical theory we are embracing, we will look at bribery issues quite differently. According to Chang et al. (2001), we can only choose between ethical universalism (universal norms of ethical conduct), or ethical relativism (each culture has its own social morality). They did not consider the possibility that both approaches could be true. The authors chose ethical relativism. They asserted that there is a grey area between gifts and bribes. If universal norms of ethical behavior do not exist, then it is certainly difficult to distinguish gifts and bribes. The confusion comes from the excessive influence exerted by cultural conditioning factors. The authors did not see the possibility to have both universal human rights and universal moral principles on one hand, and ethical issues we could consider from an ethical relativism perspective, on the other hand. If we adopt such an ethical equilibrium viewpoint, then grey areas between gifts and bribes will disappear.

12.3.1 The Myth of Grey Areas of Morality in Bribery Issues

Some authors (Tian 2008; Werner 2000; Steidlmeier 1999) presupposed that there is no clear boundary between gifts and bribes, as if both gifts and bribes were culturally-bound phenomena. Werner (2000) concluded that the most reliable criterion for distinguishing gifts and bribes is the legality of the exchange (unlike bribes, gifts are legal). The basic motive is quite different: maintaining good relationships (through gift-giving practices), or getting something done quickly (bribing activities). The basic motive for giving-bribes was not precisely identified. In bribery, the offer-side is trying to ensure he/she will have a preferential treatment, to the detriment of others (such as competitors). So, giving bribes implies to guarantee that the offer-side will have a better situation in the near future. The other way to believe that the lines between gifts and bribes are blurred is to refer to some cultural practices and norms about gift-giving. According to Tian (2008), we cannot know the nature of corruption in China without deeply understanding its philosophical and spiritual roots, that is, the influence of Daoism (and perhaps Confucianism) on the way gift-giving and bribery are understood. Steidlmeier (1999) even said that it is difficult to distinguish a bribe from a tip/commission. The author used an utilitarian principle: bribes could have good as well as bad effects. In terms of means and consequences, bribes could be as good as gifts. Does it imply a Nietzschean transmutation of social values? If we consider that bribes as well as gift-giving practices are culturally-bound, then we will suggest that the traditional distinction between rightness and wrongness is obsolete. But it would be a distortion of Nietzsche's critique of unjustified dualisms (right/wrong, good/evil, true/false). Nietzsche (1978, 24) emphasizing the need of a free spirit, that is, a spirit released from the yoke of unjustified dualisms. What is considered as good is not so good than what it seems to be. What is seen as wrong could have positive impact on reality. Nietzsche asserted that the faith in truth has nothing to do with truth itself (Nietzsche 1978, 39). A faith in moral truths is not a proof of morality (Nietzsche 1967, 246). Nietzsche was attacking the notion of morality we find in Christianity (and Buddhism) and even in traditional Western metaphysics. He was aware that ruling social classes will impose their values/principles on the working classes. But it does not imply that Nietzsche's transmutation of values has no limitations. The way Hitler has distorted Nietzsche's philosophy (in *Mein Kampf*) actually shows the dramatic consequences of such philosophical misunderstanding. Nietzsche was not really concerned with criminal issues. He was much more concerned with our representations and beliefs. He was certainly deeply aware of the social/moral impact of rulers' values/principles over citizens. Nietzsche put the emphasis on our mental and perceptual mistakes giving birth to false representations of rightness/wrongness. Such an approach could be used by moral relativistic philosophers. But it cannot be used to morally justify bribery. Bribery tends to favour the highest social classes and has deep social impact in the long-term. Nietzsche would not admit to morally justify such phenomenon. Corruption would certainly remain wrong, because of its bad consequences.

Those who claim that there are grey areas of morality in bribery issues actually reflect a consequentialist approach. They are using societal culture/morality to morally justify the phenomenon of bribery. They do not want to morally justify bribery. But in taking societal culture/morality as an absolute reality, they put bribery in the realm of good things (or at least, unavoidable events). Societal culture/morality are not means to justify bribes. But in considering them as realities that should never be morally criticized, relativistic thinkers are unconsciously justifying bribery. They seem not to be aware of the meaning of moral justification. They are explaining that bribery has cultural roots, that is, conditioning factors. Justification means that a given phenomenon is characterized by numerous motives. Such motives are suitable to a given set of moral principles as objective criteria for decision-making processes. Moral justification refers to one's values system. Moral justification also needs to describe objective principles of action (criteria for decision-making processes). Otherwise, moral justification would be the final and ultimate justification of one's values system. So, moral justification implies self-criticism and openness to a dialogue about ethical issues. Those who claim that there is a grey area of morality in bribery issues probably refer to their values system and to the moral values/principles characterizing their own society. Unfortunately, they are unable to put in place some rational/objective principles that could make bribery a moral phenomenon. They cannot finalize their moral reasoning process, since they cannot define moral principles helping us to face the phenomenon of bribery.

The grey areas of morality in bribery issues are thus implicitly self-created and described as an ultimate truth we cannot (or should not) question. But it is a mythical idea that tends to reveal the emotional and symbolic aspects of reality bribery is evoking. Myths tend to hide some dimensions of reality as if they would be sub-products of an undefinable mystery. As said Brisson (2005, 45–46), myth is providing order and organization within the realm of human action. Myths impose a coherent view on the universal and existential categories (such as space and time, substance and causality). They are even proposing an anthropological view of human existence and being. The myth of grey areas in bribery issues reflects the need to tolerate various cultural practices. In that way, a principle of philosophical anthropology is conveyed by such belief: human being and existence cannot be ordered by universal norms of ethical behavior (for instance, 'a human being has no moral essence'). As Sartre (1970, 1943) said, human being is creating himself/herself through his/her actions and decisions. He/she defines his/her own values. There are no universal values everybody should actualize in his/her daily life. Every value is existentially and personally chosen. The belief in grey areas of morality within bribery issues is conveying such an existentialist principle.

According to Cassirer (1944), without a belief in the reality of its object, the myth would lose its ground. Cassirer (1944, 81–83) asserted that a myth combines a theoretical (conceptual) element and a (perceptual) element of artistic creation. The theoretical element refers to the belief itself. The perceptual element implies that mythical perception is a perception of the self/world that is qualitatively different from the perception people generally have. Cassirer saw mythical perception as paving the way to the artistic creation. The perceptual element of myth focuses on action rather than on representation, said Cassirer (1944, 84–86). But the way actions are enhanced reveals a structural/paradigmatic outlook. Mythical thought cannot be isolated from a paradigm-created function of human spirit (Eliade 1963, 24–25). Paradigms are representations and explanations of reality, or given community's shared beliefs (Kühn 1970, 43–51), whether it the self, the world, Nature, or God. Mythical perceptions are identifying exemplary actions aiming at a unified sense of our existence. Mythical perception deepens our meaning of life. Myths focus on action: basic emotions and feelings about the mysteries of life find a way to reduce their power/influence over our peaceful state of mind. That's why Cassirer concluded that the instinct of life has created the myth-creating function (Cassirer 1944, 113). Then, mythical thought has evolved at all historical periods (including the present era). The coherence of mythical thought is guaranteed by the unity of feeling it unveils. Myth is an offspring of emotion (Cassirer 1944, 89–90).

When we consider the myth of grey areas of morality within bribery issues, we could observe that there is belief, but no element of artistic creation. However, this myth is clearly focusing on action. It implies to ensure a unity of feeling, when facing given circumstances. The myth is ensuring that there is no uncertainty, neither about social expectations, nor about morally justifiable behaviors. The myth of grey areas of morality within bribery issues is not grounded in artistic creation, but rather on social needs and expectations about human behavior. It is also the case with the myth of race (Montagu 1997, 155–174), or medical myths, or even contemporary popular myths such as the Roswell myth, or the "flying saucers" myth (Jung 1974). In those cases, we could find out a theoretical element (belief), but no artistic creation as such. Contemporary myths are desacralized and do not reflect the power of the origin. The way we look at contemporary myths has nothing to do with ethnological and anthropological viewpoints (Eliade, Levi-Strauss). Mythology actually mirrors very old narratives transmitted through historical traditions and: such narratives dealt with the intrinsic links between the present (existential) situation and the power of the origin (Kerényi 1980, 13–20). Cassirer's philosophical approach of myths is not focusing on the sacredness and the paradigmatic function of myths. It is rather reflecting myth as a part of language. As Brito (1999) said, Heidegger saw myth as a word that says something about what-is. Heidegger looked at myths in the same way as Greek philosophers actually perceived them: a part of language that unveils the process through which things and phenomena actually appear in human existence. Myth and language are not antagonistic, but rather complementary parts of human interpretation of what-is (Heidegger 1998, 1976). We are using such philosophical understanding of mythical thought to understand and reveal the structure of contemporary myths (such as the myth of grey areas of morality within bribery issues).

Following Cassirer's approach of myths, we could look at the grey areas of morality within bribery issues as mirroring a mythical idea (belief). Nothing more. Strictly speaking, we could consider those beliefs (such as the myth of race, or the Roswell myth) as mythical ideas rather than myths, since they do not convey any element of artistic creation. The mythical idea of grey areas of morality within bribery issues is unveiling the need not to see one's cultural framework being troubled by others' worldview. It is manifesting the existential troublesome situation with which we could experiment, when our symbolic system is morally questioned. The mythical idea of grey areas within bribery issues actually says a lot of things about human being. At least, it reveals existential insecurity in the face of otherness. In defining such grey areas, we are building great walls protecting us against any psychological threat, or moral questioning. We are showing how strong psychological mechanisms could be used to reduce the scope of moral questioning. We are manifesting how psychological resistance toward other worldviews could influence the way we are looking at bribery issues. We are protecting our own cultural framework, as if it could be threatened by otherness. We are falling into large ethnocentric traps. The way societal culture/morality are evoked actually reflects a resistance toward any moral questioning. But, if such reluctance to question our own moral values/principles is operating, then we cannot see reality as-it-is. We rather interpret reality in the way we would like to see it. This is an ethnocentric trap people will inevitably fall into, when referring to grey areas of morality within bribery issues.

So, grey areas of morality could be used to justify any corrupt behavior. Grey areas of morality within bribery issues could become a tool of unconscious dehumanization. As an abuse of power and an antitrust behavior, bribery is dehumanizing human relationships in the public/private sector. So, the mythical idea of grey areas of morality does not serve a noble end. It is rather emphasizing a mindset dehumanizing our world. It is a dehumanizing mythical idea. Whether people are aware or not of dehumanizing processes is not really important. *The essence of the mythical idea of grey areas of morality within bribery issues is to dehumanize human relationships.* Revealing the mythical idea is unveiling deep challenges. From the moment we become aware that a grey area of morality within bribery issues is a 'mythical idea', we are facing the challenge of demythologizing our perception of bribery. Demythologization, said Bultmann (1969), implies to unveil the myth conveyed by religious beliefs/dogmas. The context of bribery cannot be compared to the contents of sacred texts (such as the Bible). However, the idea of demythologization is quite enlightening for dealing with bribing practices. We rather use the term "demythicization" as a social process through which mythical ideas are unveiled as being an integral part of social practices/beliefs.

Demythologizing would mean to unveil myths impregnating the essence of given beliefs. Demythologizing processes have deep existential and spiritual meaning. As Bultmann (1969, 384) said, demythologizing implies to question mythological texts about their real meaning, that is, to interpret mythological assertions and beliefs. The way myths are mirroring reality provides a given interpretation of reality, and thus our given notion of human existence. Demythologizing is an existential and hermeneutic process. It implies to find out a meaning behind mythological forms and beliefs. It does not imply to get rid of them. On the other hand, demythicization has more to do with the way the symbolic power of mythical ideas tends to be lost throughout social/cultural conditioning factors. Barta (2002) analyzed the demythicization of the myth of Orphea. Unlike demythologization, demythicizing is closely linked to social/cultural processes and does not matter with any existential meaning. As Barthes (1957, 230) said, myths imply that we have lost the historical quality of things/events: we do not know how given phenomena and events have arisen in human existence. Demythicizing is a way to immerse ourselves in historical traditions. It is a way to unveil the historical determinants behind mythical ideas.

The belief that there are grey areas of morality within bribery issues would make difficult to distinguish bribes from gift-giving practices. Demythicizing would mean to reveal that grey areas of morality within bribery issues is a mythical idea having social and cultural roots. Demythicizing grey areas of morality within bribery issues would unveil the social/cultural roots of corruption (Glaeser and Goldin 2008). In doing so, moral questioning will be widened. The influence of mythical ideas will be considerably reduced. If we unveil the psychological need to have grey areas of morality within bribery issues, then we will understand bribery quite differently. Rather than emphasizing the cultural/social aspects of the phenomenon, we will focus on the nature of bribe-giving: an abuse of power and an antitrust behavior. Unlike gift-giving practices, bribe-giving has dehumanizing effects.

12.3.2   An Outlook on Bribing Practices: Between Moral Duty and Basic Human Virtues

Kantianism presupposes that an action can be considered as a moral action if as a principle it could be universalized (Kant 1959, 5–22, 40; 1971: 33). However, it is often impossible to put it into practice. Kantianism is a theory of rights; it emphasizes the crucial importance to recognize everybody as a subject, and not purely as an object. A theory of basic human rights can get a 'somewhat universal' approach, although people from some cultures/religions could claim that their worldview makes those rights either inexistent, or quite different from what the UN Declaration of Human Rights (1948) actually said. But if we deal with situations uncovered by universal human rights, how could we universalize given principles of action? In such situations, cultures and religions are so diverse that it could be almost impossible to ensure that any rational actor would accept a given principle of action. Some authors (Chang et al. 2001) believed that there are grey areas of morality within bribery issues. Kant would not agree, since the phenomenon of bribery implies a dishonest behavior. Kant was never concerned with cultural, social, economic, political, or religious/spiritual conditioning factors. Kant was rather focusing on the impartial individual using his/her reason. According to Kant, we must be honest in every situation. That's why Kantianism denies the existence of grey areas of morality within bribery issues. Kant thought that the consequences of being dishonest were too disastrous to allow someone becoming dishonest. Such preliminary (consequentialist) analyzis of dishonesty is presupposed in Kantian (non-consequentialist) moral reasoning process. It is the basis of his non-consequentialist approach of moral issues.

To be honest becomes a moral duty accomplished in every situation, without taking specific circumstances (or conditioning factors) into account. In Kantianism, bribery practices can never be moral actions, since they deny our basic moral duty to be honest in every situation. Kantianism is focusing on the primacy of moral duty. The Kantian approach is rooted in pure reason, without considering any conditioning (inner or external) factor.

In virtue ethics (particularly Aristotle's philosophy), honesty is not one of the basic human virtues. However, in his *Nicomachean Ethics* (1996), Aristotle put the emphasis on justice, prudence, courage, temperance, and wisdom (1114b19–1119b18; 1129a3–1138b14; 1140a24–1146a26). If we carefully analyze such virtues as they are defined by Aristotle, then it becomes self-evident that bribery can never be a moral action. Bribery does not enhance justice. Although partners agree to give and take bribes, it does not follow that such action is morally just. As an abuse of power and an antitrust behavior, giving, soliciting, or receiving bribes cannot be just behaviors. Could bribery be a prudent action?

Prudence implies to take into account the effects of our decision/action on all people, in the short-, middle- and long-term. Because of the nature of action (abuse of power and antitrust behavior), giving, soliciting, or receiving bribes cannot be prudent behaviors. How could courage be involved in bribery practices? There is no courage if there is no fear or risk (to suffer from negative effects), as stated by Weil (1990). Those who give, solicit, or receive bribes could assume some risks, or fear to be caught. But were they courageous when giving, soliciting, or receiving bribes? Are we courageous, when acting illegally? The fear of (legal) punishment is not what Weil had in mind. We cannot be courageous, when acting illegally - except if those laws we are breaking are immoral laws (which was clearly the case with the Apartheid legal system in South Africa). Courageous actions can only be in accordance with existing (and morally justified) laws and regulations. So, giving, soliciting, or receiving bribes cannot be courageous actions. Can temperance be involved in such bribery practices? Temperance entails never falling into extreme positions. Cupidity is certainly an extreme position we should avoid. Bribing practices cannot be in accordance with temperance, since they are reflecting the "get rich quick syndrom". The demand-side as well as the offer-side are not considering the negative effects of their actions. They are rather pursuing their self-interest. Nothing more. Finally, do bribery practices be wise actions? Certainly not. Wisdom presupposes the practice of other virtues (justice, prudence, courage, and temperance). So, nobody could rationally assert that bribery practices are wise behaviors. All other human virtues are neglected/denied by bribing practices. So, the Aristotelian perspective is focusing on the way virtues should be practiced. Aristotle would not accept an a priori approach of bribery issues. He would rather compare bribing practices with basic human virtues. He would ask the following question: Could such practices be considered as virtuous? Bribing practices cannot be considered as just, prudent, courageous, temperate, or wise actions.

Unlike non-consequentialist approaches, consequentialist approaches will tend to justify bribing practices in given circumstances. If we carefully analyze the nature of bribing practices (giving, soliciting, or receiving bribes), then it becomes self-evident that such actions have very negative effects on the business community, on the confidence people have in their public servants, and even on collective wealth. That's exactly the effects of abuse of power and of antitrust behaviors. But when we look at bribing practices in a non-consequentialist approach, we do have the choice between two sorts of different perspectives. Either the Kantian viewpoint (focusing on the use of pure reason, and thus on the primacy of moral duty), or the Aristotelian viewpoint (emphasizing the way we put basic human virtues into practice).

12.4   Relevant Strategies to Fight Bribery

At the corporate level, we could look at the implementation of codes of ethics. Bierstaker (2009) rightly said that it is useless for Western companies to translate their codes of conduct into Chinese, without taking into account Chinese social morality. Codes of conduct which have been written in USA (or in France) have no relevance in the Chinese context. If we carefully take the cultural context into account, then codes of conduct will be written in a more effective way. But how could we create bridges between a Confucianist society and the American way of life? Their moral viewpoints have very different roots. In a way or another, it is useless to spend time to write corporate codes of conduct. At least, codes could be used by foreign subsidiaries. But even in that case, the biggest challenge is to introduce a cross-cultural dialogue about ethical issues in the international business. Such dialogue is inevitably connected to the existence of corporate codes of conduct we would like to apply on the international scene. In some Asian countries, whistleblower hotlines could also be perceived as being irrelevant, since whistleblowing could give birth to social punishment and long-term retaliation. Means we could use in the home market are not necessarily useful in foreign countries. Blackburn et al. (2010) asserted that individuals are more likely to be corrupt when others are corrupt. There is a high propensity for Western companies to bribe, when operating abroad. According to Calderon et al. (2009), although they show a high level of transparency and integrity in their home market as well as in other developed countries, their ethical position is deeply modified, when operating in low-income countries. The organization seems to conform itself to the requirements of its external environment. If anticorruption regulations are very strong, Western companies will conform themselves to the laws. But when such regulations are quite soft, they will use the legislator's silence to favour their own interests. What is basically at stake is the depth of their meaning of integrity. If such meaning depends on the changing nature of the external environment, how could we the corporate moral discourse be reliable?

Kreikebaum (2008) asked a very relevant question: Does corporate ethics offer a viable concept of bribery? Does corporate moral discourse reliable, when dealing with corruption? According to Wu (2009), multinationals operating in the same country could vary in their propensity to pay bribes, not only because of their corporate culture (mainly, organizational values and norms of behavior) but also because of the various ways in which multinationals perceive their external environment. The external environment remains the same. What is changing is the way foreign business partners are interpreting its requirements. Such perceptions are necessarily grounded on organizational values and norms of behavior. We should not neglect the influence of societal culture (country of origin: influence of headquarters). Such societal influence could be more or less diffuse, depending on societies/cultures. Wu (2009) asserted that firm size and growth rate are important determinants of bribery at the firm level. The quality of corporate governance systems also plays an important role in firms' propensity to give bribes. But corporate governance systems do not necessarily mirror the essentials of organizational ethics. If it is not the case, we could hardly claim that good corporate governance systems could reduce firms' propensity to give bribes. Such systems could only be concerned with the best means to safeguard directors' independence and transparency on the board of directors. However, if corporate governance is basically linked to organizational ethics, then the way the firm will deal with bribing practices will reflect the coherence and reliability of its moral principles/values.

At the political level, a lot of things have to be done. Governments will clearly express their political commitment to get rid of bribery. According to Abdulai (2009), there needs to be a genuine commitment of political leaders to effectively fight corruption. A genuine commitment could imply to reduce the disparity between public and private sector wages. But other factors should also be taken into account: anticorruption reforms cannot succeed if all stakeholders (such as organized civil society) are not deeply involved in the process. It is not very ease to put such inclusive approach into practice. The same political will must be applied to top managers of various civil society organizations as well as of international financial institutions (IFIs). Perseverance and moral courage must be enhanced by politicians as well as managers of civil society organizations and IFIs (McCormick and Paterson 2006). Unfortunately, this is a moral adventure few people are ready to participate in.

At the international level, means and mechanisms to fight bribery are not really effective, at least in the short-term. In the long-term, they could be more effective if they actually convey a genuine commitment to get rid of bribery. If not, it will remain lip service, or window-dressing. According to Zekos (2004), introducing codes of conduct which are internationally enforceable means: (1) setting up basic ethical principles; (2) prohibiting any corrupt method/stratagem, (3) never considering corruption as a necessary tool for business purposes.

How may we define universal moral principles prohibiting corruption? The legal perspective reflects the diversity of legal treatment and means to fight corruption. Does ethics follow from philosophical and/or religious/spiritual grounds? If it is the case, how could cultural/religious pluralism create a convergence about corruption? Such way to look at international initiatives about corruption could be quite risky, because of the pitfalls of cross-cultural and inter-religious dialogue. That's why a phenomenological approach of bribery could be more efficient and effective. It is focusing on the nature of corrupt practices themselves rather than on social, cultural, economic, political, religious/spiritual aspects of the phenomenon. It is probably the only way to find out a universal principle that could justify universal norms about bribery. If rational beings would agree that bribery implies an abuse of power and an antitrust behavior, then they could more easily accept the idea that bribery can never be morally justified.

12.5 Conclusion

Financial crimes are often described from a legal/political viewpoint. When ethical dimensions of financial crimes are unveiled, then grey areas of morality could appear. Are such grey areas real, or unreal? Bribery is sometimes confused with gift-giving practices, as if cultural norms of behavior would induce such conduct. The way societal culture and morality are evoked reflects a resistance toward any moral questioning. But, when we are reluctant to question our own moral values/principles is operating, then we cannot see reality as-it-is. We rather interpret reality in the way we would like to see it. This is an ethnocentric trap people will inevitably fall into, when referring to grey areas of morality within bribery issues. If we unveil the psychological need to have grey areas of morality within bribery issues, then we will understand bribery quite differently. Rather than emphasizing the cultural/social aspects of the phenomenon, we will focus on the nature of bribe-giving practices. Bribes constitute an abuse of power and an antitrust behavior (and thus a dehumanizing phenomenon), while gift-giving practices are closely linked to cultural (and humanizing) norms of conduct. Bribery and gift-giving practices have very different contents and conditioning factors. Ethical (cultural) relativism is pertinent for gift-giving practices, not for bribery. Gift-giving practices are rooted in cultural conditioning factors. On the other hand, bribery has no cultural ground. In our view, any action expressing an abuse of power and an antitrust behavior could not be morally justified by rational agents. In sympathy with a Kantian viewpoint, we suggest that such action can never be morally justified since its premise cannot be accepted by rational human beings. Rational deliberation about corrupt practices would imply that the premise (or the inner structure) of corrupt practices cannot morally justify the action itself (soliciting, offering, or receiving bribes). Thus, there are no grey area of morality within bribery issues. Due to the nature of the phenomenon itself (its inner structure), bribery can never be morally justified.

References

Abdulai, A.-G. 2009. Political will in combating corruption in developing and transition economies. A comparative study of Singapore, Hong Kong and Ghana. *Journal of Financial Crime* 16(4): 387–417.

Aristotle, 1996. *The Nicomathean Ethics*. Ware: Wordsworth.

Arunthanes, Wiboon, Patriya Tansuhaj and David J. Lemak. 1994. Cross-cultural business gift giving. A new conceptualization and theoretical framework. *International Marketing Review* 11(4): 44–55.

Bailey, John, and Pablo Paras. 2006. Perceptions and attitudes about corruption and democracy in Mexico. *Mexican Studies* 22(1): 57–81.

Barta, Micheline. 2002. La démythification du mythe d'Orphée ou la conquête de la mort par la parole. *Religiologiques* 25: 97–117.

Barthes, Roland. 1957. *Mythologies*. Paris: Seuil.

Baughn, Christopher, Nancy L. Bodie, Mark A. Buchanan, and Michael B. Bixby. 2010. Bribery in international business transactions. *Journal of Business Ethics* 92: 15–32.

Bierstaker, James Lloyd. 2009. Differences in attitudes about fraud and corruption across cultures. Theory, examples and recommendations. *Cross Cultural Management* 16(3): 241–250.

Blackburn, Keith, Niloy Bose, and M. Emranul Haque. 2010. Endegenous corruption in economic development. *Journal of Economic Studies* 37(1): 4–25.

Brisson, Luc. 2005. *Introduction à la philosophie du mythe*. Paris: Librairie philosophique J. Vrin.

Brito, Emilio. 1999. *Heidegger et l'hymne au sacré*. Leuven: Leuven University Press.

Brown, Ed, and Jonathan Cloke. 2006. The critical business of corruption. *Critical perspectives on international business* 2(4): 275–298.

Bultmann, Rudolph. 1969. *Foi et compréhension. Eschatologie et démythologisation*, tome 2. Paris: Seuil.

Calderon, Reyes, José Luis Alvarez-Ace, and Silvia Mayoral. 2009. Corporation as a crucial ally against corruption. *Journal of Business Ethics* 87: 319–332.

Cassirer, Ernst. 1944. *An essay on man. An introduction to the philosophy of human culture*. New Haven: Yale University Press.

Chang, Chang Sop, Nahn Joo Chang, and Barbara T. Freese. 2001. Offering gifts or offering bribes? codes of ethics in South Korea. *Journal of Third World Studies* 18(1): 125–139.

Dal Bo, Ernesto, Pedro Dal Bo, and Rafael Di Tella. 2006. Plata o plomo? Bribe and punishment in a theory of political influence. *The American Political Science Review* 100(1): 41–53.

DiMaggio, Paul J. and Walter W. Powell. 1991. The iron cage revisited: institutional isomorphism and collective rationality in organizational fields. In *The New Institutionalism in Organizational Analysis*, ed. W.W. Powers and Paul J. DiMaggio, 63–82. Chicago: The University of Chicaco Press.

Eliade, Mircea. 1963. *Aspects du mythe*. Paris: Gallimard.

Glaeser, Edward L., and Claudia Goldin. 2008. *Corruption and reform: lessons from america's economic history*. Chicago: The University of Chicago Press.

Gopinath, C. 2008. Recognizing and justifying private corruption. *Journal of Business Ethics* 82: 747–754.

Gordon, Kathryn, and Maiko Miyake. 2001. Business approaches to combating bribery: A study of codes of conduct. *Journal of Business Ethics* 34(3–4): 161–173.

Heidegger, Martin. 1976. *What is called thinking?*. New York: Harper Perennial.

Heidegger, Martin. 1998. *Parmenides*. Bloomington: Indiana University Press.

Hooker, John. 2009. Corruption from a cross-cultural perspective. *Cross Cultural Management* 16(3): 251–267.

Hume, David. 1961. *Treatise on human nature*. London: Dent.

Jung, Carl-Gustav. 1974. *Un mythe moderne*. Paris: Gallimard.

Kant, Immanuel. 1959. *Foundations of the Metaphysics of Morals*. Indianapolis: Bobbs-Merrill.

Kant, Immanuel. 1971. *Critique de la raison pratique*. Paris: PUF.

Kerényi, Charles. 1980. De l'origine et du fondement de la mythologie. In *L'essence de la mythologie*, ed. Carl-Gustav Jung, and Charles Kerényi, 11–41. Paris: Petite bibliothèque Payot.

Khalil, Fahad, Jacques Lawarrée, and Sungho Yun. 2010. Bribery versus extortion: Allowing the lesser of two evils. *The Rand Journal of Economics* 41(1): 179–198.

Kreikebaum, Hartmut. 2008. Corruption as a moral issue. *Social Responsibility Journal* 4(1–2): 82–88.

Kühn, Thomas S. 1970. *The structure of scientific revolutions*. Chicago: The University of Chicago Press.

Li, Shaomin, and Ming Ouyang. 2007. A dynamic model to explain the bribery behavior of firms. *International Journal of Management* 24(3): 605–620.

McCormick, John T., and Nancy Paterson. 2006. The threat posed by transnational political corruption to global commercial and development banking. *Journal of Financial Crime* 13(2): 183–194.

Montagu, Ashley. 1997. *Man's most dangerous myth: The fallacy of race*. Walnut Creek: AltaMira Press.

Nietzsche, Friedrich. 1967. *La généalogie de la morale*. Paris: Gallimard.

Nietzsche, Friedrich. 1978. *L'antéchrist*. Paris: Gallimard.

Okogbule, Nlerum S. 2006. An appraisal of the legal and institutional framework for combating corruption in Nigeria. *Journal of Financial Crime* 13(1): 92–106.

Sanyal, Rajib, and Turgut Aguvenli. 2009. The propensity to bribe in international business: The relevance of cultural variables. *Cross Cultural Management* 16(3): 287–300.

Sartre, Jean-Paul. 1943. *L'Être et le néant*. Essai d'ontologie phénoménologique. Paris: Gallimard.

Sartre, Jean-Paul. 1970. *L'existentialisme est un humanisme*. Paris: Nagel.

Shehu, Abdullahi Y. 2004. Combating corruption in Nigeria—Bliss or bluster? *Journal of Financial Crime* 12(1): 69–87.

Steidlmeier, P. 1999. Gift giving, bribery and corruption: Ethical management of business relationships in China. *Journal of Business Ethics* 20(2): 121–132.

Tian, Qing. 2008. Perception of business bribery in China: The impact of moral philosophy. *Journal of Business Ethics* 80: 437–445.

Velasquez, Manuel. 1988. *Business ethics*. Concepts and Cases. Englewood Cliffs: Prentice Hall.

Weil, Simone. 1990. *L'enracinement*. Prélude à une déclaration des devoirs envers l'être humain. Paris: Gallimard.

Werner, Cynthia. 2000. Gifts, bribes, and development in post-soviet Kazakstan. *Human Organization* 59(1): 11–22.

Wu, Xun. 2009. Determinants of bribery in Asian firms: Evidence from the World Business Environment Survey. *Journal of Business Ethics* 87: 75–88.

Zekos, Georgios I. 2004. Ethics versus corruption in globalization. *Journal of Management Development* 23(7): 631–647.

Part IV
Tax Evasion, Money Laundering and Technological Aspect of Financial Crime

Chapter 13
Applying Evidence-Based Profiling to Disaggregated Fraud Offenders

Andreas Kapardis and Maria Krambia-Kapardis

Abstract In recent years, profiling has moved to a more evidence-based approach, and into mainstream forensic psychology as the new discipline of Behavioural Investigative Advice. Furthermore, profiling in the United Kingdom has become a recognised profession. The chapter first considers white-collar offenders, including fraud offenders, and individual differences as well as some myths about white-collar offenders before focusing on empirical (both exploratory and comparative) studies of such offenders' characteristics and their limitations. Attention then turns to the offender profiling concept as it has evolved over the years, outlining approaches to it (diagnostic evaluation, criminal investigative analysis, crime action profiling, investigative psychology and geographical profiling) before focusing on the feasibility of applying a recast notion of geographical profiling to internet fraudsters. The chapter concludes about the importance of a small number of characteristics of fraud offenders and how they could be utilized to reduce the risk of fraud but, also, makes suggestions for future research.

13.1 Introduction

Fraud is an example of *economic crime* which, in turn, is a category of white-collar crime. More specifically, the essential feature of fraud is that it entails deception. According to the Association of Certified Fraud Examiners, "fraud includes any intentional or deliberate act to deprive another of property or money by guile,

A. Kapardis (✉)
Department of Law, University of Cyprus, Nicosia, Cyprus
e-mail: Kapardis@ucy.ac.cy

M. Krambia-Kapardis
Cyprus University of Technology, Limassol, Cyprus
e-mail: Maria.kapardis@cut.ac.cy

© Springer International Publishing Switzerland 2016
M. Dion et al. (eds.), *Financial Crimes: Psychological, Technological, and Ethical Issues*, International Library of Ethics, Law, and the New Medicine 68, DOI 10.1007/978-3-319-32419-7_13

deception, or other unfair means".[1] An example would be occupational fraud whereby an accountant in collusion with a client steals money from the company employing him. 'Economic crime' refers "to illegal acts committed by an individual or a group of individuals to obtain a financial or professional advantage. In such crimes (e.g., abuse of foreign economic aid, internet fraud, tax evasion) the offender's principal motive is economic gain".[2] The term 'white-collar crime' was first defined by American sociologist-criminologist Edwin Sutherland in 1940 as "a crime committed by a person of respectability and high social status in the course of his occupation." The following are examples of white-collar crime: tax evasion, money laundering, fraud, embezzlement, insider trading, bribing, cybercrime, identity theft, Ponzi schemes, and copyright infringement, selling kangaroo meat for beef, running unsafe factories. It can be seen that the terms white-collar crime, economic crime and fraud overlap.

Fraud is but one example of white-collar crime. The cost of white-collar crime all over the world is multidimensional and substantial. In the U.S., alone, its annual financial cost has been estimated to be approximately $500 billion–$1 trillion (Friedrichs 2007). The 2014 PwC Global Economic Crime Survey that involved 5,128 respondents from organisations in 95 countries found that 65 % had experienced asset misappropriation, 29 % procurement fraud, 27 % bribery and corruption, 24 % cybercrime,[3] and 22 % accounting fraud (PwC 2014: 6). It was also found that 2 % of the respondents reported losses as a result of the fraud of more than US$ 100,000. Based on an analysis of 1,380 cases investigated worldwide, the ACFE (2012) *Report to the Nations on Occupational fraud and Abuse* found that the typical organization loses 5 % of its revenue to fraud each year, an estimated annual loss worldwide of $US 3.5 trillion (ACFE 2012: 4). Interestingly enough, nearly half of the victim organizations did not recover any losses caused by the fraud (ACFE 2012: 4). Across the Atlantic, according to the UK Office of Fair Trading (2009), 3.2 million adults in the country fall victim to mass marketed scams every year, their collective loss mounting to 3.5 billion pounds.

As the world is, at the time of writing, celebrating the 25th anniversary of the internet, there is no doubt that the internet makes electronic frauds one of the most threatening forms of economic crime. Needless to say, of course, that white-collar crime can result in both physical harm, including people getting injured at work, illnesses, and even death, as well as psychological harm such as victims being at risk of developing anxiety and depression (see Ganzini et al. 1990; Sharp et al. 2004). The 2014 PwC Global Economic Crime Survey (2014: 12) reported that for the respondents the collateral damage of fraud victimization included employee morale (28 %), reputation/brand (18 %), business relations (19 %) and share price (2 %). There were also cases of organizations completely disintegrating as a result

---

[1]Association of Certified Fraud Examiners. (2014). *What is Fraud?* http://www.acfe.com/fraud-101.aspx.

[2]http://definitions.uslegal.com/e/economic-crime/.

[3]Cyber fraud has been increasing internationally, according to Kroll's (2013/2014) *Global Fraud Report* (p. 9).

of a single incident of fraud (2014: 13). The same survey also found that almost half (48 %) of the CEOs were concerned about cyber threats and lack of data security (2014: 29).

Psychologically speaking, a number of factors facilitate fraud. Fraud at a distance perpetrated through media entails reduced social cues during interaction with the victim. Although few persons possess the degree of callousness to con a person face-to-face, a much greater number of persons are capable of the depersonalised social aggression required for indirect fraud. It has been suggested that the lack of social cues in communication such as email leads to a reduction in the influence of social norms and constraints on the average person's behaviour (Johnson 1998). Overall, these media serve to distance the fraudster from the prospective victim, making the predatory conduct less difficult for those offenders with some semblance of conscience. At the same time, fraud on the internet poses new challenges for criminologists.

An offender's motivation to commit fraud was emphasized by Cressey (1950) in his classic article on "the criminal violation of financial trust" in which discussed the concept of the 'non-shareable problem' (1950: 742–743), a factor that underpins the decision to resolve the problem (e.g., financial distress, loss of status) by stealing. Cressey's (1971) hypothesis became known as the 'fraud triangle' which subsequently was developed to comprise the components of 'pressure', 'opportunity' and 'rationalization' (i.e. self-generated reasons which justify the behaviour and ease any misgivings the offender may have-see below) to account for fraud (see Albrecht et al. 2012; Dorminey et al. 2012). The importance of rationalizations was documented in a study by Piquero and Simpson (2002) who surveyed corporate managers and managers-in-training. They found that white-collar offending is inhibited when a firm has a working compliance program, when managers do not perceive career benefits and, finally, when managers perceive the illegal act as highly immoral. As one would have predicted, white-collar offenders do not consider themselves criminals (Willott et al. 2001).

Although the fraud triangle has been adopted in auditing standards as a useful framework to analyse fraud risk and to prevent and detect fraud (see Ramamoorti 2008), it cannot be said to provide a profile per se of fraud offenders. A significant improvement on the fraud triangle was reported by Krambia-Kapardis (2001) who, for her doctoral work, examined closely fifty serious fraud cases in which the offender/s had been convicted in Melbourne, Australia. The frauds comprised mainly financial statement fraud, trust account fraud, and theft of assets. On the basis of her findings, she proposed the ROP fraud model which comprises three components: (1) **R**ationalizations, (2) **O**pportunity (in terms of situational factors and organizational characteristics), and (3) **P**erson (crime-prone and motivated to commit fraud), in addition to being under pressure and possessing rationalizations which can be considered part of a person's crime-proneness. The ROP model emphasizes the importance of a person having a crime-prone personality, a topic about which a great deal has been written by criminological psychologists (see Eysenck 1996; Jones 2006: 398–427). Thus, without ignoring the fact that sometimes it is a firm that perpetrates fraud (Hogan et al. 2008), the ROP model is more

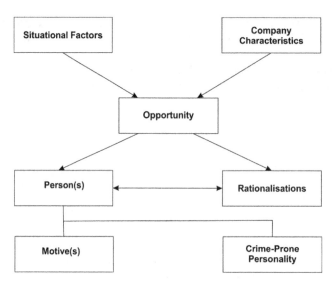

Fig. 13.1 ROP Model 1 (*Source* Krambia-Kapardis 2001: 84)

comprehensive than the fraud triangle as it integrates characteristics of the individual culprit in a separate but essential component- the person (see Fig. 13.1 from Krambia-Kapardis 2001: 82–83 for details) and also makes possible a very useful eclectic fraud detection model (see Krambia-Kapardis 2001: 84).

While a plethora of studies has been published on auditors and fraud detection and prevention (see, for example, Carpenter 2007; Dellaportas 2013; Krambia-Kapardis 2001), some researchers have focused on fraud victimization (Holtfreter et al. 2008, 2010c; Ross and Smith 2011). While others have examined whether imprisonment deters tax fraudsters (Bagaric et al. 2011), the fact is very few researchers have addressed the importance of individual differences between white-collar offenders in general and fraud offenders in particular. This neglect of a significant factor in the aetiology of fraud, namely the offender's personality, can be attributed to the impact of Edwin Sutherland's (1983) classical study *White Collar Crime*. Considering an economic crime offence as a collective act and not as an act which could be explained with reference to an individual's personality, Sutherland (1983) argued that personality has no relevance in the case of economic crime, "a crime committed by a person of respectability and high social status in the course of his occupation" (1983: 7). Not surprisingly, therefore, the organization approach to white-collar crime has been the main approach and a lot of attention has been paid to characteristics of corporations that place them at a risk of fraud victimization or as perpetrators (see, for example, Holtfreter 2005; Hogan et al. 2008) while others have emphasised the link between fraud-victimization and the American dream (Trahan et al. 2005). The present authors agree with Alalechto (2003: 336) that, by dismissing the important of personality characteristics when discussing the concept of white-collar crime, authors like Shapiro (1990) and Ruggeiro (2000) "throw the egg away with the shell…". As this paper shows below, there is no empirical justification for the view that economic offenders do not intend the crimes they perpetrate and/or that they do not act rationally. As will be shown below, available evidence documents a number of personality characteristics of economic criminals (see Bromberg 1965; Kellens 1977; Collins and Schmidt 1993; Terpstra et al. 1993; Kolz 1999; Spencer 1965). In fact, it has been known for some time now that knowing in advance how conscientious someone is on the basis of psychological tests helps to predict the likelihood of theft at work (Kolz 1999). Also, from a geographical profiling point of view (see below), according to a Dutch study by Montoya et al. (2013), 64 % of persons involved in digital fraud (i.e. online shopping, internet banking(skimming or hacking of banking systems) lived in the same geographical region as the victim compared to 27 % of traditional fraud offenders. The same study also found that: compared to digital threats, digital offenders were more likely to have a criminal record and to act alone; digital threats occur relatively more frequently between ex-partners and digital frauds occurred more often between business partners compared to traditional fraud.

When considering the literature on white-collar (mainly fraud) offenders' characteristics, it should be remembered that limited attention has been paid by fraud researchers to the very process by which a person who is motivated to commit fraud and has an opportunity to do so actually makes the decision to go ahead and do it (see Murphy and Dacin 2011). At this point it is appropriate to examine a number of popular misperceptions about white-collar offenders which have permeated the literature on white-collar offenders (Brody et al. 2012). As Perri (2011) rightly reminds us, such misperceptions have included the belief that the crimes of white-collar offenders are out of character, are isolated events (i.e. they do not reoffend), they do not really do serious harm as they are not violent, are a homogeneous populations of offenders and, finally, that their personalities are not characterised by psychopathy and/or narcissism-features of conventional street criminals. Such misperceptions have underpinned the portrayal by the media of WCCs, the limited attention paid until relatively recently to white-collar crime in general and fraud in particular by police services all over the world, and the lenient penal sanctions imposed by the courts when, on the odd occasion, someone is convicted of a white-collar crime. Furthermore, white-collar crime on the internet may be a small percentage of total crime but there is no doubt that the changes in technology that have occurred and continue to occur involving the use of information technology to perpetrate white-collar crime like fraud and identity theft have affected significantly offence, offender and victim characteristics. According to a study by the United Nations Office on Drugs and Crime (2013), cybercrime involving financial driven crime requires a high degree of organization and specialization characteristic and for this organized crime is heavily involved in such activities on the internet. Thus, the criminal activities may be traditional but the accomplices may be located in close geographical proximity, as found by the Montoya et al. (2013) study.

Of course, from the general public's point of view the risk of becoming a victim of crime is much higher as far as white-collar crime in general and fraud in particular is concerned rather than conventional street crime which is what the mass media and some well-known criminologists continuously focus on (see Wilson 2011). One need only consider the extent of financial and emotional devastation left behind by some well-known financial scandals such as Enron, WorldCom, and the case of Bernard Madoff (Ramamoorti 2008). Regarding the prevention of scams through emails, the 2009 report by the Office of Fair Trading recommends the use of filters for automatic elimination of suspect scams delivered via email since word-level text mining of scam communications can recognise accurately the content of scams in general and each particular type of scams (Office of Fair Trading 2009: 11). In this sense it is the text that is being 'profiled' and not the offender. In other words, in the same sense as the behaviour of a conventional violent offender evident in the crime (e.g. rape, armed robbery, serial homicide etc.) may well provide clues about their psychological characteristics, in the same way the behaviour of a fraudster in perpetrating his/her crime can provide us with cues about their psychological characteristics. To take an unusual example, in the case of a telemarketing fraud, the only 'crime scene' and behaviour specimen available is the text of the message sent over the internet by a scammer.

Contrary to popular belief that white-collar crime does not cause any 'real' harm like conventional crime, in fact, it is now well-established, for example, that certain fraud offenders not only resort to violence but also commit homicide to prevent their crimes from being discovered and have been termed "red-collar criminals" (Perri 2011; Perri and Lichtenwald 2007; Brody and Kiehl 2010). In more recent years, however, researchers have not only demolished the myths surrounding WCCs but some work has been done on profiling such offenders by identifying some of their distinguishing demographic and psychological characteristics (see below). Interestingly, one such characteristic, namely having a neurotic personality significantly predicts incarcerated white-collar offenders' (most had been convicted of fraud) probability of rearrest (Listwan et al. 2010), thus putting to rest one of the misperceptions about such offenders. The present authors emphasize that: (a) the concept of the 'profiler' has evolved in recent years to become the 'Behavioural Investigative Adviser' in the United Kingdom, a conceptual development which calls for a higher degree of sophistication in putting forward profiles of fraud offenders and, in order to rise to the occasion, (b) there is a need to disaggregate frauds and fraud offenders in order to construct specific offender profiles which are contextualized and, thus, of practical use. To illustrate, in a study of serious complex fraud cases against Australian Commonwealth agencies during 2000–2007 involving 852 cases and 521 suspects, Higginson (2012) used cluster analysis to identify such offenders' common characteristics. Improving our ability to predict, investigate and prevent fraud remains a major challenge because the empirical evidence is limited but any organisation that has finances runs a risk of experiencing fraud, whether from within or not.

Bearing in mind that, as Friedrichs (2007) reminds us, there exists in the literature on white-collar crime a fair number of terms being used such as white-collar crime, economic crime, corporate crime, and occupational crime, it comes as no surprise to find that definitions of fraud also vary. For Edwin Sutherland (1940: 9) white-collar crime represented "crime committed by a person respectability and high social status in the course of his occupation". Sutherland's definition is vague and it leaves out fraud committed by offenders of low socio-economic status. However, his definition must be seen in relation to his differential association theory according to which criminal behaviour is learned. Doing away with the element of status in the definition, Clinard and Quinney (1973) argued that 'white-collar crime' should be replaced by the terms corporate crime (i.e. "offenses committed by corporate officials for their corporation and the offences of the corporation itself" (p. 188) and occupational crime [i.e. "offences committed by individuals for themselves in the course of their occupations and the offenses of employees against their employers" (p. 188)].

Defining 'fraud' to mean "obtaining something of value or avoiding an obligation by means of deception", Duffield and Grabosky (2001: 1) distinguished four broad categories of fraud and give the following examples of each:

(a) Fraud committed against an organisation by a principal or senior official of that organisation (e.g., offences against shareholders, or creditors by "high flying entrepreneurs" or corrupt practices by senior officials);

(b) Fraud committed against an organisation by an "insider" or a "outsider" such as a client (e.g., embezzlement, insurance fraud, tax evasion or other types of fraud against government);

(c) Fraud committed against one individual against another in the context of face-to-face interaction (e.g., fraud by sales staff, unethical investment advisers who prey on clients and/or customers, dubious plumbers and so forth who prey on consumers); and, finally,

(d) Fraud committed against a number of individuals through print or electronic media or by other indirect means (e.g., Nigerian advance fee frauds, share market manipulation, deceptive advertising, and soliciting investments by contacting very large numbers of prospective victims).

As Duffield and Grabosky (2001) reminded their readers, the four fraud categories are neither definitive nor mutually exclusive but "provide a useful point for explanation". Regarding the (a) category of fraudster, the work of Simon (1999) is pertinent as it describes the modern business executive as a boyish egocentric individual with a reduced-capacity for empathy, bent on confirming his superiority, thus trying to reduce his strongly felt inferiority. This corresponds with Alalehto's (2003) finding that economic criminals are likely to be neurotic extroverts. Before taking a close look at the literature on characteristics of WCCs, let us next consider the well-known methods for profiling offenders (see Kapardis 2014, for detailed discussion) and the question whether contemporary notions of evidence-based offender profiling could be applied to detect and/or prevent fraud. In so doing, the question of whether claims made have been excessive and unjustified will also be addressed. It will be argued that, in the light of the assessment of the available empirical evidence, one needs to contextualize fraud-offender profiling by differentiating types of fraud, type of fraudster, the particular industry and type of organisation involved. In other words, the profile concerned needs to be tailor-made to the particular context and the aim for which it is being used. However, in the absence of evidence-based fraud profiling, a great deal of research is required before achieving reasonable fraud offender profile utility.

13.2 Offender Profiling Methods: A Case of Excessive Claims?

A number of films, CSI-type series on television and a few books by real-life profilers[4] have popularised criminal profiling (see Kapardis 2014: 364–372, for details).The notion of offender profiling refers to the use of behavioural data evident in a crime to assist a police investigation by seeking to infer attributes of probable offenders, thus narrowing the police search of suspects (Kocsis 2006; Crighton 2010). Of course, offender profiling is not new (see Kapardis 2014, for details). Let us next consider four approaches to profiling offenders and one approach to profiling places (geographical profiling).

Diagnostic evaluation: This is a clinical perspective on profiling offenders whereby a psychiatrist or clinical psychologist, for example, 'relate or diagnose possible psychopathologies indicative of the behaviours evident in a crime and from this [to] extrapolate some understanding of the probable offender'[5] (Kocsis 2009: 216). Impressive examples such as Brussel's (1968) list of characteristics of the person likely to be the 'mad bomber' George Metsky back in New York in 1956, however, should not make the reader overlook the fact that profiling offenders using the diagnostic evaluation method is largely subjective and falls short of the professionalism required in the critical environment of a major crime investigation (Rainbow 2011: 1).

Criminal investigation analysis (CIA) has also been known as 'psychological profiling' and as 'crime scene analysis' and has been the result of research into serial killers and other serious violent and sexual offenders since the 1970s by members of the Behavioral Sciences Unit at the FBI Academy in Quantico, Virginia. Drawing on a detailed examination of the crime scene and all the information available about the victim, the crime/s, the forensic evidence and autopsy reports, the aim with this method is to provide the investigators with a description of some important demographic characteristics, including lifestyle, the type of personality of the likely culprit and whether the crime was one of a series of crimes by the same offender, thus assisting in the apprehension and questioning of the

---

[4]Films such as *Silence of the Lambs*, television series like *Cracker* in the UK, *CSI: Crime Scene Investigation*, *CSI: Miami* or *Profiler*, and popular books like *The Real Cracker* by Cook (2001), *The Jigsaw Man* (Britton 1998) and *Picking Up the Pieces* (Britton 2001).

[5]See, for example, Badcock (1997), Boon (1997), Girod (2004), Palermo (2004), Proulx et al. (2007).

offender (Douglas et al. 1986). The methodology used combined low-level quantitative analysis and utilised the Unit's own collective experience over the years with constructing offender profiling. The FBI's Criminal Investigative Analysis, has been criticised for: being based on weak social science methodology (Howitt 2002: 199); relying largely on the individual profiler's intuition and, consequently, not being objective, let alone 'scientific' (Ainsworth 2001: 102); and, finally, that two profilers using the same crime scene analysis data will often produce different profiles. The criticisms levelled against the CIA method must be weighed against its contribution sometimes in bringing to justice serious criminals who terrorise whole communities. Also, we should not forget that profiling is but one tool available to police investigators. The risk of a misleading psychological profile is reduced if the expert concerned is well-versed in personality theories which alone cannot produce psychological profiles but can facilitate the profile production process (Boon 1997: 59). The usefulness of the CIA method in profiling WCCs is very doubtful indeed for reasons explained below. The next method would seem to have greater potential.

Crime action profiling[6] (CAP) is very similar to the CIA approach but uses such statistical techniques as multidimensional scaling (MDS) to develop models 'in which crime behaviours are correlated with various offender characteristics and thus operate as mechanisms by which the perpetrators of future crimes may be profiled' (Kocsis 2009: 220).

Investigative psychology (IP): Like CAP, IP is a research-based approach to profiling offenders which has, largely under the aegis of David Canter, evolved[7] in the United Kingdom to a specialised discipline (Canter 2004). IP researchers are interested in patterns in a broad range of criminal behaviour that can aid criminal investigators and not in inferring offender motivations (for an example see Santilla et al. 2008). Statistical profiling has been applied to a broader range of offences than psychological profiling. Canter and Alison (2000: 7) have argued that such statistical offender profiling can be seen as a natural part of 'investigative psychology'.

Geographic profiling: Geographic profilers, whether drawing on geography or environmental psychology, analyse related crime locations in order to identify a specific area that may be linked to the perpetrator/s of the offences (Rossmo 2000). This approach to profiling has been greatly assisted by the availability of such computer programmes as Geographical Information Systems (GIS) that generate geographic profiles. The reader should note in this context that there is *geographical profiling* (that is, spatial movement analysis of a single serial offender) and *geographical mapping* (that is, special patterns analysis pertaining to a number of offenders over a period of time).[8] The main idea behind geographical profiling is

---

[6]See Kocsis (2006) for an account of the principles and procedures inherent in the Crime Action Profiling approach to profiling crimes.

[7]Whether justifiably is debatable because of the overlap with such pre-existing specialisations as police, forensic and criminal psychology (Kocsis 2009: 219).

[8]See Ratcliff (2004).

to offer investigators probability estimates where a suspect's residence or base for offending might be. A geographic profile can be used in combination with a psychological profile to help investigators have a fairly good idea who they should be looking for. Of course, not all types of offenders or offence types can be geographically profiled. The meaning of terms like 'space', 'residence' and 'crime scene' becomes rather problematic when applied to WCCs on the internet. The 'weapon' and the 'crime scene' of a telemarketing fraudster is the computer he/she is using to access potential victims. Also, such an offender may be located in a different country from that of the victim. Consequently, when his/her location is identified, there is a need to seek the co-operation and assistance of the relevant authorities in the country concerned for any legally-sanctioned action to be taken. But how good is the validity and utility of different approaches to profiling?

Developments in offender profiling: Today, profiling has moved from the early criminal investigative analysis to a more evidence-based approach and into mainstream forensic psychology. Furthermore, profiling in the United Kingdom has become a recognised profession, namely *Behavioural Investigative Adviser* (BIA) (Rainbow 2011: 1) and the discipline that has emerged is termed *Behavioural Investigative Advice*. The term BIA has replaced 'offender profiler' and the working conditions, professional and ethical standards of BIAs are regulated at a national level by the Association of Chief Police Officers (ACPO). Regarding what a BIA actually does,[9] his/her role is "'to provide the investigating officer with an additional perspective and decision support through a serious crime investigation; an additional 'tool in the box'" rather than any magical panacea" (Rainbow and Gregory 2011: 20). The work of BIAs is greatly assisted by the existence of systematic structured electronic databases pertaining to offender characteristics such as CASMIRC[10] and VICAP[11] in the U.S and VISOR[12] in the U.K.

Utility of criminal profiling: due to the paucity of scientifically grounded research evidence concerning the utility of different offender profiling approaches, the evidence base for profiling conventional offenders[13] is 'remarkably limited' (Crighton 2010: 152) and 'Efforts to look at the accuracy of profilers empirically has yielded mixed results' (p. 153). Also, as far as it has been possible to ascertain, there has been no study comparing the predictive ability of different approaches to profiling white-collar/fraud offenders.[14] According to Kocsis (2009: 226), the evidence addressing the utility of criminal profiling in assisting with crime detection is, not surprisingly perhaps, as scant as the evidence for the accuracy of profiles. Also, while research evidence has been reported supporting the notion of

---

[9]See Rainbow and Gregory (2011), for details.

[10]Child Abduction and Serial Murder Investigative Resource Center.

[11]Violent Criminal Apprehension programme.

[12]Violent and Sexual Offender Register.

[13]See Almond et al. (2011), Crighton (2010), and Kocsis (2009), for detailed discussion of studies.

[14]See Goodwill et al. (2009), for a comparison of typological, thematic and multivariate models of rape.

behavioural consistency that is fundamental to profiling (e.g., Farrington et al. 2006; Grubin et al. 2001), the same cannot, unfortunately, be said for notions of homology (see House 1997; Mokros and Alison 2002). Nevertheless, the professionalization of profiling has no doubt added to the contribution such specialists can make to police investigations of crime (Almond et al. 2011: 262).[15] As will be shown below, the noticeable lack of adequate research into characteristics of WCCs in general and fraud offenders in particular means that the state of knowledge does not allow us to talk about reliable profiles of different types of offenders. Rather, such empirical knowledge as there is, would be better used to reduce the risk of fraud occurring (i.e. fraud prevention) rather than to identify the culprit among a number of potential suspects.

13.3 Characteristics of White-Collar Criminals, Including Fraud Offenders: General Comments

In considering characteristics of fraud offenders, it should be remembered that, contrary to what the popular media report, there is no such thing as a "typical fraud offender" or a "typical fraud offence" and, also, that many authors talk about 'white collar criminals' while others have examined a range of frauds and the perpetrators. As far as the characteristics themselves are concerned, as will be seen below, they can be grouped under different categories, including demographic and psychological. Furthermore, as Duffield and Grabosky (2001) pointed out, (a) certain psychological factors are common to different frauds while others are unique to specific types of fraud (2001: 3) and (b) the psychological factors that differentiate one type of fraud offence from another may also distinguish one type of fraud offender from another. To illustrate, a high-flying entrepreneurial CEO of a corporation who commits fraud against investors is likely to have different psychological characteristics from a compulsive gambler who defrauds his employer.

As already mentioned above, the literature on characteristics of white-collar offenders, including fraud offenders, is limited in terms of the number of relevant studies but, also, as we shall see next, the quality of such studies' methodology. Admittedly: research into such offenders is a relatively recent development; most perpetrators remain unknown or unreported; it is not easy to get access to the few that get convicted; archival data on offenders kept by police; courts, prisons and agencies responsible for the administration of non-custodial sanctions on offenders have their limitations; officially processed offenders are not representative of the general offender population; few researchers use control groups; and, finally, some researchers have utilized data collected by other researchers in earlier times. It should also be noted in this context that the demographic characteristics found by a study of fraud offenders may well reflect the particular sample of offenders used.

---

[15]See 2003b, 2004, regarding the qualities of successful profilers.

For example, if a study focuses on financial misstatement culprits, then it is likely to find a higher level of education because, generally speaking, one does not become an accountant or lawyer or doctor without tertiary qualifications. Along the same vein, if a researcher focuses on serious fraud offenders serving a term of imprisonment, then one would expect a higher representation of people over the age of 40 years, without a criminal record and with tertiary qualifications by virtue of the fact that these are credentials required for certain positions in a company. Also, since women are still not being treated as equal in society, it comes as no surprise to find that men are over-represented in some types of fraud because certain occupations remain male-dominated. The reader should note, however, that even though many studies of white-collar crime have not considered gender differences, the gender gap for some frauds has narrowed in recent decades and, contrary to previous welfarist and needs-focused explanations of fraud, women are also involved in more sophisticated and planned cases of fraud (see Goldstraw et al. 2005, for a study).[16] Furthermore, the internet offers aspiring fraudsters ample importunity to narrow any remaining gender gap in criminal offending.

Ragatz and Fremouw (2010) reported a much-needed and thorough critique of the literature on psychological profiles of white-collar offenders (see Table 13.1). Their review comprised a total of ten studies of demographic attributes of white-collar offenders (six exploratory Pogrebin et al. 1986; Daly 1989; Langton and Piguero 2007; Weisburd et al. 1990; Dodd 2004; Holtfreter 2005) and four comparative ones (Wheeler et al. 1988; Benson and Moore 1992; Mustaine and Tewksbury 2002; Poortinga et al. 2006—see Table 1, in Ragatz and Fremouw 2010: 377–378). The exploratory ones were least rigorous provided descriptive statistics and the comparative ones compared white-collar offenders to other offender types or non-offenders. Ragatz and Fremouw also evaluated six studies of personality attributes of white-collar offenders [one exploratory (Dhami 2007) and five comparative ones (Collins and Schmidt 1993; Kolz 1999; Alalehto 2003; Walters and Geyer 2004; Blickleetal. 2006—see Table 2, p. 380 in Ragatz and Fremouw 2010, for details]. The evaluation of the literature on profiles of white-collar offenders draws firstly on the detailed review by Ragatz and Fremouw (2010) before also taking a close and critical look at ten additional such studies.

Considering separately explorative and comparative studies of (a) demographic and (b) psychological characteristics of white-collar offenders,[17] Ragatz and Fremouw (2010) draw attention to a number of serious methodological weaknesses identified, including:

---

[16]For a listing of a large number of studies of fraud by four categories of fraud, see Appendix 1.1 in Hays and Prenzler (2003: 29–30).

[17]The term 'white-collar offenders' is used instead of 'white-collar criminals' because in some studies researchers have used data on suspects arrested. It is argued this term is more appropriate from a criminological point of view as many people arrested are not prosecuted and cannot justifiably be considered as confirmed offenders.

Table 13.1 Characteristics of white-collar criminals, including fraud offenders

Authors	Method and sample	Findings
Alalehto (2003) (Comparative)	Interviews of 128 businessmen as informants concerning some close friend or colleague who committed a criminal act (including tax evasion) and compared with friend or colleague who did not commit a criminal act (Sweden)	Conceited, neurotic, extrovert
Australian Institute of Criminology and PricewaterhouseCoopers (2003) (Exploratory)	183 convicted serious fraud offenders	More likely in their 40's, completed secondary education or had professional qualifications, stable employment, were directors of company or in accounting duties in organization, have no criminal record, acted alone, motivated by greed or gambling
Blickle et al. (2006)* (Comparative)	Gave personality tests to 150 active managers in German companies and 76 white-collar prison inmates in Germany who formerly held such positions	Controlling for social desirability, business white-collar crime predicted by gender (males more likely), low behavioural self-control, high hedonism, high narcissism, high conscientiousness, low integrity
Busy et al. (2008) (Exploratory)	Survey of 45 nationally-recognised experts on white-collar criminals (U.S.)	Leaders versus followers, need for control, fear of falling, narcissism, lack of social conscience
Dellaportas (2013) (Exploratory)	Unstructured group discussions with inmate accountants convicted of fraud-related offences-three panels, totalling 13 inmates	Support for the importance of fraud triangle (motivation, opportunity, rationalisations), especially opportunity
Dodd (2004)* (Exploratory)	Employee records of 103 white-collar offences kept by a United Kingdom shipment business	Differentiated a 'nothing-to-lose' offender subtype and a 'troublemaker' offender subtype, both equally likely to not to have children, be aged less than 28 years, and to be in the company's employment for less than 3.5 years
Hays and Prenzler (2003) (Exploratory)	Focus groups with four agencies: Australian Securities and Investments Commission, Australian Competition and Consumer Commission, Office of Fair Trading, Major Fraud, Queensland Police	Identified 4 categories of fraudsters (natural, accomplices, evolved and opportunistic) and 20 types of fraud

(continued)

Table 13.1 (continued)

Authors	Method and sample	Findings
Holtfreter (2005)* (Exploratory)	Surveyed 1,142 Certified Fraud Examiners focusing on occupational fraud	Age, education and gender of culprits differed depending on the type of fraud: asset misappropriation and corruption (likely to be younger, equally likely to be male or female and not to differ from each other in terms of their level of education), fraudulent financial statement (more likely to be older, educated males in managerial or executive positions)
Holtfreter et al. (2010a) (Exploratory)	10,598 young adults surveyed	Low self-control correlates with credit card and check fraud
Holtfreter et al. (2010b) (Exploratory)	Paper-and-pencil survey of 305 undergraduates about fraud offending and victimization	Fraud-offending and victimization is correlated with low self-control
Langton and Piquero (2007)* (Exploratory)	Data from pre-sentence reports on 1910 convicted white-collar offenders-originally gathered between 1976 and 1978 in Wheeler et al. (2000)	Strain (personal negative emotions associated with tax fraud, business motives associated with anti-trust and securities offences) a weak predictor of embezzlement
Marks (2012) (Exploratory)	Some executives who perpetrated massive frauds	Lack of moral compass, troubling friends, family and relationships, deception, arrogance, cleverness and creativity
Piquero et al. (2010) (Exploratory)	Vignette survey of 87 adults returning to higher education	Desire for control predicts corporate offending, controlling for degree of self-control
Poortinga et al. (2006)* (Comparative)	73 embezzlers (WCCs) compared to 73 retail fraud, larceny from a building, unarmed bank robbery and car theft	WCCs more likely to be white, more educated and less likely substance abuse
Ragatz et al. (2012). (Comparative)	Tested characteristics of inmates: 39 white-collar only, 88 white-collar versatile offenders and 86 non-white-collar inmates	White-collar offenders scored higher on psychopathology and psychopathic traits but lower on lifestyle criminality than non-white-collar offenders, white-collar versatile were the highest in criminal thinking, and substance abuse distinguished non-white-collar from white-collar offenders

(continued)

Table 13.1 (continued)

Authors	Method and sample	Findings
Shover et al. (2004)* (Exploratory)	Qualitative interviews of 47 fraudulent telemarketers	Middle-class family backgrounds, disproportionately managerial and entrepreneurial families, predisposed to economic activities requiring few credentials and providing a high income but experiencing strain when their high expectations of material success were not fulfilled legitimately
Walters and Geyer (2004)* (Comparative)	Surveyed 97 male prison inmates serving time for white-collar offences	White-collar offenders with no prior history of non-white-collar crimes registered lower levels of criminal thinking, criminal identification, and deviance than white-collar offenders previously arrested for non-white-collar crimes

(A) Studies of demographic characteristics
(A1) Exploratory studies

- All six studies failed to use a comparison group and, consequently, it is impossible to know if the characteristics reported do not also apply to other offenders or non-offenders (Ragatz and Fremouw 2010: 383).
- Three exploratory studies (Daly 1989; Langton and Piquero 2007; Weisburd et al. 1990) re-analysed archival data from the same previous studies (Weisburd et al. 1991; Wheeler et al. 1982, 1988, 2000) which had been collected in the late 1970s and, thus, may well not apply to white-collar offenders today (Ragatz and Fremouw 2010: 383–384). Furthermore, use of archival data coded by others is considered problematic because those who coded the data originally may have had their on biases (2010: 384).
- In some exploratory studies (e.g., Holtfreter 2005; Langton and Piquero 2007) only arithmetic means of the demographic characteristics concerned were provided, while in others (Daly 1989; Weisburd et al. 1990) only a percentage value was provided, measures that are not sufficiently informative (Ragatz and Fremouw 2010: 384).
- The evidence from exploratory studies does not show "whether white-collar crime should be considered a dimensional or a categorical structure", something which taxonometrics analysis could do (Ragatz and Fremouw 2010: 385).

(A2) Comparative studies

- The external validity of two (Benson and Moore 1992; Wheeler et al. 1988) out of the three comparative studies is limited because they used the same sample (convicted federal white-collar offenders on whom data had been collected in the late 1970s).

- All comparative studies failed to take offender gender into account (2010: 388), thus confounding the results.

(B) Studies of psychological characteristics of white-collar offenders [one exploratory (Dhami 2007)] and five comparative

- All studies (N = 6) used different definitions of white-collar crime, limiting the generalizability of the results obtained (Ragatz and Fremouw 2010: 392).
- Several studies provide insufficient data to enable conclusions to be drawn about the reliability of the data used (2010: 392).
- All three studies (Alalehto 2003; Dhami 2007; Kolz 1999) that used interviews to collect data do not provide pertinent information about the interviewers (Ragatz and Fremouw 2010: 393).
- While in the one exploratory study (Dhami 2007) no comparison group was used, Collins and Schmidt (1993) matched their offender and professional groups on age and ethnicity but not on gender and job position (Ragatz and Fremouw 2010: 394).
- Blickle et al. (2006) used self-report data only and, while they measured social desirability, they failed to check that self-reported offending matched the information in the offenders' court files (Ragatz and Fremouw 2010: 393).
- All three studies that claimed to have measured the five-factor model of personality (Blickle et al. 2006; Kolz 1999) in fact did not consider all five factors Ragatz and Fremouw 2010: 394–395).

On the basis of their literature review, Ragatz and Fremouw (2010) concluded that "few conclusions can be drawn from the white-collar literature as it currently stands" (2010: 396). Also, that, compared to non-white-collar offenders, white-collar offenders are older, white, employed, have a high-school diploma or equivalent, and are less likely to have a substance abuse problem or a criminal record (Ragatz and Fremouw 2010: 396). Compared to white-collar professionals, white-collar offenders score less on conscientiousness, agreeableness and behavioral self-control but score higher on anxiety and extroversion (Ragatz and Fremouw 2010: 396). It should be noted in this context that most available studies have not considered the socio-economic status of white-collar offenders.

Ragatz and Fremouw (2010: 397–399) urge researchers to work on a generally-accepted definition of white-collar crime. They also suggest that future research should investigate: the socio-economic status of white-collar offenders who commit specific white-collar offences compared to non-white-collar offenders, taking into account gender. In addition, they consider it important that work be carried out on the demographic and psychological characteristics of officially-processed compared to unreported white-collar offenders, examine such psychological attributes as psychopathic traits in different categories of offenders and in non-offenders as well as their criminal attitudes, criminal thinking and motives

(Ragatz and Fremouw 2010: 397–399). Let us next consider the evidence for WCC's characteristics reported by the seventeen studies in Table 13.1.

Excluding the seven studies (marked with *) in Table 13.1 that were also included in the Ragatz and Fremouw (2010) literature review, it leaves ten of which nine are exploratory and only one (Ragatz et al. 2012) is comparative. As Ragatz and Fremouw (2010) remind us, exploratory studies cannot tell us whether the distribution of demographic and other characteristics found among white-collar offenders is different from other categories of offenders and/or the public at large. The findings reported by such studies, therefore, are limited in their usefulness as far as profiling white-collar offenders in general and fraud offenders in particular are concerned. This is especially so when we also note that, as shown in Table 13.1, the nine studies used different methodologies (e.g., paper-and-pencil questionnaire surveys, telephone survey, focus groups, unstructured group discussion, archival data, psychometric tests, records of a private company, face-to-face interviews with fraudsters), different samples of offenders or informants (e.g., undergraduates, business executives who had committed fraud, prison inmates, fraudulent tele-marketers, adult members of the public, government agency personnel) and focused on different demographic and/or psychological characteristics. Furthermore, four studies shown in Table 13.1 collected data on how experts on white-collar crime (Busy et al. 2008; Hays and Prenzler 2003) and certified fraud examiners (Holtfreter 2005) or businessmen (Alalechto 2003) perceived white-collar offenders instead of the researchers themselves accessing such offenders.

Examination of the nine exploratory studies shows that low *self-control* has been found by Blickle et al. (2006), Holtfreter et al. (2010a, b). Interestingly, in support of Busy et al. (2008), Piquero et al. (2010) found in their vignette survey of eighty-seven adults returning to higher education that, controlling for degree of self-control, a *desire for control* predicts corporate offending. *Need for control* was also considered a characteristic of white-collar criminals by the majority of the 45 nationally-recognised experts in the Busy et al. (2008) survey. *Narcissism* is another characteristic of white-collar criminals reported by both Blickle et al. (2006) and Busy et al. (2008). The Swedish study by Alalehto (2003) reported that white-collar offenders were perceived as being conceited, neurotic and extravert.

Two well-controlled comparative studies tested prison inmates serving time for white-collar offences and compared them with active managers in German companies (Blickle et al. 2006) or with other inmates who were white-collar versatile or serving a sentence for non-white-collar offences (Ragatz et al. 2012) and reported interesting findings regarding psychological characteristics, including evidence for serious psychopathology. More specifically, focusing on prison inmates Ragatz, Fremouw and Baker found that, comparing white-collar only (WCO) to white-collar versatile offenders (WCV) and non-white collar (NWC) offenders, WCO:

- Were more socially outgoing than NWC offenders.
- Scored higher on Anxiety-Related disorders than NWC offenders.
- Reported significantly more problems with alcohol than NWC offenders.

- Had the lowest criminal thinking scores.
- Scored significantly lower on the 'Denial of Harm' factor.
- Scored lower than NWC on the 'Entitlement' factor.
- Exhibited fewer criminal attitudes (in support of Walters and Greyer 2004).
- Were less likely to adhere to a criminal lifestyle.

Regarding versatile white-collar offenders (i.e. also having convictions for non-white collar offences), they exhibited the most antisocial attitudes of all the inmates under comparison and, also, were significantly highest in Machiavellian Egocentricity when contrasted with NWC offenders.

The findings yielded by the Ragatz et al. (2012) study are very interesting but need to be replicated as all three groups comprised prisoners and especially as the NWC offender group consisted mostly of drug offenders.

According to Bucy et al. (2008), researchers have described eight personality characteristics "that fuel white collar criminal activity", namely: need for control (Simpson and Piquero 2002), bullying (Griffin 2005), charisma (DeCellers and Pfarrer 2004), "fear of falling" (Lerman 1999), company ambition/the need for corporate success (Garten 1987), narcissism (Litterick 2005), lack of integrity (Dittenhofer 1995) and lack of social conscience (Collins and Schmidt 1993). However, as Alalehto (2003) reminds us, "A personality trait is not enough on its own to trigger the commission of a crime, but it is one factor among others-environmental or situational- that may trigger criminal acting out" and, also, that it is has not been possible so far to show etiologically what effect personality has on a law-abiding person in comparison to an offender (p. 352).

Some researchers have investigated typologies of WCCs while others have looked for their personality characteristics. As far as typologies are concerned, in the U.S. Busy et al. (2008) reported the results of a survey of 47 national experts in the area of white-collar crime (experienced prosecutors and defence lawyers of at least 15 years of experience) regarding their the perceptions of white-collar offenders. The majority of the interviewees agreed that WCCs can be described as either "followers" or "leaders" and, also, that the former are "less confident, less aggressive, less ambitious, passive, subservient, dominated, gullible, prone to blindly follow others, and less likely to accept responsibility for their actions" (Bucy et al. 2008: 411). In Britain, Dodd (2004) differentiated white-collar offenders into 'nothing-to-lose' and 'troublemaker' and Hays and Prenzler (2003) in Australia identifies four categories of fraudsters: 'natural', 'accomplices', 'evolved', and 'opportunistic'. Finally, Shover et al. (2004) reported findings in support of 'strain theory' in criminology (see Agnew 2000; Broidy 2001). Their quality interviews of 47 fraudulent telemarketers who had middle-class family backgrounds (especially managerial and entrepreneurial families) experienced strain when their high expectations of material success and turned to telemarketing fraud, an easy source of high income. However, strain was a weak predictor of embezzlement in Piquero and Langton's (2007) study, a findings than needs to be treated with a great deal of caution because the data analysed had initially been obtained from pre-sentence reports on convicted white-collar offenders between

1976 and 1978 which means they are rather out of date in terms of people's material success expectations and the data itself is also limited by possible inbuilt bias of those who originally interviewed the offenders concerned in order to prepare pre-sentence reports.

13.4 Conclusion

The risk of fraud is a product of both personality and environmental or situational variables. This means individuals will vary in their propensity to commit fraud even when they are subject to similar pressures in their environment. It also means that situations will vary in their impact on individuals according to the inherent risk factors at any given time. Just as there are likely to be high-to-low-risk individuals, there are also likely to be high-to-low-risk situations. As individuals move from one environment (including the internet) to another, the probability of fraud behaviour also changes. There are likely to be situational conditions that would discourage all but the most incorrigible people from committing fraud. Conversely, there are situations that encourage fraud to the point that even the average person is at risk of engaging in it. As Marks (2012), emphasises, in addition to identifying individuals with a proclivity to commit fraud, it is vital to also identify the environment in which fraud is more likely to be committed. Such environment could promote fraud within the company by virtue of a passive weak tone at the top or because fraud committed remains hidden due to silence in the social environment concerned, as happened in the Madoff case in the United States (van de Bunt 2010).

The preceding discussion makes it clear that the fraud offenders who have constituted a significant proportion of the white-collar offenders examined by the studies in Table 13.1 is not a homogeneous population of offenders in terms of their offending as well as their demographic and psychological characteristics. Distilling the literature findings drawing on Ragatz and Fremouw's (2010) review and the additional seven studies critiqued above, it can be concluded that, the method-ological limitations of the great majority of the studies considered (which have almost all been carried out in the United States) notwithstanding, the following can be said of white-collar offenders: (a) it is disappointing that after approximately three decades of research, as Ragatz and Fremouw 2010) have concluded, "few conclusions can be drawn from the white-collar literature as it currently stands" and (b) a distinction needs to be mad between white-collar only and versatile white-collar offenders, with the latter being more likely to show serious psy-chopathology and both categories to being likely to possess a narcissistic person-ality. In view of the fact that the two adequately-controlled comparative studies involved prison inmates, the conclusions drawn about characteristics of white-collar offenders, including fraud offenders, need to be replicated by methodologically sound studies that will also include such offending on the internet.

The utility of the available profiles of white collar offenders, which in the main have focused on fraud offenders, is limited not only because of serious methodological limitations but, also, by the fact that research into such offenders has been only at one of three different levels of analysis, namely the *macro* (1) social structure theory and strain theory (e.g., Durkheim 1965; Merton 1968), (2) at the *meso* level in terms of differential association (Sutherland 1940; Clinard 1990) and (3) at the *micro* level (see Table 13.1). As no single study has considered fraudulent behavior at least at two of the levels mentioned, a profile of fraud offenders drawing on only one level of analysis is bound to be limited. Thus, it is necessary to supplement the existing literature in Table 13.1 with pertinent additional fraud-risk characteristics that form part of the ROP model of fraud aetiology proposed by Krambia-Kapardis (2001). Such fraud-risk factors at the individual micro level which pressurize, motivate someone to commit fraud because of what Cressey (1950, 1971) termed a 'non-shareable problem'. Such pressures that have been identified in the literature (see Albrecht et al. 2012; AIC & PWC 2003) are: financial pressures (e.g., to keep one's business afloat, disastrous investment), vices (e.g., drugs, compulsive gambling, alcohol, extra-marital affairs), work-related pressures (e.g., disgruntlement because one is not appreciated, desire for revenge on the company, fear of being dismissed from one's job), and additional pressures such as a strong desire, for example, for material possession beyond one's financial means in order to maintain a certain social status, or a very strong wish to have power and control over others. To the list of egocentric factors that motivate people to commit fraud, whether within or from outside a company, we should add greed and excessive ambition. Of course, as Cressey (1950, 1971) rightly argued, a fraudster needs to justify the fraud to him/herself, emphasizing the crucial importance of rationalizations which allow such white-collar offenders to perceive themselves as morally responsible individuals being forced to act unethically.

As already mentioned, the profile of white-collar offenders in general and fraud offenders in particular which is yielded by the studies examined in Table 13.1 is incomplete because it leaves out a crucial part, namely the perceived opportunity to commit the fraud and get away with it, most often also ignoring also the importance of a person's rationalizations. As stated at the outset, a great deal of fraud is nowadays committed on the internet by persons who are outsiders to companies and target large numbers of unknown (to the fraudster) potential victims. Thus, the studies reporting characteristics of convicted fraud offenders who victimized their own employer have reported interesting and useful findings for fraud forensic accountants and auditors interested in fraud prevention and detection but fall short as far as evidence-based offender profiling is concerned. It becomes clear that the key to understanding and eventually being able to largely control fraud is to consider both the individual and the environment in which they operate. Consequently, what is required is contextualized specific fraud offender profiling research that will investigate and synthesize both individual and organizational characteristics of fraud offenders within a company and by unknown outsiders who victimize government services, corporations and individuals. The fact of the matter is that the idea of generating one profile that would apply to all fraud offenders has been proven unrealistic and non-feasible in view of the heterogeneity of frauds and fraud offenders. A less ambitious but feasible undertaking would be to attempt to profile at different levels of analysis (e.g., individual and organizational) and specific types of fraud offenders perpetrating specific frauds. Also, future research should aim to obtain a more complex causal picture of what attributes separate fraud offenders from versatile fraud offenders and those committing common crime.

Identification of fraud risk is still in its infancy as far as individual perpetrators are concerned. Few categories of offences suffer from the same dearth of psychological profiles of offenders as fraud and white-collar crime in general. More research is required before conclusively defining which personality traits or disorders make up characteristic predispositions toward fraud. In the meantime, the best that can be done is to point to personality characteristics and motivating factors that may be associated with an increased risk of fraud. Unfortunately, these characteristics (e.g., narcissism) and motivations (e.g., a need to demonstrate superiority over others) also influence a great deal of legitimate, indeed desirable behaviour in professional and corporate settings. Consequently, they are not always amenable to policy intervention. Meanwhile, one policy opportunity that arises clearly from the above discussion is that of confronting techniques of neutralisation. To this end, the efforts of anti-corruption and integrity authorities and NGO's (e.g., Transparency International) in raising the standard and making it clear what constitutes unacceptable behaviour may in long run increase inhibitions against fraud. Ethics, however, will get us so far. There will always be a hard core of determined individuals who, knowing too well the difference between right and wrong, will choose the latter and commit fraud. Utilising the research findings about the importance of a few fraud offender characteristics, when selecting people for appointment or evaluating them or promotion especially to positions of financial trust, (a) psychological tests can be used to filter out persons with psychopathologies as far as self-control and such other personality characteristics as narcissistic personality and anti-social personality disorder is concerned, and (b) such persons can be interviewed to ascertain whether they have certain vices (e.g., gambling, drugs, etc.) that carry a risk of living beyond one's financial means. For their part, fraud researchers should focus on specific types of frauds in order to produce profiles with adequate predictive utility.

References

Agnew, R. 2000. Sources of criminality: Strain and subcultural theories. In *Criminology: A contemporary handbook*, ed. J.F. Shelley, 349–371. Belmont, CA: Wadsworth.

Ainsworth, P.B. 2001. *Offender profiling and crime analysis*. Cullompton: Willan.

Alalehto, T. 2003. Economic crime: Does personality matter? *International Journal of Offender Therapy and Comparative Criminology* 47(3): 335–355.

Albrecht, W.S., C.O. Albrecht, C.C. Albrecht, and M.F. Zimbelman. 2012. *Fraud examination*, 4th ed. OH, USA: South Western Cengage Learning.

Almond, L., L. Alison, and L. Porter. 2011. An evaluation and comparison of claims made in behavioural investigative advice reports compiled by the National Policing Improvement Agency in the United Kingdom. In *Professionalizing Offender profiling: Forensic and investigative psychology in practice*, ed. L. Alison, and L. Rainbow, 250–268. London: Routledge.

Association of Certified Fraud Examiners. 2012. Report to the Nations on Occupational Fraud and Abuse. 2012 global fraud study. http://www.acfe.com/uploadedFiles/ACFE_Website/Content/rttn/2012-report-to-nations.pdf. Accessed 15 Mar 2014.

Australian Institute of Criminology and PricewaterhouseCopers. 2003. Serious fraud in Australia and New Zealand, Research and Public Policy Series, no. 48, Australian Institute of Criminology. http://www.aic.gov.au/documents/3/5/F/%7B35F4BC09-08AC-46D5-AD96-C85D7DA923E7%7DRPP48.pdf. Accessed 3 Feb 2014.

Badcock, R. 1997. Developmental and clinical issues in relation to offending in the individual. In *Offender profiling: Theory, research and practice*, ed. J.L. Jackson, and D.A. Bekerian, 9–42. New York: Wiley.

Babaric, M., T. Alexander, and A. Rathinayake. 2011. The fallacy of general deterrence and the futility of imprisoning offenders for tax fraud. *Australian Tax Forum* 26(3): 511–540.

Benson, M.L., and E. Moore. 1992. Are white-collar and common offenders the same? An empirical examination and a theoretical critique of a recently proposed general theory of crime. *Journal of Research in Crime and Delinquency* 29: 251–272. doi:10.1177/0022427892029003001.

Boon, J.C.W. 1997. The contributions of personality theories to psychological profiling. In *Offender profiling: Theory, research and practice*, ed. J.L. Jackson, and D.A. Bekerian, 43–60. New York: Wiley.

Blickle, G., A. Schlegel, P. Fassbender, and U. Klein. 2006. Some personality correlates of business white-collar crime. *Applied Psychology: An International Review* 55(2): 220–233. doi:10.1111/j.1464-0597.2006.00226.x.

Britton, P. 1998. *The jigsaw man*. London: Corgi Books.

Britton, P. 2001. *Picking up the pieces*. London: Corgi Books.

Brody, R.G., and K.A. Kiehl. 2010. From white-collar crime to red-collar crime. *Journal of Financial Crime* 17(3): 351–364.

Brody, R.G., S.R. Melendy, and I. Perry. 2012. Commentary for the American accounting association's 2011 annual meeting panel on emerging issues in fraud research. *Accounting Horizons* 26(3): 513–531.

Broidy, L.M. 2001. A test of general strain theory. *Criminology* 39(1): 9–35.

Bromberg, W. 1965. Business crime and the business of crime. In *Crime and mind: A psychiatric analysis of crime and punishment*. New York: Macmillan.

Brussel, J.A. 1968. *Casebook of a crime psychiatrist*. New York: Simon and Schuster.

Bucy, P.H., E.P. Formby, M.S. Raspanti, and K.E. Rooney. 2008. Why do they do it? Motives, mores, and character of white collar criminals. *St John's Law Review* 82(2): 401–571.

Canter, D. 2004. Offender profiling and investigative psychology. *Journal of Investigative Psychology and Offender Profiling* 1: 1–15.

Canter, D.V., and L. Alison. 2000. Profiling property crimes. In *Profiling property crimes*, ed. D. Canter, and L. Alison, 1–30. Aldershot: Ashgate.

Carpenter, T.D. 2007. Audit team brainstorming: fraud risk identification, and fraud risk assessment: Implications of SAS No. 99. *The Accounting Review* 82(5): 1119–1140.

Clinard, M.B. 1990. *Corporate corruption: The abuse of power*. New York: Praeger.

Clinard, M.B., and R. Quinney. 1973. *Criminal behaviour systems: A typology*, 2nd edn. New York: Holt, Rinehart and Winston.

Collins, J.M., and F.L. Schmidt. 1993. Personality, integrity and white-collar crime—a construct validity study. *Personal Psychology* 46(2): 295–311.

Cook, S. 2001. *The real cracker: Investigating the criminal mind*. London: Channel 4 Books.

Cressey, D.R. 1950. The criminal violation of financial trust. *American Sociological Review* 15(6): 738–743.

Cressey, D.R. 1971. *Other people's money: A study in the social psychology of embezzlement.* Glencoe: Free Press.

Crighton, D.A. 2010. Offender profiling.In *Forensic psychology*, ed. G.J. Towl and D. Crighton, 148–159. Chichester, West Sussex: BPS Blackwell.

Daly, K. 1989. Gender and varieties of white-collar crime. *Criminology* 27(4): 769–794.

DeCellers, K.A., and M.D. Pfarrer. 2004. Heroes or villains? Corruption and the charismatic leader. *Journal of Leadership and Organizational Studies* 11(1): 67–77.

Dellaportas, S. 2013. Conversations with inmate accountants: Motivations, opportunity and the fraud triangle. *Accounting Forum* 37(1): 29–39.

Dhami, M.K. 2007. White-collar prisoners' perceptions of audience reaction. *Deviant Behaviour* 28(1): 57–77.

Dittenhofer, M.A. 1995. The behavioural aspects of fraud and embezzlement. *Public Money and Management* January–March 15(1): 9–14.

Dodd, N.J. 2004. 'Troublemaker' and 'nothing t loase' employee offenders identified from a corporate crime data sample. *Crime Prevention and Community Safety: An International Journal* 6(3): 23–32.

Dorminey, J., A.S. Fleming, M.J. Kranacher, and R.A. Riley. 2012. The evolution of fraud theory. *Issues in Accounting Education* 27(2): 555–579.

Douglas, J.E., R.K. Ressler, A.W. Burgess, and C.R. Hartman. 1986. Criminal profiling from crime scene analysis. *Behavioral Sciences and the Law* 4(4): 401–421.

Duffield, G., and P. Grabosky. 2001. The psychology of fraud. Canberra: Australian Institute of Criminology Trends and Issues in Crime and Criminal Justice, No. 199. http://www.anatomyfacts.com/Research/fraud.pdf. Accessed 13 Jan 2014.

Durkheim, E. 1965. *The division of labour in society. Trans. G. Simpson.* New York: Free Press.

Eysenck, H. 1996. Personality and crime: Where we stand. *Psychology, Crime and Law* 2(3): 143–152.

Farrington, D.P., J.W. Coid, L.M. Harnett, D. Jolliffe, N. Soteriou, R.E. Turner, and D.J. West. 2006. Criminal careers up to age 50 and life success up to age 48. New findings from the Cambridge Study of delinquent development. *Home Office Research Study 299*. London: Home Office Research, Development and Statistics.

Friedrichs, D.O. 2007. *Trusted criminals. White collar crime in contemporary society*, 3rd ed. Belmont, CA: Thomson Wadsworth.

Ganzini, L., B. McFarland, and J. Bloom. 1990. Victims of fraud; comparing victims of white collar and violent crime. *Bulletin of the American Academy of Psychiatry and the Law* 18(1): 55–62.

Garten, H.A. 1987. Insider trading in the corporate interest. *Wisconsin Law Review* 68(4): 573–640.

Girod, R. 2004. *Profiling the criminal mind: Behavioral investigative analysis.* New York: Universe Inc.

Goldstraw, J., R.G. Smith, and Y. Sakurai. 2005. Gender and serious fraud in Australia and New Zealand. Canberra: Australian Institute of Criminology Trends and Issues in Crime and Criminal Justice, N. 292. http://www.aic.gov.au/media_library/publications/tandi2/tandi292.pdf. Accessed 10 Jan 2014.

Goodwill, A.M., L.J. Alison, and A.R. Beech. 2009. What works in offender profiling? A comparison of typological, thematic, and multivariate models. *Behavioral Sciences and the Law* 27(4): 507–529.

Griffin, G. 2005. Criminal charges possible. *Denver Post*, March 16, at A01.

Grubin, D., P. Kelly, and C. Brunsdon. 2001. Linking serious assaults through behaviour. Home Office Research Study 215. London: Home Office Research, Development and Statistics.

Hays, H., and T. Prenzler. 2003. Profiling fraudsters: A Queensland case study in fraudster crime. Final Report to Crime Prevention Queensland. Brisbane, Australia: Griffiths University. http://www.aic.gov.au/media_library/aic/research/fraud/profilingfraudsters.pdf. Accessed 18 Jan 2014.

Higginson, A. 2012. Faces of fraud: An analysis of serious and complex fraud against Australian commonwealth agencies. Paper presented at the Australian Institute of Criminology, 3 October

2012. https://www.google.com.cy/?gws_rd=cr&ei=rfUuU-v3HoeStQa0goCoCQ#q=Higginson+
2012+Faces+of+fraud+an+analysis+of+serious+and+complex+fraud+against+Australian+
commonwealth+agencies. Accessed 15 Oct 2012.

Hogan, C.E., R. Zabihollah, R.A. Riley, and U.K. Velury. 2008. Financial statement fraud:
Insights from the academic literature. *Auditing: A Journal of Practice and Theory* 27(2):
231–252.

Holtfreter, K. 2005. Is occupational fraud "typical" white-collar crime? A comparison of
individual and organizational characteristics. *Journal of Criminal Justice* 33(4): 353–365.

Holtfreter, K., M.D. Reisig, and T.C. Pratt. 2008. Low self-control, routine activities, and fraud
victimization. *Criminology* 46(1): 189–220.

Holtfreter, K., K.M. Beaver, M.D. Reisig, and T.C. Pratt. 2010a. Low self-control and fraud
offending. *Journal of Financial Crime* 17(3): 295–307.

Holtfreter, K., M.D. Reisig, and N.L. Piquero. 2010b. Low self-control and fraud: Offending,
victimization, and their overlap. *Criminal Justice and Behavior* 37(2): 188–203.

Holtfreter, K., et al. 2010c. Low self-control and fraud: Offending, victimization, and their
overlap. *Criminal Justice and Behavior* 37: 188–203.

House, J.C. 1997. Towards a practical application of offender profiling: The RNC's criminal
suspect prioritization system. In *Offender Profiling: Theory, Research and Practice*, ed. J.L.
Jackson, and D.A. Bekerian, 177–190. New York: Wiley.

Howitt, D. 2002. *Forensic and criminal psychology*. Harlow: Pearson Education.

Johnson, A. 1998. Causes and implications of disinhibited behaviour on the internet. In
Psychology and the Internet: Intrapersonal, interpersonal and transpersonal implications, ed.
J. Grackenbach, 43–60. San Diego, California: Academic Press.

Jones, S. 2006. Criminology. Oxford University Press.

Kapardis, A. 2014. *Psychology and law: A critical introduction*, 4th ed. Melbourne, Australia:
Cambridge University Press.

Kellens, G. 1977. Sociological and psychological aspects. In *Criminological Aspects of Economic
Crime*, vol. 15. Strasbourg, Germany: European Committee on Crime Problems.

Krambia-Kapardis, M. 2001. Enhancing the auditor's fraud detection ability: An interdisciplinary
approach. Peter Lang.

Kocsis, R.N. 2006. *Criminal profiling: Principle and practice*. NJ, Tottowa: Human Press.

Kocsis, R.N. 2009. Criminal profiling. In *Applied criminal psychology: A guide to forensic
criminal sciences*, ed. R.N. Kocsis. Springfield, Il: Charles C. Thomas.

Kolz, A.R. 1999. Personality predictors off retail theft and counterproductive behaviour. *Journal of
Professional Services Marketing* 19(2): 107–114.

Kroll. 2013/2014. Global fraud report. Who's got something to hide? Searching for insider fraud.
https://www.google.com.cy/?gws_rd=cr&ei=jbAmU-SOKeaAywOCsoCABQ#q=Kroll
+2013%2F2014+Global+Fraud+Report.+Who%E2%80%99s+Got+Something+to+Hide%3F+
. Accessed 12 March 2014.

Langton, L., and N.L. Piquero. 2007. Can general strain theory explain white-collar crime? A
preliminary investigation of the relationship between strain and select white-collar offenders.
Journal of Criminal Justice 35(1): 1–15.

Lerman, L.G. 1999. Blue-chip billing: Regulation of billing and expense fraud by lawyers.
Georgetown Journal of Legal Ethics 12(2): 205–254.

Listwan, S.J., N.L. Piquero, and P. Van Voorhis. 2010. Recidivism among a white-collar sample:
Does personality matter? *Australian and New Zealand Journal of Criminology* 43(1): 156–174.

Litterick, D. 2005. Rich–but by no means beyond the dreams of avarice. Daily Telegraph
(London), November 19, at 33.

Marks, J.T. 2012. A matter of ethics: understanding the mind of a white-collar criminal. Financial
Executive, November, pp. 31–34. http://www.financialexecutives.org/KenticoCMS/Financial-
Executive-Magazine/2012_11/A-Matter-of-Ethics–Understanding-the-Mind-of-a-Wh.aspx.
Accessed 20 Feb 2013.

Merton, R.K. 1968. *Social theory and social structure*. New York: The Free Press.

Mokros, A., and L. Alison. 2002. Is profiling possible? Testing the predicted homology of crime scene actions and background characteristics in a sample of rapists. *Legal and Criminological Psychology* 7: 25–43.

Montoya Morales, A.L., M. Junger, P.H. Hartel. 2013. *How 'Digital' is Traditional Crime?* In: European Intelligence and Security Informatics Conference, EISIC 2013, 12–14 Aug 2013, Uppsala, Sweden, 31–37. IEEE Computer Society. ISBN 978-0-7695-5062-6.

Murphy, P.R., and M.T. Dacin. 2011. Psychological pathways to fraud: Understanding and preventing fraud in organizations. *Journal of Business Ethics* 101(4): 601–618.

Mustaine, E.E., and R. Tewksbury. 2002. Workplace theft: An analysis of student employee offenders and job attributes. *American Journal of Criminal Justice* 27(1): 111–127.

Office of Fair Trading. 2009. The psychology of scams: Provoking and committing errors of judgement. http://www.oft.gov.uk/shared_oft/reports/consumer_protection/oft1070.pdf. Accessed 19 Dec 2013.

Palermo, G.B. 2004. *The faces of violence*, 2nd edn. Springfield, IL: Charles C Thomas.

Perri, F.S. 2011. White-collar criminals: The 'kinder, gentler' offender? *Journal of Investigative Psychology and Offender Profiling* 8(3): 217–241.

Perri, F.S., and T.G. Lichtenwald. 2007. A proposed addition to the FBI criminal classification manual. *The Forensic Examiner* 16(4): 18–30.

Piquero, N.L., and S.S. Simpson. 2002. Low self-control, organizational theory, and corporate crime. *Law and Society review* 36(3): 509–547.

Piquero, N.L., A. Schoepfer, and L. Langton. 2010. Completely out of control or the desire to be in complete control? How does self-control and the desire for control relate to corporate offending? *Crime and Delinquency* 5(4): 627–647.

Pogrebin, M., E. Poole, and R. Regoli. 1986. Stealing money: An assessment of bank embezzlers. *Behavioral Sciences and the Law* 4(4): 481–490.

Poortinga, E., C. Lemmen, and M.D. Jibson. 2006. A case control study: White–collar defendants compared with defendants charged with other non-violent theft. *Journal of American Academy of Psychiatry and Law* 34(1): 82–89.

Proulx, J., E. Beauregard, M. Cusson, and A. Nicole. 2007. *Sexual murderers: A comparative analysis and new perspectives*. New York: Wiley.

Price Waterhouse Coopers. 2014. Global economic crime survey. https://www.google.gr/search?sourceid=navclient&ie=UTF-8&rlz=1T4NDKB_enCY512CY559&q=PWC+2014+Global +Economic+Crime+Survey. Accessed 20 March 2014.

Rainbow, L. 2011. Professionalising the process. In *Professionalizing offender profiling: Forensic and investigative psychology in practice*, ed. L. Alison, and L. Rainbow, 1–3. London: Routledge.

Rainbow, L., and A. Gregory. 2011. What behavioural investigative advisers actually do. In *Professionalizing offender profiling: Forensic and investigative psychology in practice*, ed. L. Alison, and L. Rainbow, 18–34. London: Routledge.

Ramamoorti, S. 2008. The psychology and sociology of fraud: Integrating the behavioural sciences component into fraud and forensic accounting curricula. *Issues in Accounting Education* 23(4): 521–533.

Ragatz, L.L., and W. Fremouw. 2010. A critical examination of research on the psychological profiles of white-collar criminals. *Journal of Forensic Psychology Practice* 10(5): 373–402.

Ragatz, L.L., W. Fremouw, and E. Baker. 2012. The psychological profile of white-collar offenders: Demographics, criminal thinking, psychopathic traits, and psychopathology. *Criminal Justice and Behavior* 10(5): 373–402.

Ratcliff, J.H. 2004. Crime mapping and the training needs of law enforcement. *European Journal on Criminal Policy and Research* 10(1): 65–83.

Ross, S., and R.G. Smith. 2011. Risk factors for advance fee fraud victimization. Australian Institute of Criminology, Trends and Issues in Crime and Criminal Justice, No. 420. Canberra, Australia. http://www.aic.gov.au/publications/current%20series/tandi/401-420/tandi420.html. Accessed 20 Jan 2013.

Rossmo, D.K. 2000. *Geographic profiling*. Boca Raton, FL: CRC Press.

Ruggiero, V. 2000. *Organized and corporate crime in Europe*. Ashgate, UK: Dartmouth.

Shapiro, S. 1990. Collaring the crime, not the criminal: Reconsidering the concept of white-collar crime. *American Sociological Review* 55(3): 346–365.

Santtila, P., M. Laukkanen, A. Zappalà, and D. Bosco. 2008. Behavioural crime linking in serial homicide. *Psychology, Crime and Law* 14(3): 245–265.

Sharp, T., A. Shreve-Neiger, F. Fremouw, J. Kane, and S. Hutton. 2004. Exploring the psychological and somatic impact of identity theft. *Journal of Forensic Sciences* 49(1): 131–136.

Shover, N., G.S. Coffey, and C.R. Sanders. 2004. Dialling for dollars: Opportunities, justifications, and telemarketing fraud. *Qualitative Sociology* 27(1): 59–75.

Simon, D. 1999. *Elite deviance*. Boston: Allyn & Bacon.

Spencer, J.C. 1965. White-collar crime. In *Criminology in transition*, ed. T. Grygier, H. Jones, J.C. Spencer, et al. London: Tavistock.

Sutherland, E.H. 1940. White-collar criminality. *American Sociological Review* 5(1): 1–12.

Sutherland, E.H. 1983. *White collar crime*. New Haven, CT: Yale University Press.

Terpstra, J.C., E.J. Rozell, and R.K. Robinson. 1993. The influence of personality and demographic variables on ethical decisions related to insider trading. *Journal of Psychology* 127(4): 375–389.

Trahan, A., J.W. Marquart, and J. Mullings. 2005. Fraud and the American dream: Toward an understanding of fraud victimization. *Deviant Behavior* 26(6): 601–620.

United Nations Office on Drugs and Crime [UNODC]. Feb 2013. Comprehensive study on cybercrime. http://www.unodc.org/documents/organized-crime/UNODC_CCPCJ_EG.4_2013/CYBERCRIME_STUDY_210213.pdf. Accessed 17 Feb 2014.

Van de Bunt, H. 2010. Walls of secrecy and silence: The Madoff case and cartels in the construction industry. *Criminology and Public Policy* 9(3): 435–453.

Walters, G.D., and M.D. Geyer. 2004. Criminal thinking and identity in male white-collar offenders. *Criminal Justice and Behavior* 31(3): 263–281.

Weisburd, D., E.F. Chayet, and E.J. Waring. 1990. White-collar crime and criminal careers: Some preliminary findings. *Crime and Delinquency* 36(3): 342–355.

Wheeler, S., D. Weisburd, and N. Bode. 1982. Sentencing the white-collar offenders: Rhetoric and reality. *American Sociological Review* 47(5): 641–659.

Wheeler, S., D. Weisburd, E. Waring, and N. Bode. 1988. White-collar crimes and criminals. *American Criminal Law Review* 25(3): 331–357.

Wheeler, S., D. Weisburd, E. Waring, and N. Bode. 1991. *Crimes of the middle classes: White collar offenders in the federal courts*. New Haven, CT: Yale University Press.

Wheeler, S., D. Weisburd, and N. Bode. 2000. Nature and sanctioning of white collar crime, 1976–1978: federal judicial districts. ICPRS 8989. https://www.ncjrs.gov/pdffiles1/Digitization/115308NCJRS.pdf. Accessed 15 Jan 2014.

Willott, S., C. Griffin, and M. Torrance. 2001. Snakes and ladders: Upper-middle class male offenders talk about economic crime. *Criminology* 29(2): 441–466.

Wilson, H.Q. 2011. Hard times, fewer crimes. *Wall Street Journal*. http://online.wsj.com/news/articles/SB10001424052702304066504576345553135009870. Accessed 15 Feb 2014.

Chapter 14
Globalization and the Challenge of Regulating Transnational Financial Crimes

Nlerum S. Okogbule

Abstract The chapter examines the challenges posed to the regulation of transnational financial crimes by the processes of globalization. Acknowledging that globalization has promoted greater integration of states into the international economy through interconnection of markets, financial services and capital, it argues that the products of technological advancements, such as computer and the Internet, have been increasingly used and exploited by criminals in the perpetration of transnational financial crimes. It demonstrates that the existing national and international legal instruments and mechanisms have been unable to sufficiently grapple with the problems of transnational financial crimes and suggests that more emphasis be placed on enhanced preventive measures, such as increased electronic surveillance, modernization of applicable legal rules along these lines, international co-operation and the cultivation of a global ethical consensus on the subject.

14.1   Introduction

This chapter seeks to examine the challenges posed to the regulation of transnational financial crimes by the processes of globalization. It is axiomatic that globalization has promoted greater integration of states into the international economy through interconnection of markets, financial services, and free movement of labour and capital. Today, financial transactions involving millions of dollars are easily carried out through bank transfers, the use of Visa and Credit Cards, and the Internet—avenues and mechanisms that are sometimes exploited and compromised by criminals. These developments have brought to centre-stage enormous regulatory challenges, including how to effectively deal with cross-border financial crimes. While the adoption of the United Nations Convention Against Transnational

N.S. Okogbule (✉)
Rivers State University of Science and Technology, Port Harcourt, Nigeria
e-mail: nlerumokogbule@yahoo.co.uk

© Springer International Publishing Switzerland 2016   295
M. Dion et al. (eds.), *Financial Crimes: Psychological, Technological,*
and Ethical Issues, International Library of Ethics, Law,
and the New Medicine 68, DOI 10.1007/978-3-319-32419-7_14

Organised Crime in 2000 is a bold attempt by the international community to deal with economic crimes in the broader context, the peculiarly complex nature of financial crimes has made their regulation more problematic. The instantaneous nature of some financial transactions, increasing sophistication of the financial services sector through technological advancements and innovations coupled with the development of new portfolios and products by financial institutions have all contributed to make a complex regulatory problem even more challenging. This is complicated by the web of regulatory national mechanisms governing such crimes and the disparate levels of enforcement by states.

It is therefore important to examine the normative underpinnings of these developments and how the regulatory instruments and mechanisms can effectively be deployed to combat financial crimes worldwide. It would be suggested inter alia, that from a technological perspective, greater emphasis needs to be placed on integrated collaborative preventive measures, such as electronic surveillance, in order to discourage and reduce opportunities for the commission of these crimes rather than the reactive measures underpinning some of the existing instruments and approaches. Such an approach must be sufficiently embedded in, and reinforced within the framework of a global ethical consensus.

The chapter is organized in four parts. The first part will explore the scope and ramifications of transnational financial crimes while the second part examines the nature of globalization and instantiates how it is implicated in the commission of transnational financial crimes. In the third part, the challenges impacting on the regulation of these crimes are examined, alongside the national and international efforts at combating transnational financial crimes. It will be shown that because of the complex nature of cyberspace where most financial transactions now take place, regulating such crimes effectively has been problematic. The final part of the chapter draws a number of conclusions from the analysis and suggests the way forward in dealing with transnational financial crimes.

14.2   Nature of Transnational Financial Crimes

Financial crime is a very broad subject, and it includes conducts such as money laundering, corruption, terrorist financing, financial fraud, among others. They are opportunity-driven crimes. Criminals usually take advantage of any available opportunities to commit such crimes. No doubt, such opportunities have increased with the tremendous advancements in technology, which are being used in exploiting the financial systems, procedures and structures (Michel 2008, 396). In considering what constitutes financial crime, one of the crucial elements is whether the crime involves the movement or transfer of money through the manipulation or unlawful penetration of institutions and procedures in the public or private sectors. The high yield nature of the crime, financial gain as the primary motivation and the fact that it is a form of organised crime are also important determinants in this respect. Financial crimes have over the years assumed increasing dimensions worldwide, both in terms of their volume, sophistication, complexity and debilitating impact in society.

Although there are many ways through which financial crimes are committed, one prominent avenue today for the perpetration of such crimes is through the use of computers and the Internet.[1] Indeed, the Internet has become not only a place to gather information, but where one can fulfil all of one's daily needs and activities. This is because all forms of social and financial transactions, including the purchase of goods and services, are now carried out through the Internet. To be sure, electronic commerce enables businesses to reach a market that is virtually unlimited, excluding only those that have no access to the Internet or are not computer literate (Fletcher 2007, 193). It is trite that through electronic transfers millions of dollars are easily transferred around the globe at the touch of a button. Paradoxically, the rise in usage of the Internet for carrying out financial transactions and e-business has led to an increase in transnational financial crimes.[2] Indeed, more and more persons now use computers, mobile phones, ipads, and Internet for their social contacts and financial transactions. For instance, through the medium of Internet, a financial crime can be committed against a victim in one country by a national of another country operating from an entirely different third country. This transnational dimension of financial crime carries with it immense regulatory challenges, a recognition of which eventually led to the adoption of the UN Convention Against Transnational Organized Crime (2000). The central purpose of the Convention as stated in Article 1 is "to promote cooperation to prevent and combat transnational organized crime more effectively".

In determining whether a crime is transnational in nature, it is expedient to examine the description of 'transnational' in Article 3 of the Convention. According to the Convention, "an offence is transnational in nature if: (a) it is committed in more than one State; (b) it is committed in one State but a substantial part of its preparation, planning, direction or control takes place in another State; (c) it is committed in one State but involves an organized criminal group that engages in criminal activities in more than one State; or (d) it is committed in one state but has substantial effects in another State". This shows that a complex range of activities perpetrated in several countries under different circumstances fall within the purview of transnational crime. Computers and the Internet have become key instruments of such crimes. Thus, a cyber criminal can access a person's credit card details on the Internet and use it to complete order forms through which the

---

[1]Since the Internet and computers are products of technological advancements, they will be the central focus of this contribution in examining how they have been used in the commission of financial crimes.

[2]Adebiyi (2005, 148–172).

merchant accepts the order and ships goods/services to the suspect. Another form of financial crime committed through, and facilitated by the Internet is the 'Nigerian 419 Scam', so-called because of its reference to Sect. 419 of the Nigerian Criminal Code on Advance fee fraud. This crime entails the target person receiving unsolicited fax, e-mail or letter containing a proposal concerning Nigeria, or any other African country requesting some payments to be made in advance to facilitate access to a bequest left in a will, or to purchase specified chemical substance to enable some large currency in possession of the initiator to be chemically cleaned and the money shared, or to enable the processing of documents for a crude oil supply or service contract from the government (Okonkwo 1995, 306–308; UNODC 2005, 24–25). Sadly, some innocent Internet users, businessmen and women are known to have fallen victims of these contraptions and lost millions of dollars in the process.[3]

Additionally, the fact that international computer networks can transfer huge amounts of data around the globe in a matter of seconds makes the deployment of such instruments in the commission of financial crime an object of scrutiny. This is because the process involved in this mobility of computer data can easily be compromised by criminals, and the information used to commit financial crimes such as credit card fraud, money laundering among others. It is obvious that side by side with the technological advancements represented by the use of computer and Internet, have also emerged a number of Internet security vulnerabilities. From a technological viewpoint, two of the critical points of vulnerability are through the Server and the communication pipeline or highway. According to Nigel Fletcher, cyber criminals are able to exploit these vulnerabilities either through hacking, or the use of malicious code to gain information required in carrying out the fraud (Fletcher 2007, 193). Thus, with the development of sites such as Ebay.com, Amazon.com, and PayPal.com, a fraudster can hack into their databases and access credit card and bank account details as well as the personal information that he requires in order to defraud innocent site users (Fletcher 2007, 194). Consequently, the fact that advancements in technology have brought with them more security vulnerabilities makes regulation in this area of law more challenging. It has therefore been said that e-commerce has significantly challenged the traditional way of doing business, and indeed, the general business thinking (Laudon and Guercio Traver 2004, 12). These technological advances and the new dimensions they have brought to financial crimes have also been globalized, due to the increasing interconnectivity of people worldwide. It is therefore important to examine the nature of the relationship between globalization and financial crimes.

---

[3]For example, in one famous such case Amaka Anajemba was convicted and sentenced to two and half years jail term after defrauding a Brazilian Bank and its director of $242 Millions through the e-mail scam. See, *The Guardian* (18 July 2005, 1).

14.3 Globalization and Transnational Financial Crimes

Globalization is one of the most pervasive, but deeply contested processes and developments in contemporary society. It is a multi-faceted process that has engendered an avalanche of writings and debates concerning its nature, historical origins and impact in society.[4] This has made it extremely difficult to define, categorize, and clarify the purport of globalization. Nevertheless, it can be said that globalization essentially entails the intensified movement of goods, money, technology, information, people, ideas and cultural practices across the globe as well as the interdependence of social and economic processes.[5] This comprehensive approach to the description of globalization is also evident in the definition proffered by Held et al. (2003) who defines globalization as: "A process (or a set of processes) which embodies a transformation in the spatial organisation of social relations and transactions—assessed in terms of their extensity, intensity, velocity and impact generating transcontinental or interregional flows and networks of activity, interaction, and the exercise of power" (Held et al. 2003, 68). This definition underscores the intensity and extensity of global networks and interconnectedness as well as the velocity of global flows which has been a defining feature of contemporary society. Although there are many dimensions of globalization,[6] the central focus of this chapter is on economic and technological dimensions insofar as these facilitate the commission of transnational financial crimes. This consideration is informed by the fact that the worldwide spread of industrial production and new technologies promoted by unrestricted mobility of capital and unfettered freedom of trade have concurrently also facilitated the commission of financial crimes. To be sure, the social and economic transformations taking place globally as part of the globalization process have engendered the commission of financial crimes in ways not previously contemplated. Moreover, modern technology has resulted in unprecedented communication worldwide, and its use in markets enables people from different countries to strike financial deals within minutes, often without seeing each other.

The advances in technology and the application of such innovations means that people have become interconnected at a level never seen before in history. Indeed, technology is generating global convergence, and deep interconnectivity. For instance, the Internet is helping to convey information to all corners of the globe, while advances in air transport has enabled people to cross borders in greater numbers at shorter time frames (Mahbubani 2012, 11). The introduction of Smart Card schemes to facilitate financial transactions has also been prompted by technological innovations. A Smart Card scheme is a system that permits the

---

[4]It is from this perspective that David Held and Anthony McGrew have described debates about it as one of the most fundamental debates of our time. Held and McGrew (2002, ix).

[5]Holton (2005, 15).

[6]These include political, social, legal, technological and economic dimensions with their various impacts on social and economic relations.

digitalization of cash, as well as other intangible assets. In practical terms, this scheme enables the consumer to pay for goods and services with his funds stored on a card (Ajayi 1998, 114). Smart Cards are chip based, and they ensure that "monetary value is stored or loaded into a renewable or disposable card, which can be used to purchase goods and services. Each time the card is used, the monetary value thereon is reduced, and if the card is one with an indefinite life, or one that is rechargeable, value can be loaded thereon from time to time" (Ajayi 1998, 115). The holder usually loads the card with money from his account, and uses the card to pay for goods and services, while the vendor obtains payment by downloading digital cash on to the vendor's card or a POS device. Schemes such as this which are designed to enhance commerce and increase the convenience of consumers have become avenues through which some financial crimes are perpetrated. Indeed, the use of the Internet has enabled all kinds of financial transactions, such as payments, settlements, and transfers to be effected through the use of credit and debit cards worldwide. Moreover, in order to enhance their customer base, banks and other financial institutions regularly roll out new products and portfolios to encourage their customers and investors to invest in their companies. Most of these products and portfolios are run with or facilitated through electronic transfer methods or the use of the Internet. Needless to say, these instruments have also become useful vessels for the commission of financial crimes. The borderless nature of the Internet which is revolutionizing commerce has brought with it new opportunities to commit crimes. The growth in the level of financial crimes in this era of globalization is having serious negative impact on the international economy. This is because, in general, financial crimes weaken economies and financial systems and ultimately undermines democracy and good governance. These abnormalities are usually magnified when such transactions are transnational, a situation that has given rise to a number of legal and regulatory challenges which are next considered.

14.4 Legal/Regulatory Challenges and Responses

14.4.1 Legal and Regulatory Challenges

The transnational dimension of financial crime, its impact on the global economy, and the role of globalization in deepening the intensity and extensity of such crimes make it imperative to have international regulatory mechanisms to deal with the challenge. In this connection, the advances in technology and the vulnerabilities usually exploited in the commission of financial crimes underscore the need for the modernization of legal mechanisms on the subject. This point was highlighted by a publication of the Commonwealth Secretariat, where it is stated that[7] "with the rapid advancement in computer technology over the past few years, there has been

---

[7]Commonwealth Secretariat (2001, 1).

increasing concern and focus in many countries, on the need to develop and modernise the law in order to take full advantage of technological improvements and at the same time to ensure that states can respond to computer crime and related criminal law issues associated to these developments". Such modernization will ensure that the legal mechanism follows closely, and responds adequately, to the dictates of technological changes in dealing with the associated criminal tendencies or opportunities. On this score, one of the central challenges regarding the regulation of transnational financial crime is the issue of jurisdiction. The challenge, according to Sofaer and Goodman (2001, 35) "is how to regulate a technology that permits rapid transactions across continents and hemispheres using legal and investigative instruments that are fragmented across jealously but ineffectively guarded national and jurisdictional borders" Jurisdiction which is an aspect of state sovereignty refers to the legislative, judicial and administrative competence of a state or its agencies over particular individual matters (Brownlie 2008, 229). A state may exercise jurisdiction over a particular transnational financial crime on any, or a combination of some of the following governing principles. These include territoriality, nationality, passive nationality, protective or security, or the universality principle (Brownlie 2008, 301–305). Although these principles are somewhat covered by the provisions of Article 15 of the United Nations Convention on Transnational Organized Crime, problems usually arise when the legal system or machinery of a state is unable to deal effectively with the crime or when the state is covering the prosecution of the culprit and refuses to extradite the suspect to the other state that may have the competence and functioning machinery to try the offender. A recent example of an inefficient legal system in grappling with such crimes is the conviction in London, United Kingdom of one Chief James Ibori, a former State Governor in Nigeria on a 10-count charge of fraud, corruption and money laundering involving several million pounds. Ironically, he had earlier been discharged for similar offences by a compromised court in Nigeria.[8] The jurisdictional problem arises because even the position of the Permanent Court of International Justice (PCIJ) in the *Lotus Case*[9] formulating some guiding principles has not been particularly helpful in this regard, and has accordingly been severely criticized (Brownlie 2008, 303). The Court after stating that "the territoriality of criminal law … is not an absolute principle of international law and by no means coincides with territorial sovereignty", went further to posit that: "Far from laying down a general prohibition to the effect that States may not extend the application of their laws and the jurisdiction of their courts to persons, property or acts outside their territory, it leaves them in this respect a wide measure of discretion which is only limited in certain cases by prohibitive rules; as regards other cases, every State remains free to adopt the principles which it regards as best and most suitable".

The freedom of states to adopt principles which they regard as best and most suitable has led to a measure of uncertainty concerning the scope and limits of the

---

[8]See, *This Day Newspaper* (18 April 2012, 1).
[9](1927, PCIJ, Ser. A, no.10, 20).

extra-territoriality principle. Moreover, within the context of the present discourse and the increasing use of computers and Internet in the commission of financial crimes, the jurisdictional problem becomes acute since the international scope of cyberspace makes it difficult to determine which countries have jurisdiction over particular matters. Thus, vital jurisdictional questions may arise where the criminal is in country A and uses computer there to connect his accomplice in country B, and the offence is committed against an innocent person in country C. Investigation and prosecution for such offences require that evidence be traced, preserved and collected from more than one country, which may have different procedural laws relating to such matters. Investigators therefore have to understand and comply with the various laws applicable in the countries implicated in the crime. For instance, the powers of seizure and arrest as well as the procedural laws differ markedly in different countries; and wading through such transnational procedural laws could be unduly cumbersome and unnerving (Salifu 2008, 435).

Another important challenge confronting the regulation of transnational financial crimes is the difficulty in accessing and analyzing electronic records, such as computer network logs, e-mails, and word processing files, as evidence of the commission of an offence to facilitate the prosecution of offenders. To be sure, using such electronically generated evidence to prosecute a case can raise serious issues relating to their admissibility and connection to the suspected offenders (Oni 2005, 218–228). This challenge is magnified when it is realized that anonymity is a prominent element in cyberspace to the extent that open electronic cash transactions and transfers can be made instantly from one jurisdiction to another without leaving a trail. On this score, it can be said that the use of such technologically-enabled devices poses great challenges for law enforcement much more than conventional crime. This makes the adoption of internet specific regulation imperative (Fletcher 2007, 201). With the peculiar nature of cyberspace and how it has been used to perpetrate financial crimes, it must be acknowledged that even the existence of the aforesaid regulatory mechanisms would not necessarily eliminate new types of criminal behaviour that could be contrived to challenge extant approaches to crime prevention and regulation. This requires that the fight against cybercrime must be a sustained and rapidly adjusting one to respond to new technological innovations and the criminal opportunities they create. This is particularly crucial because the criminal justice systems and international regulatory efforts have not kept pace with technological change in such a way as to effectively respond to the problems created by transnational financial crime (Adebiyi 2005, 170). In addition to the identified challenges arising from the international character of financial crime, other problems affecting the regulation of such crimes especially when committed through the Internet, include inadequate legal powers for investigation and access to intangible computer data and systems, and the lack of harmonization between the different national procedural laws concerning the investigation of computer related crimes (Adebiyi 2005, 170). There are also critical problems concerning the tracing of assets, as the use of Smart Cards makes it difficult for proper records of suspicious transactions to be kept. Accordingly, where records are unavailable to show how funds are moved from one jurisdiction to another, it becomes very difficult for the courts or other enforcement authority of the foreign government to carry out tracing (Ajayi 1998, 121). The issue of inadequate records of financial transactions by financial institutions, especially in the developing countries, makes it even more difficult to appropriately deal with transnational financial crimes.

From the above analysis, it can be said that the use of the products of technological advancements, such as computers and the Internet, to commit transnational financial crimes has brought to the fore two critical regulatory issues. First, it has underscored the imperative of concerted international co-operation in dealing with transnational financial crimes. Since financial crime is a global problem, to be effective, efforts at combating it must be global in approach. This requires the active involvement of all regions of the world in the efforts to prevent these new forms of criminality using Internet and other technology-driven mechanisms. Second, the complex nature of cyberspace and the international dimensions involved makes the creation of Internet specific regulations imperative. The objective is to ensure that the regulatory mechanism takes cognizance of the peculiarities of financial crimes committed through the use of computers and the Internet. On this score, conscious efforts must be made by the international community to ensure that the benefits of globalization are preserved through improvements of the international structures that ensure financial stability (Lagarde 2012, 26). Although globalization has helped to bring societies closer together and make them more open, it has also brought with it new and unfamiliar risks. These include the risks associated with the use of Internet to carry out financial transactions. As Lagarde (2012, 26) has opined in a related context, these risks must be kept at bay if we are to reap the rewards of integration. Since no part of our interconnected world is immune to the problems created by transnational financial crime, only this global approach in dealing with the challenges can be meaningful and effective.

Additionally, considering that the challenges of regulating financial fraud in cyberspace are more complex than regulating fraud in the real world, both conventional legal responses and novel technological approaches must be utilized (Fletcher 2007, 194). The deployment of these two response measures in dealing with transnational financial crimes raises an important problematic, namely, how to formulate effective legal and ethical rules and standards to regulate these products of technology in this era of globalization since such rules are usually predicated on extant technological procedures which are frequently discarded for more improved versions. This has been a recurring dilemma of legal regulation since law invariably follows, and strives to keep pace with, technological innovations. In this particular situation, the legal rules formulated to deal with the products of technological advancements must not be too far behind the technological innovations they seek to regulate. In light of these challenges, it becomes important to examine some of the national and international measures designed to address these challenges.

14.4.2   Current Efforts at Combating Transnational Financial Crimes

The challenges discussed in the preceeding section do not necessarily suggest lack of efforts to combat transnational financial crimes. To be sure, given the impact of such crimes on the international economy, valiant efforts have been made at national and international levels to deal with the increasing globalization of financial crime. Notable efforts in this direction include the adoption of the United Nations Convention on Transnational Organized Crime (2000), Convention Against Corruption (2003) and the United Nations' Convention Against Illicit Traffic in Narcotic Drugs and Psychotropic Substances (1988). These Conventions contain some important provisions relating to the regulation of transnational financial crimes.

For present purposes, two provisions of the Convention on Transnational Organized Crime on this subject deserve mention here. First, Article 6(1) of the Convention requires states to adopt legislative and other measures to criminalize conducts such as the conversion or transfer of property arising from the proceeds of crime with the intention of disguising the illicit origin of such property. States are also to establish as criminal offences the concealment or disguise of the true nature, source, location, disposition, movement or ownership of property which is the proceeds of crime. In the same vein, State Parties are required under Article 7 of the Convention to institute comprehensive domestic regulatory and supervisory regimes for banks and non-bank financial institutions with emphasis on customer identification, record-keeping and reporting of suspicious transactions in order to deter and detect all forms of money laundering. In furtherance of this, State Parties also agree to implement feasible measures to detect and monitor the movement of cash and appropriate negotiable instruments across their borders provided that such measures do not impede the cross-border movement of legitimate capital (Article 7 (2)). These provisions invariably encouraged states without such laws to enact comprehensive legislations covering different aspects of financial crime and how to treat the proceeds of such criminal activities. For example, a state such as Nigeria enacted the Economic and Financial Crimes Commission Act (2002) with wide-ranging provisions governing various aspects of financial crime. The second set of provisions of the Convention that merit consideration here are those on international co-operation and assistance in the fight against transnational financial crime. The provisions essentially enjoin mutual co-operation and assistance among states in the investigation and prosecution of criminal matters. Thus it is provided in Article 18(1) and (2) as follows:

> State Parties shall afford one another the widest measure of mutual assistance in investi-
> gations, prosecutions and judicial proceedings in relation to the offences covered by this
> Convention as provided for in Article 3 and shall reciprocally extend to one another similar
> assistance where the requesting State Party has reasonable grounds to suspect that the
> offence referred to in Article 3, paragraph 1(a) or (b), is transnational in nature, including
> the victims, witnesses, proceeds, instrumentalities or evidence of such offences are located
> in the requested State Party and the offence involves an organized criminal group.

2. Mutual legal assistance shall be afforded to the fullest extent possible under relevant laws, treaties, agreements and arrangements of the requested State Party with respect to investigations, prosecutions and judicial proceedings in relation to the offences for which a legal person may be held liable in accordance with Article 10 of this Convention in the requesting State Party.

It must be mentioned that these provisions on mutual legal assistance reinforce existing bilateral and multilateral agreements on measures against transnational financial crimes. For instance, among Commonwealth countries, there is the Treaty on Mutual Assistance in Criminal Matters within the Commonwealth. This treaty which has been domesticated by several Commonwealth countries is essentially designed to increase the level and scope of assistance rendered between Commonwealth Governments in criminal matters. In the case of Nigeria, for example, and concerning tracing of the proceeds of criminal activities, S.20(1) of the Mutual Assistance in Criminal Matters within the Commonwealth (Enactment and Enforcement) Act[10] provides that a request for assistance may be made in respect of: "(a) identifying, searching and locating property within the requested country believed to be acquired with the proceeds of criminal activities, and (b) the security of property in the requested country believed to be acquired with the proceeds of criminal activities".[11] In relation to money laundering, a key financial crime, there is the Financial Action Task Force (FATF) comprising European, North and South American and Asian states with the main task of co-ordinating the joint international action against money laundering. The Task Force has made some significant strides in this area. In particular, it has successfully formulated Forty-eight (48) Recommendations designed to assist states in the fight against money laundering. In the African continent, there is the Inter-Governmental Action Group Against Money Laundering in West Africa (GIABA) established in 2000 through the work of Economic Community of West African States (ECOWAS) to co-ordinate the war against money laundering and terrorism in the sub-region. On its part, the East and Southern African Anti-Money Laundering Group (ESAAMLG) co-ordinates the fight against money laundering in those sub-regions. These transnational and regional mechanisms are clearly indicative of the deployment of multi-jurisdictional task forces which combine investigative resources from several agencies to enhance the capabilities and effectiveness of measures to combat these forms of financial crimes. They also rely upon and build on collaboration between the various enforcement agencies involved in the fight against these crimes.

In addition, a number of states have also enacted statutory instruments to deal with the scourge of financial crimes in their countries in compliance with their obligations under the Convention Against Transnational Organized Crime. In this connection, reference may be made to the United States that have enacted comprehensive statutes dealing with transnational financial crimes such as money

---

[10]Cap M24, Laws of the Federation of Nigeria, 2004.

[11]See also the Treaty between the Federal Republic of Nigeria and United States of America on Mutual Legal Assistance in Criminal Matters, signed at Washington on 13 September, 1989.

laundering and official corruption. In Nigeria, where the scourge of advance fee fraud has become an international affair, the government in 2002 enacted the Economic and Financial Crimes Commission Act to tackle this scourge frontally. The government also enacted the Independent Corrupt Practices and Other Related Offences Act (2000). These statutory enactments notwithstanding, transnational financial crimes remain a fundamental problem in the Nigerian society largely because the underlying norms, value system and ethical underpinnings have not been adequately handled (Okogbule 2007, 57; Dion 2010, 241). It is our contention that in order to make the various national and international regulatory mechanisms effective in this era of globalization, appropriate mechanisms must be put in place to prevent and reduce the security vulnerabilities annexed to the technological advancements, and also enhance the ethical climate in cyberspace. This approach seems attractive because the products of technological advancements have consistently exhibited a number of vulnerabilities that have been exploited in the commission of transnational financial crimes.

14.5   Conclusion

An attempt has been made in this chapter to highlight the regulatory challenges facing the international community in dealing with transnational financial crimes. There is no doubt that globalization which has transformed the world into a global village has had phenomenal impact on the prevalence of such crimes. It has been shown that globalization and technological innovations have added a measure of complexity to the hitherto existing problem of regulating transnational financial crimes. The processes of interconnection, interaction and communication which are hallmarks of globalization have brought with them new products, portfolios, and technologies such as the Internet which are being exploited to facilitate the commission of financial crimes. While these instruments are making enormous contribution to socio-economic development, they also present new and peculiar challenges to law enforcement. Since transnational financial crimes are opportunity-driven, one of the most effective ways of combating or preventing them is through the elimination or reduction of those opportunities that are frequently exploited by criminals. Some of these opportunities stem from the security vulnerabilities that are annexed to the technologically-driven innovations and instruments and therefore require appropriate response measures. In significant respects, the response of the international community through the adoption of legal instruments, such as the United Nations' Convention Against Transnational Organised Crime, has not provided a holistic and effective answer to the challenge posed by these crimes. This stems from the fact that the peculiar nature of cyberspace engenders regulatory challenges that are completely different from those created by conventional crime. Yet, the current legal framework does not provide enough regulation specific to the challenges that cyber fraud presents (Fletcher 2007, 205). This makes it imperative for the formulation of a new legal framework to respond to the dictates of technological developments (Sofaer and Goodman 2001, 29). More efforts are therefore required especially in the area of preventive measures, which could entail designing products that are either resistant to, or facilitate the detection and investigation of financial crimes. In addition, the adoption of a Convention dealing with specific aspects of financial crime is one way of moving the fight against these crimes forward. Equally signal in this respect is the need for enhanced deployment of electronic surveillance since it represents the single and most important law enforcement weapon against an organized transnational crime such as financial crime. Electronic surveillance not only enables law enforcement officials to learn of the conspirators' plans to commit crimes before they are carried out, but also enables them to intercept and frustrate such conspirators while discussing their criminal plans with their associates in foreign countries.

Moreover, since the challenges posed by transnational financial crimes are global in nature, the adoption of a global ethic in responding to those challenges seems imperative. This is informed by the fact that "a global ethic contains the principles, rules, institutional arrangements, attitudes, and virtues required to address global issues" (Rodin 2012, 34; Kung 2004, 45). The global village must therefore come together in order to deal with the problem of transnational financial crimes. The growth of global interconnectivity as well as the spread of information and ideas engendered by such developments has made it imperative for our moral compasses to expand beyond national borders. Such global approaches will not only enable us collectively and effectively deal with these crimes, but contribute to the strengthening of the global village through the cultivation of a global ethical consensus (Mahbubani 2012, 11). Given that we now live in a world and time in which humankind is threatened by a number of activities, such as transnational financial crimes, the need for a global ethical consensus on the subject cannot be over-emphasized. It is only through such approaches that humankind can maximally benefit from the promise of globalization and effectively respond to the challenges posed by transnational financial crimes.

References

Adebiyi, T. 2005. Internet crime. *Modern Practice Journal of Finance and Investment Law* 9 (1–2): 145–172.

Ajayi, O. 1998. Leap frogging the African economy into the 21st century through electronic smart cards: The legal perspective. *Modern Practice Journal of Finance and Investment Law* 2(2): 113–131.

Brownlie, I. 2008. *Principles of public international law*, 7th ed. Oxford: Oxford University Press.

Commonwealth Secretariat. 2001. *Law in cyber space*. London: Commonwealth Secretariat.

Dion, M. 2010. Corruption and ethical relativism: What is at stake?'. *Journal of Financial Crime* 17(2): 240–250.

Fletcher, N. 2007. Challenges for regulating financial fraud in cyberspace. *Journal of Financial Crime* 14(2): 190–207.

Held, D., and A. Mcgrew. 2002. *Globalization and anti-globalization*. Cambridge: Polity Press.

Held, D., et al. 2003. Rethinking globalization. In *The global transformations reader: An introduction to the globalization debate*, 2nd ed, ed. D. Held, and A. McGrew, 67–74. Cambridge: Polity Press.

Holton, R. 2005. *Making globalization*. New York: Palgrave Macmillan.

Kung, H. 2004. A global ethic as a foundation for global society. In *The globalization reader*, ed. Frank J. Lechner, and John Boli, 44–50. Oxford: Blackwell Publishing Ltd.

Lagarde, C. 2012. Fragmentation risks. *Finance and Development* 49(3): 26.

Laudon, K.C., and C. Guercio Traver. 2004. *E-Commerce: Business, technology, society*. Reading, MA: Addison Wesley.

Mahbubani, K. 2012. The global village has arrived. *Finance and Development* 49(3): 10–11.

Michel, P. 2008. Financial crimes: The constant challenge of seeking effective preventive solutions. *Journal of Financial Crime* 15(4): 383–397.

Okogbule, N.S. 2007. Official corruption and the dynamics of money laundering in Nigeria. *Journal of Financial Crime* 14(2): 49–63.

Okonkwo, C.O. 1995. Advance fee fraud and other related offences decree, 1995: An appraisal. In *Law, justice and the nigerian society*, ed. I.A. Ayua, 306–321. Nigerian Institute of Advanced Legal Studies: Lagos.

Oni, O. 2005. Legal challenges in the admissibility of computer-generated evidence in Nigeria. *Modern Practice Journal of Finance and Investment Law* 9(1–2): 214–230.

Rodin, D. 2012. Toward a global ethic. *Ethics and International Affairs* 26(1): 33–42.

Salifu, A. 2008. The impact of internet crime on development. *Journal of Financial Crime* 15(4): 432–443.

Sofaer, A.D., and S.E. Goodman. 2001. *The transnational dimension of cyber crime and terrorism*. Stanford: Hoover Press.

UNODC, 2005. *Transnational organized crime in the West African region*. United Nations Office on Drugs and Crime.

Chapter 15
The Transnational Organisation of the Drugs Trade

Peter Enderwick

Abstract The international trade in illicit drugs, one of the largest industries in the world economy, is firmly under the control of transnational criminal organisations (TCOs). These groups have prospered under a long standing regime of drug prohibition. This chapter examines the global drugs trade with three main aims. First, it outlines the nature of the illicit drug industry, its size and methods of organisation. We find that there are marked similarities in the ways in which both legitimate and illegitimate international businesses are organised, in part because both have responded to continuing globalisation. Both types of businesses are fragmenting, partially externalising activities, and increasing locational flexibility. Second, we consider the impact of new technologies on the illicit drugs industry. It is apparent that TCOs are using such technologies to both improve the efficiency of their operations and to reduce the likelihood of their detection. This creates significant challenges for drug law enforcement agencies. Third, we consider the ethics of the global drugs industry. The key ethical challenge for an industry which generates huge social, economic and health costs is whether continuation of a 40 year war on drugs founded on prohibition, is more ethically acceptable than an evidence-based approach focusing on harm reduction. The drugs policy reform debate is a vibrant and sweeping one, currently attracting massive interest worldwide.

15.1 Introduction

The illegal drugs trade is concerned with the cultivation, production, distribution and sale of substances subject to drug prohibition laws. Trade, and increasingly transnational trade, in drugs have developed to form a large and highly profitable part of global commerce. The global drugs trade had an estimated value of more than $410 billion in 2010, equivalent to 2.3 % of legitimate global trade

P. Enderwick (✉)
Auckland University of Technology, Auckland, New Zealand
e-mail: Peter.Enderwick@aut.ac.nz

© Springer International Publishing Switzerland 2016
M. Dion et al. (eds.), *Financial Crimes: Psychological, Technological, and Ethical Issues*, International Library of Ethics, Law, and the New Medicine 68, DOI 10.1007/978-3-319-32419-7_15

(Havocscope 2012). What distinguishes the transnational drugs trade from other global industries is the highly illegal nature of its activities, the large profits earned, the immense social costs created, and the significant resources dedicated to its control and reduction. For these reasons it is an industry worthy of close study, particularly from an ethical perspective. The intention of this chapter is to provide such an analysis.

The discussion provides an overview and evaluation of the industry, with a particular focus on two key considerations. The first of these is how the industry has been impacted by technological advances. While legitimate global industries have responded to emerging technologies affecting production, organisation, communication and control, the illicit drugs industry has been no different. Technology has changed the nature of products, the organisation of the industry, and the challenges of legal enforcement. The second aspect we consider is the ethics of the drugs industry, and in particular, the ethical basis of global drugs policy. This is a timely issue. It is more than 40 years since the United States declared a "war on drugs" with the alleged aim of eliminating the trade. Four decades later and the drugs industry is more ubiquitous than ever imposing massive social costs and devouring an unsustainable level of public resources. With a widespread perception that the war has failed, there have been growing calls for new approaches to the global drugs problem (Global Commission on Drug Policy 2011). We provide an evaluation of this debate.

The chapter is organised around six substantive sections. We begin by describing the nature of the transnational drugs industry, in particular patterns of demand, supply, and the role of organised crime. This is followed by an analysis of the impact of changing technologies on the way the industry operates. Section 15.4 considers the social costs of the drugs industry and the moral implications of these. We then turn to the key ethical debate as to what constitutes an appropriate regulatory response to the drugs industry and whether prohibition should continue to be the dominant policy position. Final thoughts are offered in the conclusions section.

15.2 International Business, Organised Crime, and the Drugs Trade

The transnational drug industry is driven by the same factors as most industries— the interplay of demand and supply. However, because of its illegality, it is organised and managed in distinct ways. Demand for drugs comes from the many users around the world. Estimates suggest that globally some 210 million people use illicit drugs each year, some 5 % of the working age population. This figure is well below the number of people who use tobacco, a quarter of the world's population (UNODC 2011a). Supply depends critically on the particular drug products. In the case of cocaine and heroin, growing conditions are important and the supply of ingredients tends to be restricted to a small number of supplying countries (primarily Afghanistan in the case of heroin and Colombia in the case of cocaine). The production of marijuana is more widely distributed and in many countries much of the demand is met locally. ATS (amphetamine type stimulants) such as methamphetamines, popularly known as 'ice' and 'crystal meth', are mainly produced in highly mobile clandestine labs and again, demand is largely met locally. Existing international business frameworks such as the eclectic paradigm (Dunning 2000) provide useful frameworks for understanding the operations of transnational criminal organisations (TCOs). The eclectic paradigm argues that three sets of conditions must exist for the development of international production: organisations must possess ownership advantages, combine these with (overseas) locational advantages, and normally exploit these advantages internally.

15.2.1 Ownership Advantages

The ownership advantages developed by TCOs serve to offset the disadvantages of foreignness they may face. Just like legitimate MNEs, these firms build on domestically created advantages which, in the case of TCOs, may result from a history of narcotics cultivation, widespread corruption, or weak law enforcement. In addition, TCOs are able to exploit expatriate enclaves to establish distribution facilities for example, the Jamaican community in London, or Russian migrants to the United States. A third form of ownership advantage stems from strategies of risk reduction including operating from a low risk home base, building complex operational structures that reduce the likelihood of detection and exploiting corruptive contacts to achieve protection or gain insider information (Enderwick 2009). Increasingly important to international drug traffickers is ensuring a high level of flexibility in their operations. This can be achieved in a number of ways including dense network structures which allow rapid adjustments to changing circumstances, transient cross-border alliances, and utilisation of modern communications and information technologies. Unlike legitimate international businesses TCOs are not bound by sovereignty or legal concerns and can adjust quickly when needs dictate.

15.2.2 Locational Advantages

International drug traffickers are also able to exploit locational advantages. Unlike legitimate MNEs which generally prefer safe, secure and well developed locations, TCOs are more likely to exploit locational weaknesses. These include high levels of corruption, market and institutional failures, and even elements of state failure (Enderwick 2009). In the same way that licit MNEs may seek tax or regulatory havens, TCOs also utilize favourable location conditions. For example, cocaine production in Bolivia has increased significantly since 2007. The authorities in Bolivia have permitted increased production of coca which is "legal" under domestic law, but contrary to international conventions of which Bolivia is a signatory. Bolivia also reduced law enforcement measures against drug production and trafficking. Clearly, such operating conditions are highly attractive to organised drug traffickers. The boundaries between licit and illicit activities are also exploited in the drug trade. India, a major pharmaceutical producer, has become a significant supply hub for illegal narcotics as it is the world's largest producer of licit opium and the only authorised user of the gum method of opium production for pharmaceutical preparations. Similarly, China is emerging as an important regional hub for heroin and methamphetamine moved from the Golden Triangle in south east Asia. China offers low-cost production laboratories and since the late 1990s cooperation between mainland criminals and more experienced gangs in Hong Kong, Macao and Taiwan has become common (Yeh 2006). Like a number of legitimate industries such as clothing and textiles and electronics, it appears that the global drugs trade is becoming more fragmented with new markets and supply lines emerging in regions that traditionally were neither producer or consumer areas. West Africa, for example, has become a major transit region for cocaine destined for Europe. This is a development that has occurred in just the last 5 years or so.

Locational flexibility and substitution are also apparent in the drugs industry. There is documented evidence of a "balloon effect" in both production and transit routes whereby law enforcement success in one area drives traffickers somewhere else (U.S. Dept of State 2010). Estimates suggest that while almost a third of all cocaine destined for the United States was trafficked through the Caribbean in 1997, by 2009 this had fallen to less than 10 % (UNODC 2011b). This displacement effect helps to explain the growing use of Western African states in supply routes, and Central America as a production base as detection efforts intensify in Mexico.

15.2.3 Internalisation

The third strand of conventional explanations of international production highlights the benefits of internalising transactions. While theories emphasise the importance of market failures in driving internalisation, for TCOs there are also benefits of maintaining secrecy and effective governance (Enderwick 2009). Digital information technologies allow efficient and, in many cases encrypted, communications making interception more difficult. Internalisation is also encouraged by the absence of market prices for intermediate products including precursor chemicals and services such as drug "cooks". Such products and services may be secured more efficiently through internalisation and hierarchical structures. The enormous mark up on each step of the drug value chain also encourages internalisation in an attempt to capture these profits. One estimate suggested that the mark-up on heroin from farm to street was in excess of 3000 fold and for cocaine more than 1800 times (Economist 2001). Internalisation, or at least bounded externalisation of activities, also facilitates governance within TCOs. Lacking the conventional forms of compliance such as contract enforcement through the legal system, TCOs make greater use of mechanisms designed to increase commitment and minimize defections. These include drawing membership from similar ethnic clans or tribal groups, a variety of rituals, oaths and secret ceremonies as well as violence (Enderwick 2009). While the conventional economic literature argues that violence is a relatively inefficient mechanism for governing transactions (North et al. 2006), it remains popular with TCOs (UNODC 2002).

This discussion suggests that the global drugs industry appears to share some of the characteristics of legitimate global business: the profit objective, investment in international operations, the exploitation of market and institutional failure, use of leading edge communications technologies, and a desire for greater flexibility. Where they differ is in existence of strong demand for illicit goods like drugs, a desire to frustrate monitoring and detection, management structures and practices that stress loyalty and secrecy, and dispute resolution based on violence.

15.3   Changing Technologies and the Organisational Response

Rapidly emerging technologies have had a major impact on organisational and management practices in recent years (Lee and Clark 1996). Just as legitimate business organisations have adjusted to shifting technologies, the same has been true for transnational criminal organisations. Technology provides opportunities for, and threats to, criminal groups. We can distinguish two major groups of impacts that emerging communication and information technologies have had on transnational drug crime: indirect and direct.

15.3.1   Indirect Impacts of New Technologies

Indirect impacts on TCOs result from the significant growth in legitimate international business activity that new technologies have facilitated (Hagemann 2008). New technologies have enabled an expansion of markets and production sites and allowed the effective management and coordination of far flung operations. New trade routes have created novel opportunities for the trafficking of products and precursor chemicals. At the same time widespread deregulation of financial markets has made it easier to launder illicit profits, at least up until 2001. As the legitimate global economy has grown, so have illegitimate activities (Naim 2005).

15.3.2 Direct Impacts of New Technologies

More significant has been the direct utilisation of new technologies by TCOs. Transnational crime organisations appear to be driven by two key motives in employing such technologies. One is the conventional intention of using new technologies to improve productivity and the efficiency of consumption, production, distribution, and ancillary operations such as money laundering. The second motive, and one that distinguishes TCOs from most legitimate business, is the deployment of technologies to frustrate detection and intervention in their activities. Turning first to the efficiency effects of new technologies, these are apparent in several areas. In terms of consumption, the internet can be effective in encouraging new drug users. The "club" structure of the internet provides an efficient forum to exchange information, promote particular interests, and provide support to others. Of course this does not affect only drug taking, it is also apparent with regard to pornography (Eberstadt and Layden 2010). The internet is a powerful technology affecting drug experimentation primarily because it could encourage consumption by reducing the perceived risks of drug taking. In the virtual world there is no physical confrontation between buyers and sellers an experience which, in the real world, could act as a filter and deterrent (INCB 2001). The internet also provides opportunities to access drugs which may not be available locally. Drug production has also been affected by the growth of the internet. A huge amount of technical information is now available for those lacking specialist training to produce particularly ATS (Amphetamine type stimulants) such as methamphetamines. Evidence certainly suggests that such information is used: in the United States less than 10 % of suspects in the production of methamphetamine are trained chemists (INCB 2001). The proliferation of new types of designer drugs, the result of small molecular changes in existing controlled drugs, may also be encouraged by the availability of information on the internet.

New communications technologies have also enabled TCOs to change their strategies and structures. The internet has brought a massive rise in cyber crime which offers a low cost operating structure for criminal groups. Cyber crime operations require fewer resources, for example a physical presence may not be necessary, and the problems of clearly defining and prosecuting such offences across national borders mean that the perceived risks may be lower (INCB 2001). New low cost communication and control technologies have also enabled TCOs to diversify activities, achieving economies of scope. Drug trafficking networks can be used to move other contraband such as tobacco and counterfeit goods, even human cargo (Winterdyk et al. 2011). TCOs have also restructured their operations in ways that reflect the strategic imperatives of legitimate MNEs. Like many large organisations they have pursued greater flexibility and efficiency, decentralising and moving from hierarchical and clearly bounded structures to more cell-like configurations. Such arrangements enable greater specialisation and the opportunity to tap into the expertise of other specialist groups. Apart from their efficiency benefits, network structures offer several other advantages to the TCO. Multiple membership networks increase density which makes penetration and detection more difficult. Varying membership of networks also creates challenges for detection agencies. The profitability of the global drugs trade has created a strong demand for ancillary criminal services such as money laundering. Again, the internet has enhanced the efficiency of such activities. TCOs no longer need to use traditional money laundering centres characterised by banking secrecy, limited regulation and widespread corruption. Funds can now be moved quickly and easily to almost anywhere in the world in a range of forms including bonds, stocks and derivatives. Electronic funds transfer creates a problem for the authorities in that suspicions that might normally be raised through personal interactions or with the movement of large sums of cash can be evaded.

The second direct impact of technology is unique to criminal groups and is designed to obfuscate investigation and detection. Technologies have been used in a number of ways to frustrate detection. As well as the ability to transfer funds electronically, TCOs use encryption technologies to make the interception of communications more complex. They have engaged in electronic warfare in an attempt to detect intrusion. GPS shipping technologies can be used to determine the movement and location of shipments providing useful information on captures. For law enforcement agencies the internet in particular has made their task more testing. The rapid growth of internet pharmacies has made the monitoring of drugs sales very complex. At the same time the changing organisational structures of TCOs has created a test for the authorities.

One challenge has been the structural mismatch between protagonists. Most law enforcement agencies are conventionally structured: hierarchical organisations with clearly defined geographical scope. However, the global drugs business is now organised in ways which make such structures increasingly inappropriate (McConnell International 2000). Drug crime is global and multi-jurisdictional while TCO operating structures have become flatter, more specialised, and more fragmented. Effectively, those managing such operations increasingly 'orchestrate' and facilitate illicit global value chains (Gereffi et al. 2005), emulating the 'global factory' in the licit world (Buckley 2011). The same issues have been faced by anti-terrorist authorities (Van Cleave 2007). These changes in the strategies of TCOs will require enforcement agencies to rethink the ways in which they operate and greatly increase the need for cross-agency and cross-jurisdictional cooperation.

A second major challenge is the enforcement environment which applies to cyber crime. The novelty of such types of crimes means that there exists uncertainty in the interpretation of legal context. When crimes are committed in cyberspace it may not be clear which legal jurisdiction applies, how cross-border investigations should be conducted, and how rulings can be enforced when the accused resides overseas (Brenner and Schwerha IV 2002). Electronic evidence also creates problems since such evidence can be modified and admissibility questions may arise.

A third challenge for law enforcement agencies is the sheer pace of technological change and the resource costs of remaining at the technological forefront. Massive investments in technology and skilled manpower are required if drug law enforcement agencies are to remain germane. In particular, developing countries which are unable to make appropriate investments may present "locational advantages" to criminal groups based on their institutional failures (Enderwick 2009).

A fourth issue faced by agencies is the requirement to reconcile their need for effective regulatory powers and individual privacy rights. The extent to which communications can be legally intercepted or disrupted is by no means clear and a considerable body of legal precedents will need to be developed. Again, there is a corollary with the debates in a number of countries about possible tensions between individual rights and the effective prevention of terrorism.

These are all challenges that are not likely to be overcome easily and transnational crime seems to be increasing at a rate that exceeds cross-national cooperation and enquiry (INCB 2001).

15.4   Costs of the Drugs Trade

At the heart of most debates on drugs policy is consideration of the costs that the drugs trade brings. A key factor in the prohibition of drugs, particularly the first international attempts at narcotics control which occurred at the beginning of the twentieth century in response to growing concerns over opium, was the enormous costs that drugs impose, both on users and on society more generally. This rationale, although not always clearly articulated, also underpinned then United States President Richard Nixon's 1971 declaration of a "war on drugs". Illegal drug use imposes a wide range of costs. The most apparent are health costs. Illegal drug use is widespread with estimates suggesting that globally approximately 210 million people or almost 5 % of all adults used illicit substances in 2010 (UNODC 2011a). Such use brings obvious dangers: 200,000 people die annually from illegal drugs (UNODC 2011a), many as a result of an overdose. Obviously, different classes of drugs carry different costs and effects. Opiates such as heroin are the most damaging with the highest treatment costs, while cannabis is the most widely used drug. Those injecting drugs experience higher risks of diseases such as HIV and Hepatitis C. Estimates suggest that almost 20 % of drug users that inject are HIV-positive while the incidence rate for Hepatitis C is closer to 50 % (UNODC 2011a). In terms of numbers it is estimated that the number of people infected annually in the United States through sharing needles is 32,000 (Drug Policy Alliance 2010). Drug abuse is also related to many other social problems including family disintegration, job loss, and domestic violence. For drug users there are the obvious costs of financing a drug habit (prohibition tends to push prices up), which encourages other criminal activity, particularly property crime. Authorities in the United Kingdom estimate that drug dependency is responsible for the majority of crime, perhaps 85 % of shoplifting, 70–80 % of burglaries, and more than half of all robberies. These crimes cost the United Kingdom $25 billion a year (No 10 Strategy Unit 2003). It is suggested that half of all property crime in Britain is drug related (Travis 1998). Estimates for other countries such as New Zealand also confirm that around half of all crime is drug related (Berl economics 2009).

The global drugs trade also imposes other costs on society. The nature of illegal activities including drugs means that conventional approaches to enforcing transactions such as through contracts are not available. Rather, there is widespread resort to violence, and in the extreme case, killings. The FBI estimated that 5 % of U.S. murders in the late 1990s were drug related (FBI 2000). In Mexico, a major producer and supplier of illegal drugs, it is estimated that 90 % of murders are drug related (Carl 2009) and that more than 40,000 deaths between 2006 and 2010 were attributable to the drug wars (Hernandez 2011). It is no coincidence that globally, murder rates are highest in Central America (Honduras and El Salvador) as well as Jamaica, all centres of drug activity (UNODC 2011b). The widespread use of firearms in many of these murders is also linked to organised crime activities (UNODC 2011b). Central America is prone to violent drug crime as it is a key hub linking the supply of cocaine to both the North American and European markets, and major areas of coca production in Colombia, Peru and Bolivia. The profitability of the drugs trade, with gross profit margins of up to 300 %, creates the resources to corrupt public officials. Transnational criminal organisations contribute to political, economic and social instability through corrupt payments. When corruption becomes widespread the resulting conditions enable the growth of related forms of international crime including money laundering and human trafficking. In extreme cases the costs of corruption can be immense, threatening democratic rule and sustainable economic development, weakening regulatory controls and contributing to a perception of 'failed states' such as Afghanistan.

Further costs produced by the drugs trade are the negative externalities that arise. These are costs imposed primarily on third parties. One example is the likelihood of rising local addiction rates when a location becomes a major drugs hub. This seems to have occurred in a number of cases including the Dominican Republic (Fieser 2011). A further type of negative externality occurs in the production of illicit drugs. For example, in countries like Colombia the expansion of plantations is threatening jungle habitats. Processing in remote laboratories creates significant chemical waste and contaminated water. Efforts to eradicate illegal crops through the use of pesticides add to pollution problems. A third type of negative externality arises when the social chaos of rampant drug trafficking triggers widespread migration. In such cases costs are imposed on neighbouring destination states. For example, Ecuador is believed to have absorbed more than 150,000 Colombian refugees (AlertNet 2011). Drug prohibition may also adversely affect civil liberties, for example when banks are required to disclose information on suspected transactions or when workplace drug testing is mandatory. A particularly damaging aspect of the global drugs industry is the widespread involvement of young people. Because of the lower likelihood of imprisonment, minors are widely involved in the distribution and sale of illicit drugs (SAMHSA 2011). They may become involved in other drug-related crime, in the extreme even murder. Simply by being involved in the trade they face an increased risk of drug use and dependence (Johnston et al. 2011). Drug convictions can seriously affect future options for young people, impacting on their employment prospects, ability to obtain education funding, and access to substance abuse treatment. Such waste of young lives is extremely costly to any society.

One of the most widely criticised costs of the drugs trade is the resource costs involved. Medical and law enforcement costs in particular, mean resource scarcity elsewhere, even in related areas such as drug education, treatment, and preventative programmes. The extent of drug-related incarceration is staggering. In the United States alone the number of people imprisoned for drug violations rose from 50,000 in 1980 to more than half a million in 2010, a 1100 % increase. Drug arrests in the United States have more than tripled in the last 25 years, totalling more than 1.66 million arrests in 2009 with more than 80 % of these arrests simply for possession (Drug Policy Alliance 2010). The result is that the United States has the highest incarceration rate in the world at 743 per 100,000 people in 2009 and drug offences accounting for two-thirds of the federal prison population (Bureau of Justice Statistics 2011). The United States spends some $40 billion per year running the prison service while the war of drugs costs an estimated $51 billion each year (Drug Policy Alliance 2010). These are very considerable costs which are central to any meaningful discussion of appropriate drugs policy.

15.5   Ethics of the Global Drugs Trade

It is difficult to imagine a positive ethical case for the illegal drugs trade. This is true from either an ethical virtues position such as Aristotle, or a consequentialist position as reflected in utilitarianism. According to Aristotle, ethical virtues such as justice and temperance are fundamental to human wellbeing (Bostock 2000). Human happiness is the conscious result of virtuous activity and is not a random process. Rather, people are responsible for developing and applying such virtues. Aristotle labelled people who spurn virtuous behaviour because they see little or no value in such standards as evil. It could then be argued that those engaged in the drugs trade are intrinsically evil: they voluntarily choose actions which detract from their own, and others, happiness. In essence, they impose involuntary actions on others acting in ignorance. The drugs trade incorporates three undesirable forms of morality as highlighted by Aristotle: vice, incontinence and brutality. Vices are behavioural extremes which fall outside the bounds of virtuous behaviour. Incontinence is negative behaviour motivated by the desire for immediate gratification. As our earlier discussion suggests, brutality is a widely adopted form of governance within the drugs trade. Aristotelian ethics delineates certain emotions such as hate or spite and actions such as theft or murder as always wrong. This suggests that involvement in the illegal drugs trade is ethically wrong.

From a consequentialist perspective involvement in the drugs trade is also wrong. Utilitarianism (Lyons 1965) argues that the moral worth of an act should be determined by its impact and that any act can only be judged in the light of its consequences. The discussion in Sect. 15.4 suggests that the negative consequences of the drugs trade are both immense and enduring. Prohibition in the illegal drugs trade suggests that there are rules that should be followed to minimise the undesirable consequences created by the trade. We can also identify an analogy between what has been termed 'negative utilitarianism' (Popper 1945), the desire to minimise evil or harm, and the emerging policy perspective of harm minimisation (see below). Thus, the ethical yardstick of the global drugs trade appears straightforward: a business founded on the manufacture and trade of illegal substances known to inflict significant social and medical costs appears highly unethical. However, when we consider social and policy responses to the drugs "problem" things become less clear. While a policy of prohibition of drugs makes any involvement in the business illegal and unethical, consideration of alternative policy prescriptions such as decriminalisation of (some) drugs raises complex ethical considerations. In such instances policy decisions need to incorporate the "harm principle", that is the extent to which policy serves to reduce harmful effects. The policy focus shifts from an attempt to eliminate drug use (reducing consumption), to reducing the deaths, diseases, crime and social breakdown associated with prohibitionist policies that many judge to have failed.

The harm reduction concept could be seen as a consequentialist approach to drug policy, emphasising outcomes rather than any policy intent and adopting an amoral perspective on drug use. Supporters claim that harm reduction offers a "value-neutral" discourse which is necessary since a moral position (that drugs are always wrong), inhibits rational debate and means that drug policy can never be evidence based (Hathaway 2001). Social policy, it is argued, should be reasoned, evidence-based, and not built purely on prejudices.

15.5.1   The Case for Prohibition

The case that is made for drug prohibition has several facets. At its most basic prohibitionists highlight the nature of the product and the reasons why drugs were outlawed in the first place. Their harmful nature means that society is better off banning their use. Drugs which harm users also damage society by imposing costs on families, the economy and society. The utilitarian argument for prohibition is then simple: prohibition limits the availability and use of drugs. It does this in a number of ways: limiting supply, raising prices, imposing deterrent penalties and unambiguously denouncing drug use. In this way the associated harms of drug use are also minimised. While this appears to be a strong argument it requires some qualification. Some harm to others such as justified punishment is acceptable and not all wrongful harm, for example adultery, is deemed criminal (Smith 2002). Logically, prohibition should also be extended to other commodities such as alcohol, tobacco and fatty foods that generate significant social costs. The exceptional position of drugs is clear from estimates of such social costs. Drug abuse in the U.S. was estimated to bring annual costs of $181 billion, marginally lower than those of tobacco ($193 billion) and alcohol ($235 billion) (ONDCP 2004).

This estimate for drug expenses is only a partial one and does not include costs such as family disintegration, loss of employment, or domestic violence.

Prohibition also recognises the addictive qualities of drugs. Critics of prohibition argue that individuals should be free to make informed choices regarding drug use. However, there are doubts as to whether such choices would be rational or rather, determined by dependency. Recent evidence suggests that drug addiction is more than just a biochemical process in the brain. It has its roots in both the biology of the individual, how susceptible they are to addiction, and the environment in which they live. There is evidence to suggest that some people have an "addictive personality" (NIDA 2010). If true, this raises significant ethical issues since the "problem" is not randomly distributed and the case for protecting the vulnerable becomes a strong one, perhaps strong enough to justify prohibition. Prohibitionists argue that legalization to decriminalize drug use would be a dangerous gamble. While it might reduce the harm associated with drugs it would almost certainly expand drug use increasing harm overall. Furthermore, it would be almost impossible to reverse legalization once legalized drugs became widely used and accepted. Supporters of prohibition also argue that even if drug exclusion policies have not achieved expected results it does not follow that drugs should be decriminalised. They cite the analogy that murders still happen despite the law, but nobody supports decriminalising murder.

15.5.2   The Case Against Prohibition

The case against drug prohibition and in support of decriminalisation is one that has recently received high level endorsement (Global Commission on Drug Policy 2011; Latin American Commission on Drugs and Democracy 2009). The case against prohibition is a powerful one which draws on a number of perspectives.

The first argument is that adults should enjoy a moral freedom to use drugs (Smith 2002). In a liberal and democratic society adults should have the right to live their lives the way they choose, provided they do not infringe the rights of others. Evidence on the widespread use of drugs throughout most of recorded history suggests that eliminating drugs is probably not a realistic goal. While in principle such an argument appears to have merit, as suggested earlier, it is hard to argue that dangerous drug use impacts only on the user and not on others.

A second, and more damning case against prohibition is simply that it has failed. In 1998 the United Nations committed member states to achieve what it termed a "drug-free world" promising to eliminate or significantly reduce consumption of the three leading narcotics—heroin, cocaine and cannabis—within a decade. While a goal of zero tolerance of drug use is unrealistic—there simply are not the resources to investigate and prosecute every drug crime—the reality is drug use actually increased over this period. For example, it is estimated that production of marijuana in the United States has increased ten-fold since 1980 (Gettman 2006). A more colloquial argument often heard is if we cannot keep our prisons drug-free, then we can hardly expect a drugs free society.

Further evidence of the failure of the war on drugs is provided by detection rates. Given available resources, current detection rates are too low to enable an effective prohibition policy. United Nations estimates suggest that only 10–15 % of heroin and 30 % of cocaine shipments are intercepted worldwide. The detection rate would need to be closer to 70 % to substantially curtail supply. In part the failure of prohibition policies may be the result of a lack of understanding of the critical components of the international drugs industry. Conventional policy approaches have emphasised controlling the source, that is, eradicating crops in the field. The experience of Peru is illustrative of the challenges. A 12 year programme of eradication of coca plants was temporarily suspended because the authorities believed that it had little impact. Peru now produces almost as much coca as Colombia and the policy focus has switched to catching major traffickers (Romero 2010). Support against a prohibitionist stance is also found in the considerable social and medical costs of drug use. Despite the war on drugs there has been an increase in the number of drug overdose deaths (Girion et al. 2011) as well as drug-related epidemics including HIV, hepatitis B, and hepatitis C (Barrett et al. 2009). In addition, prohibition has spawned significant social and criminal costs with drug-related crime, widespread corruption and vast costs of incarceration (Dorsey and Middleton 2010). The Associated Press reports that the cost of the war on drugs since 1971 exceeds US$1 trillion (Associated Press 2010). This estimate is based on budgets to tackle drug crime and takes no account of the social costs. For many observers the resource costs of customs, police, and the court and prison systems, far outweigh results. Critics of prohibition also see a parallel with the failed US experiment on alcohol prohibition in the 1920s which hugely benefitted emerging organised crime (Okrent 2010). Replacing prohibition would provide opportunities to tackle the drugs problem in new ways. Of relevance is the example of tobacco where education has brought about declining use and a recognition of the significant costs of smoking, certainly in developed countries. Critics of prohibition suggest that there are also lessons to be learned from the management of alcohol where it is abuse of a lawfully available substance that attracts penalties and not supply and possession which effectively stimulates a black market and organised crime.

A third argument against prohibition is that it creates perverse effects, impacts that are contrary to policy intentions. One example is the prospect that banning drugs adds to their mystique and encourages experimentation, the so-called "forbidden fruit" effect. There are also perverse effects in the market for drugs because that market has been driven underground. Prohibition pushes up prices and inflates profit margins creating strong incentives to produce or sell illegal drugs. At the same time such a market offers no assurances on quality control and significant profits are untaxed. Because drug users do not identify as "victims" the risks of apprehension are low and deterrence is achieved by increasing the amount of resources deployed and the severity of punishments. However, research suggests that increased law enforcement leads to increased drug market violence (Werb et al. 2011). Because of the nature of incentives (and sanctions) the drugs trade is dominated by ruthless groups who readily employ violence and seek ways to minimise the probability of detection (complex network and hierarchical structures) as well as the employment of those like juveniles who may face less severe penalties (Heyne 2008). Supply by criminal groups also encourages continual expansion of the market with strategies such as giving free drugs to new users in the expectation of creating dependency.

15.5.3 The Challenges of Decriminalisation

There are strong pressures in many countries for a reconsideration of drugs policy. The most persuasive argue the need for comprehensive change and the range of problems that prohibition has created. The Global Commission (2011) provides a wide ranging attack on prohibition emphasising the need for three major, and interrelated, changes: the decriminalisation of drug use when there is no harm to others; legal regulation of the drugs market to wrest control from organised crime groups; and the adoption of education and treatment programmes. Such a view suggests that drug problems are multifaceted and exist within a complex social and health environment. However, moving from prohibition to some form of decriminalisation and regulation will present a number of challenges.

An obvious one is increased policy complexity. One of the attractions of a policy of prohibition is its simplicity. If drugs are prohibited, cultivation, trafficking, possession and use are relatively straightforward offences to define. If some form of decriminalisation were to apply then policy must embrace more subtle nuances. For example, are all drugs—recreational and medicinal—to be included? At what age are people judged to be responsible for decisions on drug use? What degree of intervention in the forms of education or treatment should the state provide? Clearly, an effective alternative to prohibition would necessitate careful design.

Second, decriminalisation would have to be accompanied by comprehensive regulation. Failure to introduce regulation would simply reinforce the already well entrenched position of organised crime. Regulation would need to ensure quality and safety of supply, to provide for anti-drug education, and to ensure hazard reduction strategies such as the provision of clean needles. In combination, such policies could work to reduce the power of organised crime, to lower demand, and to decrease social and health risks.

A third policy requirement would be the need to differentiate between different classes of drugs and to provide detailed and relevant information on the risks associated with each. One of the disadvantages of prohibition is that it treats all illegal drugs as similar, implying that they carry comparable risks. This is not the case and there is a danger that people could perceive the risks to be exaggerated promoting scepticism. A necessary condition for decriminalisation would be the creation, and acceptance, of an accurate drug classificatory system based on scientific measures of harm (Nutt et al. 2007).

Another challenge for anti-prohibitionists is their notion of the sovereign individual acting in a rational and autonomous way. Such a concept has limited applicability in the case of drugs where problems of addiction and dependency arise. The United Nations suggests that of the estimated 250 million drug users worldwide, some 10 % or 25 million people, could be classified as dependent or problem drug users (UNODC 2008). The nature of addiction means that such individuals are unable to act in rational ways and provision for their management would need to be made. This highlights the important point that emphasising the reduction of harm in society does not always equate to a reduction of harm to the drug user (Miller 2001). There is also an important morality issue here. Harm reduction advocates often portray drug users as unlucky and largely submissive victims. This abrogates individual responsibility for the condition and the likelihood of overcoming it (Fitzpatrick 2000). In essence, the authorities assume responsibility for the actions of the individual (Dalrymple 2006) which seems inconsistent with the utilitarian principle of individual liberty.

There have been experiments in both harm reduction and in legal liberalisation. A number of European countries including Switzerland, Germany and the Netherlands operate needle exchange booths providing free syringes in an attempt to limit the spread of viruses such as Hepatitis C and HIV. Similar programmes have also been adopted in parts of Canada and Australia. The sharing of equipment among injecting drug users accounts for almost one-third of new HIV infections in the world outside sub-Saharan Africa. Needle exchange programmes do seem to contribute to harm reduction (Palmateer et al. 2010). An useful overview of global programmes of harm reduction is provided in Harm Reduction International (2010). Relaxation of drugs laws has been attempted in a number of cases. Sixteen U.S. states have legalised medicinal marijuana and Britain reclassified cannabis from a Class B to a Class C drug in 2004 but reversed the decision in 2009. Perhaps the best test case is provided by Portugal which decriminalised all illicit drugs in 2001. The available evidence suggests that this did not lead to major increases in drug use and that legal system overcrowding and some drug-related harms have been reduced (Greenwald 2009; Hughes and Stevens 2010).

Despite a growing amount of evidence suggesting the possible benefits of decriminalisation and regulation, there remains significant resistance to policy change. Changing institutional structures will be a major challenge. At the country level government agencies concerned with policymaking, budget allocation and policy implementation are not designed to integrate drug policies. In most cases there is a major separation between law enforcement and public health agencies. Decriminalisation and regulation will necessitate massive organisational restructuring if policy goals are to be achieved. There is a similar separation and well entrenched criminal focus at the global level when we consider the principal agencies of the United Nations (UNODC, INCB and CND). Politicians supporting drug reform also face considerable opposition. Public attitudes fashioned over a 40 year period of the "war on drugs" see reform as a sign of weakness within political advocates. Whilst reform may make sense in terms of effective resource use, public opposition appears formidable (Newcombe 2004; Walker 1994).

While it is beyond the scope of this chapter, any move from prohibition to decriminalisation of drugs would involve far reaching institutional and policy changes. Some of the possible options have been outlined in a number of useful discussion documents (Transform 2006, 2009). There is a further immorality when we consider the distribution of the costs and "profits" of the illicit drugs trade. The drugs trade generates both huge monetary profits and social costs. Studies suggest that the vast majority of these profits are captured in predominantly drug consuming nations, principally within Europe and the United States. Profits are then laundered through the Western banking system, with a large proportion allegedly passing through the city of London. In recent years a number of major banks including HSBC and Wachovia Bank have been implicated in drug money laundering. A study of Colombia revealed that only 2.6 % of the value of cocaine produced in that country remains there. The vast majority (97.4 per cent) of profits are captured by global crime syndicates and laundered in the West (Gaviria and Mejia 2011). Prohibition works to sustain such inequality as it maintains high drug prices (and profits) while transferring the costs of the drugs trade (violent crime, high rates of incarceration, medical costs and associated crime costs) to producer and trafficking nations.

15.6 Conclusion

In this chapter we have examined the international drugs industry, a significant force in the illegal global economy. Our discussion highlights a number of conclusions. The first are the marked similarities between the global drugs industry and other, legitimate, global sectors. There is evidence of both types of business responding to the pervasive forces of globalisation and consolidating their competitive positions through strategic and structural changes. Fragmentation of activities, outsourcing, network type structures and a deepening of global reach are characteristic of both legitimate and illegitimate global industries. Second, the global drugs industry is a ready adopter of new information and communications technologies. While such technologies offer efficiency benefits to all global organisations, for organised crime they also offer new ways to avoid detection. Understanding and responding to such strategies is an ongoing challenge for law enforcement agencies. Third, our discussion makes clear that the global drugs industry has been moulded, in large part, by the operation of a policy of prohibition, and in particular, the four decade war on drugs. This stance appears to have consolidated the position of organised crime and to have produced massive economic, social and health costs. The ethical issue is the question of how best to control the drugs industry, and in particular the relative merits of prohibition versus decriminalisation and regulation. Growing discontent with the effectiveness of a policy of prohibition has pushed this debate to the political foreground but it remains an extremely divisive one.

References

Alertnet. 2011. Colombians seek refuge in Ecuador. *AlertNet* (14 January). www.trust.org/alertnet/news.

Associated Press. 2010. *After 40 years, $1 trillion, U.S. war on drugs has failed to meet any of its goals*. Associated Press (13 May).

Barrett, D., C. Cook, R. Lines, G. Stimson, and J. Bridge. 2009. *Harm reduction and human rights. The global response to drug-related HIV epidemics*. London: International Harm Reduction Association.

Berl economics. 2009. *Costs of harmful alcohol and other drug use*. Final Report to Ministry of Health and ACC BERL Economics, Wellington, New Zealand.

Bostock, D. 2000. *Aristotle's ethics*. New York: Oxford University Press.

Brenner, S.W., and J.J. Schwerha IV. 2002. Transnational evidence gathering and local prosecution of international cybercrime. *The John Marshall Journal of Computer and Information Law* 20(3): 347.

Buckley, P.J. 2011. International integration and coordination in the global factory. *Management International Review* 51(2): 269–283.

Bureau of Justice Statistics. 2011. *Office of justice programs*. www.bjs.ojp.usdoj.gov.

Carl, T. 2009. *Progress in Mexico drug war is drenched in blood*. Associated Press (Nov 3).

Dalrymple, T. 2006. *Romancing opiates: Pharmacological lies and the addiction bureaucracy*. New York: Encounter.

Dorsey, T.L., and P. Middleton. 2010. *Drugs and crime facts*. Washington DC: U.S. Department of Justice, Bureau of Justice Statistics.

Drug Policy Alliance. 2010. *Making your voice heard 2010 annual report*. New York: Drug Policy Alliance.

Dunning, J.H. 2000. The eclectic paradigm as an envelope for economic and business theories of MNE activity. *International Business Review* 9: 163–190.

Eberstadt, M., and M.A. Layden. 2010. *The social costs of pornography*. Princeton, NJ: The Witherspoon Institute.

Economist. 2001. *Stumbling in the dark: Special report on illegal drugs*. The Economist (28 July).

Enderwick, P. 2009. Applying the eclectic framework: The strategy of transnational criminal enterprises in the global era. *Critical Perspectives in International Business* 5(3): 170–186.

FBI (Federal Bureau of Investigation). 2000. *Crime in the United States, 1999*. Washington, DC: U.S. Government Printing Office.

Fieser, E. 2011. *Drug addiction surges in Dominican Republic*. GlobalPost (22 August).

Fitzpatrick, M. 2000. *The tyranny of health: Doctors and the regulation of lifestyle*. London: Routledge.

Gaviria, A., and D. Mejia. 2011. *Anti-drugs policies in Colombia: Successes, failures and wrong turns*. Bogota: Ediciones Uniandes.

Gereffi, G., J. Humphrey, and T. Sturgeon. 2005. The governance of global value chains. *Review of International Political Economy* 12(1): 78–104.

Gettman, J. 2006. Marijuana production in the United States. *The Bulletin of Cannabis Reform* 2: 1–28.

Girion, L., S. Glover, and D. Smith. 2011. *Drug deaths now outnumber traffic fatalities in the U.S., data shows*. Los Angeles Times.

Global Commission on Drug Policy. 2011. War on drugs. Report of the global commission on drug policy. www.globalcommissionondrugs.org.

Greenwald, G. 2009. *Drug decriminalization in Portugal: Lessons for creating fair and successful drug policies*. Washington: Cato Institute.

Hagemann, H. 2008. Consequences of the new information and communication technologies for growth, productivity and employment. *Competitiveness Review* 18(1/2): 57–69.

Harm Reduction International. 2010. *The global state of harm reduction 2010*. London: Harm Reduction International.

Hathaway, A. 2001. Shortcomings of harm reduction: Toward a morally invested drug reform strategy. *International Journal of Drug Policy* 12: 125–137.

Havocscope. 2012. Estimates of global drug trafficking. www.havocscope.com/black-market/drugtrafficking.

Hernandez, D. 2011. *How many have died in Mexico's drug war?* Los Angeles Times (7 June).

Heyne, P. 2008. An economic perspective on illegal drugs. In: *Are economists basically immoral? and other essays in economics, ethics and religion.* Indianapolis: Liberty fund.

Hughes, C.E., and A. Stevens. 2010. What can we learn from the Portuguese decriminalization of illicit drugs? *British Journal of Criminology* 50(6): 999–1022.

INCB. 2001. *Report of the international narcotics control board for 2001. Globalisation and new technologies: Challenges to drug law enforcement in the 21st century.* Vienna: INCB.

Johnston, L.D., P.M. O'Malley, J.G. Bachman, and J.E. Schulenberg. 2011. *Monitoring the future: National survey results on drug use 1975–2010 vol 1, secondary school students.* Ann Arbor: The University of Michigan, Institute for Social Research.

Latin American Commission on Drugs and Democracy. 2009. Drugs and democracy: Towards a paradigm shift. www.drugsanddemocracy.org.

Lee, H.G., and T.H. Clark. 1996. Impacts of the electronic marketplace on transaction cost and market structures. *International Journal of Electronic Commerce* 1(1): 127–149.

Lyons, D. 1965. *Forms and limits of utilitarianism.* New York: Oxford University Press.

McConnell International. 2000. *Cyber crime...and punishment? Archaic laws threaten global information.* Washington DC: McConnell International.

Miller, P. 2001. A critical review of the harm minimization ideology in Australia. *Critical Public Health* 11(2): 167–178.

Naim, M. 2005. *Illicit: How smugglers, traffickers and copycats are hijacking the global economy.* New York: Doubleday.

Newcombe, R. 2004. *Attitudes to drug policy and drug laws: A review of the international evidence.* www.tdpf.org.uk/newcombe2004.pdf.

NIDA. 2010. *Drugs, brains, and behavior: The science of addiction. National Institute on Drug Abuse.* Bethesda, Maryland: National Institute of Health, U.S. Department of Health and Human Services.

North, D.C., J.J. Wallis, and B.R. Weingast. 2006. *A conceptual framework for interpreting recorded human history.* NBER Working Paper No 12795. Cambridge, MA: National Bureau of Economic Research.

No 10 Strategy Unit. 2003. *No 10 strategy unit drugs report phase one—understanding the issues,* 12 May, London.

Nutt, D., L.A. King, W. Saulsbury, and C. Blakemore. 2007. Development of a rational scale to assess the harm of drugs of potential misuse. *Lancet* 369: 1047–1053.

Okrent, D. 2010. *The rise and fall of prohibition.* New York: Scribner.

ONDCP. 2004. *The economic costs of drug abuse in the United States, 1992–2002.* Washington DC: Executive Office of the President (Publication No 207303).

Palmateer, N., J. Kimber, M. Hickman, S. Hutchinson, T. Rhodes, and D. Goldberg. 2010. Evidence for the effectiveness of sterile injecting equipment provision in preventing hepatitis C and human immunodeficiency virus transmission among injecting drug users: A review of reviews. *Addiction* 105(5): 844–859.

Popper, K.R. 1945. *The open society and its enemies, vol. 1. Plato.* London: Routledge and Kegan Paul.

Romero, S. 2010. *Coca production makes a comeback in Peru.* The New York Times.

Smith, P. 2002. Drugs, morality and the law. *Journal of Applied Philosophy* 19(3): 233–244.

Substance Abuse and Mental Health Services Administration (SAMHSA). 2011. *Results of the 2010 national survey on drug use and health: Summary of national findings.* NSDUH Series H 41. Rockville, MD: US Department of Health and Human Services.

Transform. 2006. *After the war on drugs: Options for control.* Bristol: Transform Drug Policy Foundation.

Transform. 2009. *After the war on drugs: Blueprint for regulation*. Bristol: Transform Drug Policy Foundation.

Travis, A. 1998. *Drugs 'boosting property crime'*. The Guardian (22 April).

UNODC. 2002. *Results of a pilot survey of 40 selected organized criminal groups in 16 countries: Global programme against transnational organised crime*. Vienna: United Nations Office on Drugs and Crime.

UNODC. 2008. *World drug report 2008*. Vienna: United Nations Office on Drugs and Crime.

UNODC. 2011a. *World drug report 2011*. Vienna: United Nations Office on Drugs and Crime.

UNODC. 2011b. *Global study on homicides: Trends/contexts/data*. Vienna: United Nations Office on Drugs and Crime.

U.S. Department of State. 2010. *International narcotics control strategy report*. Washington, DC: U.S. Department of State, Bureau of International Narcotics and Law Enforcement Affairs.

Van Cleave, M.K. 2007. *Counterintelligence and national strategy*. Washington, DC: National Defense University Press.

Walker, S. 1994. *Sense and nonsense about crime and drugs: A policy guide*. Belmont, CA: Wadsworth Publishing.

Werb, D., G. Rowell, G. Guyatt, T. Kerr, J. Montaner, and E. Wood. 2011. Effect of drug law enforcement on drug market violence: A systematic review. *International Journal of Drug Policy* 22(2): 87–94.

Winterdyk, J., B. Perrin, and P. Reichel (eds.). 2011. *Human trafficking: Exploring the international nature, concerns and complexities*. Boca Raton, FL: CRC Press.

Yeh, A. 2006. *China becoming drawn into global drugs trade*. Financial Times (June 23).

Chapter 16
Money Laundering Compliance—The Challenges of Technology

Louis de Koker

Abstract Anti-money laundering (AML) and counter-terrorist financing (CTF) measure focus on the abuse by criminals of technology and new payment systems to hide the flows of illicit funds. The AML/CTF system itself, however, uses technology to monitor transactions, identify potential suspicious and unusual transactions and report them to the authorities. This chapter considers the AML/CTF framework, technology and ethical implications relating to customer monitoring and reporting. The AML/CTF framework, especially in relation to new payment methods such as mobile money, gives rise to privacy risks. Mobile money systems are capable of collecting and storing large amounts of data on clients. In countries that are subject to rule of law, this data is shared with the state within a legal framework. Many mobile money models are, however, operating in countries where the rule of law is weak. The ethical implications of providing access to the client data in both types of jurisdictions are often neglected by AML/CTF practitioners. This chapter discusses risk and risk management in the context of mobile money and highlights some of the complexities that face compliance officers who need to ensure compliance but also appropriate protection of legitimate interests of clients. With increasing international consensus that millions of socially vulnerable people should be included in the formal financial system, appropriate balancing of potentially competing interests is of increasing importance.

16.1 Introduction

This paper focuses on anti-money laundering (AML) and counter-terrorist financing (CTF) compliance challenges posed by technology. While much of the AML/CTF discussion regarding technology is focused on how criminals and terrorists employ new payment methods and technology to evade current controls (Financial Action

L. de Koker (✉)
Deakin Law School, Centre for Cyber Security Research,
Deakin University, Geelong, Australia
e-mail: louis.dekoker@deakin.edu.au

© Springer International Publishing Switzerland 2016
M. Dion et al. (eds.), *Financial Crimes: Psychological, Technological,
and Ethical Issues*, International Library of Ethics, Law,
and the New Medicine 68, DOI 10.1007/978-3-319-32419-7_16

329

Task Force 2010), this chapter considers the AML/CTF framework, technology and ethical implications from a monitoring and reporting perspective. New technologies, especially new payment methods, are often viewed with suspicion by law enforcement because it may give rise to money laundering and terrorist financing (ML/TF) risks. The AML/CTF framework, especially in relation to new payment methods such as mobile money, also gives rise to privacy risks. Mobile money systems are capable of collecting and storing large amounts of data on clients. In countries that are subject to rule of law, this data is shared with the state within a legal framework. Many mobile money models are, however, operating in countries where the rule of law is weak. The ethical implications of providing access to the client data in both types of jurisdictions are often neglected by AML/CTF practitioners. This chapter discusses risk and risk management in the context of mobile money and highlights some of the complexities that face compliance officers who need to ensure compliance but also appropriate protection of legitimate interests of clients. With increasing international consensus that millions of socially vulnerable people should be included in the formal financial system, appropriate balancing of potentially competing interests is of increasing importance.

16.2   The Global AML System

Money laundering refers in essence to acts performed in respect of proceeds of crime that change or hide the criminal origin of these funds, in order to allow the criminal to spend the ill-gotten gains with impunity. Criminals have engaged in laundering activity for many ages. Those who needed to hide the true nature of their ill-gotten gains were often able to rely on third parties to assist them. Thieves and robbers, for example, could rely on fences who buy stolen goods. Apart from receipt of stolen goods and general criminalisation of acts of accessories, these acts did not attract the much legal attention. These acts were often simply viewed as the natural conduct of a criminal. As drug syndicates grew in wealth and power, however, law enforcement concerns about criminals hiding behind veils of bank secrecy increased (Rider 1993). The 1970 Bank Secrecy Act of the United States heralded an important change in the traditional approach. It created a framework for new record-keeping obligations for American bankers to assist law enforcement and also introduced an obligation to report suspicious activity and certain large cash transactions (Villa 1988). This Act was adopted to facilitate the combating of organised crime and drug trafficking in the United States but it provided an example of anti-laundering action that could be taken by other countries too.

In the mid-1980s policymakers internationally began to consider co-ordinated action against money laundering (Shams 2001; Reuter and Truman 2004). This occurred in the context of increasing pressure to confiscate assets acquired through drug offences. Important voices were raised against drug-related money laundering both by criminals abusing financial institutions and by institutions turning a blind eye to the true nature of the funds that they were handling. The US and UK took the lead by criminalising the laundering of proceeds of crime, with countries such as Australia following in quick succession. Policy decisions on proceeds of crime at a national level also informed the international negotiations of the text that became the 1988 Vienna Convention. This Convention became the first international instrument to include anti-money laundering measures.

One year later the G7 plus 1 convened a task team to recommend measures to assess the results of existing international cooperation to prevent the abuse of financial institutions for money laundering and to consider additional preventative measures to enhance multilateral action (G7 1989). In 1990 this task team, known as the Financial Action Task Force, submitted a brief report with 40 recommendations on steps to be taken to take to improve national legal systems, enhance the role of the financial system and strengthen international cooperation against money laundering (Financial Action Task Force 1990). These recommendations became known as the FATF Recommendations. They soon hardened into international standards that guided the design of AML laws of all countries, coupled with a peer review mechanism to evaluate the level of compliance of countries with these standards. The Recommendations were revised in 1996 and complemented by a set of Special Recommendations of Terrorist Financing in 2001 when the global security concerns prompted the broadening of the FATF mandate to terrorist financing. The FATF Recommendations were further detailed in a 2001 revision and in 2012 both sets were revised and consolidated in a single set of Recommendations (Financial Action Task Force 2012a).

The FATF Recommendations set standards on a variety of matters including the criminalizing of money laundering; measures to be taken by regulated businesses to perform specified customer due diligence (CDD); measures to ensure that they identify their customers correctly and understand their business and business patterns; the content of legal duties to report suspicious transactions to the authorities; and the establishment and maintenance of a national financial intelligence unit (FIU) to receive and analyse suspicious transaction reports (STRs) and provide intelligence to the appropriate law enforcement agencies. The Recommendations also address appropriate regulation and supervision of financial activities as well as other high risk business and professional activities; law enforcement powers and capacity, especially relating to asset forfeiture; and powers and capacity to support cross-border cooperation in criminal matters. The FATF Recommendations are not legally binding but are authoritative. They are endorsed by more than 190 jurisdictions and are supported by key international institutions such as the United Nations Security Council, World Bank and International Monetary Fund.

Much of the impact of the FATF Recommendations stems from its system of mutual evaluation of compliance with the standards, combined with indirect economic penalties for non-compliance. The FATF, the World Bank, the International Monetary Fund and FATF-Style Regional Bodies, regional groupings of countries within the FATF framework, cooperate to publicly evaluate the level of compliance by countries with the Recommendations (International Monetary Fund 2011;

Financial Action Task Force 2013a). The names of countries that fail to comply are published and they are exposed to countermeasures by compliant countries and their financial institutions. The threat of economic penalties has proved powerful to move countries towards compliance (International Monetary Fund 2011).

16.3 The FATF Recommendations and Financial Institutions

The FATF Recommendations are mainly aimed at financial institutions although the focus was broadened in 2001 to other non-financial businesses that face a high money laundering or terrorist financing risk, the so-called "Designated Non-Financial Business and Professions" (DNFBPs).

The FATF has an activity-based definition of "financial institutions". The definition is therefore not aimed at specific types of institutions but rather at legal or natural persons who conduct as a business one or more of a range of financial activities for or on behalf of a customer. These activities include acceptance of deposits and other repayable funds from the public, lending and money or value transfer services. In general therefore banks, insurance companies, money remitters and security brokers are covered. DNFBPs on the other hand include casinos, real estate agents, dealers in precious metals and stones, lawyers, notaries, other independent legal professionals and accountants and trust and company service providers (Financial Action Task Force 2012a).

The Recommendations and consequently national laws require these institutions to adopt measures to mitigate their risk of abuse for money laundering or terrorist financing purposes. Banks therefore adopted and implemented policies to support AML/CTF processes in their organisations, especially relating to identifying and verifying the identities of their clients and ensuring that they understand the sources of income and business of their higher value clients (Dion 2012). Banks also appointed money laundering compliance officers to assist banks to meet their compliance obligations. These officers assist in the management of money laundering and terrorist financing risk. They generally ensure that employees are trained on the relevant processes, monitor compliance with CDD processes and manage AML/CTF reporting obligations (Verhage 2009).

While compliance obligations receive much attention, it is important for purposes of this chapter to note that AML/CTF laws altered the relationship between regulated institutions and their clients. Banks are private sector service providers that traditionally served their clients within a contractual private law framework. AML/CTF laws added a number of public obligations to this relationship. Banks were enlisted by the state to support crime combating by carefully selecting their clients through CDD processes, by monitoring their transactions and by confidentially filing reports with a state agency where transactions appear suspicious and unusual. The grafting of these public duties on a private relationship may give rise to legal and ethical conflict in given cases and require closer attention.

16.3.1 KYC/CDD

Banks gather extensive information on clients as part of their AML/CTF obligations. The gathering and verification of client information by regulated institutions
is generally referred to as CDD or "Know Your Customer" processes. These processes are aimed at denying services to undesirable clients and at collecting sufficient information to enable a bank to monitor a client's transactions for suspicious
and unusual transactions. Banks generally gather the following information about a
client (Basel Committee on Banking Supervision 2001; Basel Committee on
Banking Supervision 2016; Financial Action Task Force 2013b):

(a) name and any other names used;
(b) permanent address;
(c) contact particulars such as telephone numbers and an e-mail address;
(d) date and place of birth;
(e) nationality;
(f) occupation, public position held and/or name of employer;
(g) an official personal identification number or other unique identifier contained
     in an unexpired official document; and
(h) signature.

In some countries, such as Indonesia, the client's religion is also captured in
standard account opening processes (Bester et al. 2008). Additional information is
required when a client poses a higher money laundering or terrorist financing risk.
This is for example the case in respect of Politically Exposed Persons (PEPs)
(Greenberg et al. 2010). These are persons who hold prominent public functions,
senior politicians, senior government, judicial or military officials, senior executives
of state owned corporations and important political party officials (Gilligan 2009).
They hold positions that may be abused for corruption and therefore regulated
institutions must exercise greater care when dealing with them, their close associates and their family members. In practice that means that clients are screened
against lists of known PEPs and other high risk customers to ensure appropriate risk
management where a client is identified as a PEP (Geary 2010; De Koker and
Harwood 2015). In addition, clients have to be screened to ensure that they do not
appear on national or international sanctions lists, for instance lists of known terrorists linked to the Taliban or Al Qaeda or as persons who are implicated in
proliferation of weapons of mass destruction.

16.3.2 Monitoring and Reporting

The AML laws require banks to monitor the accounts of their clients. In practice
large banks divide their clients into groups based on the information that the bank
has about its clients. The risk that each group posed is assessed and, based on that
risk, a client's transaction is scanned against the information that the bank has in

respect of that client, against transaction patterns of the client's peer group and against known money laundering patterns (Financial Action Task Force 2013b). Counterparties may also be scanned against lists of high risk individuals.

Monitoring is complex and most large banks therefore use expensive automated transaction and client monitoring systems to support the monitoring processes. These systems scan transactions against client information, known patterns of money laundering and terrorism and often names of specific listed persons. Transactions that meet specified parameters, for example large cash transactions, and clients whose names appear similar to listed names, are flagged for further attention. In large institutions, depending on the sensitivity of the monitoring settings, numerous transactions are flagged daily. The flagging is merely an alert that a particular matter meets the institution's parameters for matters requiring closer attention. Transactions and clients that were flagged have to be reviewed and more information may be required before decisions regarding reportability can be made.

This review process has to be done in person, often by compliance officers and sometimes by trained analysts who support the compliance function. They need to consider the facts available to the bank to determine whether a suspicious transaction report should be filed with the FIU. The analysis is generally not particularly comprehensive. The analysts are working under pressure. Neither is the intention that the investigation should establish that a crime was committed. The objective is merely to determine whether there are grounds for a suspicion that give rise to a reporting obligation. In English law that suspicion, if entertained, is not required to be clear, firmly grounded or reasonable. (*Shah and Anor v HSBC Private Bank (UK) Ltd* [2012] EWHC 1283 (QB)). The analysts furthermore lack investigative powers and the analysis is mainly limited to the institutional data on the client (Verhage 2009). In many cases the institutional data may be outdated. Clients have little incentive to alert their banks to a change in employment or even a change of address, for example where the client receives statements electronically. Often large institutions may have different sets of data on the same client, gathered each time the client applied for another product or service. The analyst must consider this confusing picture without contacting the client as that may amount to a tip-off about money laundering concerns and a potential report to the authorities. Tipping-off is in itself a serious offence (Goldby 2012).

If a report is filed, the financial intelligence unit will generally not return and provide feedback on each report. General feedback may be provided, for example how the number of reports filed by the bank compares with those of its peers and the general value of the reports filed. Whether the decision to file a specific report was therefore correct, is not generally confirmed or denied. Occasionally there may be a request for further information. Such a request indicates that the authorities are looking into the report or a matter relating to the client or the report, but feedback as to whether that investigation actually delivered any law enforcement value is not provided. FIUs operate in confidence and information is only shared with law enforcement and intelligence partners in that country and abroad. As a consequence, analysts work largely in the dark.

The result of this fairly ineffective reporting regime is that many transactions that should be reported are probably not. This failure is of obvious interest to law enforcement (Goldby 2012). This discussion focuses, however, on the other side of the coin: many transactions that ought to remain private and confidential are disclosed to the authorities. In addition, the system is designed to keep this information from the clients. This, it is argued, puts a huge obligation on compliance officers not only to act in legally correctly but also in a manner that is ethically responsible.

As a final note, it should be pointed out that many countries compel banks not only to report suspicious and unusual transactions but all transactions involving specified cash amounts or foreign wire transfers. In these countries regulated institutions provide large blocks of client and transactional information data to the FIU. With this brief introduction and overview of key aspects of the AML/CTF system, the paper turn to banks and the impact of their surveillance role on their duty of confidentiality to their clients.

16.4   Sharing Confidential Client Information with the State

Banks generally owe a legal duty to keep a client's information confidential. This duty arises from the contract with the client and the nature of the services delivered. In a number of countries, especially tax havens, the duty is re-enforced by criminal law, making it an offence to release information of a client to third parties (Palan 2002). In most countries, however, the duty of confidentiality is not absolute. Under English law, for example, the court in *Tournier* (*Tournier v National Provincial and Union Bank of England* [1924] 1 KB 461) famously recognised the banker's duty of confidentiality and secrecy but also four exceptions where the banker may disclose such information, i.e. where the bank is compelled by law to disclose the information; if the bank has a public duty to disclose the information; if the bank's own interests require disclosure; and where the client agreed to the information being disclosed.

AML/CTF laws compel banks to report suspicious transactions. Statutory reports of suspicious transactions therefore resort under the first *Tournier* exception. This exception, however, covers reports that clearly meet the reporting requirements. As discussed above, over-reporting or defensive reporting, depending on the facts, may amount to a breach of a duty to keep the client's information confidential. In practice, given the limited information that analysts can access, many innocent transactions are reported to the authorities.

Courts have recognised that compliance officers experience difficulty to comply in good faith with their AML/CTF reporting obligations. They have therefore not imposed very high legal expectations on compliance officers making these decisions. Many countries require these reports to be filed when there are reasonable grounds for a suspicion. In the United Kingdom the law does not impose an explicit reasonable grounds threshold to be crossed before a report is filed. In *K Limited v*

National Westminster Bank, for example, Longmore LJ stated *(K Limited v National Westminster Bank plc* [2007] 1 WLR 311 par 21):

> The existence of suspicion is a subjective fact. There is no legal requirement that there should be reasonable grounds for the suspicion. The relevant bank employee either suspects or he does not. If he does suspect he must (either himself or through the bank's nominated officer) inform the authorities.

This approach was affirmed in *Shah and Anor v HSBC Private Bank (UK) Ltd* [2012] EWHC 1283 (QB)).

British compliance officers should therefore file a report when they think that there is a possibility, which is more than fanciful, that a transaction involves proceeds of crime or financing of terrorists. The suspicion must be more than a vague feeling of unease but does not need to be "clear" or "firmly grounded and targeted on specific facts"(*R v Da Silva* [2006] EWCA Crim 1654) or, as stated above, even based upon "reasonable grounds".

The British approach leaves clients of British banks with little legal protection for the confidentiality of their financial information. It is not clear whether systems that require the presence of reasonable grounds for a suspicion before a reporting duty is triggered provide clients with higher levels of protection. The compliance system is generally geared towards over-reporting (De Koker and Symington 2011; De Koker and Symington 2014). Over-reporting or defensive reporting is the result of the design of the reporting obligations. There are significant statutory penalties for money laundering and the failure to report but no statutory penalties for reporting a matter that should not have been reported. When in doubt, it is therefore safer to file a report. An avalanche of unwanted information is not necessarily appreciated by the FIU, but the data still goes into its database and remains available for future use in that country or an exchange with another country. Over-reporting may constitute a breach of the banker's duty to maintain client confidentiality but that aspect receives little legal attention. Reporting obligations, their current structure and effect become even more vexed when the information is disclosed in an environment where it may be abused by state organs.

16.4.1   Potential for Abuse of Access to Information by the State

The FATF standards are aimed at providing law enforcement access to financial information of clients. One of the FATF's main objectives was to break down bank secrecy barriers that shielded criminals. The standards are therefore not designed to ensure protection of client information against inappropriate access and usage by government agencies. Abuse of the access to information provided by the AML/CTF framework is difficult to identify and prove. Suspicious transaction reports are filed confidentially. The FATF standards enforce confidentiality to protect the institutions and its employees from retaliation by criminal clients and to allow law enforcement to investigate the matter without alerting the client. The report and any subsequent requests for further information therefore occur in confidence. Whilst this lack of transparency is justifiable, it also creates space for potential abusive practices.

Concerns have been raised in a number of cases that some countries or agencies selectively implemented AML/CTF laws against political opponents or used the laws to pursue other political or other objectives (Chaikin and Sharman 2007, 18–13, 69–72; Götz and Jonsson 2009, 68; Tang and Ai 2010, 219). While appropriately structured FIUs may withstand political pressures and take action against aberrant employees who may on rare occasions abuse their access to data, many FIUs are not in that fortunate position. These FIUs, often located in developing countries, lack sufficient and effective protective measures to ensure that their powers are exercised for proper purposes. Their governance structures are not sufficiently strong to protect them from abuse for political purposes. The Egmont Group and the World Bank undertook a survey of FIUs in 2008 to take stock of key aspects of their governance structures. 65 countries participated in the survey (Egmont Group and World Bank 2010). The results indicated that there are grounds for concern.

A significant number of FIUs reported that their heads were political appointees that lacked independence. The heads of 46 % of the administrative FIUs were appointed by a minister, by cabinet or by the head of state. The heads of 34 % of the FIUs were appointed to fixed terms of office while 62 % did not have fixed terms. Heads of FIUs are not necessarily politically neutral. Only 47 % of the FIUs reported "that membership or management of political parties or bodies are prohibited for heads of FIUs, as are other political activities as well as certain business activities or directorships."

72 % of FIUs reported that they cannot be given instructions or guidance from another state body concerning the conduct of the FIU's assignment. While this reflected well on the majority of FIUs that responded to the survey, it left questions marks about the 28 % that could not report a similar level of independence. This has to be read with the fact that 60 % of the respondent FIUs reported that they "are not governed by any oversight or review board or other governing body that determines policies of strategies with regard to operational matters, or strategies concerning non-operational matters." The data that regulated institutions disclose to FIUs is not necessarily shielded from other government agencies and functionaries. More than half of the respondent FIUs reported that some other state body or judicial authority had access to the FIU's data holdings. 62 % reported that they could (or had to) disclose their findings or the results of their analyses to a superior authority (for example a ministry, the government or a supervisory authority).

While the study confirmed that many FIUs were appropriately structured and met basic good governance requirements, it raised concerns about those that are not. A significant number of these are located in developing countries that generally have weaker protection of privacy and other civil liberties. It is furthermore important to note that disclosure of information to a well-structured FIU does not mean that it may not be shared with FIUs in other countries that are more vulnerable to political interference and abuse. The FATF standards provide a framework in which FIUs share information with each other. Although most FIUs will not share information with an FIU that does not meet basic structural criteria in terms of independence, it is clear from the Egmont survey that this bar is not necessarily set very high. Once information is released its correct usage cannot be ensured. As this happens in confidence at an international level, civil society cannot monitor or identify abuses with ease.

16.4.2 Technology Increasing the Numbers of Clients and Amount of Data

The development of the global AML/CTF system coincided with the development of mass financial services. Formal financial services have become so entrenched in modern life that those who do not have a bank account or a means to make or receive electronic payments are generally at a disadvantage.

The ability and, in some countries, the right to access basic financial services therefore began to receive more attention in the past decade. Ways had to be found to overcome obstacles that people faced when trying to access financial services. These barriers differ from country to country (Demirgüç-Kunt et al. 2008). Many of those who are excluded do not have sufficient funds to merit a savings account. However, many cite the relative high costs of services, the geographic distance to the closest service point, a lack of trust in financial services for cultural or religious reasons and a lack of documents that are required to verify identity in order to access services (De Koker 2006; Financial Action Task Force 2011; Demirguc-Kunt et al. 2015). Global attention to financial inclusion intensified when global policymakers realised that nearly a half of the world's adult population lacked access to financial services and that much can be gained socially and economically by providing them with access to appropriate products and services. According to the World Bank's 2014 Global Findex 2 billion adults worldwide did not have a bank account (Demirguc-Kunt et al. 2015). These adults are located primarily in developing and low capacity countries.

Reaching out to such a large number of potential clients is, however, not feasible or cost-effective with traditional branch-based banking. Though technology such as Automated Teller Machines would play a role, even this technology is expensive and difficult to maintain and service in remote rural areas. More promising is mobile phone-based banking services.

Mobile banking services, generally referred to as mobile money, are rendered via the mobile phones of clients (Chatain et al. 2011). This form of service, especially to enable existing clients of banks to communicate with their bank and make balance enquiries or even payments, has been available in many developed countries for some time. It parallels the use of internet banking services. In a number of developing countries where governments support financial inclusion, mobile money services have gone one step further, enabling the client to establish the business relationship or open a bank account via the mobile phone. Non face-to-face account opening is revolutionising financial services in developing countries by enabling providers to reach out to clients in remote rural areas (Groupe Speciale Mobile Association 2016).

The mobile money framework involves generally a bank, a telecommunications company that provides the mobile phone service and a network of agents, which in developing countries are often the small retailers that also sell airtime vouchers to mobile phone users. In many countries the lead role is taken by the bank or the financial service provider. In some countries, for example Kenya, the regulator allowed the telecommunications company to play the major role with the bank merely holding the account where the money of the clients is pooled (Buku and Meredith 2013). Clients are able to open an account over the phone without personal contact with any bank employees. Cash-in and cash-out services are provided by the agents and in some urban areas by ATMs too.

16.5   Mobile Money and AML

While mobile money can advance financial inclusion, it also poses money laundering and terror financing risks (FATF 2013c). A World Bank analysis (Chatain et al. 2008, 2011, 33) identified the key risks as anonymity, elusiveness, rapidity and poor oversight. Anonymity and elusiveness are closely-linked to non face-to-face-account opening processes combined with the lack of public sources of information that could verify the identity of users in many developing countries. Even where a client's identity is established upfront, the phone and user details can be handed to another who may operate that account unbeknown to the provider. Many mobile phone users in developing countries share the use of a single phone and the true identity of a person who performed a specific transaction may therefore be elusive. Rapidity is the risk relating to the fast transfer of funds. The sheer speed of transactions complicates attempts to interdict transactions and confiscate proceeds of crime or financing of terrorism. Poor oversight is the risk that the traditional financial services and telecommunications regulators fail to work together to identify and mitigate the risks of mobile money through effective regulation and appropriate oversight.

These financial integrity risks must be weighed against financial integrity benefits that can be advanced by mobile money. People who do not have access to formal financial services often rely on informal service providers, for example hawaladars, to send and receive remittance or informal credit providers. If funds are stolen, these clients generally have little recourse. In addition, they sustain informal financial services that can in turn be abused to launder money or fund terror. Formalisation therefore promotes integrity objectives and support effective AML/CTF frameworks (Financial Action Task Force 2011, 2012b). The FATF provided space for the development of appropriate new payment methods and mobile money when it introduced a risk-based approach (RBA) to certain elements of AML/CTF regulation and compliance. This approach was optional when it was first acknowledged in 2003, but certain aspects have become mandatory when the Recommendations were revised in 2012.

The cornerstone of the RBA is risk assessment. Under Recommendation 1 countries are expected to "identify, assess and understand" their money laundering and terrorist financing risks. That assessment will then inform appropriate regulatory and other risk mitigation measures. Countries should also require their AML/CTF regulated institutions to undertake risk assessments to mitigate their institutional ML/TF risks. These institutional assessments determine the intensity of the CDD measures that are adopted (De Koker 2013). The FATF's risk-based approach allows countries to exclude activity from AML/CTF regulation where the activity is limited and pose a low level of ML/TF risk. Regulated institutions on the other hand are urged to follow a risk-based approach to manage their compliance obligations. They need to undertake institutional risk assessments to distinguish their high and lower risk customers, transactions and services. Enhanced due diligence is required in relation to high risk customers, transactions and services. In cases where the level of risk was assessed as lower, regulators could allow, and institutions may consider employing, simplified due diligence measures. This FATF scheme therefore allows simplified due diligence in relation to mobile money services provided that the money laundering and terror financing risks are assessed as lower. The assessment should focus on the residual risk of the model, that is the level of risk that remains after the imposition of controls. In the case of mobile money, such controls often include strict usage control limits, for example allowing only low value transactions to be concluded, reinforced by daily and monthly limits to prevent the laundering of a large amount by splitting it amongst a series of smaller transactions.

Many mobile money models were therefore developed with appropriate controls to justify simplified due diligence measures (Solin and Zerzan 2010). Simplified due diligence measures may, however, undermine the effectiveness of account monitoring (De Koker 2011) and, as a result, may lead both to fewer reports of actual criminal activity and more disclosure of information of innocent clients to the authorities. This is of particular concern given the ability of mobile money to generate client data and the fact that this data is often held by more than one party in the mobile money provider chain.

16.5.1 Extensive Data

Mobile money generates far more data about clients than normal financial services do. Although the formal client records of the financial service provider may hold limited information about a client, the communication data and other data produced by the client and his handset may reveal much about the client (Naef et al.

2014). Communication data reflects social patterns and contacts of the client. If the phone is used for transactions, the client profile is enriched by data about the client's financial transactions and spending patterns (De Koker and Jentzsch 2013). The data itself can be sufficiently rich to enable analysts to correctly identify an unidentified client. In addition, the mobile phone handset can act as a tracking device enabling analysts to track the movements of the user and, if required, to locate and apprehend the user (Chatain et al. 2011).

16.5.2 Records Held by Both the Bank and the Telecommunications Provider

The data generated by mobile money is furthermore in the hands of more than one provider. While the bank may hold extensive client records, client data held by the mobile telecommunications operator will often be richer. Although they also owe duties of confidentiality to their clients, they do not share the banker's tradition and culture of client confidentiality. In practice, therefore, telecommunication providers often provide information to law enforcement more freely and informally than bankers would. This does not happen in the public eye but according to the evidence of three different South African telecommunication providers in *S v Agliotti* (*S v Agliotti* 2011 (2) SACR 437 (GSJ) (S. Afr.) such practices are not necessarily isolated.

   The Agliotti prosecution was a particularly important organized crime prosecution in South Africa's modern legal history. It was also politically sensitive as it involved a former South African Police Commissioner who was imprisoned for corruption and links to organised crime. The Agliotti prosecution failed, amongst others, because the integrity of important mobile phone records was questioned. During an examination of these records and the way in which information was exchanged with law enforcement, it came to light that several South African mobile phone service providers had not been protective of client privacy when law enforcement requested information, sometimes releasing information on the promise that due legal processes will be followed and providing data of clients that are not subject to any criminal investigation. Three senior fraud and forensic representatives from three different telecommunication service providers testified. They were called by the prosecution to tender evidence about certain cellular phone calls which were made to or from certain cellular phones registered to or in the names of the accused and related parties. Although they assured the court that mobile phone records were only issued out upon receipt of a court-issued subpoena, cross-examination of the representative of one company revealed instances where records were provided merely on the promise that the police official will apply for such a subpoena. The representative of another mobile service provider testified that they had furnished the police with about fifty lever arch files filled with mobile phone records in respect of various people. Nobody could explain in court what had happened to all the data as only a small portion was handed in and used as exhibits in the case.

Abuse of the system by the police was also demonstrated by the defence team during the cross-examination of the three representatives. For example, it transpired that the police subpoenaed and obtained, amongst many others, mobile phone records of the accused's attorney, the accused's advocate and counsel, the counsel's father and some of his clients and even of a lawyer who was not linked to the case. In these cases the police did not have sufficient grounds to justify a subpoena and either misrepresented facts to the judicial officer who issued it, or that officer failed to scrutinise the application. The mobile telecommunications representatives testified that they did not consider the evidence on which subpoenas were obtained and whether the reach of the subpoena was justified. If the investigators produce a subpoena, they will provide the information. This was often done in a spirit of goodwill and based on a long-standing relationship with law enforcement. The interests of the client and whether investigators were acting beyond the law was not being considered.

16.5.3 Increased Chances of Errors in the Filing of STRs

The simplified due diligence measures that are employed in relation to mobile money increases the chances of errors. If automated monitoring systems identify unusual transactions, analysts have less client information at their disposal to determine whether a suspicious transaction report is warranted (De Koker 2011). Less information decreases the chances that actual criminal transactions are identified and increases the chances of unnecessary or incorrect reports of innocent transactions.

16.6 Ethical Perspectives

Reporting occurs within a legal framework, but is it ethical to submit such reports on clients? Legal and ethical obligations tend to overlap as the law generally reflects moral principles of society. Legal rules, however, do not necessarily express ethical principles and hence what is legal may not always be ethical. For purposes of this paper it is submitted that a distinction should be made between filing a statutory suspicious transaction report on conduct that is clearly linked, or reasonably suspected to be linked, to criminal behaviour and the filing of such reports transactions without reasonable grounds. I restrict this analysis to the reporting of suspicious transactions rather than the routine reporting of higher value transactions. The latter has primarily an administrative purpose while the former is explicitly aimed at combating crime.

In general, the filing of a statutory report on clear or reasonably suspected criminal conduct would be ethical. Private information of the client is being disclosed but it is done to protect society against crime. Applying a utilitarian ethical approach, the harm to the individual is justified by the advancement of the legitimate interests of the greater number of law-abiding citizens. The decision to file such a report would also qualify as ethical in terms of a Kantian approach as the compliance officer is striving to ensure that the bank does not support criminal actions that may harm vulnerable people. By alerting the authorities to criminal acts and potential threats to abuse the bank, the compliance officer promotes honesty and respect for society. The courage, good faith and wisdom displayed by such a decision would also meet the Aristotelian requirements for ethical conduct.

The issue is more complicated when the bank has legitimate reasons to fear the political abuse of such a disclosure, for example where the client is a leader of the opposition and the transaction is linked to conduct that may be illegal but not unethical, for example, humanitarian assistance to a person who is being persecuted by the country's authoritarian government. If the bank files a report, it would be acting as an agent of an oppressive regime. Such a decision may be legal in terms of the laws passed by, or abused by, that government but is unlikely to qualify as ethical in terms of the tests outlined above. The question whether to file a report is, however, best considered more holistically in conjunction with all the other ethical questions that arise when business is done in such a political environment (Holliday 2005).

The second group of reports are those that are filed because they display some element of a potentially suspicious transaction, but not sufficient reasonable grounds to suspect that the transaction involves proceeds of crime or financing of terrorism. These often comprise the bulk of suspicious transaction reports that are filed. They are filed because banks lack the time and resources to look deeper into the issues, the reporting framework prevents them from contacting the customer for more information and because the fear of penalties and often the desire to impress the regulator tend to weigh the decision in favour of reporting (De Koker and Symington 2014). It is submitted that it is unlikely that such reports are filed ethically. From a utilitarian perspective it is cannot be argued that they advance the greater good. They may have a negative impact on the client but they tend to clog the law enforcement system with reports that add little value. From an Aristotelian perspective a decisions to file a report in these cases primarily to protect the reporter and the bank against penalties and despite the absence of reasonable grounds for a suspicion do not display personal virtues of courage, good faith and wisdom. Also from a Kantian perspective these reports cannot be said to reflect moral rights and duties such a respect for customers, honesty and the duty to assist vulnerable people.

16.7   Conclusion

Technology enables financial institutions and governments to gather more data on clients than ever before and also to mine the data more effectively than in the past. Financial inclusion initiatives are broadening the reach of this system to millions of socially vulnerable clients in developing economies. These countries often lack strong legal and institutional mechanisms to protect privacy and client confidentiality. This raises concerns regarding responsible and ethical corporate compliance with statutory information-sharing responsibilities.

Financial institutions should comply with the law and should support legitimate state action against crime by preventing the abuse of their services by criminals and terrorists and by reporting such instances where they occur. Although financial institutions owe a duty of confidentiality to their clients, such disclosures are both legal and ethical. Both as compelled disclosures and as disclosures in the public interest they also fall within the recognised *Tournier* exceptions to bank secrecy. Unfortunately, however, many of the transactions that are reported do not involve proceeds of crime or funding of terror and do not support crime combating. The reality is that it is generally very difficult for a bank to determine whether an unusual transaction involves money laundering or terrorist financing or not. They have limited information at their disposal and limited powers and means to investigate such a transaction. More information is therefore being shared than what was envisaged by the designers of the AML/CTF framework.

When determining whether to report a transaction or not, banks are often viewed as balancing their own commercial and risk management interests against the public interest to combat crime and terrorism. There is however a third party to this process: the client. As the AML/CTF framework focuses on crime and criminal clients, little attention is given to this party. However, most clients whose information is disclosed in terms of this framework are honest, law-abiding citizens whose transactions happen to meet the very general criteria for potentially suspicious transactions.

It is submitted that privacy and the interests of law-abiding clients should receive more protection. However, the decisions that affect them are taken in backroom operations far from scrutinising eyes. The law and business practice entrusted these decisions to compliance officers. They are therefore best placed to increase the level of protection of innocent clients. In order to do that, they need the support of the senior management of the business. They also need a thorough understanding not only of the legal framework but also of their ethical obligations to the institution and the state. They need to appreciate the conflicts that arise in this area and the impact of their decisions on society and on the clients of the institutions in general.

The FATF can also play an important role to ensure a balanced approach. It is however, unlikely that the law enforcement-oriented bodies such as the FATF will emerge as champions of the privacy rights of law-abiding clients. The FATF does however have an interest in ensuring that information disclosed in an STR or shared cross-border is not abused for political purposes. Such abuse will threaten the sustainability of the STR system and of international exchanges of AML/CTF disclosures. The FATF's mutual evaluation methodology that is applied to determine the extent to which a country complies with the global AML/CTF standards, can assess the political independence of an FIU as well as the arrangements to ensure that data released by the FIU is used for law enforcement purposes. The enquiry could extend to the structures and processes that protect privacy and the mechanisms at the disposal of clients that suspect that their financial privacy was breached by an AML/CTF-related report or disclosure.

Bank supervisors should also pay closer attention to banks' AML/CTF policies and processes regarding reporting of transactions to ensure that only those transactions that fall within the ambit of the AML/CTF laws are reported and that banks take appropriate steps to protect the confidentiality of their clients.

All stakeholders should furthermore ensure that clients understand the legal rules regarding AML/CTF disclosures. This is especially important in respect of new clients who are first generation users of formal financial services. The routine reporting of non-criminal client data where clients are unaware of the risks of such disclosure is difficult to defend on ethical grounds. It is submitted that knowledge and privacy oversight mechanisms will be of even greater importance as millions of socially vulnerable people are provided with, and encouraged to take up, formal financial services.

References

Basel Committee on Banking Supervision. 2001. *Customer due diligence for banks*. Basel: Basel Committee on Banking Supervision.

Basel Committee on Banking Supervision. 2016. *Sound management of risks related to money laundering and financing of terrorism*. Basel: Basel Committee on Banking Supervision.

Bester, H., D. Chamberlain, L. de Koker, C. Hougaard, R. Short, A. Smith, and R. Walker. 2008. *Implementing FATF standards in developing countries and financial inclusion: Findings and guidelines*. Washington DC: FIRST Initiative, The World Bank.

Buku, M., and M. Meredith. 2013. Safaricom and M-PESA in Kenya: Financial inclusion and financial integrity. *Washington Journal of Law, Technology & Arts* 8(3): 375–400.

Chaikin, D., and J. Sharman, 2007. *APG/FATF anti-corruption/AML/CTF*, FATF/APG. Research Paper. Sydney: Asia-Pacific Group on Money Laundering.

Chatain. P.-L., R. Hernández-Coss, K. Borowik, and A. Zerzan. 2008. *Integrity in mobile phone financial services: Measures for mitigating risks from money laundering and terrorist financing*. World Banking Working Paper 146. Washington, DC: The World Bank.

Chatain, P.-L., A. Zerzan, W. Noor, N. Dannaoui, and L. de Koker. 2011. *Protecting mobile money against financial crimes: Global policy challenges and solutions*. Washington, DC: The World Bank.

De Koker, L. 2006. Money laundering control and suppression of financing of terrorism: Some thoughts on the impact of customer due diligence measures on financial exclusion. *Journal of Financial Crime* 13(1): 26–50.

De Koker, L. 2011. Aligning anti-money laundering, combating of financing of terror and financial inclusion: Questions to consider when FATF standards are clarified. *Journal of Financial Crime* 18(4): 361–386.

De Koker, L., and J. Symington. 2011. *Conservative compliance behaviour: Drivers of compliance responses to AML/CFT laws in the financial services industry in South Africa*. Midrand: FinMark Trust, Centre for Financial Regulation and Inclusion.

De Koker, L. 2013. The 2012 revised FATF recommendations: Assessing and mitigating mobile money integrity risks within the new standards framework. *Washington Journal of Law, Technology & Arts* 8(3):165–196.

De Koker, L., and N. Jentzsch. 2013. Financial inclusion and financial integrity: Aligned incentives? *World Development* 44: 267–280.

De Koker, L., and J.W.G. Symington. 2014. Conservative corporate compliance: Reflections on a study of compliance responses by South African banks. *Law in Context* 30: 228–254.

De Koker, L., and K. Harwood. 2015. Supplier integrity due diligence in public procurement: Limiting the criminal risk to Australia. *Sydney Law Review* 37(2): 217–241.

Demirgüç-Kunt, A., T. Beck, and P. Honohan. 2008. *Finance for all? Policies and pitfalls in expanding access*. Washington, DC: The World Bank.

Demirguc-Kunt, A., L. Klapper, D. Singer, and P. Van Oudheusden. 2015. *The Global Findex database 2014: Measuring financial inclusion around the world*. Policy Research Working Paper 7255. Washington, DC: World Bank Group.

Dion, M. 2012. The moral discourse of banks about money laundering: An analysis of the narrative from Paul Ricoeur's philosophical perspective. *Business Ethics: A European Review* 21(3): 251–262.

Egmont Group, World Bank. 2010. *Executive summary of the final report on survey of FIU governance arrangements*. http://www.egmontgroup.org/library/egmont-documents. Accessed 28 August 2012.

Financial Action Task Force. 1990. *Report*. Paris: Financial Action Task Force.

Financial Action Task Force. 2010. *Money laundering using new payment methods*. Paris: Financial Action Task Force.

Financial Action Task Force. 2011. *Anti-money laundering and terrorist financing measures and financial inclusion*. Paris: Financial Action Task Force.

Financial Action Task Force. 2012a. *The FATF recommendations*. Paris: Financial Action Task Force.

Financial Action Task Force. 2012b. *Declaration of the ministers and representatives of the financial action task*. Paris: Financial Action Task Force.

Financial Action Task Force. 2013a. *Methodology for assessing technical compliance with the FATF Recommendations and the effectiveness of AML/CFT systems*. Paris: Financial Action Task Force.

Financial Action Task Force. 2013b. *Anti-money laundering and terrorist financing measures and financial inclusion*. Paris: Financial Action Task Force.

Financial Action Task Force. 2013c. *Guidance for a risk-based approach to pre-paid cards, mobile payments and internet-based payment services*. Paris: Financial Action Task Force.

G7. 1989. *Paris economic declaration*. Paris: G7.

Geary, J.M. 2010. PEPs—Let's get serious. *Journal of Money Laundering Control* 13(4): 103–108.

Gilligan, G. 2009. PEEPing at PEPs. *Journal of Financial Crime* 16(2): 137–143.

Goldby, M. 2012. Anti-money laundering reporting requirements imposed by english law: Measuring effectiveness and gauging the need for reform. *Journal of Business Law* (forthcoming).

Götz, E., and M. Jonsson. 2009. Political factors affecting AML/CTF efforts in post-communist Eurasia: The case of Georgia. *Journal of Money Laundering Control* 12(1): 59–73.

Greenberg, T.S., L. Grey, D. Schantz, C. Gardner, and M. Latham. 2010. *Politically exposed persons: A guide on preventive measures for the banking sector*. Washington, DC: The World Bank.

Groupe Speciale Mobile Association. 2016. *2015 State of the industry report: Mobile money*. London: GSMA.

Holliday, I. 2005. Doing business with rights violating regimes corporate social responsibility and Myanmar's military junta. *Journal of Business Ethics* 61(4): 329–342.

International Monetary Fund. 2011. *Anti-money laundering and combating the financing of terrorism (AML/CTF): Report on the effectiveness of the program*. Washington, DC: International Monetary Fund.

Naef, E., P. Muelbert, S. Raza, R. Frederick, J. Kendall, and N. Gupta. 2014. *Using mobile data for development*. Boston: Cartesian and Bill & Melinda Gates Foundation.

Palan, R. 2002. Tax havens and the commercialization of state sovereignty. *International Organization* 56(1): 151–176.

Reuter, P., and E. Truman. 2004. *Chasing dirty money: The fight against money laundering*. Washington, DC: Institute for International Economics.

Rider, B.A.K. 1993. The practical and legal aspects of interdicting the flow of dirty money. *Journal of Financial Crime* 3(3): 234–253.

Shams, H. 2001. The fight against extra-territorial corruption and the use of money laundering control. *NAFTA: Law and Business Review of the Americas* 85: 85–133.

Solin, M., and A. Zerzan. 2010. *Mobile money: Methodology for assessing money laundering and terrorist financing risks*. London: GSMA.

Tang, J., and L. Ai. 2010. Combating money laundering in transition countries: The inherent limitations and practical issues. *Journal of Money Laundering Control* 13(3): 215–225.

Verhage, A. 2009. Between the hammer and the anvil? The anti-money laundering-complex and its interaction with the compliance industry. *Crime Law and Social Change* 52(1): 9–32.

Villa, J.K. 1988. A critical view of bank secrecy act enforcement and the money laundering statutes. *Catholic University Law Review* 37: 489–509.

Chapter 17
New Technologies and Money Laundering Vulnerabilities

Jun Tang and Lishan Ai

Abstract As the Internet becomes more and more a worldwide phenomenon, prepaid card system, internet payment services, and mobile payment services are potentially subject to a wide range of vulnerabilities that can be exploited for money laundering. Numerous third-party payment service providers offer individuals the ability to make online purchases, funding accounts with wire transfers, money orders, and even cash. In most cases, the provider of this service will not have a face-to-face relationship with its customers and may even allow anonymous accounts. As the development of new technologies of information and communication has created opportunities for criminals to misuse such technologies for the purposes of money laundering. On the other hand, new technology can also be applied to increasing anti-money laundering efficiency and quality. This chapter aims to demonstrate money laundering risks associated with new technology-based financial activities, to introduce enterprise-wide AML information solution, to explain basic principles of risk-based approach, and to demonstrate Chinese practice regarding on money laundering vulnerabilities related to new-tech payment system.

17.1 Emerging Money Laundering Risks

Businesses are becoming increasingly global and interconnected as they continue to engage in E-commerce. This will enhance the risks of identity-related financial crime through use of modern technology. International AML theory holds that money launderers universally want to use the weaknesses of financial regulation system to combine the dirty money into legitimate economic system, and the

J. Tang (✉)
School of Statistics and Mathematics, Zhongnan University of Economics and Law,
Wuhan, Hubei 430073, China
e-mail: James_tang97@yahoo.com.cn

L. Ai
School of Political and Social Inquiry, Monash University, Melbourne, Australia
e-mail: Ali_shane1127@hotmail.com

© Springer International Publishing Switzerland 2016   349
M. Dion et al. (eds.), *Financial Crimes: Psychological, Technological,*
and Ethical Issues, International Library of Ethics, Law,
and the New Medicine 68, DOI 10.1007/978-3-319-32419-7_17

possibility of being monitored and detected in the regulatory blind pot or regulatory weak point where is relatively low. Thus, emerging payment instrument with loose regulation can be exploited in any step of the three stages of money laundering, namely placement, layering and integration.

The Australia Institute of Criminology (AIC) identified some elements that will facilitate technology-enabled crime, including developments in the digitisation of information, especially relating to the widespread use of broadband services and mobile and wireless technologies, and the evolution of electronic and internet payment systems (AIC 2007, 36), creating a number of vulnerabilities. Key among these is that networks and their data can be accessed remotely without physical access being required, and this facility assists both the user and the criminal. Indeed, the most significant emerging money laundering risks are identified in funds transfers, including stored value cards (or prepaid cards), mobile payments and internet payments.

There are a number of features of the internet which attract criminals, including anonymity, lack of 'face to face' contact, speed of transactions, access to globalised processes and new payment technologies, and the cross border activity (Filipkowski 2008, 18). The adoption of encryption techniques and the facility for remote transfer increase extraordinarily the anonymity of electronic money. It is difficult to adequately implement customer identification and record keeping on electronic transactions, let alone carry out the obligations of suspicious transaction report (STR) on them.

Indeed, Recommendation 8 of the 2003 Financial Action Task Force on Money Laundering *Forty Recommendations* (FATF 2004, 4) states that

> [F]inancial institutions should pay special attention to any ML threats that may arise from new or developing technologies that might favour anonymity, and take measures, if needed, to prevent their use in money laundering schemes. In particular, financial institutions should have policies and procedures in place to address any specific risks associated with non-face-to-face business relationships or transactions.

Moving to June 2008, FATF published another specific report named *Money Laundering & Terrorist Financing Vulnerabilities of Commercial Websites and Internet Payment Systems* to re-emphasize the importance of regulating internet payment systems. Based on the investigations from over twenty countries and regions, the report provides main characteristics and actual case studies of money laundering activities through commercial websites and internet payment systems, and proposed associated risk management measures (FATF 2008, 12). In addition, FATF first delivered the specific *Report on New Payment Methods* in 2006, and then revised this to present a new version in October 2010, which noted new payment methods are substantially different from traditional transactions, and all countries should closely monitor these (FATF 2010). Indeed, the report concludes that potential vulnerabilities associated with commercial website and internet payment systems may not necessarily constitute a higher risk for the online sector than for the offline sector, as long as the sector and the relevant competent authorities understand the potential risk, and appropriate risk-based measures with regard to customer identification, record keeping and transaction reporting are taken.

17.2 Customer Identification in Non-face-to-Face Transactions

New payment methods (NPM) and technological innovation have brought financial service industries into a new era. Increasingly, transactions are conducted via non-traditional channels. Customers do not have to physically contact financial service providers, and can even perform transactions beyond geographic limits. As the only proof of customer identity, the registered information left by customers on the occasion of opening an account is absolutely inconsistent with the accuracy and adequacy of customer due diligence (CDD) requirements. Unfortunately, a set of feasible methods for determining the real identification of online customers and controlling their online transactions has not yet been determined in many jurisdictions.

Linked with a specific bank account, internet payment services may come from different parts of the world, and there are no geographic restrictions (FATF 2008, 23). Both the registration and transactions could in certain circumstances be performed anonymously. On certain websites, an anonymous email address is enough to make registration and operate transactions. Connections to commercial websites and internet payment systems are available everywhere in the world, and if one owns a legal bank account in a country it can be used to conduct transactions across international borders at any time. This can create problems when screening and monitoring account activities, and information technologies enable internet payment transactions to be performed automatically and with little human intervention in the process, making it more difficult for law enforcement to locate and to pursue criminals and money launderers. Indeed, the mentioned issues can be abused for laundering illicit fund at the placement stage.

Increasing money laundering risks and challenges for reporting regulated, regulators and supervisors may be involved when the customer is absent for the purpose of physical identification. Indeed, it has been observed that 'the more automated the banking and financial system becomes, the less 'face to face' contact between clients and employees and the greater the holes in the detection net' (McCusker 2004, 47). Financial institutions and other reporting entities should therefore, have measures to cope with non-face-to-face transactions, and must ensure that the customer's identity is established properly and adequately, such as through the provision of additional documentary evidence by the customer. The institutions should also ensure that the first operational payments are carried out through an account opened in the customer's name (Handoll 2006, 152).

17.3 Anti-money Laundering Risk Management

The movement for the adoption of practical AML policies was influenced by a growing awareness of money laundering vulnerabilities that had previously lain hidden in every possible aspect of financial transactions, from the customer, transaction interface, payment instruments, financial services and products, and so on. These emerging challenges and potential money laundering risks placed financial sectors and non-financial payment industry in a difficult position, and forced them to keep reviewing previous AML arrangements, trying to recognise and offset the weaknesses and eliminate loopholes, and proposing revised approaches. Local financial institutions and non-financial payment institutions will encounter more opportunities, as well as greater risks, of being used as vehicles for money laundering with the development of the economy, and, as a result, AML risk management needs to be strengthened by AML regulators.

In analyses of money laundering issues and in evaluations, there has been too much focus historically upon the "front end" of customer identification rather than the more challenging "back end" customer monitoring compliance issues deduced from patterns of trading and other aspects of the conduct of accounts (Levi 2009, 543). As cyber laundering was believed to be the latest and most advanced technique in money laundering typology (Filipkowski 2008, 19), AML regulation on internet payment services is required to developed on the basis of risk management, and pay enough attentions to "back end" controls relating to preventing online money laundering activities.

In regards to the increased money laundering vulnerability that accompanies these new methods of payment in the financial industry, the following aspects of risks should be considered (FATF 2010):

Customer due diligence—Absence of 'face to face' contact is particularly common among technology based payment businesses. As recognised by FATF Recommendation 8, non 'face to face' transactions increase the risk of the product being used for illicit purposes by third parties.

Recording keeping—According to FATF Recommendation 10, both data related to identification and transaction records should be maintained for at least 5 years. These recommendations do not explicitly suggest the collection of Internet Protocol (IP) addresses of customers initiating a payment transaction through a personal computer.

Value limit—The higher the value and/or frequency of transactions, the greater the risk of money laundering [1].

Geographical limits—Cross-border functionality of NPM enables transactions to be conducted from jurisdictions where they may not be subject to adequate AML regulation and supervision, and where they may be outside the reach of foreign law enforcement investigations.

All financial entities and non-financial reporting institutions that by the nature of their business are vulnerable to money laundering should have effective AML programs in place. This would enable them: (i) to determine the true identity of existing and prospective customers and, where there are transactions involving an entity acting on behalf of another, to take steps to verify the identity of the underlying principal; (ii) to recognise and report suspicious transactions to the law enforcement authorities and financial supervisors; (iii) to ensure that compliance departments regularly monitor the implementation and operation of AML systems; (iv) to ensure cooperation across different sectors; (v) to prevent the money laundering risks from spreading from one sector to another; and (vi) to develop practical AML approaches on the basis of risk consideration.

Indeed, efforts should be made to ensure that the new payment systems have appropriate security measures in place and include a watching brief on the potential impact of new technologies. Following this trend, the effective AML countermeasures should be presented as risk management plans, involving the procedure of customer risk-rating, establishment of enterprise-wide AML information solution, and the application of risk-based approach (RBA).

17.3.1 Enterprise-Wide AML Information System

An enterprise-wide AML information system consists of all kinds of ML risk assessment systems, ranging from the 'front end' client reception to the background analysis.

17.3.1.1 Customer Risk-Rating

As the first step of the risk analysis process, customer reception in reporting institutions is subject to strict examination by regulatory bodies, and it is the basic instrument in the implementation of know your customer (KYC) rules. The *BSA Manual* published by the FFIEC emphasises the purpose of CDD. FFIEC (2010, 24) states that:

> [T]he objective of CDD should be to enable the bank to predict with relative certainty the types of transactions in which a customer is likely to engage, and these processes assist the bank in determining when transactions are potentially suspicious.

An effective AML compliance program includes due diligence around the account opening process. This must meet the requirements identified in the customer identification program (CIP), including customer identity verification, and determination of the actual beneficial owner and the actual account holder. Reporting institutions should comply with due diligence legislation to verify the identification of the customer, and, if necessary, check the watch lists of high risk customers. Based on determining the nature and purpose of transactions, the CDD system should be able to anticipate account activity according to the amount transacted, the frequency of transactions, the objectives of capital flow, and the geographic factors. Apart from the basic compliance requirements in due diligence and account opening, this module should combine the enterprise's internal control, internal audit, and customer relationship management.

Apart from conducting a multi-tiered CIP from simple account opening, record keeping procedures and enhanced due diligence (EDD) for higher risk accounts, proactive account monitoring for suspicious activities should also be undertaken. Indeed, identification of customers with a high money laundering risk and investigating their associated operations, covering at the least non-face-to-face transactions, cross-frontier correspondent banking, and politically exposed persons (PEPs) is necessary (Handoll 2006, 158).

From the practical perspective, reporting institutions are required to keep updating customer information collected under CDD processes and to undertake reviews of existing records of their customers, in particular those in higher risk categories of product/services, designated services, country/jurisdiction, and business delivery methods/channels (see Table 17.1). Lower risk customers are also categorised so that reporting institutions can improve AML efficiency by taking simplified CDD procedures for these.

Table 17.1 Examples of high money laundering risk categories

Products and services	Designated services
• private banking; • offshore activities; • deposit taking; • wire transfers an international activities; • transactions with undisclosed beneficiaries; • loan guarantee schemes; • traveller checks; • bank checks; • money orders; • foreign exchange transactions; • trade finance; • payable through accounts; and • pre-paid credit cards	• opening an account; • accepting deposits or allowing withdrawals; • making a loan; • issuing a debit or credit card; • supplying goods through a finance lease; • supplying goods by way of hire purchase; • issuing traveler's cheques; • providing remittances services which transfer money or property; • certain superannuation-related transactions or services; • issuing or accepting liability under life insurance policies; • issuing or selling securities and derivatives; and • exchanging foreign currency
Country/jurisdiction	Business delivery methods/channels
• any country or particular region of a country in which you may do business; • any country subject to trade sanctions; and • any country known to be a tax haven, source of narcotics or other significant criminal activity	• online/internet; • phone; • fax; • email; and • third-party agent or broker

17.3.1.2 Watch List

A relevant watch list should be carefully checked both at the due diligence stage
and the link analysis stage. It represents an important reference for the case management module in the workflow tools. Watch lists are periodically released by law
enforcement agencies or related international organisations. The primary functions
of watch lists are:

- Allowing organisations to monitor all transactions involving certain individuals,
  relationships, products, organisations, or countries;
- Identifying and generating automatic reports on particularly risky entities, such
  as high-risk and non-cooperative jurisdictions determined by FATF, countries
  under international sanction, PEPs, and high-risk transaction activities performed by particular individuals or organisations which are under investigation
  or penalties from law enforcement agencies; and
- Establishing "zero risk" or "no problem absolutely customers"—Since it is
  common to involve frequent transactions with large amount of funds for a
  large-scale enterprise, a "zero risk" or "no problem absolutely customers" list
  can exempt some big enterprises with high reputation from reporting during a
  certain time period. Enterprises on the zero risk list may be changed from time
  to time according to their actual business behaviour.

17.3.1.3 Transaction Risks

Abnormal account transaction analysis is an analytical methodology based on
in-depth experiences. This requires staff carrying out the analysis to have a sound
knowledge of all kinds of normal trading behaviours, such as normal trading patterns in the real estate industry and the usual payment methods for senior managers
of a corporate body. The idea is that the staff involved in analysis, would be more
knowledgeable than counter staff, and would be immediately aware when abnormal
behaviour occurs.

Generally, transaction risks can be summarised into the following three
categories:

(1) Fund-Related Behaviours—Transactions that are possibly involved with
    money-laundering activities or transactions that evidently disguise the origin
    of funds. For example, internal transfers between different accounts in the
    same enterprise, rapid fund movement, and the sudden activity of a previously
    dormant account need to be paid to enough attention as they may be used in
    money laundering;

(2). Transaction-Related Behaviours—Behaviour where transaction value exceed
    specified limits, or there is an apparent structuring of large-value funds into
    small amounts of money (also known as 'smurfing') should be paid extra

attention. This behaviour normally poses higher risks of money laundering activity, and are typically marked for further investigation; and

(3) Miscellaneous Behaviours—Frequent changes to an account can often be regarded as a signal that money laundering is occurring. Activities that would fall into this category include the settlement and/or standing instructions of an account, the movement of funds without a corresponding business, and the indirect deposit in excess of a designated amount into an account. These types of offsetting trades can increase the potential risk for money laundering.

There are numerous parameters used in the transaction risk assessment process, including transaction amounts, cash amounts in transaction, the number of transactions, the highest amount of a single transaction, transaction frequency coefficients, payment balance coefficients, dispersion coefficients of the transaction amount, the number of accounts, the number of branches in which an account is opened, the number of foreign currency accounts, the number of transaction counterparties, the number of accounts held by transaction counterparties, the number of transaction counterparties to the inflow/outflow of funds, the number of regions in the inflow/outflow of funds, and the number of foreign currencies involved. The pre-condition for the feasibility of this method is a sufficient understanding of local economic development, local industry distribution, transaction patter in the specific industry, and counter staff awareness of the usual transaction behaviour of certain groups of customers.

17.3.1.4   Scenario Detection

This refers to traditional monitoring systems utilising a rules based approach to detect known patterns of money laundering behaviours. Scenario detection creates statistical data based on specific characteristics extracted from previous money laundering cases, and interpret these data via a set of regular indicators. If the upper limits of these regular indicators are triggered, the information system will determine as 'recurrence' of money laundering activity, resulting in an alert for the recurrence. Although scenario detection is still based on objective standards, it is a meaningful reference as well as an important component of the risk ranking process.

17.3.1.5   Behaviour Profiling

As traditional monitoring systems can only operate based on statistical profiles derived from previously known suspicious behaviour and customer activities across all lines of business, they can be evaded by money launderers. This has resulted in behaviour profiling becoming a core module of second generation AML compliance systems at the international level. This module anticipates the customer's behaviour through behaviour profiling and generates continuous analysis. It has the ability to build and understand each individual customer's profile, compare activities with expectations, and provide alerts when profiles thresholds are exceeded. In detail, profile engine can automatically update behavioural profiles for every account that is maintained. The system is able to intelligently process every transaction and analyse behaviour in the context of the behavioural profiles, both on an individual basis, and against the defined peer group. When unusual or irregular activity is detected, alerts are triggered, signalling the need for investigation. Behaviour profiling provides further analysis and allows a reporting institution to map previously unknown patterns of behaviour through a complete knowledge of a customer's activities, and can even detect suspicious links between seemingly unrelated accounts.

17.3.1.6 Link Analysis

Link analysis is a powerful tool for uncovering complex money laundering operations and is designed to identify hidden relationships between transactions, accounts, customers, and even associated organisations. An effective link analysis module is tightly connected to 'watch list modules', that conduct comprehensive analysis on the basis of notifications of suspicious behaviour provided by law enforcement agencies. When combating money laundering, a link analysis module can highlight high risk geographic locations, which represent a key element in the risk ranking process. In general, link analysis operates at three fundamental levels:

(1) Business Relationships
    The system should be able to identify an actual beneficial owner, and defines unusual business relationships between underlying accounts, including relatives' relationships, relationships between affiliated companies, and special relationships involving risk sensitive persons. Under this category, there are three subsidiary aspects, namely, funds link analysis [2], geographical link analysis [3], and specific industry and occupation link analysis [4];
(2) Data Consistency
    If money launderers attempt to disguise their behaviour by changing important details such as name, address, and reference details when opening an account, the system should be able to identify these data inconsistencies by checking other referencing data links, and generate alert reports; and
(3) Inter-Related Transactions
    The *modus operandi* for a sophisticated money laundering operation nearly always involves multiple financial institutions. The system should be capable of identifying possible associations between inter-related transaction patterns across accounts, both internal and external to the institution.

17.3.1.7 Risk Ranking

This is a module that collects all submitted risks from different risk assessment processes, and according to designated risk weighted values, gives a final risk ranking score for each transaction and its associated account, customer, and organisation, and produces a suspects list ranked by their risk scores. Along with the suspects list, the system also outlines reasonable grounds and explanations for each suspicious activity. In a comprehensive database system, if the money laundering risk posed by a customer scores as medium level or high level in a number of sub-systems, the overall risk score of this customer should have a higher co-efficient as the final ranking. Risk rating codes are classified as follows:

- Extreme Risk (requires management approval)—this could include accounts for PEPs, such as diplomats from foreign countries; money service businesses owned by aliens; foreign correspondent accounts and so on;
- High Risk—non-resident aliens; accounts with high currency activity or high wire activity (particularly foreign wires);
- Moderate Risk—limited private banking or trust services; established multi-faceted business that also provide limited money services businesses (MSB) services; new customer relationships with limited higher risk services (such as wires) or higher risk nature of business (such as cash intensive restaurant, jewellery store, pawnbroker, and so on);
- Low Risk—known customer; stable account activity such as cheque account; secured loans; few if any higher risk services.

17.3.1.8 Workflow Tools

An efficient workflow tools module is critical for the entire enterprise-wide AML solution. This process must be flexible, auditable, and have the ability to maintain, retrieve and report case management activities. It is the most important link and combines systems of the regulators and of other co-operating institutions, and integrates all business links within an enterprise as an automatic solution body. The main functions of workflow tools are:

(1) Information Reporting and Investigation—Reporting systems should provide an 'end to end' AML SARs or STRs reporting process to the FIU, and guide the staff writing the filing reports in 'wizards' format, and encrypt the results during the automatic delivery process. Investigating tools assist the compliance staff to further investigate and verify the alerts submitted by the system before these results are reported to the regulators. It also provides a summary of filing or reporting reasons, including account summaries, customer backgrounds, current status, and transaction history. If necessary, visual or graphic documents can be supported to investigate the hidden relationship between different accounts;

(2) Case Management—An effective case management system can reduce false positives and bring together the output from disparate systems. It allows for the staff keep adding false alert cases to the case library. Case management is helpful in allowing the system to learn new money laundering rules, and is also useful for training staff about working processes of enterprises;

(3) Record Keeping—This tool should meet key requirements of current international AML regulations, that is, all the transaction records generated over at least the previous 5 years should be kept as searchable data.

An Enterprise-Wide AML Solution Diagram

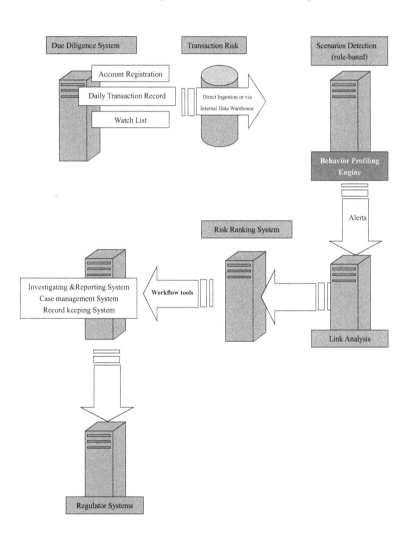

Key functions of an enterprise-wide AML information system solution include CDD, watch lists, transaction risks, scenario detection, behaviour profiling, link analysis, risk ranking and workflow tools (see above diagram). However, in order to achieve greater success in combating money laundering, the enterprise-wide AML information solution also needs supplementary support and assistance from the external environment, improvement of related regulatory guidance, maintenance of watch list databases, and the development of inter-relationships between different financial institutions. As an undertaking that provides more benefits to the public interest over private interests, AML activities cannot be successfully accomplished without any one of the above-mentioned elements.

17.3.2 Automatic Analysis and Manual Examination of Suspicious Transactions

The information technology (IT) industry is a facilitator and has proved to be a powerful engine for the development of AML practices. As a key part of an entire risk management mechanism, enterprise-wide AML information systems can assist financial institutions to identify, access, and control legal risks, operational risks, and reputational risks, and safeguard the soundness of financial institutions. However, results produced by an enterprise-wide AML risk-assessment process are dynamic, which only provide an indication or possibility. Just like any human endeavour, technical data-mining models may make mistakes. Indeed, two types of mistakes may be generated from the data mining model, namely false positives and true negatives. False positives refer to a data mining model that recognises a normal transaction as an money laundering activity, which in fact it is not, and the latter refers to data mining results that fail to identify a genuine money laundering activity and assesses it as a 'normal transaction' (see Table 17.2). These two types of errors cannot be completely avoided in the data mining process; thus, further checks of the technical results should be undertaken manually.

From the technical perspective, challenges concerning AML reporting therefore include the difficulty of distinguishing between 'true positive' or 'false positive' reports, and how can reporting authorities distinguish between 'true positive' and current non reported 'true negative' reports? To reduce the false positive rate (FPR), reporting entities should employ adequate techniques, including statistical analysis, neural networks, decision trees, fuzzy logic, and genetic algorithms, and create internal talent pools containing multi-disciplinary staff who specialise in informatics and computer science, thus improving not only the quantity of reporting but also the

Table 17.2 Types of money laundering (ML) control reporting

	ML	Non-ML
Reporting	True positive	False positive
Non-reporting	False negative	True negative

quality (Gao and Ye 2007, 174). Research shows that data-mining can help AML analysis by reducing data preparation time, and determine detection priorities, improve FPR, and lessen the pressure on personnel, training, and budgets (Gao and Ye 2007, 170). As data-mining in the context of AML is still a young and challenging field, both the FIU and financial institutions need to further enhance the technical capacity to use these new techniques (such as rule-based reasoning, blackboard, and many other aspects of AI technology) to separate genuine suspect transactions regarding money laundering offences from irrelevant information, strengthen the training in AI models, and build a strong financial database supported by all AML-related institutions without legal or competitive hurdles.

The most important factors in AML procedures are human resources and technical resources. International KYC rules have become increasingly rigorous, and the determination of suspicious transactions requires subjective standards, which result in a heavy workload for AML staff, who often have to deal with excessive numbers of customers, transactions, and associated reports. Due to the amount and complexity of information, suspicious information is hard to detect through staff vigilance. In this regard, AML technical systems can supplement manual work to a degree, and increase the overall efficiency of the system. However, in AML practice, decision-making cannot depend fully on automatic analysis. Risk management strategies must be applied by both public and private sector organisations if efficient and effective AML systems are to operate.

The real problem is that IT based solutions are not a real solution but a means to an end. Technology may create a false sense of security that leads the staff rely on the system to find possible money laundering. Further human analysis is also required on those transactions that have been identified by the systems. AML staff determine the direction of research and development, decide on purchases, optimise AML techniques, plan how to apply technical advances to AML practice, and identify and fix any problems with AML technical deficiency. It is critical that human ability remains the key factor in successful risk control to prevent money laundering, and this human judgement is irreplaceable in AML work.

17.4 Basic Principles of AML Risk-Based Approach (RBA)

Although analysis of 'risk' has been the fundamental element in financial industries for more than two decades, it is only since 2007 that concepts of risk, risk assessment and risk management have become central elements in the context of AML strategies. Previous AML experiences have overwhelmingly focused on the compliance side, but the compliance regulation is not sensitive enough to reflect the money laundering vulnerabilities in a timely manner. Thus, the AML regulatory direction is gradually shifting from compliance requirement to risk consideration. Indeed, international AML standard-makers encouraged regulated entities to carry out RBA on the basis of risk assessment, to increase the awareness of money laundering risks, and to eventually perform AML practice in an effective way.

Indeed, RBA requires the AML regulated entities to scientifically assess money laundering risks confronted by the institution, the department, and the entire sector, and conduct primary and subsidiary AML measures to effectively monitor and prevent potential money laundering activities. The ultimate goal of RBA is to ensure that resources are allocated in the most efficient manner so that the greatest money laundering risks receive the highest attention. Compared with traditional rule-based approach, both of the regulator and the regulated should change their performance concerning AML compliance examination and incentive program. The changes are as follows:

- *Uneven efforts*—Differentiated with rule-based approach, RBA no longer mainly focuses on meeting all the rules, instead of that, RBA aims to recognize and mitigate money laundering risks faced by specific sector, and to pour resources into the most risky area. Regulated institutions tailor the different levels of AML measures according to distinct risk consideration, for example, standard customer due diligence and enhanced customer due diligence. Regulators and examiners, on the other hand, pay more attentions to the vulnerable part of the AML procedures, rather than conduct even assessment for every AML process.
- *Keep the manner of risk adjustment*—It is utmost important that the RBA remains dynamic to risk, and is able to revolve to match a changed threat, and therefore flexible. Money Business Services (MBs) should be able to show how their strategy and approach meet the changing threats as identified by their own staff or external public sector parties (FATF 2009, 7).
- *Encourage subjectivity of reporting entities*—Recognizing the subjectivity of suspicious transaction identification is a practicable solution for the over-reporting problem of the suspicious reporting system. Recent AML development requires the obliged entities to gradually reduce objective criteria for suspicious activity reporting (SARs), intensify the capability for financial institutions to subjectively determine the money-laundering suspicious activities. Subjective determination should perform on the basis of objective criteria, that is, suspicious activity should be identified mainly according to subjective analysis, and supplemented by objective indicators. In this way, the value of SAR reporting intelligence will be increased.

As the subjective identification will act significant role in determining suspicious activity, the examination principle for assessing the quality of reporting system should be changed accordingly. FATF (2009, 8) indicates that regardless of the strength and effectiveness of AML controls established by MSBs, criminals will continue to attempt to move illicit funds through the financial sector undetected and will, from time to time, succeed. It must be recognized that any reasonably applied controls, including controls implemented as a result of a reasonably implemented risk-based approach will not identify and detect all instances of money laundering.

Therefore, regulators, law enforcement and judicial authorities must take into account and give due consideration to a MSB's well-reasoned risk-based approach. When MSBs do not effectively mitigate the risks due to a failure to implement an adequate risk-based approach or failure of a risk-based programme that was not adequate in its design, regulators, law enforcement or judicial authorities should take necessary action, including imposing penalties, or other appropriate enforcement/regulatory remedies.

Developed to cope with "defensive SAR filings", the BSA Manual instructs that examiners should focus on evaluating a bank's policies, procedures, and processes to identify and analyse suspicious activity, rather than on a bank's decision with respect to any individual case. Thus, bank should not be criticized for the failure to file a SAR unless the failure is significant or accompanied by evidence of intentionally bad faith (Kini 2005, 946).

- *Combination of rule-based approach and risk-based approach*—Promotion and application of risk-based approach does not mean to ignore or even to destroy the old rule-based approach, but to encourage obliged entities to develop their own AML internal control system according to the business characteristics after meeting the minimum standards of AML program. The minimum requirements include customer due diligence system, transaction monitoring and large-value transaction reporting, record-keeping system, etc. The obliged entities have more flexibility to make their own internal control system, but they must meet the minimum standards before that. Explicit rules for regulating low-risk money laundering activities are still necessary for the regulated side. These rules should be developed and published by the regulatory bodies, and the rule-based approach should be remained for assessing the minimum standard of AML compliance, for example, the tick-the-box approach.
- To put it somewhat differently, the RBA for combating ML aims to provide control to the organisation itself so that it can design an AML program that best suits it, changing the approach from following 'the letter of the law' to an approach that embodies the practical management of risk. This transfer of control from regulatory body to the regulated entity provides flexibility but requires the organisations to be knowledgeable of the money laundering risks they face.

Risk-based AML principles include two core requirements (1) an AML system must be able to fully reflect the money laundering risks of customers and associated financial businesses, (2) the AML system should consider the greater money laundering risks posed by non-contact transactions. Under a risk-based regulatory system, the regulated entity must be proactive in the mitigation of money laundering risk, and must be provided with the most appropriate regulatory strategies on specified risk.

The rationale of implementing RBA looks sound, however, the practical application of an RBA requires resources to gather and interpret information on risk, develop AML procedures and systems, as well as well-trained personnel with a sound understanding of the risk and who are capable of making sound judgements. Three of the most important conditions in RBA implementation are (Ross and Hannan 2007, 110):

(i) There has to be agreement about the basis on which risk is determined or what the risks are.
(ii) There must be an explicit, agreed model of the attributes what will contribute to the assessment of risk.
(iii) There must be a model of accessing to knowledge about the outcomes of assessments in order to develop and refine a risk-based decision.

These conditions are not readily found in either government or private sectors in many developing economies, and even some of developed countries.

17.5 China's AML Countermeasures Towards NPM Vulnerabilities

With the rapid development of the Chinese financial industry, various products and services based on new or developing technologies are being increasingly introduced. For example, internet users and E-Commerce have increased explosively in China during past few years, with an extremely large number of Chinese online users and an unbelievable growth in transaction volume. According to the China Internet Network Information Centre, in 2006 the population of internet users in China rose by 30 % to 132 million at December 2006 (AIC 2007, 15), and the annual growth rate was about 19 %. This figure has been estimated to have risen to 485 million in 2011 (Reuters 2011).

New economy developed on the basis of internet website and information technology was launched 1990s. Developed countries enacted sets of strategic plan to promote rapid development in this sector, and accordingly escalate national competitive advantage. China turned its eyes on the new business model and new technology development since 1999 [5]. From then on, Chinese government adopted active supports and loose regulations towards the electronic business, especially regarding on the innovation of business model and business expansion of the privately-owned enterprises (POE). "In China, the internet economy is actually the pronoun for the private economy. To be more blunt, Chinese internet economy is equal to Chinese private economy in nature" (Liu 2010). As the result of government supports and lax regulation, internet payment services in China have developed and expanded rapidly.

Internet users and E-Commerce have increased in an explosive way in China during past few years, and it brought an extremely large cardinal number of Chinese online users. Taken the Alipay (Zhi Fu Bao in Chinese) [6] as an example, the number of Alipay registered users has already outnumbered three hundreds million within just 6 years. This number, actually, exceeds the customer number of the biggest Chinese commercial bank, Industrial and Commercial Bank of China

(ICBC). It is evident that the massive number of transaction volume is a hard problem faced by the regulators. Internet payment systems associated with E-commerce leave spaces for money launderers to use the trade-based money laundering techniques, for example fake transactions or transfer-pricing [7]. Due to the nature of swift online transactions, internet payment systems are vulnerable to money laundering at the layering stage.

The complicated nature and characteristics of the internet payment services [8] makes the effective AML regulation in this area hard to meet (Filipkowski 2008, 18). According to 2008's report, there were no regulations in place addressing Electronic Commerce or Internet payment systems in China. Nevertheless, on 13 December 2007, the Chinese Ministry of Commerce issued an opinion on enhancing the regularised development of electronic commerce. The objectives of the guidance were to help the third-party electronic payment service providers to improve the reputation of the industry, operate in a prudent and stable manner, prevent blind business expansion and out-of-order competition, and ensure the safety of users' funds. The guidance encouraged measures like standardised operation and management, overseeing business flow, securing electronic payment, keeping transaction data, and preventing online illegal financial transactions (FATF 2008, 29).

In response to the new challenge, the People's Bank of China (PBC) required Chinese financial institutions to strengthen customer identification in non-face-to-face transactions such as transactions conducted by using telephone, internet and ATM services, and enacted *Administrative Measures for the Payment Services Provided by Non-Financial Institutions* on 21st June, 2010 (hereafter referred to as Administrative Measures 2010), officially putting the third-party payment under the Chinese AML regulation and supervision. Article 2 of the *Administrative Measures 2010* provides four categories of the payment services provided by non-financial institutions in China, including internet payment services, prepaid-card services, POS machine business, and other payment services designated by PBC. In fact, internet payment services occupy the largest proportion among all the third-party payment services (PBC 2010). Concerning non-face-to-face transactions, reporting institutions shall strengthen internal management measures, update technical means to ensure integrated transmission of relevant information of transactions and customers and thus feed monitoring and analysis of suspicious transactions.

Regrading on the third-party payment services for E-commerce industry, individual vendors should be guided to develop their own AML measures. In fact, Article 11 of the *Administrative Measures 2010* clearly requires that non-financial institutions applicants for the payment services should prepare documents with regard to anti-money laundering measures for qualification examination (PBC 2010). If the AML measures made by the E-commerce vendors are not sound enough, the business opening qualification will not be permitted by related authority. In March 2012, PBC newly published the *Administrative Measures for Anti-Money Laundering and Combating Terrorist Financing by Payment Institutions* requiring all Chinese payment institutions to establish AML internal control system before the application for the business licence, and to conduct proper identification and verification of customer identity (PBC 2012).

As the transacted products include high value goods, precious metals, real estate, and negotiable securities via internet websites, which all happen to be good choices for integrating illicit fund into the legitimate economy, it is a real challenge for AML regulators to tell how many transactions relating to money laundering activities are among the massive number of online transactions. In fact, according to the FATF's latest examination report on China, the customer identification and record keeping in precious metals and stones, layers, notaries, real estate agents and company service providers are still very weak (FATF 2012, 42). Consequently, regulatory measures and technical plans with regard to regulating new technology related transactions should be established and constantly updated.

The wider the geographical reach of a NPM product, the higher the money-laundering risk will be. Cross-border functionality enables payment service providers to conduct their business from jurisdictions where they may not be subject to adequate AML regulation and supervision, and where they may be outside the reach of foreign law enforcement investigations (FATF 2010, 7). In response to this, China has amended its legislation to require financial institutions to give special attention to customers from countries or regions with weak AML regimes, and transactions which have anything to do with countries or regions that the Chinese authorities have identified as being of AML concern (FATF 2012, 49). However, these requirements should be extended to the non-financial payment institutions as well.

Apart from risk rating associated with new technology-based money laundering activities, China also faces challenges and difficulties in applying AML information solution in a certain degree. Due to a lack of staff experience and deficiencies in technical assistance, the challenge faced by reporting entities in China currently is their high FPR resulting in the inefficiencies due to voluminous data sets. For example, the 18 indicators of suspicious transactions in the banking sector listed by the PBC are quantified as (at most) 8 or 9 indicators in the automatic process, meaning there has to be 'manual' analysis. It is said that the automatic system, via 'blacklist' database filters, targets around 10,000 transactions everyday, of which 99 % are determined as 'false hits' with manual analysis (Geng 2010) [9].

For most reporting institutions in China, data quality remains a challenge. Chinese banks have invested in IT software and process modification when mandated by regulators. Generally most banks opt for cheap and basic 'off the shelf' systems which only satisfy the basic regulatory requirements and put the regulator at ease (Asian Banker White Paper 2009, 9). However, these low-tech monitoring tools, which focus on detecting and flagging but not on the accuracy of these alerts, do not assure comprehensive suspicious transactions reporting, and where reports are made they are often useless because the underlying data is incorrect. Reporting institutions should fully understand money laundering vulnerabilities and risks in the industry or sectors they are practicing in, and should foster a money laundering risk-rating system and an enterprise-wide AML information solution system based on practical analysis and existing real conditions.

In addition, RBA implementation would need to ensure that appropriate software is installed within its IT systems to enable it to identify unusual transactions. It is vital to tackle the problem using an RBA, as well as the technology that is adaptable, so that systems can be dynamic in the way that they respond to changes in the patterns of money laundering. Although Chinese AML programs have made such improvements, the capacity and readiness of reporting institutions to fully implement RBA in the short term is still doubtful.

Under the RBA environment, regulators should be the drivers behind the adoption of customised solutions that mitigate the real risks facing a firm, by giving back to senior management the responsibility for their design and implementation while at the same time as holding them accountable for this(Killick and Parody 2007, 215). More importantly, both the regulators and the regulated should determine the most applicable way to implement risk management strategies for every step of AML programs.

Thus, when deciding to carry out the risk-based AML approach as an AML national strategy, Chinese authorities should carefully evaluate whether the preconditions for conducting a full implementation of the RBA are in place (PBC 2009). Not only are there the issues of adequate resources and sound staff training, but there is also a need for efficient information sharing systems and cooperative arrangements among AML shareholders. Adequate internal control systems and comprehensive legal framework are also demanded.

17.6   Conclusion

Main typologies related to the misuse of NPMs for money laundering purposes were identified include third party funding and exploitation of the non-face-to-face nature of NPM accounts (FATF 2008, 7). Besides, electronic commerce together with the online payment system is an emerging industry entirely established on the internet platform. Compared to the traditional business model and offline financial services, the emerging industry and new technology bring new concept of business operation with the characteristics of swiftness and convenience. However, at the meantime, it also creates potential channels for illicit activities. There are few features of the internet which attract criminals, including anonymity, non face-to-face contacts, speed of the transactions, globalization process and new payment technologies, and cross border activity (Filipkowski 2008, p.18).

New payment technologies and digital currencies have been identified as possessing risk characteristics which pose a threat to traditional due diligence systems in the international campaign against money laundering, and limit the effectiveness of implementing internal controls in numerous areas. Indeed, anonymity increases the attractiveness of NPMs for money launderers, however the risk factor could be mitigated by implementing robust CDD and verification procedures, and other measures such as imposing value limits and strict monitoring systems. Obvious gap exists between the rapid development of the internet payment industry and the lagged financial regulation and counter-measures in this field. The securities issues and risk issues hidden in the online payment services eventually raised a great and wide attention at both the national and international level.

Versatile financial activities conducted via different channels, especially high-tech methods, will require a higher capacity for managing money laundering risks in financial institutions and non-financial payment institutions. All regulated institutions need to have processes and procedures in place for assessing the money laundering risk in providing designated services, customer identification and verification, ongoing CDD [10], and EDD [11]. They also should conduct training sessions on how to complete the risk rating procedures and how to better understand the risk rating process.

Thus, it is plausible to adopt money laundering risk management mechanisms which acts against the likelihood of money laundering risks faced by individual regulated institutions and involve financial services. The risk management mechanism contains three main components: the ML risk rating system, which measures the existing risk of money laundering in the regulated institution under the regulation of the AML program, the enterprise-wide AML information solution that measures the effects of an enterprise-wide AML program quality on the vulnerability of the regulated institution to money laundering, and the application of RBA which allows regulated institutions to associate risk levels with customers and products and produce an appropriate system, one that suits their own risk profiles.

To sum up, new technologies bring the challenges in combating money laundering not only to the financial institutions and third-party payment industry, but also to the regulatory agencies, law-makers and police officers. It is shown in the China's example that each country or region may face constraints and difficulties when setting up a sound AML system dealing with new technology-based money laundering activities. This constraint has two dimensions. First is the level of human resources employed at government bodies and private sector entities. Second is the level of technical expertise of such human resources as compared with their counterparts in developed countries.[1] However, if AML competent authorities can help financial institutions and internet payment service providers to fully understand emerging money laundering risks, develop comprehensive risk management program, adequately monitor the financial transactions of their customers, and monitor for and act on deviations from the customer transaction profile, the lack of face-to-face contact may not constitute a problem.

Notes

1. The term 'value limits' refers to limitations on the maximum amount that can be held in an account or product; or limitations on the maximum amount per single payment transaction; or limitations on the frequency or cumulative value of permitted transactions per day/week/month/year; or a combination of the aforementioned limitations. Also the number of accounts or cards allowed per customer can be considered a type of value limit.

---

[1]Neil Jensen and Cheong-Ann Png. 2011. Implementation of the FATF 40 + 9 Recommendations: A Prospective from Developing Countries. *Journal of Money Laundering Control* 14(2): 110, 115.

2. Funds link analysis is designed to use available data and information analysing the link between upstream and downstream sources of the funds and searching out the hidden relationship between seemingly superficial data.

3. Geographical link analysis compares the funds flow situation with the local economic structure and development level and conducting statistical analysis on transaction data generated from geographic jurisdictions with high risk.

4. Specific industry and occupation link analysis is used to extract indicators of business scale, business frequency, transaction time and settlement methods in specific industries and occupations with high reliance on data and to use these indicators to analyse abnormal business behaviours in individual cases.

5. In August 1999, Chinese government firstly published *the decisions on enhancing technical Innovation, developing high-technology, and realizing the industrialization.*

6. Alipay (支付宝) is the internet payment service for one of the biggest E-commerce companies in China—Alibaba (阿里巴巴), just like the PayPal for eBay.

7. Transfer pricing, refers to pricing agreements established by mutual agreement rather than free market forces.

8. Internet payment services include mobile payments, micro-payments or digital precious metals. The process of internet payment systems is that companies provide so called electronic cash or e-cash services to their customers. It is sort of replacement for physical cash. Usually, software which stores value on the computers of their clients (merchants and consumers) is provided to them. This stored value can then be transmitted via the internet between personal computers in order to buy and sell goods or services.

9. This is from presentation at the Chinese Anti-Money Laundering Annual Forum hosted by the China Centre for Anti-Money Laundering Studies (Fudan University) in Shanghai on 26 November 2010. Geng Wei is the chief compliance officer at the head office of Bank of China.

10. It refers to measures for checking the identity of customers and checking that their financial activity matches that identity.

11. It refers to measures for screening employees to ensure they do not expose your business to money laundering risk, for example, checking their identity and their background to ensure they are of good character, ensuring they are suitable.

References

Asian Banker White Paper. 2009. *Identifying anti-money laundering issues in chinese banks.*
Australian Institute of Criminology. 2007. Future direction in technology-enabled crime: 2007–2009. *Research and Public Policy Series* 78: 1–131.
Federal Financial Institutions Examination Council. 2010. *Bank secrecy act/anti-money laundering examination manual.* vol. 24.

Filipkowski, Wojciech. 2008. Cyber laundering: an analysis of typology and techniques. *International Journal of Criminal Justice Sciences* 3: 15–27.

Financial Action Task Force on Money Laundering. 2004. *Methodology for assessing compliance with the FATF 40 recommendations and the FATF 9 special recommendations.*

Financial Action Task Force on Money Laundering. 2008. *Money laundering & terrorist financing vulnerabilities of commercial websites and internet payment systems.*

Financial Action Task Force on Money Laundering. 2009. *Risk-based approach guidance for money service businesses.*

Financial Action Task Force on Money Laundering. 2010. *Money laundering using new payment methods.*

Financial Action Task Force on Money Laundering. 2012. *Mutual evaluation 8th follow-up report: Anti-money laundering and combating the financing of terrorism-China.*

Gao, Zengan, and Mao Ye. 2007. A framework for data mining-based anti-money laundering research. *Journal of Money Laundering Control* 10: 170–179.

Handoll, John. 2006. *Capital, payments and money laundering in the European union.* London: Oxford University Press.

Killick, Marcus, and David Parody. 2007. Implementing AML/CFT measures that address the risks and not tick boxes. *Journal of Financial Regulation and Compliance* 15: 210–216.

Kini, Satish M. 2005. Federal bank regulatory agencies issue long-awaited anti-money laundering examination manual. *The Banking Law Journal* 122: 940–952.

Levi, Michael. 2009. E-gaming and money laundering risks: A European overview. *ERA Forum* 10: 533–546.

McCusker, Rob. 2004. China, globalisation and crime: A potential victim of its own prospective success? *Journal of Financial Crime* 12: 44–52.

Reuters. 2011. China web users hit 485 million. http://www.reuters.com/article/2011/07/19/us-china-internet-idUSTRE76I12020110719. Accessed July 19.

Ross, Stuart, and Michelle Hannan. 2007. Money laundering regulation and risk-based decision-making. *Journal of Money Laundering Control* 10: 106–115.

Other Materials in Chinese

Liu, Zhiming. 2010. Internet website: The gluttonous feast for the chinese private economy. http://tech.sina.com.cn/i/2010-01-06/18263744376.shtml. Accessed January 06.

The People's Bank of China. 2009. *Chinese anti-money laundering strategic development guideline.*

The People's Bank of China. 2010. *The administrative measures for the payment services provided by non-financial institutions.*

The People's Bank of China. 2012. *The administrative measures for anti-money laundering and combating terrorist financing by payment institutions.*

Wei, Geng. 2010. The interaction of AML staff and AML techniques. In *Paper presented at the Chinese anti-money laundering annual forum.* Shanghai, 26 November 2010.

Concluding Remarks—Financial Crimes Research, Theoretical and Practical Implications

New theories have been presented to address myriad aspects of white collar crime, in addition to which practical guidelines have been established for the legitimate implementation of research-backed legislative and practical actions to combat the aforementioned areas of white collar crime. These recommendations can be integrated into the EU in an effort to lend aid to the current fraudulency embedded in Cyprus and Greece. It can be integrated into anti-money laundering, anti-corruption and drug trade efforts by legal bodies around the world.

Chapter 1 reflects on anti-corruption measures needed in Cyprus and Greece and presents data on how corruption resulted in reduced investment and reduced growth in addition to which it acted as a disincentive for innovation, development, and capital investment. Furthermore, corruption has evidently a negative impact on socio-political factors such as democratization by undermining "citizens" confidence in democratic institutions and the rule of law. Corruption has an impact on society and environment. In the social area, moral values and principles are destroyed, democracy is undermined and institutions are corroded. Tax evasion is just one area where corruption stems, one area where current research indicates methods for removing the source of corruption. Indeed, Chap. 2 in this volume indicates that non-economic determinants have the strongest impact on tax evasion. In particular, complexity is the most important determinant of tax evasion, followed by education, income source, fairness and tax morale. That information in mind, attempts could be made by governments to make improvements to the levels of complexity in the tax system. By enhancing the general educational knowledge of taxpayers, tax evasion is also reduced. Wage and salary income subject to withholding also represents another important curb on tax evasion. This could lead to improvements in tax revenue collection by governments. Chapter 3 also highlights the fact that reciprocity is one of the main drivers of information sharing among countries—tax treaties have been found to contribute as well to the flow of information across borders.

As financial institutions face the threat of liability from both the regulators and customers, it is reasonable to ask whether whose that service the public sector's financial needs are acting out of dedicated support for a common goal or principally

© Springer International Publishing Switzerland 2016

M. Dion et al. (eds.), *Financial Crimes: Psychological, Technological, and Ethical Issues*, International Library of Ethics, Law, and the New Medicine 68, DOI 10.1007/978-3-319-32419-7

to avoid penalty. The current approach to these concerns are designed to make criminal activities unprofitable and to keep the proceeds of crime out of the hands of criminals and terrorist. These goals cannot be achieved without proactive confiscation mechanisms. Financial institutions are required to report suspicious transactions within 30–60 days and if necessary refuse to complete the transaction. The result is that either the transaction occurs (with potentially illegitimate money entering the financial system), or the funds walk away, free to search for an alternative entry point. Chapter 4 emphasize this issue: what is absent from the current system is the ability to immediately seize the funds without delay as recommended, pending determination of the legitimacy of the funds involved. Providing a financial incentive to those complying institutions could not only change the course of the problem quickly but help to grow a legitimate response to money laundering.

Theoretical research frameworks constitute the cornerstone of legitimate legislative measures, and the psychology of white collar crime is just as important a component to understand when trying to combat criminal activities such as bribery, corruption, and money laundering. It is by way of forensic psychiatric evaluation and consultation that a significant contribution to understanding, preventing, and responding to financial crimes can be made. There are, however, individual psychological dimensions of financial crimes in a given social context, the group dynamics of corrupt organizations, and the interrelationship between the two, all of which are explored in this volume. Chapters in this volume presents (1) the limitations of rational choice theory as a foundation for the legal approaches to preventing acts of financial crime, understanding their meaning, responding in accordance with the fundamentals of justice; (2) the limitations of classic actuarial responses to the prevention and postvention acts of financial crime. It is critical that the forensic psychiatric evaluation of any act of financial crime ask how it is most likely to be the product of individual or institutional psychopathology, character traits, or states of desire. Chapter 5 highlights opportunities to set forth a psychodynamically informed forensic psychiatric perspective as an aid for sentencing of white-collar crime.

Another important concept is that of cognitive factors that result in susceptibility to financial crimes including financial literacy, numeracy, and deliberative reasoning. Chapter 6 support the fact that financial literacy has been found to be a strong predictor of retirement savings, FICO scores, and savings accounts. But perhaps more important, it has been found to be a strong predictor of debt and vulnerability to predatory lending. Those individuals who have low financial literacy are more likely to employ loss aversion, sunk costs, and confirmatory bias in the financial decision making. Dual process models of decision making are used to explain that decision making can be deliberative and analytical or emotional and impulsive but in cases of investment schemes, Chap. 6 suggests that emotional and impulsive decision making are key. That impulsive decision making can be increased through stress, cognitive impairment, or ego depletion. Decision making can occur in or out of awareness. While anyone can be the victim of fraud, factors that impact our ability to deliberate and "do the math" increase our susceptibility to financial predators. Chapter 7 four-factor theory of investor gullibility (induced social risk-unawareness) also shed light on this issue.

That being said, white collar crimes cause more pain to investors, employees, and national economies compared to blue collar theft with violence. These financial crimes are often undertaken by well-educated, charming, softly spoken and socially adroit peers as opposed to those whose appearance embodies the stereotypes of violent offenders. It is for this reason that white collar crime has received less attention from psychologists and criminologists. And yet Chaps. 6–8 in this volume offer an overview of theories of what motivates the criminals, why some people are receptive to exploitation, and why systems of belief in gatekeeper institutions result in regulatory incapacity that inhibits effective risk identification and action to minimize that crime. The psychology of financial crime is diverse, inducing caution about explanations purportedly enabling systematic prediction and prevention of large-scale offences. One alternative way to understand the psychology of financial crime suggested by Chap. 8 would be to adapt the seven deadly sins, i.e, opportunity, rationalization, need, greed, emulation, anger, pleasure, fear and misjudgment. Understanding financial crime requires awareness that it involves victims and bystanders, rather than merely offenders. But this awareness has shed light on the fact that there is still great need for comprehensive empirical data that would enable more confident assessments of the psychology of financial crime and thence more effective responses. To date there are no comprehensive, culturally-independent profiling mechanisms for identification of potential and active financial criminals.

Corruption and white collar crime occurs on global and local levels, among individuals and corporations alike. While etymologically the concept of integrity doesn't refers to virtue, Chap. 11 criticize several misconceptions with regards to this concept and articulates the different degrees of responsibility in corruption—it emphasize the importance and need for virtuous communities where individuals will be supported in their quest for integrity. Sociological research in organizational deviance, specifically in the area of corporate crime, has shown how deviant behaviors (frauds and unethical behaviors) are not only restricted to individuals but also to organizations. Deviant organizations and their leaders use unethical and pressured management practice in their internal and institutional environment so as to change the norms of individuals' behaviors and also to transform societal norms in order for their actions to be legal and even be perceived as being legitimate. Chapter 9 in this volume explore the way to increase resistance capacity of internal and external actors faced with unethical pressures in order to prevent the perpetuation of organizational deviance, but further research would be needed on the mechanisms that enable deviant organizations to obtain the complicity of their employees and of the actors of their socio-institutional environment.

Globalization also poses both the opportunities and challenges to the fight against corruption in developing countries. On one hand, globalization can accelerate the convergence of governance to international standards; on the other hand, however, globalization can increase the competition for a large number of inefficient domestic firms and thus may create high pressure for them to bribe in order to survive. Chapter 10 explores how the corporate sector is an important source of rampant corruption problems in many developing countries due to a vicious cycle of bribery practices and corruption. Improvement in corporate governance can be a critical ingredient to break the vicious cycle of bribery practices and corruption. Firms controlled by individual owners and family are more likely to pay bribes than are firms governed by corporate boards, and that firms reporting higher percentage of their sales for tax purpose are less likely to be involved in corrupt exchanges. Chapter 12 questions our ethnocentrism when referring to grey areas of morality within bribery issues and improves our understanding of the concept of bribery. Through a comparison between bribe-giving and gift-giving practices, the author argue that bribery is an abuse of power and an antitrust behavior that could not be morally justified. In term of practical implications of bribery research in this volume, measures adopted by government, business community and individual firms in improving corporate governance can be effective anti-corruption strategies in an environment with high level of corruption. Public policies targeting improved corporate governance could be effective anti-corruption strategies. More important, such efforts are likely to be sustained because it is self-motivated and self-driven from the perspective of firms. Government, the business community, and individual firms all have respective roles to play in combating bribery activities in the corporate sector. Government can significantly reduce bribery by targeting areas where firms are most prone to bribery practices, such as integrity of court systems, business licensing requirements, quality of government service delivery, and taxation. The business community can reduce incidence of bribery by setting up rules of market competition so that bribery will not automatically increase as the level of competition rises. Individual firms can shoulder their share of responsibility through improvements in corporate governance, such as broadening the basis of ownership.

Chapter 13 suggests that the key to understanding and eventually being able to largely control fraud is to consider both the individual and the environment in which they operate. Consequently, what is required is contextualized specific fraud offender profiling research that will investigate and synthesize both individual and organizational characteristics of fraud offenders within a company and by unknown outsiders who victimize government services, corporations and individuals. A less ambitious but feasible undertaking would be to attempt to profile at different levels of analysis (e.g., individual and organizational) and specific types of fraud offenders perpetrating specific frauds. Also, future research should aim to obtain a more complex causal picture of what attributes separate fraud offenders from versatile fraud offenders and those committing common crime. More research is also required before conclusively defining which personality traits or disorders make up characteristic predispositions toward fraud.

There are challenges posed to the regulation of transnational financial crimes by the processes of globalization. Chapter 14 argues that the products of technological advancements, such as computer and the Internet, have been increasingly used and exploited by criminals in the perpetration of transnational financial crimes. More research is needed on enhanced preventive measures, such as increased electronic surveillance, modernization of applicable legal rules along these lines, international co-operation and the cultivation of a global ethical consensus on the subject. Since transnational financial crimes are opportunity-driven, one of the most effective ways of combating or preventing them is through the elimination or reduction of those opportunities that are frequently exploited by criminals. Currently it is imperative that there be a formulation of a new legal framework to respond to the dictates of technological developments. In addition, the adoption of a Convention dealing with specific aspects of financial crime is one way of moving the fight against these crimes forward. It is only through such approaches that humankind can maximally benefit from the promise of globalization and effectively respond to the challenges posed by transnational financial crimes. Chapter 15 explores the transnational organization of the drug trade and reflect on whether continuation of a 40 year war on drugs founded on prohibition, is more ethically acceptable than an evidence-based approach focusing on harm reduction. The author suggests that the global drugs industry is an early adopter of new information and communications technologies, offering organized crime new ways to avoid detection and argues that the global drugs industry has been bolstered by the operation of a policy of prohibition. More research is needed on this ethical issue of how best to control the drugs industry, and in particular the relative merits of prohibition versus decriminalisation and regulation. Chapter 16 discusses risk and risk management in the globalized context of mobile money and highlights practical, ethical and regulatory issues. While technology enables financial institutions and governments to gather more data on clients, developing economies often lack strong legal and institutional mechanisms to protect privacy and client confidentiality. This chapter raises concerns regarding responsible and ethical corporate compliance with statutory information-sharing responsibilities. New payment technologies and digital currencies have been identified as possessing risk characteristics which pose a threat to traditional due diligence systems in the international campaign against money laundering, and limit the effectiveness of implementing internal controls in numerous areas. Chapter 17 presents money laundering risks associated with new technology-based financial activities while introducing enterprise-wide AML information solution, and explaining principles of risk-based approach. In order to mitigate these risks, implementing robust customer due diligence (CDD) and verification procedures, and other measures such as imposing value limits and strict monitoring systems need to take place. The findings of Chaps. 15–17 have a number of important implications for practice: a key policy priority should be to focus on regulatory agencies, law-makers and police officers training and threat awareness. International campaigns need to be raised to (1) increase law-makers awareness and understand of emerging money laundering risks; (2) develop comprehensive and transnational risk management program, (3) support local financial institutions in the adequate monitor of financial transactions of their customers and in the monitor for deviations from the customer transaction profile.

Designing strategies to fight/prevent financial crimes is a hard task, which implies two basic steps. Firstly, we must know who the enemy is: not only the criminals but also the weakness in laws and regulations, and the way international organisations and governments cooperate. The identity of the 'enemy' could vary from crime to crime. It is not exactly the same in cases of bribery, tax evasion, and money laundering. Secondly, we must identify the most efficient means to rid of the enemy, or to reduce its powerful influence on social institutions. Fighting transnational crimes requires a multidimensional strategy: (1) international collaboration between police organisations and between countries; cooperation between governments and international organisations; (2) national criminal regulations (including strong penalties); (3) consciousness-raising activities to be realised in (more vulnerable) institutional settings (e.g. business milieu); (4) organisational norms of behaviour (which could reduce the probability of crimes); (5) various ways to make citizens internalise their moral duties when facing the possibility of participating in criminal acts. Such a multidimensional strategy must focus on both sanctions and prevention, and include short- to middle-term as well as long-run objectives. This volume addressed the transnational nature of financial crime. In each category, we saw how technological means were used to improve criminal schemes and unveil ethical questions that are implied in either the financial crimes or in the strategies to fight them.